The
Wedding

		DATE DUE		

Other Books by Cathy Guisewite

Recent *Cathy*® Collections

Food
Love
Mom
Work
Cathy Twentieth Anniversary Collection
Shoes: Chocolate for the Feet
I'd Scream Except I Look So Fabulous
I Am Woman, Hear Me Snore
Abs of Steel, Buns of Cinnamon
Understanding the "Why" Chromosome

Cathy® Gift Books

Confessions to My Mother
Like Mother, Like Daughter
Commiserations
Shop Till You Drop Then Sit Down and Buy Shoes

Cookbook

Girl Food: Cathy's Cookbook for the Well-Balanced Woman (with Barbara Albright)

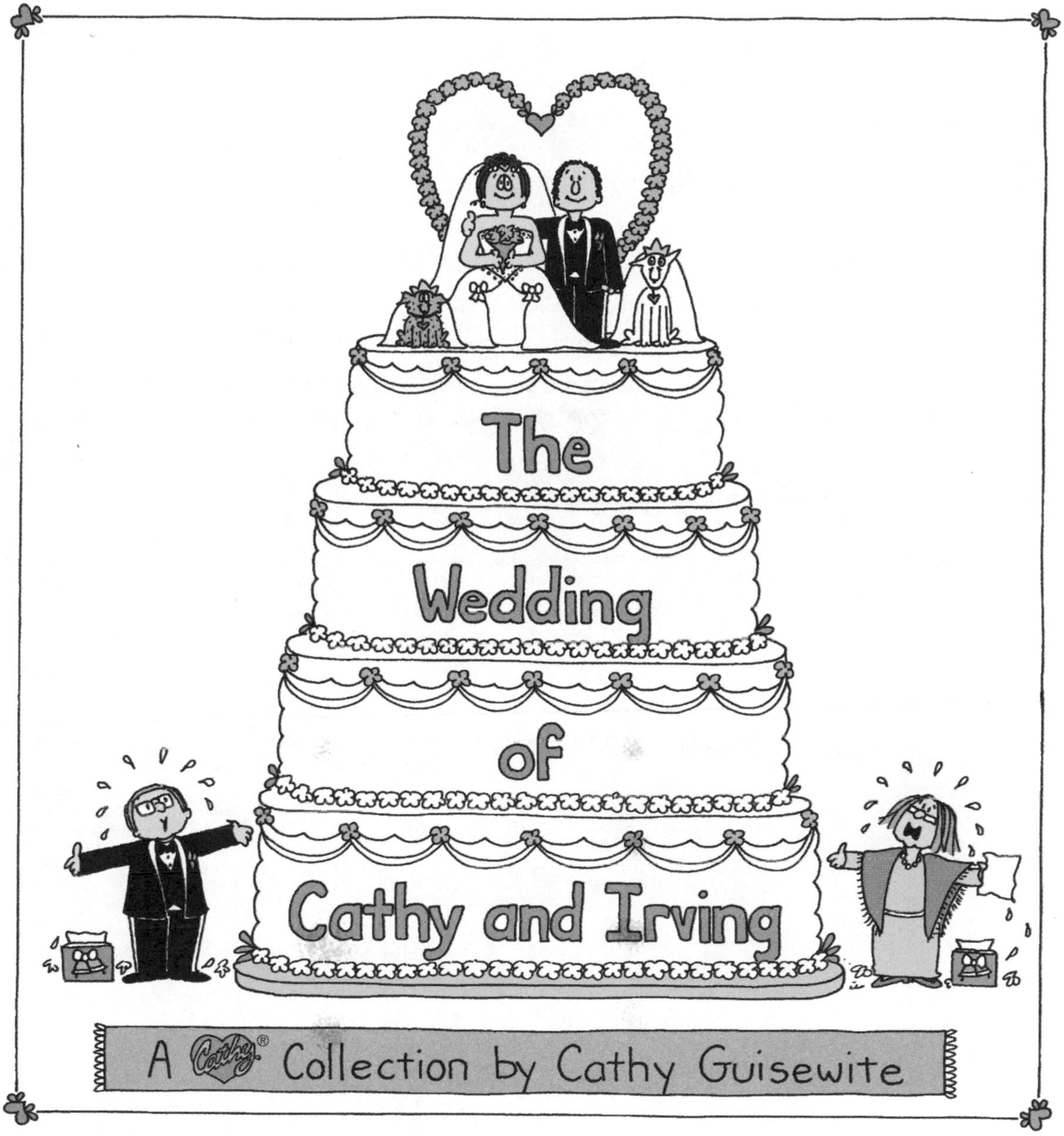
The Wedding of Cathy and Irving
A Cathy® Collection by Cathy Guisewite

Andrews McMeel Publishing

Kansas City

The Wedding of Cathy and Irving copyright © 2005 by Cathy Guisewite. All rights reserved. Printed in the United States of America. No part of this book may be used or reproduced in any manner whatsoever without written permission except in the case of reprints in the context of reviews. For permission information, write Andrews McMeel Publishing, an Andrews McMeel Universal company, 4520 Main Street, Kansas City, Missouri 64111.

05 06 07 08 09 WLS 10 9 8 7 6 5 4 3 2 1

ISBN-13: 978-0-7407-2668-2

ISBN-10: 0-7407-2668-4

Library of Congress Control Number: 2004115396

www.ucomics.com

Contents

Introduction

They dated for 27 years, two months, three weeks, and one day.
She was devoted, he was a pig.
She became enlightened, he remained oblivious.
She aspired to "goddess," he clung to "king."
She walked, he wooed her back.
She came back, he ran away.
She studied books, tapes, and astrological charts to understand him.
He watched sports.
She went to workshops, retreats, psychics, seminars, and shrinks.
He took up golf.

And yet . . .
He kept sliding back into her life, each time a little bit changed.
He gained weight, lost hair, changed careers, suffered midlife sports injuries
and severe sprains to all major ego groups.
He got open, vulnerable, and available. She got disgusted, indignant, and left.

He had his heart broken by a woman named Lydia.
She almost married a man named Alex.
They each found true love at the animal shelter.

They survived the most divisive years in history between men and women.
They weathered the "Me" decade, the "We" decade, the information age, the digital revolution,
the communication explosion, the militancy of the '70s, the greed
of the '80s, the regrouping of the '90s, the humility of the '00s, at least 9,865 diets,
and many, many, many total eclipses of the sense of humor.

Behind the scenes, they fell in love.
Between the strips, there remained something unsettled.
Until finally, after 27 years, two months, three weeks, and one day they were,
for the very first time, in the exact same place at the exact same time:
completely, utterly, with all their hearts,
ready to give up.

The Engagement

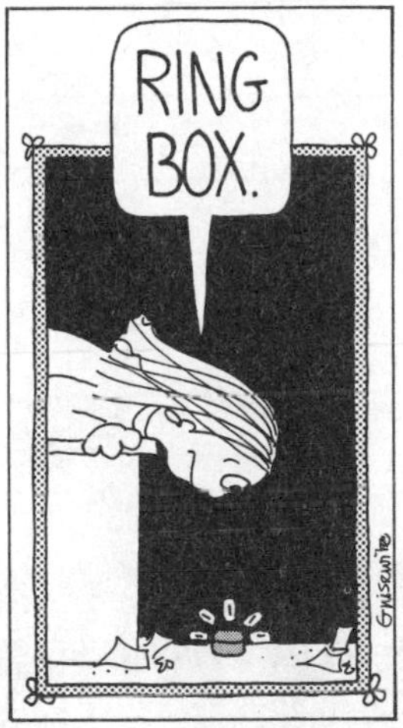
RING BOX.
Guisewite

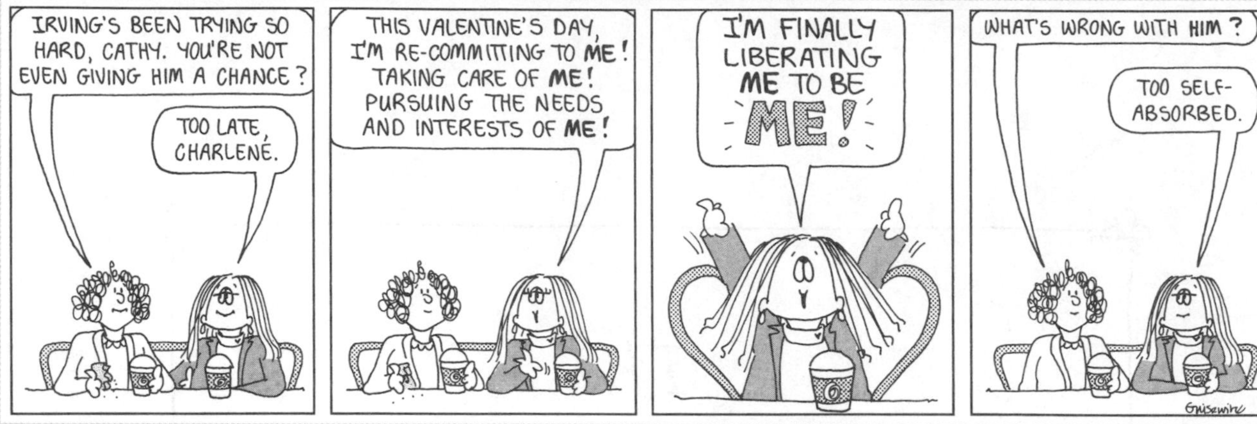
IRVING'S BEEN TRYING SO HARD, CATHY. YOU'RE NOT EVEN GIVING HIM A CHANCE?
TOO LATE, CHARLENE.
THIS VALENTINE'S DAY, I'M RE-COMMITTING TO **ME**! TAKING CARE OF **ME**! PURSUING THE NEEDS AND INTERESTS OF **ME**!
I'M FINALLY LIBERATING **ME** TO BE **ME**!
WHAT'S WRONG WITH **HIM**?
TOO SELF-ABSORBED.

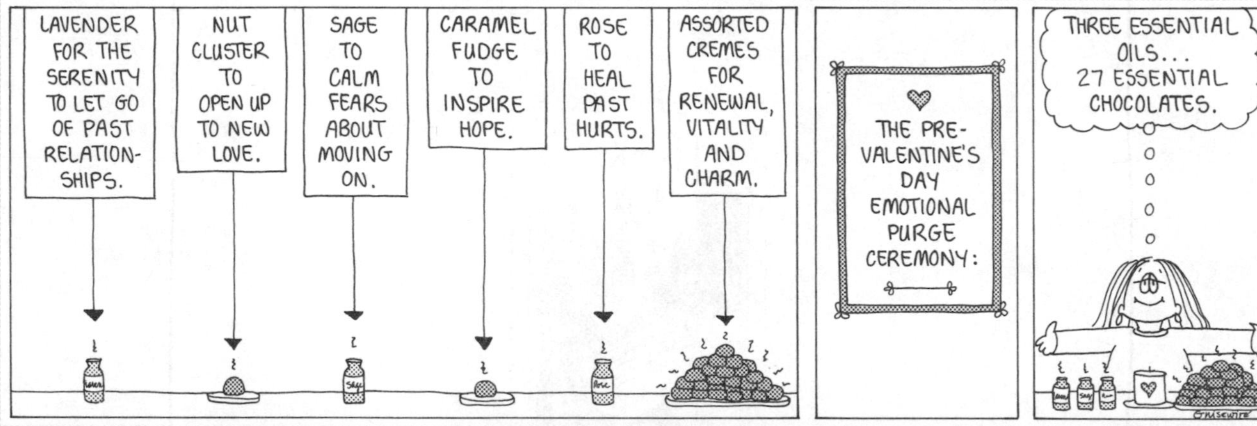
LAVENDER FOR THE SERENITY TO LET GO OF PAST RELATIONSHIPS.
NUT CLUSTER TO OPEN UP TO NEW LOVE.
SAGE TO CALM FEARS ABOUT MOVING ON.
CARAMEL FUDGE TO INSPIRE HOPE.
ROSE TO HEAL PAST HURTS.
ASSORTED CREMES FOR RENEWAL, VITALITY AND CHARM.
THE PRE-VALENTINE'S DAY EMOTIONAL PURGE CEREMONY:
THREE ESSENTIAL OILS... 27 ESSENTIAL CHOCOLATES.

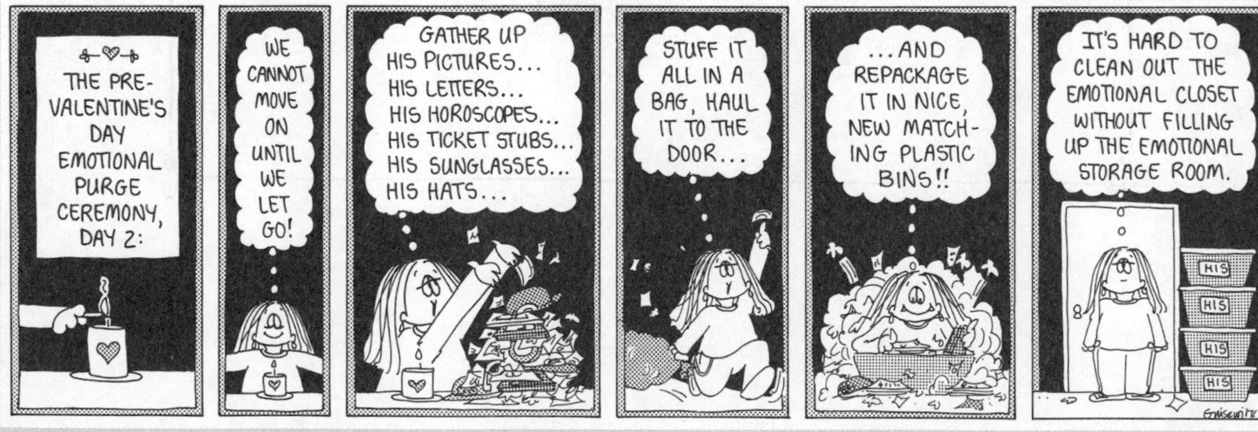
THE PRE-VALENTINE'S DAY EMOTIONAL PURGE CEREMONY, DAY 2:
WE CANNOT MOVE ON UNTIL WE LET GO!
GATHER UP HIS PICTURES... HIS LETTERS... HIS HOROSCOPES... HIS TICKET STUBS... HIS SUNGLASSES... HIS HATS...
STUFF IT ALL IN A BAG, HAUL IT TO THE DOOR...
...AND REPACKAGE IT IN NICE, NEW MATCHING PLASTIC BINS!!
IT'S HARD TO CLEAN OUT THE EMOTIONAL CLOSET WITHOUT FILLING UP THE EMOTIONAL STORAGE ROOM.
HIS
HIS
HIS
HIS

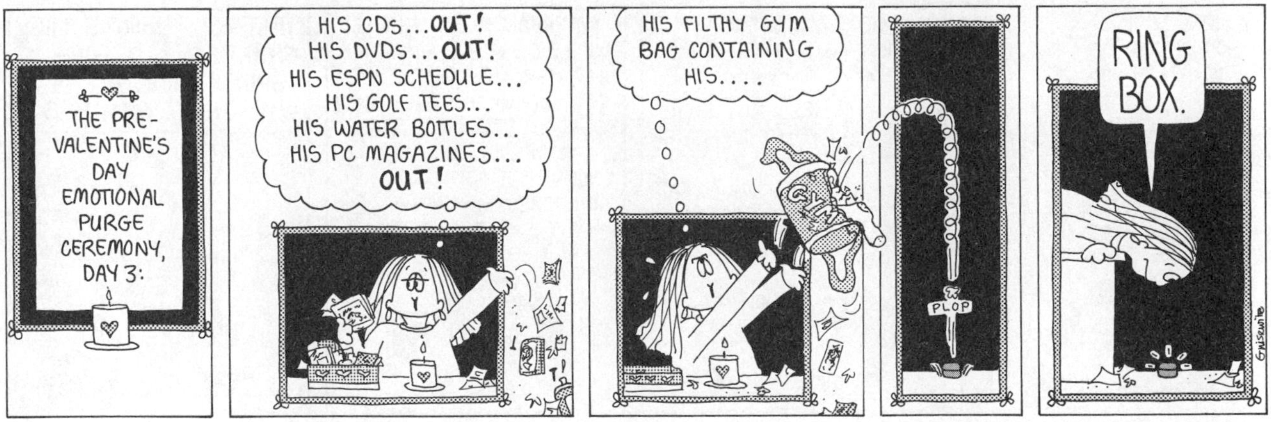
THE PRE-VALENTINE'S DAY EMOTIONAL PURGE CEREMONY, DAY 3:
HIS CDs... OUT! HIS DVDs... OUT! HIS ESPN SCHEDULE... HIS GOLF TEES... HIS WATER BOTTLES... HIS PC MAGAZINES... OUT!
HIS FILTHY GYM BAG CONTAINING HIS....
PLOP
RING BOX.

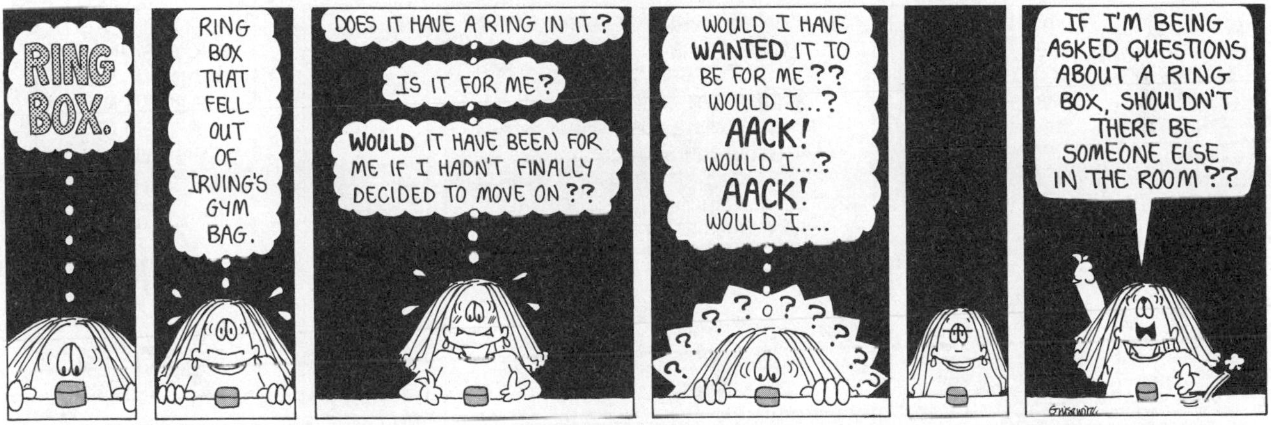
RING BOX.
RING BOX THAT FELL OUT OF IRVING'S GYM BAG.
DOES IT HAVE A RING IN IT?
IS IT FOR ME?
WOULD IT HAVE BEEN FOR ME IF I HADN'T FINALLY DECIDED TO MOVE ON??
WOULD I HAVE WANTED IT TO BE FOR ME?? WOULD I...? AACK! WOULD I...? AACK! WOULD I....
IF I'M BEING ASKED QUESTIONS ABOUT A RING BOX, SHOULDN'T THERE BE SOMEONE ELSE IN THE ROOM??

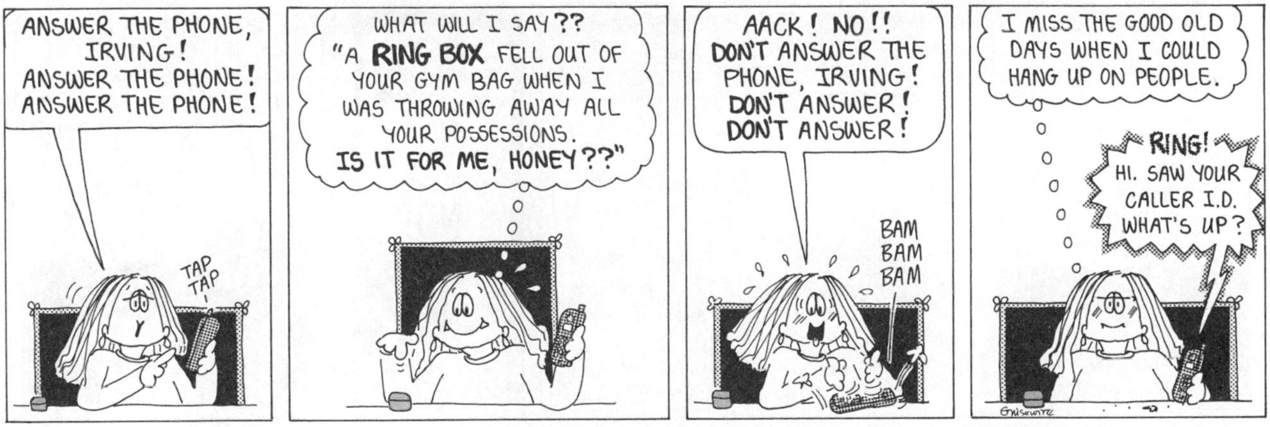
ANSWER THE PHONE, IRVING! ANSWER THE PHONE! ANSWER THE PHONE!
TAP TAP
WHAT WILL I SAY?? "A RING BOX FELL OUT OF YOUR GYM BAG WHEN I WAS THROWING AWAY ALL YOUR POSSESSIONS. IS IT FOR ME, HONEY??"
AACK! NO!! DON'T ANSWER THE PHONE, IRVING! DON'T ANSWER! DON'T ANSWER!
BAM BAM BAM
I MISS THE GOOD OLD DAYS WHEN I COULD HANG UP ON PEOPLE.
RING! HI. SAW YOUR CALLER I.D. WHAT'S UP?

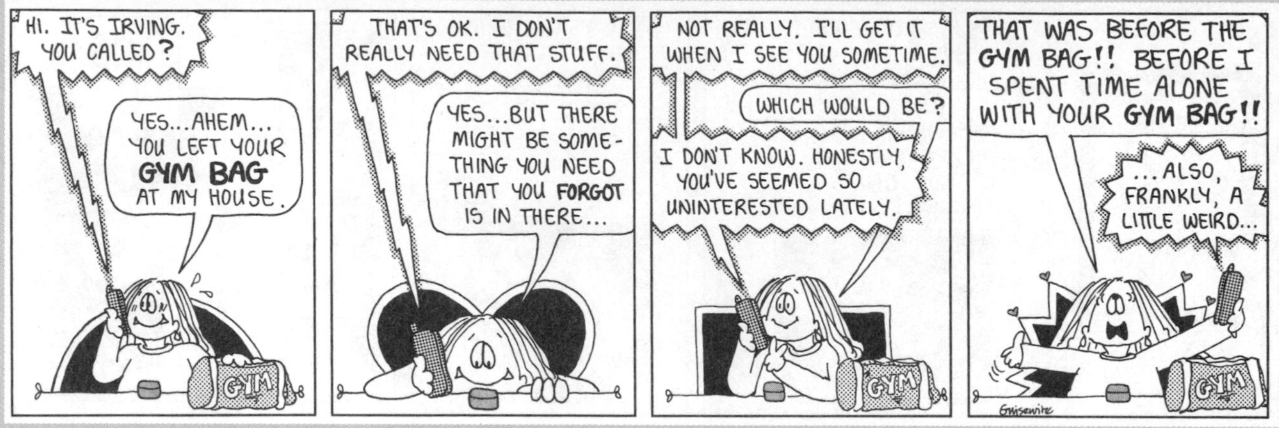
HI. IT'S IRVING. YOU CALLED?
YES...AHEM... YOU LEFT YOUR GYM BAG AT MY HOUSE.
GYM
THAT'S OK. I DON'T REALLY NEED THAT STUFF.
YES...BUT THERE MIGHT BE SOMETHING YOU NEED THAT YOU FORGOT IS IN THERE...
NOT REALLY. I'LL GET IT WHEN I SEE YOU SOMETIME.
WHICH WOULD BE?
I DON'T KNOW. HONESTLY, YOU'VE SEEMED SO UNINTERESTED LATELY.
GYM
THAT WAS BEFORE THE GYM BAG!! BEFORE I SPENT TIME ALONE WITH YOUR GYM BAG!!
...ALSO, FRANKLY, A LITTLE WEIRD...
GYM
Guisewite

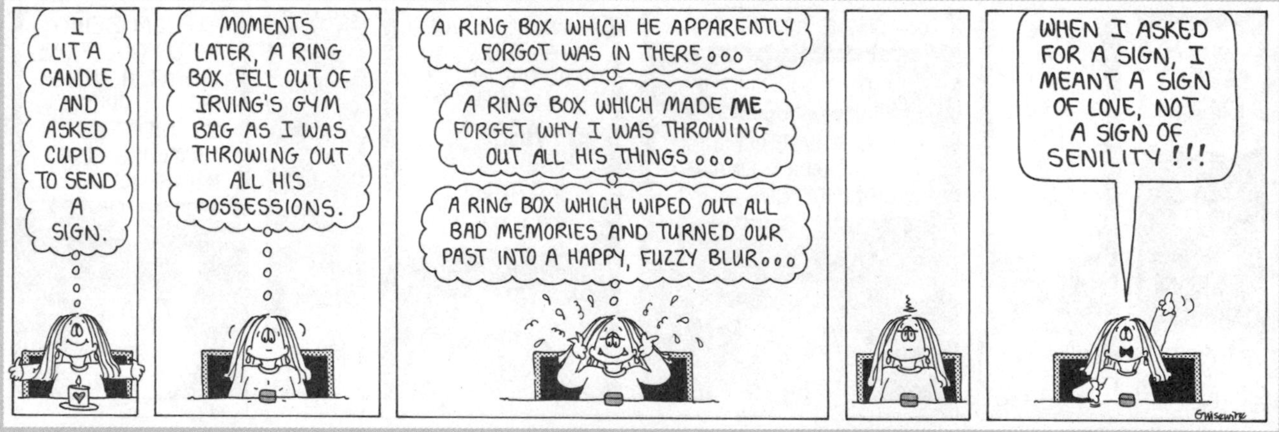
I LIT A CANDLE AND ASKED CUPID TO SEND A SIGN.
MOMENTS LATER, A RING BOX FELL OUT OF IRVING'S GYM BAG AS I WAS THROWING OUT ALL HIS POSSESSIONS.
A RING BOX WHICH HE APPARENTLY FORGOT WAS IN THERE...
A RING BOX WHICH MADE ME FORGET WHY I WAS THROWING OUT ALL HIS THINGS...
A RING BOX WHICH WIPED OUT ALL BAD MEMORIES AND TURNED OUR PAST INTO A HAPPY, FUZZY BLUR...
WHEN I ASKED FOR A SIGN, I MEANT A SIGN OF LOVE, NOT A SIGN OF SENILITY!!!
Guisewite

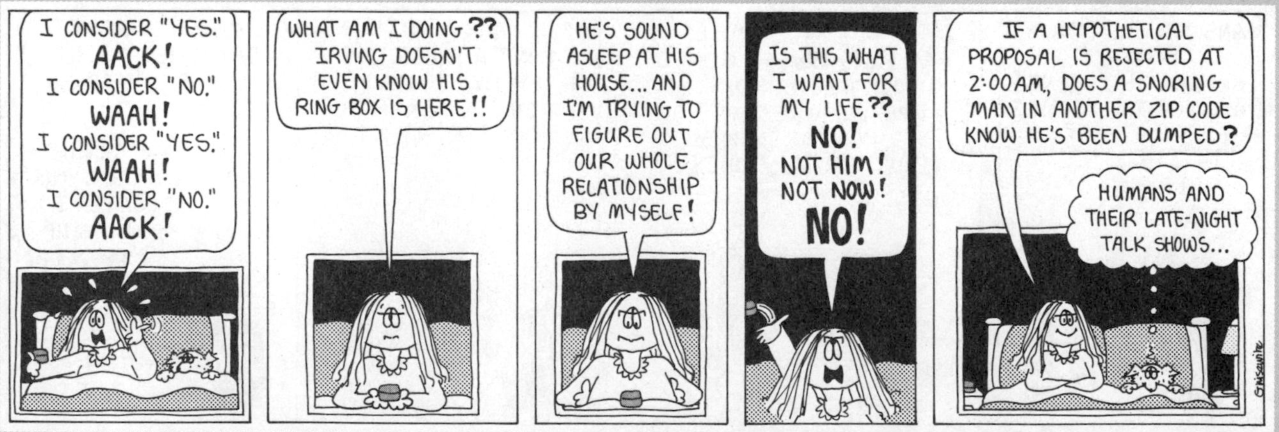
I CONSIDER "YES." AACK! I CONSIDER "NO." WAAH! I CONSIDER "YES." WAAH! I CONSIDER "NO." AACK!
WHAT AM I DOING?? IRVING DOESN'T EVEN KNOW HIS RING BOX IS HERE!!
HE'S SOUND ASLEEP AT HIS HOUSE...AND I'M TRYING TO FIGURE OUT OUR WHOLE RELATIONSHIP BY MYSELF!
IS THIS WHAT I WANT FOR MY LIFE?? NO! NOT HIM! NOT NOW! NO!
IF A HYPOTHETICAL PROPOSAL IS REJECTED AT 2:00 A.M., DOES A SNORING MAN IN ANOTHER ZIP CODE KNOW HE'S BEEN DUMPED?
HUMANS AND THEIR LATE-NIGHT TALK SHOWS...
Guisewite

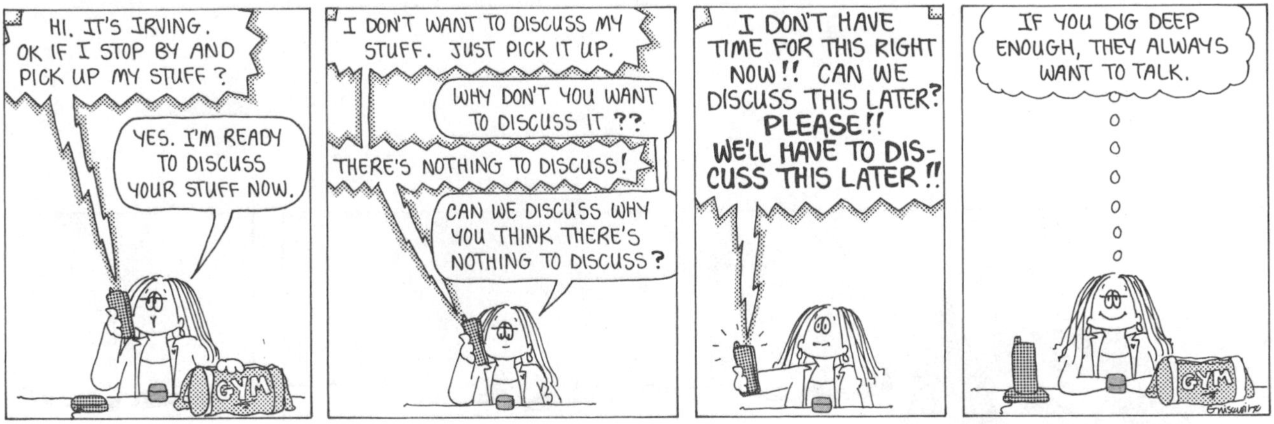
HI. IT'S IRVING. OK IF I STOP BY AND PICK UP MY STUFF ?
YES. I'M READY TO DISCUSS YOUR STUFF NOW.
I DON'T WANT TO DISCUSS MY STUFF. JUST PICK IT UP.
WHY DON'T YOU WANT TO DISCUSS IT ??
THERE'S NOTHING TO DISCUSS!
CAN WE DISCUSS WHY YOU THINK THERE'S NOTHING TO DISCUSS?
I DON'T HAVE TIME FOR THIS RIGHT NOW!! CAN WE DISCUSS THIS LATER? PLEASE!! WE'LL HAVE TO DISCUSS THIS LATER!!
IF YOU DIG DEEP ENOUGH, THEY ALWAYS WANT TO TALK.
GYM

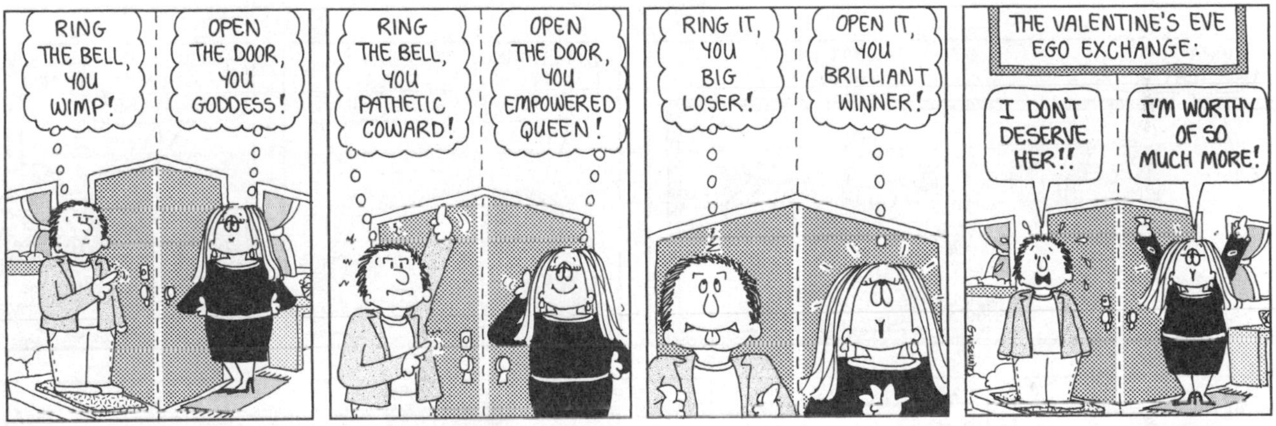
RING THE BELL, YOU WIMP!
OPEN THE DOOR, YOU GODDESS!
RING THE BELL, YOU PATHETIC COWARD!
OPEN THE DOOR, YOU EMPOWERED QUEEN!
RING IT, YOU BIG LOSER!
OPEN IT, YOU BRILLIANT WINNER!
THE VALENTINE'S EVE EGO EXCHANGE:
I DON'T DESERVE HER!!
I'M WORTHY OF SO MUCH MORE!

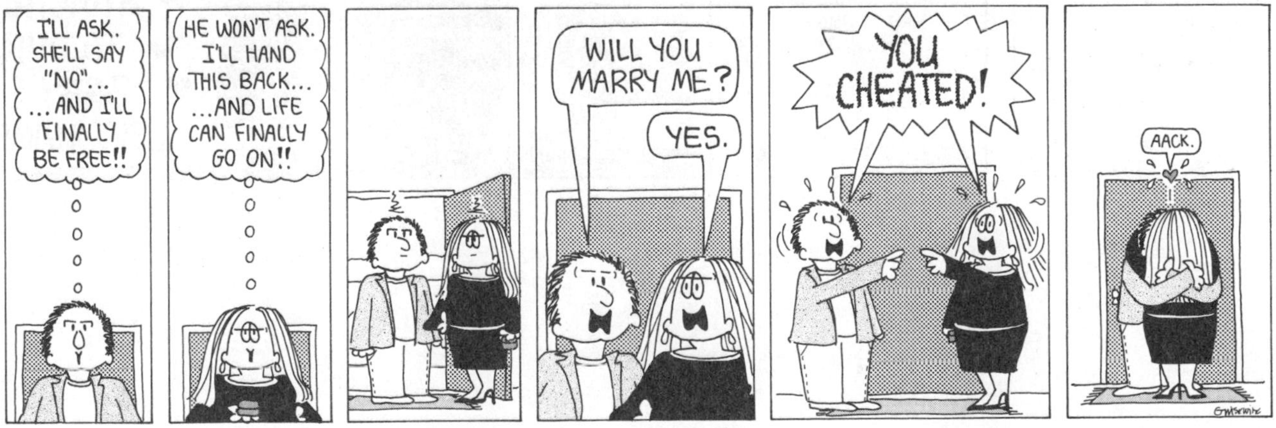
I'LL ASK. SHE'LL SAY "NO"... ...AND I'LL FINALLY BE FREE!!
HE WON'T ASK. I'LL HAND THIS BACK... ...AND LIFE CAN FINALLY GO ON!!
WILL YOU MARRY ME?
YES.
YOU CHEATED!
AACK.

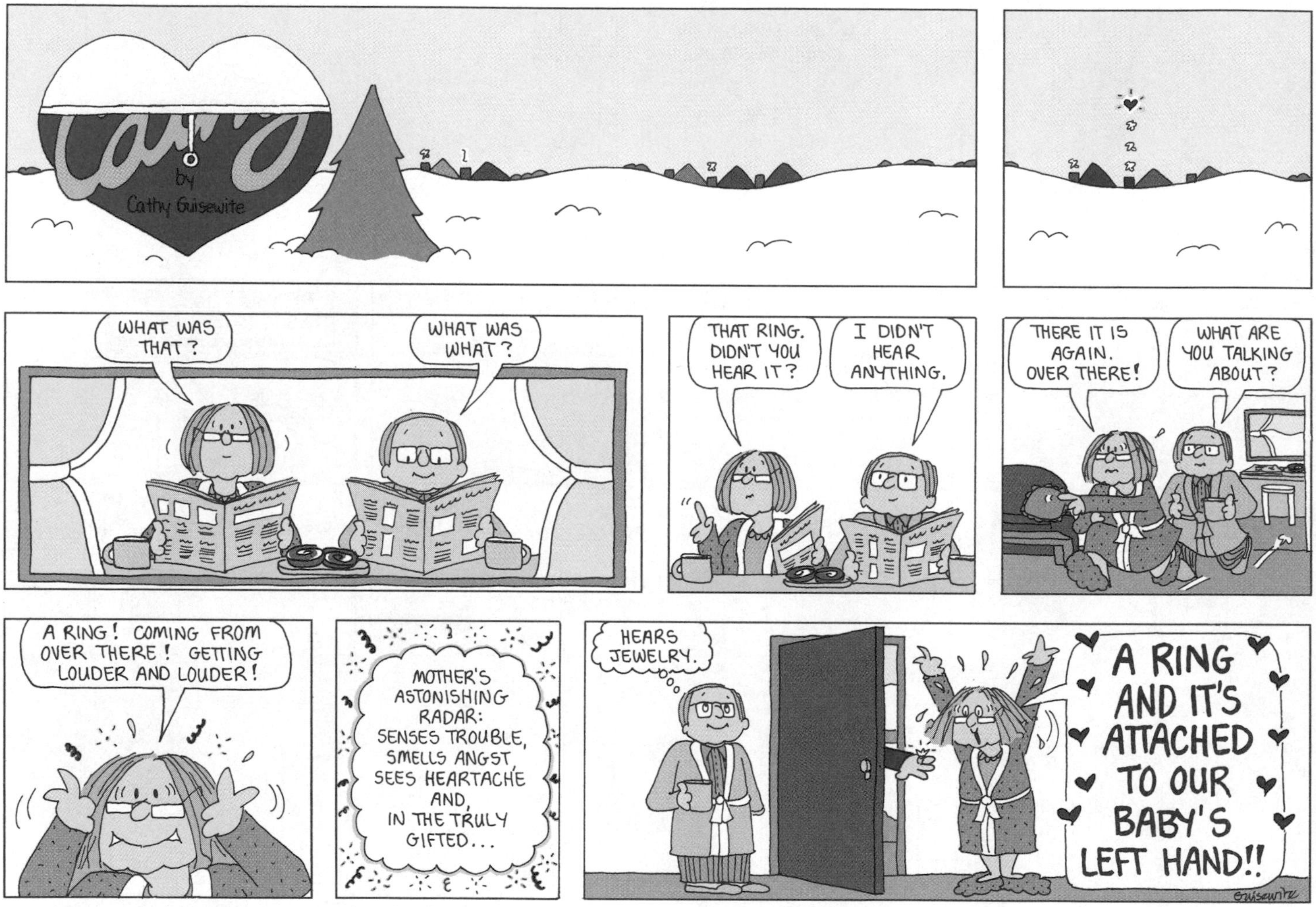
by
Cathy Guisewite
WHAT WAS THAT?
WHAT WAS WHAT?
THAT RING. DIDN'T YOU HEAR IT?
I DIDN'T HEAR ANYTHING.
THERE IT IS AGAIN. OVER THERE!
WHAT ARE YOU TALKING ABOUT?
A RING! COMING FROM OVER THERE! GETTING LOUDER AND LOUDER!
MOTHER'S ASTONISHING RADAR: SENSES TROUBLE, SMELLS ANGST, SEES HEARTACHE AND, IN THE TRULY GIFTED...
HEARS JEWELRY.
A RING AND IT'S ATTACHED TO OUR BABY'S LEFT HAND!!
Guisewite

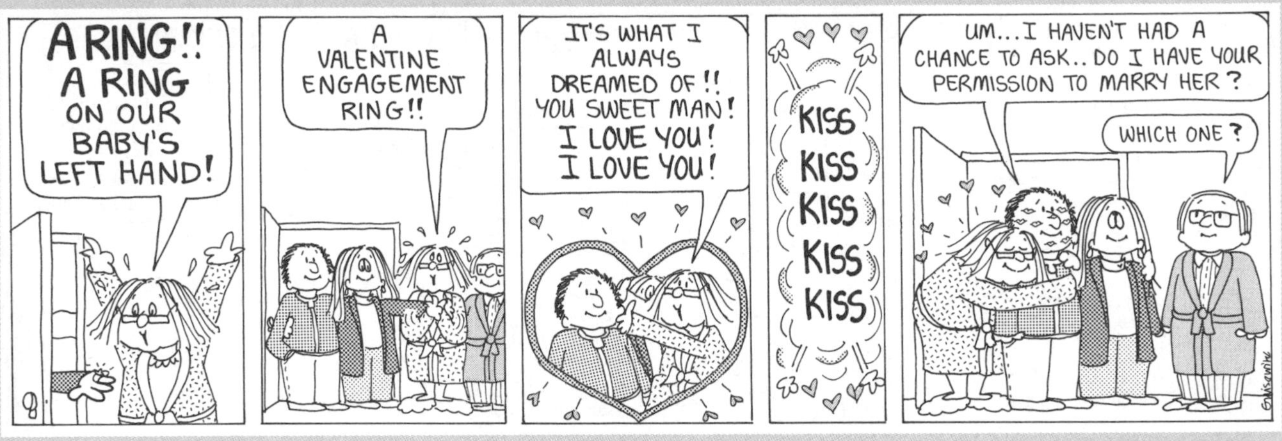

A RING!! A RING ON OUR BABY'S LEFT HAND!
A VALENTINE ENGAGEMENT RING!!
IT'S WHAT I ALWAYS DREAMED OF!! YOU SWEET MAN! I LOVE YOU! I LOVE YOU!
KISS KISS KISS KISS KISS
UM... I HAVEN'T HAD A CHANCE TO ASK.. DO I HAVE YOUR PERMISSION TO MARRY HER?
WHICH ONE?

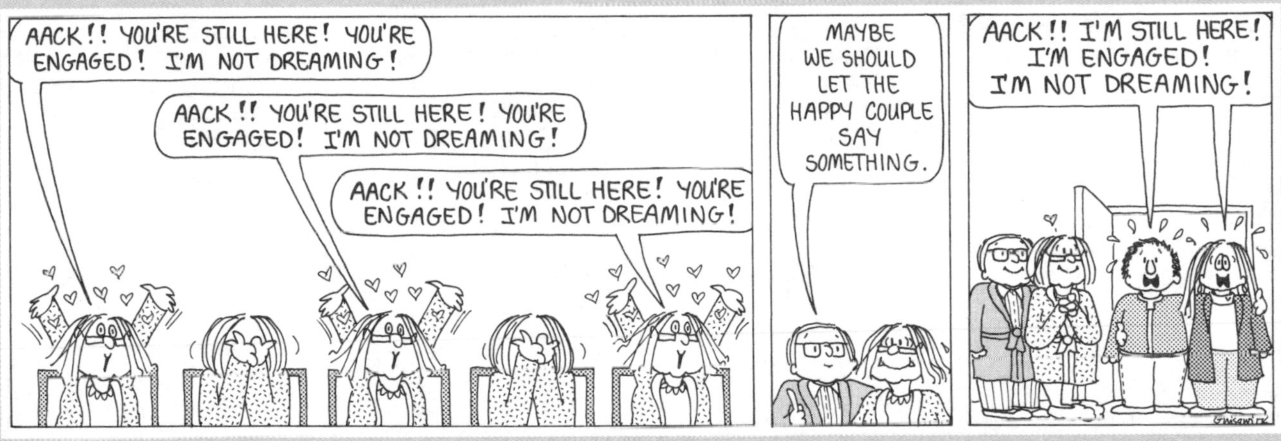

AACK!! YOU'RE STILL HERE! YOU'RE ENGAGED! I'M NOT DREAMING!
AACK!! YOU'RE STILL HERE! YOU'RE ENGAGED! I'M NOT DREAMING!
AACK!! YOU'RE STILL HERE! YOU'RE ENGAGED! I'M NOT DREAMING!
MAYBE WE SHOULD LET THE HAPPY COUPLE SAY SOMETHING.
AACK!! I'M STILL HERE! I'M ENGAGED! I'M NOT DREAMING!

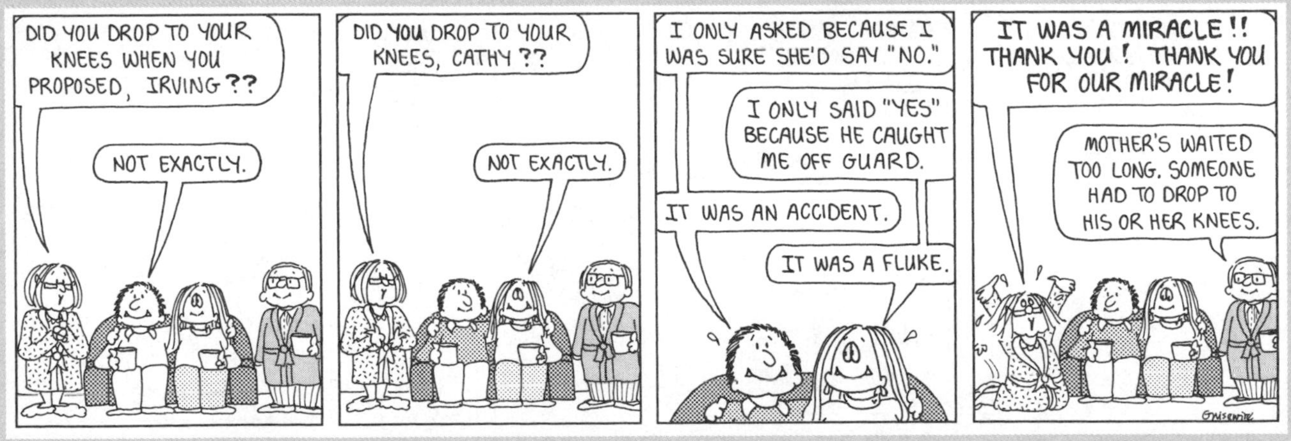

DID YOU DROP TO YOUR KNEES WHEN YOU PROPOSED, IRVING??
NOT EXACTLY.
DID YOU DROP TO YOUR KNEES, CATHY??
NOT EXACTLY.
I ONLY ASKED BECAUSE I WAS SURE SHE'D SAY "NO."
I ONLY SAID "YES" BECAUSE HE CAUGHT ME OFF GUARD.
IT WAS AN ACCIDENT.
IT WAS A FLUKE.
IT WAS A MIRACLE!! THANK YOU! THANK YOU FOR OUR MIRACLE!
MOTHER'S WAITED TOO LONG. SOMEONE HAD TO DROP TO HIS OR HER KNEES.

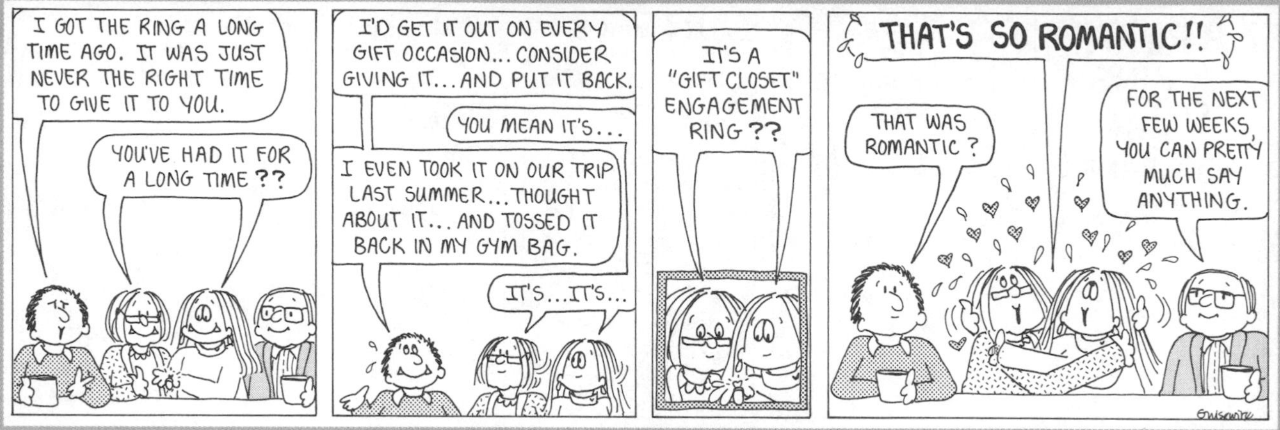
I GOT THE RING A LONG TIME AGO. IT WAS JUST NEVER THE RIGHT TIME TO GIVE IT TO YOU.
YOU'VE HAD IT FOR A LONG TIME??
I'D GET IT OUT ON EVERY GIFT OCCASION... CONSIDER GIVING IT... AND PUT IT BACK.
YOU MEAN IT'S...
I EVEN TOOK IT ON OUR TRIP LAST SUMMER... THOUGHT ABOUT IT... AND TOSSED IT BACK IN MY GYM BAG.
IT'S...IT'S...
IT'S A "GIFT CLOSET" ENGAGEMENT RING??
THAT'S SO ROMANTIC!!
THAT WAS ROMANTIC?
FOR THE NEXT FEW WEEKS, YOU CAN PRETTY MUCH SAY ANYTHING.

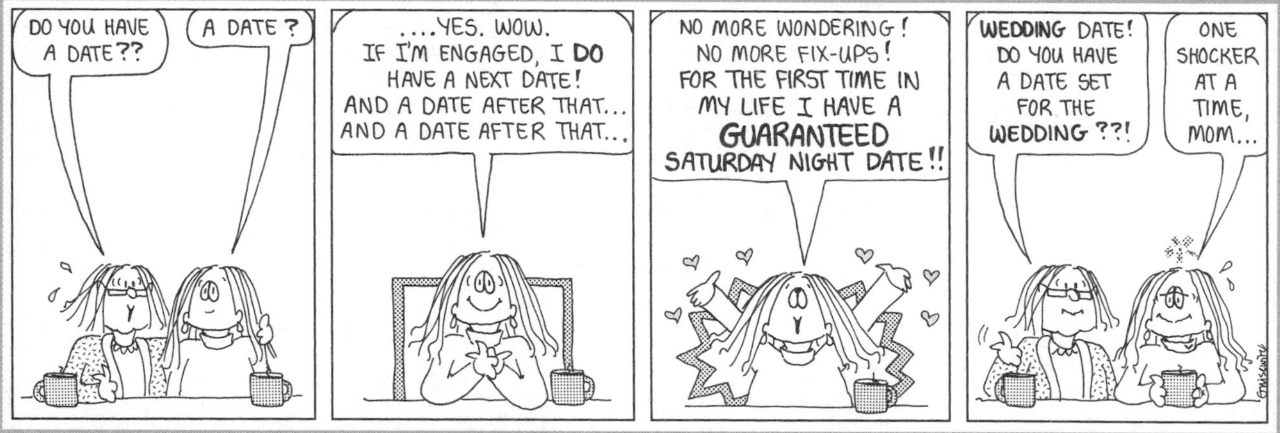
DO YOU HAVE A DATE??
A DATE?
....YES. WOW. IF I'M ENGAGED, I DO HAVE A NEXT DATE! AND A DATE AFTER THAT... AND A DATE AFTER THAT...
NO MORE WONDERING! NO MORE FIX-UPS! FOR THE FIRST TIME IN MY LIFE I HAVE A GUARANTEED SATURDAY NIGHT DATE!!
WEDDING DATE! DO YOU HAVE A DATE SET FOR THE WEDDING??!
ONE SHOCKER AT A TIME, MOM...

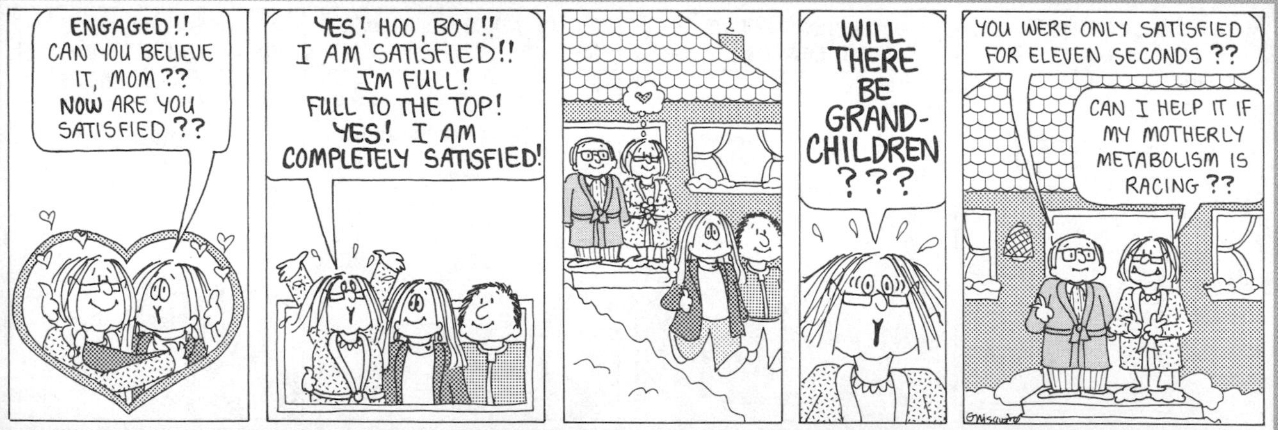
ENGAGED!! CAN YOU BELIEVE IT, MOM?? NOW ARE YOU SATISFIED??
YES! HOO, BOY!! I AM SATISFIED!! I'M FULL! FULL TO THE TOP! YES! I AM COMPLETELY SATISFIED!
WILL THERE BE GRAND-CHILDREN???
YOU WERE ONLY SATISFIED FOR ELEVEN SECONDS??
CAN I HELP IT IF MY MOTHERLY METABOLISM IS RACING??

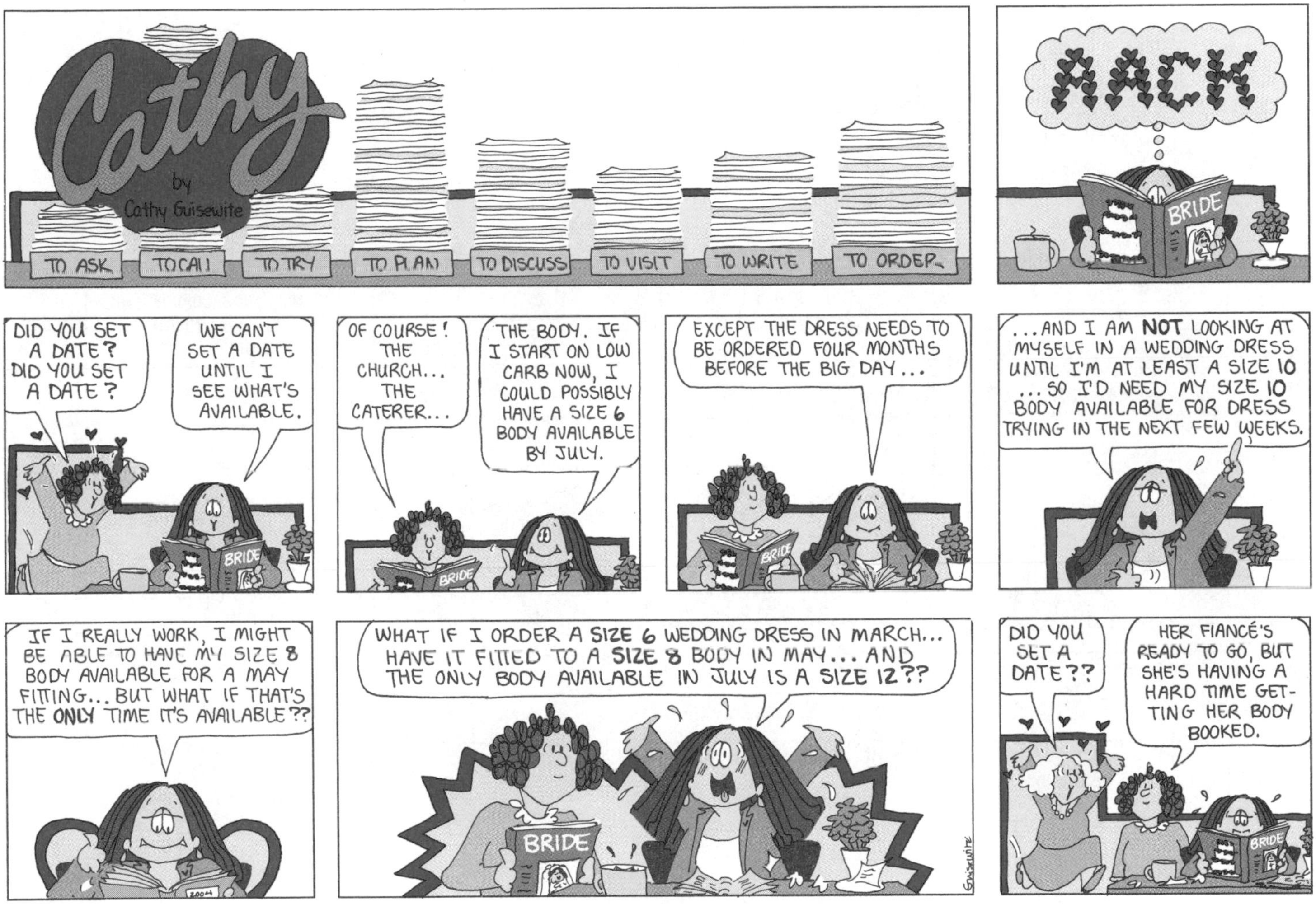

Cathy
by
Cathy Guisewite
TO ASK
TO CALL
TO TRY
TO PLAN
TO DISCUSS
TO VISIT
TO WRITE
TO ORDER
AACK
BRIDE
DID YOU SET A DATE? DID YOU SET A DATE?
WE CAN'T SET A DATE UNTIL I SEE WHAT'S AVAILABLE.
OF COURSE! THE CHURCH... THE CATERER...
THE BODY. IF I START ON LOW CARB NOW, I COULD POSSIBLY HAVE A SIZE 6 BODY AVAILABLE BY JULY.
EXCEPT THE DRESS NEEDS TO BE ORDERED FOUR MONTHS BEFORE THE BIG DAY...
...AND I AM NOT LOOKING AT MYSELF IN A WEDDING DRESS UNTIL I'M AT LEAST A SIZE 10 ...SO I'D NEED MY SIZE 10 BODY AVAILABLE FOR DRESS TRYING IN THE NEXT FEW WEEKS.
IF I REALLY WORK, I MIGHT BE ABLE TO HAVE MY SIZE 8 BODY AVAILABLE FOR A MAY FITTING... BUT WHAT IF THAT'S THE ONLY TIME IT'S AVAILABLE??
WHAT IF I ORDER A SIZE 6 WEDDING DRESS IN MARCH... HAVE IT FITTED TO A SIZE 8 BODY IN MAY... AND THE ONLY BODY AVAILABLE IN JULY IS A SIZE 12??
BRIDE
DID YOU SET A DATE??
HER FIANCÉ'S READY TO GO, BUT SHE'S HAVING A HARD TIME GETTING HER BODY BOOKED.

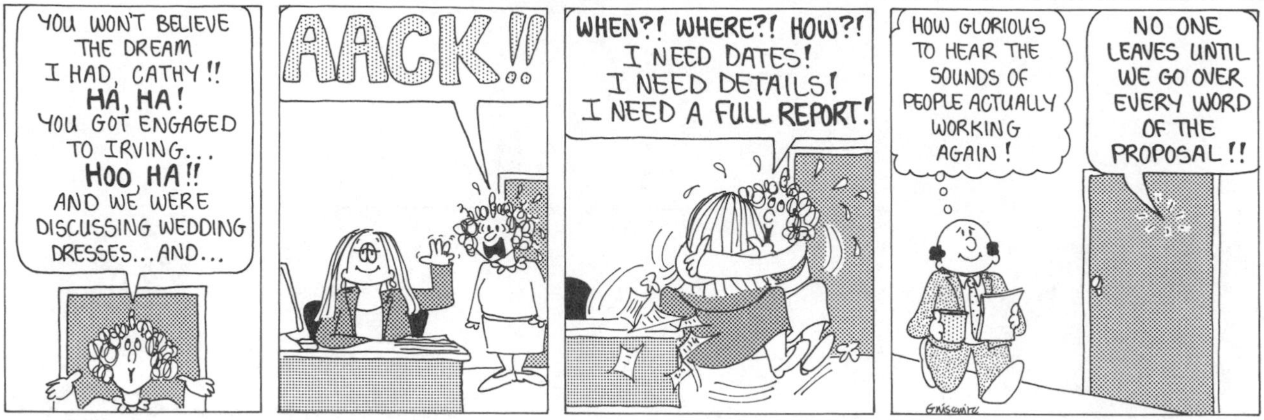
YOU WON'T BELIEVE THE DREAM I HAD, CATHY!! HA, HA! YOU GOT ENGAGED TO IRVING... HOO, HA!! AND WE WERE DISCUSSING WEDDING DRESSES...AND...
AACK!!
WHEN?! WHERE?! HOW?! I NEED DATES! I NEED DETAILS! I NEED A FULL REPORT!
HOW GLORIOUS TO HEAR THE SOUNDS OF PEOPLE ACTUALLY WORKING AGAIN!
NO ONE LEAVES UNTIL WE GO OVER EVERY WORD OF THE PROPOSAL!!

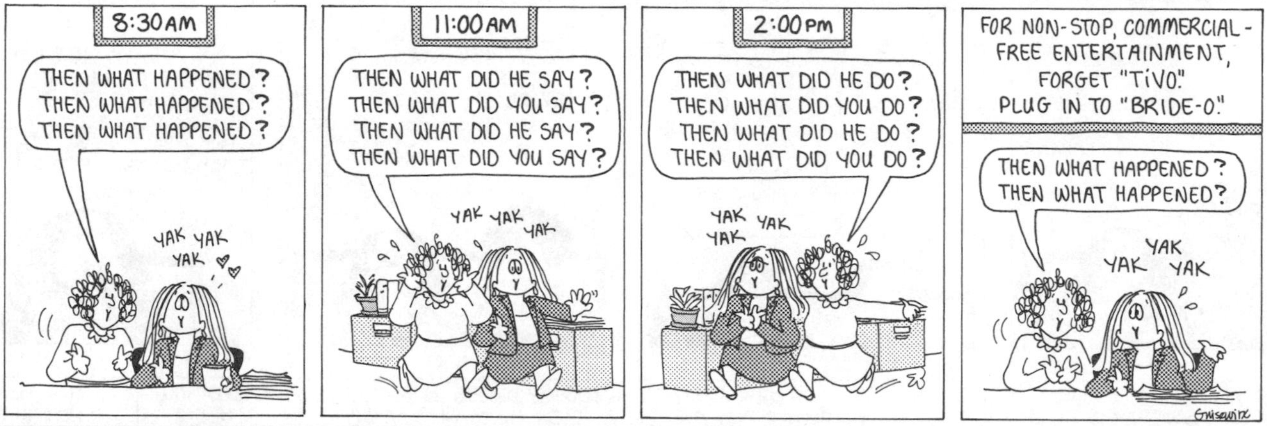
8:30 AM
THEN WHAT HAPPENED? THEN WHAT HAPPENED? THEN WHAT HAPPENED?
YAK YAK YAK
11:00 AM
THEN WHAT DID HE SAY? THEN WHAT DID YOU SAY? THEN WHAT DID HE SAY? THEN WHAT DID YOU SAY?
YAK YAK YAK
2:00 PM
THEN WHAT DID HE DO? THEN WHAT DID YOU DO? THEN WHAT DID HE DO? THEN WHAT DID YOU DO?
YAK YAK YAK
FOR NON-STOP, COMMERCIAL-FREE ENTERTAINMENT, FORGET "TiVO." PLUG IN TO "BRIDE-O."
THEN WHAT HAPPENED? THEN WHAT HAPPENED?
YAK YAK YAK

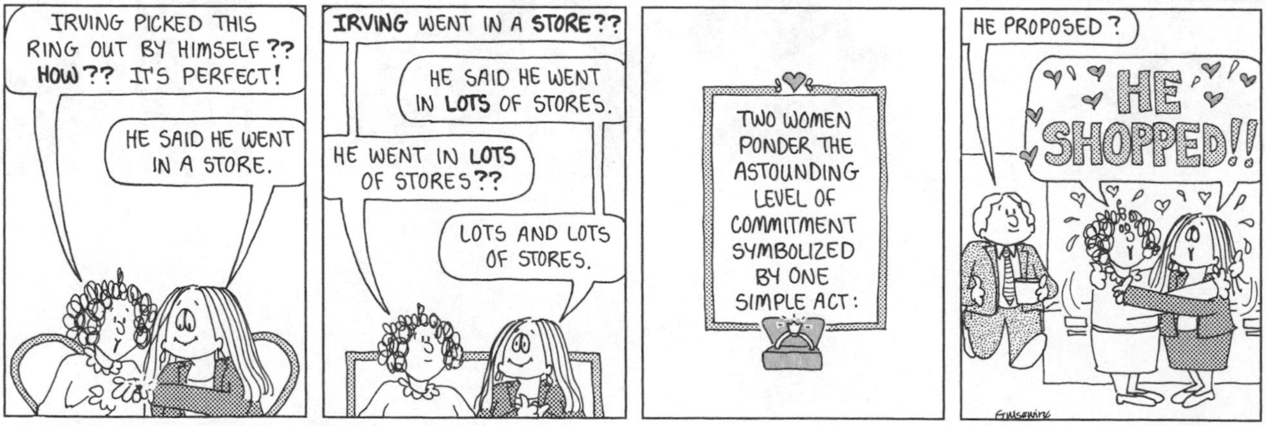
IRVING PICKED THIS RING OUT BY HIMSELF?? HOW?? IT'S PERFECT!
HE SAID HE WENT IN A STORE.
IRVING WENT IN A STORE??
HE SAID HE WENT IN LOTS OF STORES.
HE WENT IN LOTS OF STORES??
LOTS AND LOTS OF STORES.
TWO WOMEN PONDER THE ASTOUNDING LEVEL OF COMMITMENT SYMBOLIZED BY ONE SIMPLE ACT:
HE PROPOSED?
HE SHOPPED!!

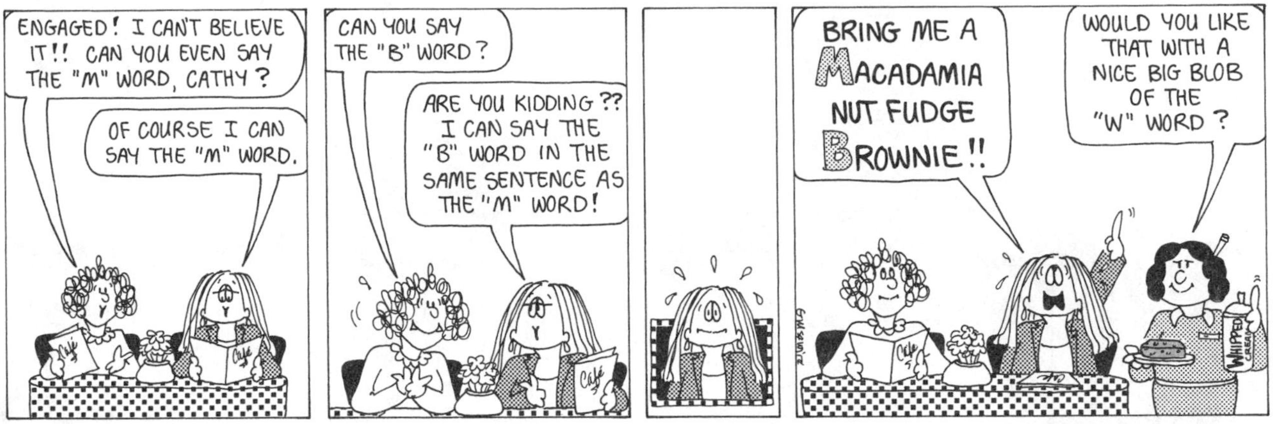
ENGAGED! I CAN'T BELIEVE IT!! CAN YOU EVEN SAY THE "M" WORD, CATHY?
OF COURSE I CAN SAY THE "M" WORD.
CAN YOU SAY THE "B" WORD?
ARE YOU KIDDING?? I CAN SAY THE "B" WORD IN THE SAME SENTENCE AS THE "M" WORD!
BRING ME A MACADAMIA NUT FUDGE BROWNIE!!
WOULD YOU LIKE THAT WITH A NICE BIG BLOB OF THE "W" WORD?

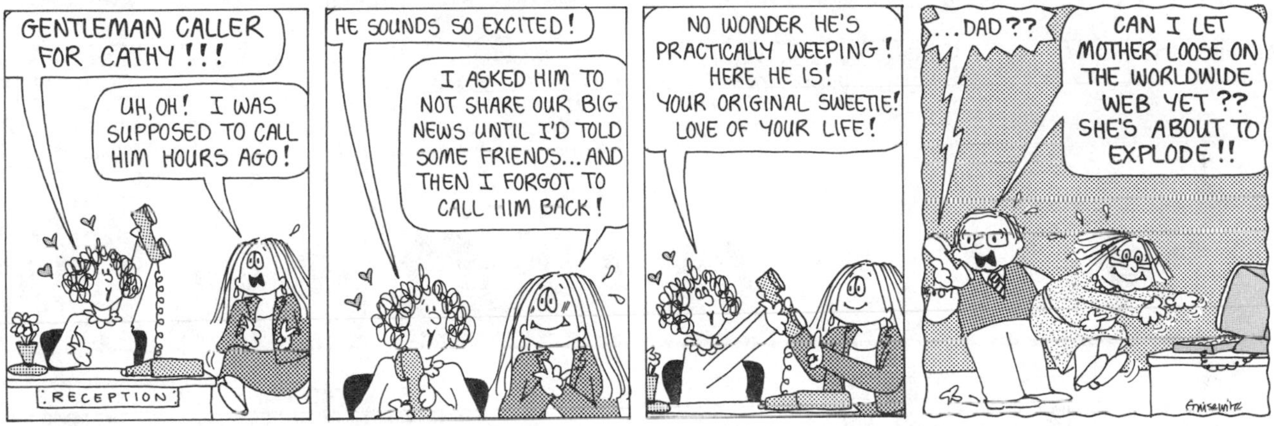
GENTLEMAN CALLER FOR CATHY!!!
UH, OH! I WAS SUPPOSED TO CALL HIM HOURS AGO!
RECEPTION
HE SOUNDS SO EXCITED!
I ASKED HIM TO NOT SHARE OUR BIG NEWS UNTIL I'D TOLD SOME FRIENDS... AND THEN I FORGOT TO CALL HIM BACK!
NO WONDER HE'S PRACTICALLY WEEPING! HERE HE IS! YOUR ORIGINAL SWEETIE! LOVE OF YOUR LIFE!
...DAD??
CAN I LET MOTHER LOOSE ON THE WORLDWIDE WEB YET?? SHE'S ABOUT TO EXPLODE!!

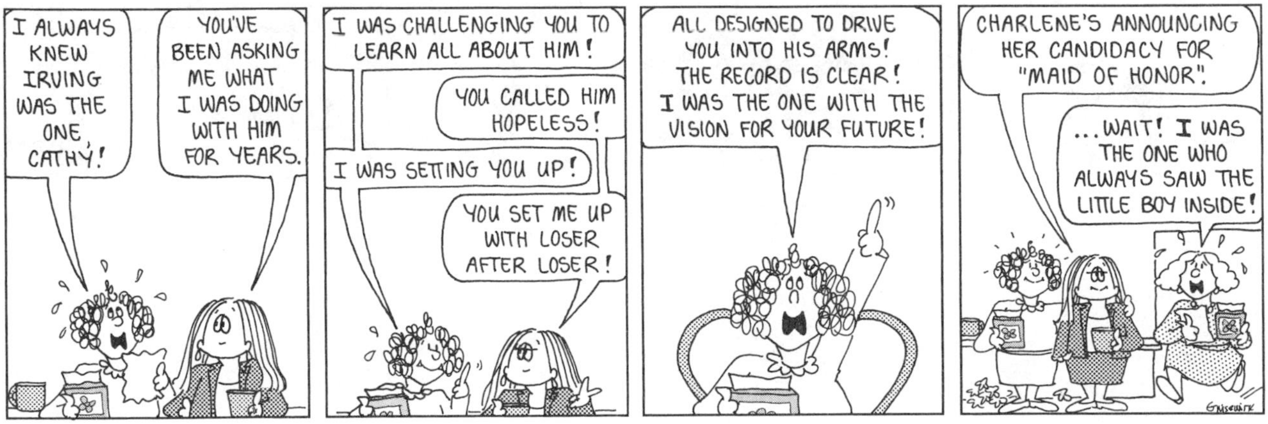
I ALWAYS KNEW IRVING WAS THE ONE, CATHY!
YOU'VE BEEN ASKING ME WHAT I WAS DOING WITH HIM FOR YEARS.
I WAS CHALLENGING YOU TO LEARN ALL ABOUT HIM!
YOU CALLED HIM HOPELESS!
I WAS SETTING YOU UP!
YOU SET ME UP WITH LOSER AFTER LOSER!
ALL DESIGNED TO DRIVE YOU INTO HIS ARMS! THE RECORD IS CLEAR! I WAS THE ONE WITH THE VISION FOR YOUR FUTURE!
CHARLENE'S ANNOUNCING HER CANDIDACY FOR "MAID OF HONOR".
...WAIT! I WAS THE ONE WHO ALWAYS SAW THE LITTLE BOY INSIDE!

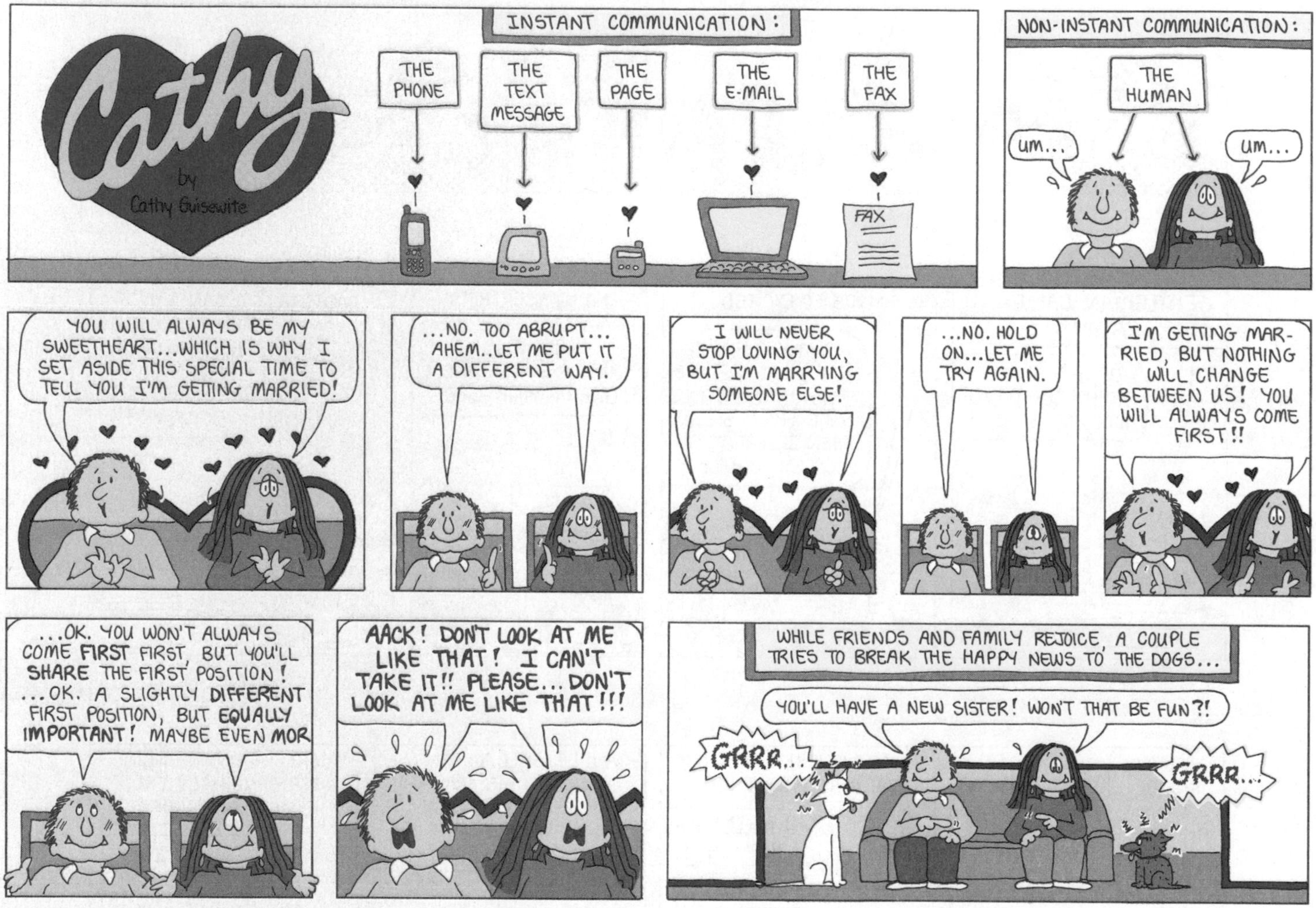

Cathy
by
Cathy Guisewite
INSTANT COMMUNICATION:
THE PHONE
THE TEXT MESSAGE
THE PAGE
THE E-MAIL
THE FAX
FAX
NON-INSTANT COMMUNICATION:
THE HUMAN
um...
um...
YOU WILL ALWAYS BE MY SWEETHEART...WHICH IS WHY I SET ASIDE THIS SPECIAL TIME TO TELL YOU I'M GETTING MARRIED!
...NO. TOO ABRUPT... AHEM..LET ME PUT IT A DIFFERENT WAY.
I WILL NEVER STOP LOVING YOU, BUT I'M MARRYING SOMEONE ELSE!
...NO. HOLD ON...LET ME TRY AGAIN.
I'M GETTING MARRIED, BUT NOTHING WILL CHANGE BETWEEN US! YOU WILL ALWAYS COME FIRST!!
...OK. YOU WON'T ALWAYS COME FIRST FIRST, BUT YOU'LL SHARE THE FIRST POSITION! ...OK. A SLIGHTLY DIFFERENT FIRST POSITION, BUT EQUALLY IMPORTANT! MAYBE EVEN MOR
AACK! DON'T LOOK AT ME LIKE THAT! I CAN'T TAKE IT!! PLEASE... DON'T LOOK AT ME LIKE THAT!!!
WHILE FRIENDS AND FAMILY REJOICE, A COUPLE TRIES TO BREAK THE HAPPY NEWS TO THE DOGS...
YOU'LL HAVE A NEW SISTER! WON'T THAT BE FUN?!
GRRR...
GRRR...

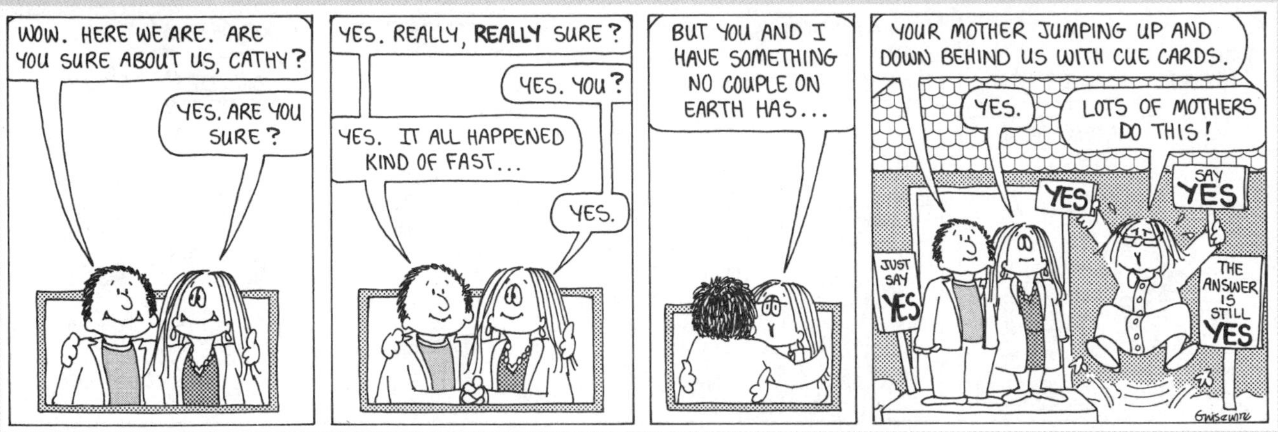
WOW. HERE WE ARE. ARE YOU SURE ABOUT US, CATHY?
YES. ARE YOU SURE?
YES. REALLY, REALLY SURE?
YES. YOU?
YES. IT ALL HAPPENED KIND OF FAST...
YES.
BUT YOU AND I HAVE SOMETHING NO COUPLE ON EARTH HAS...
YOUR MOTHER JUMPING UP AND DOWN BEHIND US WITH CUE CARDS.
YES.
LOTS OF MOTHERS DO THIS!
YES
SAY YES
JUST SAY YES
THE ANSWER IS STILL YES

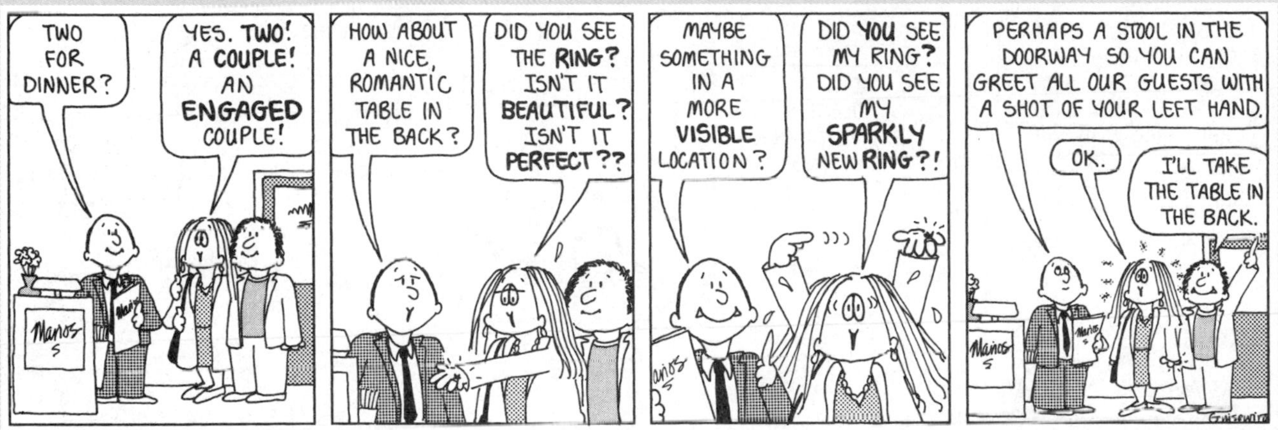
TWO FOR DINNER?
YES. TWO! A COUPLE! AN ENGAGED COUPLE!
HOW ABOUT A NICE, ROMANTIC TABLE IN THE BACK?
DID YOU SEE THE RING? ISN'T IT BEAUTIFUL? ISN'T IT PERFECT??
MAYBE SOMETHING IN A MORE VISIBLE LOCATION?
DID YOU SEE MY RING? DID YOU SEE MY SPARKLY NEW RING?!
PERHAPS A STOOL IN THE DOORWAY SO YOU CAN GREET ALL OUR GUESTS WITH A SHOT OF YOUR LEFT HAND.
OK.
I'LL TAKE THE TABLE IN THE BACK.

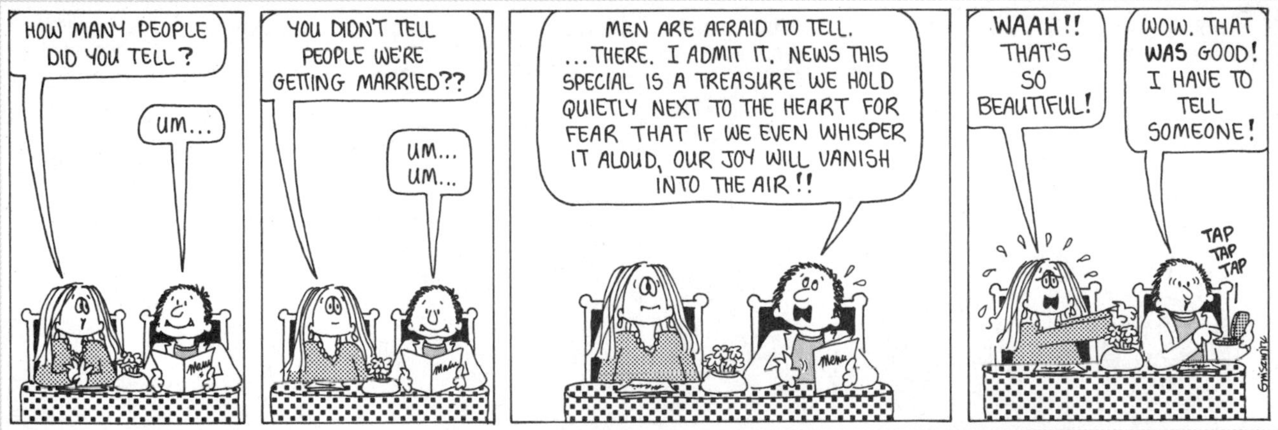
HOW MANY PEOPLE DID YOU TELL?
UM...
YOU DIDN'T TELL PEOPLE WE'RE GETTING MARRIED??
UM... UM...
MEN ARE AFRAID TO TELL. ...THERE. I ADMIT IT. NEWS THIS SPECIAL IS A TREASURE WE HOLD QUIETLY NEXT TO THE HEART FOR FEAR THAT IF WE EVEN WHISPER IT ALOUD, OUR JOY WILL VANISH INTO THE AIR!!
WAAH!! THAT'S SO BEAUTIFUL!
WOW. THAT WAS GOOD! I HAVE TO TELL SOMEONE!
TAP TAP TAP

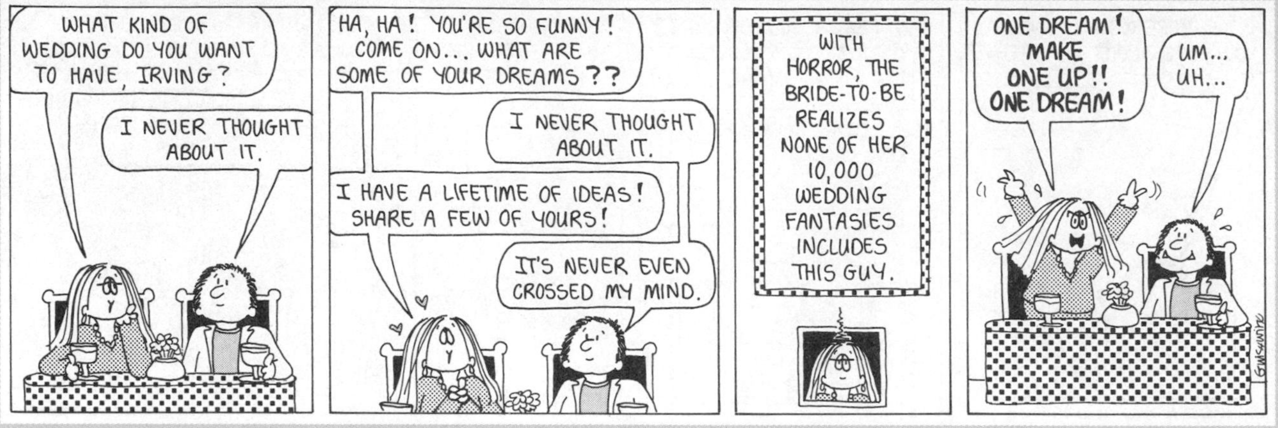
WHAT KIND OF WEDDING DO YOU WANT TO HAVE, IRVING?
I NEVER THOUGHT ABOUT IT.
HA, HA! YOU'RE SO FUNNY! COME ON... WHAT ARE SOME OF YOUR DREAMS??
I NEVER THOUGHT ABOUT IT.
I HAVE A LIFETIME OF IDEAS! SHARE A FEW OF YOURS!
IT'S NEVER EVEN CROSSED MY MIND.
WITH HORROR, THE BRIDE-TO-BE REALIZES NONE OF HER 10,000 WEDDING FANTASIES INCLUDES THIS GUY.
ONE DREAM! MAKE ONE UP!! ONE DREAM!
UM... UH...

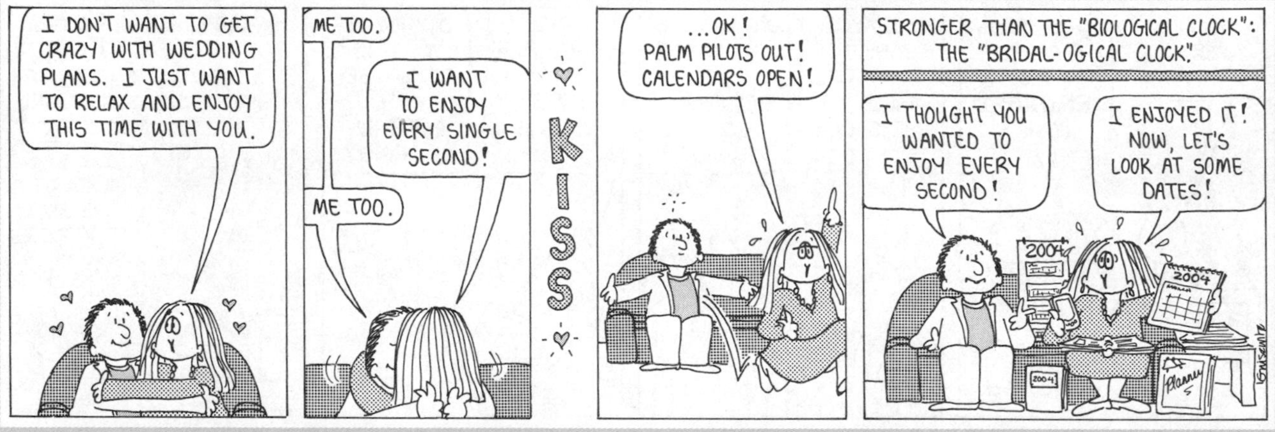
I DON'T WANT TO GET CRAZY WITH WEDDING PLANS. I JUST WANT TO RELAX AND ENJOY THIS TIME WITH YOU.
ME TOO.
I WANT TO ENJOY EVERY SINGLE SECOND!
ME TOO.
KISS
...OK! PALM PILOTS OUT! CALENDARS OPEN!
STRONGER THAN THE "BIOLOGICAL CLOCK": THE "BRIDAL-OGICAL CLOCK."
I THOUGHT YOU WANTED TO ENJOY EVERY SECOND!
I ENJOYED IT! NOW, LET'S LOOK AT SOME DATES!

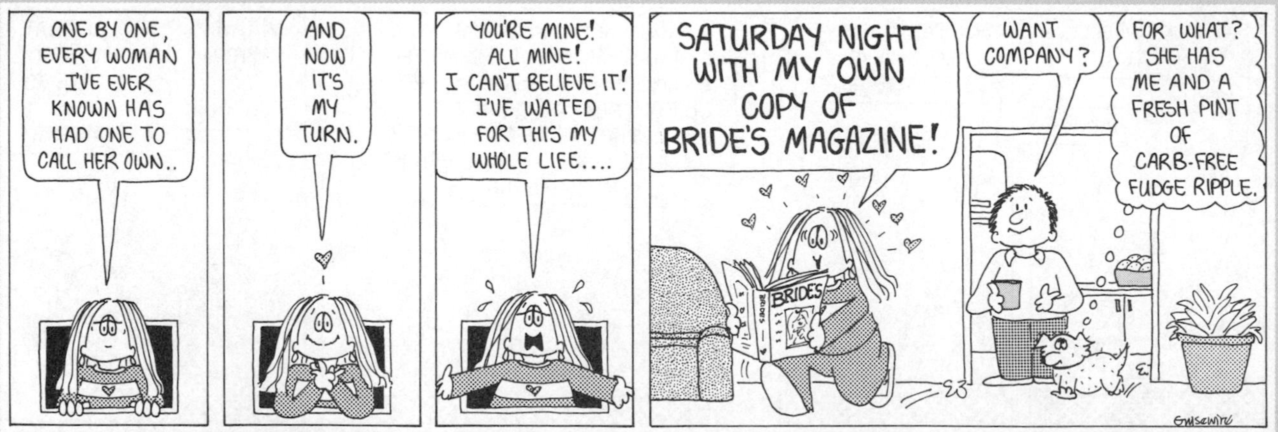
ONE BY ONE, EVERY WOMAN I'VE EVER KNOWN HAS HAD ONE TO CALL HER OWN..
AND NOW IT'S MY TURN.
YOU'RE MINE! ALL MINE! I CAN'T BELIEVE IT! I'VE WAITED FOR THIS MY WHOLE LIFE....
SATURDAY NIGHT WITH MY OWN COPY OF BRIDE'S MAGAZINE!
WANT COMPANY?
FOR WHAT? SHE HAS ME AND A FRESH PINT OF CARB-FREE FUDGE RIPPLE.

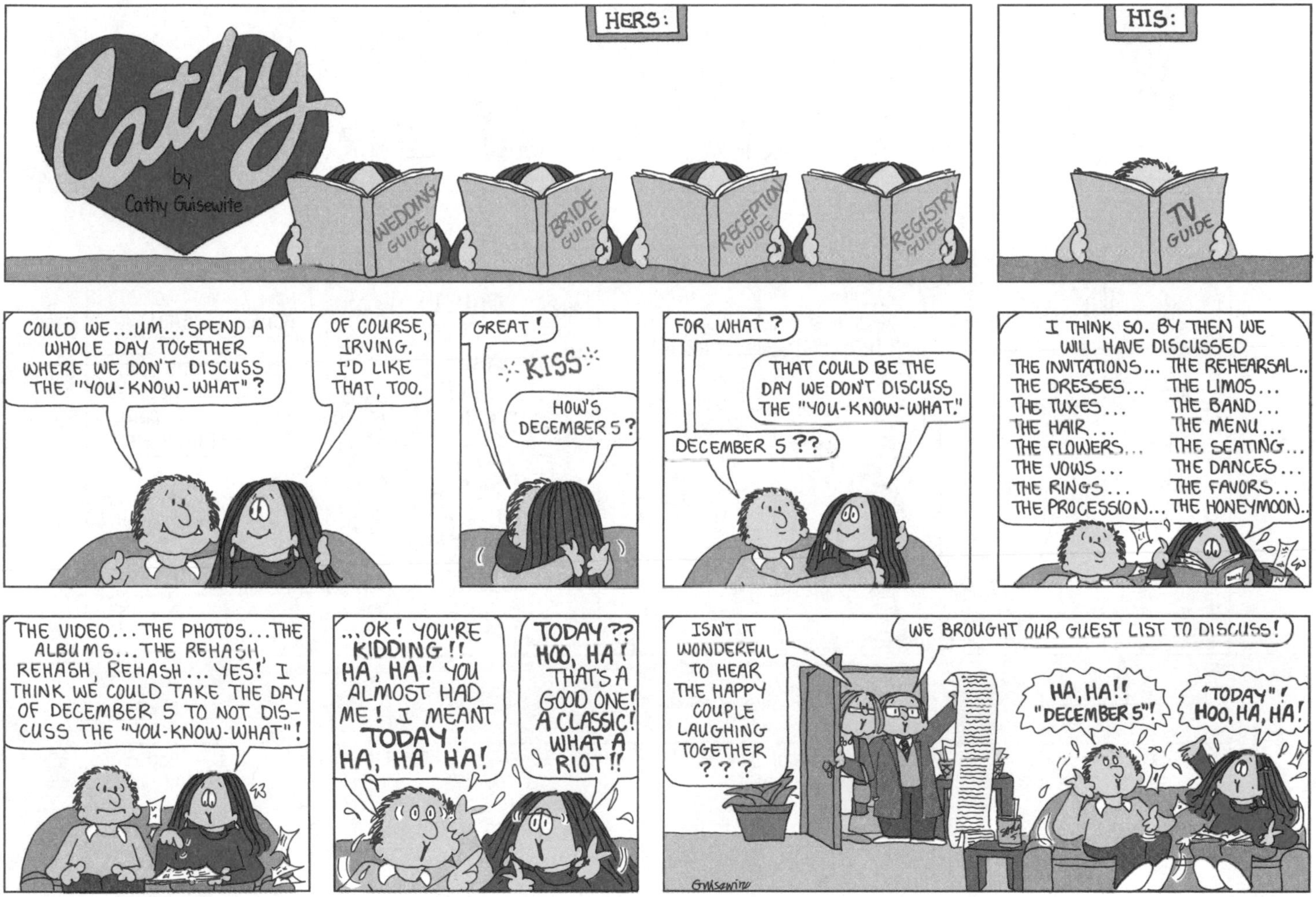
Cathy
by
Cathy Guisewite
HERS:
WEDDING GUIDE
BRIDE GUIDE
RECEPTION GUIDE
REGISTRY GUIDE
HIS:
TV GUIDE
COULD WE...UM...SPEND A WHOLE DAY TOGETHER WHERE WE DON'T DISCUSS THE "YOU-KNOW-WHAT"?
OF COURSE, IRVING. I'D LIKE THAT, TOO.
GREAT!
KISS
HOW'S DECEMBER 5?
FOR WHAT?
THAT COULD BE THE DAY WE DON'T DISCUSS THE "YOU-KNOW-WHAT."
DECEMBER 5??
I THINK SO. BY THEN WE WILL HAVE DISCUSSED THE INVITATIONS... THE DRESSES... THE TUXES... THE HAIR... THE FLOWERS... THE VOWS... THE RINGS... THE PROCESSION... THE REHEARSAL... THE LIMOS... THE BAND... THE MENU... THE SEATING... THE DANCES... THE FAVORS... THE HONEYMOON...
THE VIDEO... THE PHOTOS... THE ALBUMS... THE REHASH, REHASH, REHASH... YES! I THINK WE COULD TAKE THE DAY OF DECEMBER 5 TO NOT DISCUSS THE "YOU-KNOW-WHAT"!
...OK! YOU'RE KIDDING!! HA, HA! YOU ALMOST HAD ME! I MEANT TODAY! HA, HA, HA!
TODAY?? HOO, HA! THAT'S A GOOD ONE! A CLASSIC! WHAT A RIOT!!
ISN'T IT WONDERFUL TO HEAR THE HAPPY COUPLE LAUGHING TOGETHER???
WE BROUGHT OUR GUEST LIST TO DISCUSS!
HA, HA!! "DECEMBER 5"!
"TODAY"! HOO, HA, HA!
Guisewite

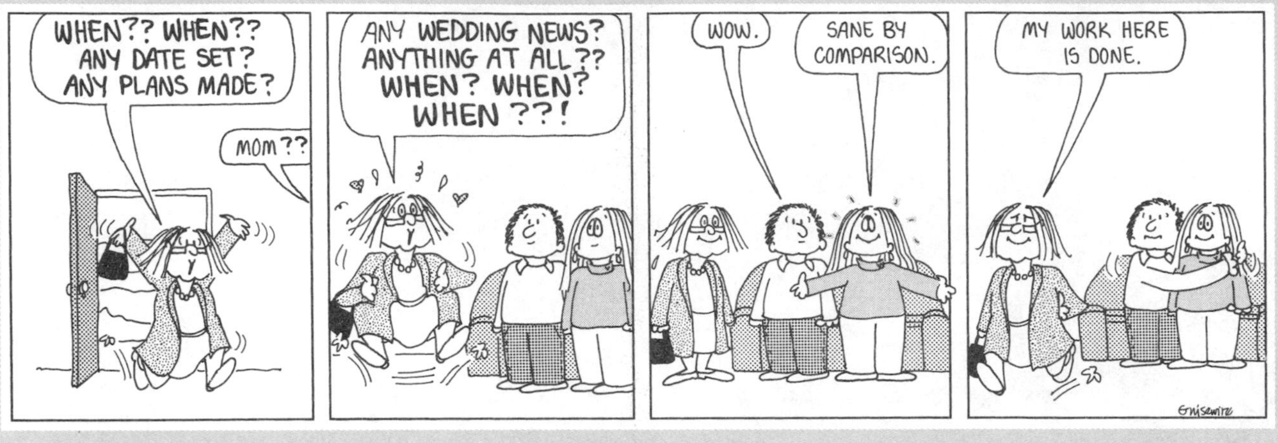
WHEN?? WHEN?? ANY DATE SET? ANY PLANS MADE?
MOM??
ANY WEDDING NEWS? ANYTHING AT ALL?? WHEN? WHEN? WHEN??!
WOW.
SANE BY COMPARISON.
MY WORK HERE IS DONE.
Guisewite

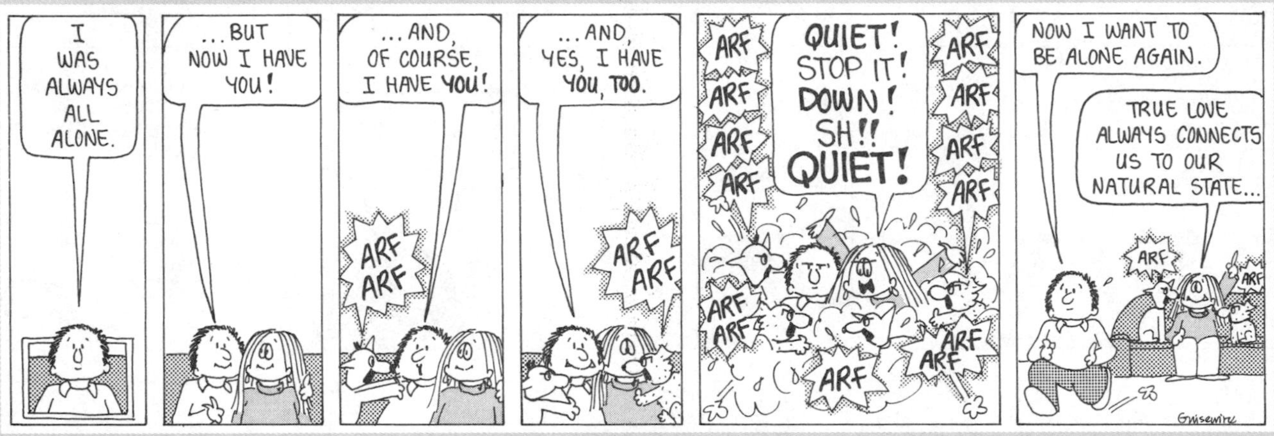
I WAS ALWAYS ALL ALONE.
...BUT NOW I HAVE YOU!
...AND, OF COURSE, I HAVE YOU!
ARF ARF
...AND, YES, I HAVE YOU, TOO.
ARF ARF
QUIET! STOP IT! DOWN! SH!! QUIET!
ARF ARF ARF ARF ARF ARF ARF ARF ARF ARF ARF ARF
NOW I WANT TO BE ALONE AGAIN.
TRUE LOVE ALWAYS CONNECTS US TO OUR NATURAL STATE...
ARF
ARF
Guisewite

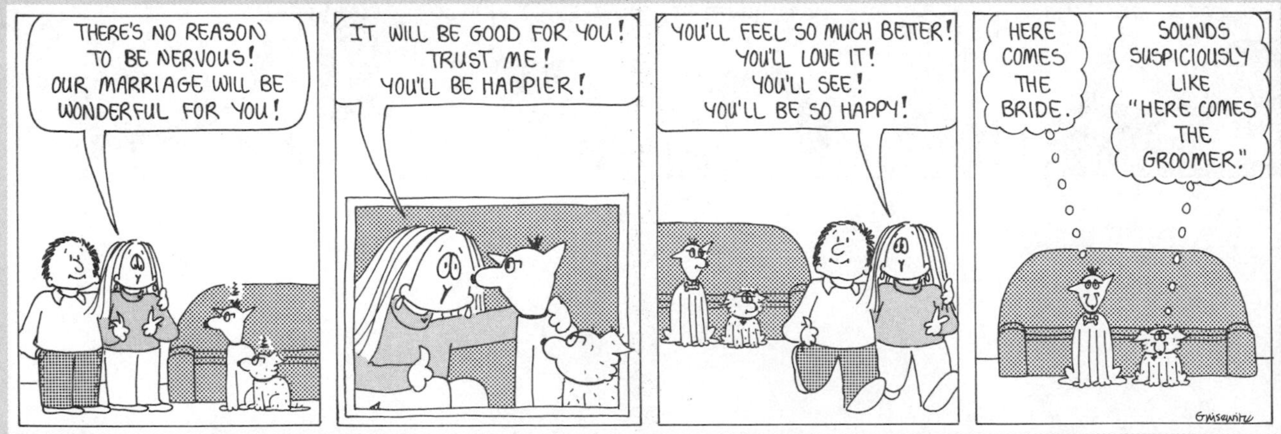
THERE'S NO REASON TO BE NERVOUS! OUR MARRIAGE WILL BE WONDERFUL FOR YOU!
IT WILL BE GOOD FOR YOU! TRUST ME! YOU'LL BE HAPPIER!
YOU'LL FEEL SO MUCH BETTER! YOU'LL LOVE IT! YOU'LL SEE! YOU'LL BE SO HAPPY!
HERE COMES THE BRIDE.
SOUNDS SUSPICIOUSLY LIKE "HERE COMES THE GROOMER."
Guisewite

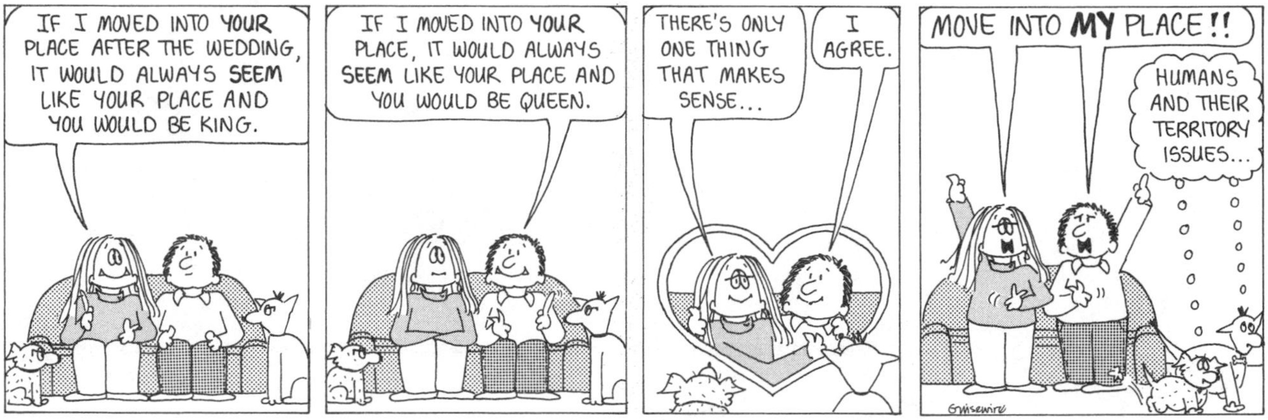
IF I MOVED INTO YOUR PLACE AFTER THE WEDDING, IT WOULD ALWAYS SEEM LIKE YOUR PLACE AND YOU WOULD BE KING.
IF I MOVED INTO YOUR PLACE, IT WOULD ALWAYS SEEM LIKE YOUR PLACE AND YOU WOULD BE QUEEN.
THERE'S ONLY ONE THING THAT MAKES SENSE...
I AGREE.
MOVE INTO MY PLACE!!
HUMANS AND THEIR TERRITORY ISSUES...

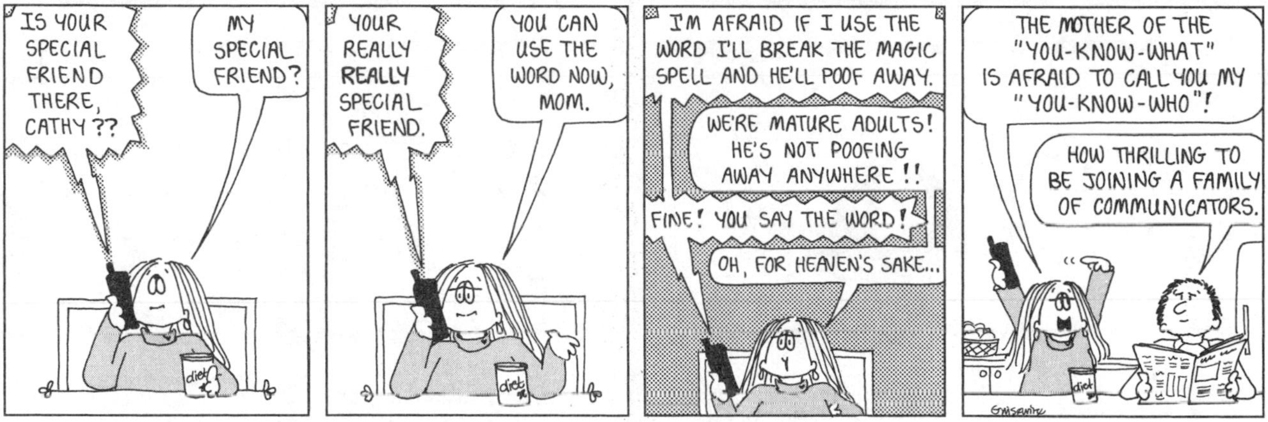
IS YOUR SPECIAL FRIEND THERE, CATHY??
MY SPECIAL FRIEND?
YOUR REALLY REALLY SPECIAL FRIEND.
YOU CAN USE THE WORD NOW, MOM.
I'M AFRAID IF I USE THE WORD I'LL BREAK THE MAGIC SPELL AND HE'LL POOF AWAY.
WE'RE MATURE ADULTS! HE'S NOT POOFING AWAY ANYWHERE!!
FINE! YOU SAY THE WORD!
OH, FOR HEAVEN'S SAKE...
THE MOTHER OF THE "YOU-KNOW-WHAT" IS AFRAID TO CALL YOU MY "YOU-KNOW-WHO"!
HOW THRILLING TO BE JOINING A FAMILY OF COMMUNICATORS.

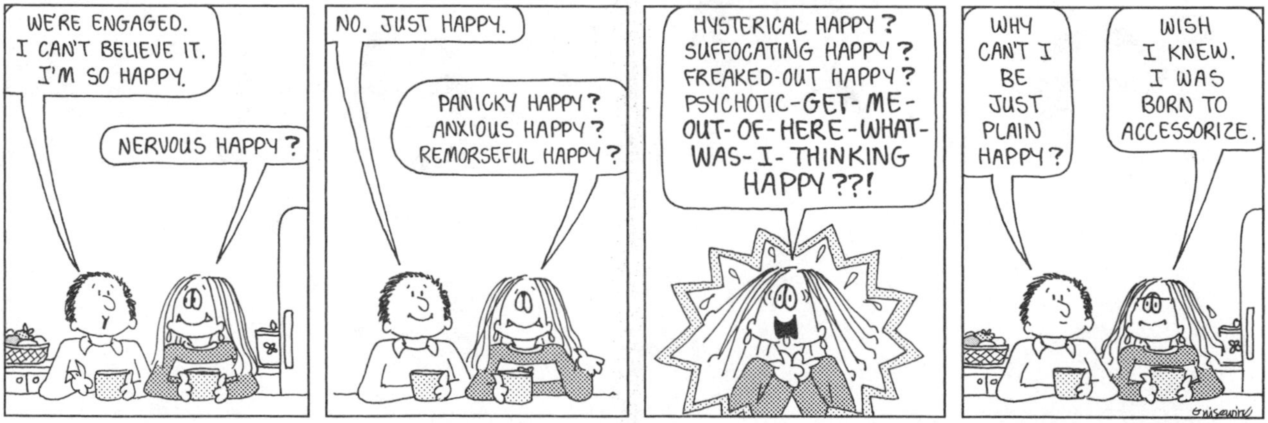
WE'RE ENGAGED. I CAN'T BELIEVE IT. I'M SO HAPPY.
NERVOUS HAPPY?
NO. JUST HAPPY.
PANICKY HAPPY? ANXIOUS HAPPY? REMORSEFUL HAPPY?
HYSTERICAL HAPPY? SUFFOCATING HAPPY? FREAKED-OUT HAPPY? PSYCHOTIC-GET-ME-OUT-OF-HERE-WHAT-WAS-I-THINKING HAPPY??!
WHY CAN'T I BE JUST PLAIN HAPPY?
WISH I KNEW. I WAS BORN TO ACCESSORIZE.

Cathy
by Cathy Guisewite
WOW. SOMEONE NEEDS TO LEARN TO DELEGATE.
I'LL DO IT.
LET'S CHECK SOME OF THIS OFF, CATHY. I'LL LINE UP THE FLOWERS.
WHAT ?? OH, NO! I KNOW EXACTLY HOW I WANT THE FLOWERS! I'LL DO THE FLOWERS!
Wedding
I'LL ORDER THE CAKE.
THE CAKE?? HOO, BOY, NO! I'LL DO THE CAKE!!
I'LL DO THE INVITATIONS. I'LL DO THE MENU. I'LL DO THE FAVORS.
I'LL DO THE PHOTOGRAPHER! I'LL DO THE GUEST BOOK! I'LL DO THE SEATING CHART! I'LL DO THE MUSIC! I'LL DO THE CLOTHES!
...TYPICAL. FOR THE MAN, A WEDDING IS ONE "I DO." FOR THE WOMAN, IT'S FIVE HUNDRED "I'LL DOS."
COULD SOMEONE EXPLAIN WHY YOU GET TO BE A CONTROL FREAK AND A VICTIM ??
I'LL DO IT.

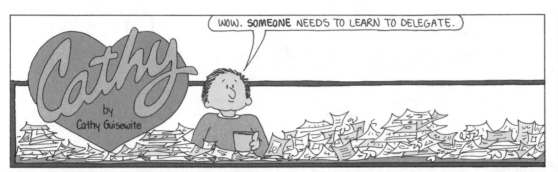

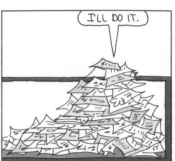

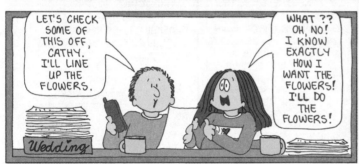

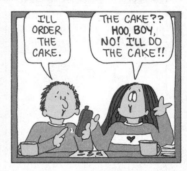

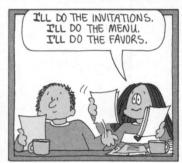

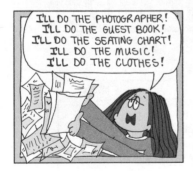

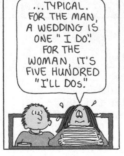

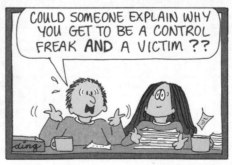

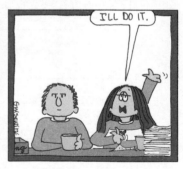

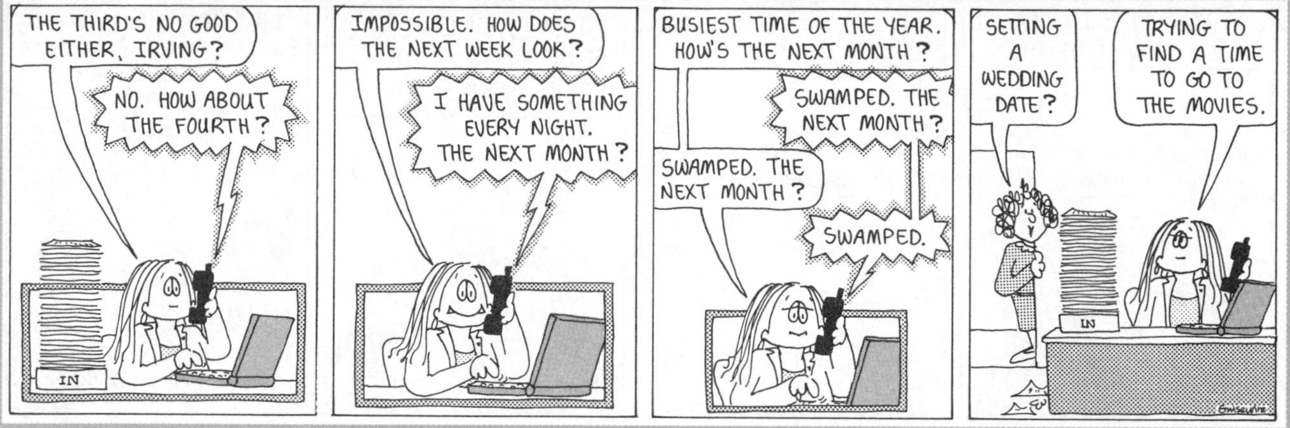
THE THIRD'S NO GOOD EITHER, IRVING?
NO. HOW ABOUT THE FOURTH?
IMPOSSIBLE. HOW DOES THE NEXT WEEK LOOK?
I HAVE SOMETHING EVERY NIGHT. THE NEXT MONTH?
BUSIEST TIME OF THE YEAR. HOW'S THE NEXT MONTH?
SWAMPED. THE NEXT MONTH?
SWAMPED. THE NEXT MONTH?
SWAMPED.
SETTING A WEDDING DATE?
TRYING TO FIND A TIME TO GO TO THE MOVIES.
IN

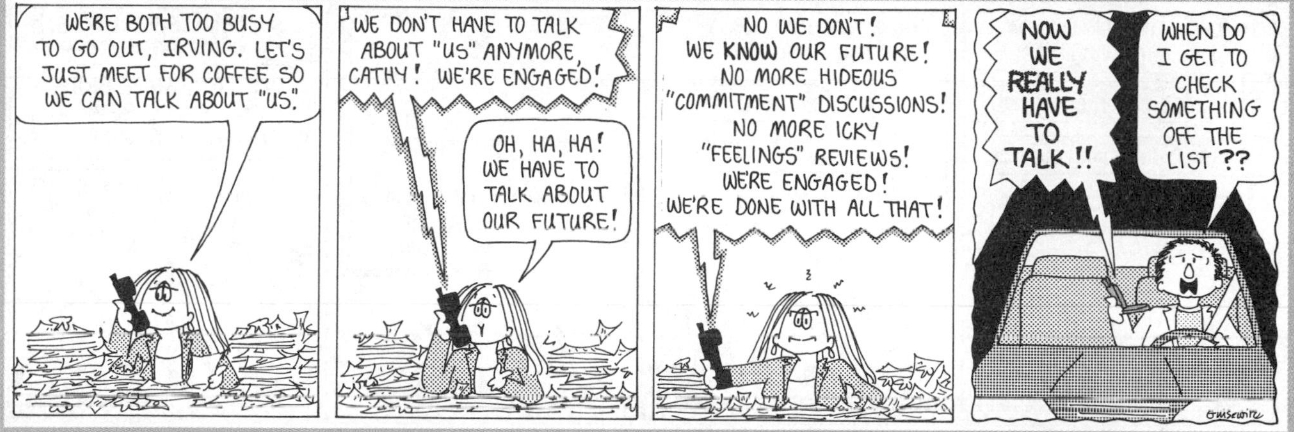
WE'RE BOTH TOO BUSY TO GO OUT, IRVING. LET'S JUST MEET FOR COFFEE SO WE CAN TALK ABOUT "US."
WE DON'T HAVE TO TALK ABOUT "US" ANYMORE, CATHY! WE'RE ENGAGED!
OH, HA, HA! WE HAVE TO TALK ABOUT OUR FUTURE!
NO WE DON'T! WE KNOW OUR FUTURE! NO MORE HIDEOUS "COMMITMENT" DISCUSSIONS! NO MORE ICKY "FEELINGS" REVIEWS! WE'RE ENGAGED! WE'RE DONE WITH ALL THAT!
NOW WE REALLY HAVE TO TALK!!
WHEN DO I GET TO CHECK SOMETHING OFF THE LIST??

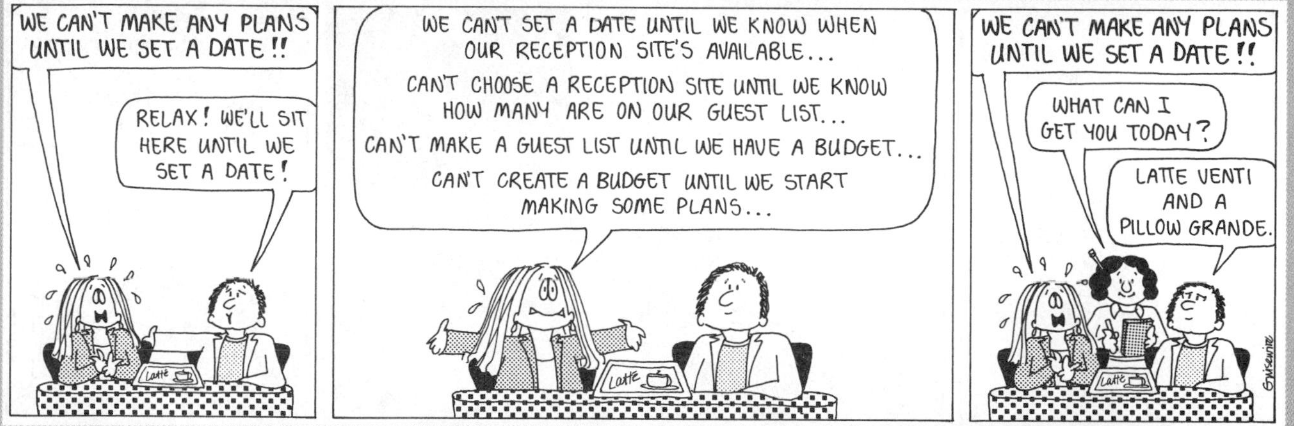
WE CAN'T MAKE ANY PLANS UNTIL WE SET A DATE!!
RELAX! WE'LL SIT HERE UNTIL WE SET A DATE!
WE CAN'T SET A DATE UNTIL WE KNOW WHEN OUR RECEPTION SITE'S AVAILABLE...
CAN'T CHOOSE A RECEPTION SITE UNTIL WE KNOW HOW MANY ARE ON OUR GUEST LIST...
CAN'T MAKE A GUEST LIST UNTIL WE HAVE A BUDGET...
CAN'T CREATE A BUDGET UNTIL WE START MAKING SOME PLANS...
WE CAN'T MAKE ANY PLANS UNTIL WE SET A DATE!!
WHAT CAN I GET YOU TODAY?
LATTE VENTI AND A PILLOW GRANDE.
LATTE

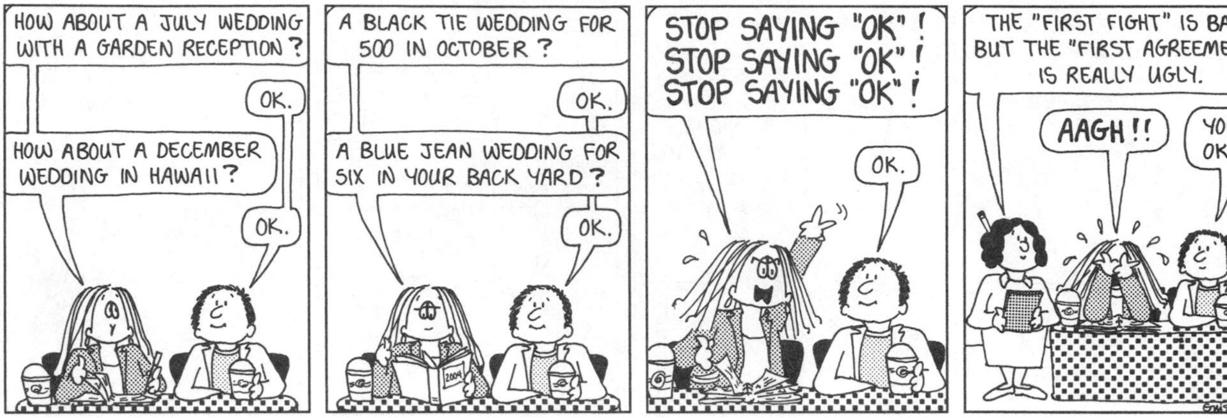
HOW ABOUT A JULY WEDDING WITH A GARDEN RECEPTION?
OK.
HOW ABOUT A DECEMBER WEDDING IN HAWAII?
OK.
A BLACK TIE WEDDING FOR 500 IN OCTOBER?
OK.
A BLUE JEAN WEDDING FOR SIX IN YOUR BACK YARD?
OK.
2004
STOP SAYING "OK"! STOP SAYING "OK"! STOP SAYING "OK"!
OK.
THE "FIRST FIGHT" IS BAD, BUT THE "FIRST AGREEMENT" IS REALLY UGLY.
AAGH!!
YOU OK?

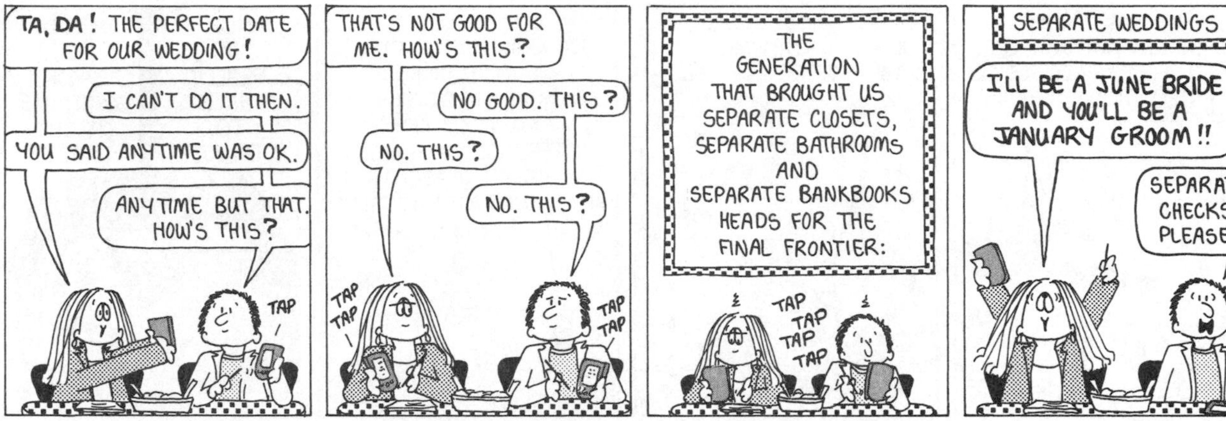
TA, DA! THE PERFECT DATE FOR OUR WEDDING!
I CAN'T DO IT THEN.
YOU SAID ANYTIME WAS OK.
ANYTIME BUT THAT. HOW'S THIS?
TAP
THAT'S NOT GOOD FOR ME. HOW'S THIS?
NO GOOD. THIS?
NO. THIS?
NO. THIS?
TAP TAP
TAP TAP
THE GENERATION THAT BROUGHT US SEPARATE CLOSETS, SEPARATE BATHROOMS AND SEPARATE BANKBOOKS HEADS FOR THE FINAL FRONTIER:
TAP TAP TAP TAP
SEPARATE WEDDINGS
I'LL BE A JUNE BRIDE AND YOU'LL BE A JANUARY GROOM!!
SEPARATE CHECKS, PLEASE!

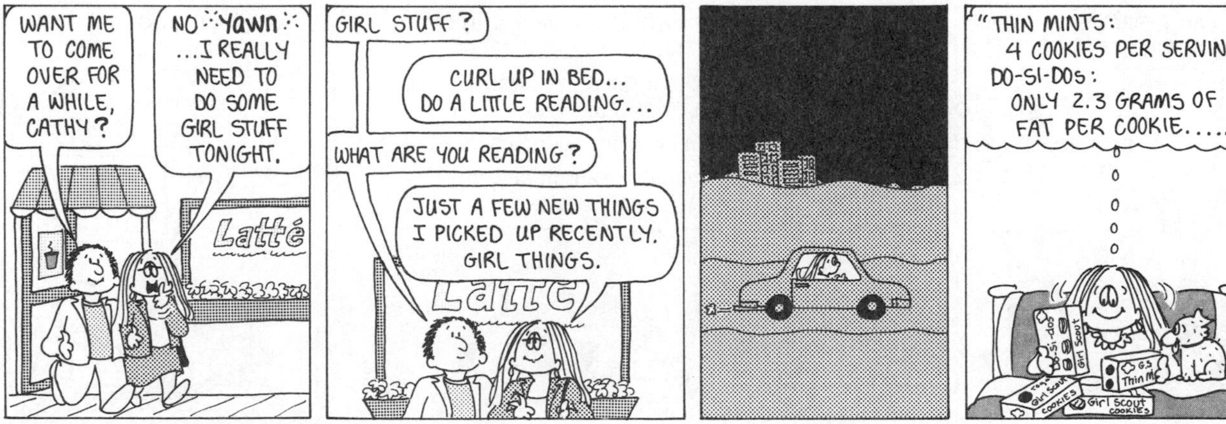
WANT ME TO COME OVER FOR A WHILE, CATHY?
NO ·:·Yawn·:· ...I REALLY NEED TO DO SOME GIRL STUFF TONIGHT.
Latté
GIRL STUFF?
CURL UP IN BED... DO A LITTLE READING...
WHAT ARE YOU READING?
JUST A FEW NEW THINGS I PICKED UP RECENTLY. GIRL THINGS.
Latté
"THIN MINTS: 4 COOKIES PER SERVING... DO-SI-DOS: ONLY 2.3 GRAMS OF FAT PER COOKIE....."
Girl Scout COOKIES
Thin M

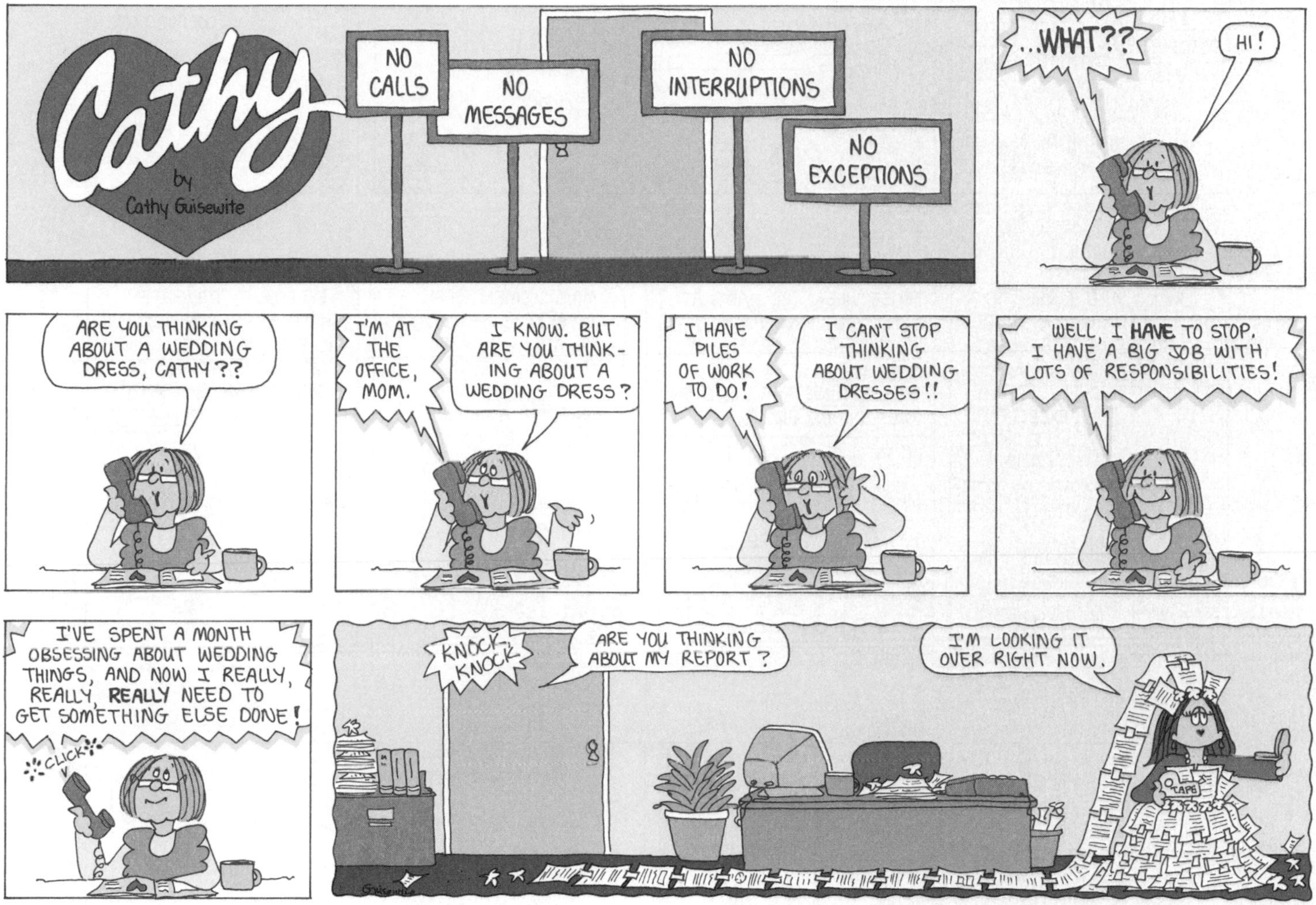
Cathy
by
Cathy Guisewite
NO CALLS
NO MESSAGES
NO INTERRUPTIONS
NO EXCEPTIONS
...WHAT??
HI!
ARE YOU THINKING ABOUT A WEDDING DRESS, CATHY??
I'M AT THE OFFICE, MOM.
I KNOW. BUT ARE YOU THINKING ABOUT A WEDDING DRESS?
I HAVE PILES OF WORK TO DO!
I CAN'T STOP THINKING ABOUT WEDDING DRESSES!!
WELL, I HAVE TO STOP. I HAVE A BIG JOB WITH LOTS OF RESPONSIBILITIES!
I'VE SPENT A MONTH OBSESSING ABOUT WEDDING THINGS, AND NOW I REALLY, REALLY, REALLY NEED TO GET SOMETHING ELSE DONE!
CLICK
KNOCK KNOCK
ARE YOU THINKING ABOUT MY REPORT?
I'M LOOKING IT OVER RIGHT NOW.

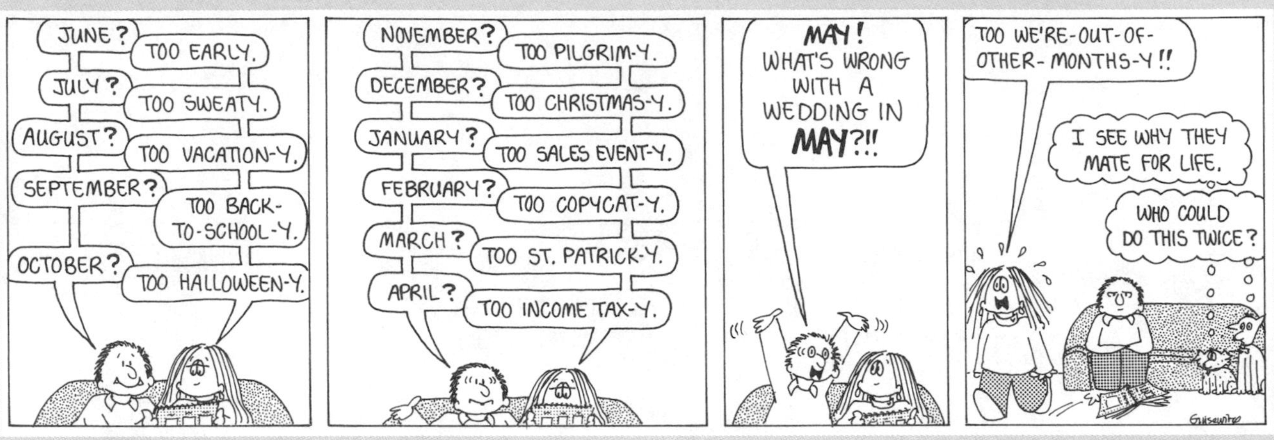
JUNE?
TOO EARLY.
JULY?
TOO SWEATY.
AUGUST?
TOO VACATION-Y.
SEPTEMBER?
TOO BACK-TO-SCHOOL-Y.
OCTOBER?
TOO HALLOWEEN-Y.
NOVEMBER?
TOO PILGRIM-Y.
DECEMBER?
TOO CHRISTMAS-Y.
JANUARY?
TOO SALES EVENT-Y.
FEBRUARY?
TOO COPYCAT-Y.
MARCH?
TOO ST. PATRICK-Y.
APRIL?
TOO INCOME TAX-Y.
MAY! WHAT'S WRONG WITH A WEDDING IN MAY?!!
TOO WE'RE-OUT-OF-OTHER-MONTHS-Y!!
I SEE WHY THEY MATE FOR LIFE.
WHO COULD DO THIS TWICE?

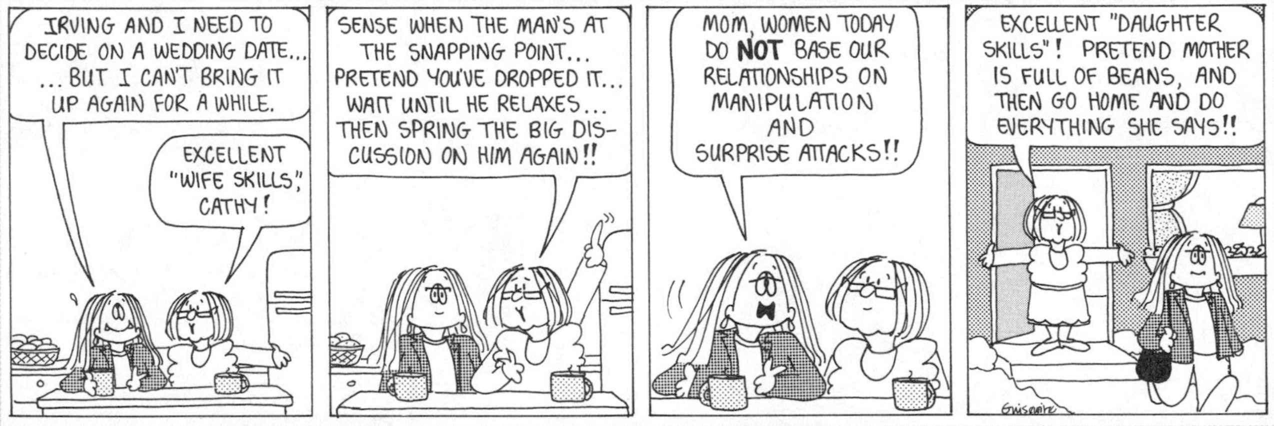
IRVING AND I NEED TO DECIDE ON A WEDDING DATE... ...BUT I CAN'T BRING IT UP AGAIN FOR A WHILE.
EXCELLENT "WIFE SKILLS," CATHY!
SENSE WHEN THE MAN'S AT THE SNAPPING POINT... PRETEND YOU'VE DROPPED IT... WAIT UNTIL HE RELAXES... THEN SPRING THE BIG DISCUSSION ON HIM AGAIN!!
MOM, WOMEN TODAY DO NOT BASE OUR RELATIONSHIPS ON MANIPULATION AND SURPRISE ATTACKS!!
EXCELLENT "DAUGHTER SKILLS"! PRETEND MOTHER IS FULL OF BEANS, AND THEN GO HOME AND DO EVERYTHING SHE SAYS!!

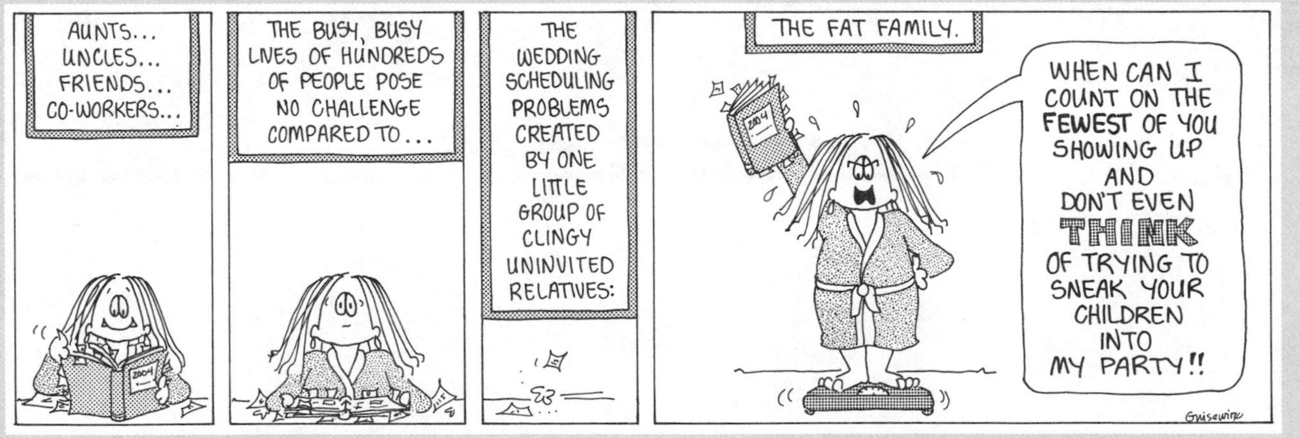
AUNTS... UNCLES... FRIENDS... CO-WORKERS...
THE BUSY, BUSY LIVES OF HUNDREDS OF PEOPLE POSE NO CHALLENGE COMPARED TO...
THE WEDDING SCHEDULING PROBLEMS CREATED BY ONE LITTLE GROUP OF CLINGY UNINVITED RELATIVES:
THE FAT FAMILY.
WHEN CAN I COUNT ON THE FEWEST OF YOU SHOWING UP AND DON'T EVEN THINK OF TRYING TO SNEAK YOUR CHILDREN INTO MY PARTY!!

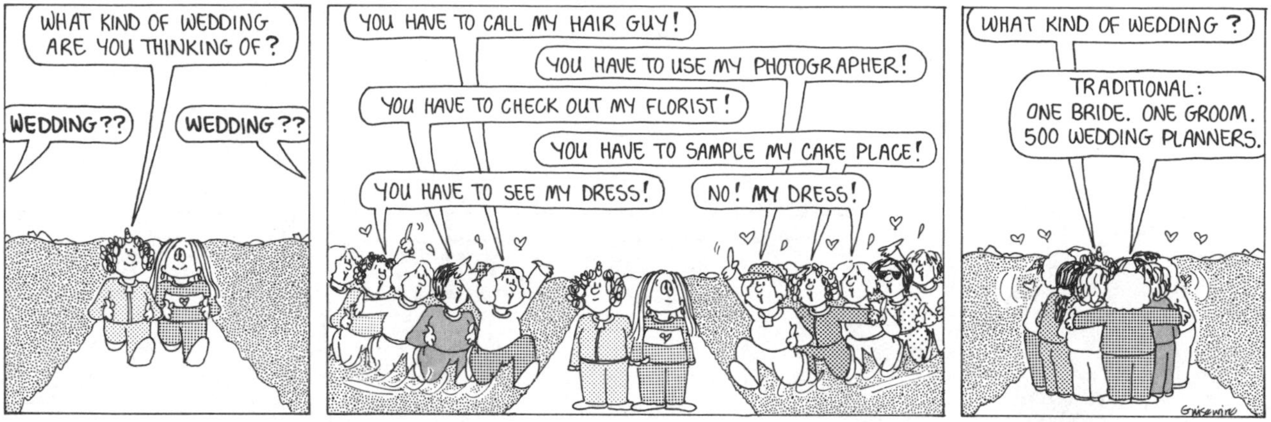
WHAT KIND OF WEDDING ARE YOU THINKING OF?
WEDDING??
WEDDING??
YOU HAVE TO CALL MY HAIR GUY!
YOU HAVE TO USE MY PHOTOGRAPHER!
YOU HAVE TO CHECK OUT MY FLORIST!
YOU HAVE TO SAMPLE MY CAKE PLACE!
YOU HAVE TO SEE MY DRESS!
NO! MY DRESS!
WHAT KIND OF WEDDING?
TRADITIONAL: ONE BRIDE. ONE GROOM. 500 WEDDING PLANNERS.

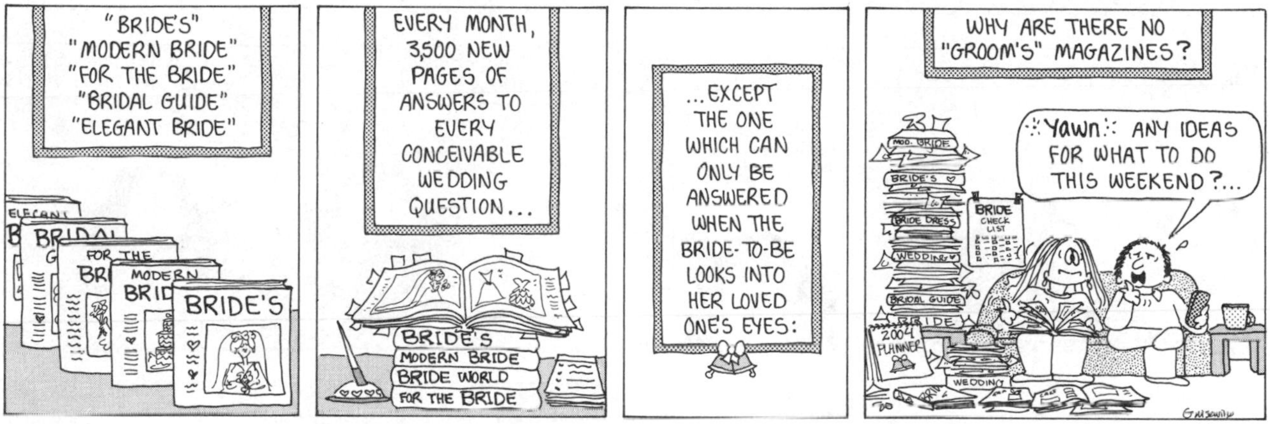
"BRIDE'S" "MODERN BRIDE" "FOR THE BRIDE" "BRIDAL GUIDE" "ELEGANT BRIDE"
BRIDE'S
EVERY MONTH, 3,500 NEW PAGES OF ANSWERS TO EVERY CONCEIVABLE WEDDING QUESTION...
BRIDE'S
MODERN BRIDE
BRIDE WORLD
FOR THE BRIDE
...EXCEPT THE ONE WHICH CAN ONLY BE ANSWERED WHEN THE BRIDE-TO-BE LOOKS INTO HER LOVED ONE'S EYES:
WHY ARE THERE NO "GROOM'S" MAGAZINES?
YAWN ANY IDEAS FOR WHAT TO DO THIS WEEKEND?...
BRIDE CHECK LIST
2004 PLANNER

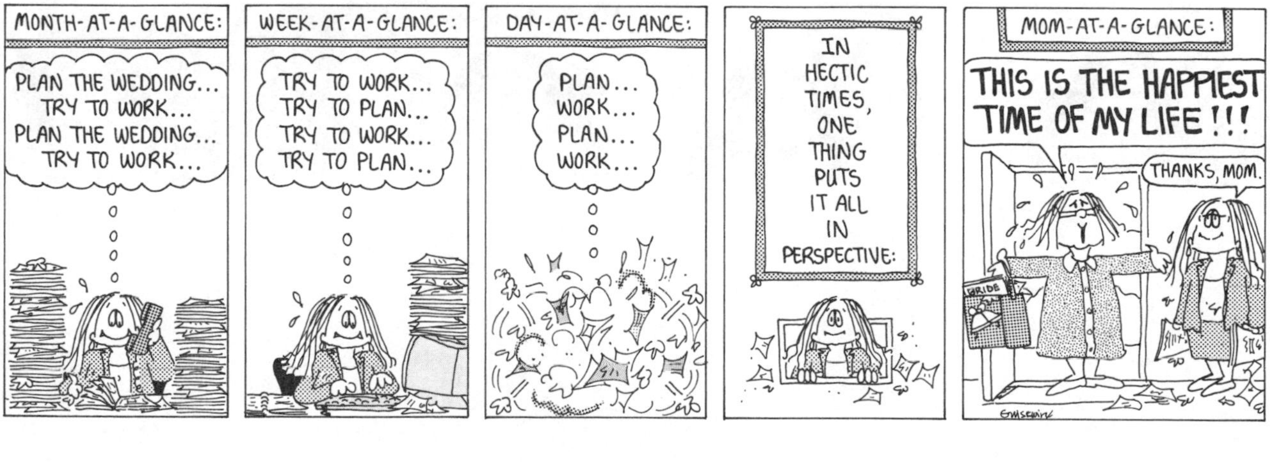
MONTH-AT-A-GLANCE:
PLAN THE WEDDING... TRY TO WORK... PLAN THE WEDDING... TRY TO WORK...
WEEK-AT-A-GLANCE:
TRY TO WORK... TRY TO PLAN... TRY TO WORK... TRY TO PLAN...
DAY-AT-A-GLANCE:
PLAN... WORK... PLAN... WORK...
IN HECTIC TIMES, ONE THING PUTS IT ALL IN PERSPECTIVE:
MOM-AT-A-GLANCE:
THIS IS THE HAPPIEST TIME OF MY LIFE!!!
THANKS, MOM.

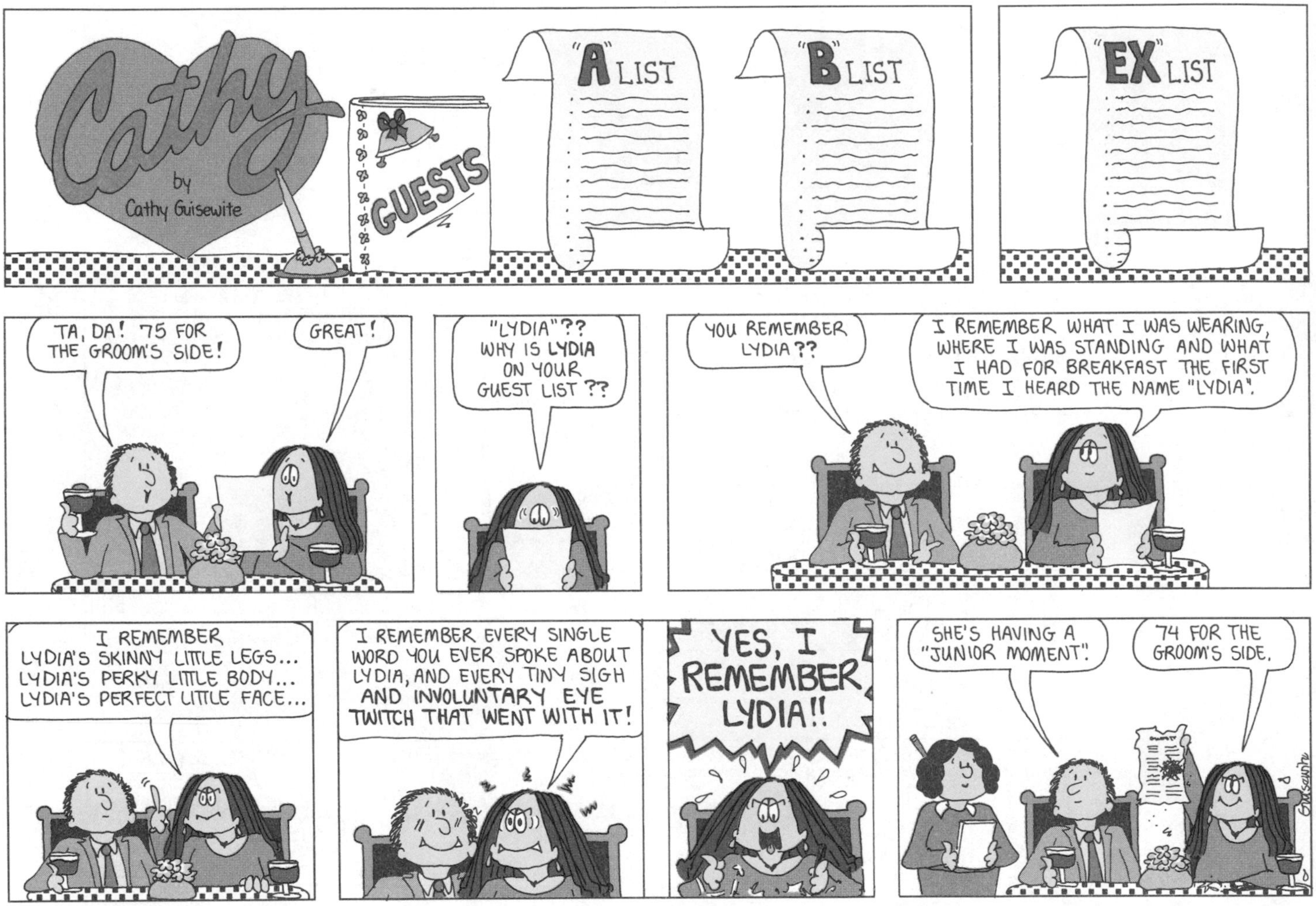
Cathy
by
Cathy Guisewite
GUESTS
"A" LIST
"B" LIST
"EX" LIST
TA, DA! 75 FOR THE GROOM'S SIDE!
GREAT!
"LYDIA"?? WHY IS LYDIA ON YOUR GUEST LIST ??
YOU REMEMBER LYDIA??
I REMEMBER WHAT I WAS WEARING, WHERE I WAS STANDING AND WHAT I HAD FOR BREAKFAST THE FIRST TIME I HEARD THE NAME "LYDIA".
I REMEMBER LYDIA'S SKINNY LITTLE LEGS... LYDIA'S PERKY LITTLE BODY... LYDIA'S PERFECT LITTLE FACE...
I REMEMBER EVERY SINGLE WORD YOU EVER SPOKE ABOUT LYDIA, AND EVERY TINY SIGH AND INVOLUNTARY EYE TWITCH THAT WENT WITH IT!
YES, I REMEMBER LYDIA!!
SHE'S HAVING A "JUNIOR MOMENT".
74 FOR THE GROOM'S SIDE.

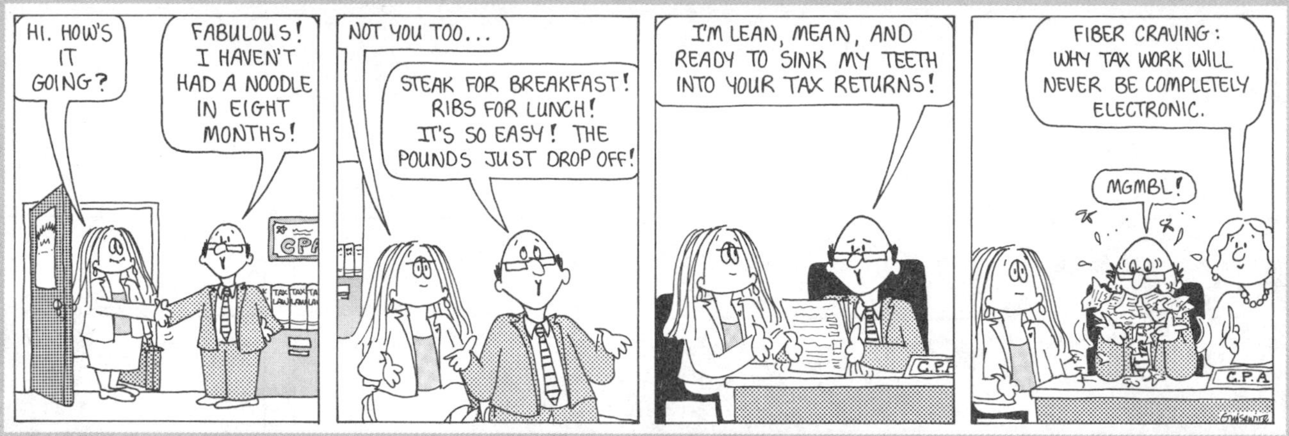
HI. HOW'S IT GOING?
FABULOUS! I HAVEN'T HAD A NOODLE IN EIGHT MONTHS!
CPA
NOT YOU TOO...
STEAK FOR BREAKFAST! RIBS FOR LUNCH! IT'S SO EASY! THE POUNDS JUST DROP OFF!
I'M LEAN, MEAN, AND READY TO SINK MY TEETH INTO YOUR TAX RETURNS!
FIBER CRAVING: WHY TAX WORK WILL NEVER BE COMPLETELY ELECTRONIC.
MGMBL!
C.P.A.

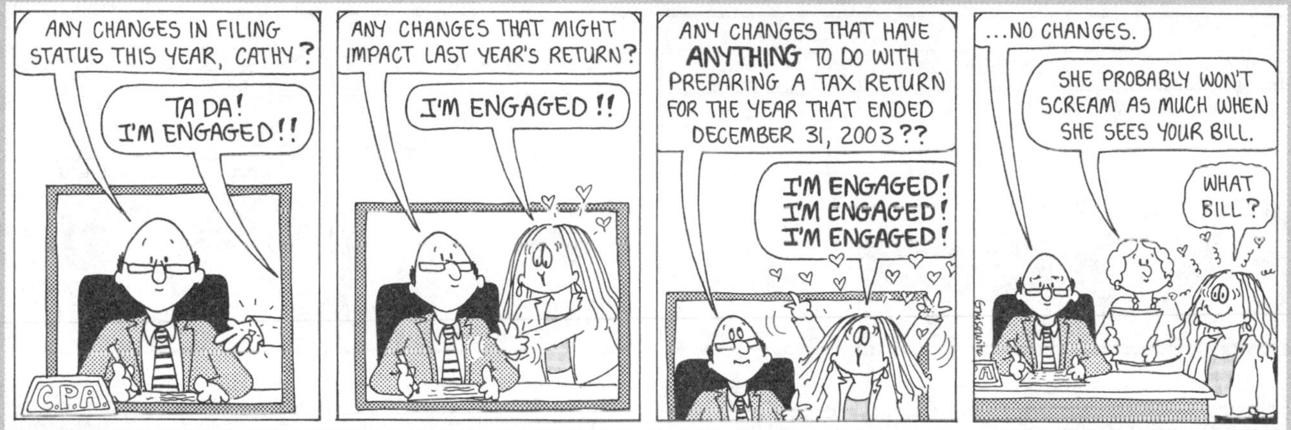
ANY CHANGES IN FILING STATUS THIS YEAR, CATHY?
TA DA! I'M ENGAGED!!
C.P.A.
ANY CHANGES THAT MIGHT IMPACT LAST YEAR'S RETURN?
I'M ENGAGED!!
ANY CHANGES THAT HAVE **ANYTHING** TO DO WITH PREPARING A TAX RETURN FOR THE YEAR THAT ENDED DECEMBER 31, 2003??
I'M ENGAGED! I'M ENGAGED! I'M ENGAGED!
...NO CHANGES.
SHE PROBABLY WON'T SCREAM AS MUCH WHEN SHE SEES YOUR BILL.
WHAT BILL?

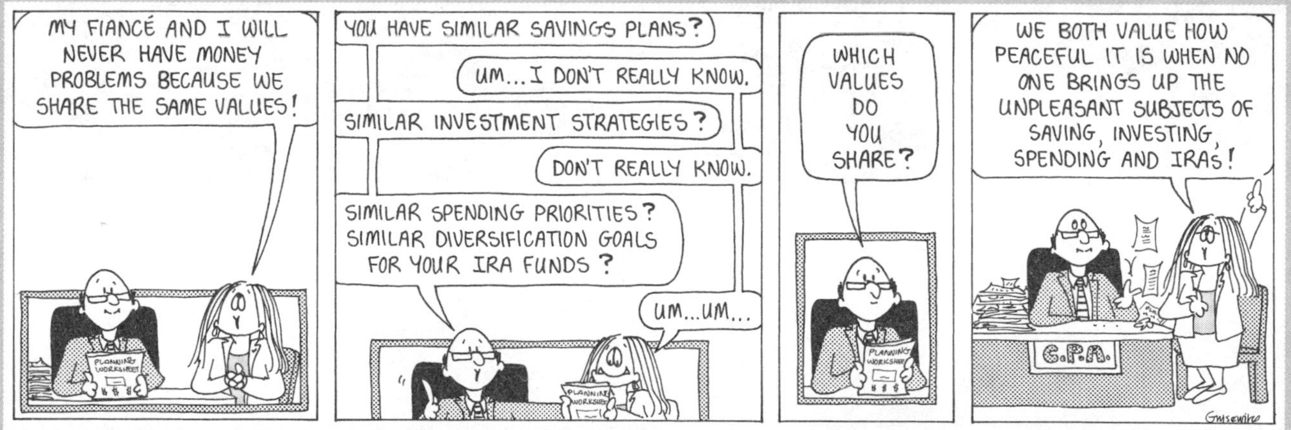
MY FIANCÉ AND I WILL NEVER HAVE MONEY PROBLEMS BECAUSE WE SHARE THE SAME VALUES!
YOU HAVE SIMILAR SAVINGS PLANS?
UM...I DON'T REALLY KNOW.
SIMILAR INVESTMENT STRATEGIES?
DON'T REALLY KNOW.
SIMILAR SPENDING PRIORITIES? SIMILAR DIVERSIFICATION GOALS FOR YOUR IRA FUNDS?
UM...UM...
WHICH VALUES DO YOU SHARE?
WE BOTH VALUE HOW PEACEFUL IT IS WHEN NO ONE BRINGS UP THE UNPLEASANT SUBJECTS OF SAVING, INVESTING, SPENDING AND IRAS!
C.P.A.

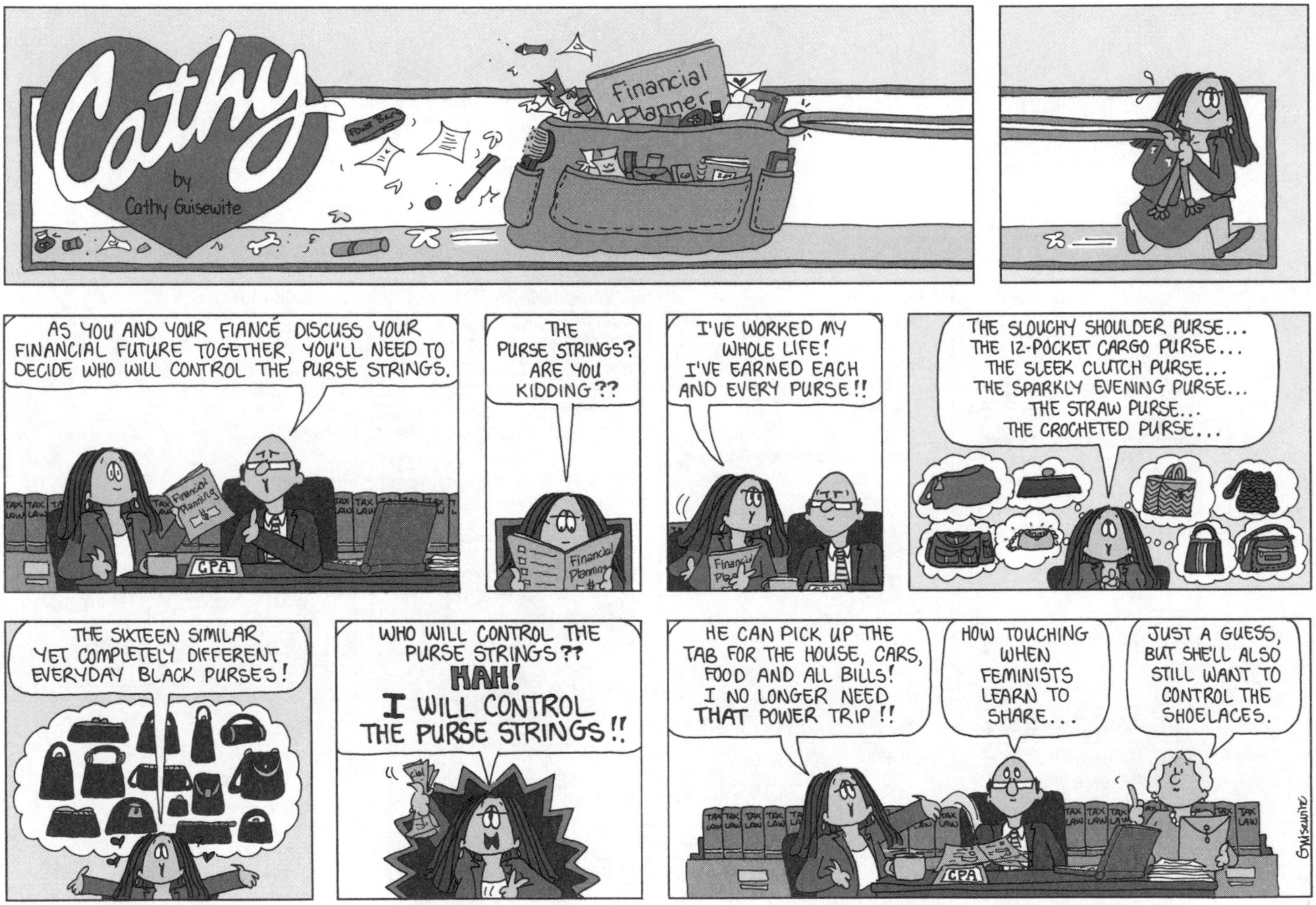
Cathy
by
Cathy Guisewite
Financial Planner
AS YOU AND YOUR FIANCÉ DISCUSS YOUR FINANCIAL FUTURE TOGETHER, YOU'LL NEED TO DECIDE WHO WILL CONTROL THE PURSE STRINGS.
THE PURSE STRINGS? ARE YOU KIDDING??
I'VE WORKED MY WHOLE LIFE! I'VE EARNED EACH AND EVERY PURSE!!
THE SLOUCHY SHOULDER PURSE... THE 12-POCKET CARGO PURSE... THE SLEEK CLUTCH PURSE... THE SPARKLY EVENING PURSE... THE STRAW PURSE... THE CROCHETED PURSE...
THE SIXTEEN SIMILAR YET COMPLETELY DIFFERENT EVERYDAY BLACK PURSES!
WHO WILL CONTROL THE PURSE STRINGS?? HAH! I WILL CONTROL THE PURSE STRINGS!!
HE CAN PICK UP THE TAB FOR THE HOUSE, CARS, FOOD AND ALL BILLS! I NO LONGER NEED THAT POWER TRIP!!
HOW TOUCHING WHEN FEMINISTS LEARN TO SHARE...
JUST A GUESS, BUT SHE'LL ALSO STILL WANT TO CONTROL THE SHOELACES.
CPA
Guisewite

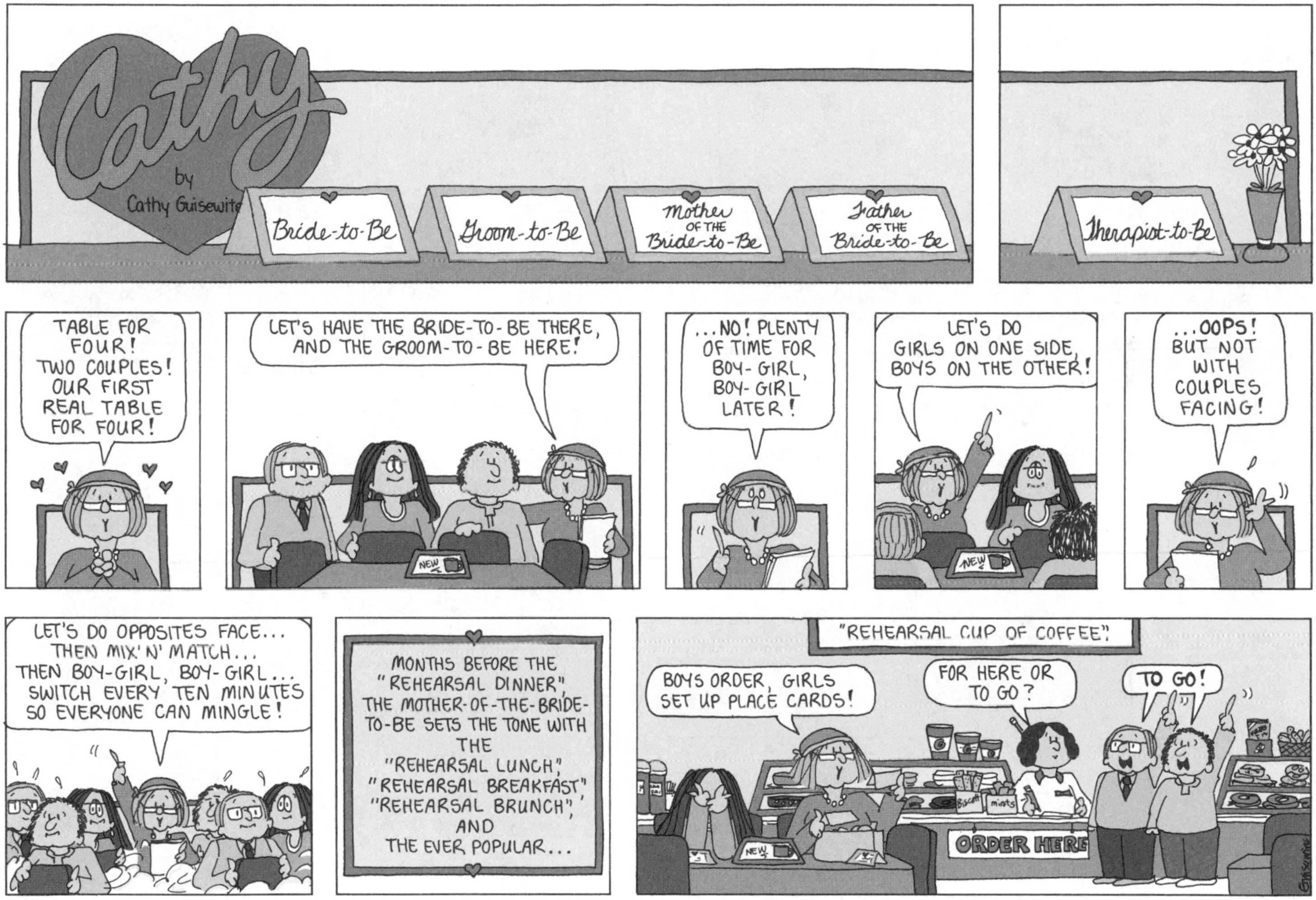
Cathy
by
Cathy Guisewite
Bride-to-Be
Groom-to-Be
Mother OF THE Bride-to-Be
Father OF THE Bride-to-Be
Therapist-to-Be
TABLE FOR FOUR! TWO COUPLES! OUR FIRST REAL TABLE FOR FOUR!
LET'S HAVE THE BRIDE-TO-BE THERE, AND THE GROOM-TO-BE HERE!
...NO! PLENTY OF TIME FOR BOY-GIRL, BOY-GIRL LATER!
LET'S DO GIRLS ON ONE SIDE, BOYS ON THE OTHER!
...OOPS! BUT NOT WITH COUPLES FACING!
LET'S DO OPPOSITES FACE... THEN MIX'N'MATCH... THEN BOY-GIRL, BOY-GIRL... SWITCH EVERY TEN MINUTES SO EVERYONE CAN MINGLE!
MONTHS BEFORE THE "REHEARSAL DINNER", THE MOTHER-OF-THE-BRIDE-TO-BE SETS THE TONE WITH THE "REHEARSAL LUNCH", "REHEARSAL BREAKFAST" "REHEARSAL BRUNCH", AND THE EVER POPULAR...
"REHEARSAL CUP OF COFFEE".
BOYS ORDER, GIRLS SET UP PLACE CARDS!
FOR HERE OR TO GO?
TO GO!
ORDER HERE

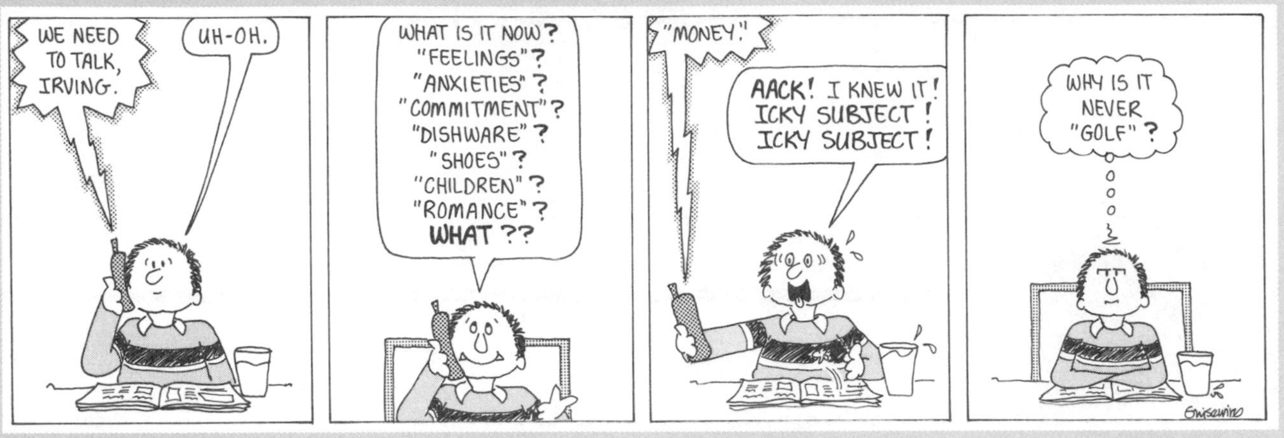
WE NEED TO TALK, IRVING.
UH-OH.
WHAT IS IT NOW? "FEELINGS"? "ANXIETIES"? "COMMITMENT"? "DISHWARE"? "SHOES"? "CHILDREN"? "ROMANCE"? WHAT??
"MONEY."
AACK! I KNEW IT! ICKY SUBJECT! ICKY SUBJECT!
WHY IS IT NEVER "GOLF"?

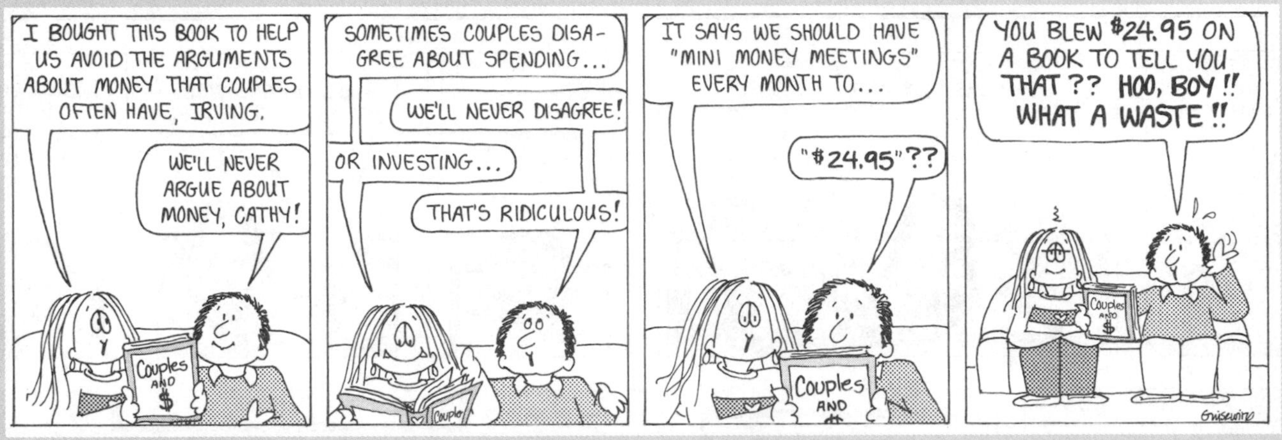
I BOUGHT THIS BOOK TO HELP US AVOID THE ARGUMENTS ABOUT MONEY THAT COUPLES OFTEN HAVE, IRVING.
WE'LL NEVER ARGUE ABOUT MONEY, CATHY!
Couples AND $
SOMETIMES COUPLES DISA-GREE ABOUT SPENDING...
WE'LL NEVER DISAGREE!
OR INVESTING...
THAT'S RIDICULOUS!
IT SAYS WE SHOULD HAVE "MINI MONEY MEETINGS" EVERY MONTH TO...
"$24.95"??
YOU BLEW $24.95 ON A BOOK TO TELL YOU THAT?? HOO, BOY!! WHAT A WASTE!!

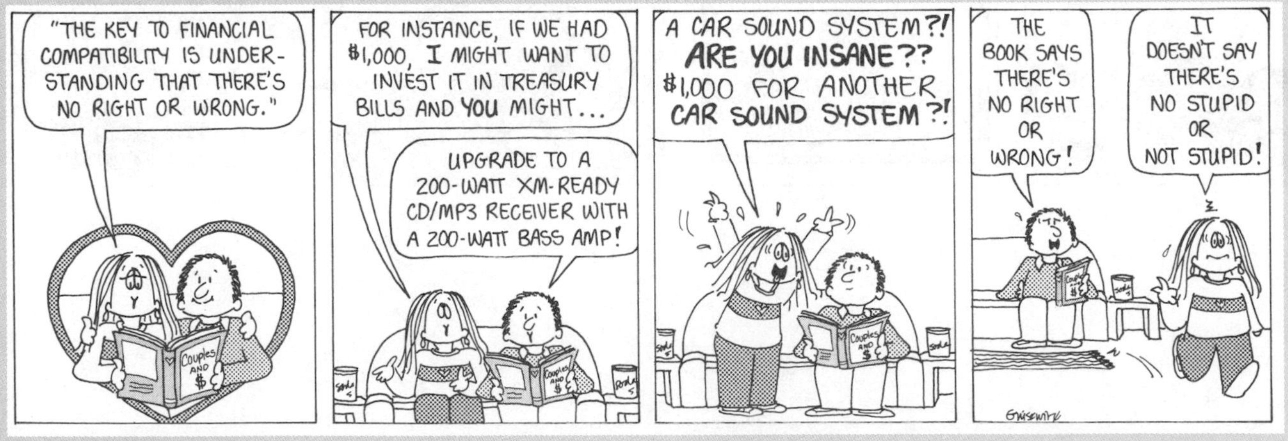
"THE KEY TO FINANCIAL COMPATIBILITY IS UNDER-STANDING THAT THERE'S NO RIGHT OR WRONG."
FOR INSTANCE, IF WE HAD $1,000, I MIGHT WANT TO INVEST IT IN TREASURY BILLS AND YOU MIGHT...
UPGRADE TO A 200-WATT XM-READY CD/MP3 RECEIVER WITH A 200-WATT BASS AMP!
A CAR SOUND SYSTEM?! ARE YOU INSANE?? $1,000 FOR ANOTHER CAR SOUND SYSTEM?!
THE BOOK SAYS THERE'S NO RIGHT OR WRONG!
IT DOESN'T SAY THERE'S NO STUPID OR NOT STUPID!

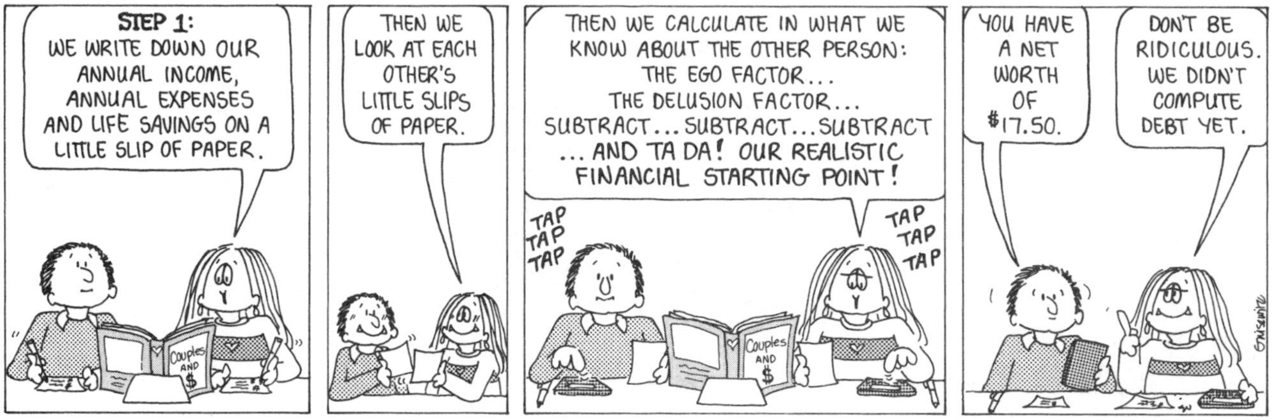
STEP 1: WE WRITE DOWN OUR ANNUAL INCOME, ANNUAL EXPENSES AND LIFE SAVINGS ON A LITTLE SLIP OF PAPER.
THEN WE LOOK AT EACH OTHER'S LITTLE SLIPS OF PAPER.
THEN WE CALCULATE IN WHAT WE KNOW ABOUT THE OTHER PERSON: THE EGO FACTOR... THE DELUSION FACTOR... SUBTRACT... SUBTRACT... SUBTRACT ... AND TA DA! OUR REALISTIC FINANCIAL STARTING POINT!
TAP TAP TAP
TAP TAP TAP
YOU HAVE A NET WORTH OF $17.50.
DON'T BE RIDICULOUS. WE DIDN'T COMPUTE DEBT YET.

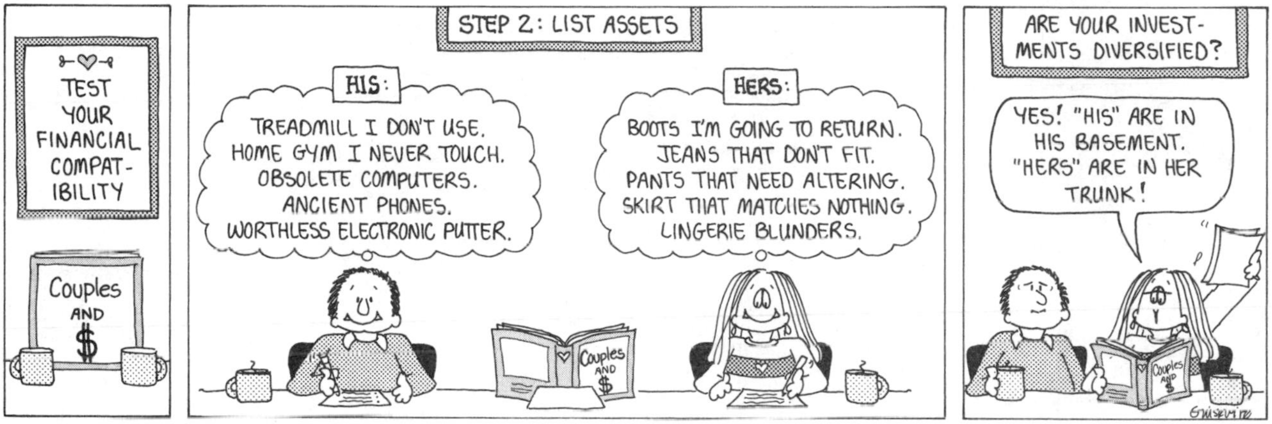
TEST YOUR FINANCIAL COMPATIBILITY
Couples AND $
STEP 2: LIST ASSETS
HIS:
TREADMILL I DON'T USE. HOME GYM I NEVER TOUCH. OBSOLETE COMPUTERS. ANCIENT PHONES. WORTHLESS ELECTRONIC PUTTER.
HERS:
BOOTS I'M GOING TO RETURN. JEANS THAT DON'T FIT. PANTS THAT NEED ALTERING. SKIRT THAT MATCHES NOTHING. LINGERIE BLUNDERS.
ARE YOUR INVESTMENTS DIVERSIFIED?
YES! "HIS" ARE IN HIS BASEMENT. "HERS" ARE IN HER TRUNK!

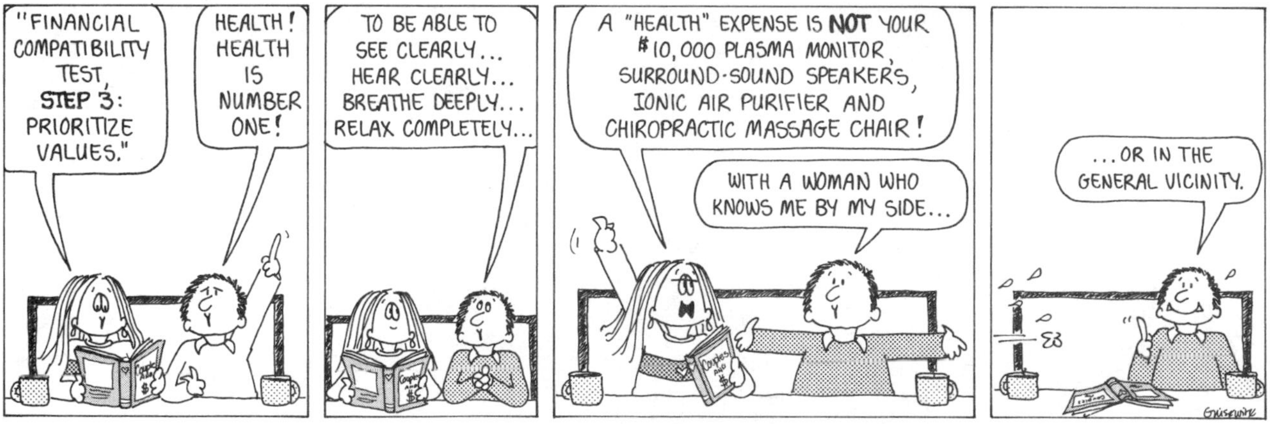
"FINANCIAL COMPATIBILITY TEST, STEP 3: PRIORITIZE VALUES."
HEALTH! HEALTH IS NUMBER ONE!
TO BE ABLE TO SEE CLEARLY... HEAR CLEARLY... BREATHE DEEPLY... RELAX COMPLETELY...
A "HEALTH" EXPENSE IS NOT YOUR $10,000 PLASMA MONITOR, SURROUND-SOUND SPEAKERS, IONIC AIR PURIFIER AND CHIROPRACTIC MASSAGE CHAIR!
WITH A WOMAN WHO KNOWS ME BY MY SIDE...
...OR IN THE GENERAL VICINITY.

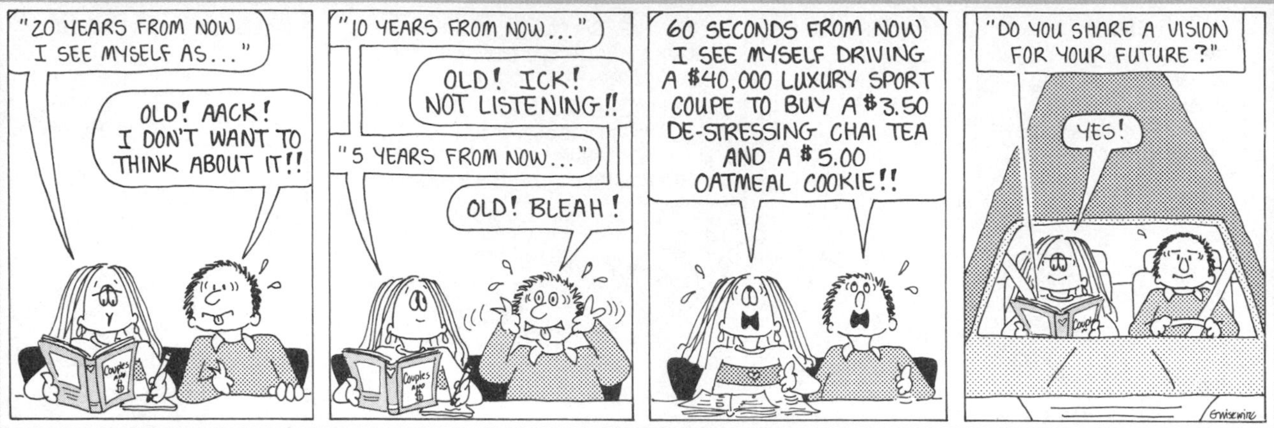
"20 YEARS FROM NOW I SEE MYSELF AS..."
OLD! AACK! I DON'T WANT TO THINK ABOUT IT!!
"10 YEARS FROM NOW..."
OLD! ICK! NOT LISTENING!!
"5 YEARS FROM NOW..."
OLD! BLEAH!
60 SECONDS FROM NOW I SEE MYSELF DRIVING A $40,000 LUXURY SPORT COUPE TO BUY A $3.50 DE-STRESSING CHAI TEA AND A $5.00 OATMEAL COOKIE!!
"DO YOU SHARE A VISION FOR YOUR FUTURE?"
YES!

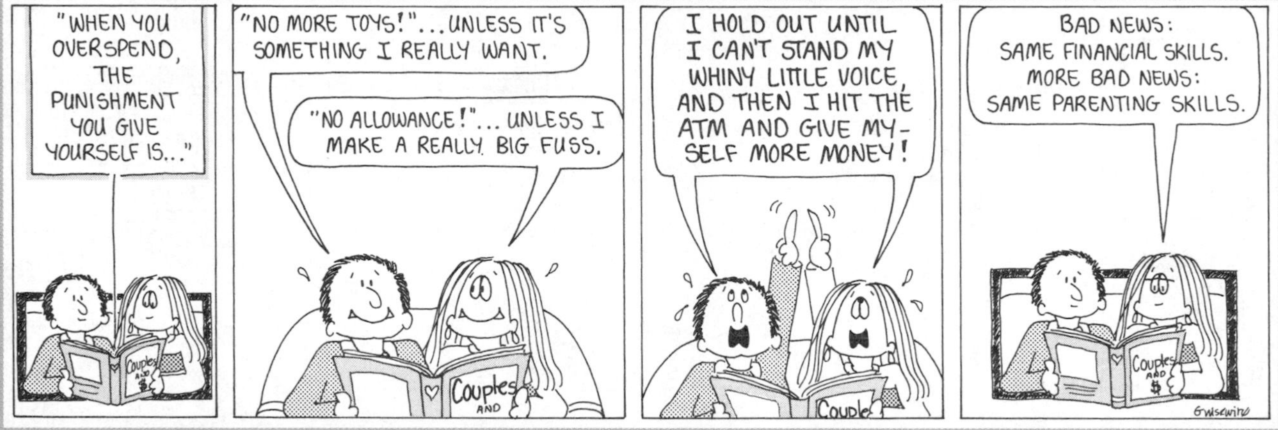
"WHEN YOU OVERSPEND, THE PUNISHMENT YOU GIVE YOURSELF IS..."
"NO MORE TOYS!"... UNLESS IT'S SOMETHING I REALLY WANT.
"NO ALLOWANCE!"... UNLESS I MAKE A REALLY BIG FUSS.
I HOLD OUT UNTIL I CAN'T STAND MY WHINY LITTLE VOICE, AND THEN I HIT THE ATM AND GIVE MY-SELF MORE MONEY!
BAD NEWS: SAME FINANCIAL SKILLS. MORE BAD NEWS: SAME PARENTING SKILLS.

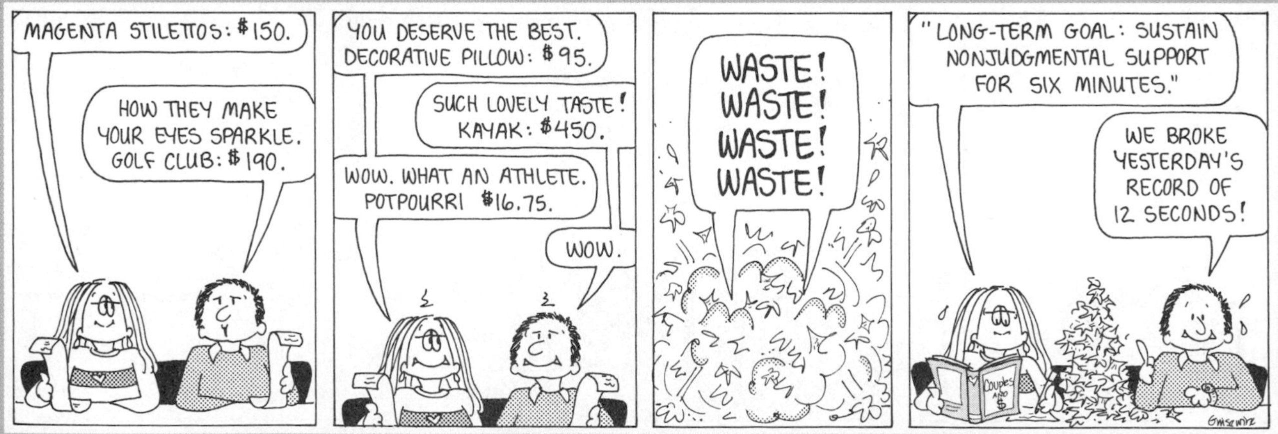
MAGENTA STILETTOS: $150.
HOW THEY MAKE YOUR EYES SPARKLE. GOLF CLUB: $190.
YOU DESERVE THE BEST. DECORATIVE PILLOW: $95.
SUCH LOVELY TASTE! KAYAK: $450.
WOW. WHAT AN ATHLETE. POTPOURRI $16.75.
WOW.
WASTE! WASTE! WASTE! WASTE!
"LONG-TERM GOAL: SUSTAIN NONJUDGMENTAL SUPPORT FOR SIX MINUTES."
WE BROKE YESTERDAY'S RECORD OF 12 SECONDS!

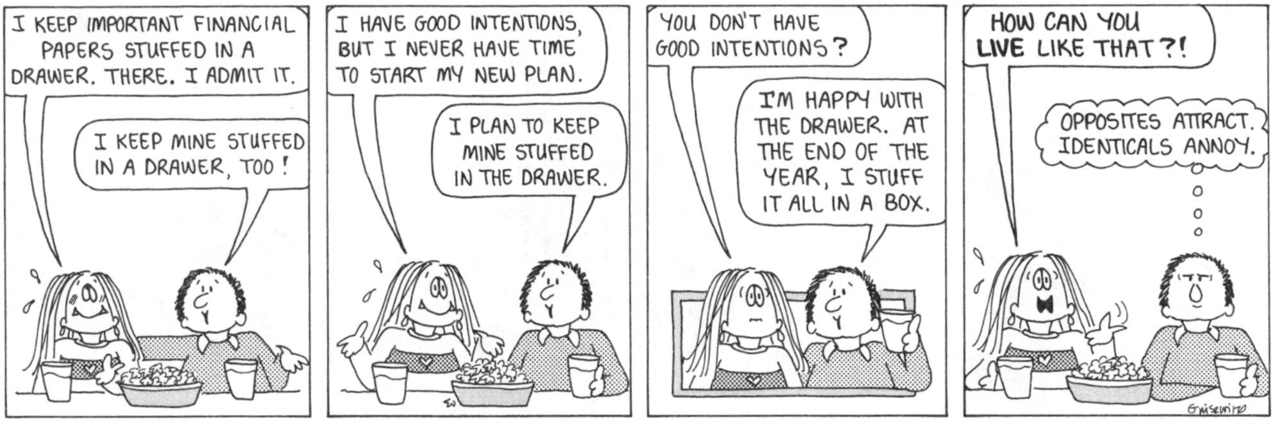
I KEEP IMPORTANT FINANCIAL PAPERS STUFFED IN A DRAWER. THERE. I ADMIT IT.
I KEEP MINE STUFFED IN A DRAWER, TOO!
I HAVE GOOD INTENTIONS, BUT I NEVER HAVE TIME TO START MY NEW PLAN.
I PLAN TO KEEP MINE STUFFED IN THE DRAWER.
YOU DON'T HAVE GOOD INTENTIONS?
I'M HAPPY WITH THE DRAWER. AT THE END OF THE YEAR, I STUFF IT ALL IN A BOX.
HOW CAN YOU LIVE LIKE THAT?!
OPPOSITES ATTRACT. IDENTICALS ANNOY.

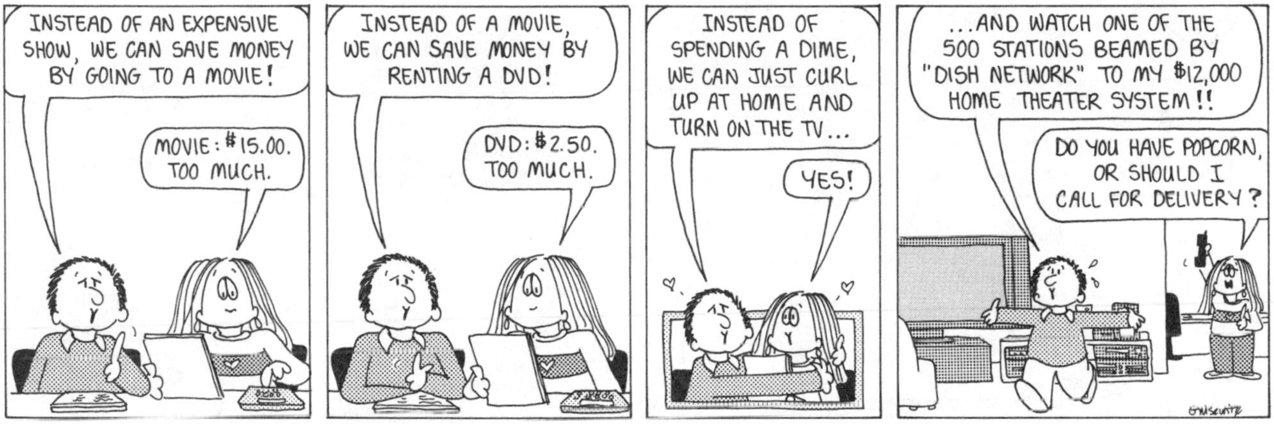
INSTEAD OF AN EXPENSIVE SHOW, WE CAN SAVE MONEY BY GOING TO A MOVIE!
MOVIE: $15.00. TOO MUCH.
INSTEAD OF A MOVIE, WE CAN SAVE MONEY BY RENTING A DVD!
DVD: $2.50. TOO MUCH.
INSTEAD OF SPENDING A DIME, WE CAN JUST CURL UP AT HOME AND TURN ON THE TV...
YES!
...AND WATCH ONE OF THE 500 STATIONS BEAMED BY "DISH NETWORK" TO MY $12,000 HOME THEATER SYSTEM!!
DO YOU HAVE POPCORN, OR SHOULD I CALL FOR DELIVERY?

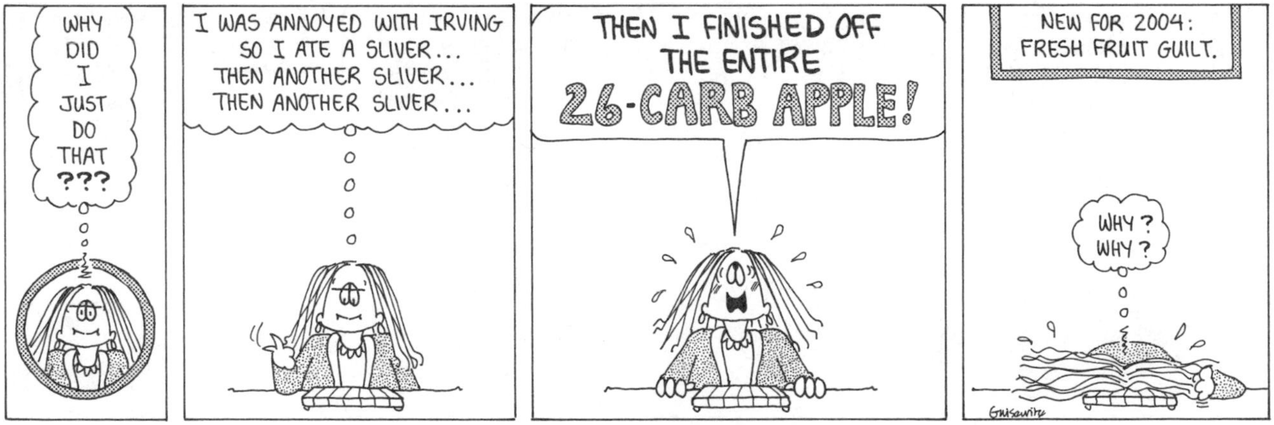
WHY DID I JUST DO THAT???
I WAS ANNOYED WITH IRVING SO I ATE A SLIVER... THEN ANOTHER SLIVER... THEN ANOTHER SLIVER...
THEN I FINISHED OFF THE ENTIRE 26-CARB APPLE!
NEW FOR 2004: FRESH FRUIT GUILT.
WHY? WHY?

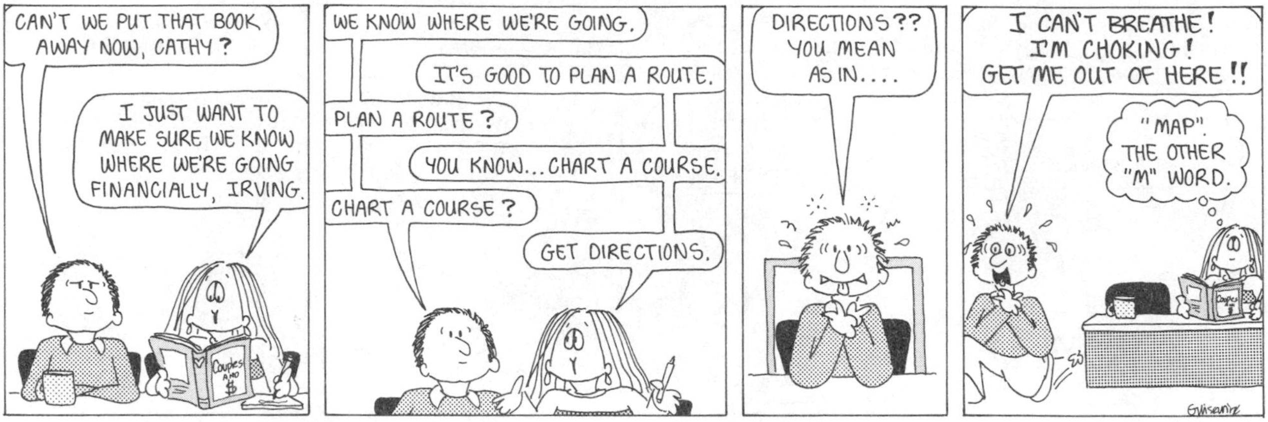
CAN'T WE PUT THAT BOOK AWAY NOW, CATHY?
I JUST WANT TO MAKE SURE WE KNOW WHERE WE'RE GOING FINANCIALLY, IRVING.
WE KNOW WHERE WE'RE GOING.
IT'S GOOD TO PLAN A ROUTE.
PLAN A ROUTE?
YOU KNOW... CHART A COURSE.
CHART A COURSE?
GET DIRECTIONS.
DIRECTIONS?? YOU MEAN AS IN....
I CAN'T BREATHE! I'M CHOKING! GET ME OUT OF HERE!!
"MAP". THE OTHER "M" WORD.

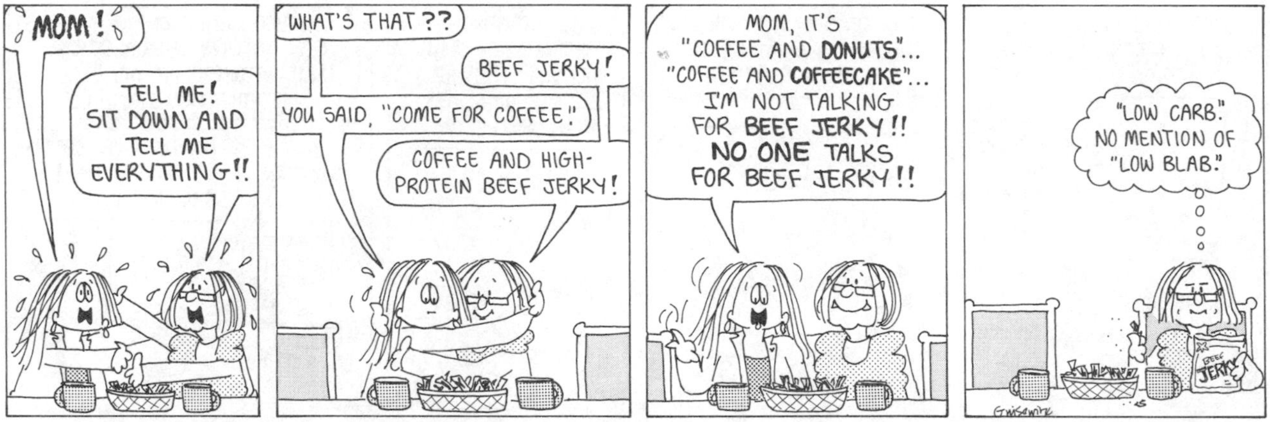
MOM!
TELL ME! SIT DOWN AND TELL ME EVERYTHING!!
WHAT'S THAT??
BEEF JERKY!
YOU SAID, "COME FOR COFFEE."
COFFEE AND HIGH-PROTEIN BEEF JERKY!
MOM, IT'S "COFFEE AND DONUTS"... "COFFEE AND COFFEECAKE"... I'M NOT TALKING FOR BEEF JERKY!! NO ONE TALKS FOR BEEF JERKY!!
"LOW CARB." NO MENTION OF "LOW BLAB."
BEEF JERKY

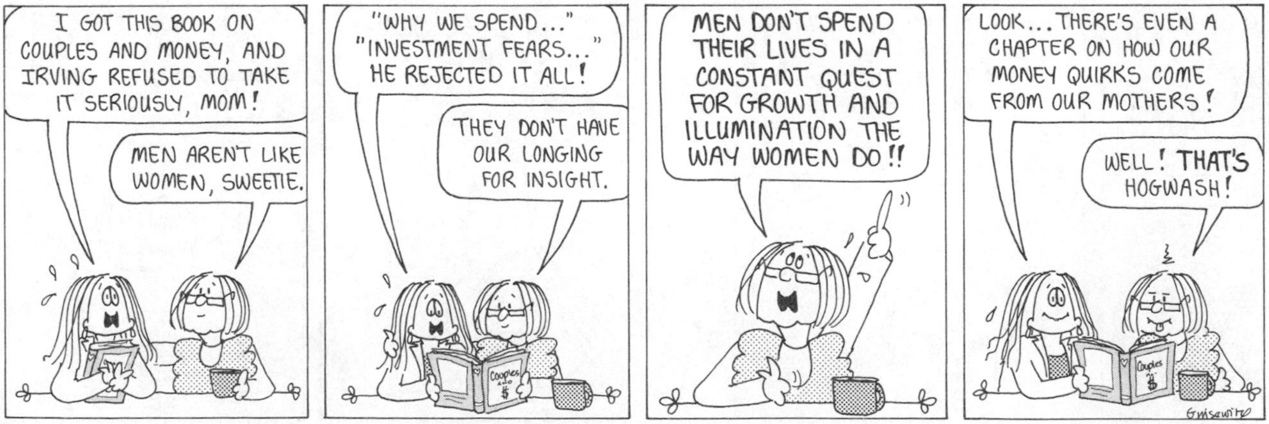
I GOT THIS BOOK ON COUPLES AND MONEY, AND IRVING REFUSED TO TAKE IT SERIOUSLY, MOM!
MEN AREN'T LIKE WOMEN, SWEETIE.
"WHY WE SPEND..." "INVESTMENT FEARS..." HE REJECTED IT ALL!
THEY DON'T HAVE OUR LONGING FOR INSIGHT.
MEN DON'T SPEND THEIR LIVES IN A CONSTANT QUEST FOR GROWTH AND ILLUMINATION THE WAY WOMEN DO!!
LOOK... THERE'S EVEN A CHAPTER ON HOW OUR MONEY QUIRKS COME FROM OUR MOTHERS!
WELL! THAT'S HOGWASH!

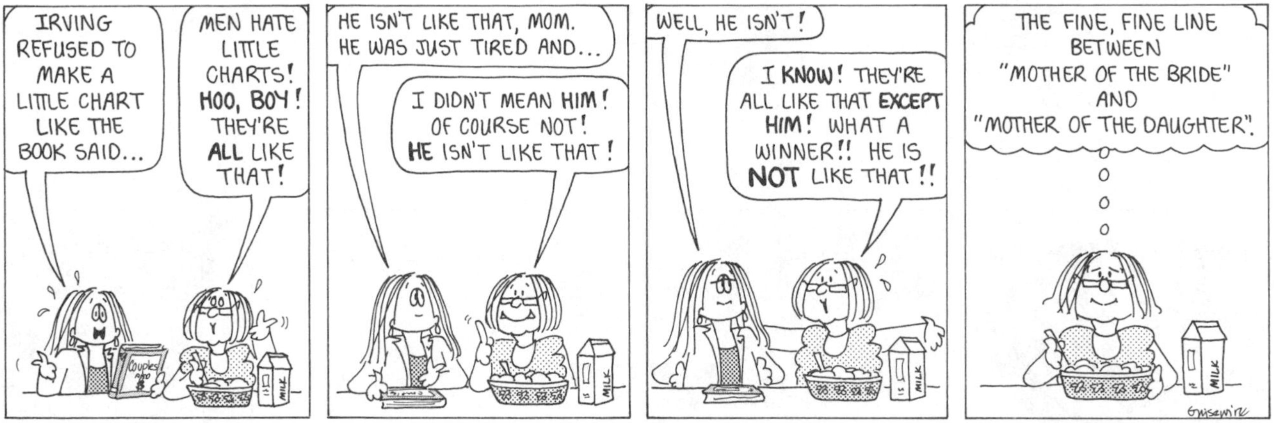
IRVING REFUSED TO MAKE A LITTLE CHART LIKE THE BOOK SAID...
MEN HATE LITTLE CHARTS! HOO, BOY! THEY'RE ALL LIKE THAT!
HE ISN'T LIKE THAT, MOM. HE WAS JUST TIRED AND...
I DIDN'T MEAN HIM! OF COURSE NOT! HE ISN'T LIKE THAT!
WELL, HE ISN'T!
I KNOW! THEY'RE ALL LIKE THAT EXCEPT HIM! WHAT A WINNER!! HE IS NOT LIKE THAT!!
THE FINE, FINE LINE BETWEEN "MOTHER OF THE BRIDE" AND "MOTHER OF THE DAUGHTER".

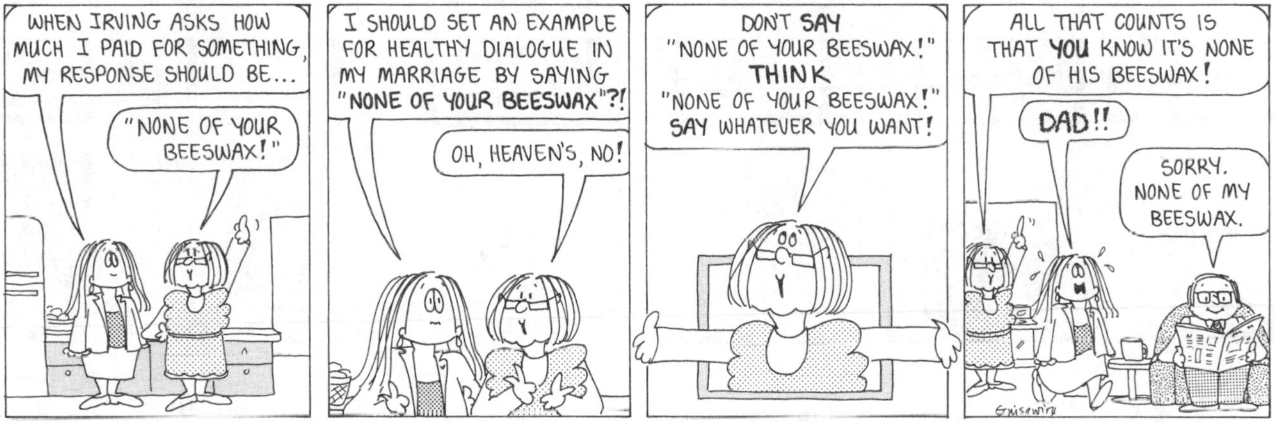
WHEN IRVING ASKS HOW MUCH I PAID FOR SOMETHING, MY RESPONSE SHOULD BE...
"NONE OF YOUR BEESWAX!"
I SHOULD SET AN EXAMPLE FOR HEALTHY DIALOGUE IN MY MARRIAGE BY SAYING "NONE OF YOUR BEESWAX"?!
OH, HEAVEN'S, NO!
DON'T SAY "NONE OF YOUR BEESWAX!" THINK "NONE OF YOUR BEESWAX!" SAY WHATEVER YOU WANT!
ALL THAT COUNTS IS THAT YOU KNOW IT'S NONE OF HIS BEESWAX!
DAD!!
SORRY. NONE OF MY BEESWAX.

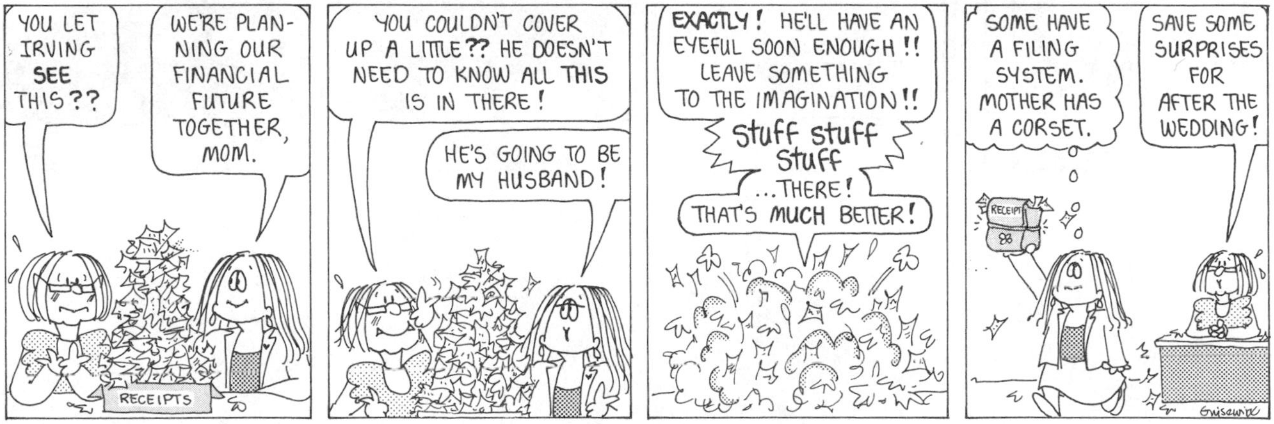
YOU LET IRVING SEE THIS??
WE'RE PLANNING OUR FINANCIAL FUTURE TOGETHER, MOM.
RECEIPTS
YOU COULDN'T COVER UP A LITTLE?? HE DOESN'T NEED TO KNOW ALL THIS IS IN THERE!
HE'S GOING TO BE MY HUSBAND!
EXACTLY! HE'LL HAVE AN EYEFUL SOON ENOUGH!! LEAVE SOMETHING TO THE IMAGINATION!!
stuff stuff stuff
...THERE!
THAT'S MUCH BETTER!
SOME HAVE A FILING SYSTEM. MOTHER HAS A CORSET.
SAVE SOME SURPRISES FOR AFTER THE WEDDING!

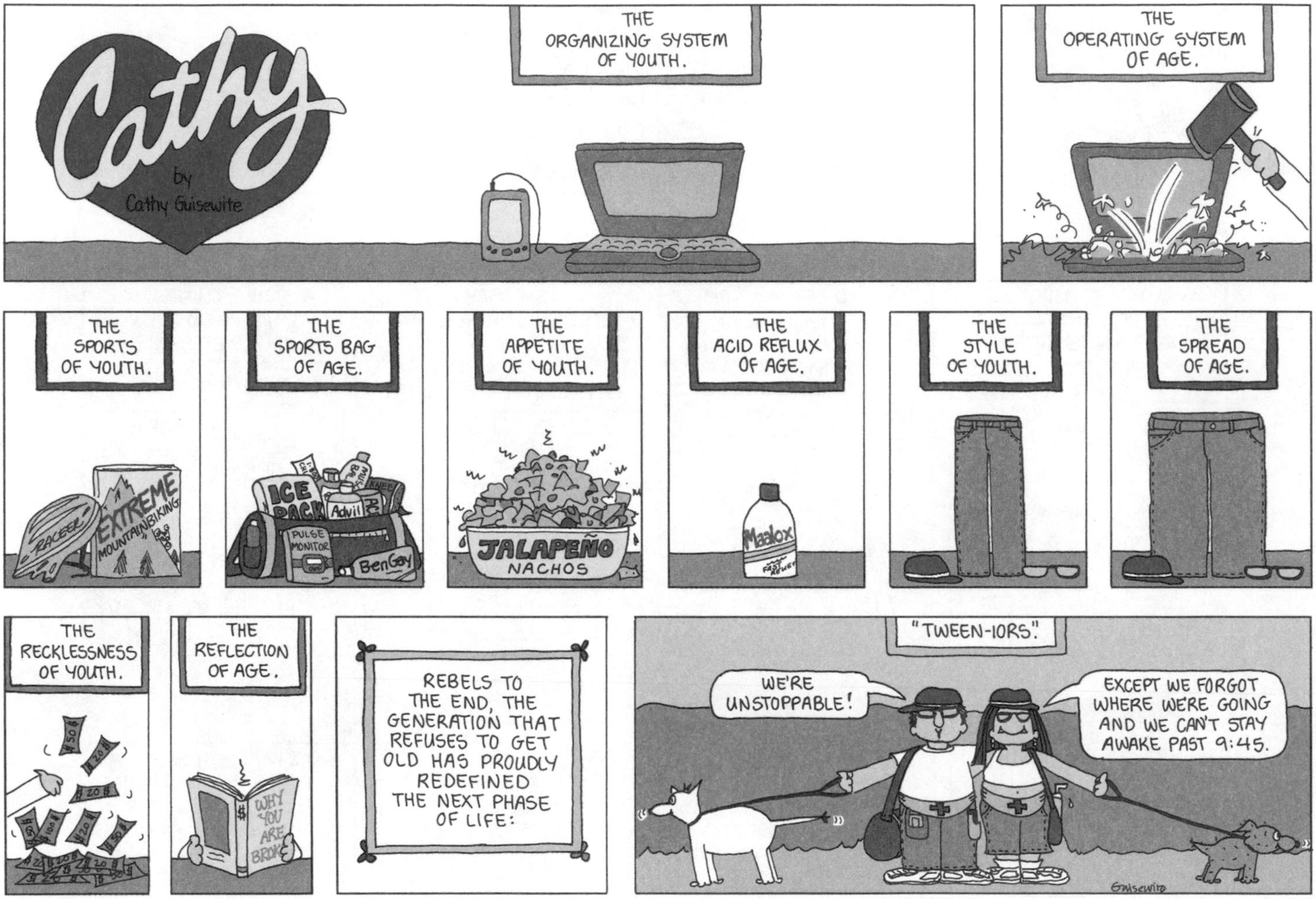
Cathy
by
Cathy Guisewite
THE ORGANIZING SYSTEM OF YOUTH.
THE OPERATING SYSTEM OF AGE.
THE SPORTS OF YOUTH.
RACER
EXTREME MOUNTAINBIKING
THE SPORTS BAG OF AGE.
ICE PACK
Advil
PULSE MONITOR
BenGay
THE APPETITE OF YOUTH.
JALAPEÑO NACHOS
THE ACID REFLUX OF AGE.
Maalox
THE STYLE OF YOUTH.
THE SPREAD OF AGE.
THE RECKLESSNESS OF YOUTH.
THE REFLECTION OF AGE.
WHY YOU ARE BROKE
REBELS TO THE END, THE GENERATION THAT REFUSES TO GET OLD HAS PROUDLY REDEFINED THE NEXT PHASE OF LIFE:
"TWEEN-IORS."
WE'RE UNSTOPPABLE!
EXCEPT WE FORGOT WHERE WE'RE GOING AND WE CAN'T STAY AWAKE PAST 9:45.
Guisewite

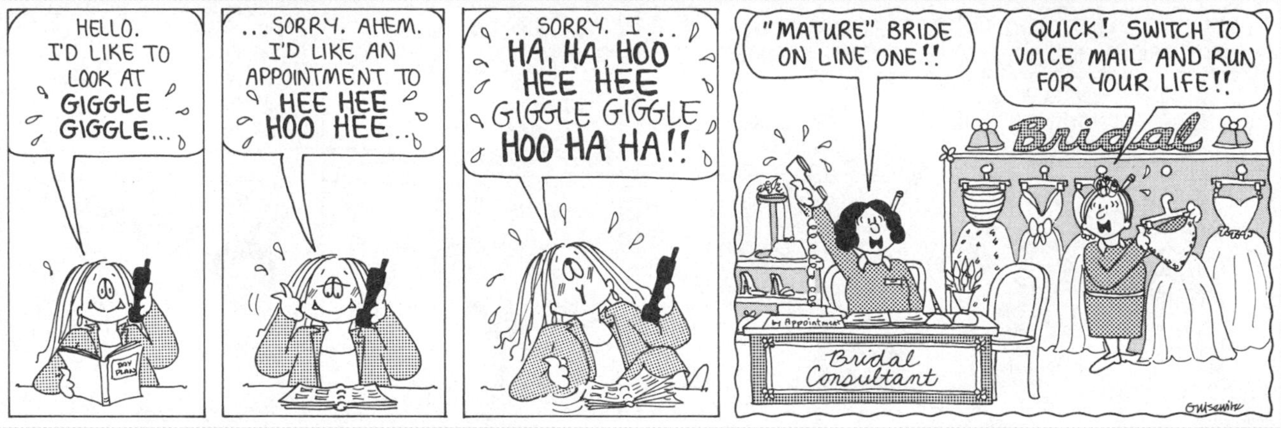
HELLO. I'D LIKE TO LOOK AT GIGGLE GIGGLE...
...SORRY. AHEM. I'D LIKE AN APPOINTMENT TO HEE HEE HOO HEE...
...SORRY. I... HA, HA, HOO HEE HEE GIGGLE GIGGLE HOO HA HA!!
"MATURE" BRIDE ON LINE ONE!!
QUICK! SWITCH TO VOICE MAIL AND RUN FOR YOUR LIFE!!
Bridal
Bridal Consultant

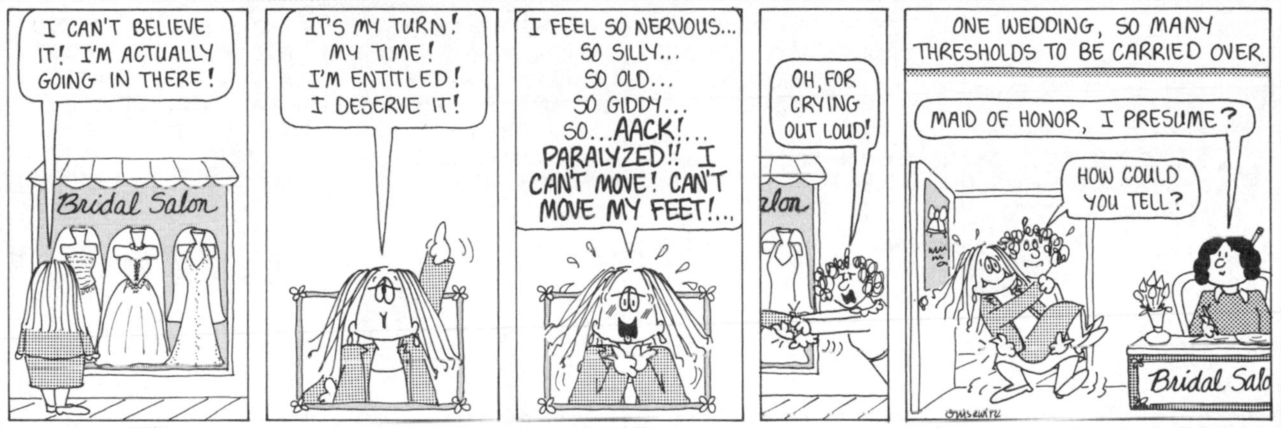
I CAN'T BELIEVE IT! I'M ACTUALLY GOING IN THERE!
Bridal Salon
IT'S MY TURN! MY TIME! I'M ENTITLED! I DESERVE IT!
I FEEL SO NERVOUS... SO SILLY... SO OLD... SO GIDDY... SO...AACK!... PARALYZED!! I CAN'T MOVE! CAN'T MOVE MY FEET!...
OH, FOR CRYING OUT LOUD!
ONE WEDDING, SO MANY THRESHOLDS TO BE CARRIED OVER.
MAID OF HONOR, I PRESUME?
HOW COULD YOU TELL?
Bridal Salo

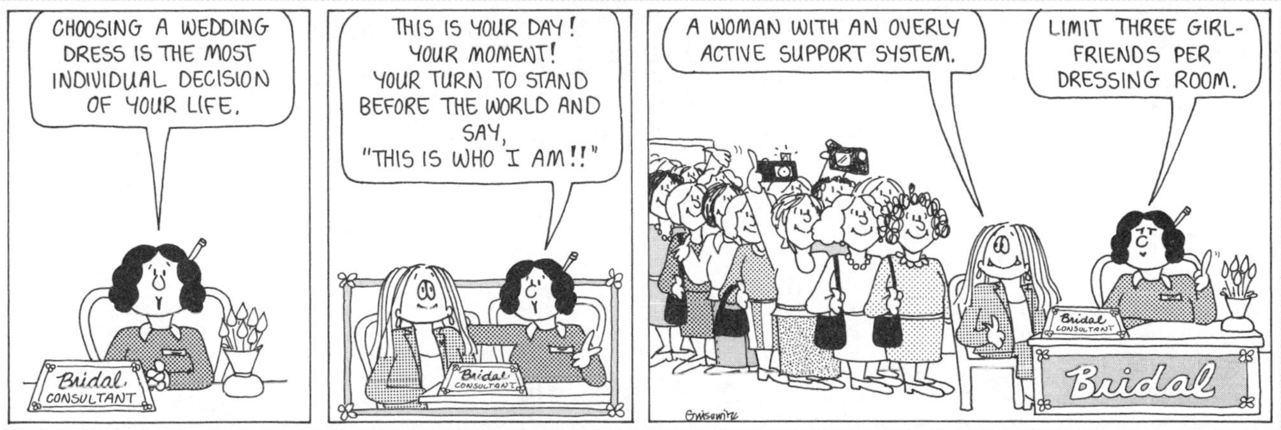
CHOOSING A WEDDING DRESS IS THE MOST INDIVIDUAL DECISION OF YOUR LIFE.
Bridal CONSULTANT
THIS IS YOUR DAY! YOUR MOMENT! YOUR TURN TO STAND BEFORE THE WORLD AND SAY, "THIS IS WHO I AM!!"
A WOMAN WITH AN OVERLY ACTIVE SUPPORT SYSTEM.
LIMIT THREE GIRLFRIENDS PER DRESSING ROOM.
Bridal

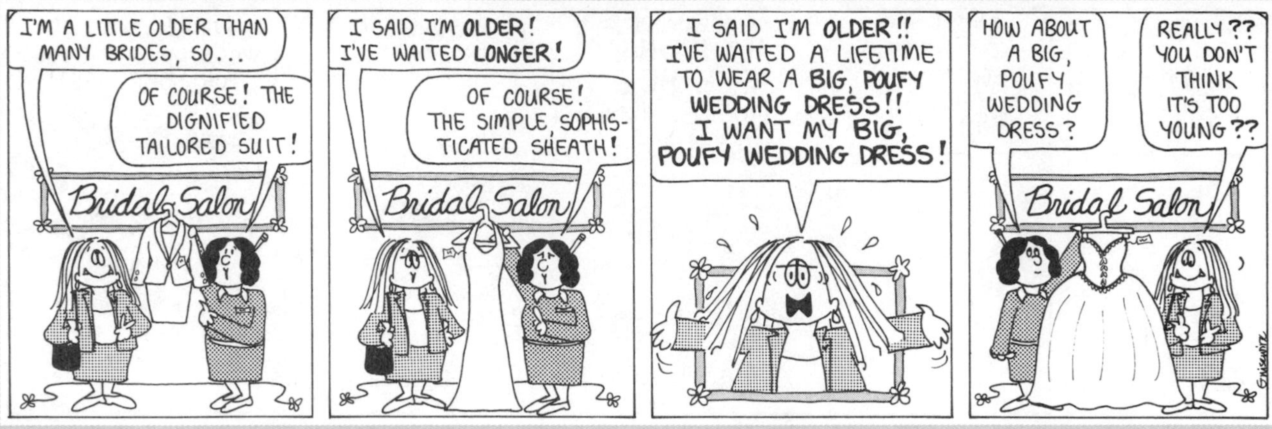
I'M A LITTLE OLDER THAN MANY BRIDES, SO...
OF COURSE! THE DIGNIFIED TAILORED SUIT!
Bridal Salon
I SAID I'M OLDER! I'VE WAITED LONGER!
OF COURSE! THE SIMPLE, SOPHISTICATED SHEATH!
Bridal Salon
I SAID I'M OLDER!! I'VE WAITED A LIFETIME TO WEAR A BIG, POUFY WEDDING DRESS!! I WANT MY BIG, POUFY WEDDING DRESS!
HOW ABOUT A BIG, POUFY WEDDING DRESS?
REALLY?? YOU DON'T THINK IT'S TOO YOUNG??
Bridal Salon

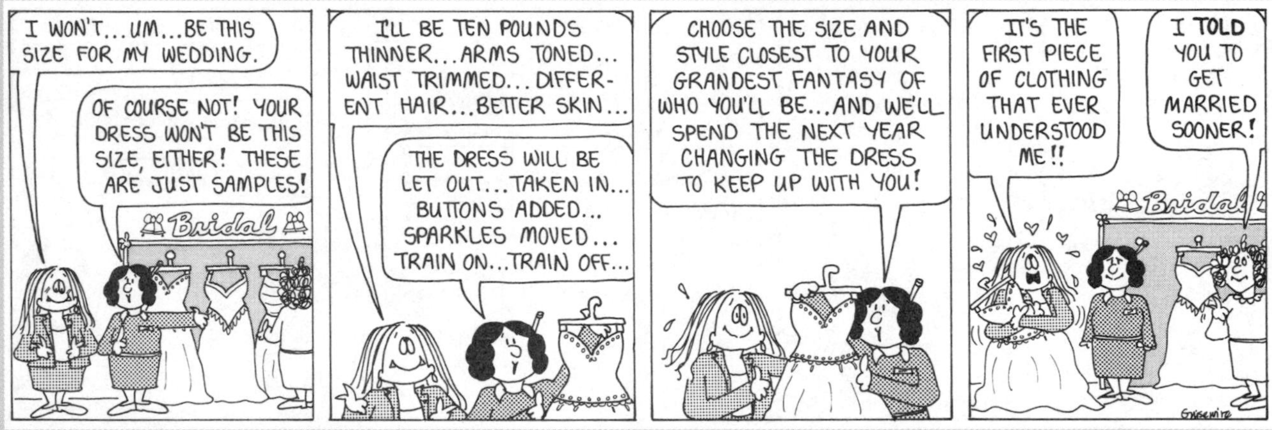
I WON'T...UM...BE THIS SIZE FOR MY WEDDING.
OF COURSE NOT! YOUR DRESS WON'T BE THIS SIZE, EITHER! THESE ARE JUST SAMPLES!
Bridal
I'LL BE TEN POUNDS THINNER...ARMS TONED... WAIST TRIMMED... DIFFERENT HAIR...BETTER SKIN...
THE DRESS WILL BE LET OUT...TAKEN IN... BUTTONS ADDED... SPARKLES MOVED... TRAIN ON...TRAIN OFF...
CHOOSE THE SIZE AND STYLE CLOSEST TO YOUR GRANDEST FANTASY OF WHO YOU'LL BE...AND WE'LL SPEND THE NEXT YEAR CHANGING THE DRESS TO KEEP UP WITH YOU!
IT'S THE FIRST PIECE OF CLOTHING THAT EVER UNDERSTOOD ME!!
I TOLD YOU TO GET MARRIED SOONER!
Bridal

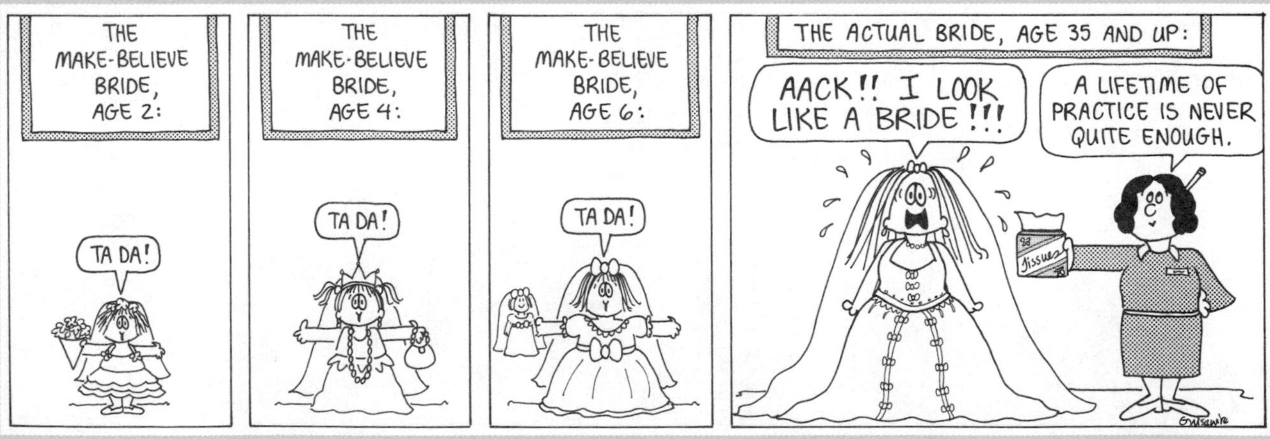
THE MAKE-BELIEVE BRIDE, AGE 2:
TA DA!
THE MAKE-BELIEVE BRIDE, AGE 4:
TA DA!
THE MAKE-BELIEVE BRIDE, AGE 6:
TA DA!
THE ACTUAL BRIDE, AGE 35 AND UP:
AACK!! I LOOK LIKE A BRIDE!!!
A LIFETIME OF PRACTICE IS NEVER QUITE ENOUGH.
Tissues

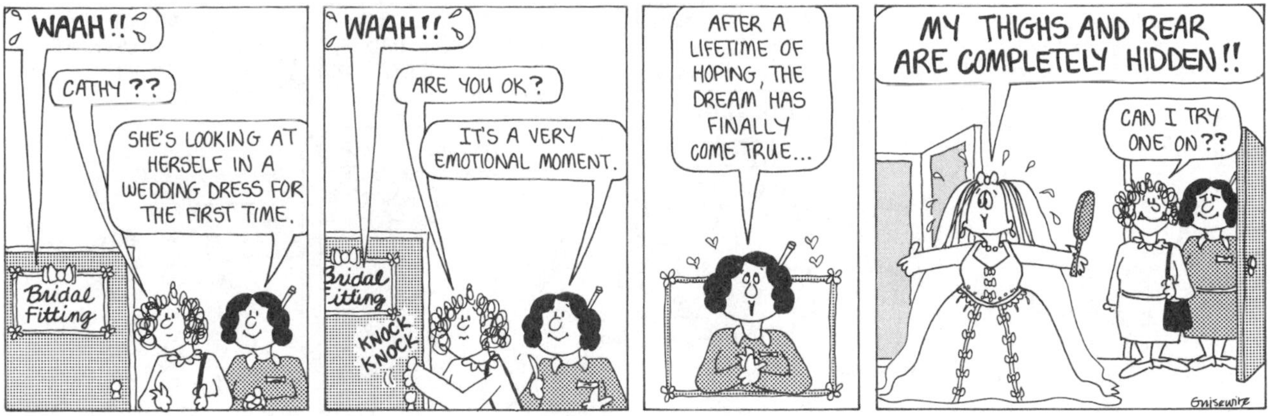
WAAH!!
CATHY??
SHE'S LOOKING AT HERSELF IN A WEDDING DRESS FOR THE FIRST TIME.
Bridal Fitting
WAAH!!
ARE YOU OK?
IT'S A VERY EMOTIONAL MOMENT.
Bridal Fitting
KNOCK KNOCK
AFTER A LIFETIME OF HOPING, THE DREAM HAS FINALLY COME TRUE...
MY THIGHS AND REAR ARE COMPLETELY HIDDEN!!
CAN I TRY ONE ON??
Guisewite

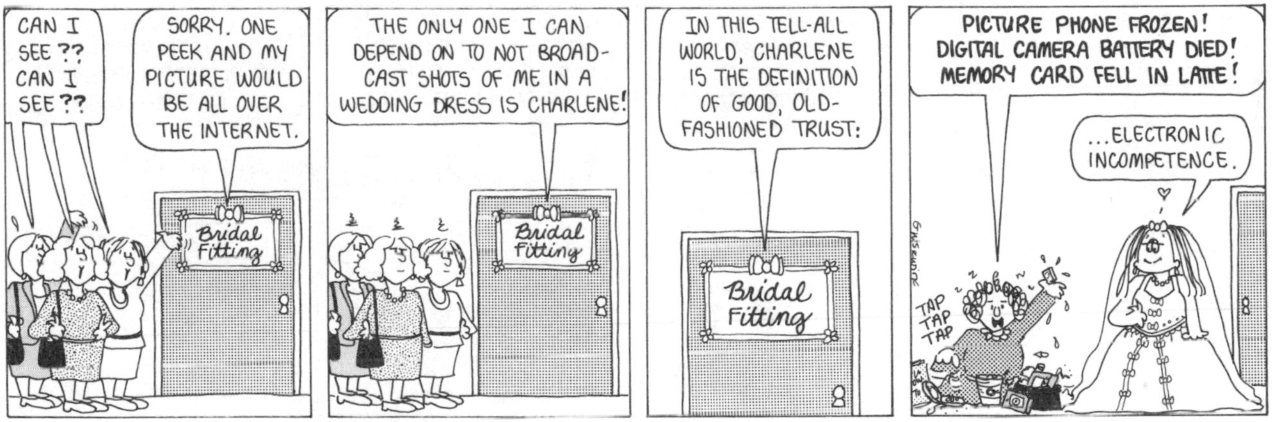
CAN I SEE?? CAN I SEE??
SORRY. ONE PEEK AND MY PICTURE WOULD BE ALL OVER THE INTERNET.
Bridal Fitting
THE ONLY ONE I CAN DEPEND ON TO NOT BROADCAST SHOTS OF ME IN A WEDDING DRESS IS CHARLENE!
Bridal Fitting
IN THIS TELL-ALL WORLD, CHARLENE IS THE DEFINITION OF GOOD, OLD-FASHIONED TRUST:
Bridal Fitting
PICTURE PHONE FROZEN! DIGITAL CAMERA BATTERY DIED! MEMORY CARD FELL IN LATTE!
...ELECTRONIC INCOMPETENCE.
TAP TAP TAP
Guisewite

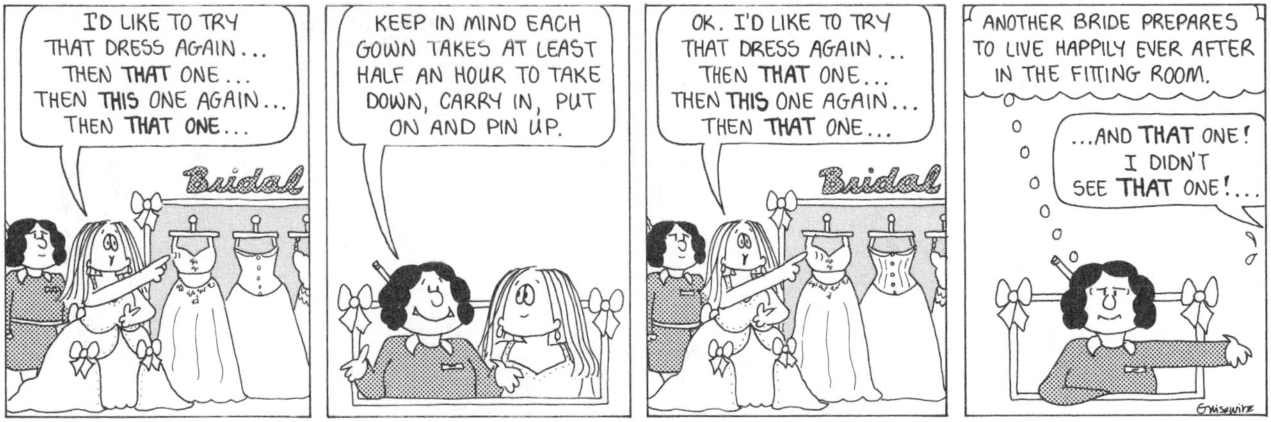
I'D LIKE TO TRY THAT DRESS AGAIN... THEN THAT ONE... THEN THIS ONE AGAIN... THEN THAT ONE...
Bridal
KEEP IN MIND EACH GOWN TAKES AT LEAST HALF AN HOUR TO TAKE DOWN, CARRY IN, PUT ON AND PIN UP.
OK. I'D LIKE TO TRY THAT DRESS AGAIN... THEN THAT ONE... THEN THIS ONE AGAIN... THEN THAT ONE...
Bridal
ANOTHER BRIDE PREPARES TO LIVE HAPPILY EVER AFTER IN THE FITTING ROOM.
...AND THAT ONE! I DIDN'T SEE THAT ONE!...
Guisewite

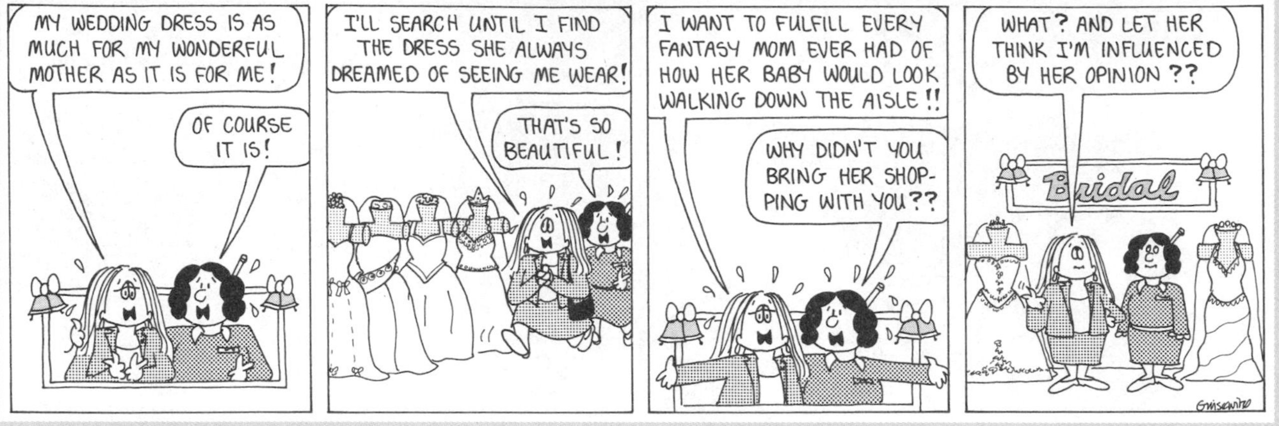
MY WEDDING DRESS IS AS MUCH FOR MY WONDERFUL MOTHER AS IT IS FOR ME!
OF COURSE IT IS!
I'LL SEARCH UNTIL I FIND THE DRESS SHE ALWAYS DREAMED OF SEEING ME WEAR!
THAT'S SO BEAUTIFUL!
I WANT TO FULFILL EVERY FANTASY MOM EVER HAD OF HOW HER BABY WOULD LOOK WALKING DOWN THE AISLE!!
WHY DIDN'T YOU BRING HER SHOPPING WITH YOU??
WHAT? AND LET HER THINK I'M INFLUENCED BY HER OPINION??
Bridal

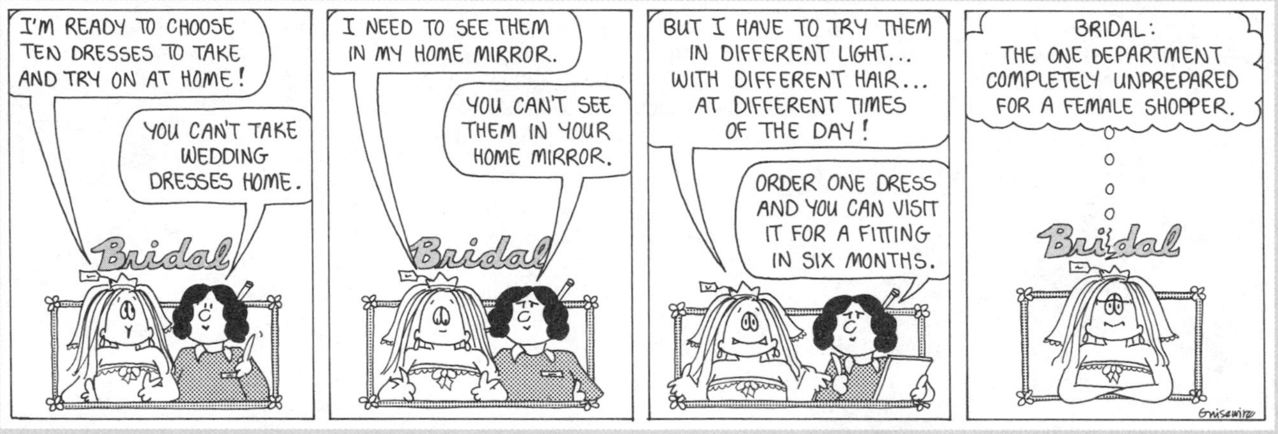
I'M READY TO CHOOSE TEN DRESSES TO TAKE AND TRY ON AT HOME!
YOU CAN'T TAKE WEDDING DRESSES HOME.
Bridal
I NEED TO SEE THEM IN MY HOME MIRROR.
YOU CAN'T SEE THEM IN YOUR HOME MIRROR.
Bridal
BUT I HAVE TO TRY THEM IN DIFFERENT LIGHT... WITH DIFFERENT HAIR... AT DIFFERENT TIMES OF THE DAY!
ORDER ONE DRESS AND YOU CAN VISIT IT FOR A FITTING IN SIX MONTHS.
BRIDAL: THE ONE DEPARTMENT COMPLETELY UNPREPARED FOR A FEMALE SHOPPER.
Bridal

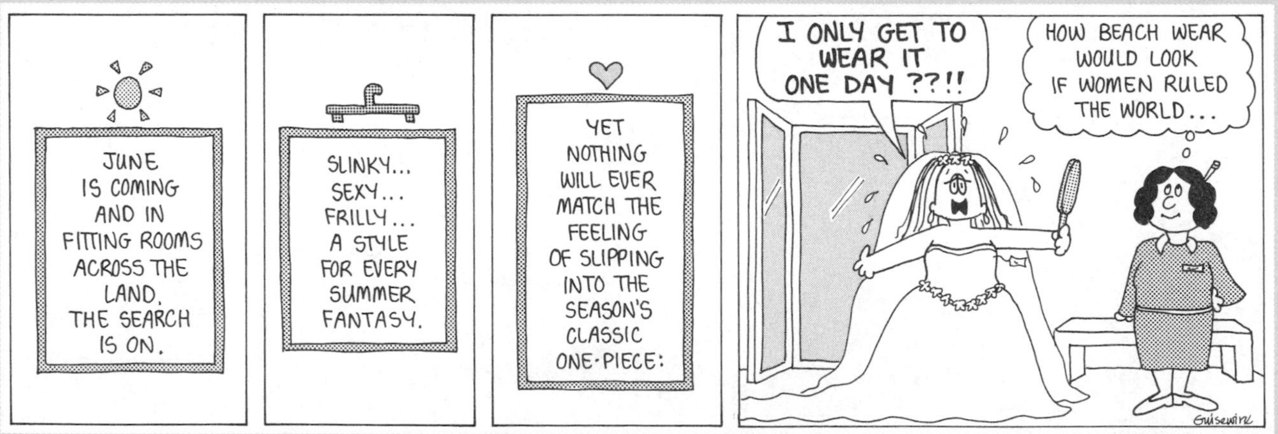
JUNE IS COMING AND IN FITTING ROOMS ACROSS THE LAND, THE SEARCH IS ON.
SLINKY... SEXY... FRILLY... A STYLE FOR EVERY SUMMER FANTASY.
YET NOTHING WILL EVER MATCH THE FEELING OF SLIPPING INTO THE SEASON'S CLASSIC ONE-PIECE:
I ONLY GET TO WEAR IT ONE DAY??!!
HOW BEACH WEAR WOULD LOOK IF WOMEN RULED THE WORLD...

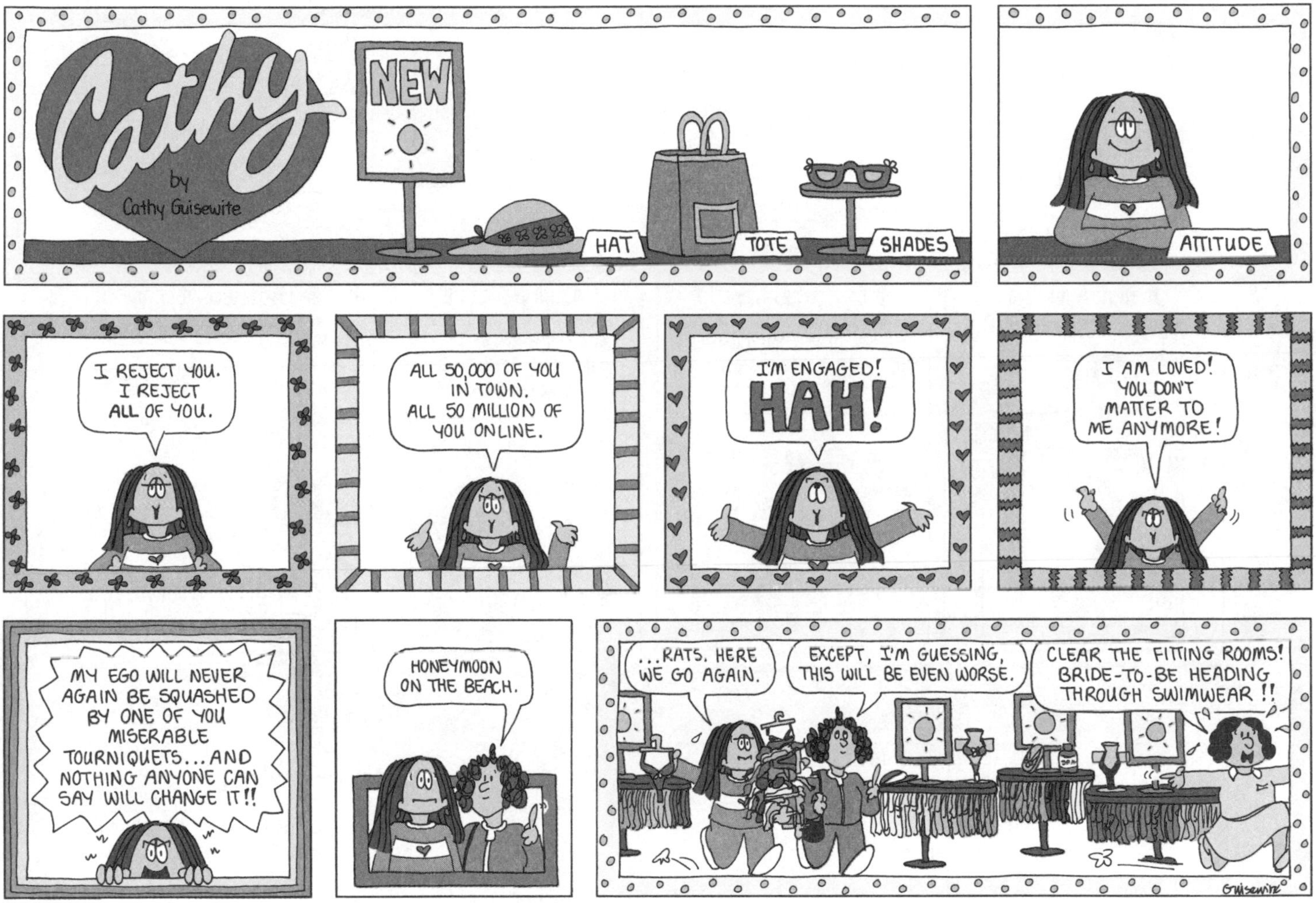
Cathy
by
Cathy Guisewite
NEW
HAT
TOTE
SHADES
ATTITUDE
I REJECT YOU. I REJECT ALL OF YOU.
ALL 50,000 OF YOU IN TOWN. ALL 50 MILLION OF YOU ONLINE.
I'M ENGAGED! HAH!
I AM LOVED! YOU DON'T MATTER TO ME ANYMORE!
MY EGO WILL NEVER AGAIN BE SQUASHED BY ONE OF YOU MISERABLE TOURNIQUETS... AND NOTHING ANYONE CAN SAY WILL CHANGE IT!!
HONEYMOON ON THE BEACH.
...RATS. HERE WE GO AGAIN.
EXCEPT, I'M GUESSING, THIS WILL BE EVEN WORSE.
CLEAR THE FITTING ROOMS! BRIDE-TO-BE HEADING THROUGH SWIMWEAR!!
Guisewite

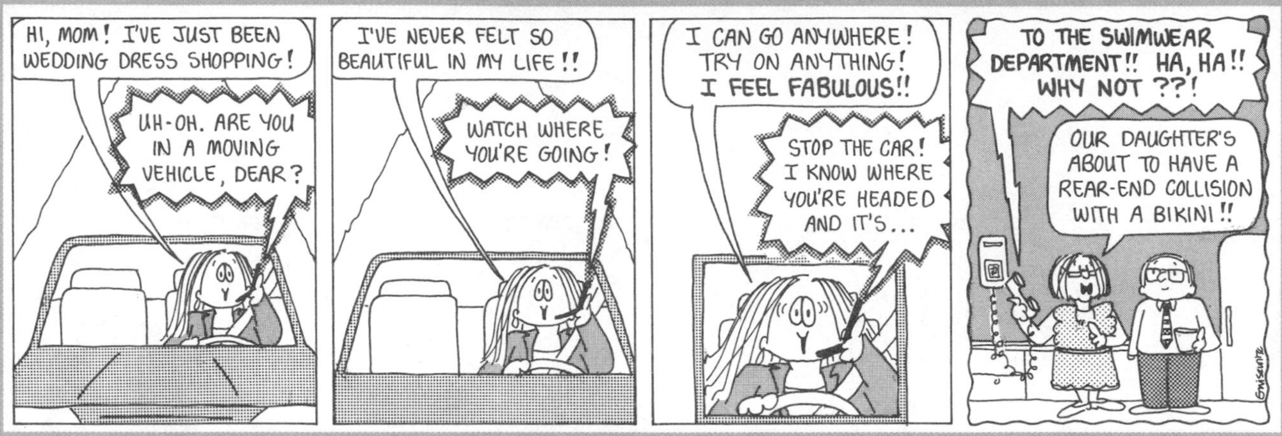
HI, MOM! I'VE JUST BEEN WEDDING DRESS SHOPPING!
UH-OH. ARE YOU IN A MOVING VEHICLE, DEAR?
I'VE NEVER FELT SO BEAUTIFUL IN MY LIFE!!
WATCH WHERE YOU'RE GOING!
I CAN GO ANYWHERE! TRY ON ANYTHING! I FEEL FABULOUS!!
STOP THE CAR! I KNOW WHERE YOU'RE HEADED AND IT'S...
TO THE SWIMWEAR DEPARTMENT!! HA, HA!! WHY NOT??!
OUR DAUGHTER'S ABOUT TO HAVE A REAR-END COLLISION WITH A BIKINI!!

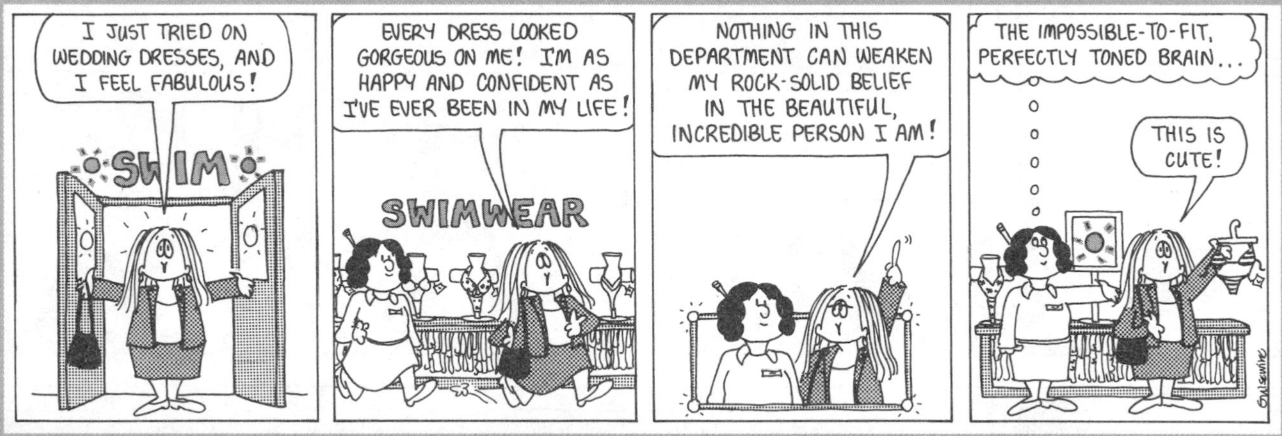
I JUST TRIED ON WEDDING DRESSES, AND I FEEL FABULOUS!
SWIM
EVERY DRESS LOOKED GORGEOUS ON ME! I'M AS HAPPY AND CONFIDENT AS I'VE EVER BEEN IN MY LIFE!
SWIMWEAR
NOTHING IN THIS DEPARTMENT CAN WEAKEN MY ROCK-SOLID BELIEF IN THE BEAUTIFUL, INCREDIBLE PERSON I AM!
THE IMPOSSIBLE-TO-FIT, PERFECTLY TONED BRAIN...
THIS IS CUTE!

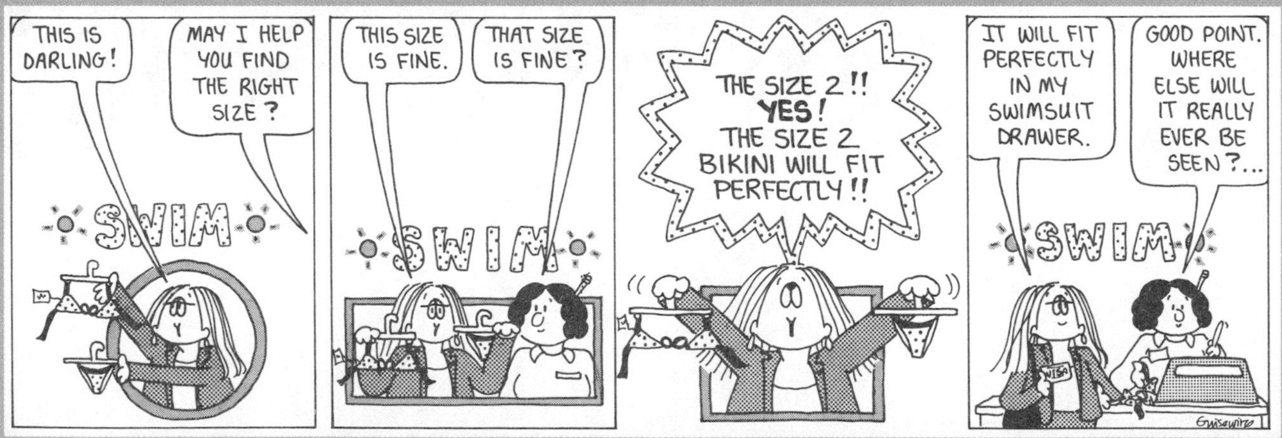
THIS IS DARLING!
MAY I HELP YOU FIND THE RIGHT SIZE?
SWIM
THIS SIZE IS FINE.
THAT SIZE IS FINE?
SWIM
THE SIZE 2!! YES! THE SIZE 2 BIKINI WILL FIT PERFECTLY!!
IT WILL FIT PERFECTLY IN MY SWIMSUIT DRAWER.
GOOD POINT. WHERE ELSE WILL IT REALLY EVER BE SEEN?...
SWIM
VISA

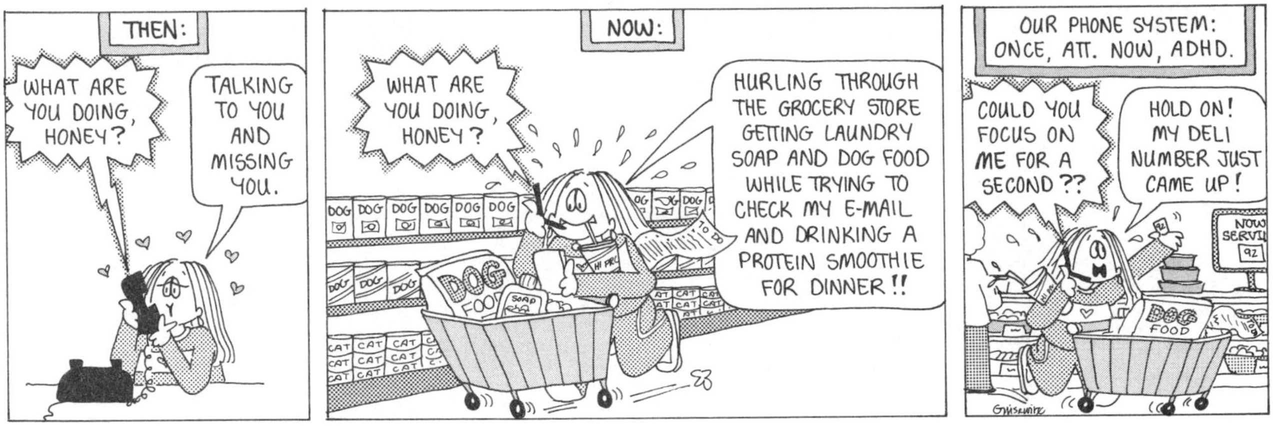
THEN:
WHAT ARE YOU DOING, HONEY?
TALKING TO YOU AND MISSING YOU.
NOW:
WHAT ARE YOU DOING, HONEY?
HURLING THROUGH THE GROCERY STORE GETTING LAUNDRY SOAP AND DOG FOOD WHILE TRYING TO CHECK MY E-MAIL AND DRINKING A PROTEIN SMOOTHIE FOR DINNER!!
OUR PHONE SYSTEM: ONCE, ATT. NOW, ADHD.
COULD YOU FOCUS ON ME FOR A SECOND??
HOLD ON! MY DELI NUMBER JUST CAME UP!

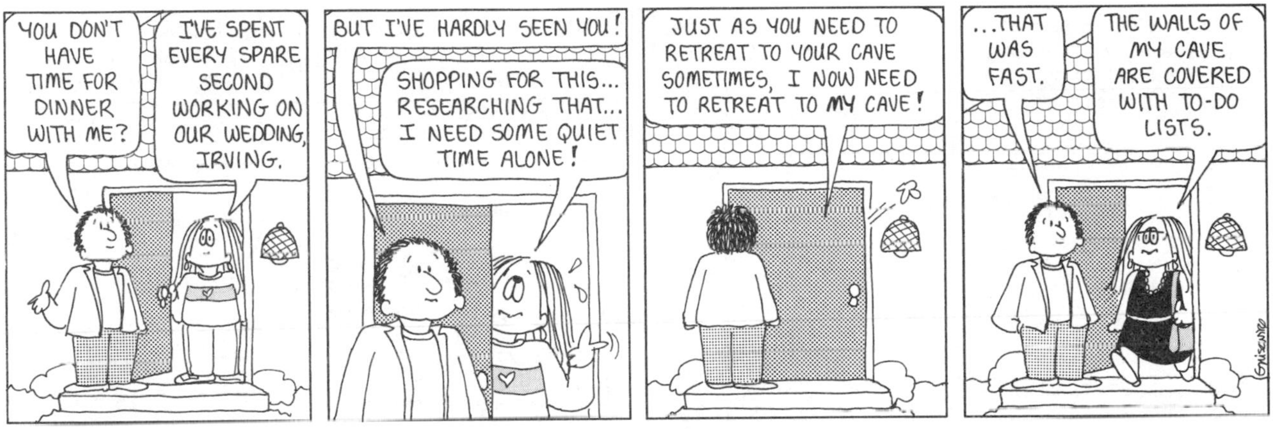
YOU DON'T HAVE TIME FOR DINNER WITH ME?
I'VE SPENT EVERY SPARE SECOND WORKING ON OUR WEDDING, IRVING.
BUT I'VE HARDLY SEEN YOU!
SHOPPING FOR THIS... RESEARCHING THAT... I NEED SOME QUIET TIME ALONE!
JUST AS YOU NEED TO RETREAT TO YOUR CAVE SOMETIMES, I NOW NEED TO RETREAT TO MY CAVE!
...THAT WAS FAST.
THE WALLS OF MY CAVE ARE COVERED WITH TO-DO LISTS.

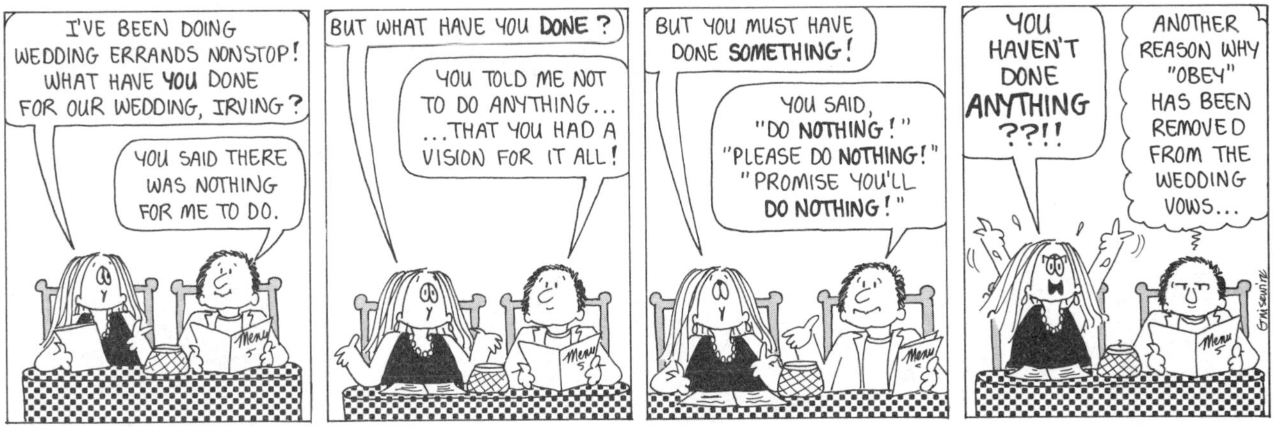
I'VE BEEN DOING WEDDING ERRANDS NONSTOP! WHAT HAVE YOU DONE FOR OUR WEDDING, IRVING?
YOU SAID THERE WAS NOTHING FOR ME TO DO.
BUT WHAT HAVE YOU DONE?
YOU TOLD ME NOT TO DO ANYTHING... ...THAT YOU HAD A VISION FOR IT ALL!
BUT YOU MUST HAVE DONE SOMETHING!
YOU SAID, "DO NOTHING!" "PLEASE DO NOTHING!" "PROMISE YOU'LL DO NOTHING!"
YOU HAVEN'T DONE ANYTHING??!!
ANOTHER REASON WHY "OBEY" HAS BEEN REMOVED FROM THE WEDDING VOWS...

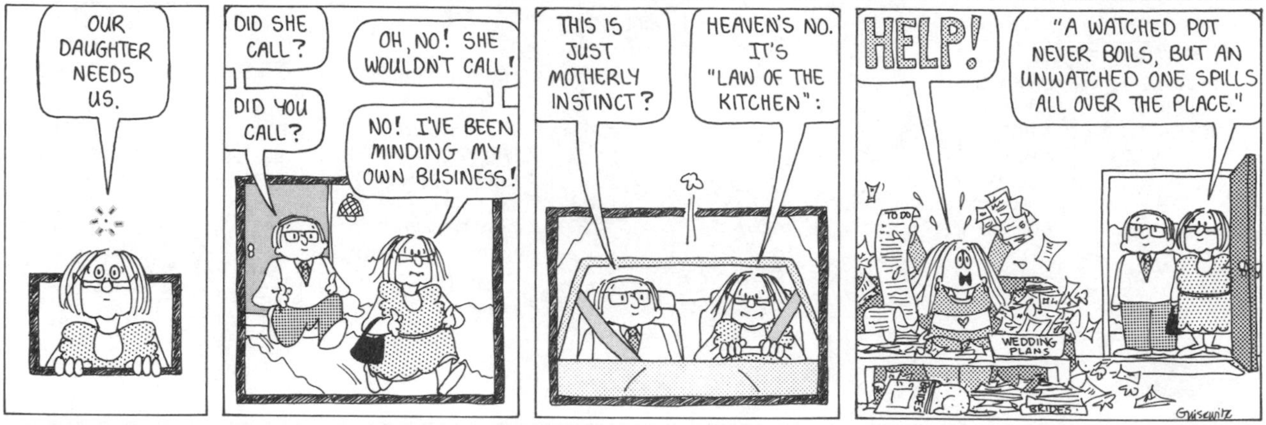
OUR DAUGHTER NEEDS US.
DID SHE CALL?
DID YOU CALL?
OH, NO! SHE WOULDN'T CALL!
NO! I'VE BEEN MINDING MY OWN BUSINESS!
THIS IS JUST MOTHERLY INSTINCT?
HEAVEN'S NO. IT'S "LAW OF THE KITCHEN":
HELP!
"A WATCHED POT NEVER BOILS, BUT AN UNWATCHED ONE SPILLS ALL OVER THE PLACE."
TO DO
WEDDING PLANS
BRIDES

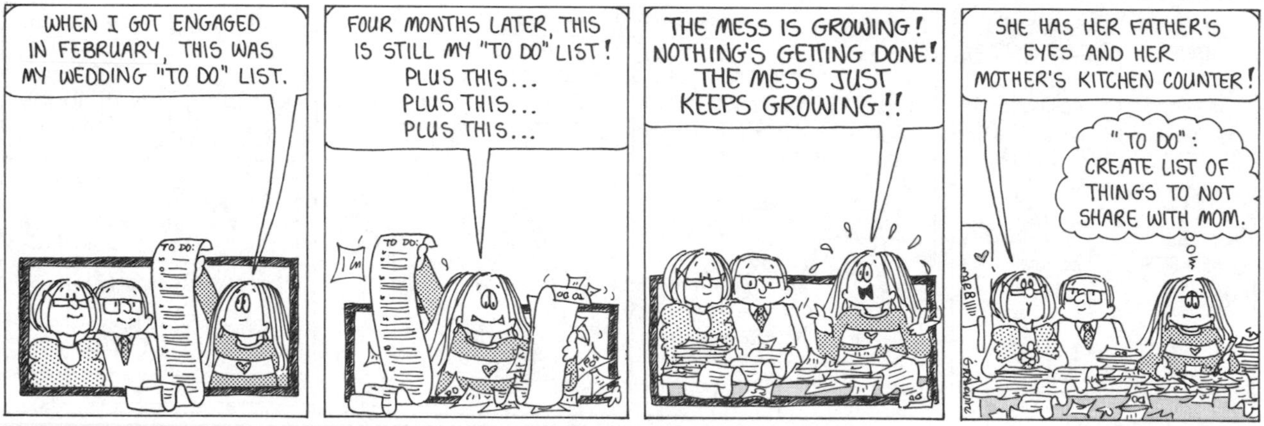
WHEN I GOT ENGAGED IN FEBRUARY, THIS WAS MY WEDDING "TO DO" LIST.
TO DO:
FOUR MONTHS LATER, THIS IS STILL MY "TO DO" LIST! PLUS THIS... PLUS THIS... PLUS THIS...
TO DO:
THE MESS IS GROWING! NOTHING'S GETTING DONE! THE MESS JUST KEEPS GROWING!!
SHE HAS HER FATHER'S EYES AND HER MOTHER'S KITCHEN COUNTER!
"TO DO": CREATE LIST OF THINGS TO NOT SHARE WITH MOM.

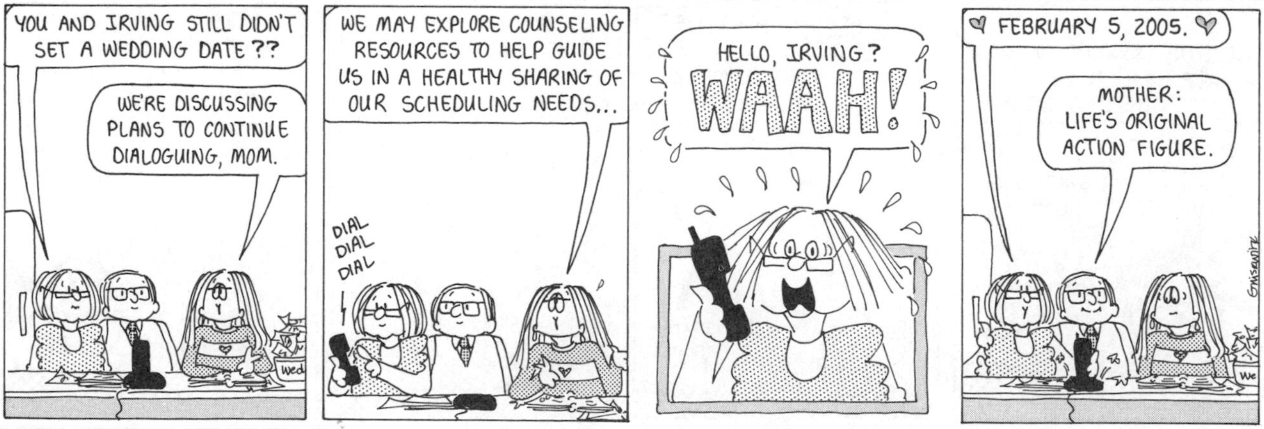
YOU AND IRVING STILL DIDN'T SET A WEDDING DATE??
WE'RE DISCUSSING PLANS TO CONTINUE DIALOGUING, MOM.
WE MAY EXPLORE COUNSELING RESOURCES TO HELP GUIDE US IN A HEALTHY SHARING OF OUR SCHEDULING NEEDS...
DIAL DIAL DIAL
HELLO, IRVING? WAAH!
FEBRUARY 5, 2005.
MOTHER: LIFE'S ORIGINAL ACTION FIGURE.

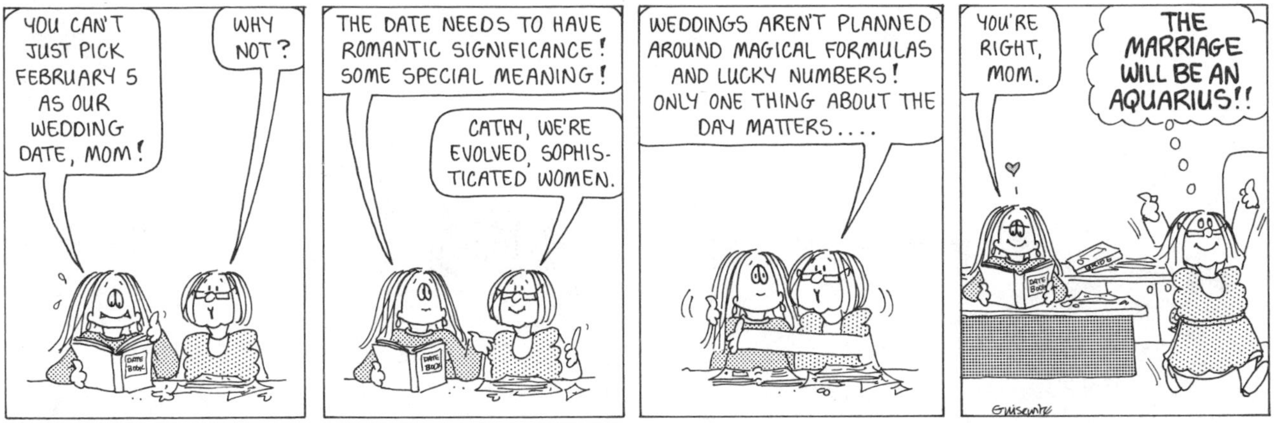
YOU CAN'T JUST PICK FEBRUARY 5 AS OUR WEDDING DATE, MOM!
WHY NOT?
THE DATE NEEDS TO HAVE ROMANTIC SIGNIFICANCE! SOME SPECIAL MEANING!
CATHY, WE'RE EVOLVED, SOPHISTICATED WOMEN.
WEDDINGS AREN'T PLANNED AROUND MAGICAL FORMULAS AND LUCKY NUMBERS! ONLY ONE THING ABOUT THE DAY MATTERS....
YOU'RE RIGHT, MOM.
THE MARRIAGE WILL BE AN AQUARIUS!!

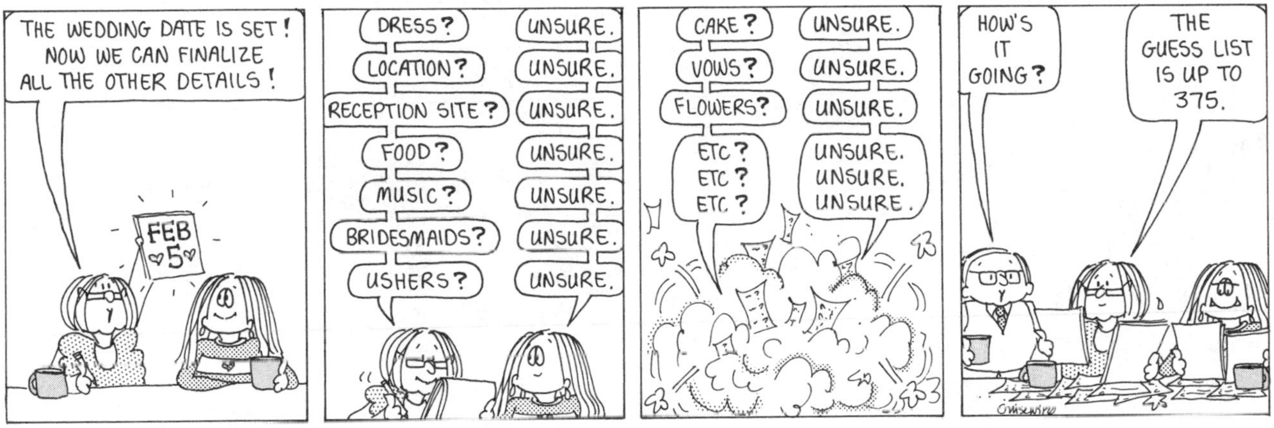
THE WEDDING DATE IS SET! NOW WE CAN FINALIZE ALL THE OTHER DETAILS!
FEB 5
DRESS?
UNSURE.
LOCATION?
UNSURE.
RECEPTION SITE?
UNSURE.
FOOD?
UNSURE.
MUSIC?
UNSURE.
BRIDESMAIDS?
UNSURE.
USHERS?
UNSURE.
CAKE?
UNSURE.
VOWS?
UNSURE.
FLOWERS?
UNSURE.
ETC? ETC? ETC?
UNSURE. UNSURE. UNSURE.
HOW'S IT GOING?
THE GUESS LIST IS UP TO 375.

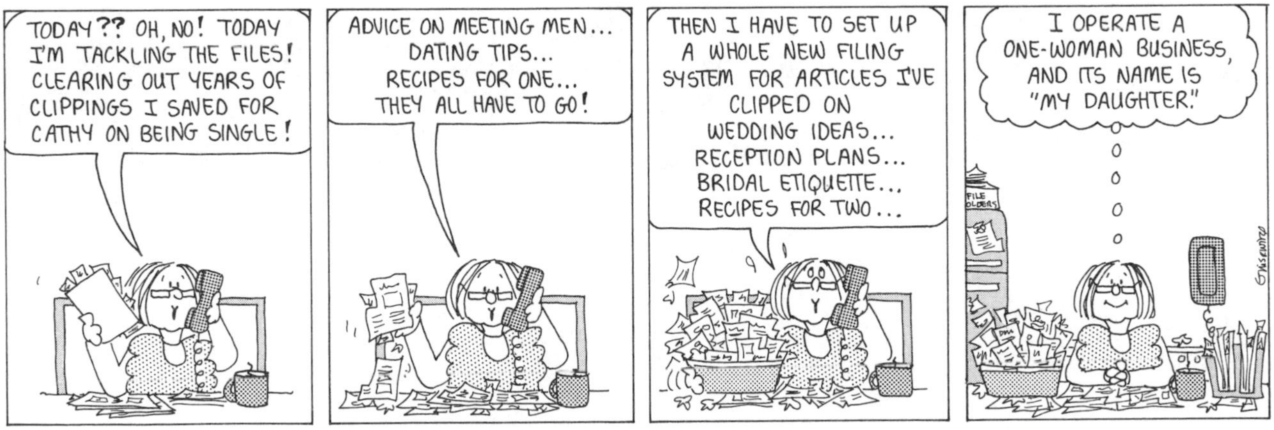
TODAY?? OH, NO! TODAY I'M TACKLING THE FILES! CLEARING OUT YEARS OF CLIPPINGS I SAVED FOR CATHY ON BEING SINGLE!
ADVICE ON MEETING MEN... DATING TIPS... RECIPES FOR ONE... THEY ALL HAVE TO GO!
THEN I HAVE TO SET UP A WHOLE NEW FILING SYSTEM FOR ARTICLES I'VE CLIPPED ON WEDDING IDEAS... RECEPTION PLANS... BRIDAL ETIQUETTE... RECIPES FOR TWO...
I OPERATE A ONE-WOMAN BUSINESS, AND ITS NAME IS "MY DAUGHTER."

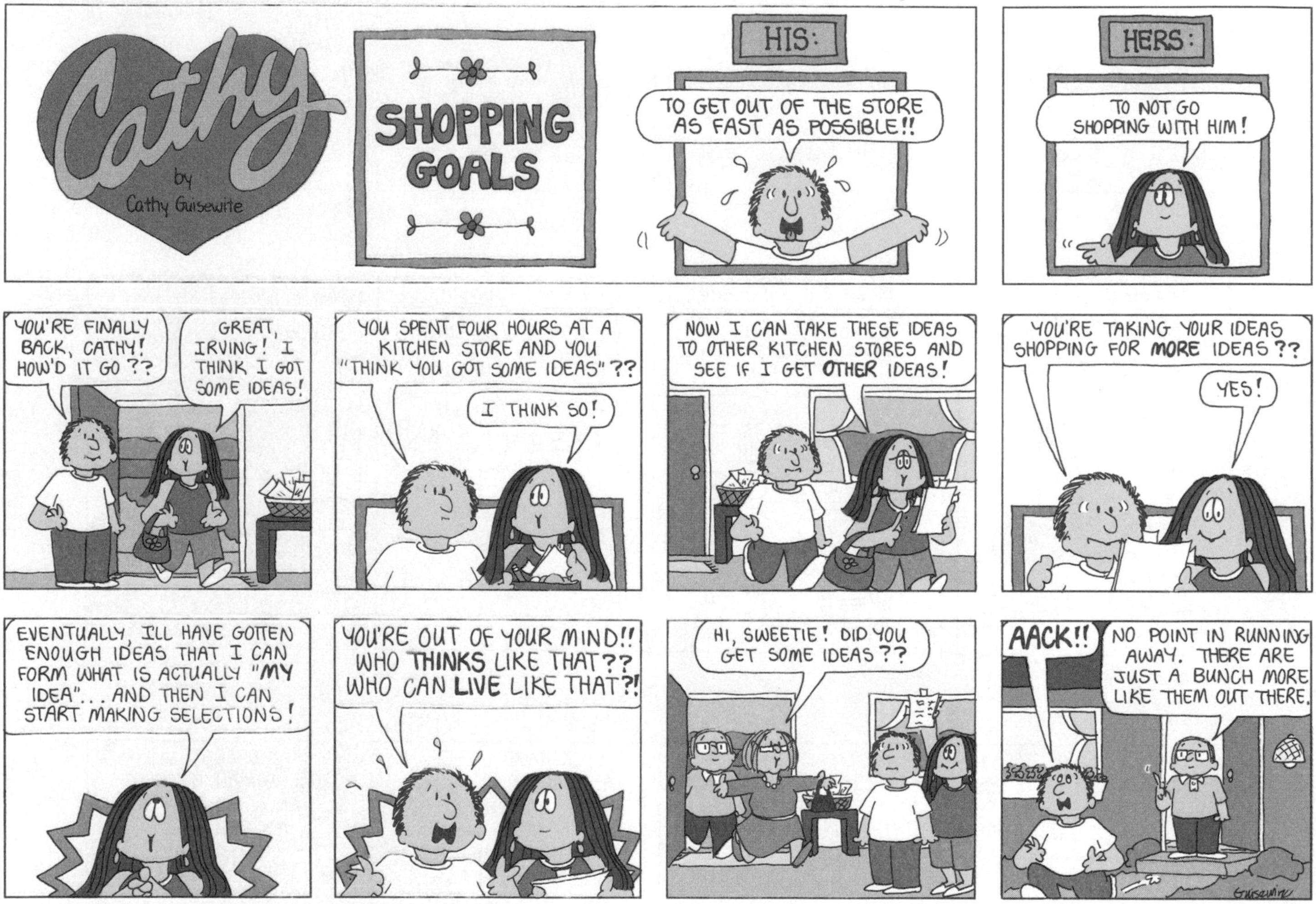
Cathy
by Cathy Guisewite
SHOPPING GOALS
HIS:
TO GET OUT OF THE STORE AS FAST AS POSSIBLE!!
HERS:
TO NOT GO SHOPPING WITH HIM!
YOU'RE FINALLY BACK, CATHY! HOW'D IT GO??
GREAT, IRVING! I THINK I GOT SOME IDEAS!
YOU SPENT FOUR HOURS AT A KITCHEN STORE AND YOU "THINK YOU GOT SOME IDEAS"??
I THINK SO!
NOW I CAN TAKE THESE IDEAS TO OTHER KITCHEN STORES AND SEE IF I GET OTHER IDEAS!
YOU'RE TAKING YOUR IDEAS SHOPPING FOR MORE IDEAS??
YES!
EVENTUALLY, I'LL HAVE GOTTEN ENOUGH IDEAS THAT I CAN FORM WHAT IS ACTUALLY "MY IDEA"... AND THEN I CAN START MAKING SELECTIONS!
YOU'RE OUT OF YOUR MIND!! WHO THINKS LIKE THAT?? WHO CAN LIVE LIKE THAT?!
HI, SWEETIE! DID YOU GET SOME IDEAS??
AACK!!
NO POINT IN RUNNING AWAY. THERE ARE JUST A BUNCH MORE LIKE THEM OUT THERE.
GUISEWITE

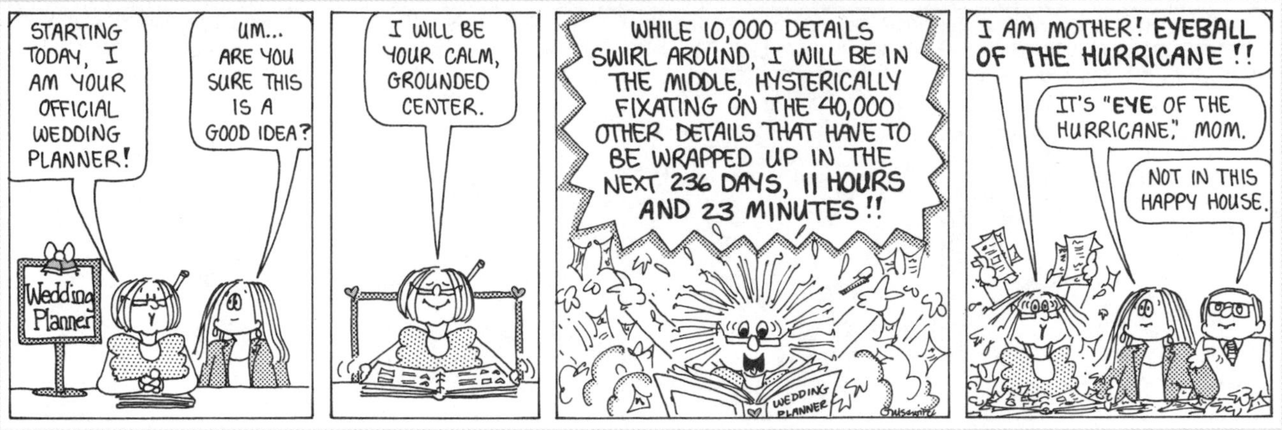
STARTING TODAY, I AM YOUR OFFICIAL WEDDING PLANNER!
UM... ARE YOU SURE THIS IS A GOOD IDEA?
Wedding Planner
I WILL BE YOUR CALM, GROUNDED CENTER.
WHILE 10,000 DETAILS SWIRL AROUND, I WILL BE IN THE MIDDLE, HYSTERICALLY FIXATING ON THE 40,000 OTHER DETAILS THAT HAVE TO BE WRAPPED UP IN THE NEXT 236 DAYS, 11 HOURS AND 23 MINUTES!!
WEDDING PLANNER
I AM MOTHER! EYEBALL OF THE HURRICANE!!
IT'S "EYE OF THE HURRICANE," MOM.
NOT IN THIS HAPPY HOUSE.

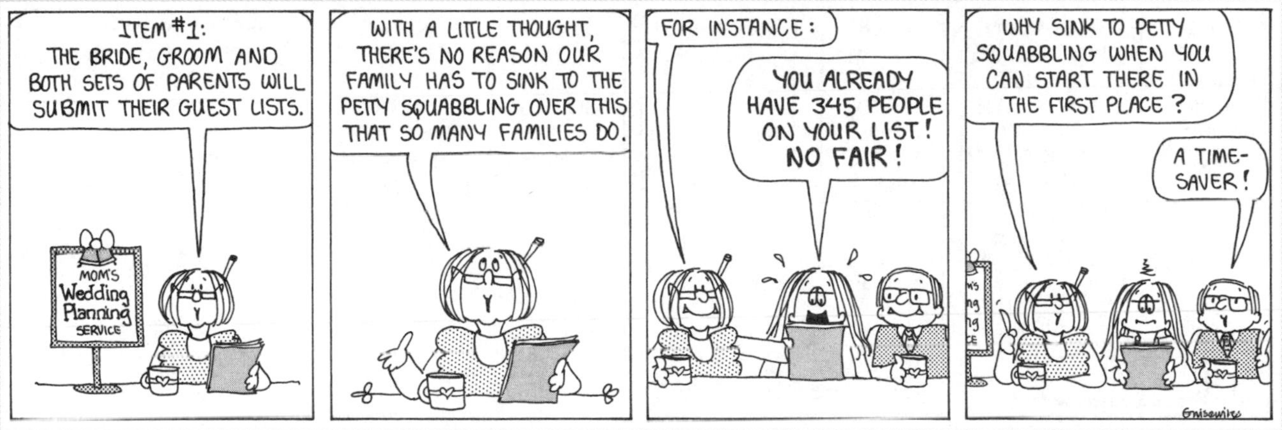
ITEM #1: THE BRIDE, GROOM AND BOTH SETS OF PARENTS WILL SUBMIT THEIR GUEST LISTS.
MOM'S Wedding Planning SERVICE
WITH A LITTLE THOUGHT, THERE'S NO REASON OUR FAMILY HAS TO SINK TO THE PETTY SQUABBLING OVER THIS THAT SO MANY FAMILIES DO.
FOR INSTANCE:
YOU ALREADY HAVE 345 PEOPLE ON YOUR LIST! NO FAIR!
WHY SINK TO PETTY SQUABBLING WHEN YOU CAN START THERE IN THE FIRST PLACE?
A TIME-SAVER!

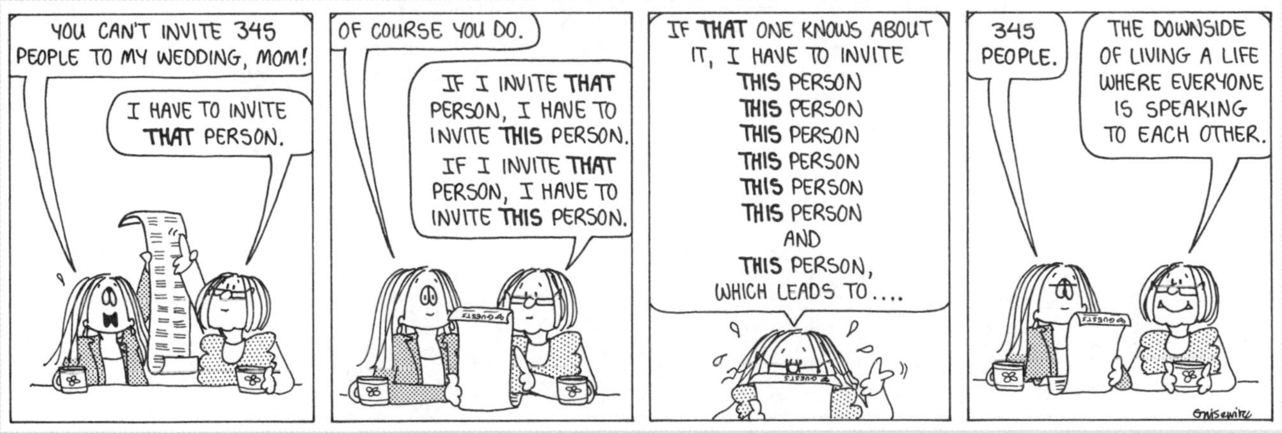
YOU CAN'T INVITE 345 PEOPLE TO MY WEDDING, MOM!
I HAVE TO INVITE THAT PERSON.
OF COURSE YOU DO.
IF I INVITE THAT PERSON, I HAVE TO INVITE THIS PERSON. IF I INVITE THAT PERSON, I HAVE TO INVITE THIS PERSON.
IF THAT ONE KNOWS ABOUT IT, I HAVE TO INVITE THIS PERSON THIS PERSON THIS PERSON THIS PERSON THIS PERSON THIS PERSON AND THIS PERSON, WHICH LEADS TO....
345 PEOPLE.
THE DOWNSIDE OF LIVING A LIFE WHERE EVERYONE IS SPEAKING TO EACH OTHER.

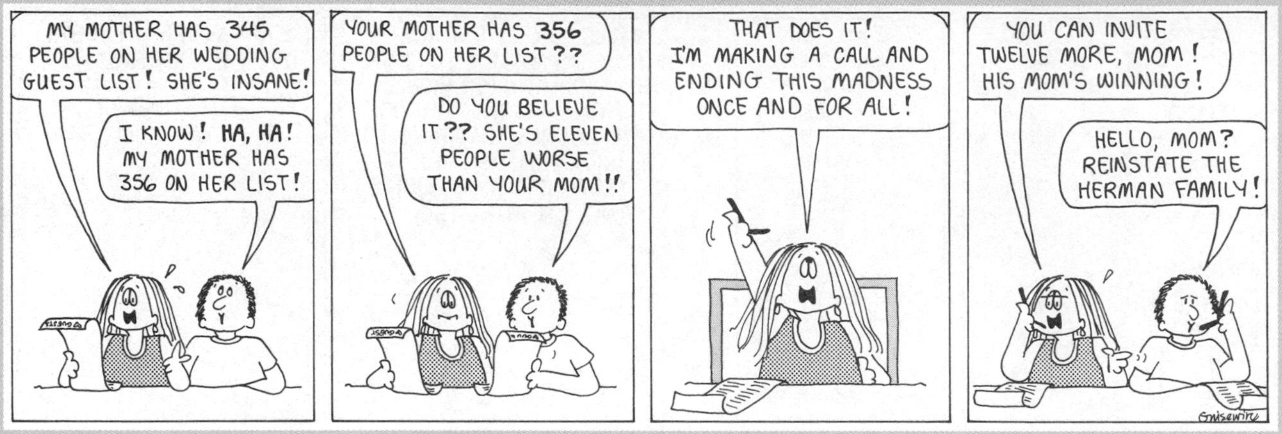
MY MOTHER HAS 345 PEOPLE ON HER WEDDING GUEST LIST! SHE'S INSANE!
I KNOW! HA, HA! MY MOTHER HAS 356 ON HER LIST!
YOUR MOTHER HAS 356 PEOPLE ON HER LIST??
DO YOU BELIEVE IT?? SHE'S ELEVEN PEOPLE WORSE THAN YOUR MOM!!
THAT DOES IT! I'M MAKING A CALL AND ENDING THIS MADNESS ONCE AND FOR ALL!
YOU CAN INVITE TWELVE MORE, MOM! HIS MOM'S WINNING!
HELLO, MOM? REINSTATE THE HERMAN FAMILY!

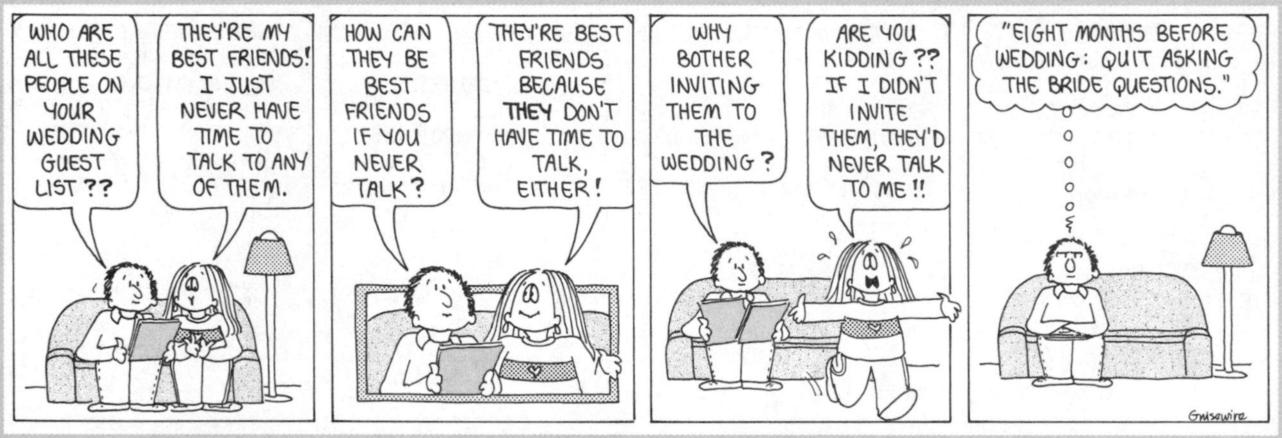
WHO ARE ALL THESE PEOPLE ON YOUR WEDDING GUEST LIST??
THEY'RE MY BEST FRIENDS! I JUST NEVER HAVE TIME TO TALK TO ANY OF THEM.
HOW CAN THEY BE BEST FRIENDS IF YOU NEVER TALK?
THEY'RE BEST FRIENDS BECAUSE THEY DON'T HAVE TIME TO TALK, EITHER!
WHY BOTHER INVITING THEM TO THE WEDDING?
ARE YOU KIDDING?? IF I DIDN'T INVITE THEM, THEY'D NEVER TALK TO ME!!
"EIGHT MONTHS BEFORE WEDDING: QUIT ASKING THE BRIDE QUESTIONS."

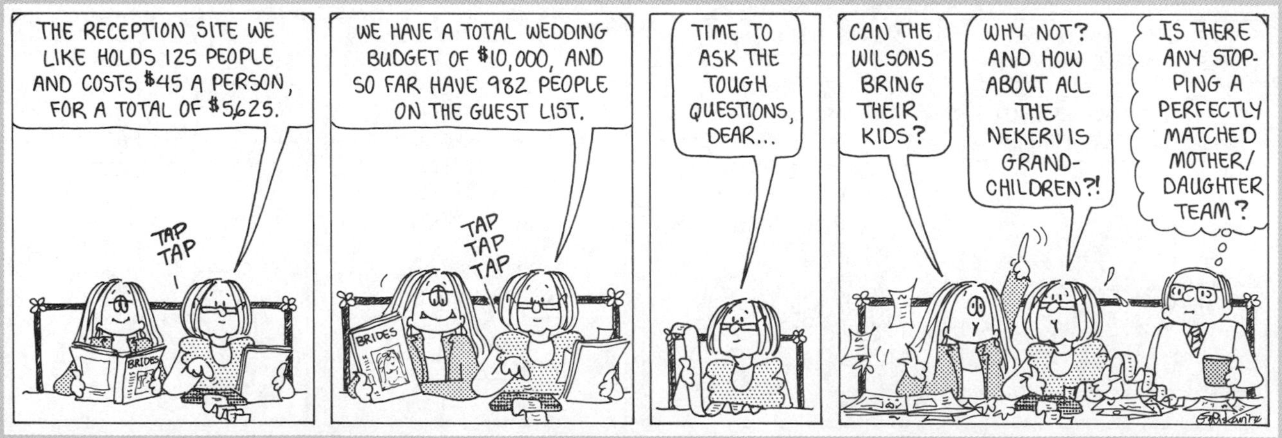
THE RECEPTION SITE WE LIKE HOLDS 125 PEOPLE AND COSTS $45 A PERSON, FOR A TOTAL OF $5,625.
TAP TAP
BRIDES
WE HAVE A TOTAL WEDDING BUDGET OF $10,000, AND SO FAR HAVE 982 PEOPLE ON THE GUEST LIST.
TAP TAP TAP
BRIDES
TIME TO ASK THE TOUGH QUESTIONS, DEAR...
CAN THE WILSONS BRING THEIR KIDS?
WHY NOT? AND HOW ABOUT ALL THE NEKERVIS GRAND-CHILDREN?!
IS THERE ANY STOP-PING A PERFECTLY MATCHED MOTHER/DAUGHTER TEAM?

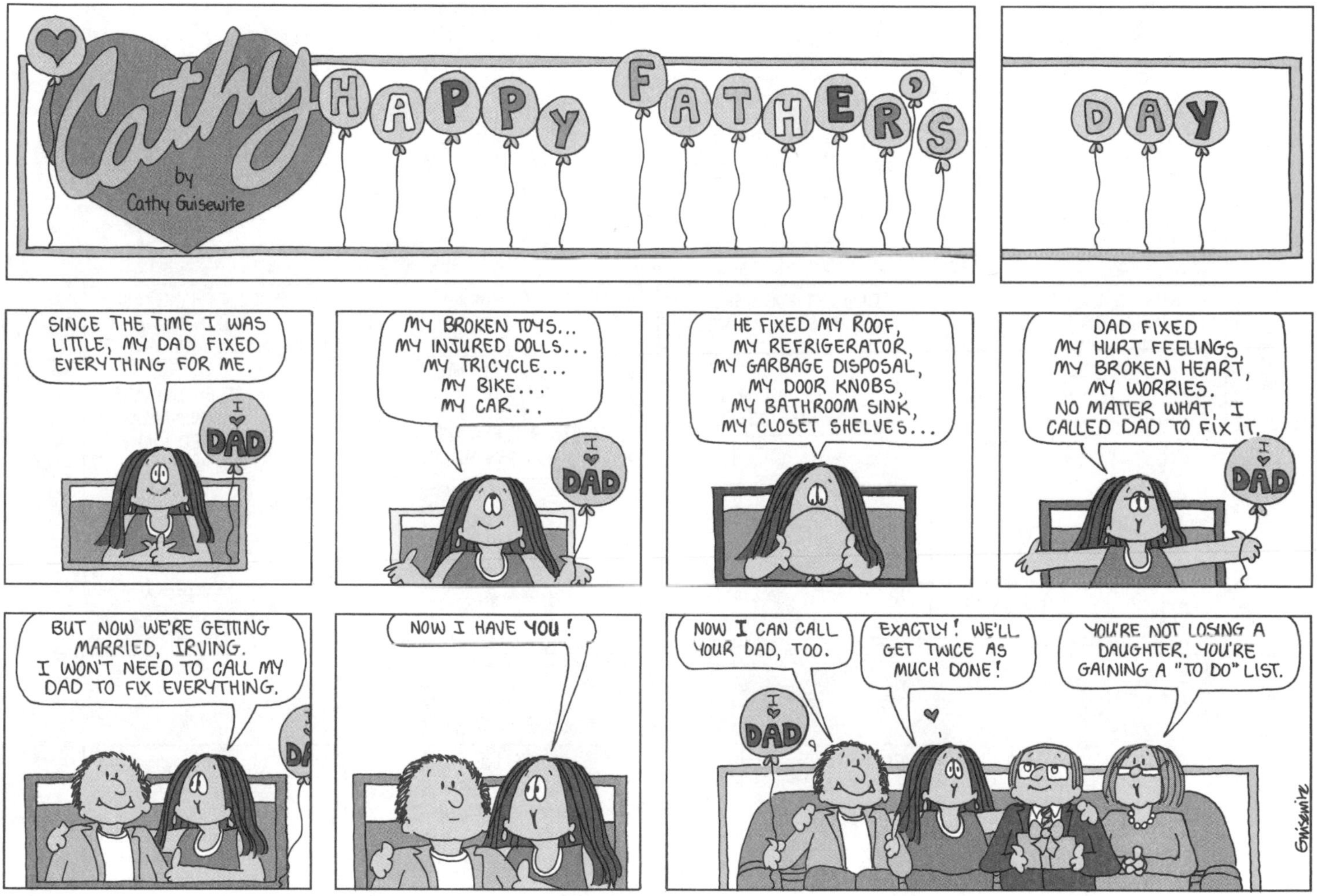
Cathy
by
Cathy Guisewite
HAPPY FATHER'S DAY
SINCE THE TIME I WAS LITTLE, MY DAD FIXED EVERYTHING FOR ME.
I ♥ DAD
MY BROKEN TOYS... MY INJURED DOLLS... MY TRICYCLE... MY BIKE... MY CAR...
I ♥ DAD
HE FIXED MY ROOF, MY REFRIGERATOR, MY GARBAGE DISPOSAL, MY DOOR KNOBS, MY BATHROOM SINK, MY CLOSET SHELVES...
DAD FIXED MY HURT FEELINGS, MY BROKEN HEART, MY WORRIES. NO MATTER WHAT, I CALLED DAD TO FIX IT.
I ♥ DAD
BUT NOW WE'RE GETTING MARRIED, IRVING. I WON'T NEED TO CALL MY DAD TO FIX EVERYTHING.
NOW I HAVE YOU!
NOW I CAN CALL YOUR DAD, TOO.
EXACTLY! WE'LL GET TWICE AS MUCH DONE!
YOU'RE NOT LOSING A DAUGHTER. YOU'RE GAINING A "TO DO" LIST.
I ♥ DAD
Guisewite

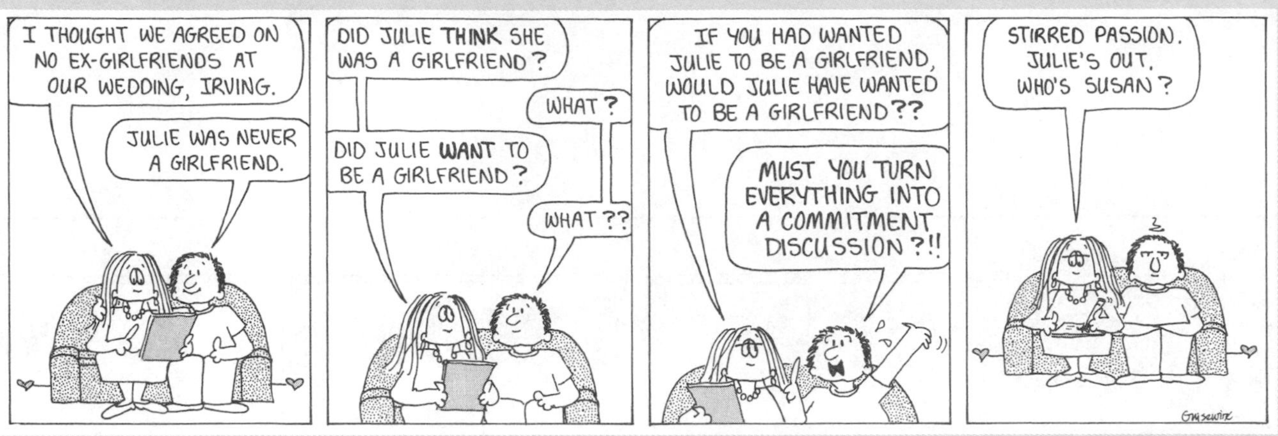
I THOUGHT WE AGREED ON NO EX-GIRLFRIENDS AT OUR WEDDING, IRVING.
JULIE WAS NEVER A GIRLFRIEND.
DID JULIE THINK SHE WAS A GIRLFRIEND?
DID JULIE WANT TO BE A GIRLFRIEND?
WHAT?
WHAT??
IF YOU HAD WANTED JULIE TO BE A GIRLFRIEND, WOULD JULIE HAVE WANTED TO BE A GIRLFRIEND??
MUST YOU TURN EVERYTHING INTO A COMMITMENT DISCUSSION?!!
STIRRED PASSION. JULIE'S OUT. WHO'S SUSAN?

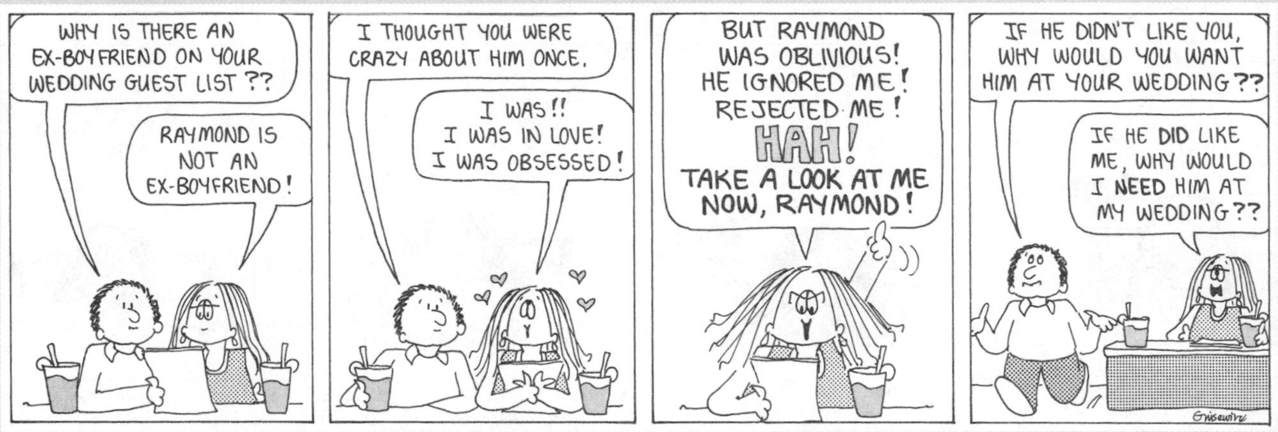
WHY IS THERE AN EX-BOYFRIEND ON YOUR WEDDING GUEST LIST??
RAYMOND IS NOT AN EX-BOYFRIEND!
I THOUGHT YOU WERE CRAZY ABOUT HIM ONCE.
I WAS!! I WAS IN LOVE! I WAS OBSESSED!
BUT RAYMOND WAS OBLIVIOUS! HE IGNORED ME! REJECTED ME! HAH! TAKE A LOOK AT ME NOW, RAYMOND!
IF HE DIDN'T LIKE YOU, WHY WOULD YOU WANT HIM AT YOUR WEDDING??
IF HE DID LIKE ME, WHY WOULD I NEED HIM AT MY WEDDING??

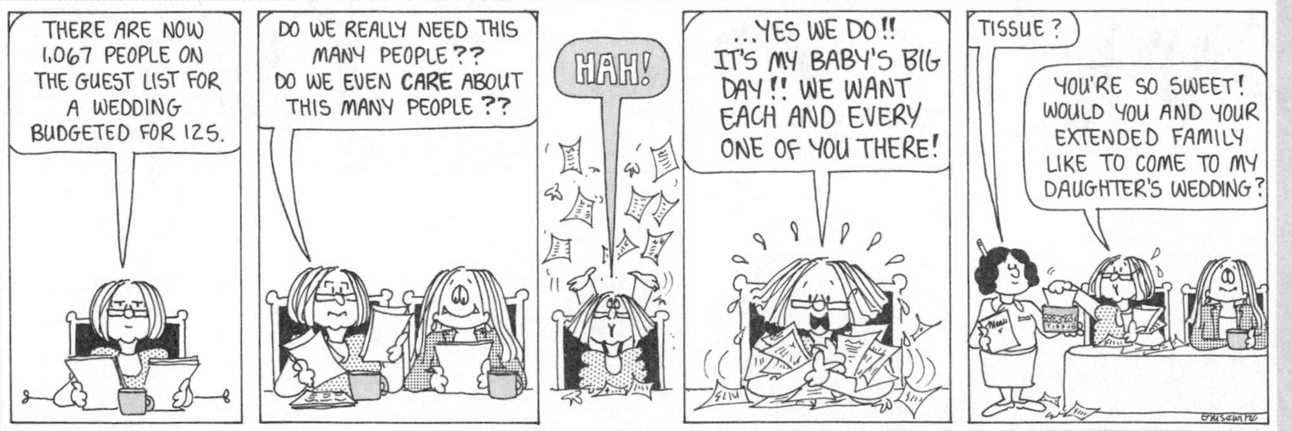
THERE ARE NOW 1,067 PEOPLE ON THE GUEST LIST FOR A WEDDING BUDGETED FOR 125.
DO WE REALLY NEED THIS MANY PEOPLE?? DO WE EVEN CARE ABOUT THIS MANY PEOPLE??
HAH!
...YES WE DO!! IT'S MY BABY'S BIG DAY!! WE WANT EACH AND EVERY ONE OF YOU THERE!
TISSUE?
YOU'RE SO SWEET! WOULD YOU AND YOUR EXTENDED FAMILY LIKE TO COME TO MY DAUGHTER'S WEDDING?

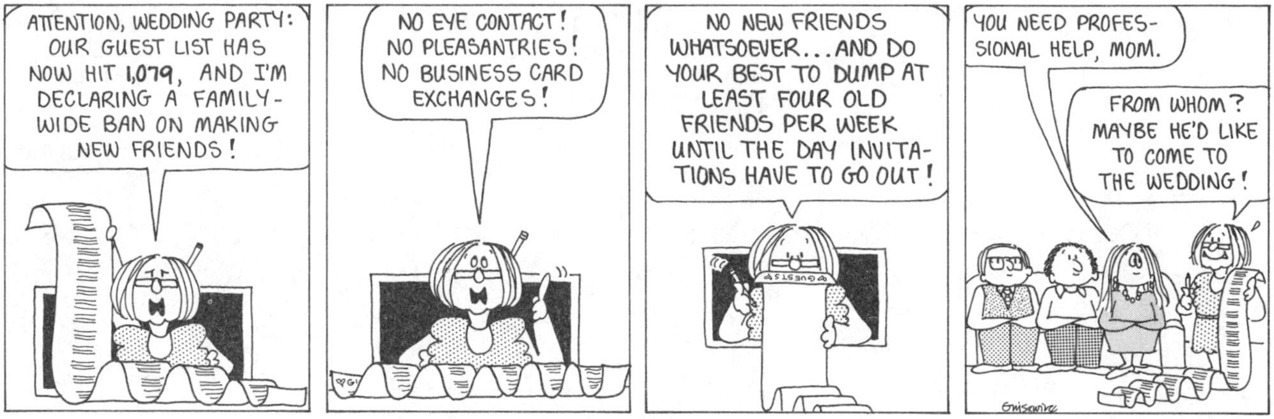
ATTENTION, WEDDING PARTY: OUR GUEST LIST HAS NOW HIT 1,079, AND I'M DECLARING A FAMILY-WIDE BAN ON MAKING NEW FRIENDS!
NO EYE CONTACT! NO PLEASANTRIES! NO BUSINESS CARD EXCHANGES!
NO NEW FRIENDS WHATSOEVER...AND DO YOUR BEST TO DUMP AT LEAST FOUR OLD FRIENDS PER WEEK UNTIL THE DAY INVITATIONS HAVE TO GO OUT!
YOU NEED PROFESSIONAL HELP, MOM.
FROM WHOM? MAYBE HE'D LIKE TO COME TO THE WEDDING!
Guisewite

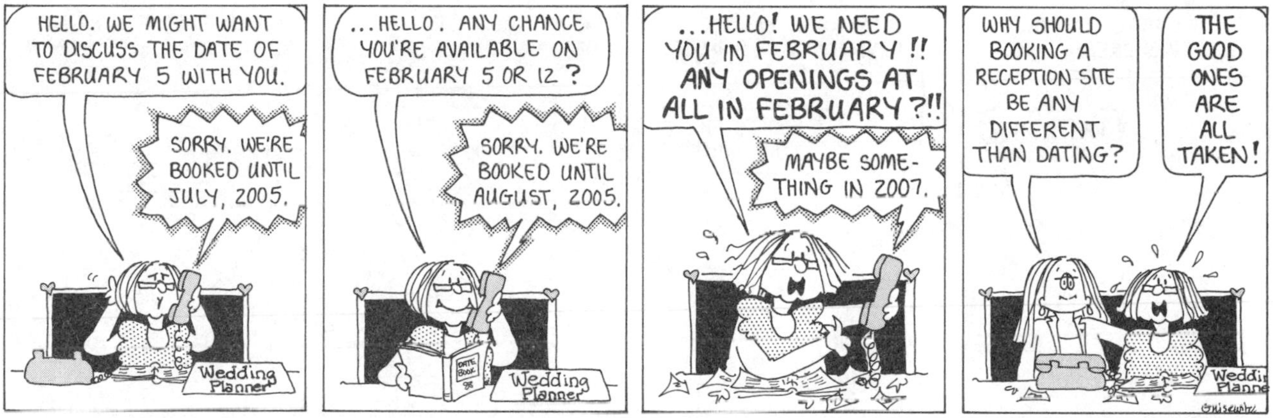
HELLO. WE MIGHT WANT TO DISCUSS THE DATE OF FEBRUARY 5 WITH YOU.
SORRY. WE'RE BOOKED UNTIL JULY, 2005.
Wedding Planner
...HELLO. ANY CHANCE YOU'RE AVAILABLE ON FEBRUARY 5 OR 12?
SORRY. WE'RE BOOKED UNTIL AUGUST, 2005.
Wedding Planner
...HELLO! WE NEED YOU IN FEBRUARY!! ANY OPENINGS AT ALL IN FEBRUARY?!!
MAYBE SOMETHING IN 2007.
WHY SHOULD BOOKING A RECEPTION SITE BE ANY DIFFERENT THAN DATING?
THE GOOD ONES ARE ALL TAKEN!
Guisewite

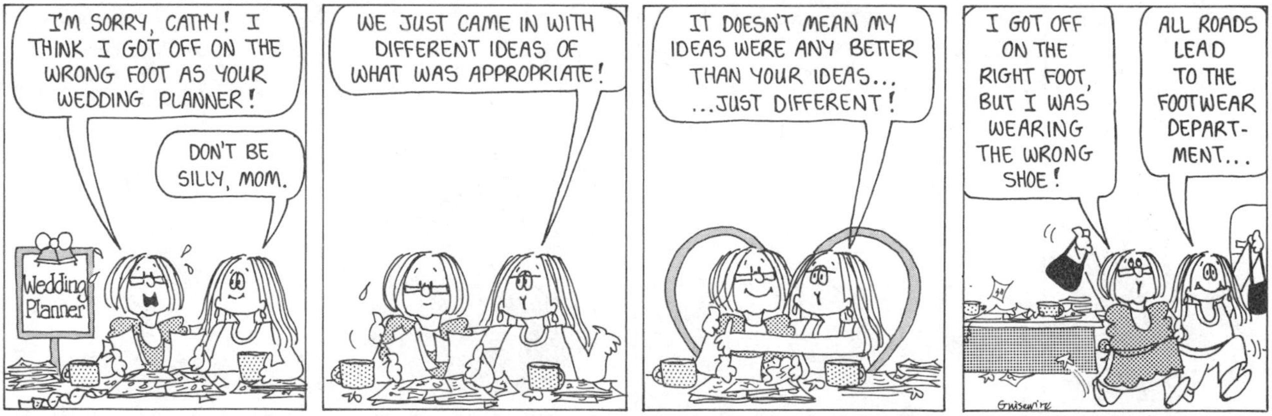
I'M SORRY, CATHY! I THINK I GOT OFF ON THE WRONG FOOT AS YOUR WEDDING PLANNER!
DON'T BE SILLY, MOM.
Wedding Planner
WE JUST CAME IN WITH DIFFERENT IDEAS OF WHAT WAS APPROPRIATE!
IT DOESN'T MEAN MY IDEAS WERE ANY BETTER THAN YOUR IDEAS... ...JUST DIFFERENT!
I GOT OFF ON THE RIGHT FOOT, BUT I WAS WEARING THE WRONG SHOE!
ALL ROADS LEAD TO THE FOOTWEAR DEPARTMENT...
Guisewite

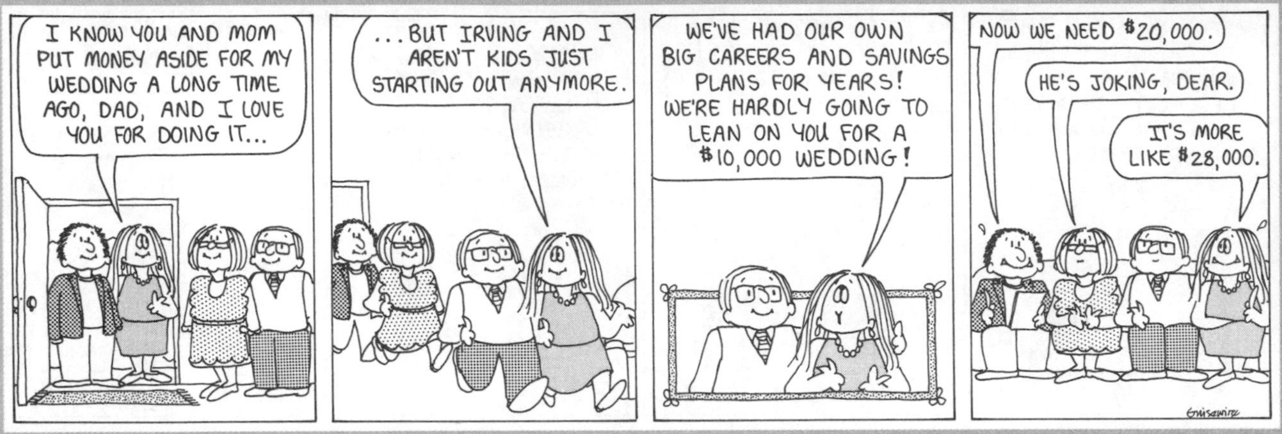
I KNOW YOU AND MOM PUT MONEY ASIDE FOR MY WEDDING A LONG TIME AGO, DAD, AND I LOVE YOU FOR DOING IT...
...BUT IRVING AND I AREN'T KIDS JUST STARTING OUT ANYMORE.
WE'VE HAD OUR OWN BIG CAREERS AND SAVINGS PLANS FOR YEARS! WE'RE HARDLY GOING TO LEAN ON YOU FOR A $10,000 WEDDING!
NOW WE NEED $20,000.
HE'S JOKING, DEAR.
IT'S MORE LIKE $28,000.

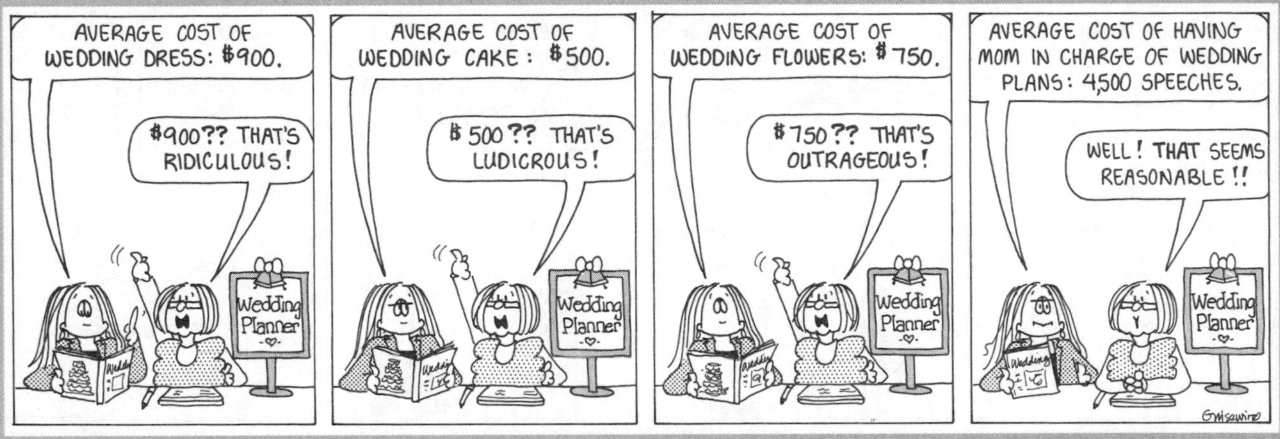
AVERAGE COST OF WEDDING DRESS: $900.
$900?? THAT'S RIDICULOUS!
Wedding Planner
AVERAGE COST OF WEDDING CAKE: $500.
$500?? THAT'S LUDICROUS!
Wedding Planner
AVERAGE COST OF WEDDING FLOWERS: $750.
$750?? THAT'S OUTRAGEOUS!
Wedding Planner
AVERAGE COST OF HAVING MOM IN CHARGE OF WEDDING PLANS: 4,500 SPEECHES.
WELL! THAT SEEMS REASONABLE!!
Wedding Planner

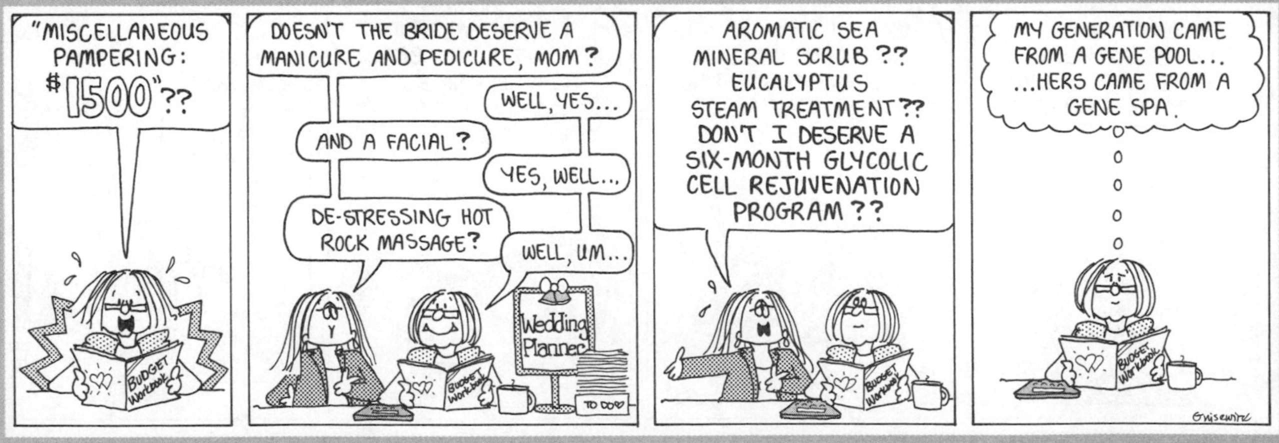
"MISCELLANEOUS PAMPERING: $1500"??
BUDGET Workbook
DOESN'T THE BRIDE DESERVE A MANICURE AND PEDICURE, MOM?
WELL, YES...
AND A FACIAL?
YES, WELL...
DE-STRESSING HOT ROCK MASSAGE?
WELL, UM...
Wedding Planner
TO DO
AROMATIC SEA MINERAL SCRUB?? EUCALYPTUS STEAM TREATMENT?? DON'T I DESERVE A SIX-MONTH GLYCOLIC CELL REJUVENATION PROGRAM??
MY GENERATION CAME FROM A GENE POOL... ...HERS CAME FROM A GENE SPA.

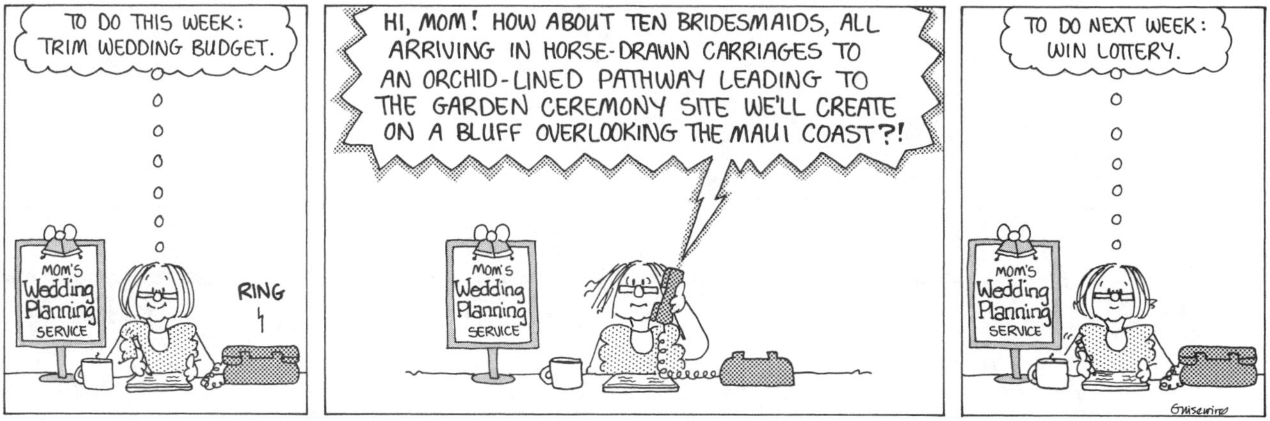
TO DO THIS WEEK: TRIM WEDDING BUDGET.
MOM'S Wedding Planning SERVICE
RING
HI, MOM! HOW ABOUT TEN BRIDESMAIDS, ALL ARRIVING IN HORSE-DRAWN CARRIAGES TO AN ORCHID-LINED PATHWAY LEADING TO THE GARDEN CEREMONY SITE WE'LL CREATE ON A BLUFF OVERLOOKING THE MAUI COAST?!
MOM'S Wedding Planning SERVICE
TO DO NEXT WEEK: WIN LOTTERY.
MOM'S Wedding Planning SERVICE

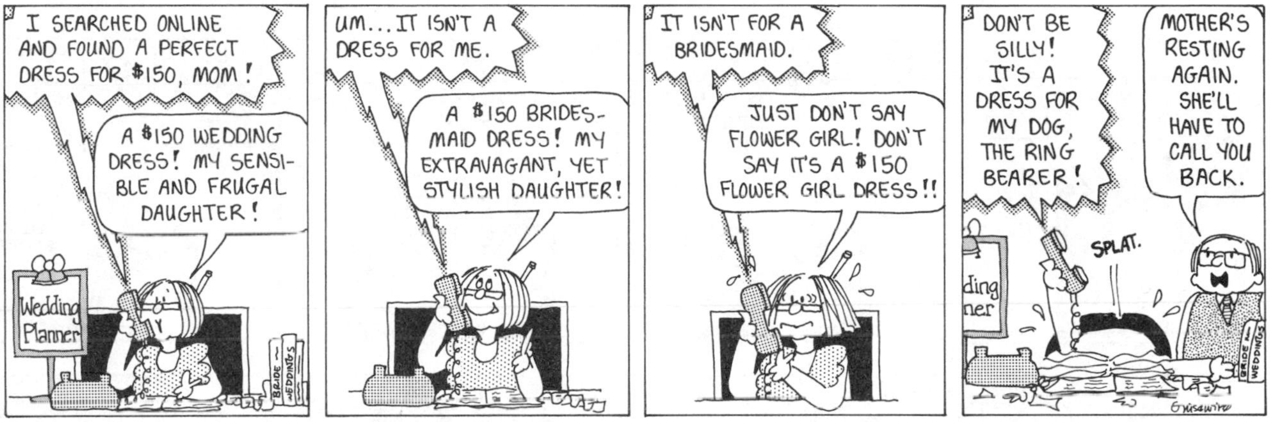
I SEARCHED ONLINE AND FOUND A PERFECT DRESS FOR $150, MOM!
A $150 WEDDING DRESS! MY SENSIBLE AND FRUGAL DAUGHTER!
Wedding Planner
UM... IT ISN'T A DRESS FOR ME.
A $150 BRIDESMAID DRESS! MY EXTRAVAGANT, YET STYLISH DAUGHTER!
IT ISN'T FOR A BRIDESMAID.
JUST DON'T SAY FLOWER GIRL! DON'T SAY IT'S A $150 FLOWER GIRL DRESS!!
DON'T BE SILLY! IT'S A DRESS FOR MY DOG, THE RING BEARER!
MOTHER'S RESTING AGAIN. SHE'LL HAVE TO CALL YOU BACK.
SPLAT.

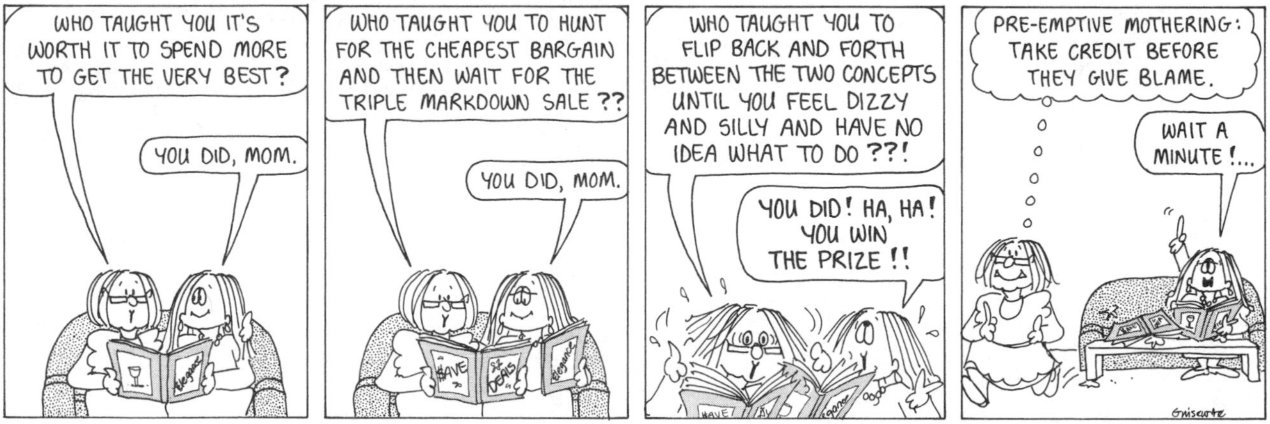
WHO TAUGHT YOU IT'S WORTH IT TO SPEND MORE TO GET THE VERY BEST?
YOU DID, MOM.
WHO TAUGHT YOU TO HUNT FOR THE CHEAPEST BARGAIN AND THEN WAIT FOR THE TRIPLE MARKDOWN SALE??
YOU DID, MOM.
WHO TAUGHT YOU TO FLIP BACK AND FORTH BETWEEN THE TWO CONCEPTS UNTIL YOU FEEL DIZZY AND SILLY AND HAVE NO IDEA WHAT TO DO??!
YOU DID! HA, HA! YOU WIN THE PRIZE!!
PRE-EMPTIVE MOTHERING: TAKE CREDIT BEFORE THEY GIVE BLAME.
WAIT A MINUTE!...

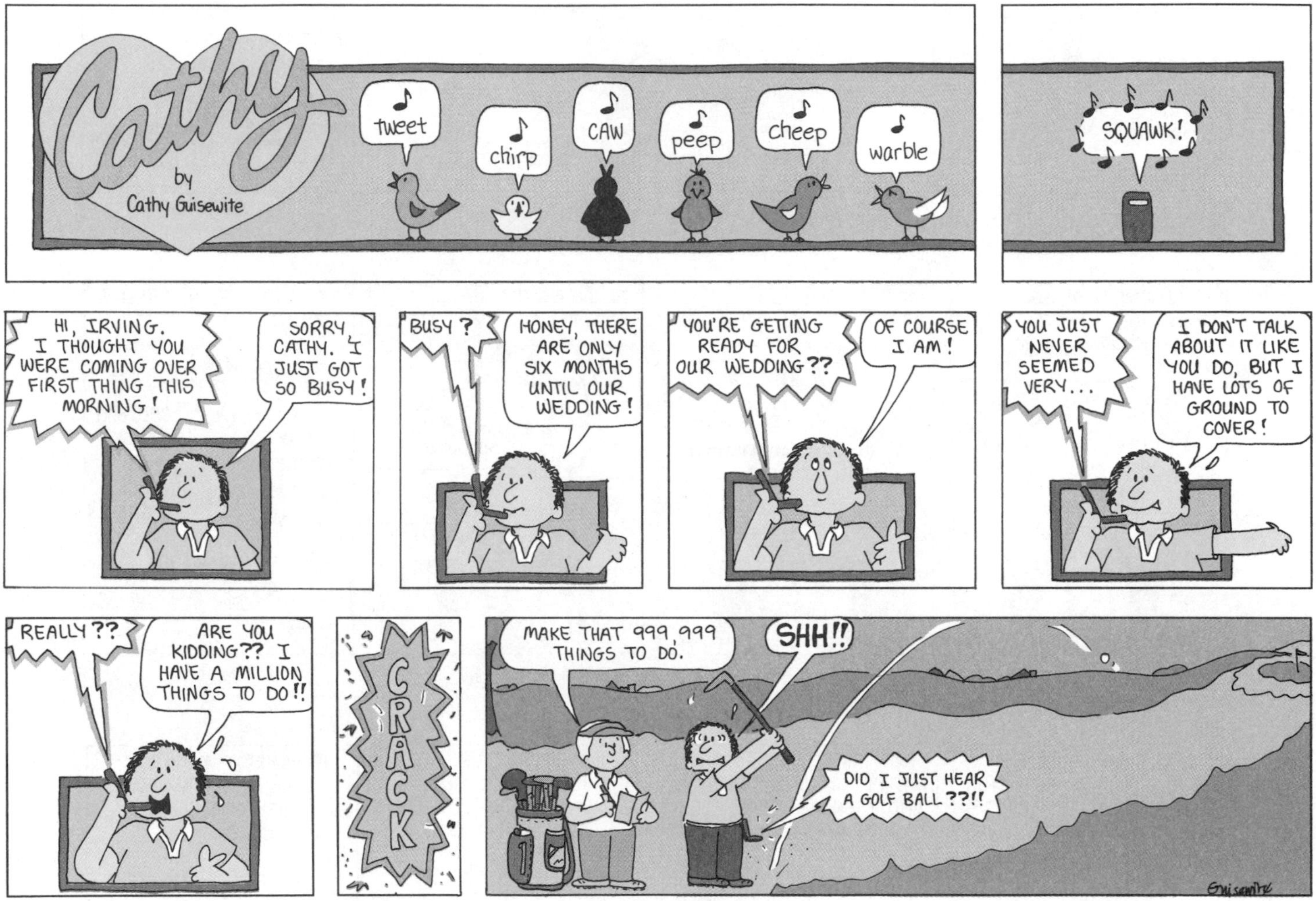
Cathy
by Cathy Guisewite
tweet
chirp
CAW
peep
cheep
warble
SQUAWK!
HI, IRVING. I THOUGHT YOU WERE COMING OVER FIRST THING THIS MORNING!
SORRY, CATHY. I JUST GOT SO BUSY!
BUSY?
HONEY, THERE ARE ONLY SIX MONTHS UNTIL OUR WEDDING!
YOU'RE GETTING READY FOR OUR WEDDING??
OF COURSE I AM!
YOU JUST NEVER SEEMED VERY...
I DON'T TALK ABOUT IT LIKE YOU DO, BUT I HAVE LOTS OF GROUND TO COVER!
REALLY??
ARE YOU KIDDING?? I HAVE A MILLION THINGS TO DO!!
CRACK
MAKE THAT 999,999 THINGS TO DO.
SHH!!
DID I JUST HEAR A GOLF BALL??!!
Guisewite

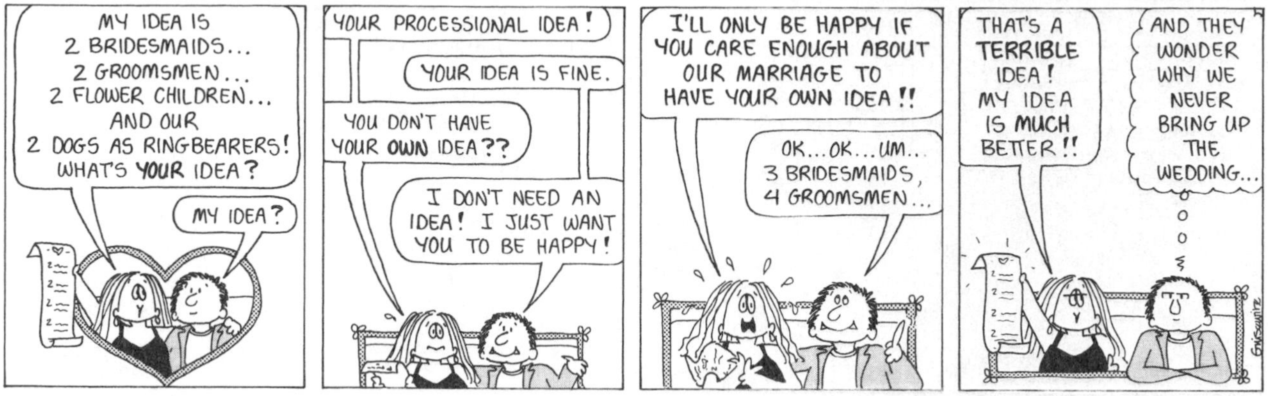
MY IDEA IS 2 BRIDESMAIDS... 2 GROOMSMEN... 2 FLOWER CHILDREN... AND OUR 2 DOGS AS RINGBEARERS! WHAT'S YOUR IDEA?
MY IDEA?
YOUR PROCESSIONAL IDEA!
YOUR IDEA IS FINE.
YOU DON'T HAVE YOUR OWN IDEA??
I DON'T NEED AN IDEA! I JUST WANT YOU TO BE HAPPY!
I'LL ONLY BE HAPPY IF YOU CARE ENOUGH ABOUT OUR MARRIAGE TO HAVE YOUR OWN IDEA!!
OK...OK...UM... 3 BRIDESMAIDS, 4 GROOMSMEN...
THAT'S A TERRIBLE IDEA! MY IDEA IS MUCH BETTER!!
AND THEY WONDER WHY WE NEVER BRING UP THE WEDDING...

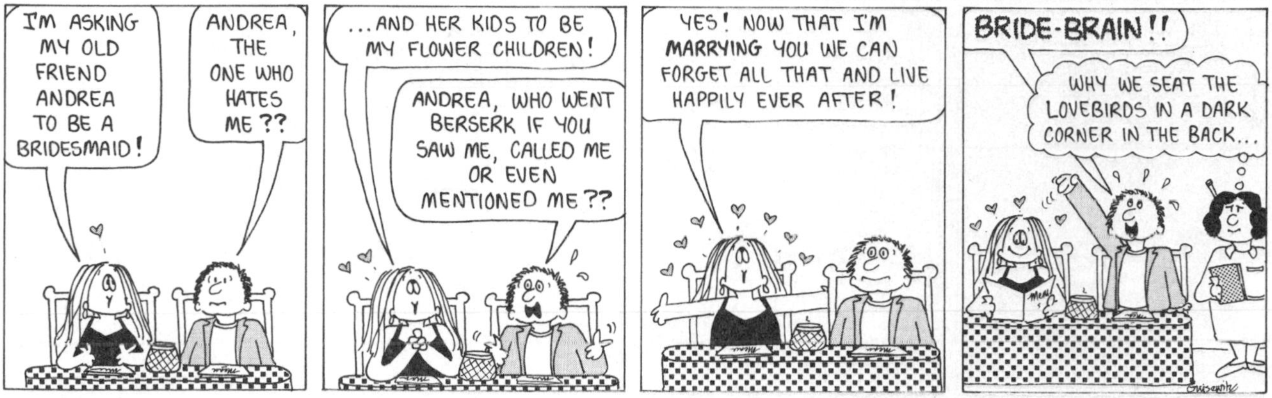
I'M ASKING MY OLD FRIEND ANDREA TO BE A BRIDESMAID!
ANDREA, THE ONE WHO HATES ME??
...AND HER KIDS TO BE MY FLOWER CHILDREN!
ANDREA, WHO WENT BERSERK IF YOU SAW ME, CALLED ME OR EVEN MENTIONED ME??
YES! NOW THAT I'M MARRYING YOU WE CAN FORGET ALL THAT AND LIVE HAPPILY EVER AFTER!
BRIDE-BRAIN!!
WHY WE SEAT THE LOVEBIRDS IN A DARK CORNER IN THE BACK...

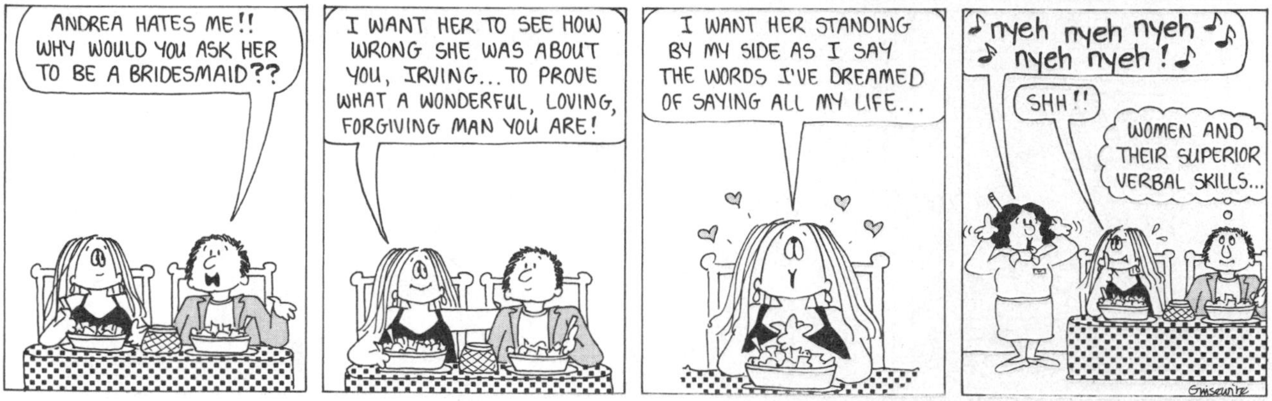
ANDREA HATES ME!! WHY WOULD YOU ASK HER TO BE A BRIDESMAID??
I WANT HER TO SEE HOW WRONG SHE WAS ABOUT YOU, IRVING... TO PROVE WHAT A WONDERFUL, LOVING, FORGIVING MAN YOU ARE!
I WANT HER STANDING BY MY SIDE AS I SAY THE WORDS I'VE DREAMED OF SAYING ALL MY LIFE...
nyeh nyeh nyeh nyeh nyeh!
SHH!!
WOMEN AND THEIR SUPERIOR VERBAL SKILLS...

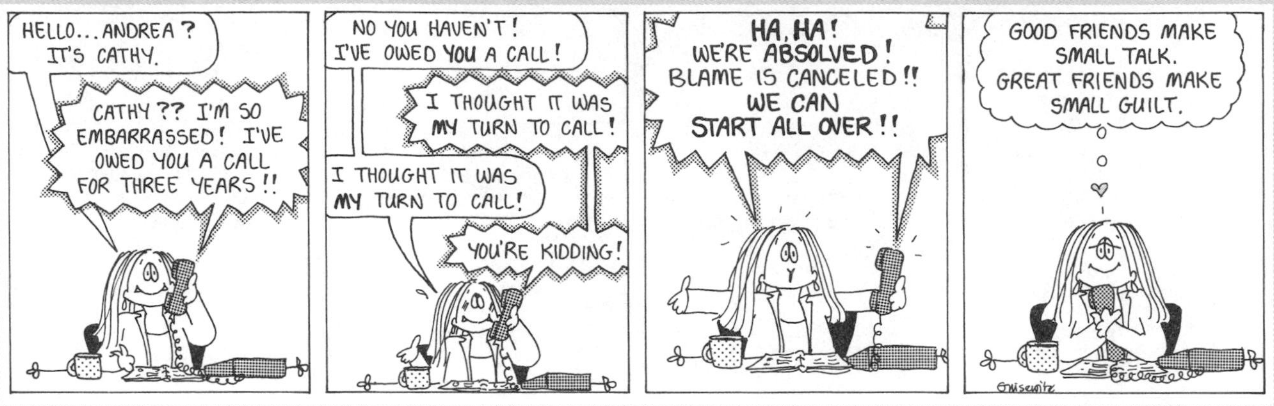
HELLO... ANDREA? IT'S CATHY.
CATHY?? I'M SO EMBARRASSED! I'VE OWED YOU A CALL FOR THREE YEARS!!
NO YOU HAVEN'T! I'VE OWED YOU A CALL!
I THOUGHT IT WAS MY TURN TO CALL!
I THOUGHT IT WAS MY TURN TO CALL!
YOU'RE KIDDING!
HA, HA! WE'RE ABSOLVED! BLAME IS CANCELED!! WE CAN START ALL OVER!!
GOOD FRIENDS MAKE SMALL TALK. GREAT FRIENDS MAKE SMALL GUILT.

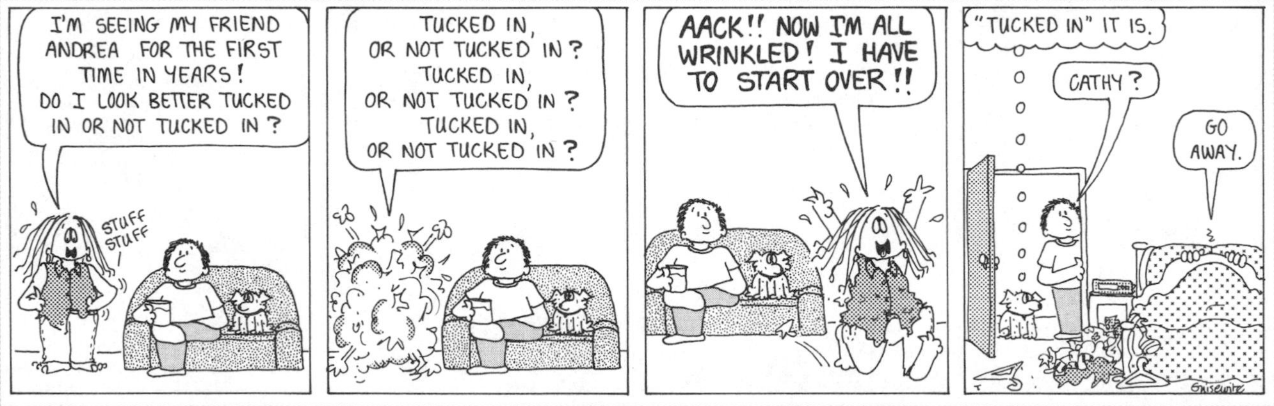
I'M SEEING MY FRIEND ANDREA FOR THE FIRST TIME IN YEARS! DO I LOOK BETTER TUCKED IN OR NOT TUCKED IN?
STUFF STUFF
TUCKED IN, OR NOT TUCKED IN? TUCKED IN, OR NOT TUCKED IN? TUCKED IN, OR NOT TUCKED IN?
AACK!! NOW I'M ALL WRINKLED! I HAVE TO START OVER!!
"TUCKED IN" IT IS.
CATHY?
GO AWAY.

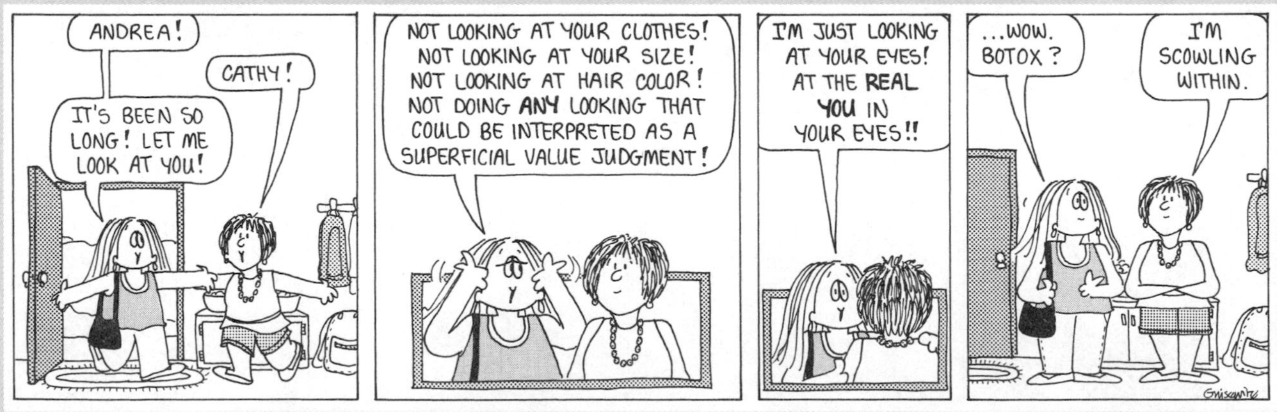
ANDREA!
CATHY!
IT'S BEEN SO LONG! LET ME LOOK AT YOU!
NOT LOOKING AT YOUR CLOTHES! NOT LOOKING AT YOUR SIZE! NOT LOOKING AT HAIR COLOR! NOT DOING ANY LOOKING THAT COULD BE INTERPRETED AS A SUPERFICIAL VALUE JUDGMENT!
I'M JUST LOOKING AT YOUR EYES! AT THE REAL YOU IN YOUR EYES!!
...WOW. BOTOX?
I'M SCOWLING WITHIN.

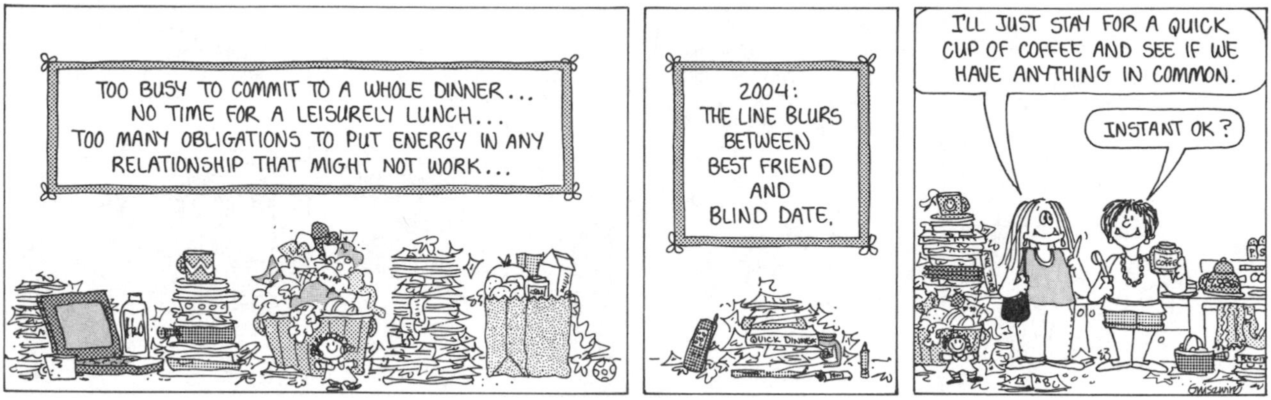
TOO BUSY TO COMMIT TO A WHOLE DINNER... NO TIME FOR A LEISURELY LUNCH... TOO MANY OBLIGATIONS TO PUT ENERGY IN ANY RELATIONSHIP THAT MIGHT NOT WORK...
2004: THE LINE BLURS BETWEEN BEST FRIEND AND BLIND DATE.
I'LL JUST STAY FOR A QUICK CUP OF COFFEE AND SEE IF WE HAVE ANYTHING IN COMMON.
INSTANT OK?

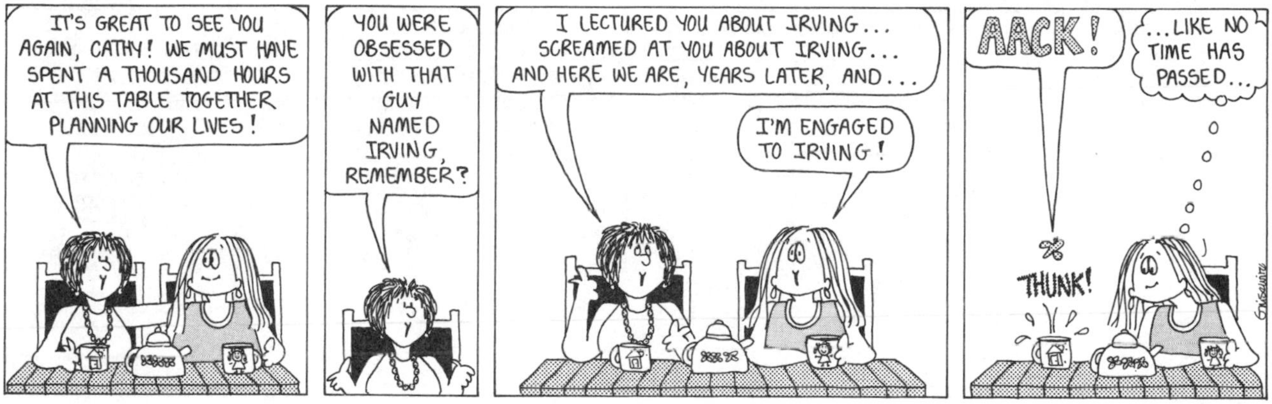
IT'S GREAT TO SEE YOU AGAIN, CATHY! WE MUST HAVE SPENT A THOUSAND HOURS AT THIS TABLE TOGETHER PLANNING OUR LIVES!
YOU WERE OBSESSED WITH THAT GUY NAMED IRVING, REMEMBER?
I LECTURED YOU ABOUT IRVING... SCREAMED AT YOU ABOUT IRVING... AND HERE WE ARE, YEARS LATER, AND...
I'M ENGAGED TO IRVING!
AACK!
THUNK!
...LIKE NO TIME HAS PASSED...

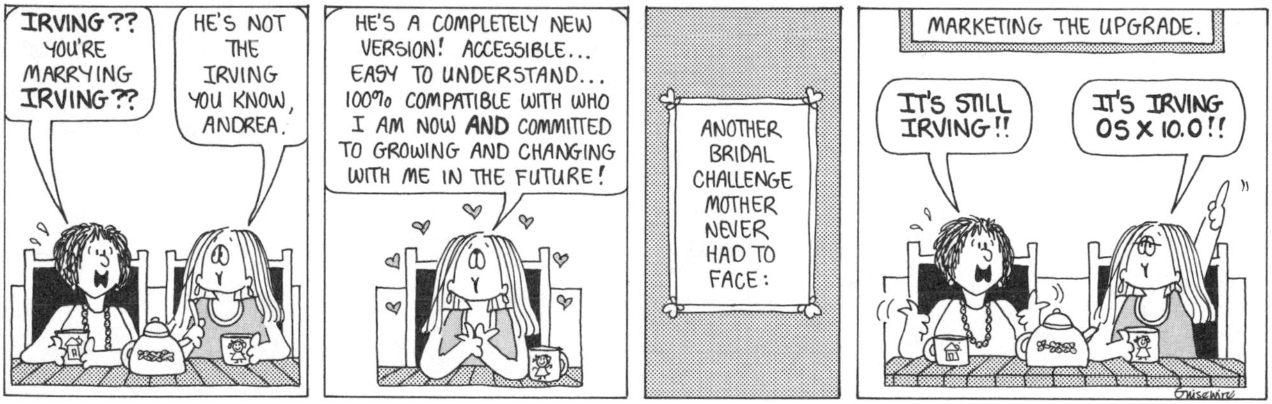
IRVING?? YOU'RE MARRYING IRVING??
HE'S NOT THE IRVING YOU KNOW, ANDREA.
HE'S A COMPLETELY NEW VERSION! ACCESSIBLE... EASY TO UNDERSTAND... 100% COMPATIBLE WITH WHO I AM NOW AND COMMITTED TO GROWING AND CHANGING WITH ME IN THE FUTURE!
ANOTHER BRIDAL CHALLENGE MOTHER NEVER HAD TO FACE:
MARKETING THE UPGRADE.
IT'S STILL IRVING!!
IT'S IRVING OS X 10.0!!

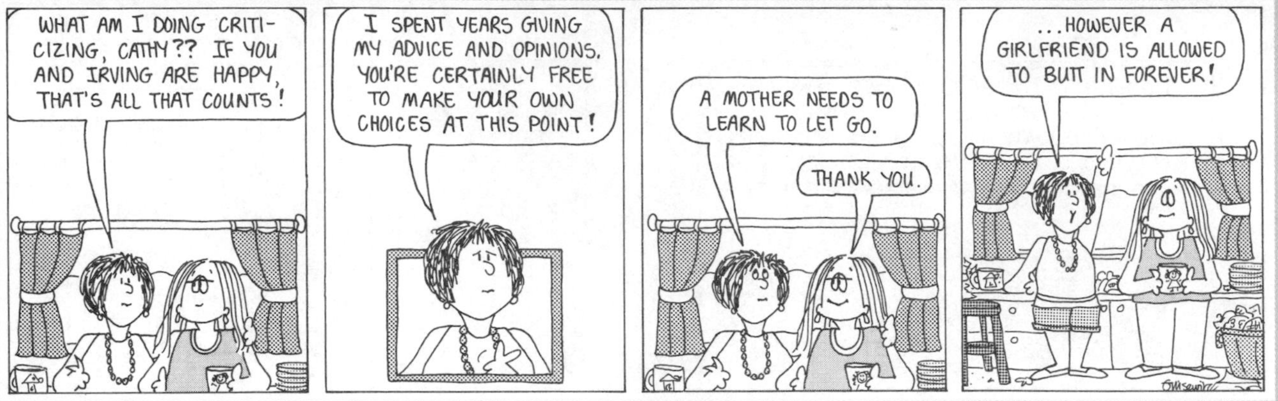
WHAT AM I DOING CRITICIZING, CATHY?? IF YOU AND IRVING ARE HAPPY, THAT'S ALL THAT COUNTS!
I SPENT YEARS GIVING MY ADVICE AND OPINIONS. YOU'RE CERTAINLY FREE TO MAKE YOUR OWN CHOICES AT THIS POINT!
A MOTHER NEEDS TO LEARN TO LET GO.
THANK YOU.
...HOWEVER A GIRLFRIEND IS ALLOWED TO BUTT IN FOREVER!

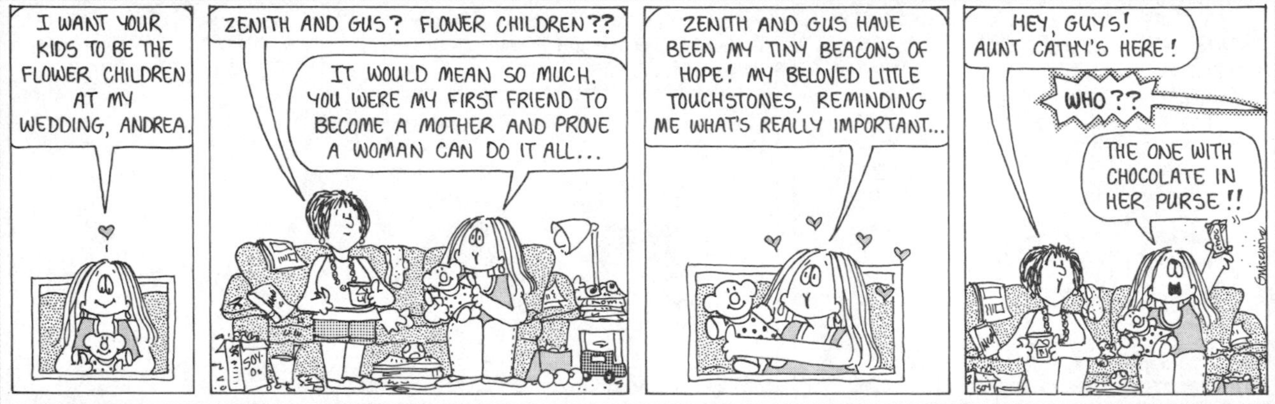
I WANT YOUR KIDS TO BE THE FLOWER CHILDREN AT MY WEDDING, ANDREA.
ZENITH AND GUS? FLOWER CHILDREN??
IT WOULD MEAN SO MUCH. YOU WERE MY FIRST FRIEND TO BECOME A MOTHER AND PROVE A WOMAN CAN DO IT ALL...
ZENITH AND GUS HAVE BEEN MY TINY BEACONS OF HOPE! MY BELOVED LITTLE TOUCHSTONES, REMINDING ME WHAT'S REALLY IMPORTANT...
HEY, GUYS! AUNT CATHY'S HERE!
WHO??
THE ONE WITH CHOCOLATE IN HER PURSE!!

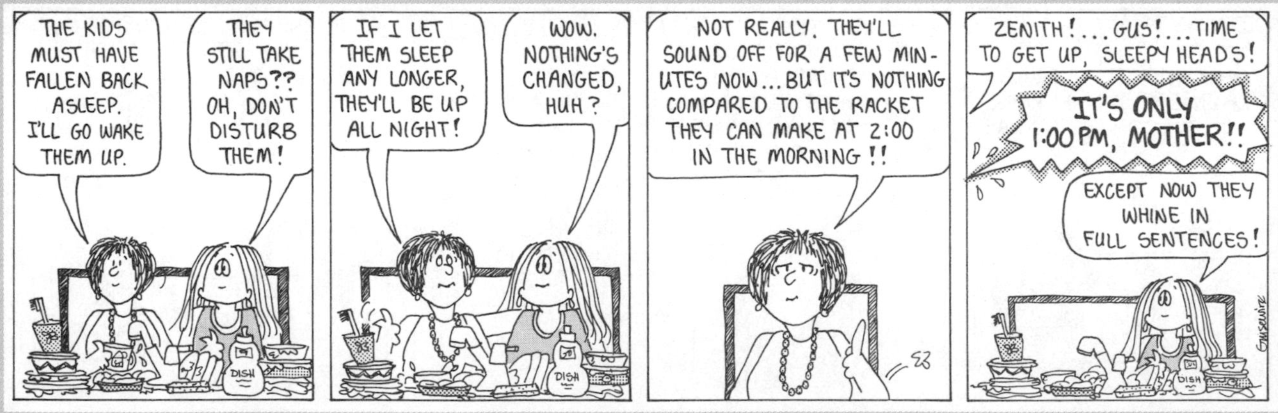
THE KIDS MUST HAVE FALLEN BACK ASLEEP. I'LL GO WAKE THEM UP.
THEY STILL TAKE NAPS?? OH, DON'T DISTURB THEM!
IF I LET THEM SLEEP ANY LONGER, THEY'LL BE UP ALL NIGHT!
WOW. NOTHING'S CHANGED, HUH?
NOT REALLY. THEY'LL SOUND OFF FOR A FEW MINUTES NOW...BUT IT'S NOTHING COMPARED TO THE RACKET THEY CAN MAKE AT 2:00 IN THE MORNING!!
ZENITH!...GUS!...TIME TO GET UP, SLEEPY HEADS!
IT'S ONLY 1:00 PM, MOTHER!!
EXCEPT NOW THEY WHINE IN FULL SENTENCES!

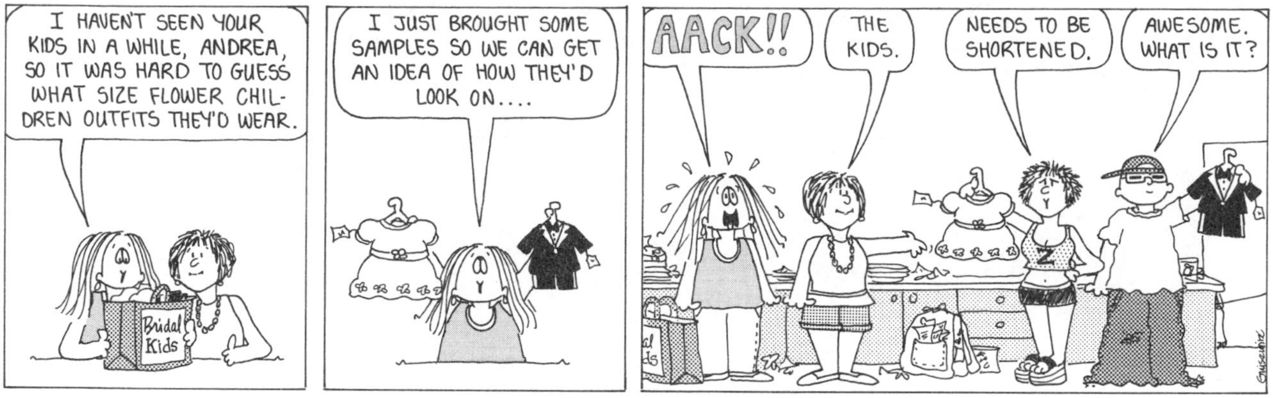
I HAVEN'T SEEN YOUR KIDS IN A WHILE, ANDREA, SO IT WAS HARD TO GUESS WHAT SIZE FLOWER CHIL-DREN OUTFITS THEY'D WEAR.
Bridal Kids
I JUST BROUGHT SOME SAMPLES SO WE CAN GET AN IDEA OF HOW THEY'D LOOK ON....
AACK!!
THE KIDS.
NEEDS TO BE SHORTENED.
AWESOME. WHAT IS IT?

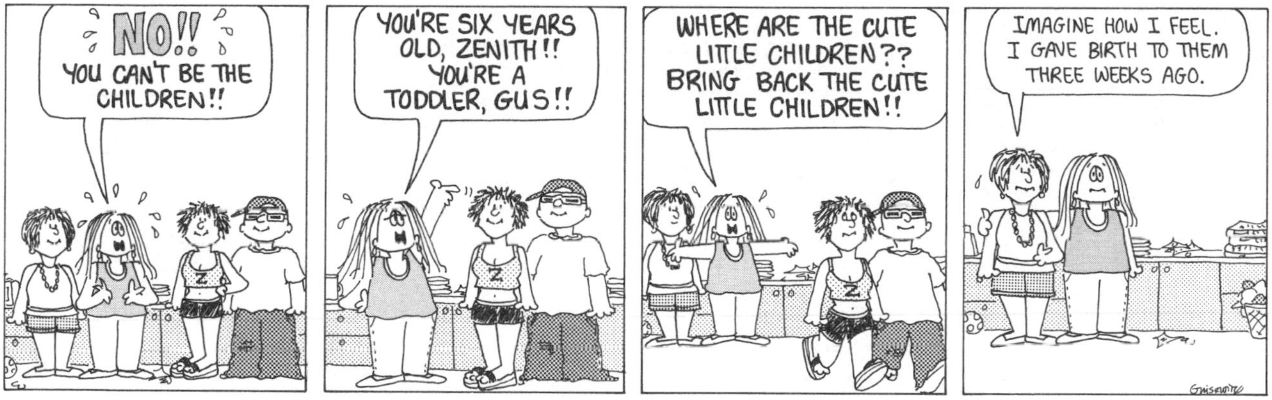
NO!! YOU CAN'T BE THE CHILDREN!!
YOU'RE SIX YEARS OLD, ZENITH!! YOU'RE A TODDLER, GUS!!
WHERE ARE THE CUTE LITTLE CHILDREN?? BRING BACK THE CUTE LITTLE CHILDREN!!
IMAGINE HOW I FEEL. I GAVE BIRTH TO THEM THREE WEEKS AGO.

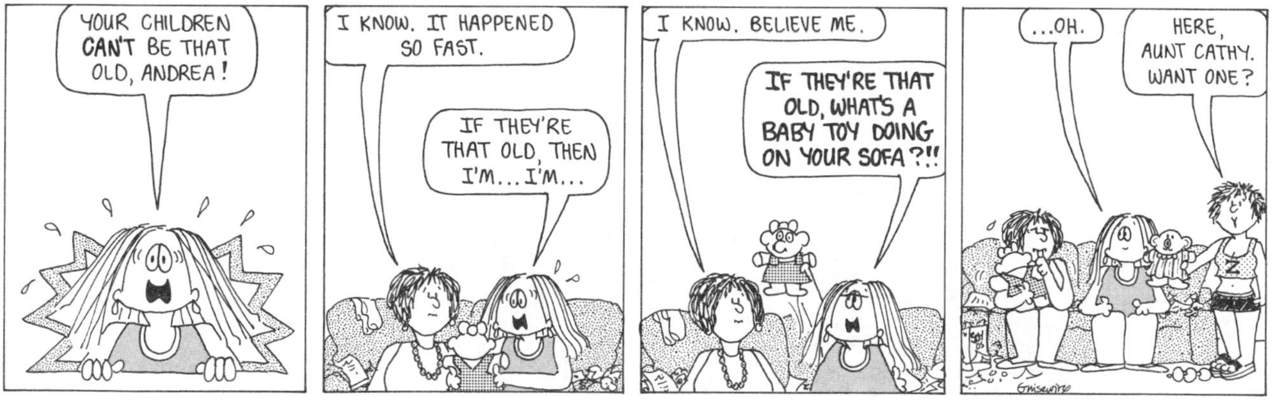
YOUR CHILDREN CAN'T BE THAT OLD, ANDREA!
I KNOW. IT HAPPENED SO FAST.
IF THEY'RE THAT OLD, THEN I'M... I'M...
I KNOW. BELIEVE ME.
IF THEY'RE THAT OLD, WHAT'S A BABY TOY DOING ON YOUR SOFA?!!
...OH.
HERE, AUNT CATHY. WANT ONE?

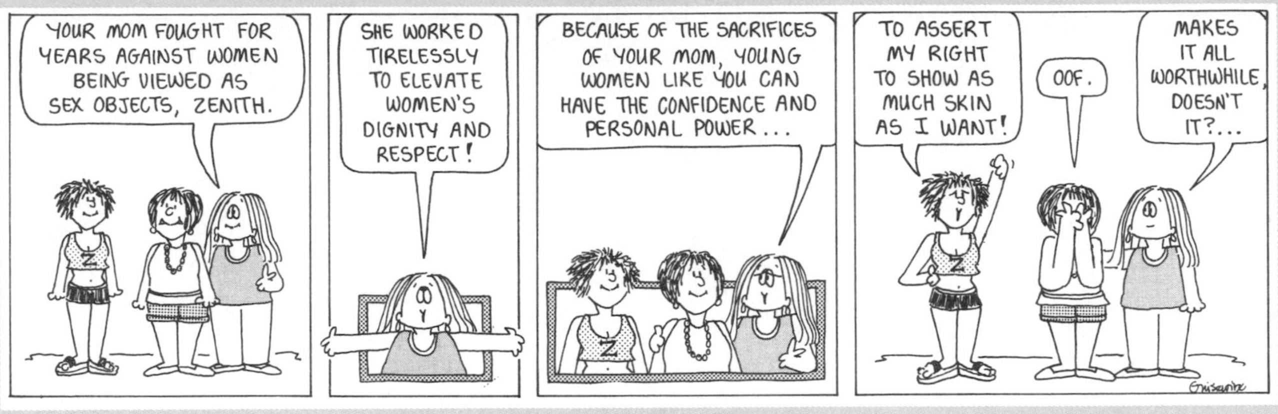
YOUR MOM FOUGHT FOR YEARS AGAINST WOMEN BEING VIEWED AS SEX OBJECTS, ZENITH.
SHE WORKED TIRELESSLY TO ELEVATE WOMEN'S DIGNITY AND RESPECT!
BECAUSE OF THE SACRIFICES OF YOUR MOM, YOUNG WOMEN LIKE YOU CAN HAVE THE CONFIDENCE AND PERSONAL POWER...
TO ASSERT MY RIGHT TO SHOW AS MUCH SKIN AS I WANT!
OOF.
MAKES IT ALL WORTHWHILE, DOESN'T IT?...

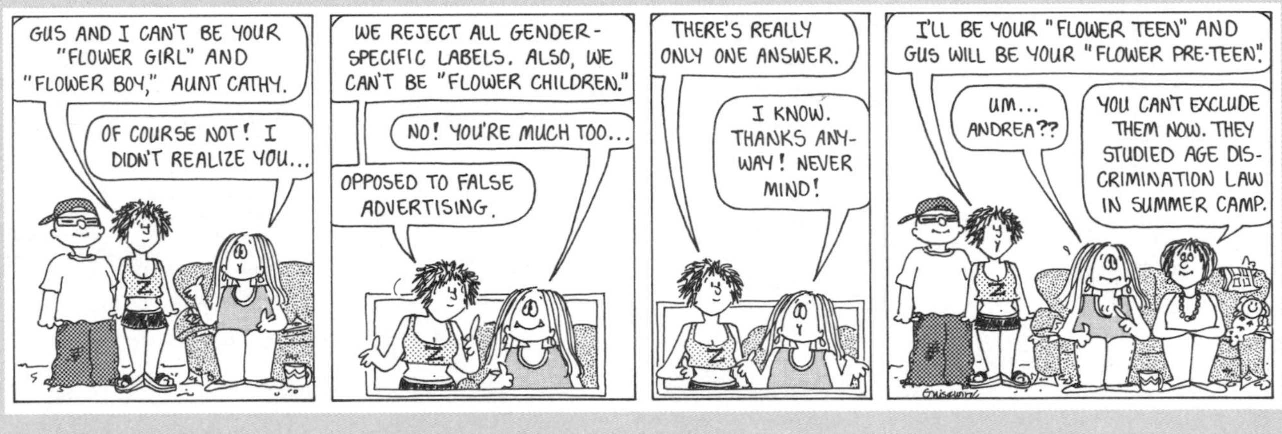
GUS AND I CAN'T BE YOUR "FLOWER GIRL" AND "FLOWER BOY," AUNT CATHY.
OF COURSE NOT! I DIDN'T REALIZE YOU...
WE REJECT ALL GENDER-SPECIFIC LABELS. ALSO, WE CAN'T BE "FLOWER CHILDREN."
NO! YOU'RE MUCH TOO...
OPPOSED TO FALSE ADVERTISING.
THERE'S REALLY ONLY ONE ANSWER.
I KNOW. THANKS ANY-WAY! NEVER MIND!
I'LL BE YOUR "FLOWER TEEN" AND GUS WILL BE YOUR "FLOWER PRE-TEEN."
UM... ANDREA??
YOU CAN'T EXCLUDE THEM NOW. THEY STUDIED AGE DIS-CRIMINATION LAW IN SUMMER CAMP.

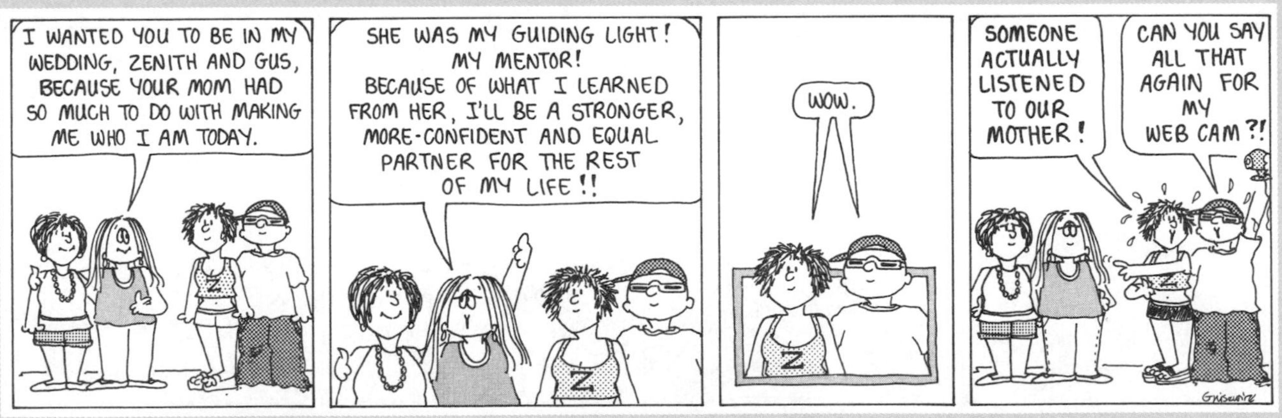
I WANTED YOU TO BE IN MY WEDDING, ZENITH AND GUS, BECAUSE YOUR MOM HAD SO MUCH TO DO WITH MAKING ME WHO I AM TODAY.
SHE WAS MY GUIDING LIGHT! MY MENTOR! BECAUSE OF WHAT I LEARNED FROM HER, I'LL BE A STRONGER, MORE-CONFIDENT AND EQUAL PARTNER FOR THE REST OF MY LIFE!!
WOW.
SOMEONE ACTUALLY LISTENED TO OUR MOTHER!
CAN YOU SAY ALL THAT AGAIN FOR MY WEB CAM?!

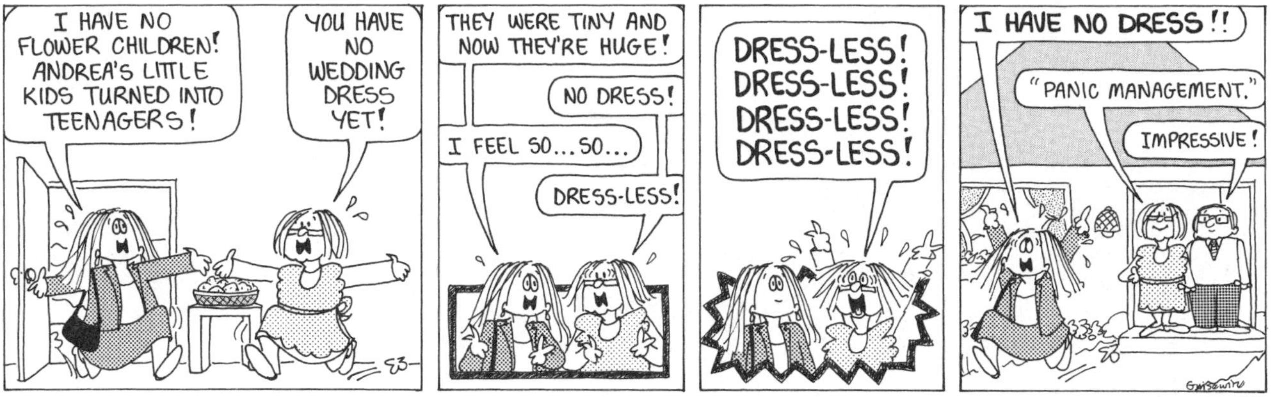
I HAVE NO FLOWER CHILDREN! ANDREA'S LITTLE KIDS TURNED INTO TEENAGERS!
YOU HAVE NO WEDDING DRESS YET!
THEY WERE TINY AND NOW THEY'RE HUGE!
NO DRESS!
I FEEL SO... SO...
DRESS-LESS!
DRESS-LESS! DRESS-LESS! DRESS-LESS! DRESS-LESS!
I HAVE NO DRESS!!
"PANIC MANAGEMENT."
IMPRESSIVE!

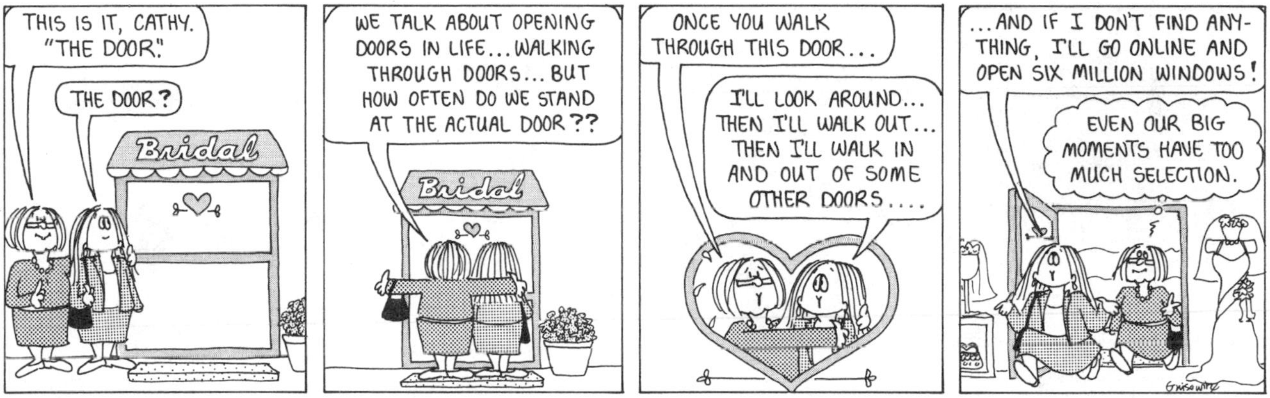
THIS IS IT, CATHY. "THE DOOR."
THE DOOR?
Bridal
WE TALK ABOUT OPENING DOORS IN LIFE... WALKING THROUGH DOORS... BUT HOW OFTEN DO WE STAND AT THE ACTUAL DOOR??
Bridal
ONCE YOU WALK THROUGH THIS DOOR...
I'LL LOOK AROUND... THEN I'LL WALK OUT... THEN I'LL WALK IN AND OUT OF SOME OTHER DOORS....
...AND IF I DON'T FIND ANYTHING, I'LL GO ONLINE AND OPEN SIX MILLION WINDOWS!
EVEN OUR BIG MOMENTS HAVE TOO MUCH SELECTION.

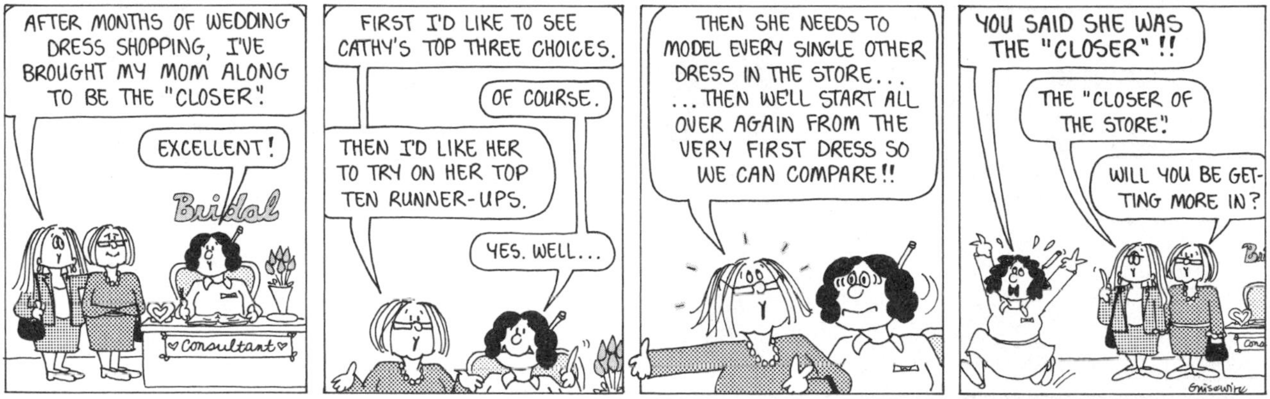
AFTER MONTHS OF WEDDING DRESS SHOPPING, I'VE BROUGHT MY MOM ALONG TO BE THE "CLOSER."
EXCELLENT!
Bridal
Consultant
FIRST I'D LIKE TO SEE CATHY'S TOP THREE CHOICES.
OF COURSE.
THEN I'D LIKE HER TO TRY ON HER TOP TEN RUNNER-UPS.
YES. WELL...
THEN SHE NEEDS TO MODEL EVERY SINGLE OTHER DRESS IN THE STORE... ...THEN WE'LL START ALL OVER AGAIN FROM THE VERY FIRST DRESS SO WE CAN COMPARE!!
YOU SAID SHE WAS THE "CLOSER"!!
THE "CLOSER OF THE STORE."
WILL YOU BE GETTING MORE IN?

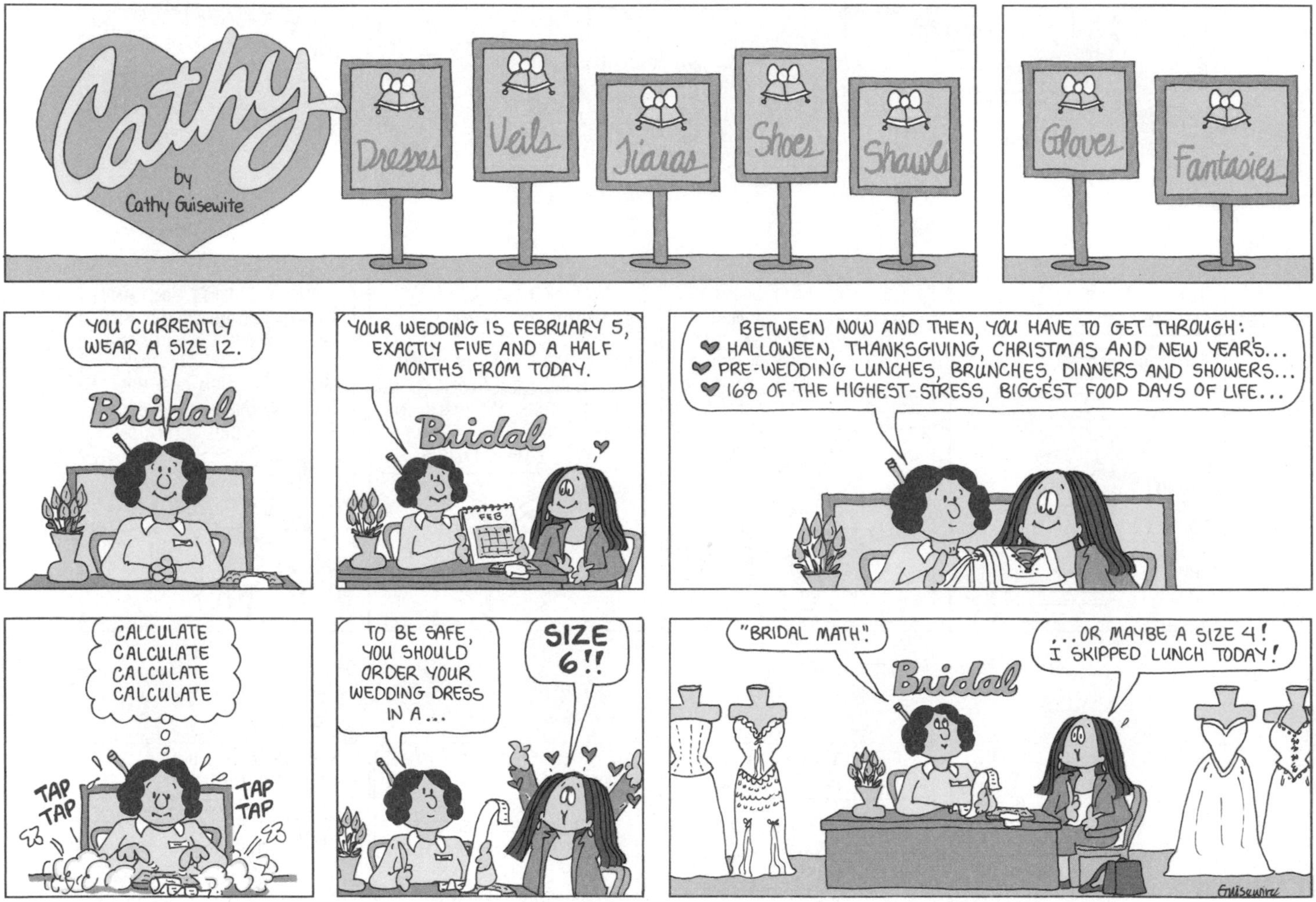
Cathy
by
Cathy Guisewite
Dresses
Veils
Tiaras
Shoes
Shawls
Gloves
Fantasies
YOU CURRENTLY WEAR A SIZE 12.
Bridal
YOUR WEDDING IS FEBRUARY 5, EXACTLY FIVE AND A HALF MONTHS FROM TODAY.
FEB
BETWEEN NOW AND THEN, YOU HAVE TO GET THROUGH:
HALLOWEEN, THANKSGIVING, CHRISTMAS AND NEW YEAR'S...
PRE-WEDDING LUNCHES, BRUNCHES, DINNERS AND SHOWERS...
168 OF THE HIGHEST-STRESS, BIGGEST FOOD DAYS OF LIFE...
CALCULATE CALCULATE CALCULATE CALCULATE
TAP TAP
TAP TAP
TO BE SAFE, YOU SHOULD ORDER YOUR WEDDING DRESS IN A...
SIZE 6!!
"BRIDAL MATH."
...OR MAYBE A SIZE 4! I SKIPPED LUNCH TODAY!
GUISEWITE

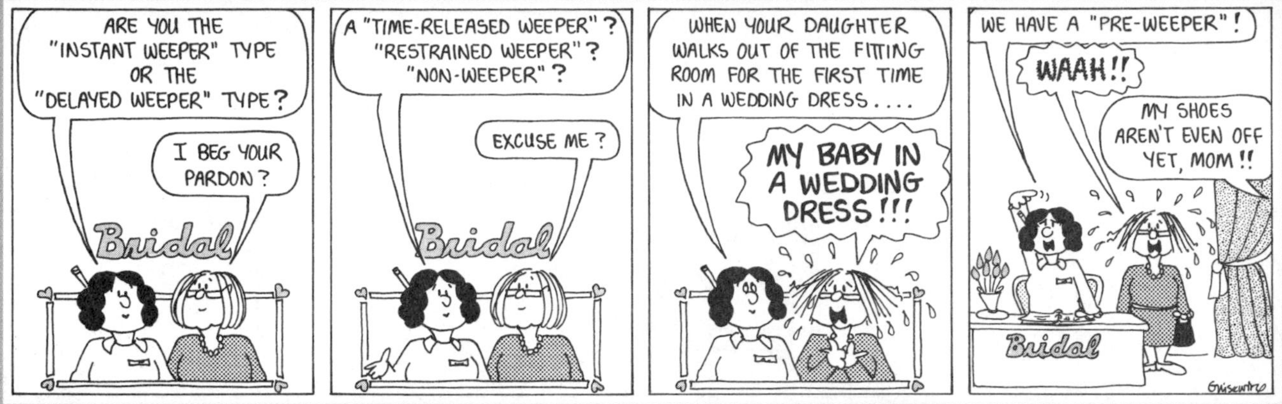
ARE YOU THE "INSTANT WEEPER" TYPE OR THE "DELAYED WEEPER" TYPE?
I BEG YOUR PARDON?
Bridal
A "TIME-RELEASED WEEPER"? "RESTRAINED WEEPER"? "NON-WEEPER"?
EXCUSE ME?
Bridal
WHEN YOUR DAUGHTER WALKS OUT OF THE FITTING ROOM FOR THE FIRST TIME IN A WEDDING DRESS....
MY BABY IN A WEDDING DRESS!!!
WE HAVE A "PRE-WEEPER"!
WAAH!!
MY SHOES AREN'T EVEN OFF YET, MOM!!
Bridal

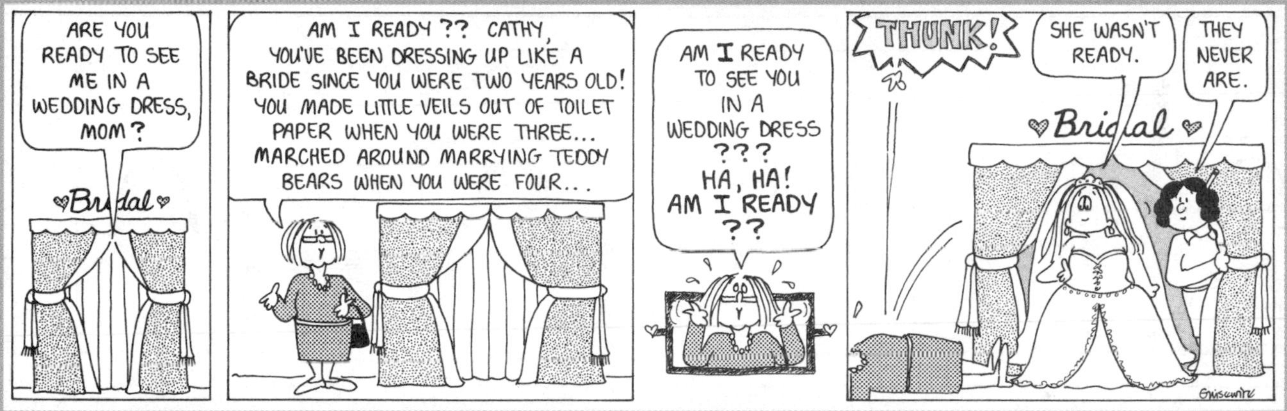
ARE YOU READY TO SEE ME IN A WEDDING DRESS, MOM?
Bridal
AM I READY?? CATHY, YOU'VE BEEN DRESSING UP LIKE A BRIDE SINCE YOU WERE TWO YEARS OLD! YOU MADE LITTLE VEILS OUT OF TOILET PAPER WHEN YOU WERE THREE... MARCHED AROUND MARRYING TEDDY BEARS WHEN YOU WERE FOUR...
AM I READY TO SEE YOU IN A WEDDING DRESS??? HA, HA! AM I READY??
THUNK!
SHE WASN'T READY.
THEY NEVER ARE.
Bridal

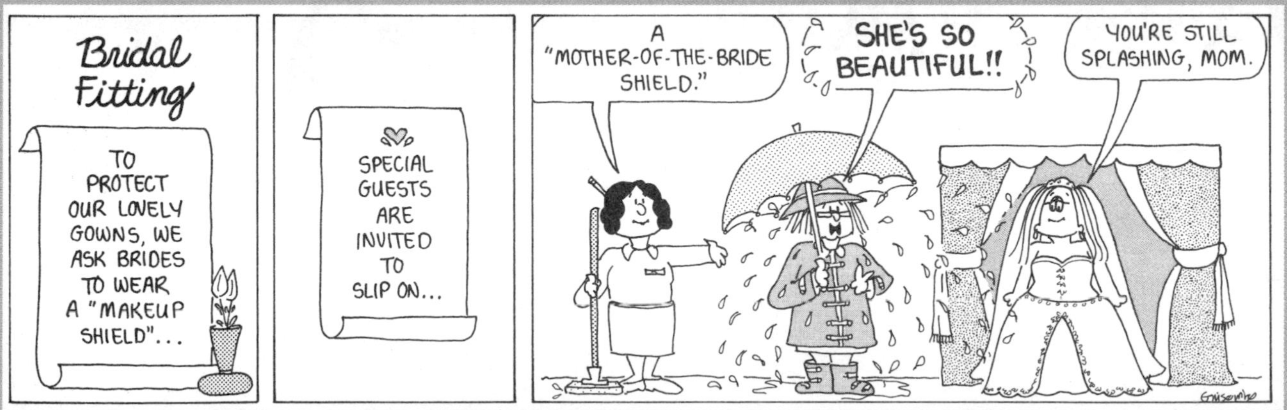
Bridal Fitting
TO PROTECT OUR LOVELY GOWNS, WE ASK BRIDES TO WEAR A "MAKEUP SHIELD"...
SPECIAL GUESTS ARE INVITED TO SLIP ON...
A "MOTHER-OF-THE-BRIDE SHIELD."
SHE'S SO BEAUTIFUL!!
YOU'RE STILL SPLASHING, MOM.

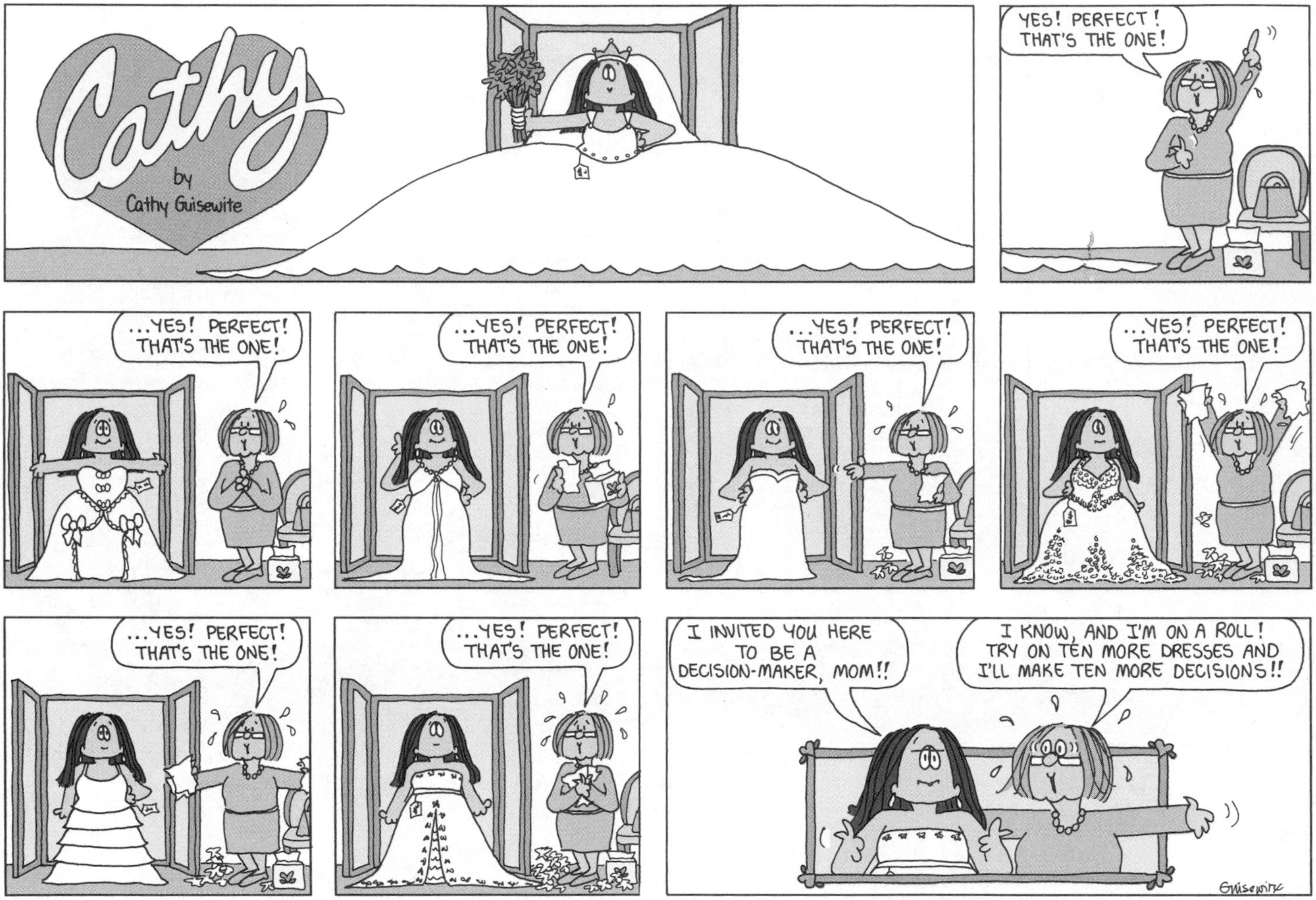
Cathy
by
Cathy Guisewite
YES! PERFECT! THAT'S THE ONE!
...YES! PERFECT! THAT'S THE ONE!
...YES! PERFECT! THAT'S THE ONE!
...YES! PERFECT! THAT'S THE ONE!
...YES! PERFECT! THAT'S THE ONE!
...YES! PERFECT! THAT'S THE ONE!
...YES! PERFECT! THAT'S THE ONE!
I INVITED YOU HERE TO BE A DECISION-MAKER, MOM!!
I KNOW, AND I'M ON A ROLL! TRY ON TEN MORE DRESSES AND I'LL MAKE TEN MORE DECISIONS!!
Guisewite

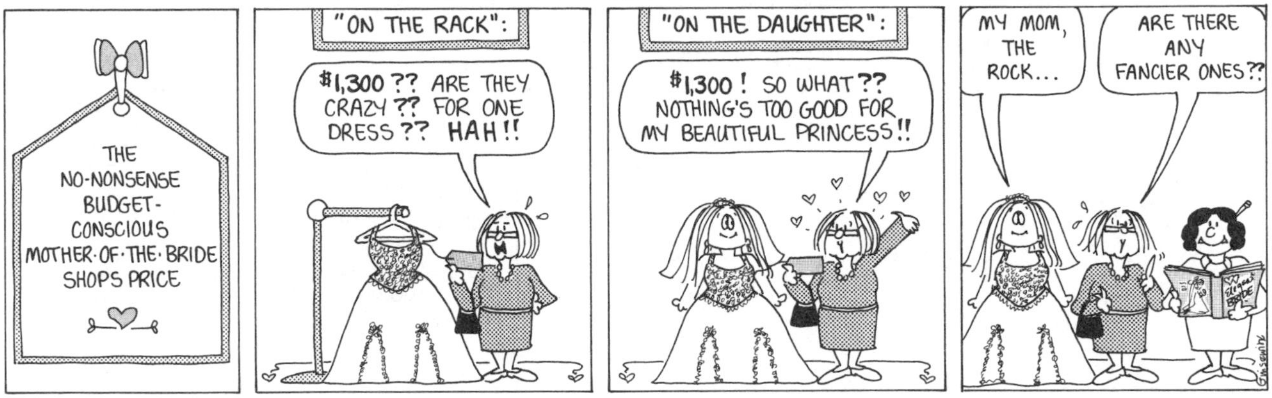
THE NO-NONSENSE BUDGET-CONSCIOUS MOTHER-OF-THE-BRIDE SHOPS PRICE
"ON THE RACK":
$1,300 ?? ARE THEY CRAZY ?? FOR ONE DRESS ?? HAH !!
"ON THE DAUGHTER":
$1,300 ! SO WHAT ?? NOTHING'S TOO GOOD FOR MY BEAUTIFUL PRINCESS !!
MY MOM, THE ROCK...
ARE THERE ANY FANCIER ONES ??

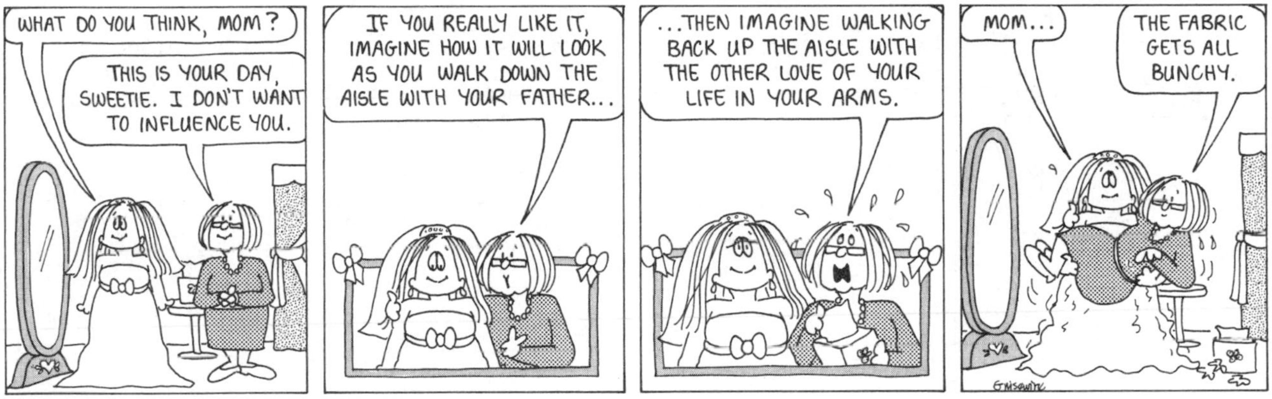
WHAT DO YOU THINK, MOM?
THIS IS YOUR DAY, SWEETIE. I DON'T WANT TO INFLUENCE YOU.
IF YOU REALLY LIKE IT, IMAGINE HOW IT WILL LOOK AS YOU WALK DOWN THE AISLE WITH YOUR FATHER...
...THEN IMAGINE WALKING BACK UP THE AISLE WITH THE OTHER LOVE OF YOUR LIFE IN YOUR ARMS.
MOM...
THE FABRIC GETS ALL BUNCHY.

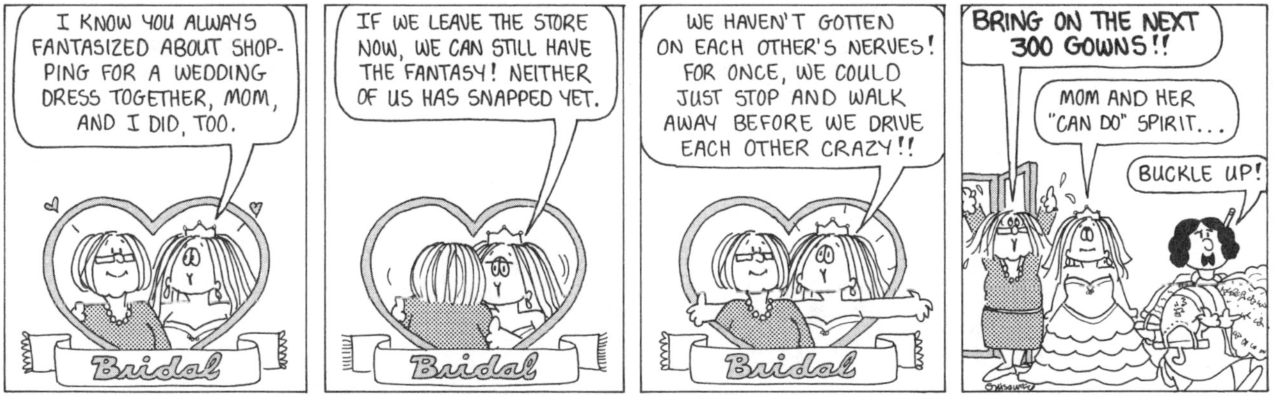
I KNOW YOU ALWAYS FANTASIZED ABOUT SHOPPING FOR A WEDDING DRESS TOGETHER, MOM, AND I DID, TOO.
Bridal
IF WE LEAVE THE STORE NOW, WE CAN STILL HAVE THE FANTASY! NEITHER OF US HAS SNAPPED YET.
Bridal
WE HAVEN'T GOTTEN ON EACH OTHER'S NERVES! FOR ONCE, WE COULD JUST STOP AND WALK AWAY BEFORE WE DRIVE EACH OTHER CRAZY !!
Bridal
BRING ON THE NEXT 300 GOWNS !!
MOM AND HER "CAN DO" SPIRIT...
BUCKLE UP!

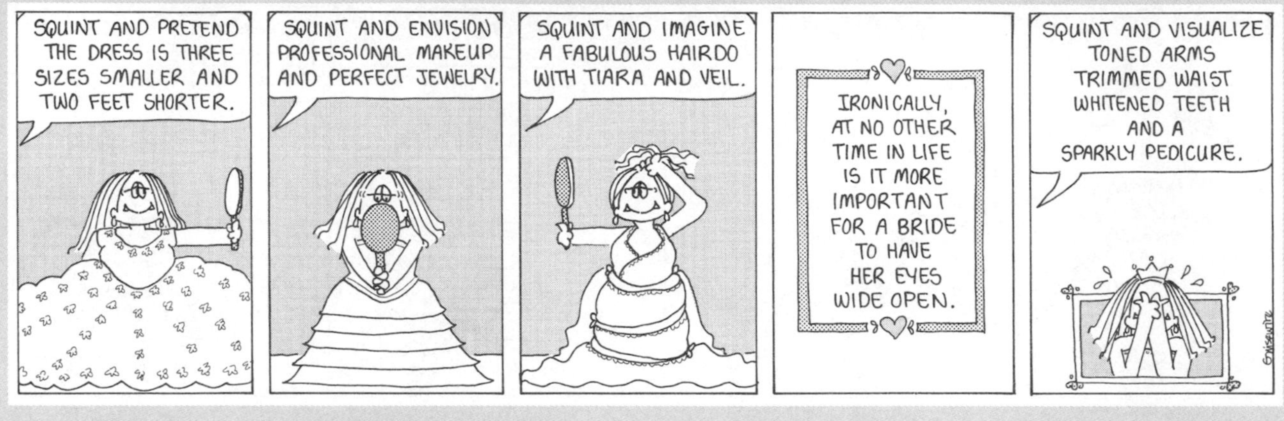
SQUINT AND PRETEND THE DRESS IS THREE SIZES SMALLER AND TWO FEET SHORTER.
SQUINT AND ENVISION PROFESSIONAL MAKEUP AND PERFECT JEWELRY.
SQUINT AND IMAGINE A FABULOUS HAIRDO WITH TIARA AND VEIL.
IRONICALLY, AT NO OTHER TIME IN LIFE IS IT MORE IMPORTANT FOR A BRIDE TO HAVE HER EYES WIDE OPEN.
SQUINT AND VISUALIZE TONED ARMS TRIMMED WAIST WHITENED TEETH AND A SPARKLY PEDICURE.

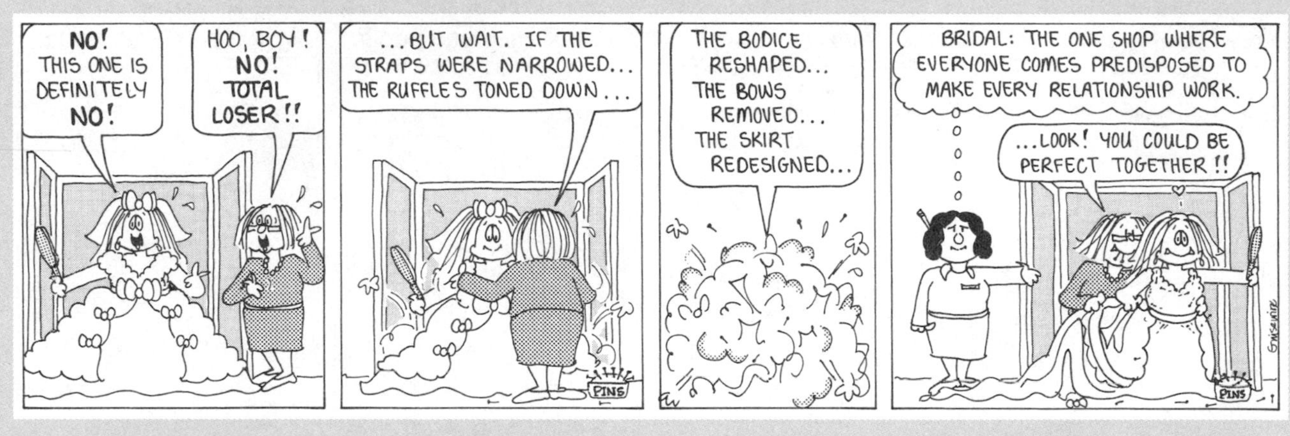
NO! THIS ONE IS DEFINITELY NO!
HOO, BOY! NO! TOTAL LOSER!!
...BUT WAIT. IF THE STRAPS WERE NARROWED... THE RUFFLES TONED DOWN...
PINS
THE BODICE RESHAPED... THE BOWS REMOVED... THE SKIRT REDESIGNED...
BRIDAL: THE ONE SHOP WHERE EVERYONE COMES PREDISPOSED TO MAKE EVERY RELATIONSHIP WORK.
...LOOK! YOU COULD BE PERFECT TOGETHER!!
PINS

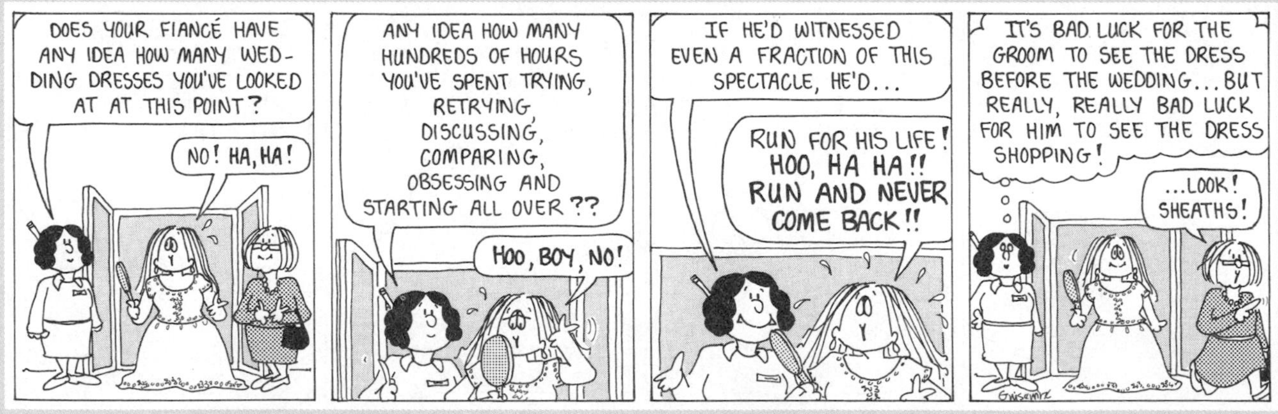
DOES YOUR FIANCÉ HAVE ANY IDEA HOW MANY WEDDING DRESSES YOU'VE LOOKED AT AT THIS POINT?
NO! HA, HA!
ANY IDEA HOW MANY HUNDREDS OF HOURS YOU'VE SPENT TRYING, RETRYING, DISCUSSING, COMPARING, OBSESSING AND STARTING ALL OVER??
HOO, BOY, NO!
IF HE'D WITNESSED EVEN A FRACTION OF THIS SPECTACLE, HE'D...
RUN FOR HIS LIFE! HOO, HA HA!! RUN AND NEVER COME BACK!!
IT'S BAD LUCK FOR THE GROOM TO SEE THE DRESS BEFORE THE WEDDING... BUT REALLY, REALLY BAD LUCK FOR HIM TO SEE THE DRESS SHOPPING!
...LOOK! SHEATHS!

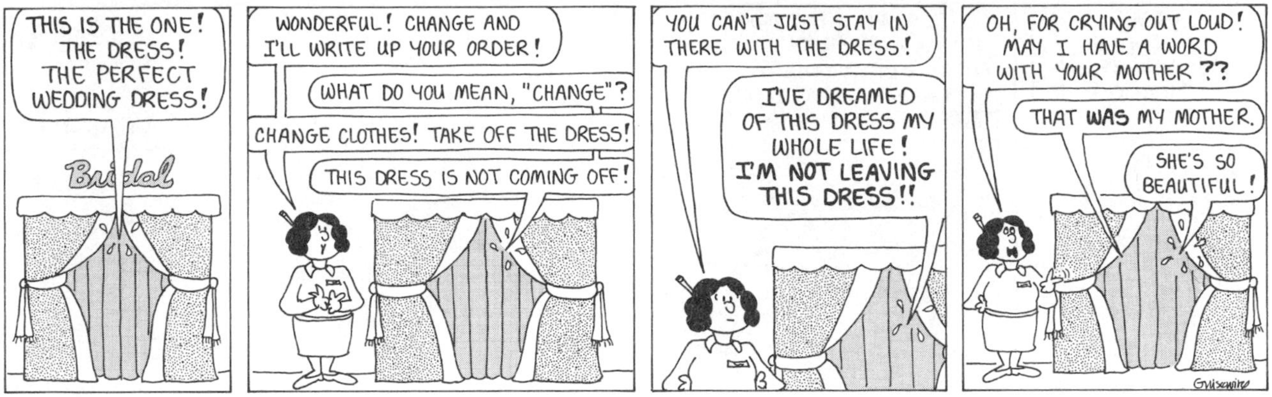
THIS IS THE ONE! THE DRESS! THE PERFECT WEDDING DRESS!
Bridal
WONDERFUL! CHANGE AND I'LL WRITE UP YOUR ORDER!
WHAT DO YOU MEAN, "CHANGE"?
CHANGE CLOTHES! TAKE OFF THE DRESS!
THIS DRESS IS NOT COMING OFF!
YOU CAN'T JUST STAY IN THERE WITH THE DRESS!
I'VE DREAMED OF THIS DRESS MY WHOLE LIFE! I'M NOT LEAVING THIS DRESS!!
OH, FOR CRYING OUT LOUD! MAY I HAVE A WORD WITH YOUR MOTHER??
THAT WAS MY MOTHER.
SHE'S SO BEAUTIFUL!
Guisewite

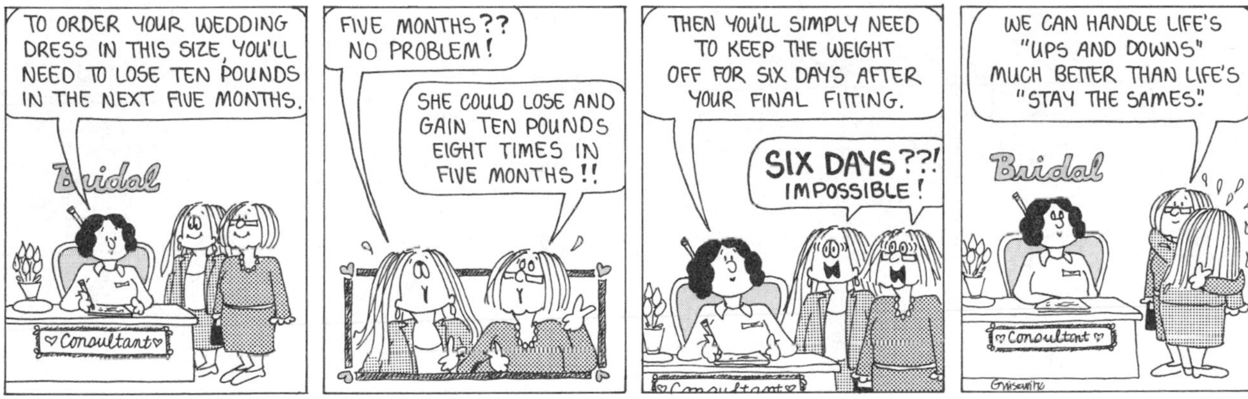
TO ORDER YOUR WEDDING DRESS IN THIS SIZE, YOU'LL NEED TO LOSE TEN POUNDS IN THE NEXT FIVE MONTHS.
Bridal
Consultant
FIVE MONTHS?? NO PROBLEM!
SHE COULD LOSE AND GAIN TEN POUNDS EIGHT TIMES IN FIVE MONTHS!!
THEN YOU'LL SIMPLY NEED TO KEEP THE WEIGHT OFF FOR SIX DAYS AFTER YOUR FINAL FITTING.
SIX DAYS??! IMPOSSIBLE!
WE CAN HANDLE LIFE'S "UPS AND DOWNS" MUCH BETTER THAN LIFE'S "STAY THE SAMES."
Bridal
Consultant
Guisewite

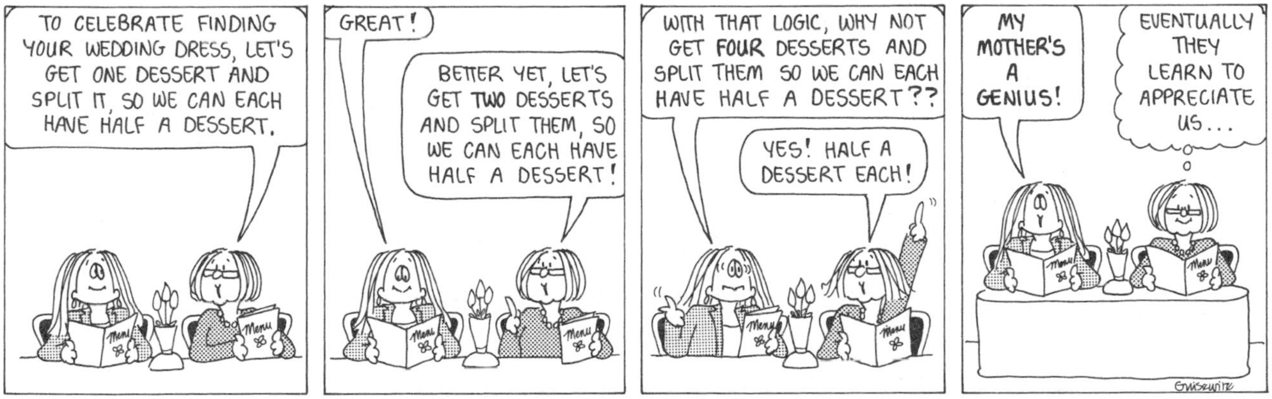
TO CELEBRATE FINDING YOUR WEDDING DRESS, LET'S GET ONE DESSERT AND SPLIT IT, SO WE CAN EACH HAVE HALF A DESSERT.
GREAT!
BETTER YET, LET'S GET TWO DESSERTS AND SPLIT THEM, SO WE CAN EACH HAVE HALF A DESSERT!
WITH THAT LOGIC, WHY NOT GET FOUR DESSERTS AND SPLIT THEM SO WE CAN EACH HAVE HALF A DESSERT??
YES! HALF A DESSERT EACH!
MY MOTHER'S A GENIUS!
EVENTUALLY THEY LEARN TO APPRECIATE US...
Guisewite

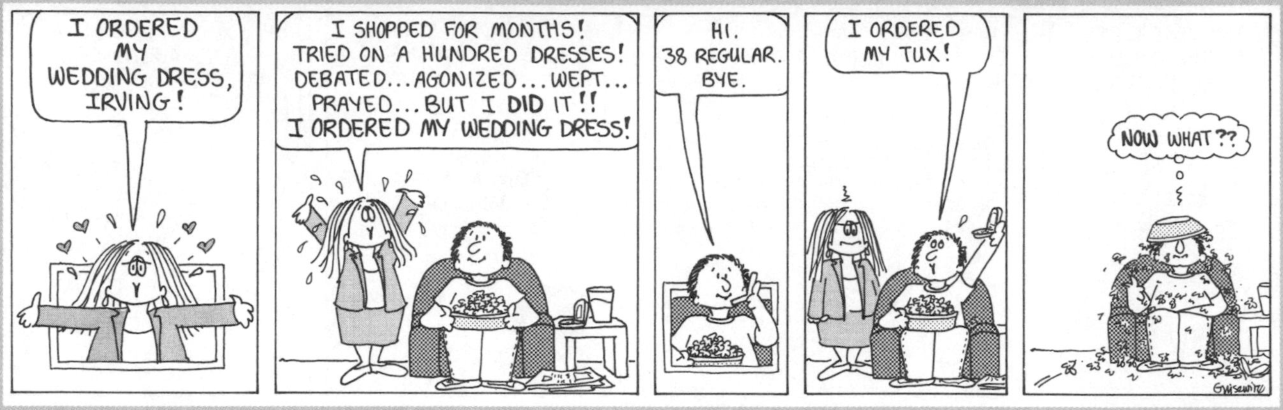

I ORDERED MY WEDDING DRESS, IRVING!
I SHOPPED FOR MONTHS! TRIED ON A HUNDRED DRESSES! DEBATED... AGONIZED... WEPT... PRAYED... BUT I DID IT!! I ORDERED MY WEDDING DRESS!
HI. 38 REGULAR. BYE.
I ORDERED MY TUX!
NOW WHAT??

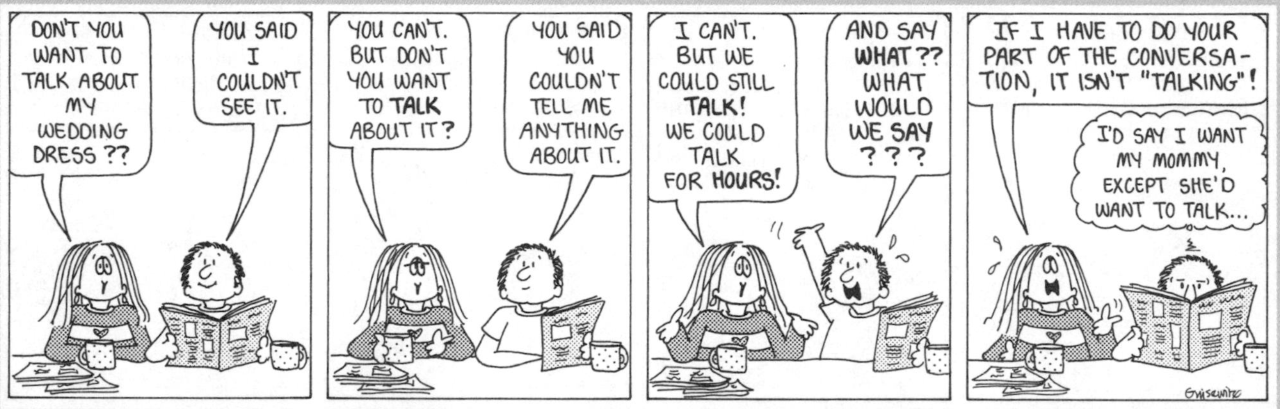

DON'T YOU WANT TO TALK ABOUT MY WEDDING DRESS??
YOU SAID I COULDN'T SEE IT.
YOU CAN'T. BUT DON'T YOU WANT TO TALK ABOUT IT?
YOU SAID YOU COULDN'T TELL ME ANYTHING ABOUT IT.
I CAN'T. BUT WE COULD STILL TALK! WE COULD TALK FOR HOURS!
AND SAY WHAT?? WHAT WOULD WE SAY???
IF I HAVE TO DO YOUR PART OF THE CONVERSA-TION, IT ISN'T "TALKING"!
I'D SAY I WANT MY MOMMY, EXCEPT SHE'D WANT TO TALK...

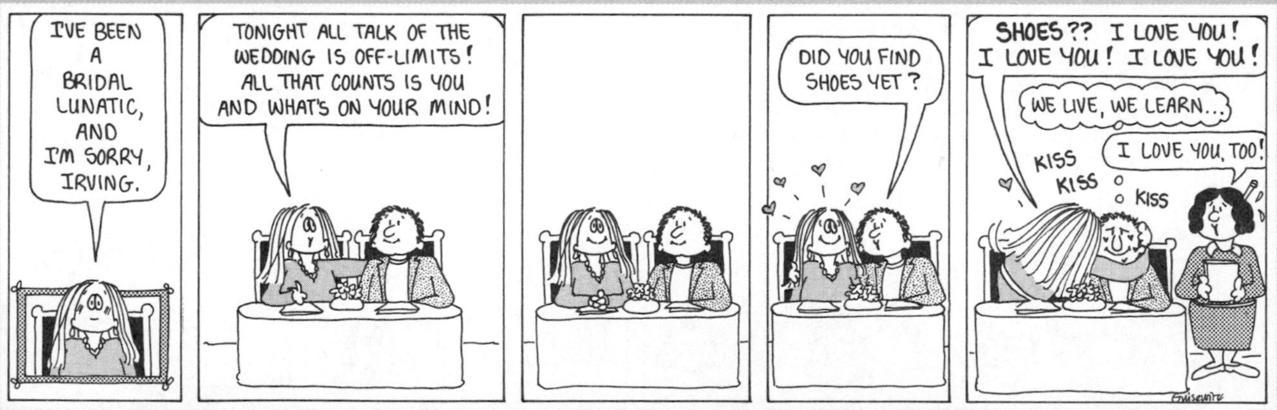

I'VE BEEN A BRIDAL LUNATIC, AND I'M SORRY, IRVING.
TONIGHT ALL TALK OF THE WEDDING IS OFF-LIMITS! ALL THAT COUNTS IS YOU AND WHAT'S ON YOUR MIND!
DID YOU FIND SHOES YET?
SHOES?? I LOVE YOU! I LOVE YOU! I LOVE YOU!
WE LIVE, WE LEARN...
KISS KISS
KISS
I LOVE YOU, TOO!

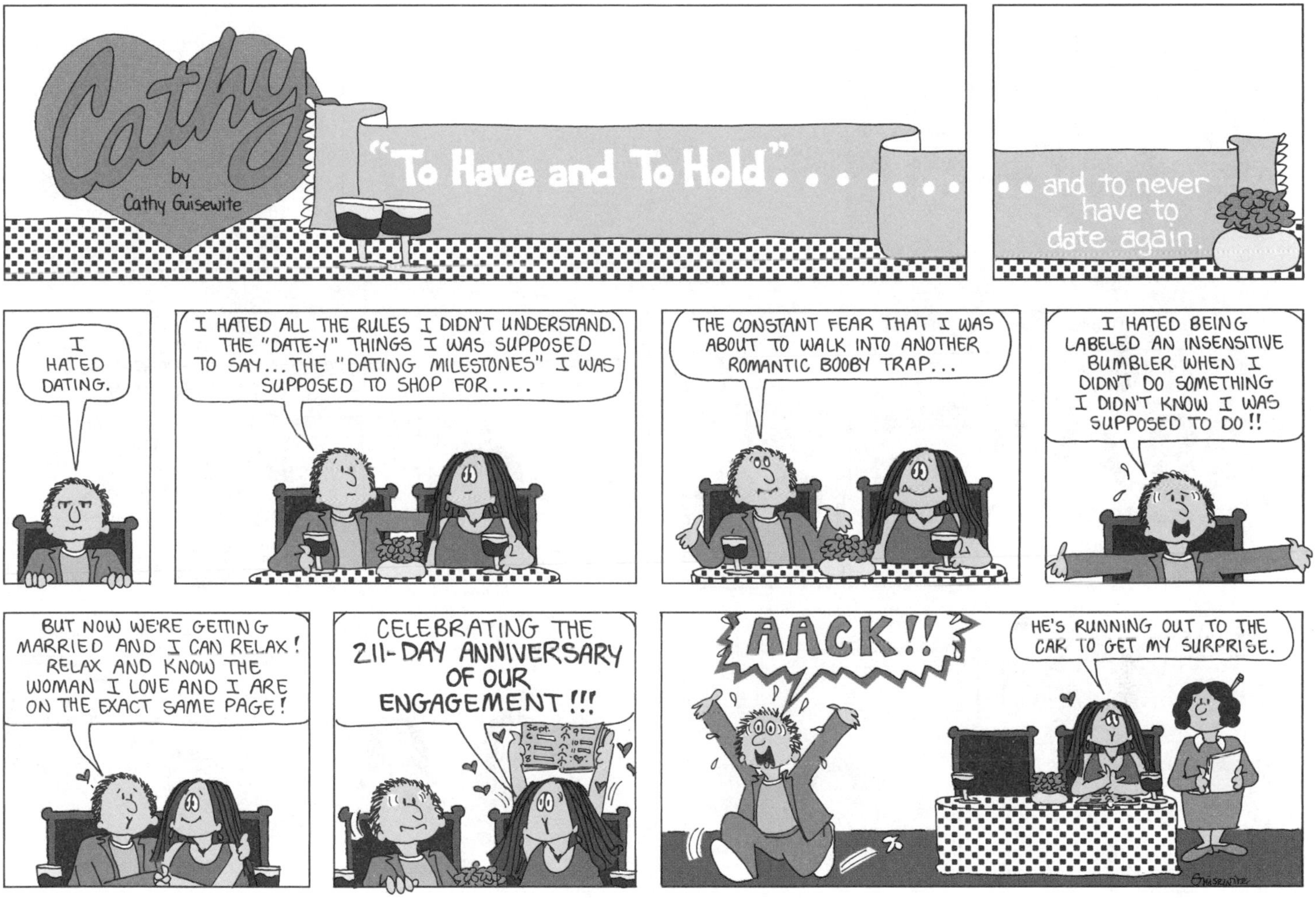
Cathy
by Cathy Guisewite
"To Have and To Hold". . . . . and to never have to date again.
I HATED DATING.
I HATED ALL THE RULES I DIDN'T UNDERSTAND. THE "DATE-Y" THINGS I WAS SUPPOSED TO SAY... THE "DATING MILESTONES" I WAS SUPPOSED TO SHOP FOR....
THE CONSTANT FEAR THAT I WAS ABOUT TO WALK INTO ANOTHER ROMANTIC BOOBY TRAP...
I HATED BEING LABELED AN INSENSITIVE BUMBLER WHEN I DIDN'T DO SOMETHING I DIDN'T KNOW I WAS SUPPOSED TO DO!!
BUT NOW WE'RE GETTING MARRIED AND I CAN RELAX! RELAX AND KNOW THE WOMAN I LOVE AND I ARE ON THE EXACT SAME PAGE!
CELEBRATING THE 211-DAY ANNIVERSARY OF OUR ENGAGEMENT!!!
AACK!!
HE'S RUNNING OUT TO THE CAR TO GET MY SURPRISE.

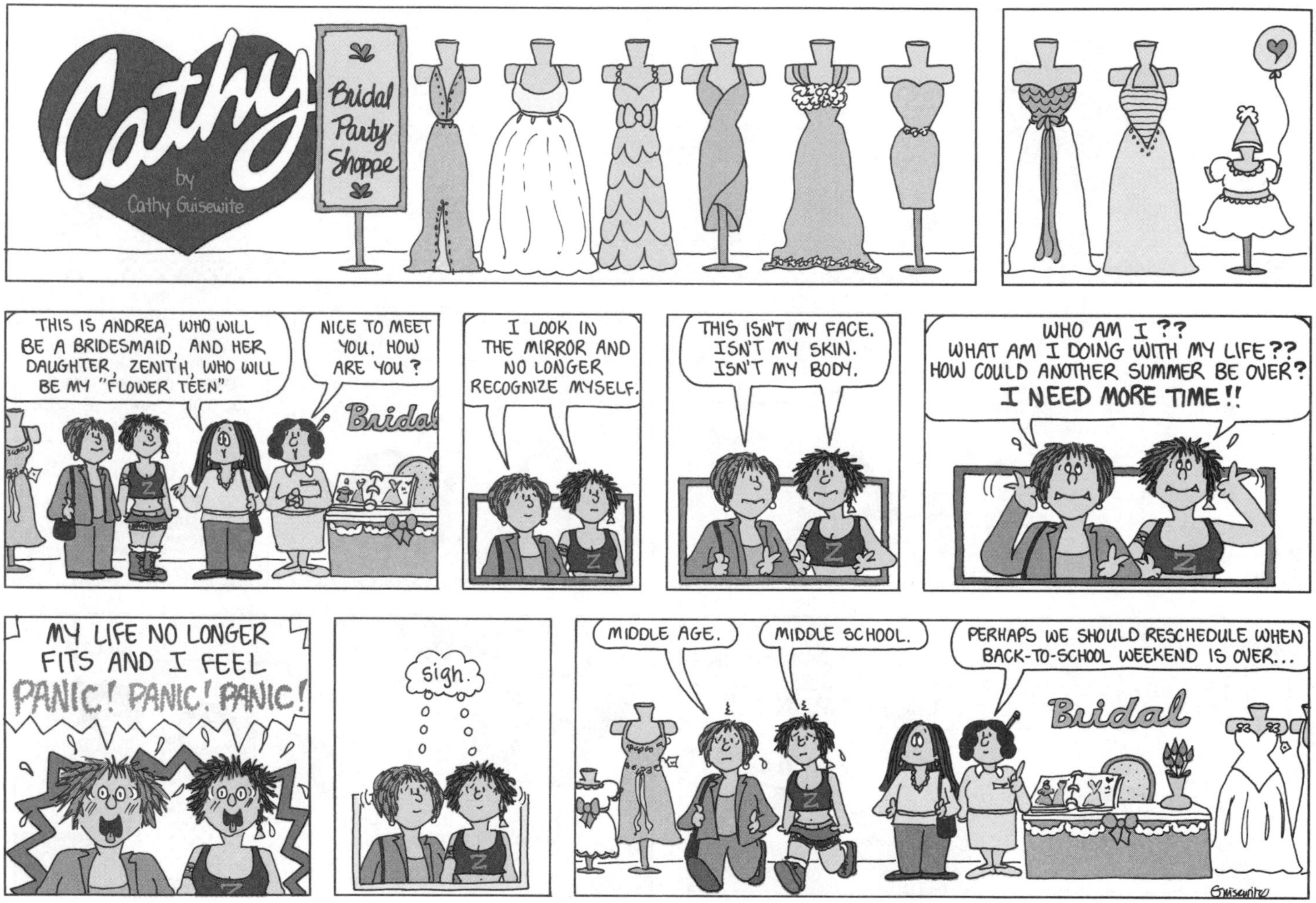
Cathy
by
Cathy Guisewite
Bridal Party Shoppe
THIS IS ANDREA, WHO WILL BE A BRIDESMAID, AND HER DAUGHTER, ZENITH, WHO WILL BE MY "FLOWER TEEN."
NICE TO MEET YOU. HOW ARE YOU?
Bridal
I LOOK IN THE MIRROR AND NO LONGER RECOGNIZE MYSELF.
THIS ISN'T MY FACE. ISN'T MY SKIN. ISN'T MY BODY.
WHO AM I ?? WHAT AM I DOING WITH MY LIFE?? HOW COULD ANOTHER SUMMER BE OVER?
I NEED MORE TIME!!
MY LIFE NO LONGER FITS AND I FEEL
PANIC! PANIC! PANIC!
sigh.
MIDDLE AGE.
MIDDLE SCHOOL.
PERHAPS WE SHOULD RESCHEDULE WHEN BACK-TO-SCHOOL WEEKEND IS OVER...
Bridal
Guisewite

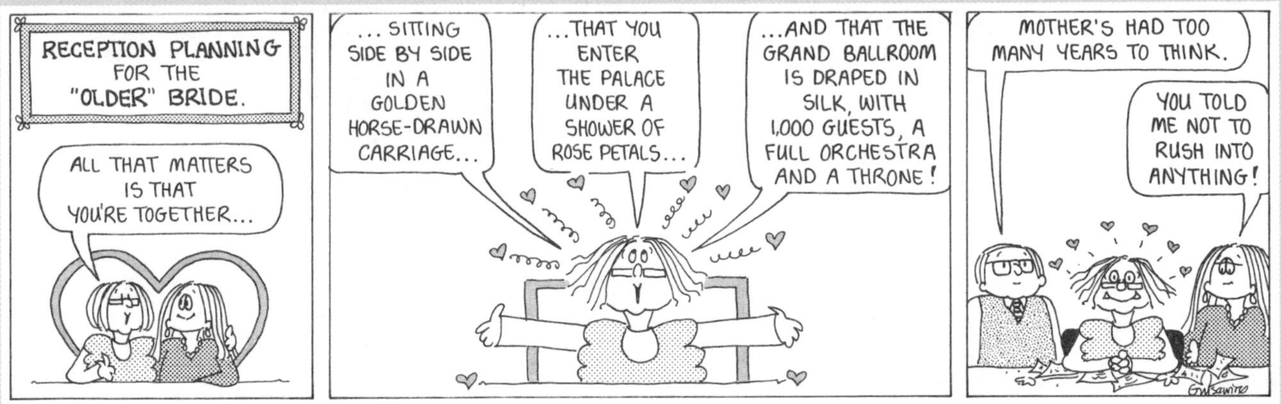
RECEPTION PLANNING FOR THE "OLDER" BRIDE.
ALL THAT MATTERS IS THAT YOU'RE TOGETHER...
... SITTING SIDE BY SIDE IN A GOLDEN HORSE-DRAWN CARRIAGE...
...THAT YOU ENTER THE PALACE UNDER A SHOWER OF ROSE PETALS...
...AND THAT THE GRAND BALLROOM IS DRAPED IN SILK, WITH 1,000 GUESTS, A FULL ORCHESTRA AND A THRONE!
MOTHER'S HAD TOO MANY YEARS TO THINK.
YOU TOLD ME NOT TO RUSH INTO ANYTHING!

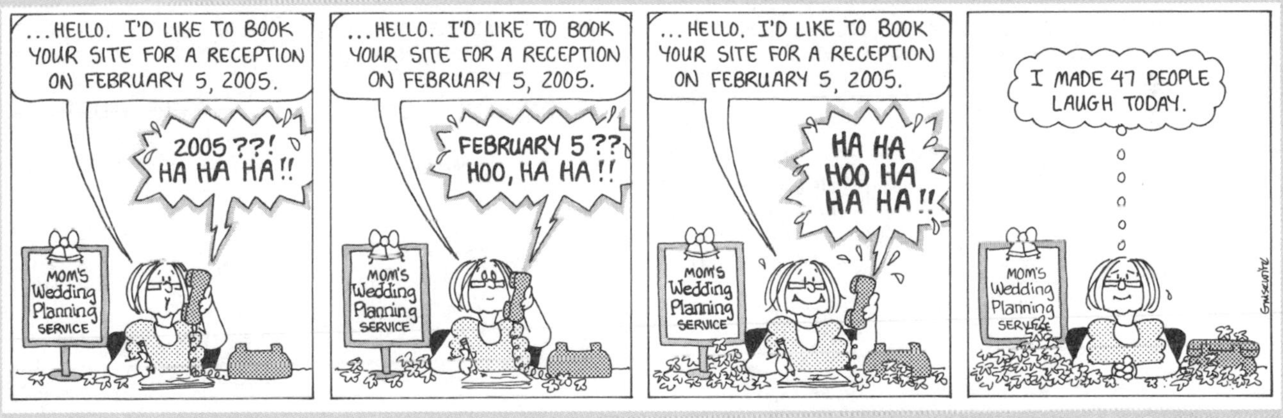
...HELLO. I'D LIKE TO BOOK YOUR SITE FOR A RECEPTION ON FEBRUARY 5, 2005.
2005??! HA HA HA!!
MOM'S Wedding Planning SERVICE
...HELLO. I'D LIKE TO BOOK YOUR SITE FOR A RECEPTION ON FEBRUARY 5, 2005.
FEBRUARY 5?? HOO, HA HA!!
...HELLO. I'D LIKE TO BOOK YOUR SITE FOR A RECEPTION ON FEBRUARY 5, 2005.
HA HA HOO HA HA HA!!
I MADE 47 PEOPLE LAUGH TODAY.

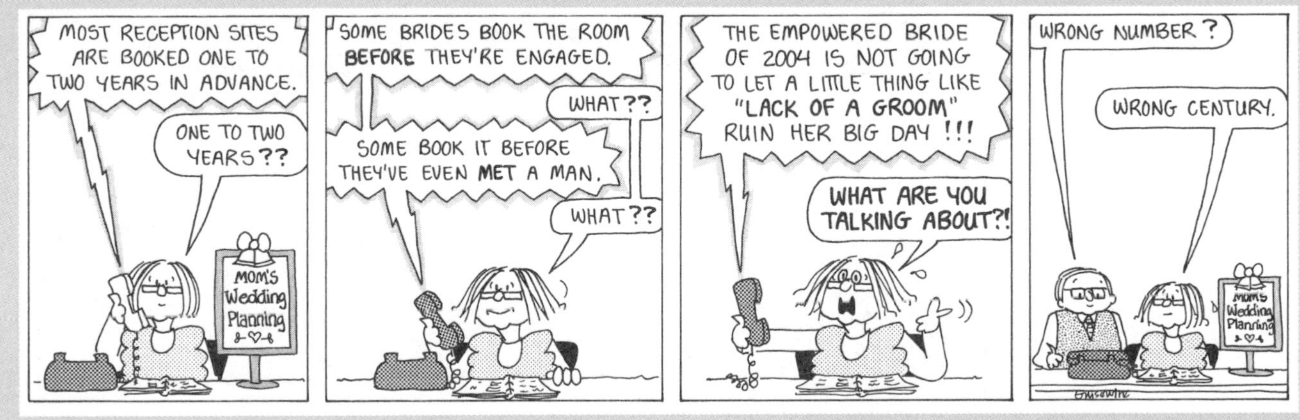
MOST RECEPTION SITES ARE BOOKED ONE TO TWO YEARS IN ADVANCE.
ONE TO TWO YEARS??
MOM'S Wedding Planning
SOME BRIDES BOOK THE ROOM BEFORE THEY'RE ENGAGED.
WHAT??
SOME BOOK IT BEFORE THEY'VE EVEN MET A MAN.
WHAT??
THE EMPOWERED BRIDE OF 2004 IS NOT GOING TO LET A LITTLE THING LIKE "LACK OF A GROOM" RUIN HER BIG DAY!!!
WHAT ARE YOU TALKING ABOUT?!
WRONG NUMBER?
WRONG CENTURY.

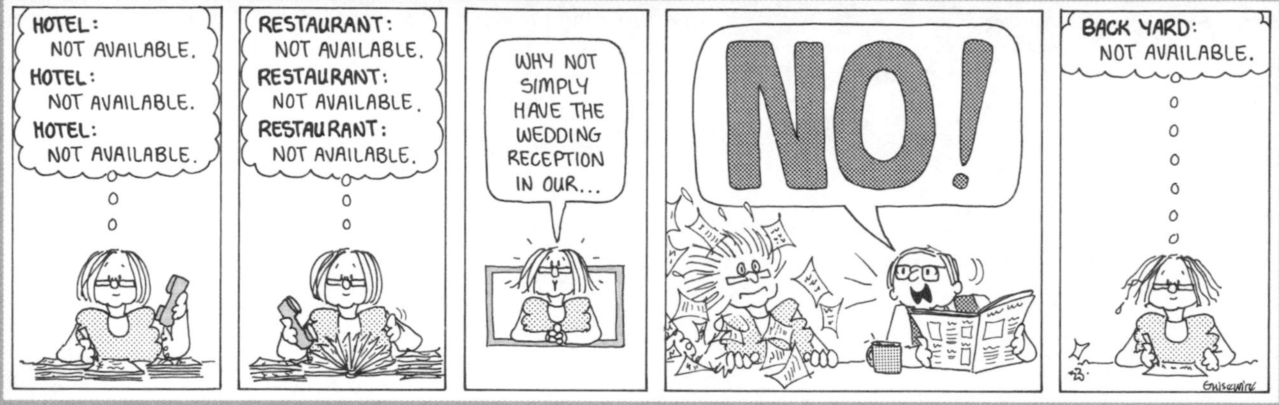
HOTEL:
NOT AVAILABLE.
HOTEL:
NOT AVAILABLE.
HOTEL:
NOT AVAILABLE.
RESTAURANT:
NOT AVAILABLE.
RESTAURANT:
NOT AVAILABLE.
RESTAURANT:
NOT AVAILABLE.
WHY NOT SIMPLY HAVE THE WEDDING RECEPTION IN OUR...
NO!
BACK YARD:
NOT AVAILABLE.

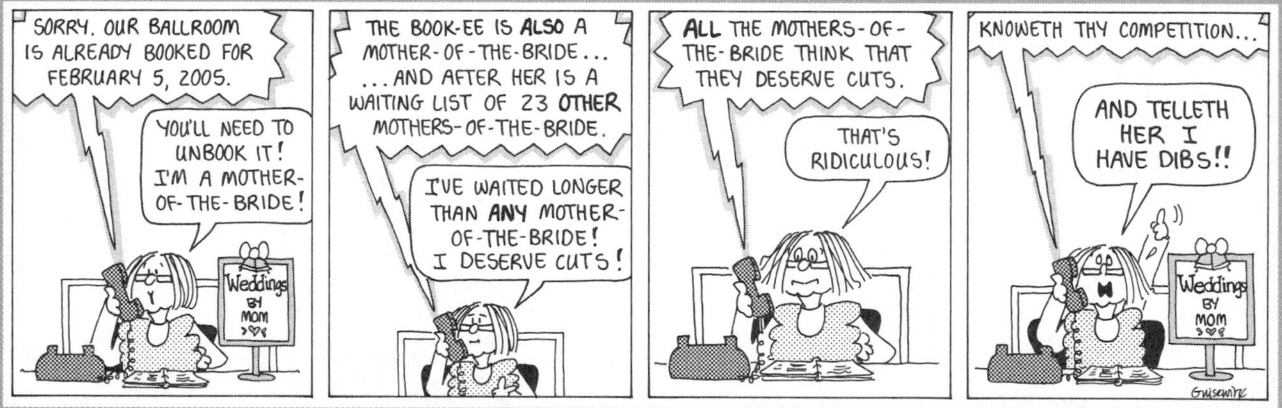
SORRY. OUR BALLROOM IS ALREADY BOOKED FOR FEBRUARY 5, 2005.
YOU'LL NEED TO UNBOOK IT! I'M A MOTHER-OF-THE-BRIDE!
Weddings BY MOM
THE BOOK-EE IS ALSO A MOTHER-OF-THE-BRIDE... ...AND AFTER HER IS A WAITING LIST OF 23 OTHER MOTHERS-OF-THE-BRIDE.
I'VE WAITED LONGER THAN ANY MOTHER-OF-THE-BRIDE! I DESERVE CUTS!
ALL THE MOTHERS-OF-THE-BRIDE THINK THAT THEY DESERVE CUTS.
THAT'S RIDICULOUS!
KNOWETH THY COMPETITION...
AND TELLETH HER I HAVE DIBS!!
Weddings BY MOM

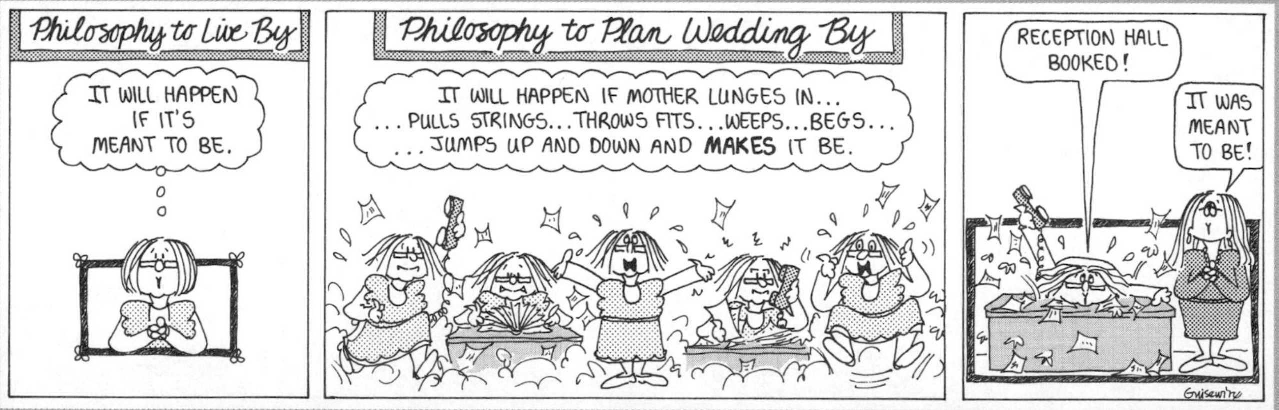
Philosophy to Live By
IT WILL HAPPEN IF IT'S MEANT TO BE.
Philosophy to Plan Wedding By
IT WILL HAPPEN IF MOTHER LUNGES IN... ...PULLS STRINGS...THROWS FITS...WEEPS...BEGS... ...JUMPS UP AND DOWN AND MAKES IT BE.
RECEPTION HALL BOOKED!
IT WAS MEANT TO BE!

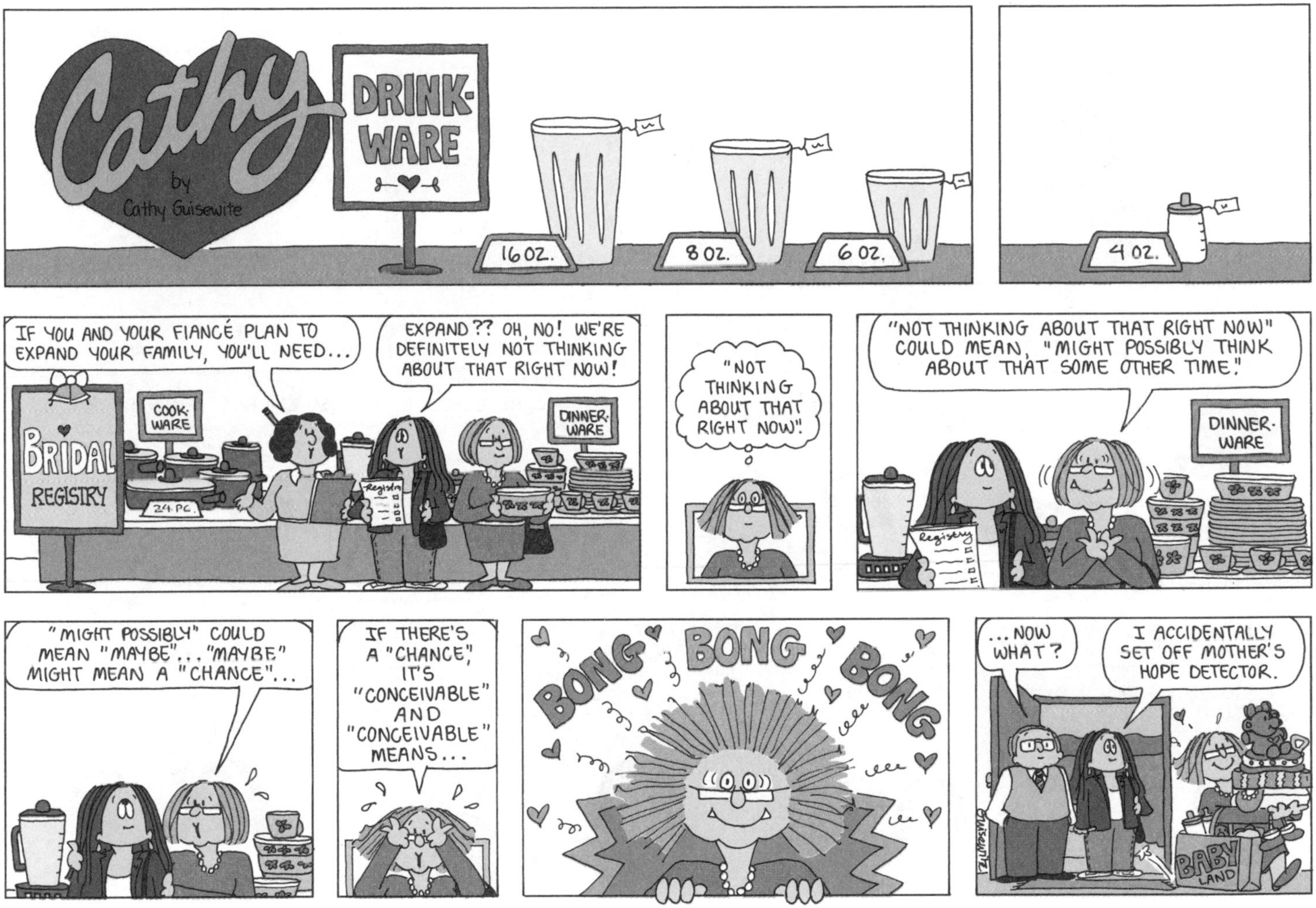
Cathy
by
Cathy Guisewite
DRINK-
WARE
16 OZ.
8 OZ.
6 OZ.
4 OZ.
IF YOU AND YOUR FIANCÉ PLAN TO EXPAND YOUR FAMILY, YOU'LL NEED...
EXPAND?? OH, NO! WE'RE DEFINITELY NOT THINKING ABOUT THAT RIGHT NOW!
BRIDAL REGISTRY
COOK-WARE
24 PC.
DINNER-WARE
"NOT THINKING ABOUT THAT RIGHT NOW".
"NOT THINKING ABOUT THAT RIGHT NOW" COULD MEAN, "MIGHT POSSIBLY THINK ABOUT THAT SOME OTHER TIME."
DINNER-WARE
"MIGHT POSSIBLY" COULD MEAN "MAYBE"... "MAYBE" MIGHT MEAN A "CHANCE"...
IF THERE'S A "CHANCE," IT'S "CONCEIVABLE" AND "CONCEIVABLE" MEANS...
BONG BONG BONG
...NOW WHAT?
I ACCIDENTALLY SET OFF MOTHER'S HOPE DETECTOR.
BABY LAND

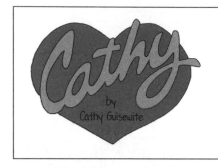

Cathy by Cathy Guisewite

TO "YOU"!

TO "US"!

TO "I"!

"A KEY TO A HAPPY MARRIAGE IS LEARNING TO ADDRESS COMPLAINTS IN A LOVING WAY".

"IF YOUR SWEETHEART IS DOING SOMETHING ANNOY-ING, BRING IT UP USING AN 'I' SENTENCE, NOT A 'YOU' SENTENCE."

INSTEAD OF SAYING, "**YOU'RE** ALWAYS LATE"... SAY, "**I** WORRY WHEN YOU'RE NOT HOME ON TIME".

INSTEAD OF SAYING, "**YOU** NEVER LISTEN"... SAY, "**I** FEEL REJECTED IF I THINK I'M NOT BEING HEARD."

INSTEAD OF SAYING, "**YOU'RE** A SLOB"... SAY, "**I'M** EXTREMELY SENSITIVE TO CLUTTER".

"**YOU**" SENTENCES MAKE IT ALL THE OTHER PERSON'S FAULT... "**I**" SENTENCES MAKE US PARTNERS IN RESPONSIBILITY.

"**YOU**" CREATES DISTANCE... "**I**" INVITES CLOSENESS!

I GET OVERWHELMED WITH FEELINGS OF INADEQUACY WHEN SOMEONE I LOVE THINKS I NEED INSTRUCTIONS ON HOW TO TALK!!

YOU CHEAT!!

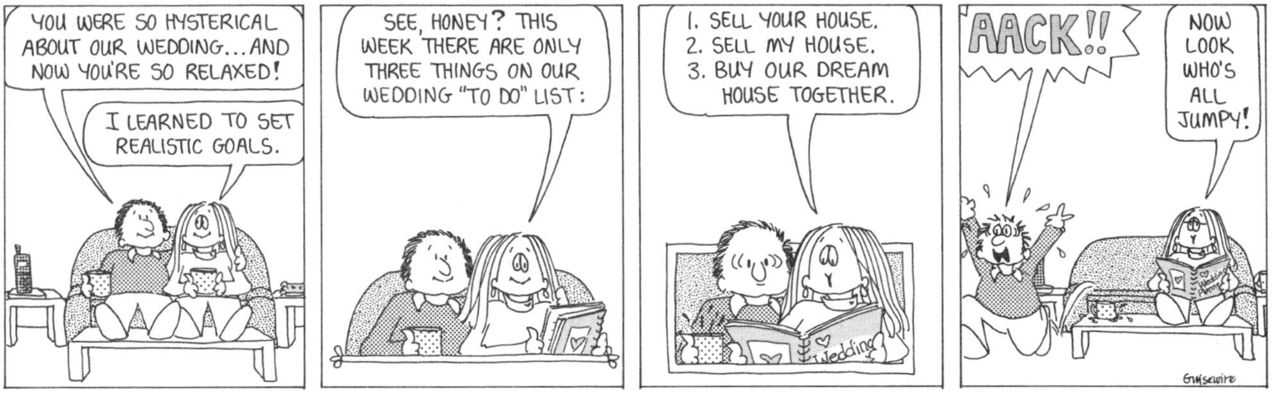
YOU WERE SO HYSTERICAL ABOUT OUR WEDDING... AND NOW YOU'RE SO RELAXED!
I LEARNED TO SET REALISTIC GOALS.
SEE, HONEY? THIS WEEK THERE ARE ONLY THREE THINGS ON OUR WEDDING "TO DO" LIST:
1. SELL YOUR HOUSE.
2. SELL MY HOUSE.
3. BUY OUR DREAM HOUSE TOGETHER.
AACK!!
NOW LOOK WHO'S ALL JUMPY!

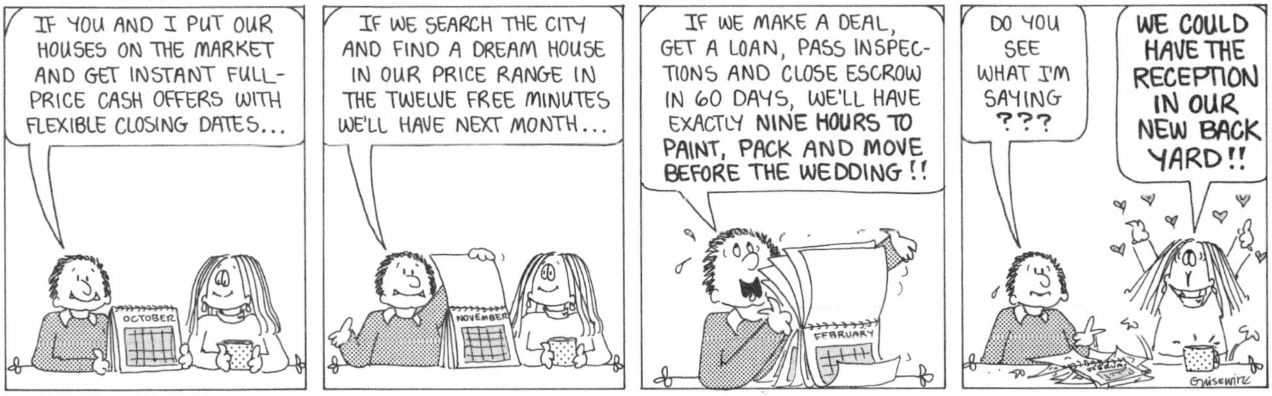
IF YOU AND I PUT OUR HOUSES ON THE MARKET AND GET INSTANT FULL-PRICE CASH OFFERS WITH FLEXIBLE CLOSING DATES...
OCTOBER
IF WE SEARCH THE CITY AND FIND A DREAM HOUSE IN OUR PRICE RANGE IN THE TWELVE FREE MINUTES WE'LL HAVE NEXT MONTH...
NOVEMBER
IF WE MAKE A DEAL, GET A LOAN, PASS INSPECTIONS AND CLOSE ESCROW IN 60 DAYS, WE'LL HAVE EXACTLY NINE HOURS TO PAINT, PACK AND MOVE BEFORE THE WEDDING!!
FEBRUARY
DO YOU SEE WHAT I'M SAYING???
WE COULD HAVE THE RECEPTION IN OUR NEW BACK YARD!!

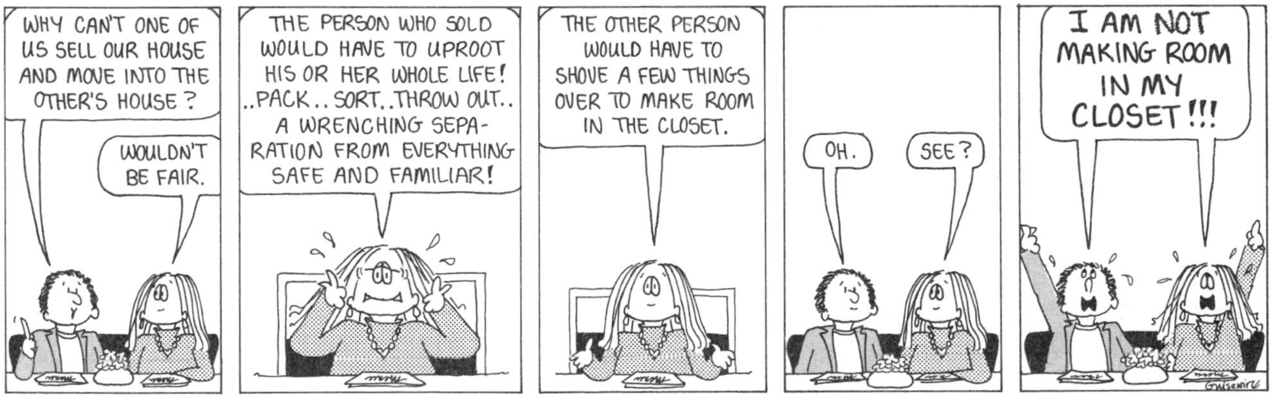
WHY CAN'T ONE OF US SELL OUR HOUSE AND MOVE INTO THE OTHER'S HOUSE?
WOULDN'T BE FAIR.
THE PERSON WHO SOLD WOULD HAVE TO UPROOT HIS OR HER WHOLE LIFE! ..PACK.. SORT..THROW OUT.. A WRENCHING SEPARATION FROM EVERYTHING SAFE AND FAMILIAR!
THE OTHER PERSON WOULD HAVE TO SHOVE A FEW THINGS OVER TO MAKE ROOM IN THE CLOSET.
OH.
SEE?
I AM NOT MAKING ROOM IN MY CLOSET!!!

Strip 1

Panel 1: THE MARRIAGE WON'T FEEL EQUAL IF IT'S ME MOVING INTO YOUR HOUSE OR YOU MOVING INTO MY HOUSE.

Panel 2: IT NEEDS TO BE YOU AND ME TOGETHER, MAKING THE EXACT SAME COMMITMENT TO OUR NEW LIFE.

Panel 3: IT WILL BE **US** MOVING INTO THEIR HOUSE. / PRETTY MUCH. / FIND ONE WITH A NICE BIG TUB! / DIBS ON ALL UPHOLSTERED FURNITURE!

Strip 2

Panel 1: ALL MY LIFE I DREAMED OF SHOPPING FOR A HOME WITH MY FIANCÉ! / OH, NO. NOT ANOTHER ONE.

Panel 2: THE DRESS SHOPPING DREAM... REGISTRY PICKING DREAM... VOW-WRITING DREAM...

Panel 3: EVERY TIME I START TO RELAX YOU COME UP WITH SOME OTHER LIFELONG DREAM THAT INCLUDES A WHOLE SET OF FANTASIES FOR WHAT I'M SUPPOSED TO DO OR SAY !!!

Panel 4: HOO, BOY ! **THAT** WAS ALL WRONG! YOUR PART GOES: "OH, DARLING, LET'S MAKE COCOA AND SNUGGLE UP WITH THE HOUSE ADS!!"

Strip 3

Panel 1: THERE'S AN OPEN HOUSE, IRVING! LET'S STOP! / WE'RE NOT READY TO SHOP FOR HOUSES YET, CATHY!

Panel 2: WE'RE NOT SHOPPING-SHOPPING. WE'RE WARM-UP SHOPPING. / WARM-UP SHOPPING?

Panel 3: YOU HAVE TO DO LOTS OF WARM-UP SHOPPING BEFORE YOU START PRACTICE SHOPPING... OTHERWISE, WHEN YOU GET TO THE **SERIOUS** SHOPPING YOU'LL... / AACK!!

Panel 4: WOW. BRAIN SPRAIN ALREADY. YOU ARE **SO** OUT OF SHAPE! / OUCH.

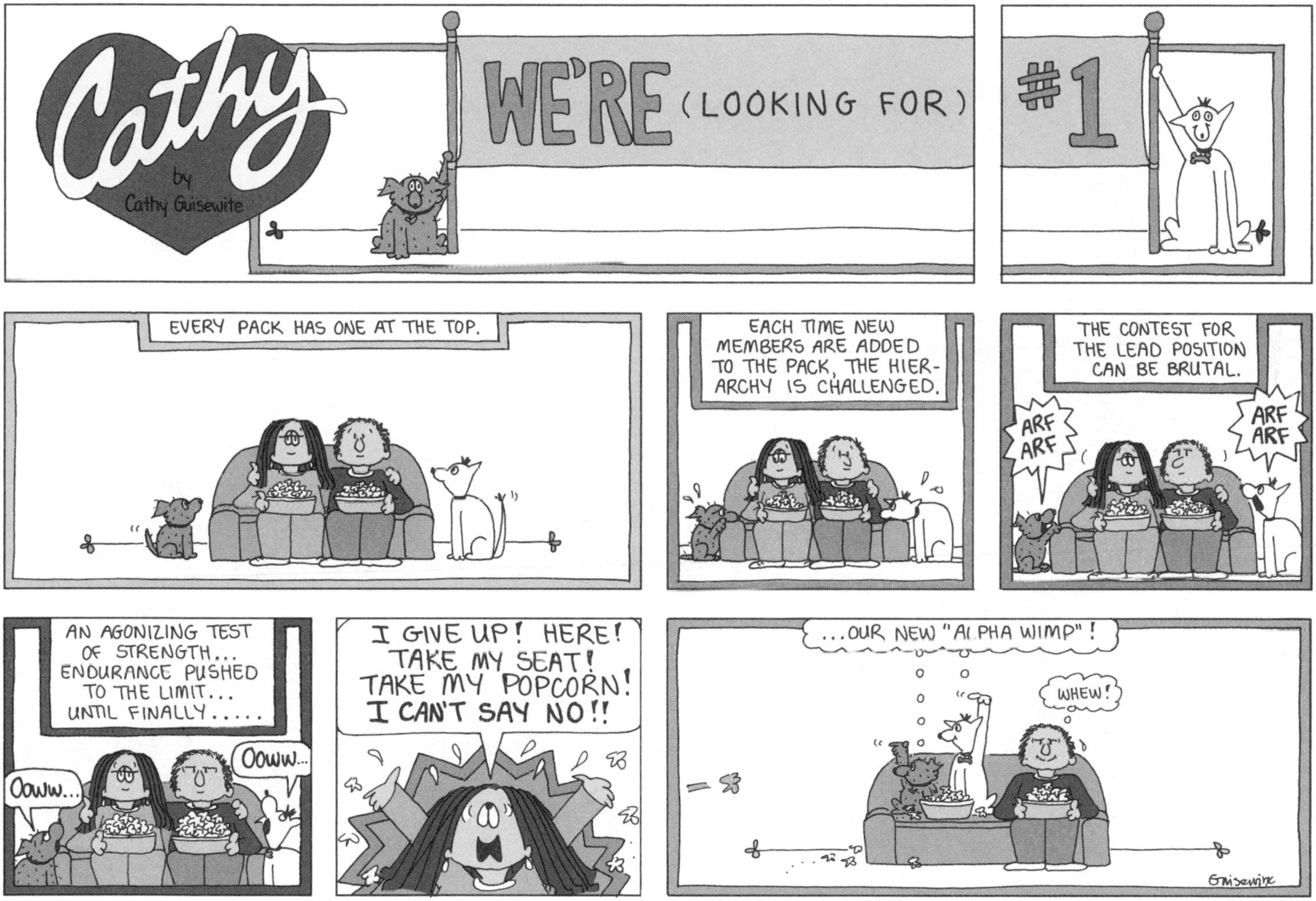
Cathy
by
Cathy Guisewite
WE'RE (LOOKING FOR) #1
EVERY PACK HAS ONE AT THE TOP.
EACH TIME NEW MEMBERS ARE ADDED TO THE PACK, THE HIERARCHY IS CHALLENGED.
THE CONTEST FOR THE LEAD POSITION CAN BE BRUTAL.
ARF ARF
ARF ARF
AN AGONIZING TEST OF STRENGTH... ENDURANCE PUSHED TO THE LIMIT... UNTIL FINALLY.....
Ooww...
Ooww...
I GIVE UP! HERE! TAKE MY SEAT! TAKE MY POPCORN! I CAN'T SAY NO!!
...OUR NEW "ALPHA WIMP"!
WHEW!
Guisewite

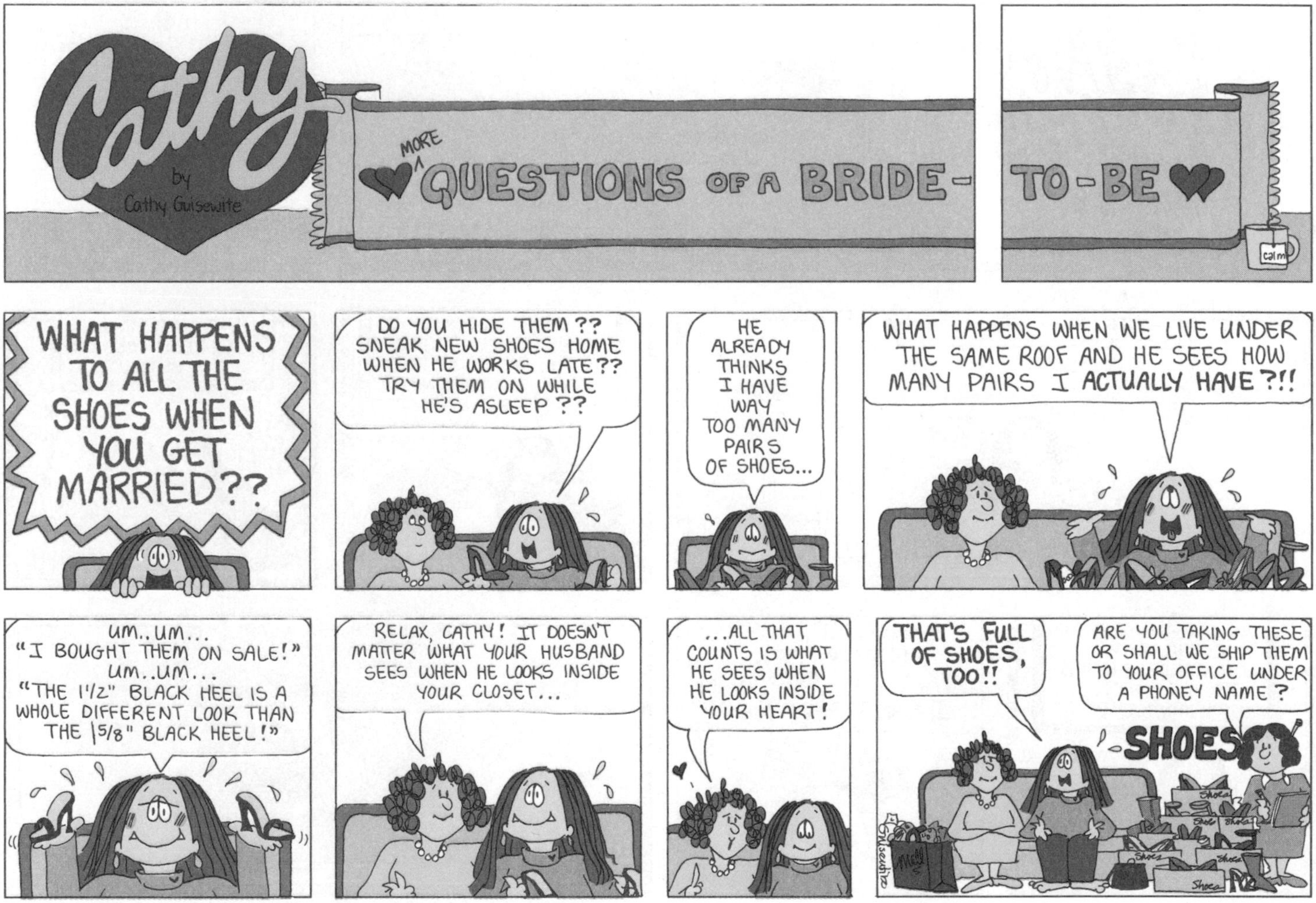
Cathy
by
Cathy Guisewite
MORE QUESTIONS OF A BRIDE-TO-BE
calm
WHAT HAPPENS TO ALL THE SHOES WHEN YOU GET MARRIED??
DO YOU HIDE THEM?? SNEAK NEW SHOES HOME WHEN HE WORKS LATE?? TRY THEM ON WHILE HE'S ASLEEP??
HE ALREADY THINKS I HAVE WAY TOO MANY PAIRS OF SHOES...
WHAT HAPPENS WHEN WE LIVE UNDER THE SAME ROOF AND HE SEES HOW MANY PAIRS I ACTUALLY HAVE?!!
UM..UM... "I BOUGHT THEM ON SALE!" UM..UM... "THE 1 1/2" BLACK HEEL IS A WHOLE DIFFERENT LOOK THAN THE 1 5/8" BLACK HEEL!"
RELAX, CATHY! IT DOESN'T MATTER WHAT YOUR HUSBAND SEES WHEN HE LOOKS INSIDE YOUR CLOSET...
...ALL THAT COUNTS IS WHAT HE SEES WHEN HE LOOKS INSIDE YOUR HEART!
THAT'S FULL OF SHOES, TOO!!
ARE YOU TAKING THESE OR SHALL WE SHIP THEM TO YOUR OFFICE UNDER A PHONEY NAME?
SHOES

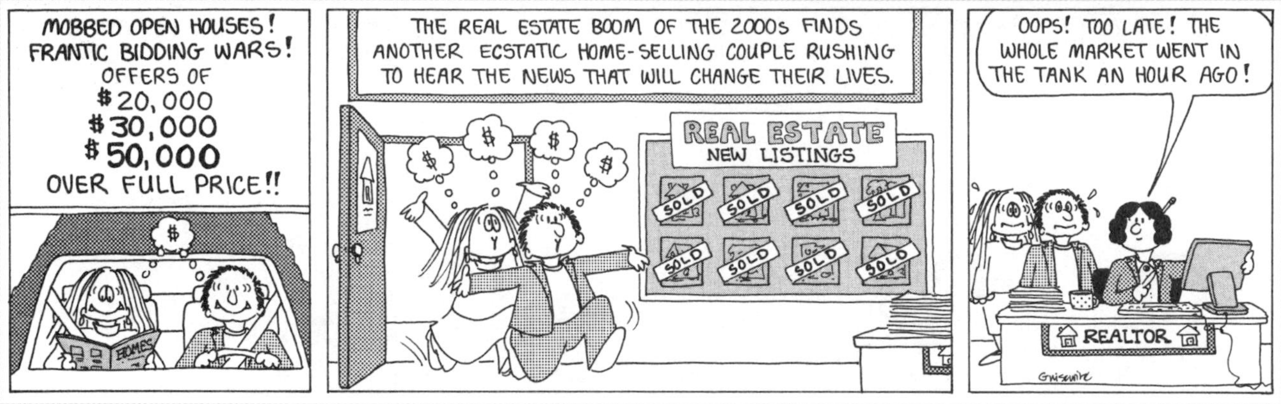
MOBBED OPEN HOUSES! FRANTIC BIDDING WARS! OFFERS OF $20,000 $30,000 $50,000 OVER FULL PRICE!!
$
HOMES
THE REAL ESTATE BOOM OF THE 2000s FINDS ANOTHER ECSTATIC HOME-SELLING COUPLE RUSHING TO HEAR THE NEWS THAT WILL CHANGE THEIR LIVES.
$
REAL ESTATE
NEW LISTINGS
SOLD
OOPS! TOO LATE! THE WHOLE MARKET WENT IN THE TANK AN HOUR AGO!
REALTOR

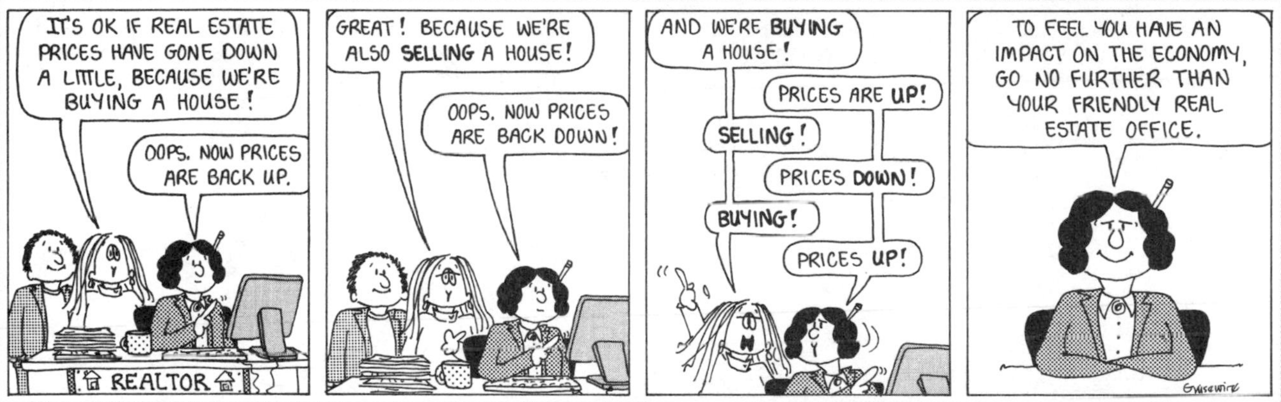
IT'S OK IF REAL ESTATE PRICES HAVE GONE DOWN A LITTLE, BECAUSE WE'RE BUYING A HOUSE!
OOPS. NOW PRICES ARE BACK UP.
REALTOR
GREAT! BECAUSE WE'RE ALSO SELLING A HOUSE!
OOPS. NOW PRICES ARE BACK DOWN!
AND WE'RE BUYING A HOUSE!
PRICES ARE UP!
SELLING!
PRICES DOWN!
BUYING!
PRICES UP!
TO FEEL YOU HAVE AN IMPACT ON THE ECONOMY, GO NO FURTHER THAN YOUR FRIENDLY REAL ESTATE OFFICE.

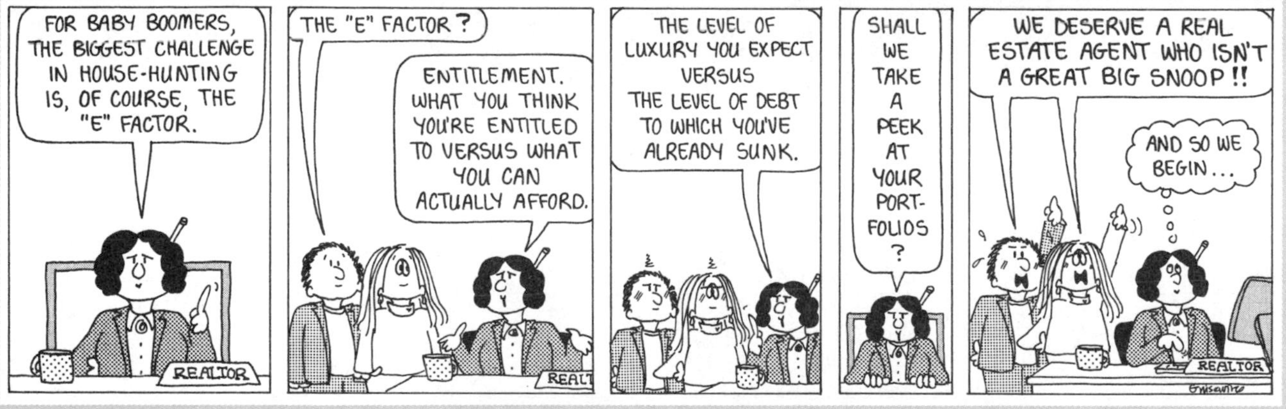
FOR BABY BOOMERS, THE BIGGEST CHALLENGE IN HOUSE-HUNTING IS, OF COURSE, THE "E" FACTOR.
REALTOR
THE "E" FACTOR?
ENTITLEMENT. WHAT YOU THINK YOU'RE ENTITLED TO VERSUS WHAT YOU CAN ACTUALLY AFFORD.
THE LEVEL OF LUXURY YOU EXPECT VERSUS THE LEVEL OF DEBT TO WHICH YOU'VE ALREADY SUNK.
SHALL WE TAKE A PEEK AT YOUR PORT-FOLIOS?
WE DESERVE A REAL ESTATE AGENT WHO ISN'T A GREAT BIG SNOOP!!
AND SO WE BEGIN...
REALTOR

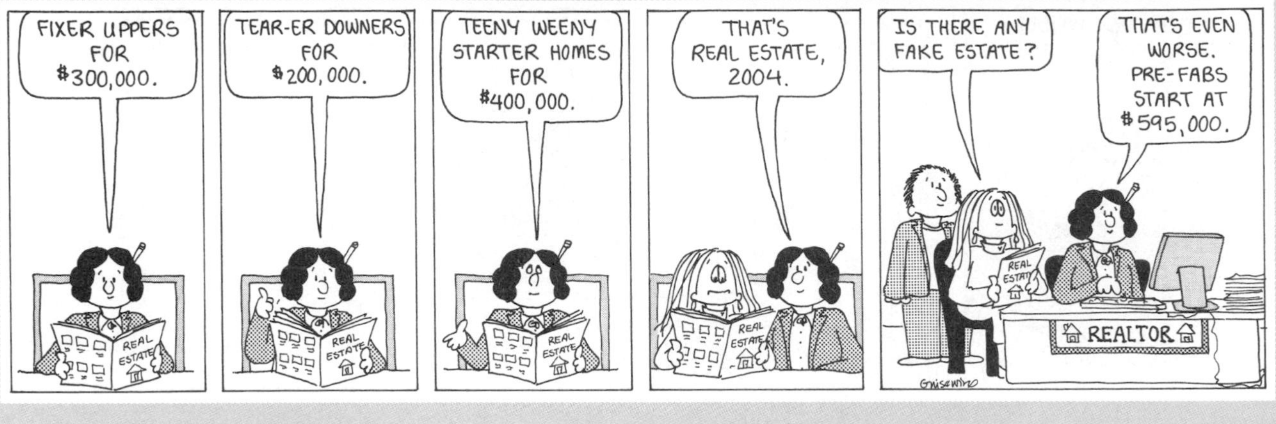
FIXER UPPERS FOR $300,000.
TEAR-ER DOWNERS FOR $200,000.
TEENY WEENY STARTER HOMES FOR $400,000.
THAT'S REAL ESTATE, 2004.
IS THERE ANY FAKE ESTATE?
THAT'S EVEN WORSE. PRE-FABS START AT $595,000.
REALTOR

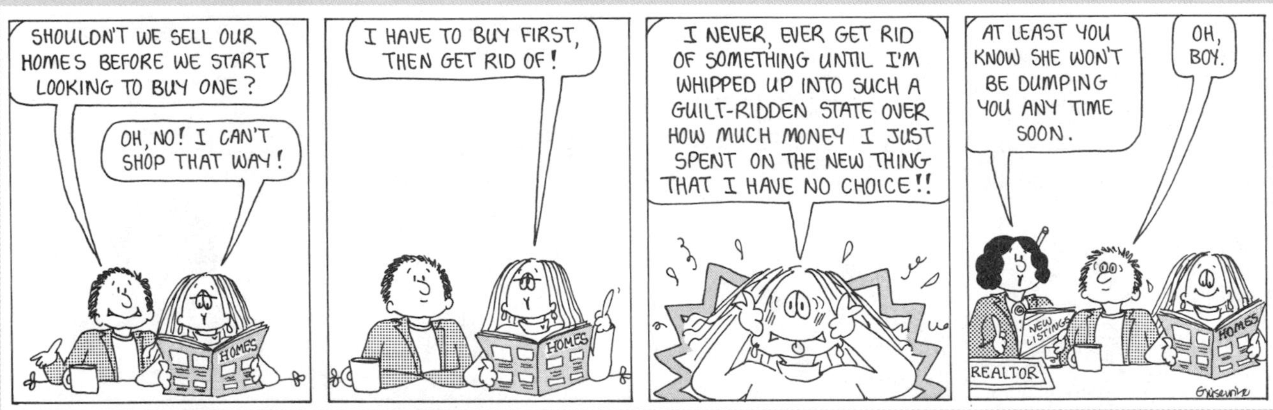
SHOULDN'T WE SELL OUR HOMES BEFORE WE START LOOKING TO BUY ONE?
OH, NO! I CAN'T SHOP THAT WAY!
I HAVE TO BUY FIRST, THEN GET RID OF!
I NEVER, EVER GET RID OF SOMETHING UNTIL I'M WHIPPED UP INTO SUCH A GUILT-RIDDEN STATE OVER HOW MUCH MONEY I JUST SPENT ON THE NEW THING THAT I HAVE NO CHOICE!!
AT LEAST YOU KNOW SHE WON'T BE DUMPING YOU ANY TIME SOON.
OH, BOY.
REALTOR

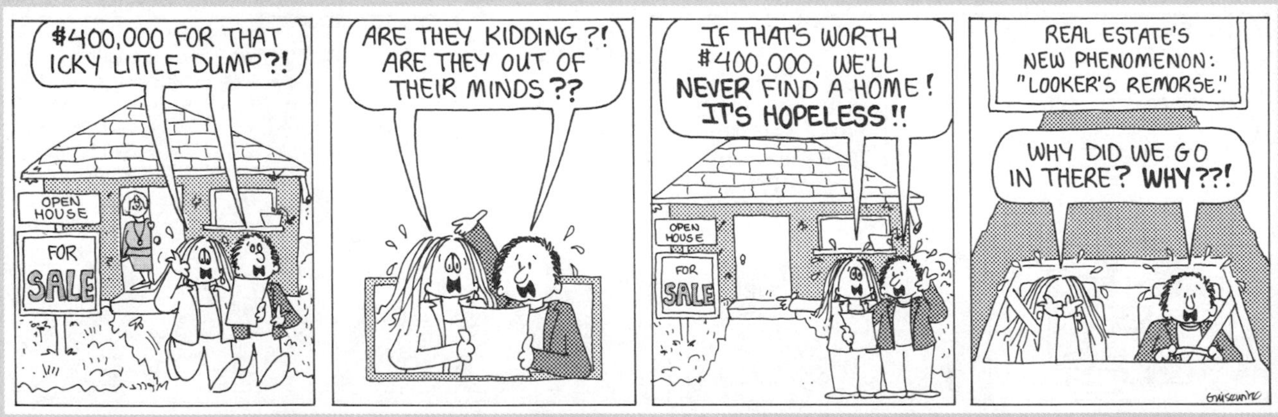
$400,000 FOR THAT ICKY LITTLE DUMP?!
OPEN HOUSE
FOR SALE
ARE THEY KIDDING?! ARE THEY OUT OF THEIR MINDS??
IF THAT'S WORTH $400,000, WE'LL NEVER FIND A HOME! IT'S HOPELESS!!
OPEN HOUSE
FOR SALE
REAL ESTATE'S NEW PHENOMENON: "LOOKER'S REMORSE."
WHY DID WE GO IN THERE? WHY??!

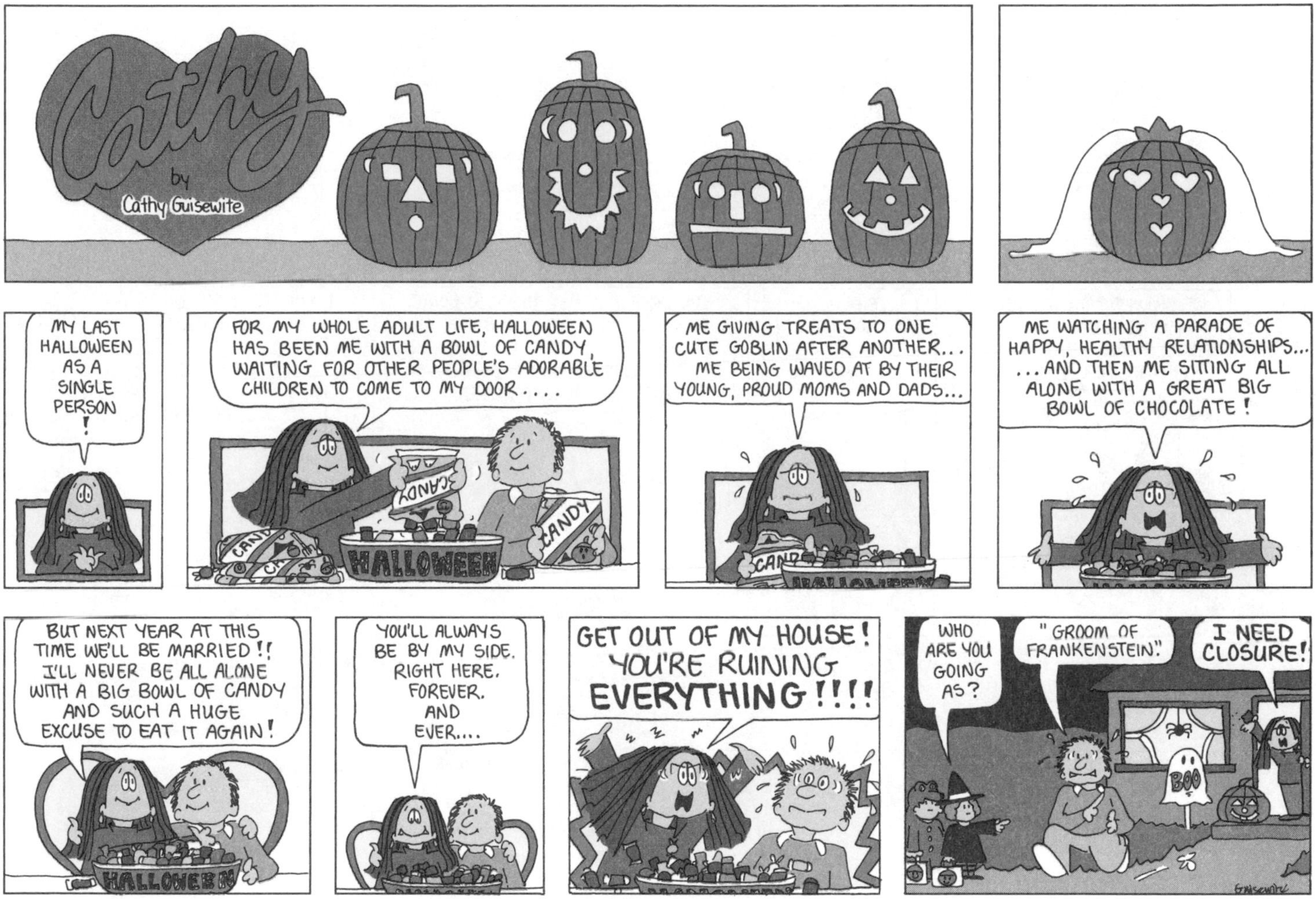
Cathy
by
Cathy Guisewite
MY LAST HALLOWEEN AS A SINGLE PERSON!
FOR MY WHOLE ADULT LIFE, HALLOWEEN HAS BEEN ME WITH A BOWL OF CANDY, WAITING FOR OTHER PEOPLE'S ADORABLE CHILDREN TO COME TO MY DOOR....
CANDY
HALLOWEEN
ME GIVING TREATS TO ONE CUTE GOBLIN AFTER ANOTHER... ME BEING WAVED AT BY THEIR YOUNG, PROUD MOMS AND DADS...
ME WATCHING A PARADE OF HAPPY, HEALTHY RELATIONSHIPS... ...AND THEN ME SITTING ALL ALONE WITH A GREAT BIG BOWL OF CHOCOLATE!
BUT NEXT YEAR AT THIS TIME WE'LL BE MARRIED!! I'LL NEVER BE ALL ALONE WITH A BIG BOWL OF CANDY AND SUCH A HUGE EXCUSE TO EAT IT AGAIN!
HALLOWEEN
YOU'LL ALWAYS BE BY MY SIDE. RIGHT HERE. FOREVER. AND EVER....
GET OUT OF MY HOUSE! YOU'RE RUINING EVERYTHING!!!!
WHO ARE YOU GOING AS?
"GROOM OF FRANKENSTEIN."
I NEED CLOSURE!
BOO
Guisewite

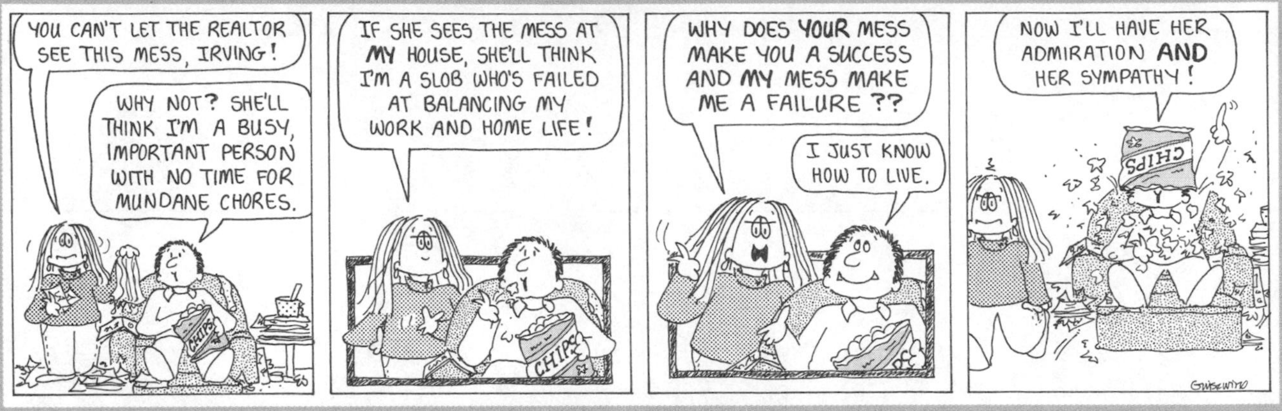
YOU CAN'T LET THE REALTOR SEE THIS MESS, IRVING!
WHY NOT? SHE'LL THINK I'M A BUSY, IMPORTANT PERSON WITH NO TIME FOR MUNDANE CHORES.
CHIPS
IF SHE SEES THE MESS AT MY HOUSE, SHE'LL THINK I'M A SLOB WHO'S FAILED AT BALANCING MY WORK AND HOME LIFE!
CHIPS
WHY DOES YOUR MESS MAKE YOU A SUCCESS AND MY MESS MAKE ME A FAILURE??
I JUST KNOW HOW TO LIVE.
NOW I'LL HAVE HER ADMIRATION AND HER SYMPATHY!
CHIPS

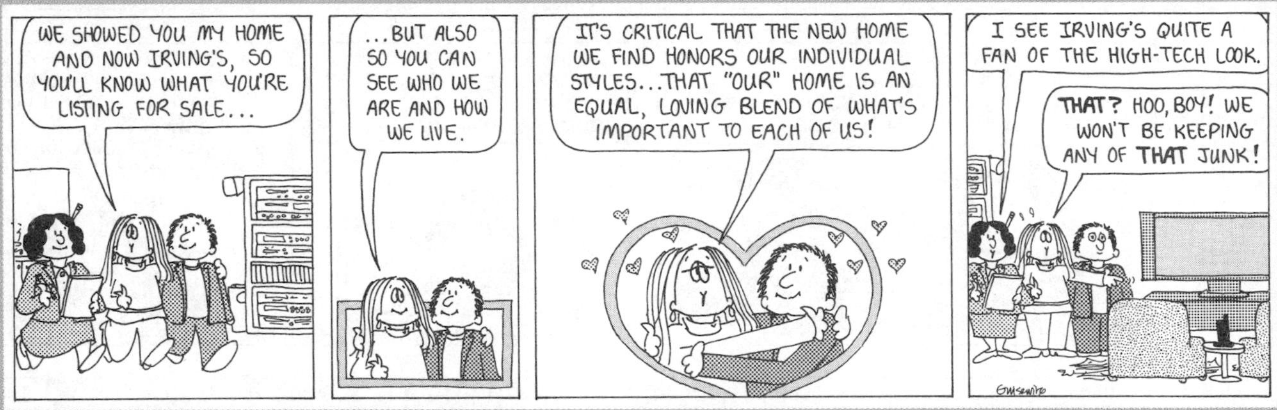
WE SHOWED YOU MY HOME AND NOW IRVING'S, SO YOU'LL KNOW WHAT YOU'RE LISTING FOR SALE...
...BUT ALSO SO YOU CAN SEE WHO WE ARE AND HOW WE LIVE.
IT'S CRITICAL THAT THE NEW HOME WE FIND HONORS OUR INDIVIDUAL STYLES...THAT "OUR" HOME IS AN EQUAL, LOVING BLEND OF WHAT'S IMPORTANT TO EACH OF US!
I SEE IRVING'S QUITE A FAN OF THE HIGH-TECH LOOK.
THAT? HOO, BOY! WE WON'T BE KEEPING ANY OF THAT JUNK!

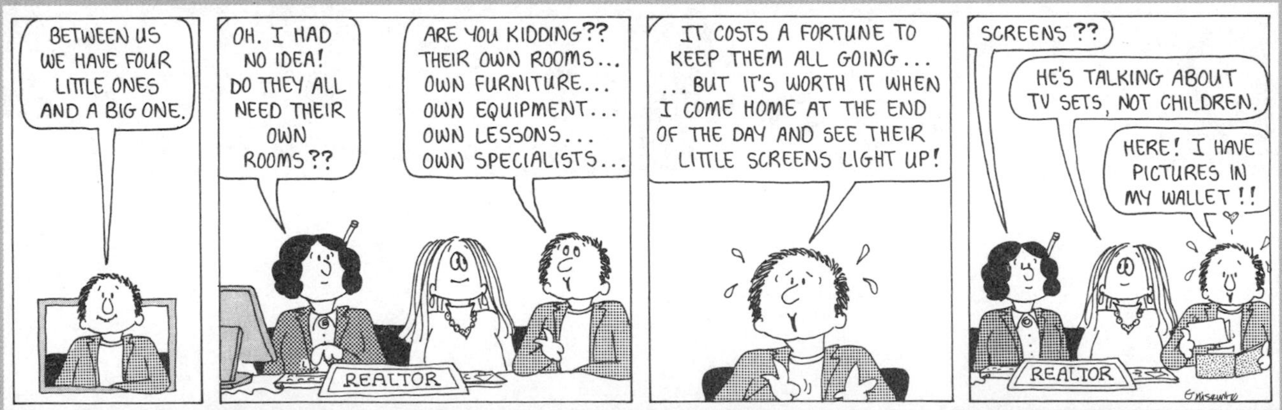
BETWEEN US WE HAVE FOUR LITTLE ONES AND A BIG ONE.
OH. I HAD NO IDEA! DO THEY ALL NEED THEIR OWN ROOMS??
ARE YOU KIDDING?? THEIR OWN ROOMS... OWN FURNITURE... OWN EQUIPMENT... OWN LESSONS... OWN SPECIALISTS...
REALTOR
IT COSTS A FORTUNE TO KEEP THEM ALL GOING... ...BUT IT'S WORTH IT WHEN I COME HOME AT THE END OF THE DAY AND SEE THEIR LITTLE SCREENS LIGHT UP!
SCREENS??
HE'S TALKING ABOUT TV SETS, NOT CHILDREN.
HERE! I HAVE PICTURES IN MY WALLET!!
REALTOR

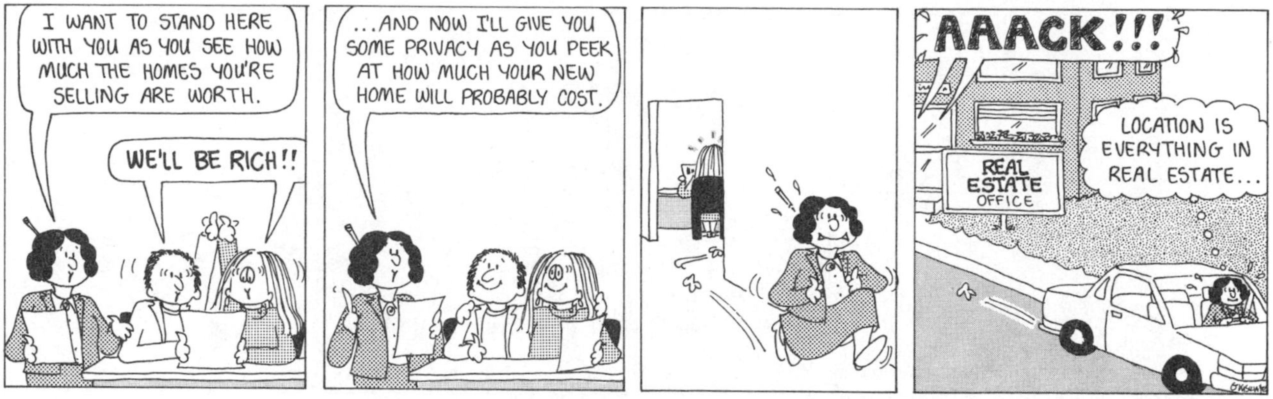
I WANT TO STAND HERE WITH YOU AS YOU SEE HOW MUCH THE HOMES YOU'RE SELLING ARE WORTH.
WE'LL BE RICH!!
...AND NOW I'LL GIVE YOU SOME PRIVACY AS YOU PEEK AT HOW MUCH YOUR NEW HOME WILL PROBABLY COST.
AAACK!!!
REAL ESTATE OFFICE
LOCATION IS EVERYTHING IN REAL ESTATE...

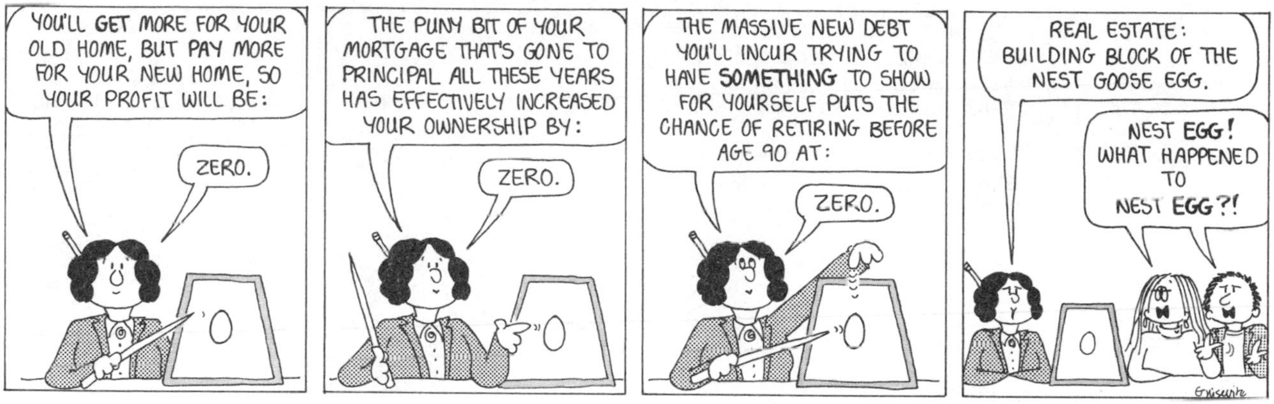
YOU'LL GET MORE FOR YOUR OLD HOME, BUT PAY MORE FOR YOUR NEW HOME, SO YOUR PROFIT WILL BE:
ZERO.
THE PUNY BIT OF YOUR MORTGAGE THAT'S GONE TO PRINCIPAL ALL THESE YEARS HAS EFFECTIVELY INCREASED YOUR OWNERSHIP BY:
ZERO.
THE MASSIVE NEW DEBT YOU'LL INCUR TRYING TO HAVE SOMETHING TO SHOW FOR YOURSELF PUTS THE CHANCE OF RETIRING BEFORE AGE 90 AT:
ZERO.
REAL ESTATE: BUILDING BLOCK OF THE NEST GOOSE EGG.
NEST EGG! WHAT HAPPENED TO NEST EGG?!

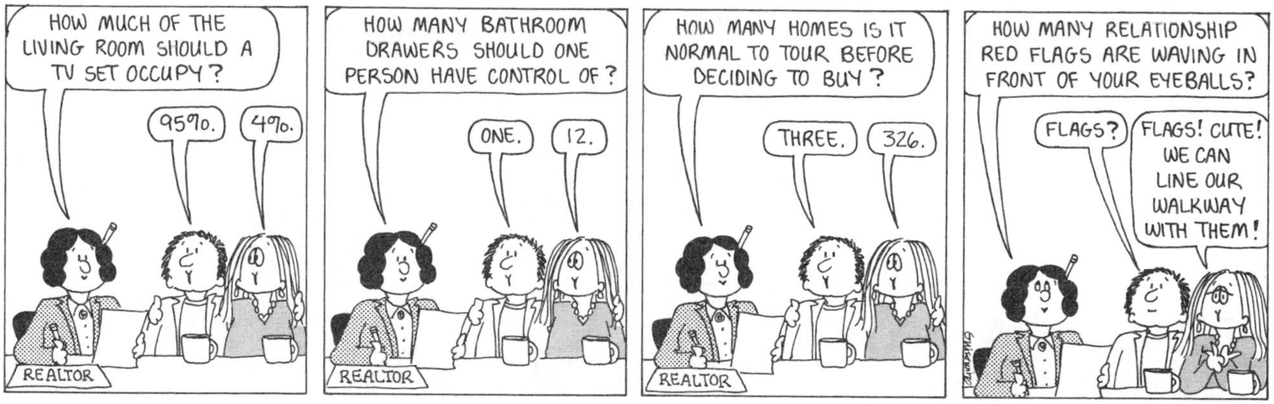
HOW MUCH OF THE LIVING ROOM SHOULD A TV SET OCCUPY?
95%.
4%.
REALTOR
HOW MANY BATHROOM DRAWERS SHOULD ONE PERSON HAVE CONTROL OF?
ONE.
12.
REALTOR
HOW MANY HOMES IS IT NORMAL TO TOUR BEFORE DECIDING TO BUY?
THREE.
326.
REALTOR
HOW MANY RELATIONSHIP RED FLAGS ARE WAVING IN FRONT OF YOUR EYEBALLS?
FLAGS?
FLAGS! CUTE! WE CAN LINE OUR WALKWAY WITH THEM!

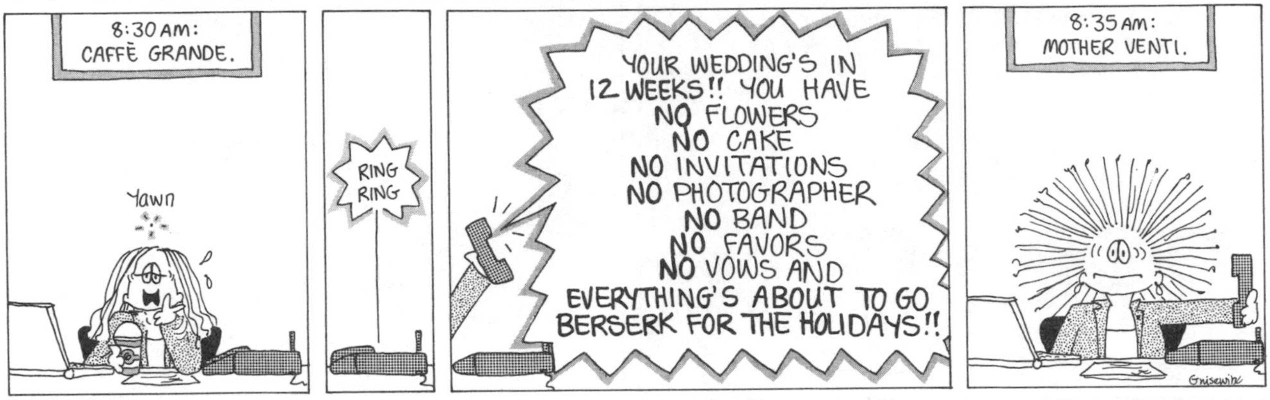
8:30 AM:
CAFFÈ GRANDE.
Yawn
RING RING
YOUR WEDDING'S IN 12 WEEKS!! YOU HAVE NO FLOWERS NO CAKE NO INVITATIONS NO PHOTOGRAPHER NO BAND NO FAVORS NO VOWS AND EVERYTHING'S ABOUT TO GO BERSERK FOR THE HOLIDAYS!!
8:35 AM:
MOTHER VENTI.
GUISEWITE

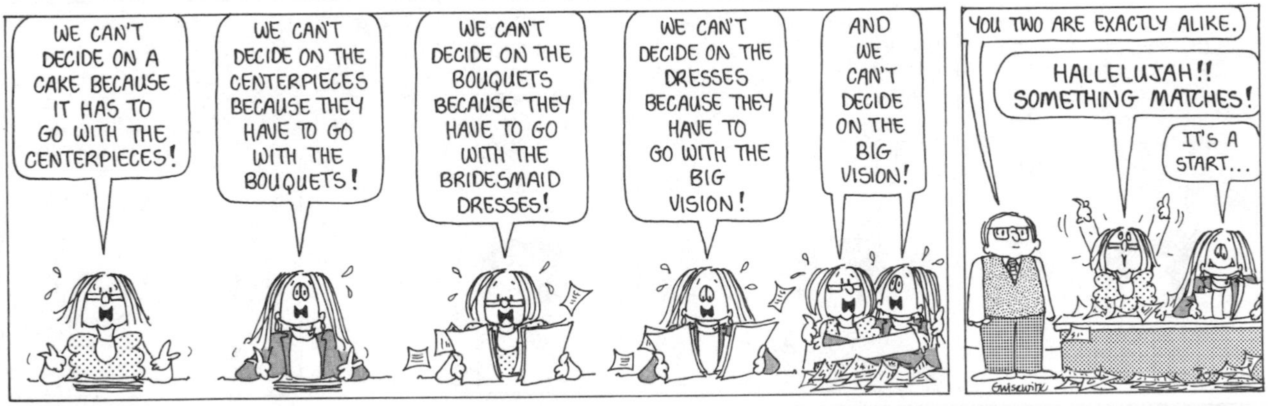
WE CAN'T DECIDE ON A CAKE BECAUSE IT HAS TO GO WITH THE CENTERPIECES!
WE CAN'T DECIDE ON THE CENTERPIECES BECAUSE THEY HAVE TO GO WITH THE BOUQUETS!
WE CAN'T DECIDE ON THE BOUQUETS BECAUSE THEY HAVE TO GO WITH THE BRIDESMAID DRESSES!
WE CAN'T DECIDE ON THE DRESSES BECAUSE THEY HAVE TO GO WITH THE BIG VISION!
AND WE CAN'T DECIDE ON THE BIG VISION!
YOU TWO ARE EXACTLY ALIKE.
HALLELUJAH!! SOMETHING MATCHES!
IT'S A START...
GUISEWITE

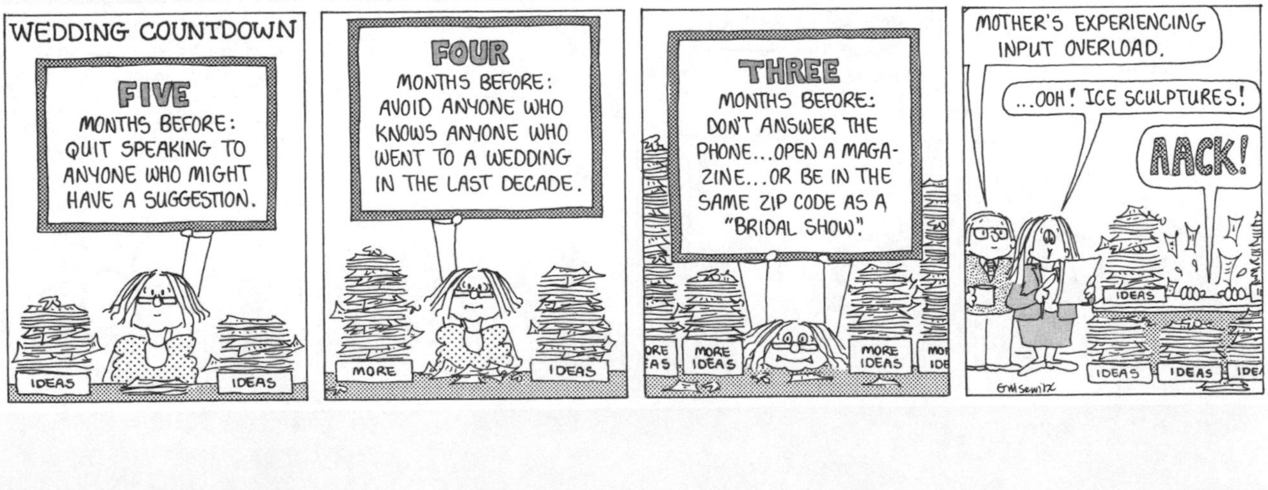
WEDDING COUNTDOWN
FIVE
MONTHS BEFORE: QUIT SPEAKING TO ANYONE WHO MIGHT HAVE A SUGGESTION.
IDEAS
IDEAS
FOUR
MONTHS BEFORE: AVOID ANYONE WHO KNOWS ANYONE WHO WENT TO A WEDDING IN THE LAST DECADE.
MORE
IDEAS
THREE
MONTHS BEFORE: DON'T ANSWER THE PHONE...OPEN A MAGAZINE...OR BE IN THE SAME ZIP CODE AS A "BRIDAL SHOW".
MORE IDEAS
MORE IDEAS
MOTHER'S EXPERIENCING INPUT OVERLOAD.
...OOH! ICE SCULPTURES!
AACK!
IDEAS
IDEAS
IDEAS
GUISEWITE

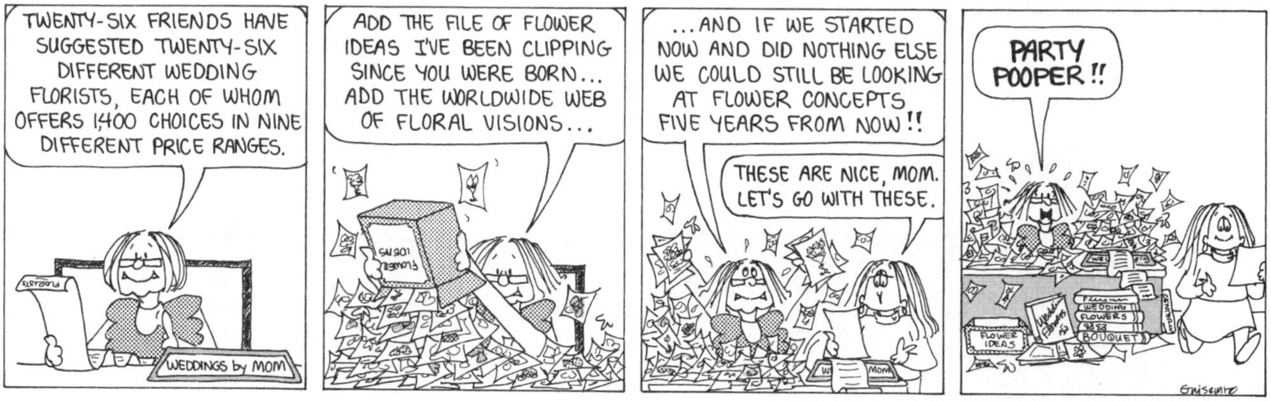
TWENTY-SIX FRIENDS HAVE SUGGESTED TWENTY-SIX DIFFERENT WEDDING FLORISTS, EACH OF WHOM OFFERS 1,400 CHOICES IN NINE DIFFERENT PRICE RANGES.
WEDDINGS by MOM
ADD THE FILE OF FLOWER IDEAS I'VE BEEN CLIPPING SINCE YOU WERE BORN... ADD THE WORLDWIDE WEB OF FLORAL VISIONS...
...AND IF WE STARTED NOW AND DID NOTHING ELSE WE COULD STILL BE LOOKING AT FLOWER CONCEPTS FIVE YEARS FROM NOW!!
THESE ARE NICE, MOM. LET'S GO WITH THESE.
PARTY POOPER!!
FLOWER IDEAS
WEDDING FLOWERS
BOUQUET

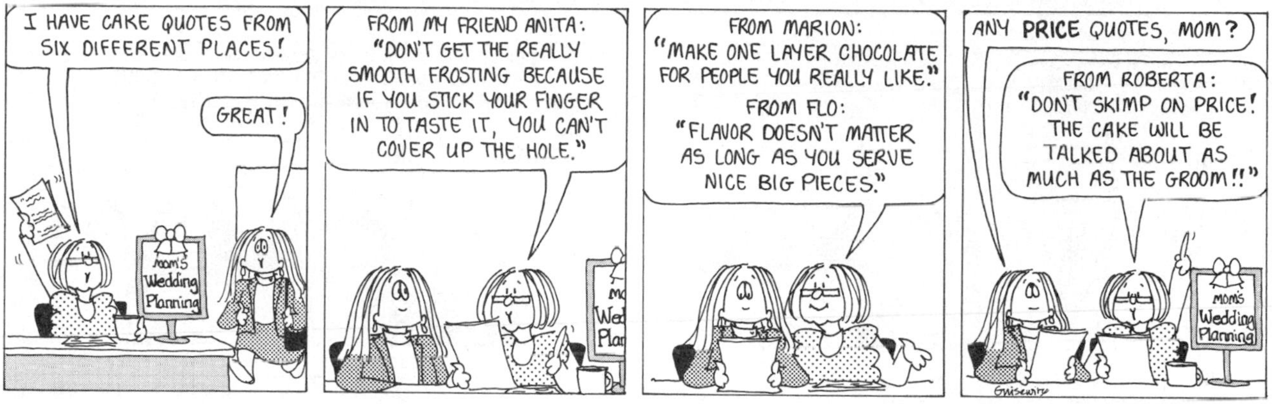
I HAVE CAKE QUOTES FROM SIX DIFFERENT PLACES!
GREAT!
Mom's Wedding Planning
FROM MY FRIEND ANITA: "DON'T GET THE REALLY SMOOTH FROSTING BECAUSE IF YOU STICK YOUR FINGER IN TO TASTE IT, YOU CAN'T COVER UP THE HOLE."
FROM MARION: "MAKE ONE LAYER CHOCOLATE FOR PEOPLE YOU REALLY LIKE."
FROM FLO: "FLAVOR DOESN'T MATTER AS LONG AS YOU SERVE NICE BIG PIECES."
ANY PRICE QUOTES, MOM?
FROM ROBERTA: "DON'T SKIMP ON PRICE! THE CAKE WILL BE TALKED ABOUT AS MUCH AS THE GROOM!!"
Mom's Wedding Planning

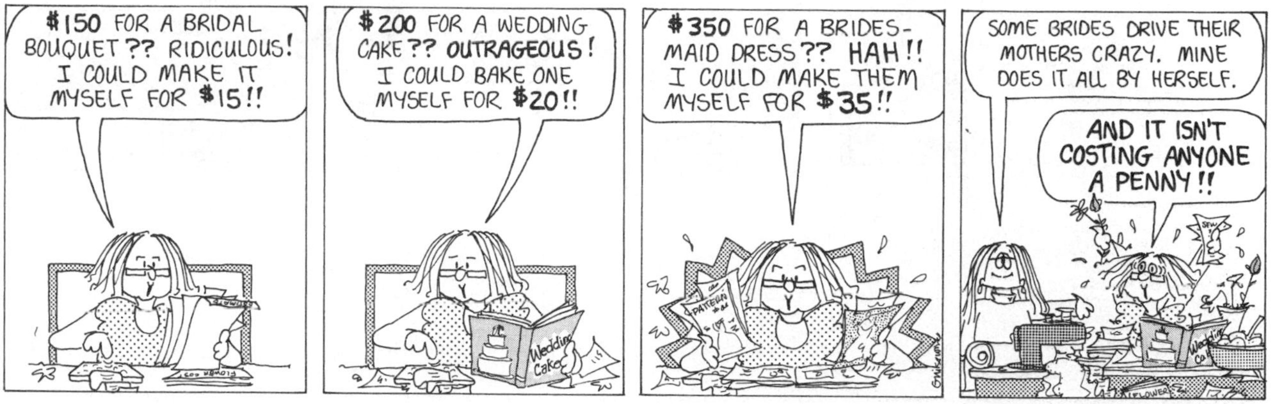
$150 FOR A BRIDAL BOUQUET?? RIDICULOUS! I COULD MAKE IT MYSELF FOR $15!!
$200 FOR A WEDDING CAKE?? OUTRAGEOUS! I COULD BAKE ONE MYSELF FOR $20!!
Wedding Cake
$350 FOR A BRIDESMAID DRESS?? HAH!! I COULD MAKE THEM MYSELF FOR $35!!
SOME BRIDES DRIVE THEIR MOTHERS CRAZY. MINE DOES IT ALL BY HERSELF.
AND IT ISN'T COSTING ANYONE A PENNY!!

Cathy

by Cathy Guisewite

RECIPE FOR HAPPINESS
- ♥ ONE BRIDE
- ♥ ONE GROOM
- ♥ TWO SETS OF ADORING IN-LAWS

RECIPE FOR DISASTER
- ♥ ONE BRIDE
- ♥ ONE GROOM
- ♥ TWO SETS OF ADORING IN-LAWS

I KNOW THAT CATHY'S HAD EVERY THANKSGIVING DINNER OF HER LIFE WITH YOU...

...BUT THIS YEAR MY PARENTS HAVE INVITED CATHY AND ME TO FLY TO THEIR HOME FOR THANKSGIVING.

IT'S THEIR WAY OF BLESSING OUR ENGAGEMENT AND WELCOMING CATHY INTO THE FAMILY... A CHANCE FOR THEM TO GET TO KNOW YOUR AMAZING, GORGEOUS DAUGHTER A LITTLE BETTER...

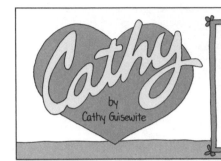

A CHANCE TO START WHAT THEY HOPE WILL BE A LONG, LOVING TRADITION OF TAKING TURNS WITH THE HOLIDAYS!

THAT'S SO BEAUTIFUL!!

DOES YOUR MOTHER MAKE HER SWEET POTATOES WITH THOSE GOOEY LITTLE MARSHMALLOWS??

NO.

SORRY, HONEY.

I WIN!

YOU HAVE HER HEART, BUT MOTHER OWNS THE STOMACH.

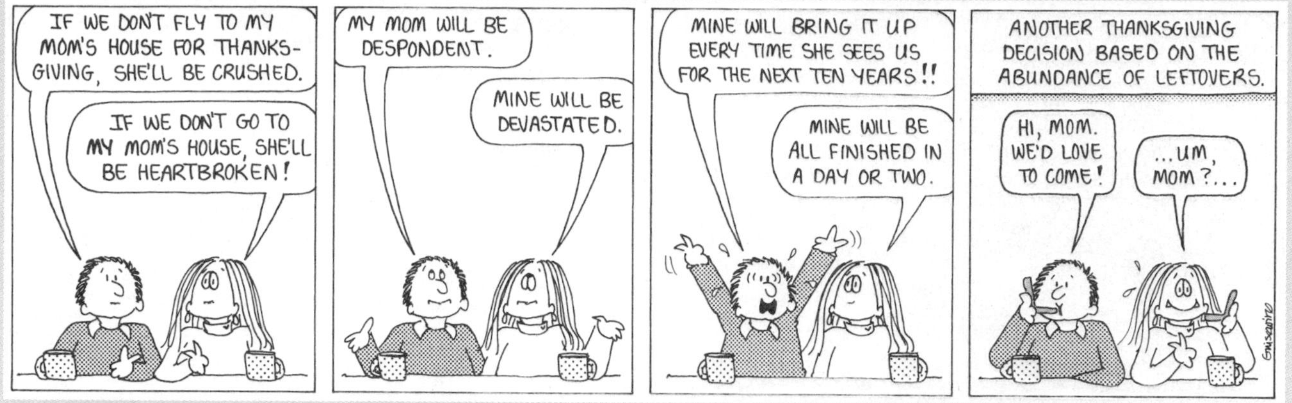
IF WE DON'T FLY TO MY MOM'S HOUSE FOR THANKSGIVING, SHE'LL BE CRUSHED.
IF WE DON'T GO TO MY MOM'S HOUSE, SHE'LL BE HEARTBROKEN!
MY MOM WILL BE DESPONDENT.
MINE WILL BE DEVASTATED.
MINE WILL BRING IT UP EVERY TIME SHE SEES US FOR THE NEXT TEN YEARS!!
MINE WILL BE ALL FINISHED IN A DAY OR TWO.
ANOTHER THANKSGIVING DECISION BASED ON THE ABUNDANCE OF LEFTOVERS.
HI, MOM. WE'D LOVE TO COME!
...UM, MOM?...

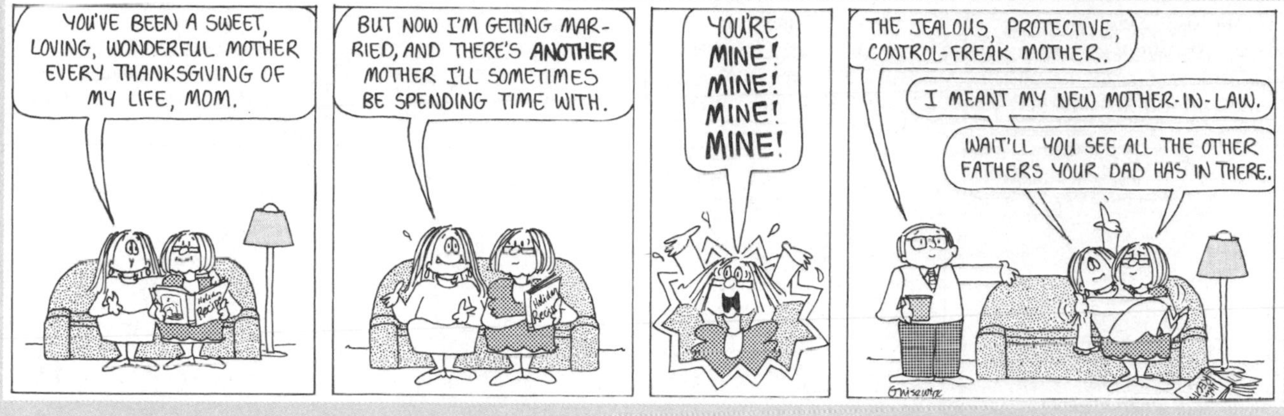
YOU'VE BEEN A SWEET, LOVING, WONDERFUL MOTHER EVERY THANKSGIVING OF MY LIFE, MOM.
Holiday Recipes
BUT NOW I'M GETTING MARRIED, AND THERE'S ANOTHER MOTHER I'LL SOMETIMES BE SPENDING TIME WITH.
YOU'RE MINE! MINE! MINE! MINE!
THE JEALOUS, PROTECTIVE, CONTROL-FREAK MOTHER.
I MEANT MY NEW MOTHER-IN-LAW.
WAIT'LL YOU SEE ALL THE OTHER FATHERS YOUR DAD HAS IN THERE.

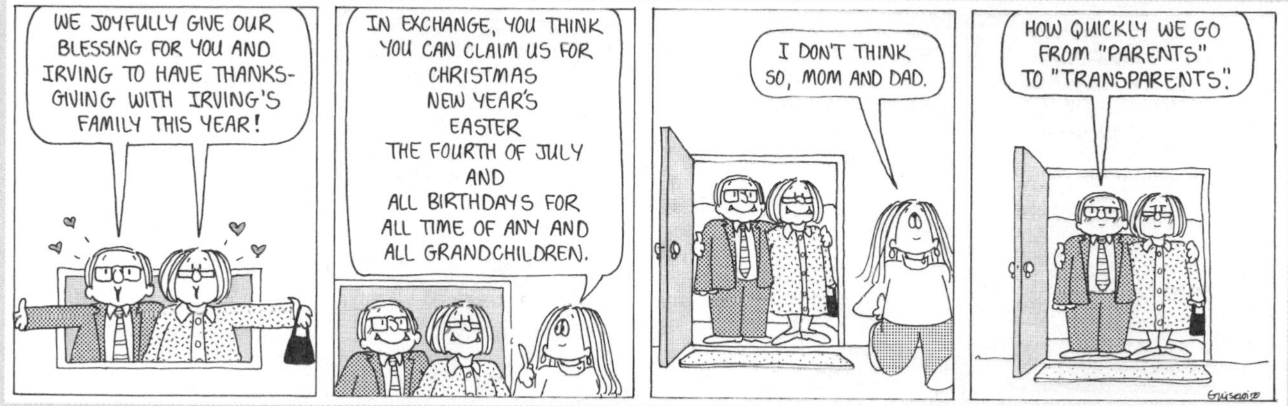
WE JOYFULLY GIVE OUR BLESSING FOR YOU AND IRVING TO HAVE THANKSGIVING WITH IRVING'S FAMILY THIS YEAR!
IN EXCHANGE, YOU THINK YOU CAN CLAIM US FOR CHRISTMAS NEW YEAR'S EASTER THE FOURTH OF JULY AND ALL BIRTHDAYS FOR ALL TIME OF ANY AND ALL GRANDCHILDREN.
I DON'T THINK SO, MOM AND DAD.
HOW QUICKLY WE GO FROM "PARENTS" TO "TRANSPARENTS".

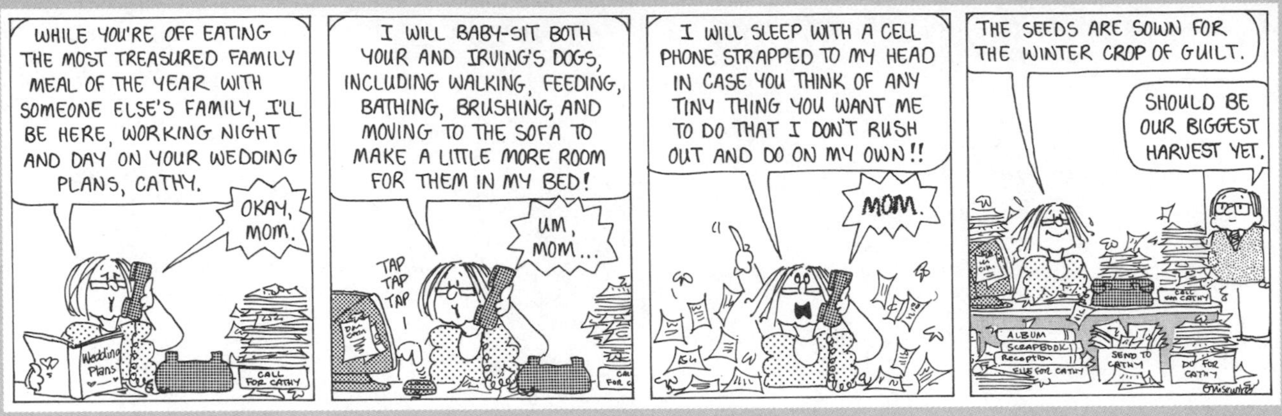
WHILE YOU'RE OFF EATING THE MOST TREASURED FAMILY MEAL OF THE YEAR WITH SOMEONE ELSE'S FAMILY, I'LL BE HERE, WORKING NIGHT AND DAY ON YOUR WEDDING PLANS, CATHY.
OKAY, MOM.
I WILL BABY-SIT BOTH YOUR AND IRVING'S DOGS, INCLUDING WALKING, FEEDING, BATHING, BRUSHING, AND MOVING TO THE SOFA TO MAKE A LITTLE MORE ROOM FOR THEM IN MY BED!
TAP TAP TAP
UM, MOM...
I WILL SLEEP WITH A CELL PHONE STRAPPED TO MY HEAD IN CASE YOU THINK OF ANY TINY THING YOU WANT ME TO DO THAT I DON'T RUSH OUT AND DO ON MY OWN!!
MOM.
THE SEEDS ARE SOWN FOR THE WINTER CROP OF GUILT.
SHOULD BE OUR BIGGEST HARVEST YET.

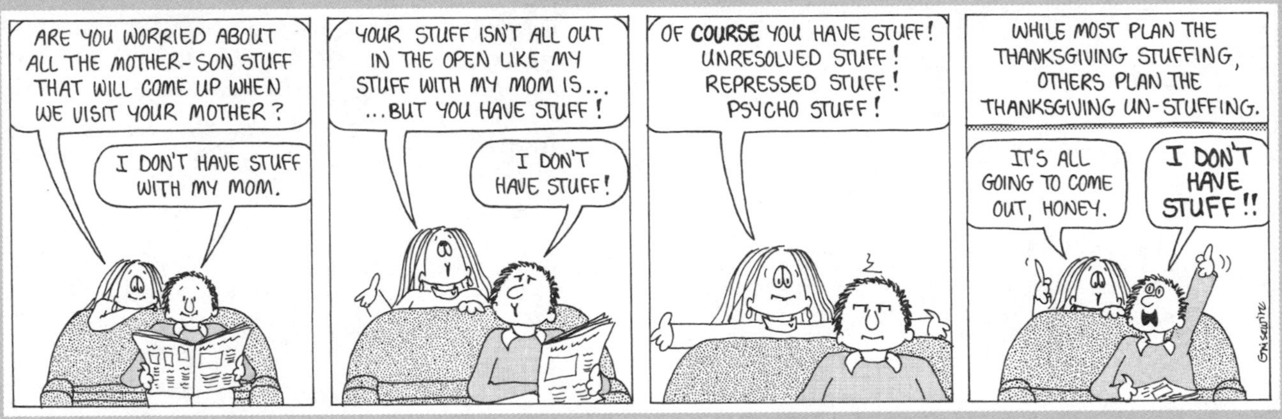
ARE YOU WORRIED ABOUT ALL THE MOTHER-SON STUFF THAT WILL COME UP WHEN WE VISIT YOUR MOTHER?
I DON'T HAVE STUFF WITH MY MOM.
YOUR STUFF ISN'T ALL OUT IN THE OPEN LIKE MY STUFF WITH MY MOM IS... ...BUT YOU HAVE STUFF!
I DON'T HAVE STUFF!
OF COURSE YOU HAVE STUFF! UNRESOLVED STUFF! REPRESSED STUFF! PSYCHO STUFF!
WHILE MOST PLAN THE THANKSGIVING STUFFING, OTHERS PLAN THE THANKSGIVING UN-STUFFING.
IT'S ALL GOING TO COME OUT, HONEY.
I DON'T HAVE STUFF!!

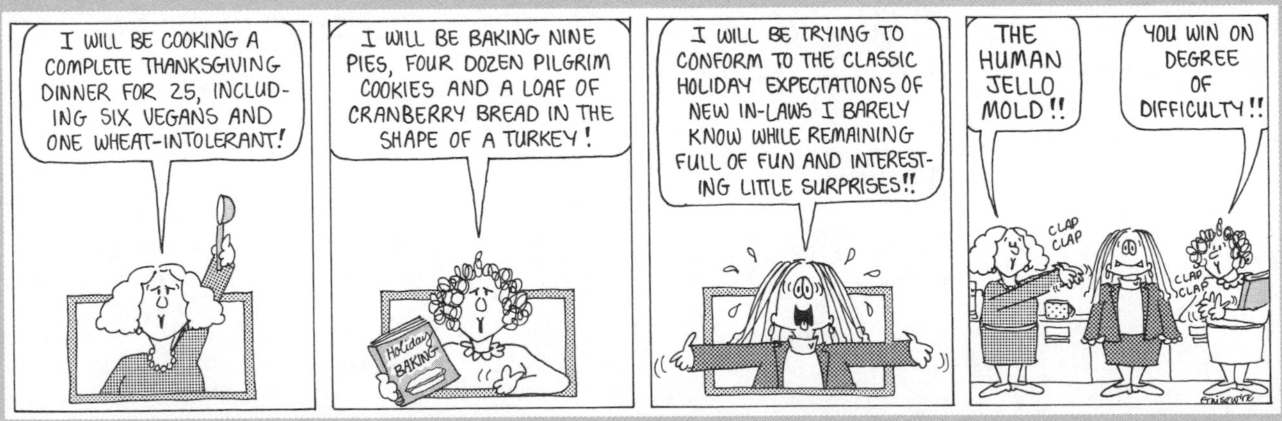
I WILL BE COOKING A COMPLETE THANKSGIVING DINNER FOR 25, INCLUDING SIX VEGANS AND ONE WHEAT-INTOLERANT!
I WILL BE BAKING NINE PIES, FOUR DOZEN PILGRIM COOKIES AND A LOAF OF CRANBERRY BREAD IN THE SHAPE OF A TURKEY!
Holiday BAKING
I WILL BE TRYING TO CONFORM TO THE CLASSIC HOLIDAY EXPECTATIONS OF NEW IN-LAWS I BARELY KNOW WHILE REMAINING FULL OF FUN AND INTERESTING LITTLE SURPRISES!!
THE HUMAN JELLO MOLD!!
YOU WIN ON DEGREE OF DIFFICULTY!!
CLAP CLAP
CLAP CLAP

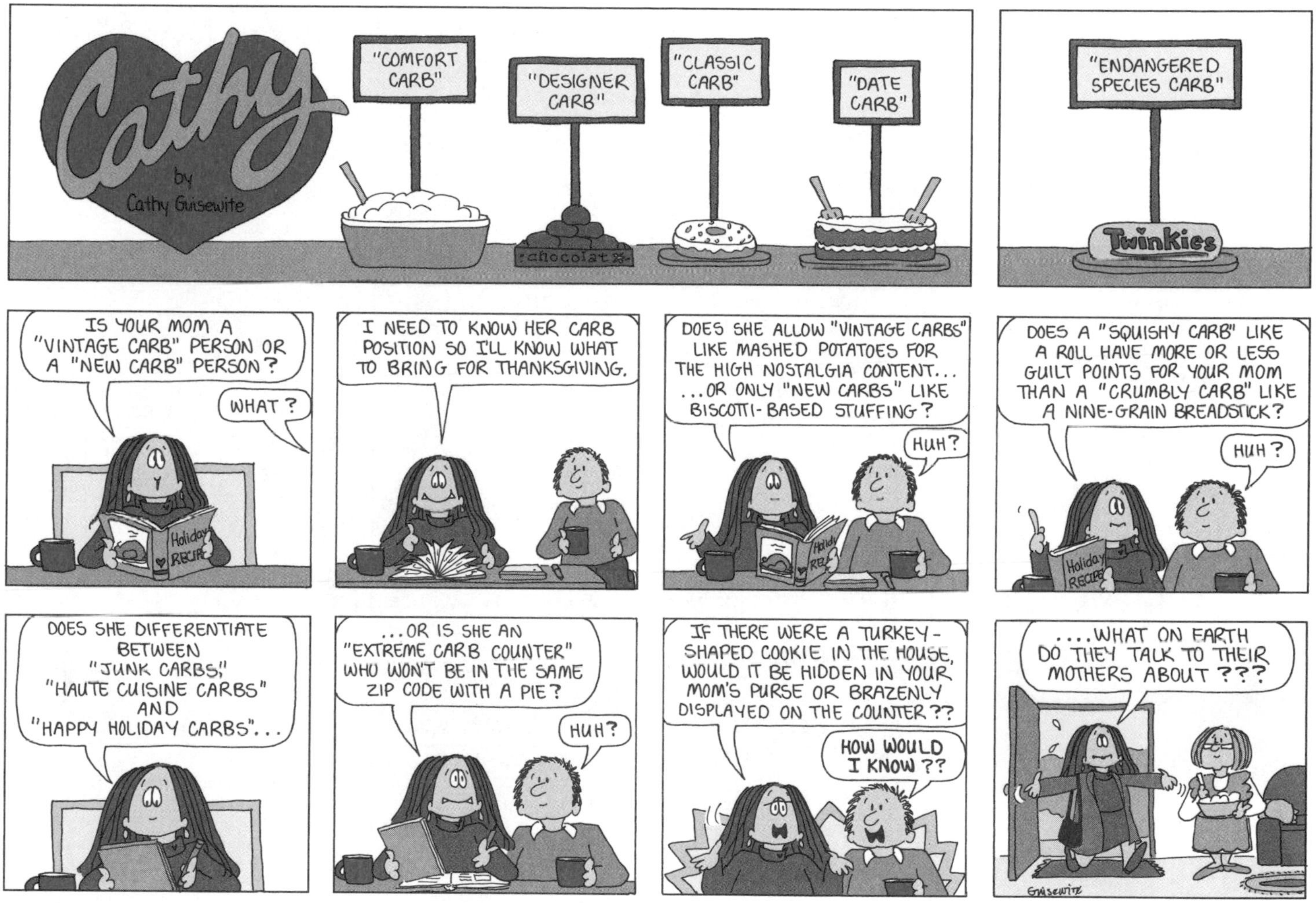
Cathy
by
Cathy Guisewite
"COMFORT CARB"
"DESIGNER CARB"
chocolat
"CLASSIC CARB"
"DATE CARB"
"ENDANGERED SPECIES CARB"
Twinkies
IS YOUR MOM A "VINTAGE CARB" PERSON OR A "NEW CARB" PERSON?
WHAT?
I NEED TO KNOW HER CARB POSITION SO I'LL KNOW WHAT TO BRING FOR THANKSGIVING.
DOES SHE ALLOW "VINTAGE CARBS" LIKE MASHED POTATOES FOR THE HIGH NOSTALGIA CONTENT... ...OR ONLY "NEW CARBS" LIKE BISCOTTI-BASED STUFFING?
HUH?
DOES A "SQUISHY CARB" LIKE A ROLL HAVE MORE OR LESS GUILT POINTS FOR YOUR MOM THAN A "CRUMBLY CARB" LIKE A NINE-GRAIN BREADSTICK?
HUH?
DOES SHE DIFFERENTIATE BETWEEN "JUNK CARBS," "HAUTE CUISINE CARBS" AND "HAPPY HOLIDAY CARBS"...
...OR IS SHE AN "EXTREME CARB COUNTER" WHO WON'T BE IN THE SAME ZIP CODE WITH A PIE?
HUH?
IF THERE WERE A TURKEY-SHAPED COOKIE IN THE HOUSE, WOULD IT BE HIDDEN IN YOUR MOM'S PURSE OR BRAZENLY DISPLAYED ON THE COUNTER??
HOW WOULD I KNOW??
....WHAT ON EARTH DO THEY TALK TO THEIR MOTHERS ABOUT???
GUISEWITE

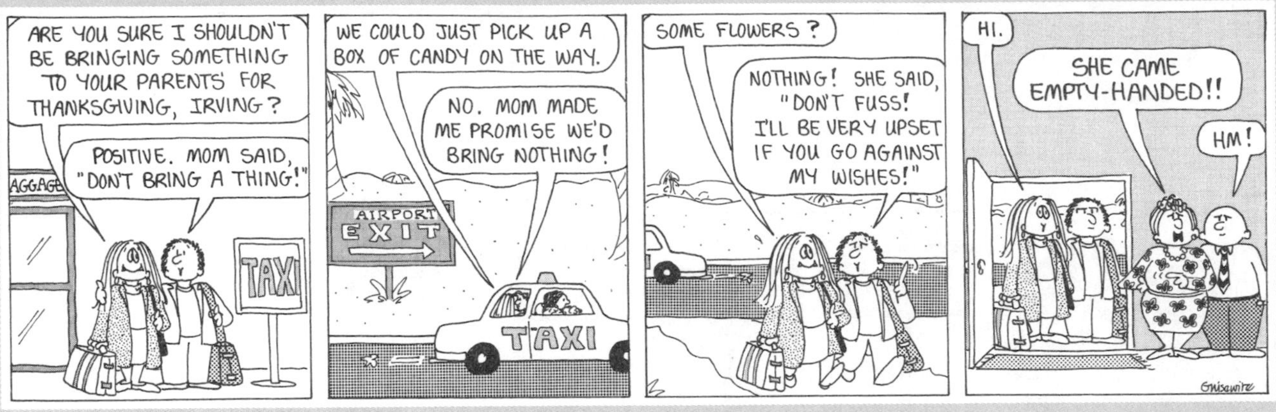
ARE YOU SURE I SHOULDN'T BE BRINGING SOMETHING TO YOUR PARENTS' FOR THANKSGIVING, IRVING?
POSITIVE. MOM SAID, "DON'T BRING A THING!"
TAXI
WE COULD JUST PICK UP A BOX OF CANDY ON THE WAY.
NO. MOM MADE ME PROMISE WE'D BRING NOTHING!
AIRPORT EXIT
TAXI
SOME FLOWERS?
NOTHING! SHE SAID, "DON'T FUSS! I'LL BE VERY UPSET IF YOU GO AGAINST MY WISHES!"
HI.
SHE CAME EMPTY-HANDED!!
HM!

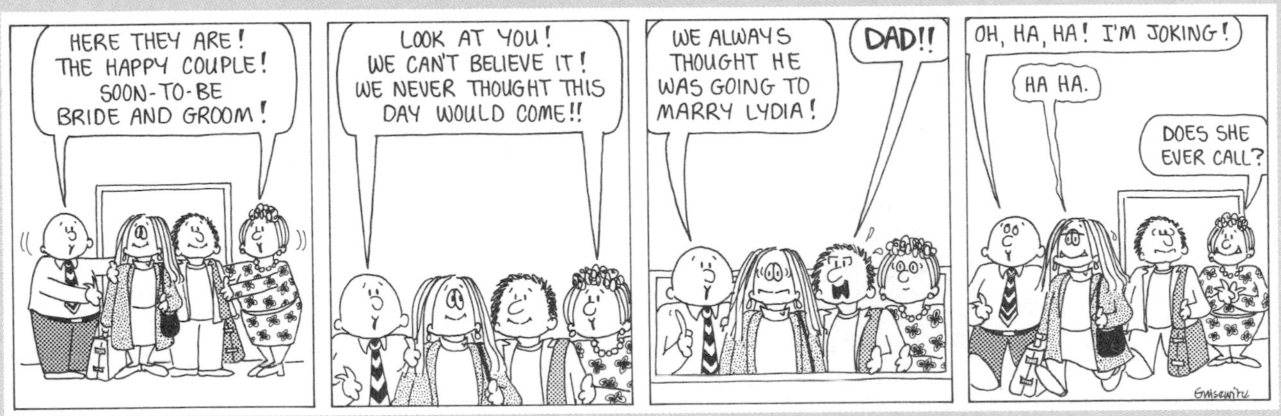
HERE THEY ARE! THE HAPPY COUPLE! SOON-TO-BE BRIDE AND GROOM!
LOOK AT YOU! WE CAN'T BELIEVE IT! WE NEVER THOUGHT THIS DAY WOULD COME!!
WE ALWAYS THOUGHT HE WAS GOING TO MARRY LYDIA!
DAD!!
OH, HA, HA! I'M JOKING!
HA HA.
DOES SHE EVER CALL?

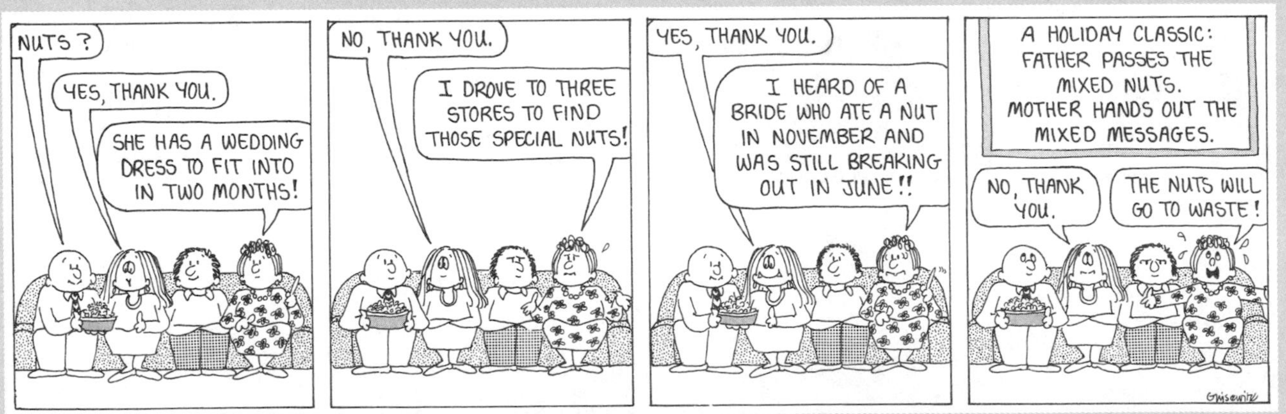
NUTS?
YES, THANK YOU.
SHE HAS A WEDDING DRESS TO FIT INTO IN TWO MONTHS!
NO, THANK YOU.
I DROVE TO THREE STORES TO FIND THOSE SPECIAL NUTS!
YES, THANK YOU.
I HEARD OF A BRIDE WHO ATE A NUT IN NOVEMBER AND WAS STILL BREAKING OUT IN JUNE!!
A HOLIDAY CLASSIC: FATHER PASSES THE MIXED NUTS. MOTHER HANDS OUT THE MIXED MESSAGES.
NO, THANK YOU.
THE NUTS WILL GO TO WASTE!

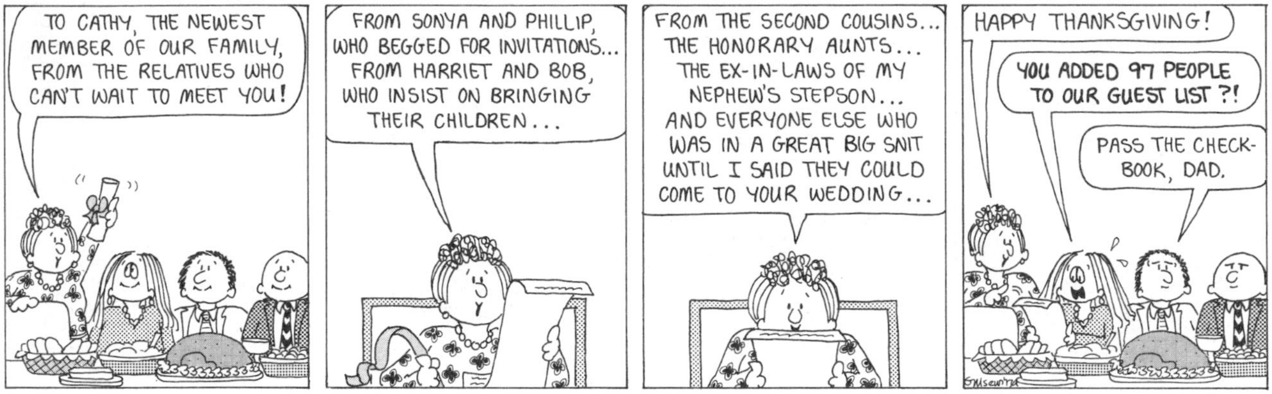
TO CATHY, THE NEWEST MEMBER OF OUR FAMILY, FROM THE RELATIVES WHO CAN'T WAIT TO MEET YOU!
FROM SONYA AND PHILLIP, WHO BEGGED FOR INVITATIONS... FROM HARRIET AND BOB, WHO INSIST ON BRINGING THEIR CHILDREN...
FROM THE SECOND COUSINS... THE HONORARY AUNTS... THE EX-IN-LAWS OF MY NEPHEW'S STEPSON... AND EVERYONE ELSE WHO WAS IN A GREAT BIG SNIT UNTIL I SAID THEY COULD COME TO YOUR WEDDING...
HAPPY THANKSGIVING!
YOU ADDED 97 PEOPLE TO OUR GUEST LIST ?!
PASS THE CHECK-BOOK, DAD.

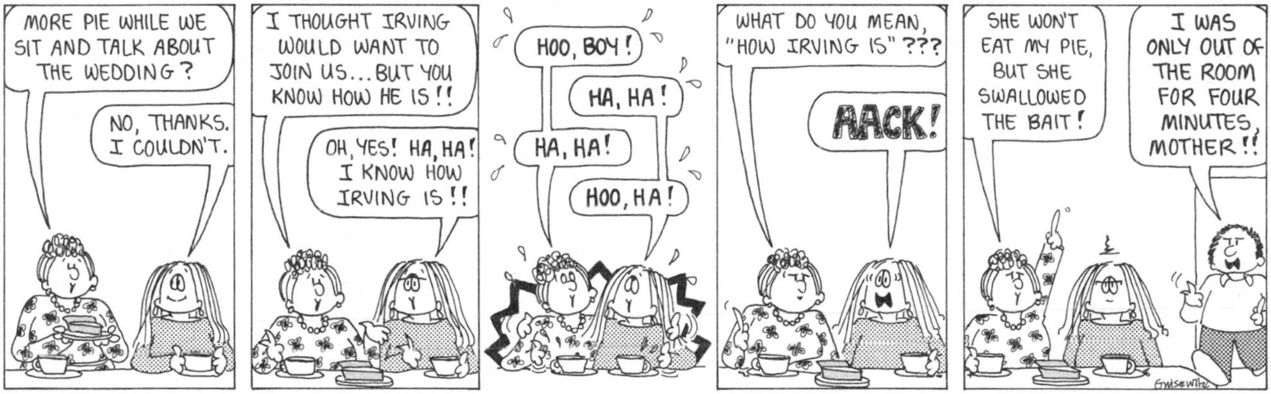
MORE PIE WHILE WE SIT AND TALK ABOUT THE WEDDING?
NO, THANKS. I COULDN'T.
I THOUGHT IRVING WOULD WANT TO JOIN US... BUT YOU KNOW HOW HE IS!!
OH, YES! HA, HA! I KNOW HOW IRVING IS!!
HOO, BOY!
HA, HA!
HA, HA!
HOO, HA!
WHAT DO YOU MEAN, "HOW IRVING IS"???
AACK!
SHE WON'T EAT MY PIE, BUT SHE SWALLOWED THE BAIT!
I WAS ONLY OUT OF THE ROOM FOR FOUR MINUTES, MOTHER!!

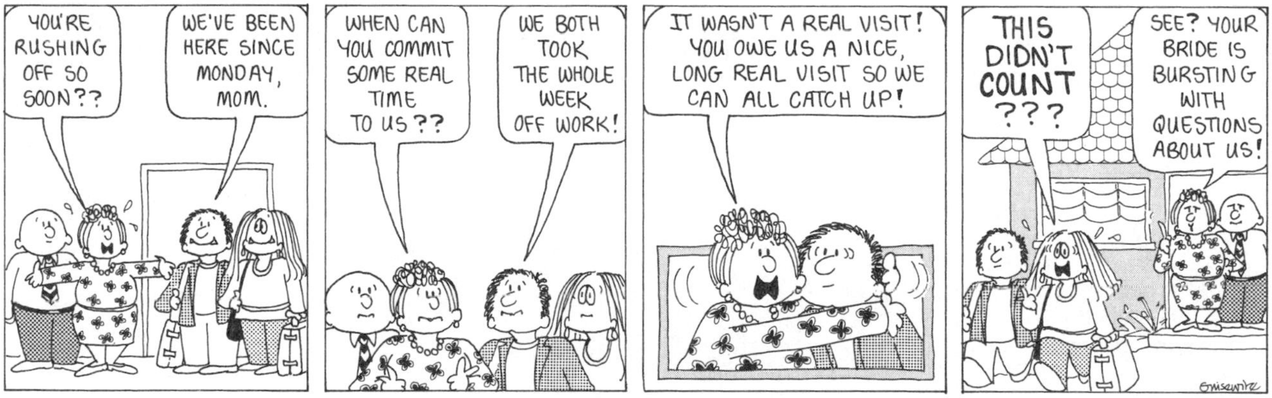
YOU'RE RUSHING OFF SO SOON??
WE'VE BEEN HERE SINCE MONDAY, MOM.
WHEN CAN YOU COMMIT SOME REAL TIME TO US??
WE BOTH TOOK THE WHOLE WEEK OFF WORK!
IT WASN'T A REAL VISIT! YOU OWE US A NICE, LONG REAL VISIT SO WE CAN ALL CATCH UP!
THIS DIDN'T COUNT???
SEE? YOUR BRIDE IS BURSTING WITH QUESTIONS ABOUT US!

HOW WAS THANKS-GIVING WITH THE NEW IN-LAWS, CATHY?

GREAT.

GREAT-WONDERFUL?
GREAT-HIDEOUS?
GREAT-AWKWARD?
GREAT-SO-SO?
GREAT-ICKY?
GREAT-PLEASANT?
GREAT-WEIRD?
GREAT-YOU-CAN'T-TELL-YOUR-MOM-BECAUSE-YOU'RE-AFRAID-I'LL-MAKE-SUGGESTIONS-FOR-THE-NEXT-20-YEARS??

HOW WAS THANKS-GIVING WITH THE NEW IN-LAWS?

GREAT.

GREAT!

WHAT MUST IT BE LIKE TO LIVE LIFE WITHOUT THE IN-BRAIN THESAURUS??

IRVING'S MOTHER...UM.. ADDED A FEW PEOPLE TO OUR GUEST LIST, MOM.

WHAT FUN! THE MORE THE MERRIER!

SHE WANTS TO USE HER FRIEND'S FLORIST INSTEAD OF THE ONE YOU BOOKED.

OUT WITH THE OLD! IN WITH THE NEW!

SHE WANTS TO CHANGE THE RECEPTION SITE, INVITATION TYPEFACE AND WEDDING DATE!

WHEE!!

MOM??...

YOUR MOTHER LEFT THE PLANET LAST WEEK. I'M HERE WITH MRS. BOBBLE-HEAD.

I FEEL ALL SILLY AND DIZZY!

Wedding Planning BY MOM

THE MOTHER'S FRAZZLED...

THE FIANCÉ'S FRIED...

THE BRIDE TURNS TO HER BELOVED BRIDAL PARTY FOR SUPPORT IN THE LAST GIDDY MONTHS BEFORE THE WEDDING...

I'M NOT WEARING THIS!!

EVERYONE'S AGREEING ON SOMETHING!!

BRIDAL "PARTY" MAY BE AN OVER-STATEMENT...

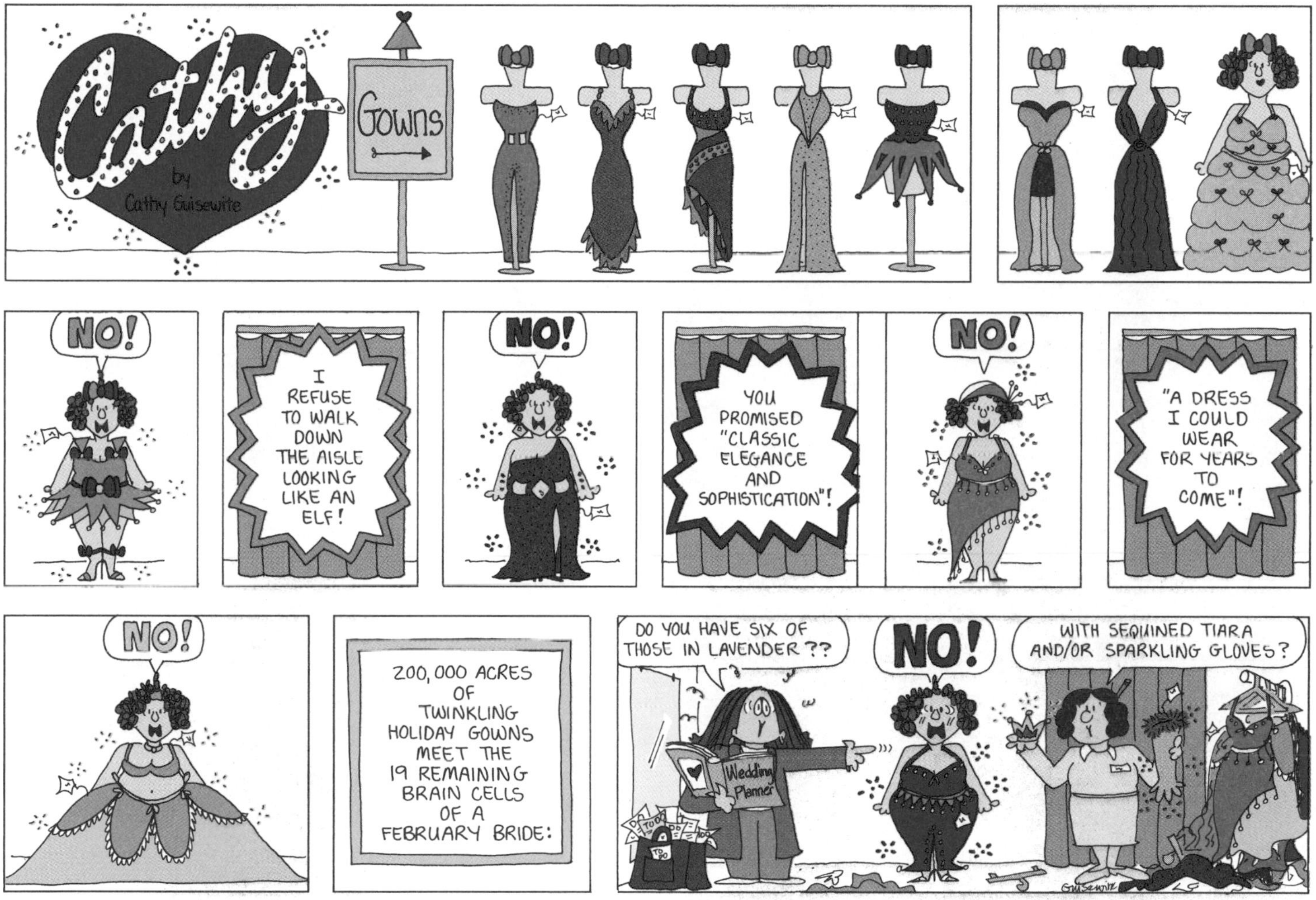
Cathy
by Cathy Guisewite
Gowns
NO!
I REFUSE TO WALK DOWN THE AISLE LOOKING LIKE AN ELF!
NO!
YOU PROMISED "CLASSIC ELEGANCE AND SOPHISTICATION"!
NO!
"A DRESS I COULD WEAR FOR YEARS TO COME"!
NO!
200,000 ACRES OF TWINKLING HOLIDAY GOWNS MEET THE 19 REMAINING BRAIN CELLS OF A FEBRUARY BRIDE:
DO YOU HAVE SIX OF THOSE IN LAVENDER??
NO!
WITH SEQUINED TIARA AND/OR SPARKLING GLOVES?
Wedding Planner

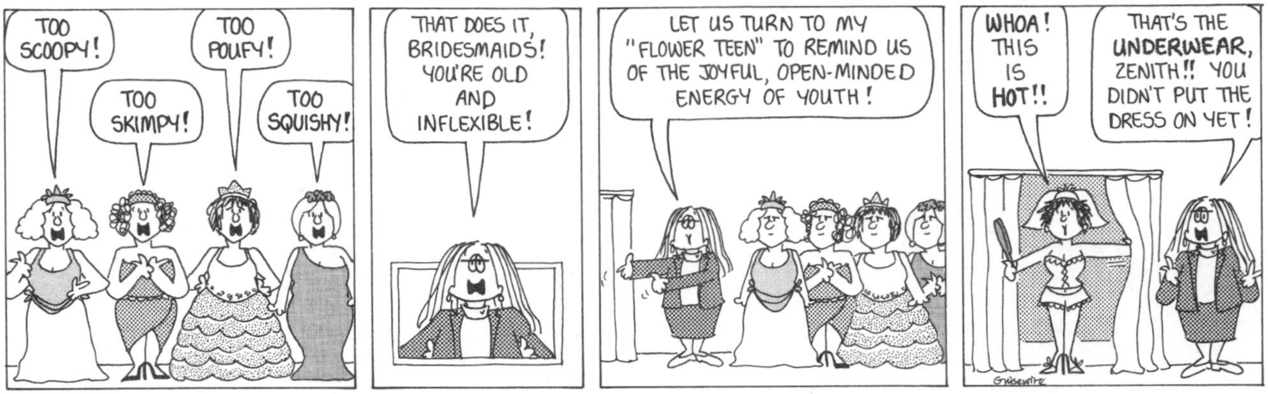
TOO SCOOPY!
TOO SKIMPY!
TOO POUFY!
TOO SQUISHY!
THAT DOES IT, BRIDESMAIDS! YOU'RE OLD AND INFLEXIBLE!
LET US TURN TO MY "FLOWER TEEN" TO REMIND US OF THE JOYFUL, OPEN-MINDED ENERGY OF YOUTH!
WHOA! THIS IS HOT!!
THAT'S THE UNDERWEAR, ZENITH!! YOU DIDN'T PUT THE DRESS ON YET!

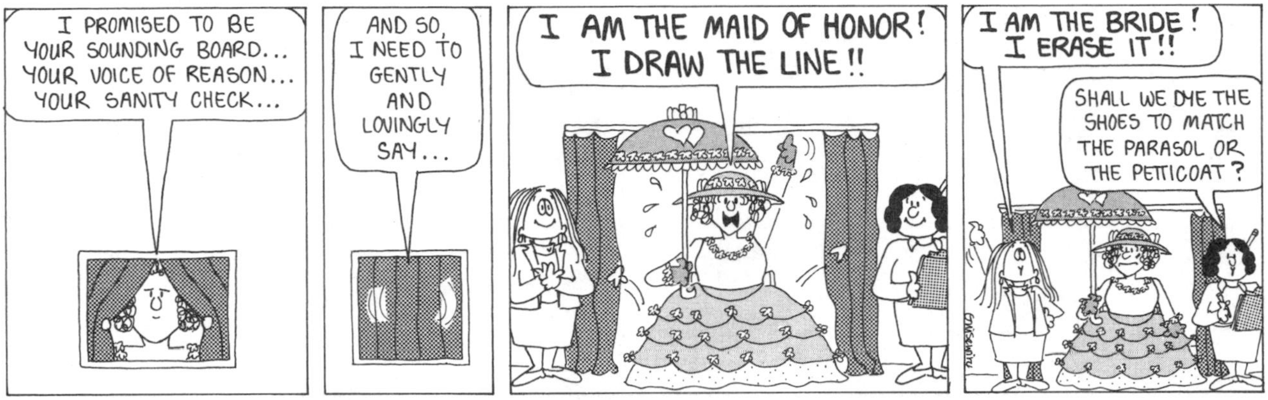
I PROMISED TO BE YOUR SOUNDING BOARD... YOUR VOICE OF REASON... YOUR SANITY CHECK...
AND SO, I NEED TO GENTLY AND LOVINGLY SAY...
I AM THE MAID OF HONOR! I DRAW THE LINE!!
I AM THE BRIDE! I ERASE IT!!
SHALL WE DYE THE SHOES TO MATCH THE PARASOL OR THE PETTICOAT?

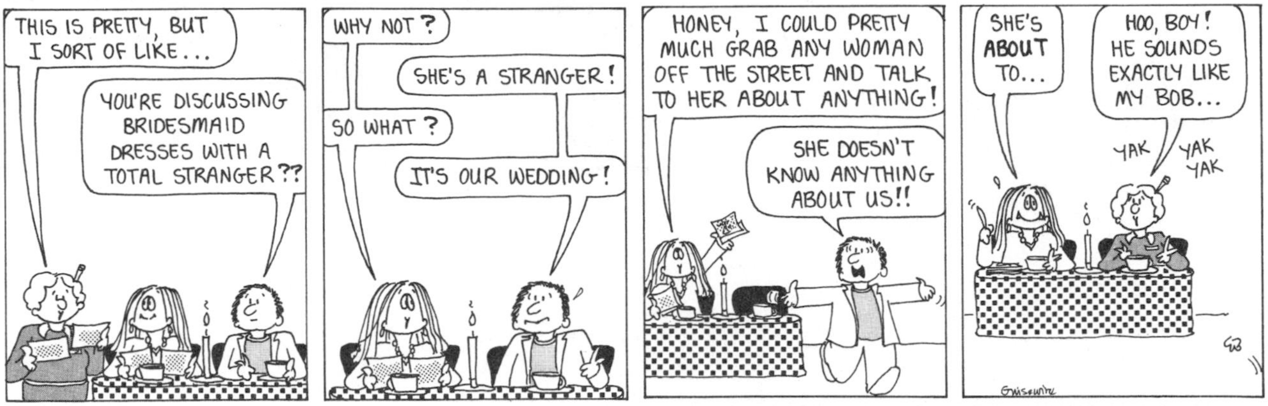
THIS IS PRETTY, BUT I SORT OF LIKE...
YOU'RE DISCUSSING BRIDESMAID DRESSES WITH A TOTAL STRANGER??
WHY NOT?
SHE'S A STRANGER!
SO WHAT?
IT'S OUR WEDDING!
HONEY, I COULD PRETTY MUCH GRAB ANY WOMAN OFF THE STREET AND TALK TO HER ABOUT ANYTHING!
SHE DOESN'T KNOW ANYTHING ABOUT US!!
SHE'S ABOUT TO...
HOO, BOY! HE SOUNDS EXACTLY LIKE MY BOB...
YAK
YAK YAK

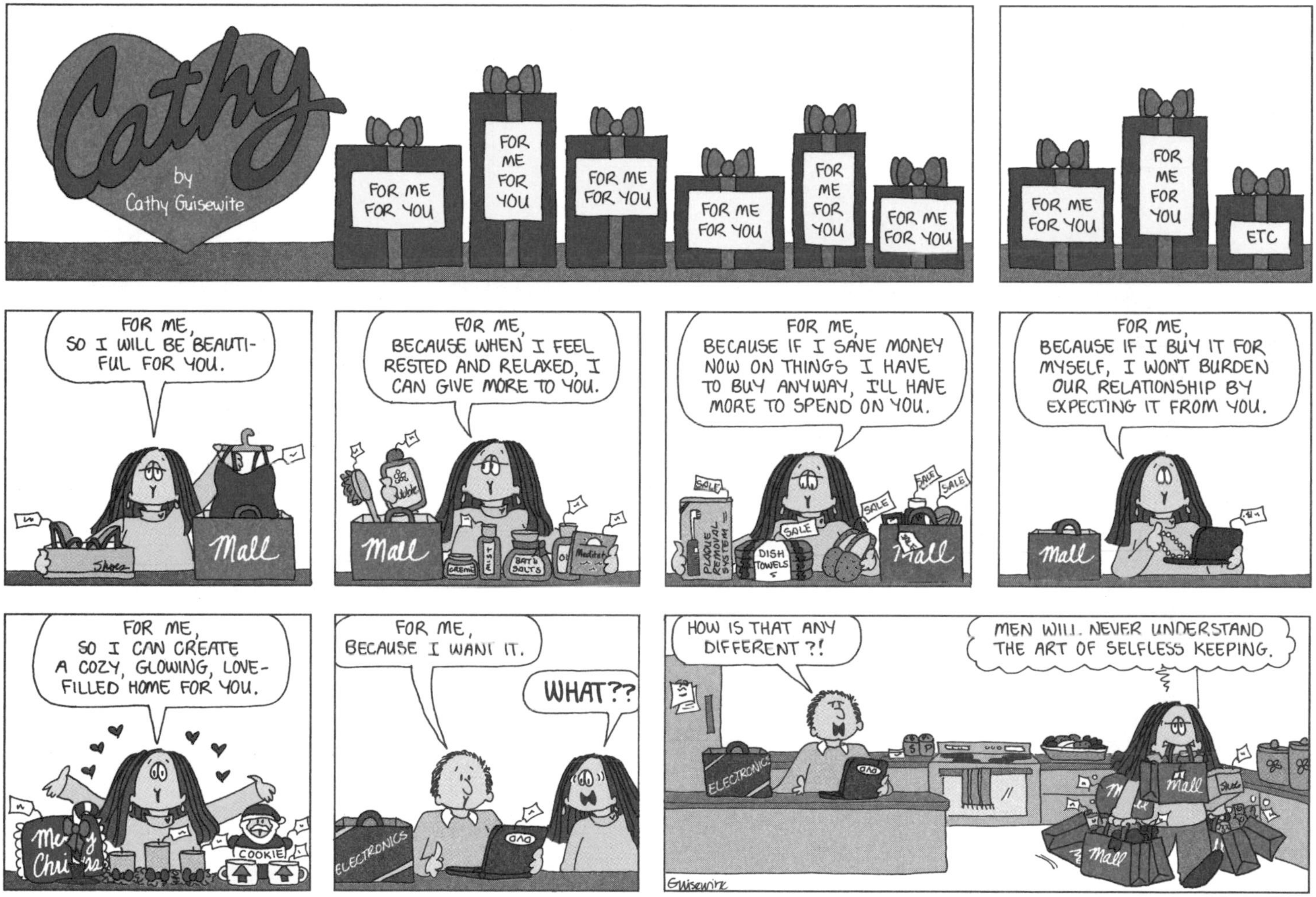
Cathy
by Cathy Guisewite
FOR ME FOR YOU
FOR ME FOR YOU
FOR ME FOR YOU
FOR ME FOR YOU
FOR ME FOR YOU
FOR ME FOR YOU
FOR ME FOR YOU
FOR ME FOR YOU
ETC
FOR ME, SO I WILL BE BEAUTIFUL FOR YOU.
Mall
FOR ME, BECAUSE WHEN I FEEL RESTED AND RELAXED, I CAN GIVE MORE TO YOU.
Mall
BATH SALTS
FOR ME, BECAUSE IF I SAVE MONEY NOW ON THINGS I HAVE TO BUY ANYWAY, I'LL HAVE MORE TO SPEND ON YOU.
SALE
PLAQUE REMOVAL SYSTEM
DISH TOWELS
Mall
FOR ME, BECAUSE IF I BUY IT FOR MYSELF, I WON'T BURDEN OUR RELATIONSHIP BY EXPECTING IT FROM YOU.
Mall
FOR ME, SO I CAN CREATE A COZY, GLOWING, LOVE-FILLED HOME FOR YOU.
COOKIE
FOR ME, BECAUSE I WANT IT.
WHAT??
ELECTRONICS
DVD
HOW IS THAT ANY DIFFERENT?!
MEN WILL NEVER UNDERSTAND THE ART OF SELFLESS KEEPING.
ELECTRONICS
Mall
Guisewite

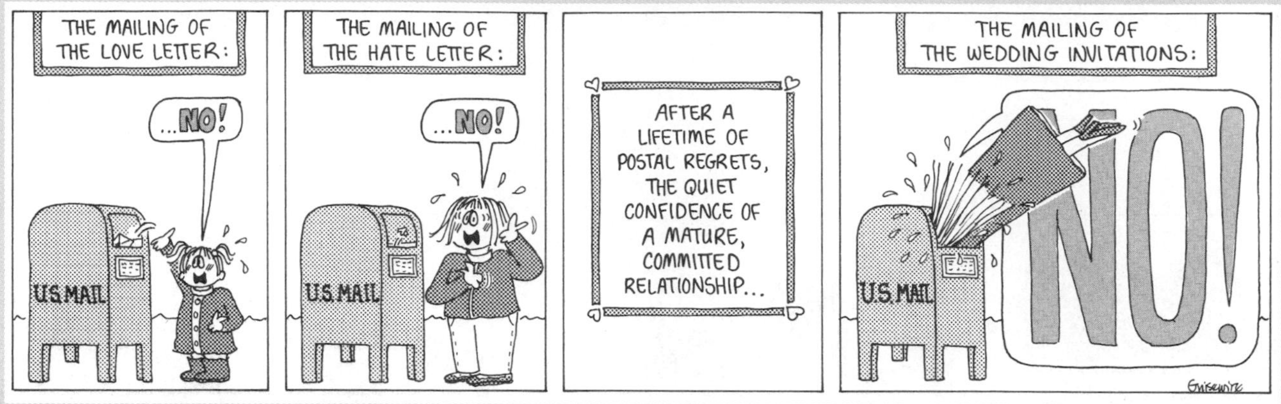

THE MAILING OF THE LOVE LETTER:
...NO!
U.S. MAIL
THE MAILING OF THE HATE LETTER:
...NO!
U.S. MAIL
AFTER A LIFETIME OF POSTAL REGRETS, THE QUIET CONFIDENCE OF A MATURE, COMMITTED RELATIONSHIP...
THE MAILING OF THE WEDDING INVITATIONS:
U.S. MAIL
NO!

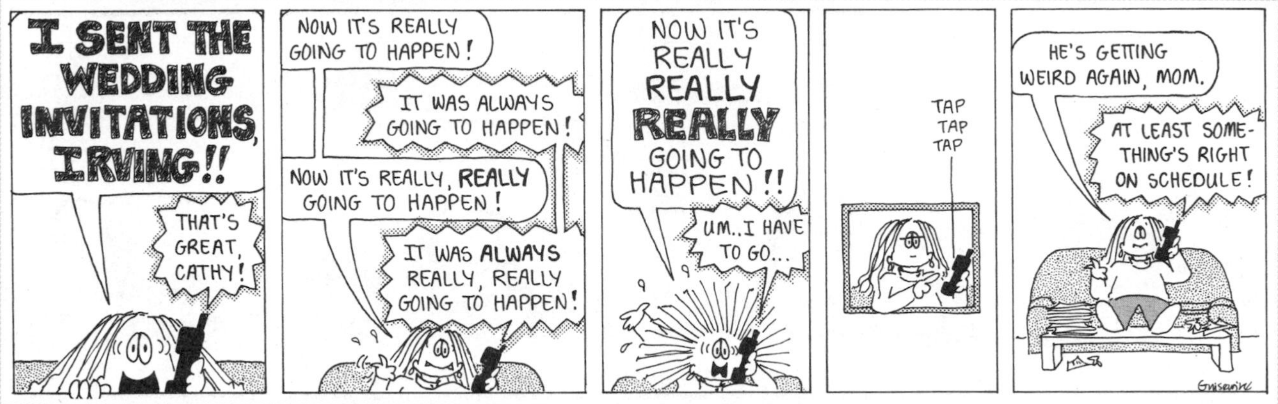

I SENT THE WEDDING INVITATIONS, IRVING!!
THAT'S GREAT, CATHY!
NOW IT'S REALLY GOING TO HAPPEN!
IT WAS ALWAYS GOING TO HAPPEN!
NOW IT'S REALLY, REALLY GOING TO HAPPEN!
IT WAS ALWAYS REALLY, REALLY GOING TO HAPPEN!
NOW IT'S REALLY REALLY REALLY GOING TO HAPPEN!!
UM..I HAVE TO GO...
TAP TAP TAP
HE'S GETTING WEIRD AGAIN, MOM.
AT LEAST SOME-THING'S RIGHT ON SCHEDULE!

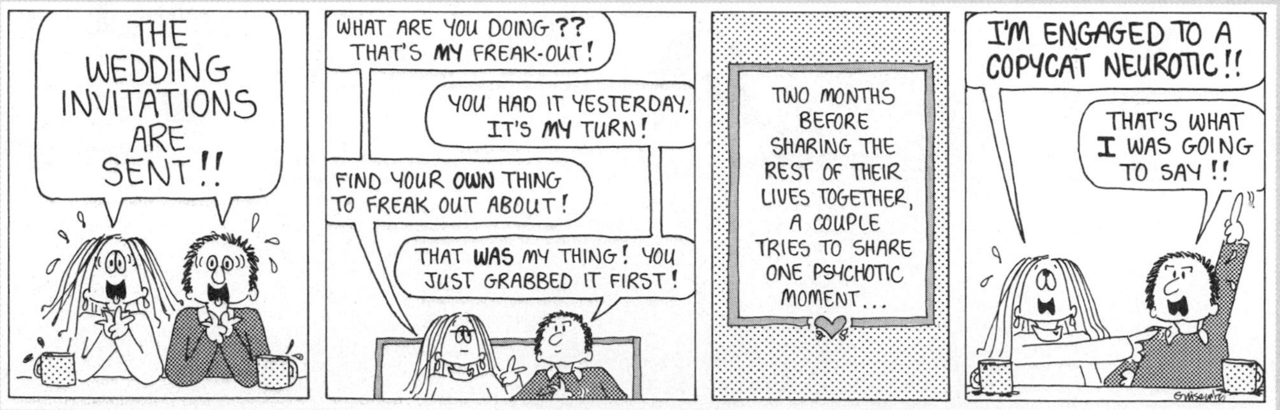

THE WEDDING INVITATIONS ARE SENT!!
WHAT ARE YOU DOING?? THAT'S MY FREAK-OUT!
YOU HAD IT YESTERDAY. IT'S MY TURN!
FIND YOUR OWN THING TO FREAK OUT ABOUT!
THAT WAS MY THING! YOU JUST GRABBED IT FIRST!
TWO MONTHS BEFORE SHARING THE REST OF THEIR LIVES TOGETHER, A COUPLE TRIES TO SHARE ONE PSYCHOTIC MOMENT...
I'M ENGAGED TO A COPYCAT NEUROTIC!!
THAT'S WHAT I WAS GOING TO SAY!!

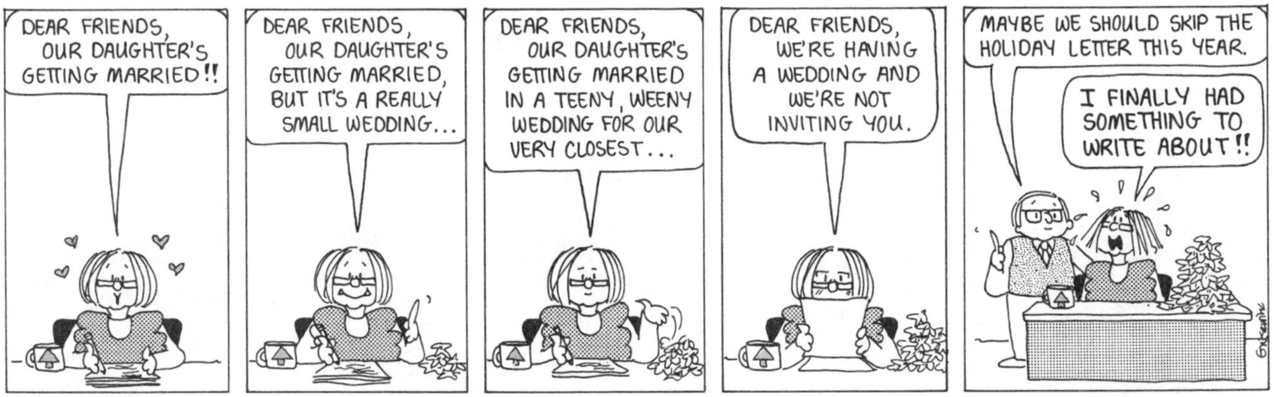
DEAR FRIENDS, OUR DAUGHTER'S GETTING MARRIED!!
DEAR FRIENDS, OUR DAUGHTER'S GETTING MARRIED, BUT IT'S A REALLY SMALL WEDDING...
DEAR FRIENDS, OUR DAUGHTER'S GETTING MARRIED IN A TEENY, WEENY WEDDING FOR OUR VERY CLOSEST...
DEAR FRIENDS, WE'RE HAVING A WEDDING AND WE'RE NOT INVITING YOU.
MAYBE WE SHOULD SKIP THE HOLIDAY LETTER THIS YEAR.
I FINALLY HAD SOMETHING TO WRITE ABOUT!!

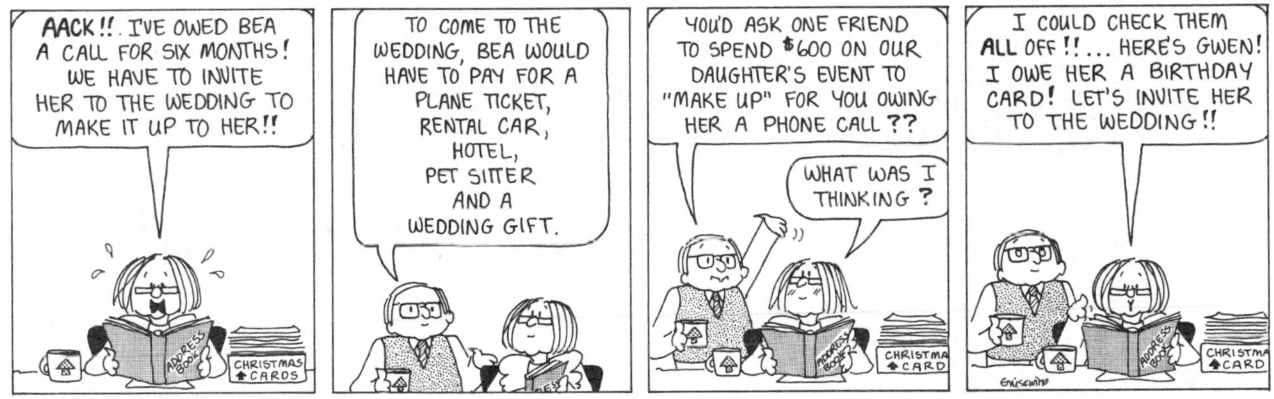
AACK!! I'VE OWED BEA A CALL FOR SIX MONTHS! WE HAVE TO INVITE HER TO THE WEDDING TO MAKE IT UP TO HER!!
ADDRESS BOOK
CHRISTMAS CARDS
TO COME TO THE WEDDING, BEA WOULD HAVE TO PAY FOR A PLANE TICKET, RENTAL CAR, HOTEL, PET SITTER AND A WEDDING GIFT.
YOU'D ASK ONE FRIEND TO SPEND $600 ON OUR DAUGHTER'S EVENT TO "MAKE UP" FOR YOU OWING HER A PHONE CALL??
WHAT WAS I THINKING?
I COULD CHECK THEM ALL OFF!!... HERE'S GWEN! I OWE HER A BIRTHDAY CARD! LET'S INVITE HER TO THE WEDDING!!

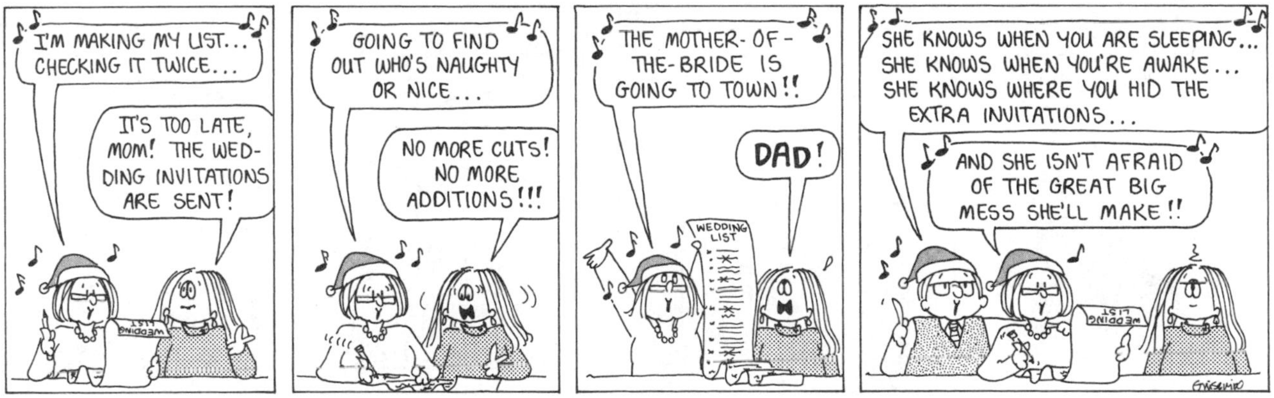
I'M MAKING MY LIST... CHECKING IT TWICE...
IT'S TOO LATE, MOM! THE WEDDING INVITATIONS ARE SENT!
GOING TO FIND OUT WHO'S NAUGHTY OR NICE...
NO MORE CUTS! NO MORE ADDITIONS!!!
THE MOTHER-OF-THE-BRIDE IS GOING TO TOWN!!
WEDDING LIST
DAD!
SHE KNOWS WHEN YOU ARE SLEEPING... SHE KNOWS WHEN YOU'RE AWAKE... SHE KNOWS WHERE YOU HID THE EXTRA INVITATIONS...
AND SHE ISN'T AFRAID OF THE GREAT BIG MESS SHE'LL MAKE!!

Strip 1:

A SERENE, PERFECT, PRE-WEDDING, PRE-CHRISTMAS MOMENT, AND THEN...

GIFT EXCHANGE AT 10:00! HOUSE SHOWING AT 3:00! CONFERENCE CALL AT 2:45! CLIENT LUNCH AT 1:00! CAKE TASTING AT 11:30! TREE TRIMMING AT 5:15!

MY LIFE AS A HUMAN SNOW GLOBE.

Strip 2:

BETWEEN WEDDING AND CHRISTMAS PLANS, WE BOTH WENT A LITTLE CRAZY LAST WEEK, IRVING.

IT'S GOOD TO JUST STOP. STOP AND NOTICE THIS MOMENT... THIS TIME... THIS SPECIAL PLACE WE ARE TOGETHER....

THIRTY-SIXTH AND THIRTY-SEVENTH IN LINE AT "THE COFFEE BEAN"!

MOVE IT! WE'VE HAD ALL THE DOWN TIME WE CAN TAKE!!

COFFEE

Strip 3:

OUR WEDDING IS OUR GIFT TO EACH OTHER, SO ABSOLUTELY NO CHRISTMAS GIFTS THIS YEAR...RIGHT?

RIGHT! JUST LITTLE NON-GIFTS.

NON-GIFTS?

LITTLE "I COULDN'T STAND TO NOT GET YOU ANYTHING" GIFTS.

JUST A COUPLE TINY "YOU KNOW I CAN'T RESIST WHEN IT'S FOR YOU" GIFTS!

WHAT ABOUT A "FOR-ONCE-WE-COULD-BE-COMPLETELY-OFF-THE-HOOK-NO-GIFT-AT-ALL" GIFT??

...WITH A TEENSY "LAST-MINUTE SURPRISE" GIFT! SWEET!

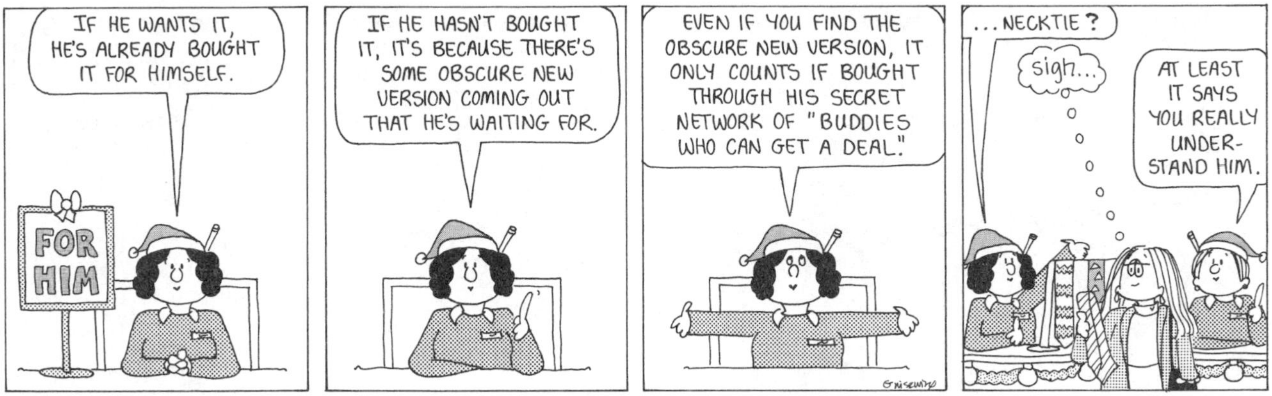
IF HE WANTS IT, HE'S ALREADY BOUGHT IT FOR HIMSELF.
FOR HIM
IF HE HASN'T BOUGHT IT, IT'S BECAUSE THERE'S SOME OBSCURE NEW VERSION COMING OUT THAT HE'S WAITING FOR.
EVEN IF YOU FIND THE OBSCURE NEW VERSION, IT ONLY COUNTS IF BOUGHT THROUGH HIS SECRET NETWORK OF "BUDDIES WHO CAN GET A DEAL."
...NECKTIE?
sigh...
AT LEAST IT SAYS YOU REALLY UNDER-STAND HIM.

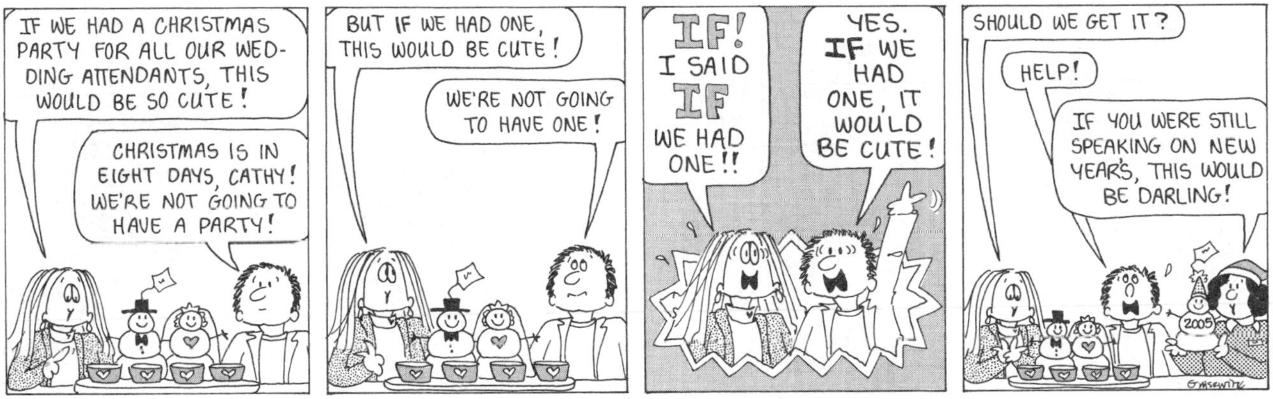
IF WE HAD A CHRISTMAS PARTY FOR ALL OUR WED-DING ATTENDANTS, THIS WOULD BE SO CUTE!
CHRISTMAS IS IN EIGHT DAYS, CATHY! WE'RE NOT GOING TO HAVE A PARTY!
BUT IF WE HAD ONE, THIS WOULD BE CUTE!
WE'RE NOT GOING TO HAVE ONE!
IF! I SAID IF WE HAD ONE!!
YES. IF WE HAD ONE, IT WOULD BE CUTE!
SHOULD WE GET IT?
HELP!
IF YOU WERE STILL SPEAKING ON NEW YEAR'S, THIS WOULD BE DARLING!
2005

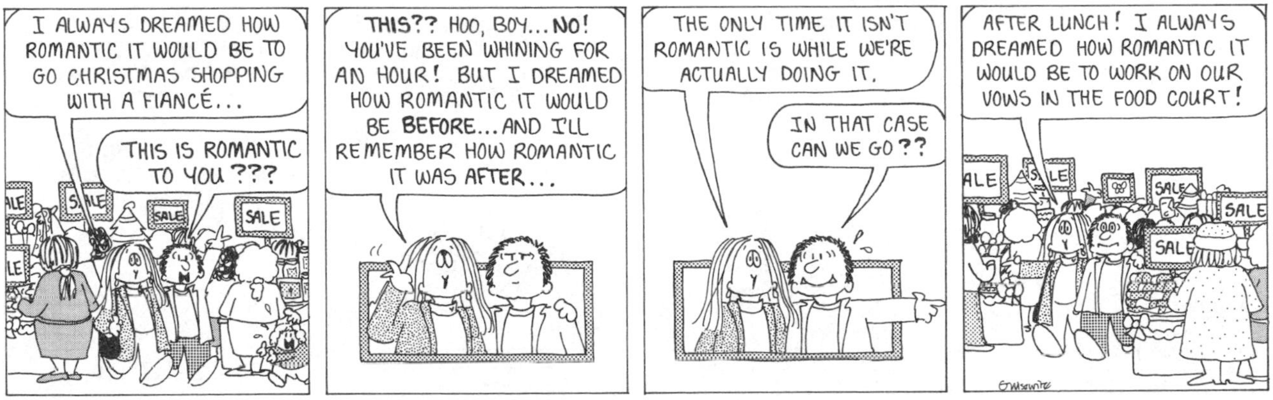
I ALWAYS DREAMED HOW ROMANTIC IT WOULD BE TO GO CHRISTMAS SHOPPING WITH A FIANCÉ...
THIS IS ROMANTIC TO YOU???
SALE
THIS?? HOO, BOY... NO! YOU'VE BEEN WHINING FOR AN HOUR! BUT I DREAMED HOW ROMANTIC IT WOULD BE BEFORE... AND I'LL REMEMBER HOW ROMANTIC IT WAS AFTER...
THE ONLY TIME IT ISN'T ROMANTIC IS WHILE WE'RE ACTUALLY DOING IT.
IN THAT CASE CAN WE GO??
AFTER LUNCH! I ALWAYS DREAMED HOW ROMANTIC IT WOULD BE TO WORK ON OUR VOWS IN THE FOOD COURT!
SALE

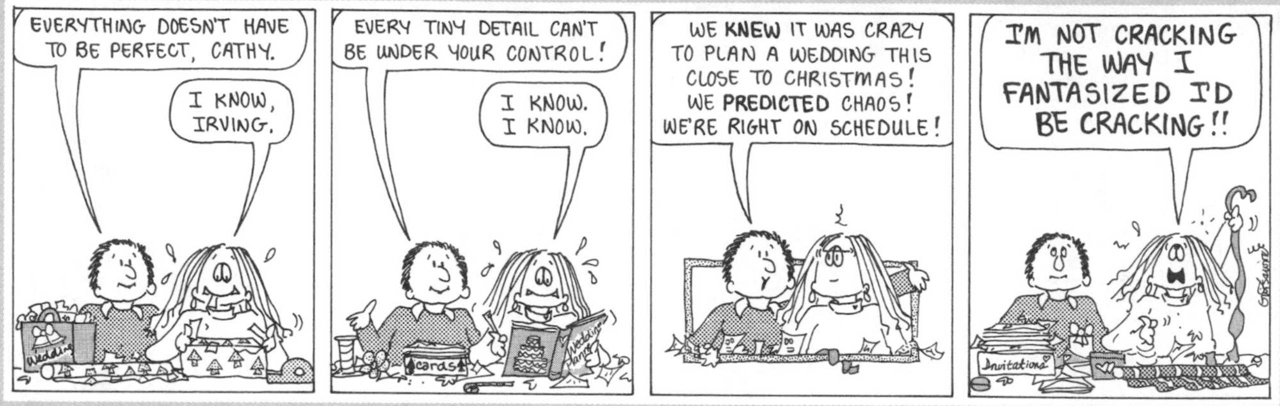
EVERYTHING DOESN'T HAVE TO BE PERFECT, CATHY.
I KNOW, IRVING.
EVERY TINY DETAIL CAN'T BE UNDER YOUR CONTROL!
I KNOW. I KNOW.
WE **KNEW** IT WAS CRAZY TO PLAN A WEDDING THIS CLOSE TO CHRISTMAS! WE **PREDICTED** CHAOS! WE'RE RIGHT ON SCHEDULE!
I'M NOT CRACKING THE WAY I FANTASIZED I'D BE CRACKING!!

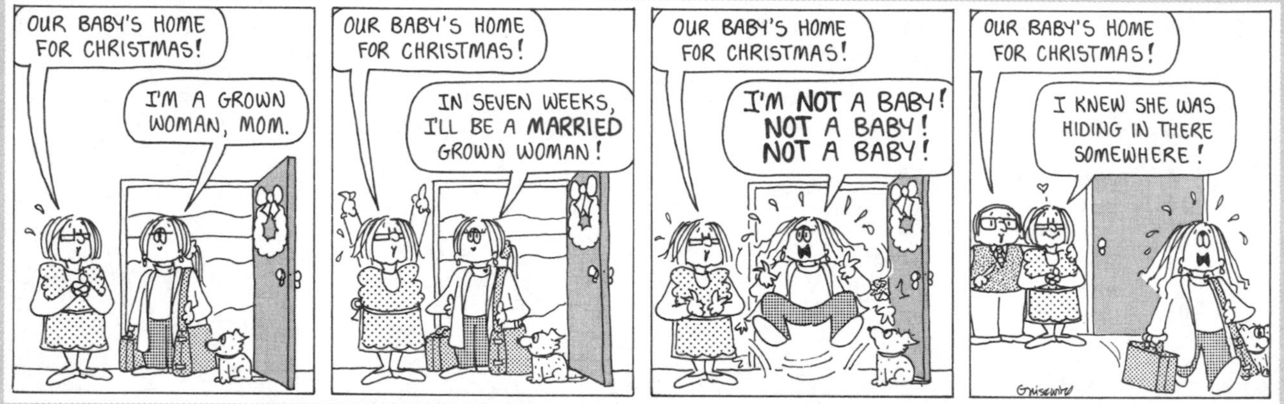
OUR BABY'S HOME FOR CHRISTMAS!
I'M A GROWN WOMAN, MOM.
OUR BABY'S HOME FOR CHRISTMAS!
IN SEVEN WEEKS, I'LL BE A **MARRIED** GROWN WOMAN!
OUR BABY'S HOME FOR CHRISTMAS!
I'M **NOT** A BABY! **NOT** A BABY! **NOT** A BABY!
OUR BABY'S HOME FOR CHRISTMAS!
I KNEW SHE WAS HIDING IN THERE SOMEWHERE!

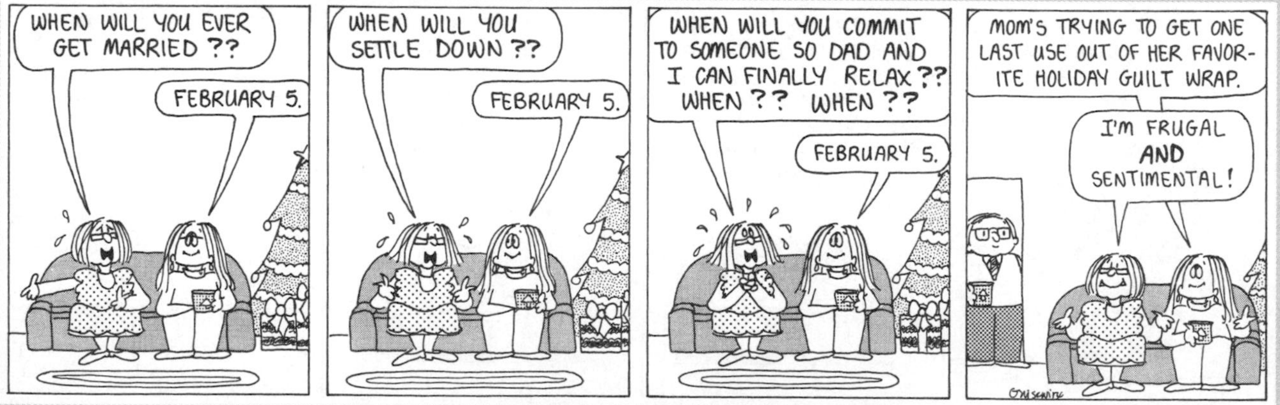
WHEN WILL YOU EVER GET MARRIED??
FEBRUARY 5.
WHEN WILL YOU SETTLE DOWN??
FEBRUARY 5.
WHEN WILL YOU COMMIT TO SOMEONE SO DAD AND I CAN FINALLY RELAX?? WHEN?? WHEN??
FEBRUARY 5.
MOM'S TRYING TO GET ONE LAST USE OUT OF HER FAVORITE HOLIDAY GUILT WRAP.
I'M FRUGAL **AND** SENTIMENTAL!

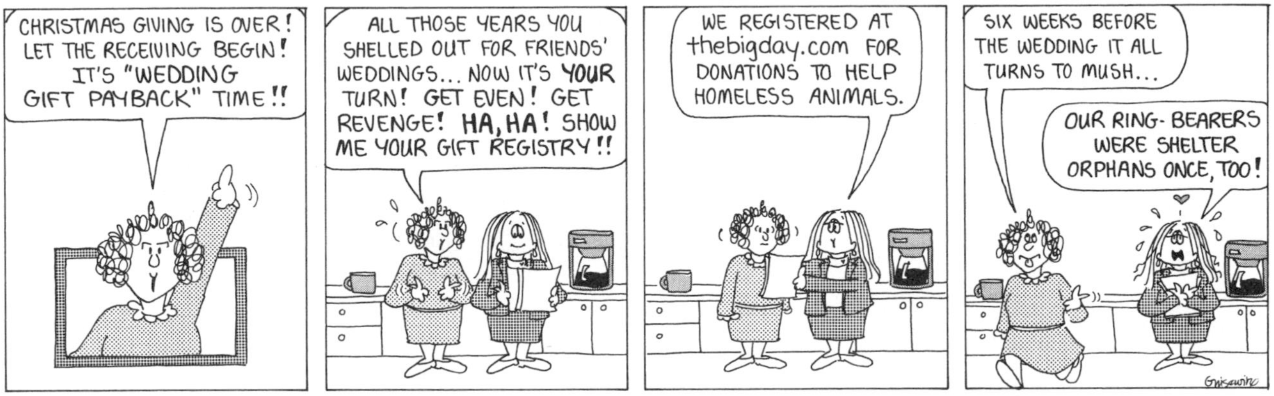
CHRISTMAS GIVING IS OVER! LET THE RECEIVING BEGIN! IT'S "WEDDING GIFT PAYBACK" TIME!!
ALL THOSE YEARS YOU SHELLED OUT FOR FRIENDS' WEDDINGS... NOW IT'S YOUR TURN! GET EVEN! GET REVENGE! HA, HA! SHOW ME YOUR GIFT REGISTRY!!
WE REGISTERED AT thebigday.com FOR DONATIONS TO HELP HOMELESS ANIMALS.
SIX WEEKS BEFORE THE WEDDING IT ALL TURNS TO MUSH...
OUR RING-BEARERS WERE SHELTER ORPHANS ONCE, TOO!

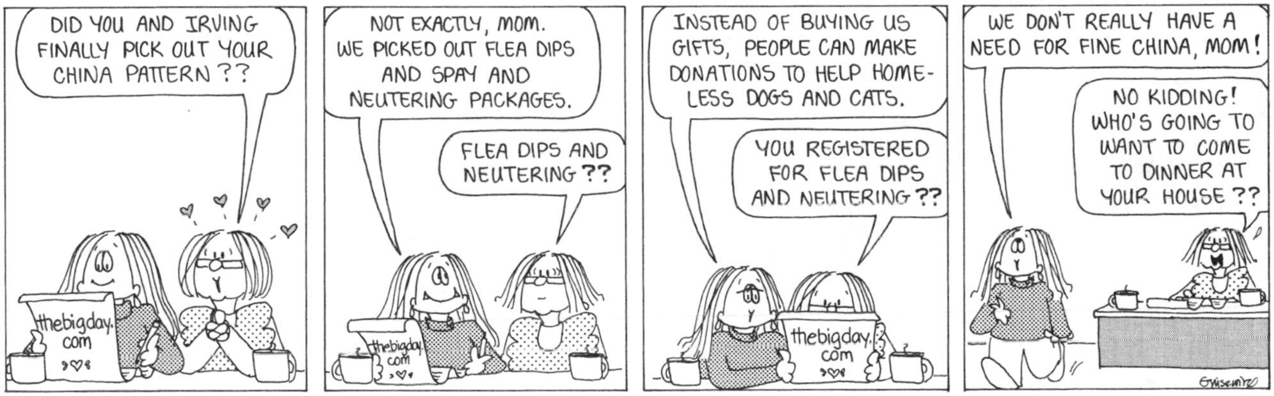
DID YOU AND IRVING FINALLY PICK OUT YOUR CHINA PATTERN??
thebigday.com
NOT EXACTLY, MOM. WE PICKED OUT FLEA DIPS AND SPAY AND NEUTERING PACKAGES.
FLEA DIPS AND NEUTERING??
INSTEAD OF BUYING US GIFTS, PEOPLE CAN MAKE DONATIONS TO HELP HOMELESS DOGS AND CATS.
YOU REGISTERED FOR FLEA DIPS AND NEUTERING??
thebigday.com
WE DON'T REALLY HAVE A NEED FOR FINE CHINA, MOM!
NO KIDDING! WHO'S GOING TO WANT TO COME TO DINNER AT YOUR HOUSE??

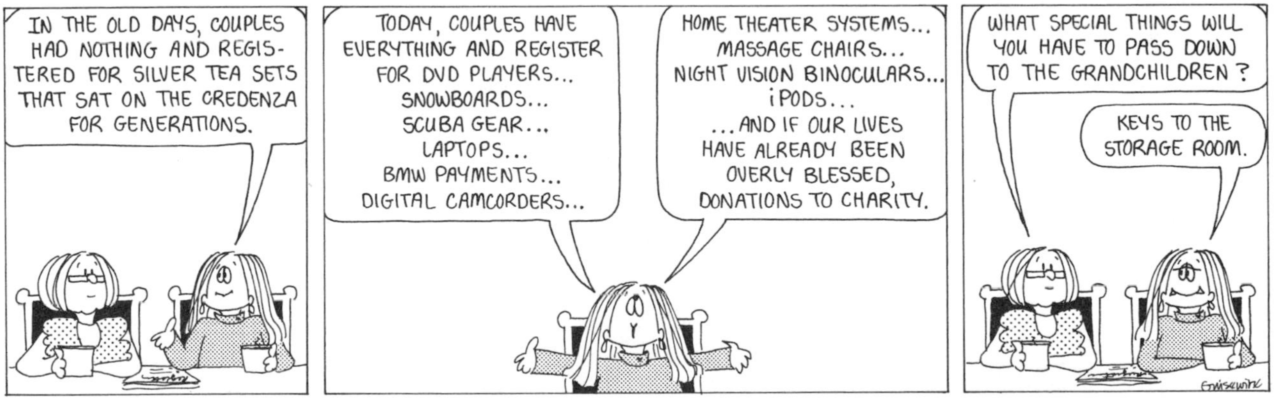
IN THE OLD DAYS, COUPLES HAD NOTHING AND REGISTERED FOR SILVER TEA SETS THAT SAT ON THE CREDENZA FOR GENERATIONS.
TODAY, COUPLES HAVE EVERYTHING AND REGISTER FOR DVD PLAYERS... SNOWBOARDS... SCUBA GEAR... LAPTOPS... BMW PAYMENTS... DIGITAL CAMCORDERS...
HOME THEATER SYSTEMS... MASSAGE CHAIRS... NIGHT VISION BINOCULARS... iPODS... ...AND IF OUR LIVES HAVE ALREADY BEEN OVERLY BLESSED, DONATIONS TO CHARITY.
WHAT SPECIAL THINGS WILL YOU HAVE TO PASS DOWN TO THE GRANDCHILDREN?
KEYS TO THE STORAGE ROOM.

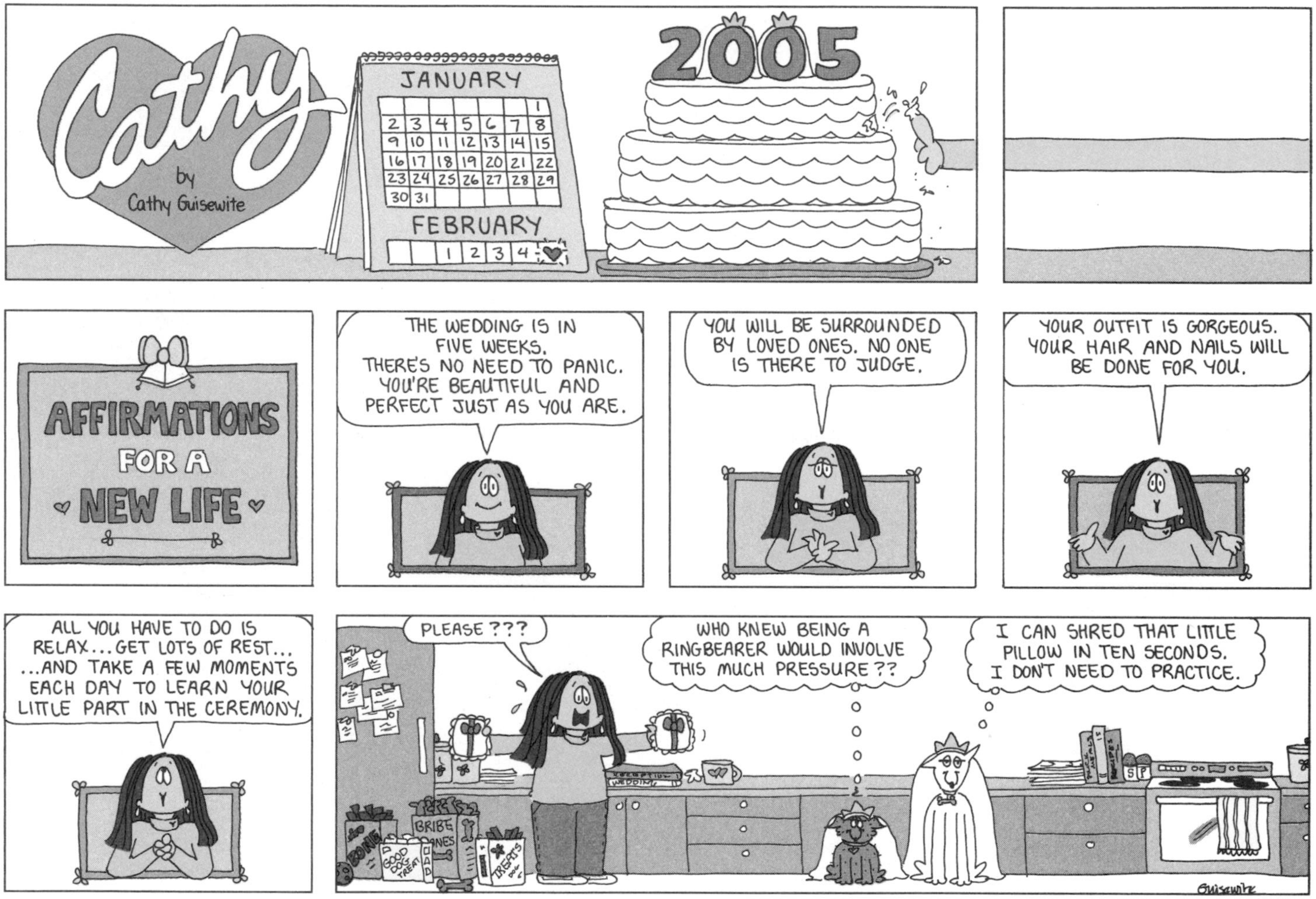
Cathy
by
Cathy Guisewite
JANUARY
FEBRUARY
2005
AFFIRMATIONS FOR A NEW LIFE
THE WEDDING IS IN FIVE WEEKS. THERE'S NO NEED TO PANIC. YOU'RE BEAUTIFUL AND PERFECT JUST AS YOU ARE.
YOU WILL BE SURROUNDED BY LOVED ONES. NO ONE IS THERE TO JUDGE.
YOUR OUTFIT IS GORGEOUS. YOUR HAIR AND NAILS WILL BE DONE FOR YOU.
ALL YOU HAVE TO DO IS RELAX... GET LOTS OF REST... ...AND TAKE A FEW MOMENTS EACH DAY TO LEARN YOUR LITTLE PART IN THE CEREMONY.
PLEASE???
WHO KNEW BEING A RINGBEARER WOULD INVOLVE THIS MUCH PRESSURE??
I CAN SHRED THAT LITTLE PILLOW IN TEN SECONDS. I DON'T NEED TO PRACTICE.
GOOD DOG TREATS
Guisewite

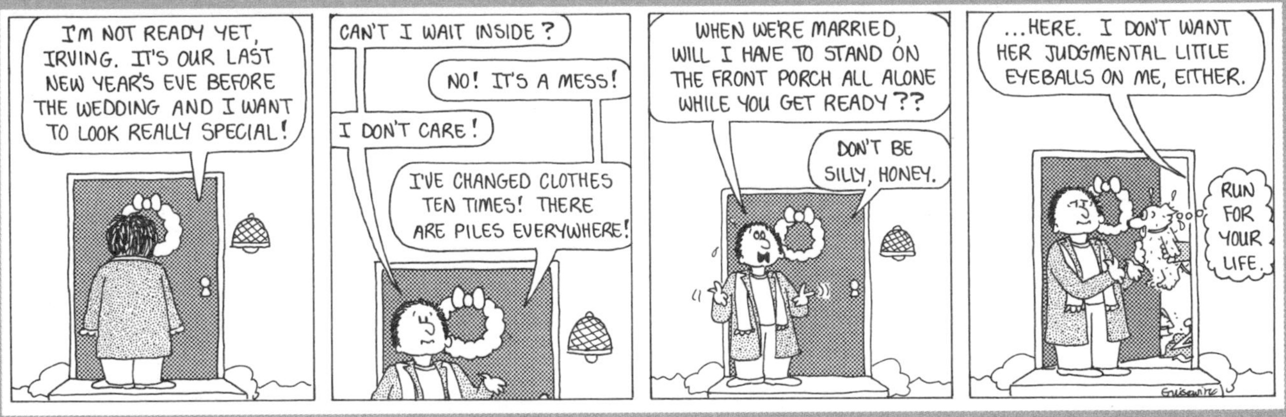
I'M NOT READY YET, IRVING. IT'S OUR LAST NEW YEAR'S EVE BEFORE THE WEDDING AND I WANT TO LOOK REALLY SPECIAL!
CAN'T I WAIT INSIDE?
NO! IT'S A MESS!
I DON'T CARE!
I'VE CHANGED CLOTHES TEN TIMES! THERE ARE PILES EVERYWHERE!
WHEN WE'RE MARRIED, WILL I HAVE TO STAND ON THE FRONT PORCH ALL ALONE WHILE YOU GET READY??
DON'T BE SILLY, HONEY.
...HERE. I DON'T WANT HER JUDGMENTAL LITTLE EYEBALLS ON ME, EITHER.
RUN FOR YOUR LIFE.
GUISEWITE

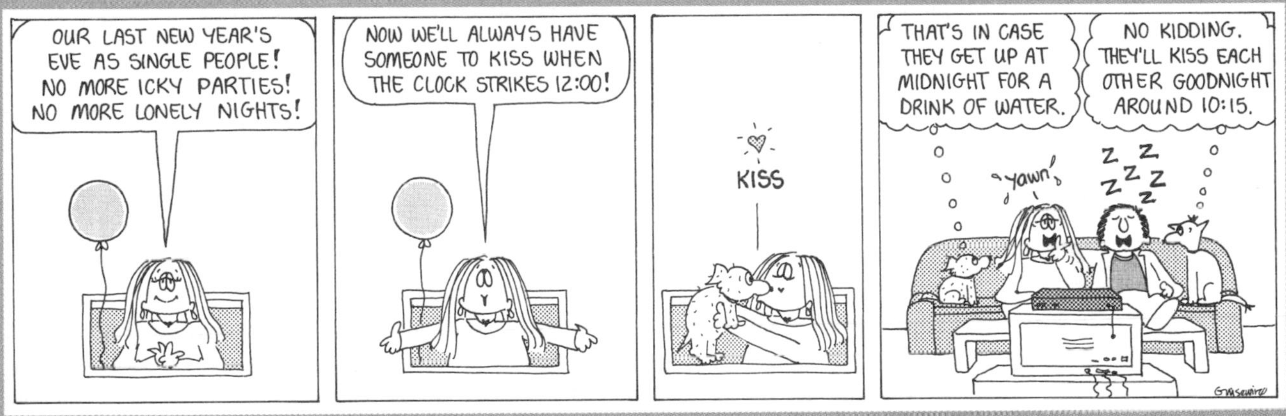
OUR LAST NEW YEAR'S EVE AS SINGLE PEOPLE! NO MORE ICKY PARTIES! NO MORE LONELY NIGHTS!
NOW WE'LL ALWAYS HAVE SOMEONE TO KISS WHEN THE CLOCK STRIKES 12:00!
KISS
THAT'S IN CASE THEY GET UP AT MIDNIGHT FOR A DRINK OF WATER.
NO KIDDING. THEY'LL KISS EACH OTHER GOODNIGHT AROUND 10:15.
yawn
Z Z Z Z Z Z
GUISEWITE

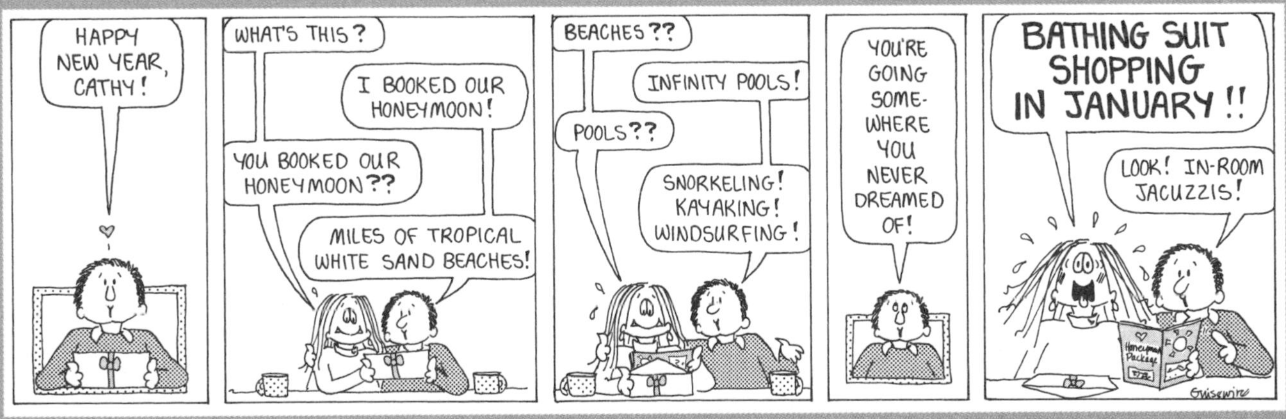
HAPPY NEW YEAR, CATHY!
WHAT'S THIS?
I BOOKED OUR HONEYMOON!
YOU BOOKED OUR HONEYMOON??
MILES OF TROPICAL WHITE SAND BEACHES!
BEACHES??
INFINITY POOLS!
POOLS??
SNORKELING! KAYAKING! WINDSURFING!
YOU'RE GOING SOME-WHERE YOU NEVER DREAMED OF!
BATHING SUIT SHOPPING IN JANUARY!!
LOOK! IN-ROOM JACUZZIS!
GUISEWITE

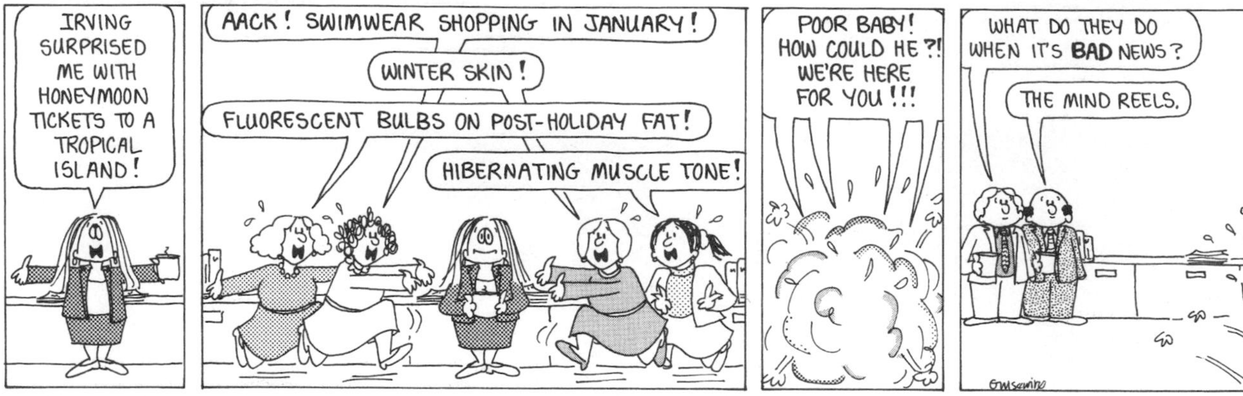
IRVING SURPRISED ME WITH HONEYMOON TICKETS TO A TROPICAL ISLAND!
AACK! SWIMWEAR SHOPPING IN JANUARY!
WINTER SKIN!
FLUORESCENT BULBS ON POST-HOLIDAY FAT!
HIBERNATING MUSCLE TONE!
POOR BABY! HOW COULD HE?! WE'RE HERE FOR YOU!!!
WHAT DO THEY DO WHEN IT'S **BAD** NEWS?
THE MIND REELS.

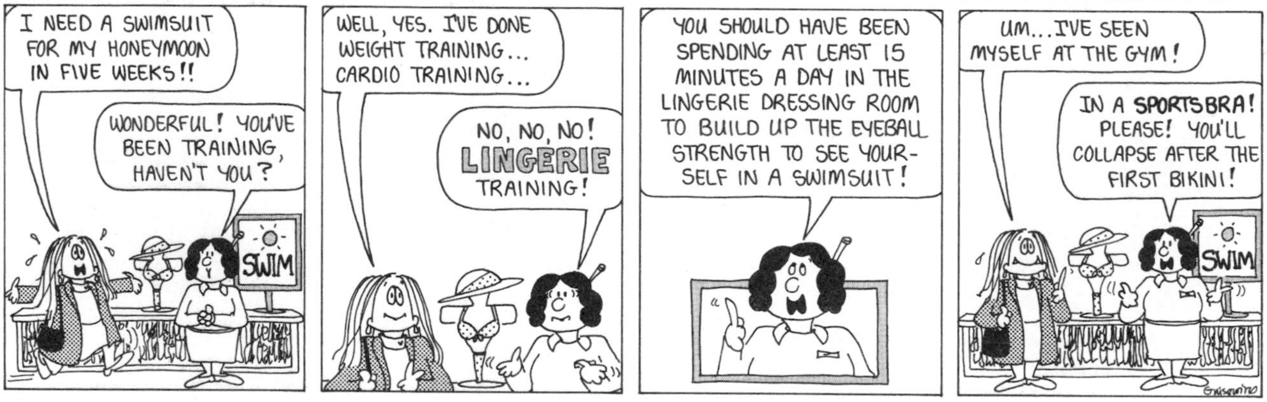
I NEED A SWIMSUIT FOR MY HONEYMOON IN FIVE WEEKS!!
WONDERFUL! YOU'VE BEEN TRAINING, HAVEN'T YOU?
SWIM
WELL, YES. I'VE DONE WEIGHT TRAINING... CARDIO TRAINING...
NO, NO, NO! **LINGERIE** TRAINING!
YOU SHOULD HAVE BEEN SPENDING AT LEAST 15 MINUTES A DAY IN THE LINGERIE DRESSING ROOM TO BUILD UP THE EYEBALL STRENGTH TO SEE YOURSELF IN A SWIMSUIT!
UM... I'VE SEEN MYSELF AT THE GYM!
IN A **SPORTS BRA**! PLEASE! YOU'LL COLLAPSE AFTER THE FIRST BIKINI!
SWIM

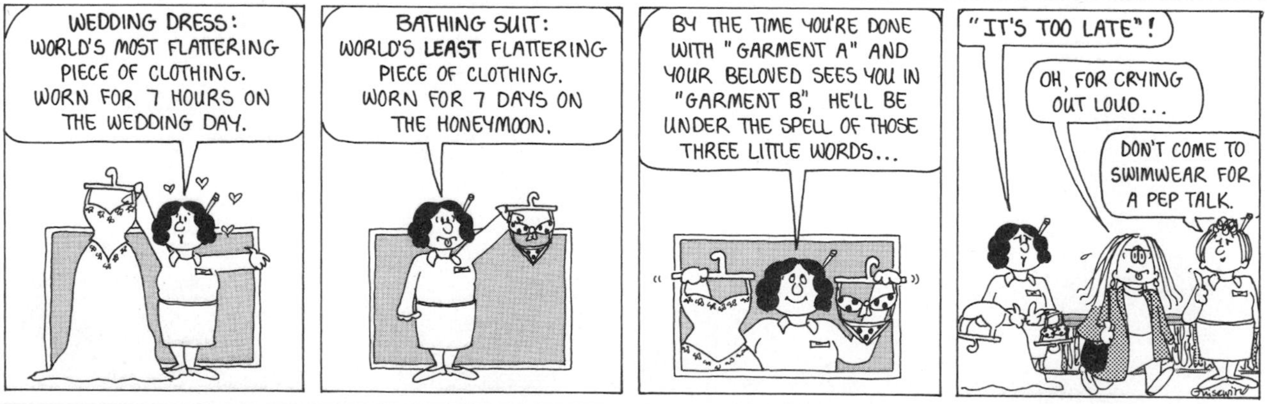
WEDDING DRESS: WORLD'S MOST FLATTERING PIECE OF CLOTHING. WORN FOR 7 HOURS ON THE WEDDING DAY.
BATHING SUIT: WORLD'S **LEAST** FLATTERING PIECE OF CLOTHING. WORN FOR 7 DAYS ON THE HONEYMOON.
BY THE TIME YOU'RE DONE WITH "GARMENT A" AND YOUR BELOVED SEES YOU IN "GARMENT B", HE'LL BE UNDER THE SPELL OF THOSE THREE LITTLE WORDS...
"IT'S TOO LATE"!
OH, FOR CRYING OUT LOUD...
DON'T COME TO SWIMWEAR FOR A PEP TALK.

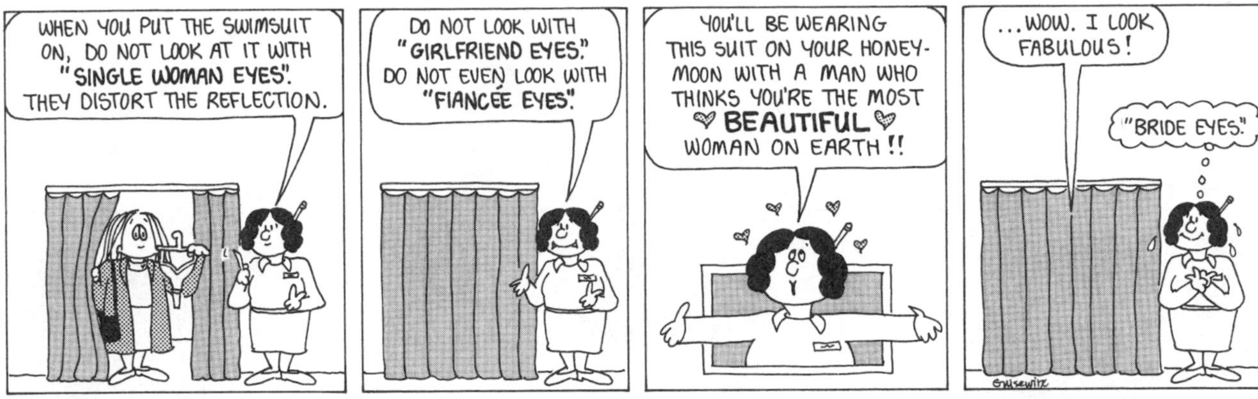
WHEN YOU PUT THE SWIMSUIT ON, DO NOT LOOK AT IT WITH "SINGLE WOMAN EYES". THEY DISTORT THE REFLECTION.
DO NOT LOOK WITH "GIRLFRIEND EYES." DO NOT EVEN LOOK WITH "FIANCÉE EYES."
YOU'LL BE WEARING THIS SUIT ON YOUR HONEYMOON WITH A MAN WHO THINKS YOU'RE THE MOST BEAUTIFUL WOMAN ON EARTH!!
...WOW. I LOOK FABULOUS!
"BRIDE EYES."

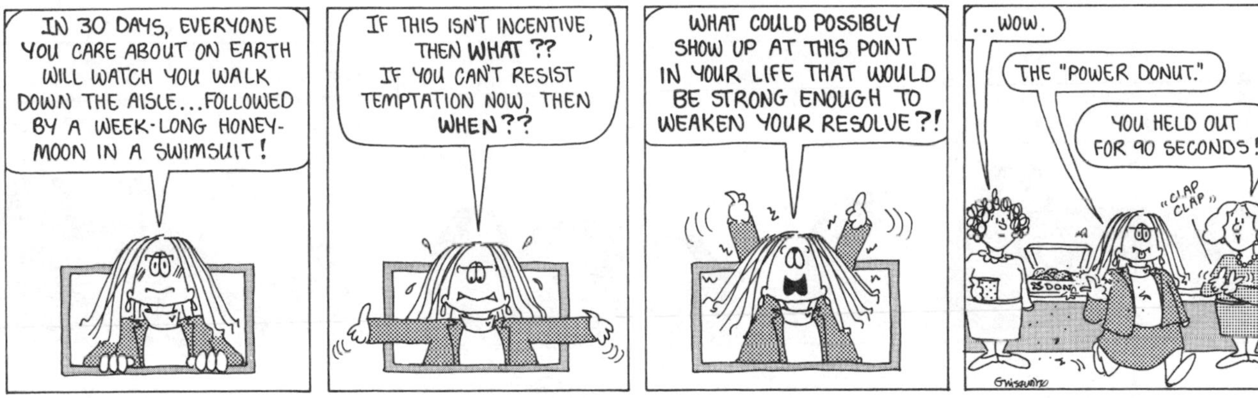
IN 30 DAYS, EVERYONE YOU CARE ABOUT ON EARTH WILL WATCH YOU WALK DOWN THE AISLE...FOLLOWED BY A WEEK-LONG HONEYMOON IN A SWIMSUIT!
IF THIS ISN'T INCENTIVE, THEN WHAT?? IF YOU CAN'T RESIST TEMPTATION NOW, THEN WHEN??
WHAT COULD POSSIBLY SHOW UP AT THIS POINT IN YOUR LIFE THAT WOULD BE STRONG ENOUGH TO WEAKEN YOUR RESOLVE?!
...WOW.
THE "POWER DONUT."
"CLAP CLAP"
YOU HELD OUT FOR 90 SECONDS!

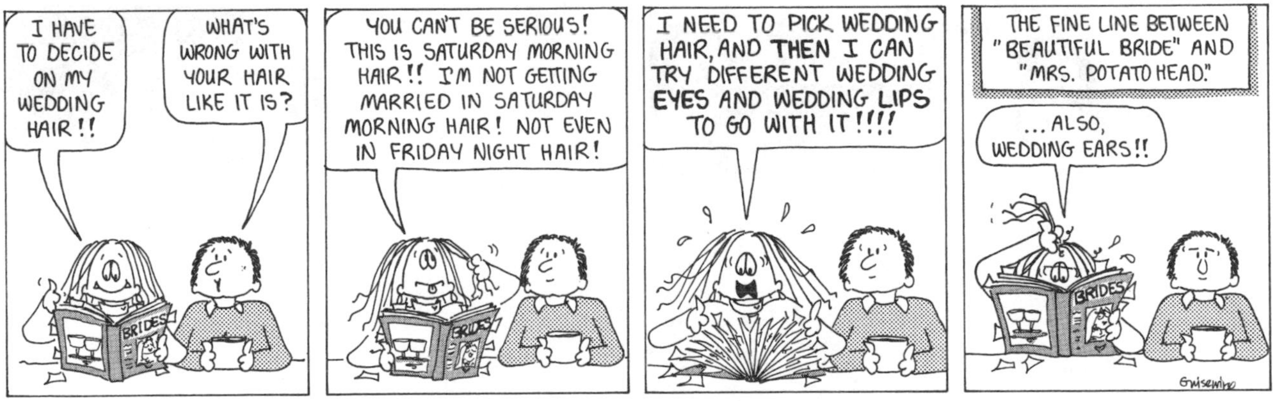
I HAVE TO DECIDE ON MY WEDDING HAIR!!
WHAT'S WRONG WITH YOUR HAIR LIKE IT IS?
BRIDES
YOU CAN'T BE SERIOUS! THIS IS SATURDAY MORNING HAIR!! I'M NOT GETTING MARRIED IN SATURDAY MORNING HAIR! NOT EVEN IN FRIDAY NIGHT HAIR!
I NEED TO PICK WEDDING HAIR, AND THEN I CAN TRY DIFFERENT WEDDING EYES AND WEDDING LIPS TO GO WITH IT!!!!
THE FINE LINE BETWEEN "BEAUTIFUL BRIDE" AND "MRS. POTATO HEAD."
...ALSO, WEDDING EARS!!

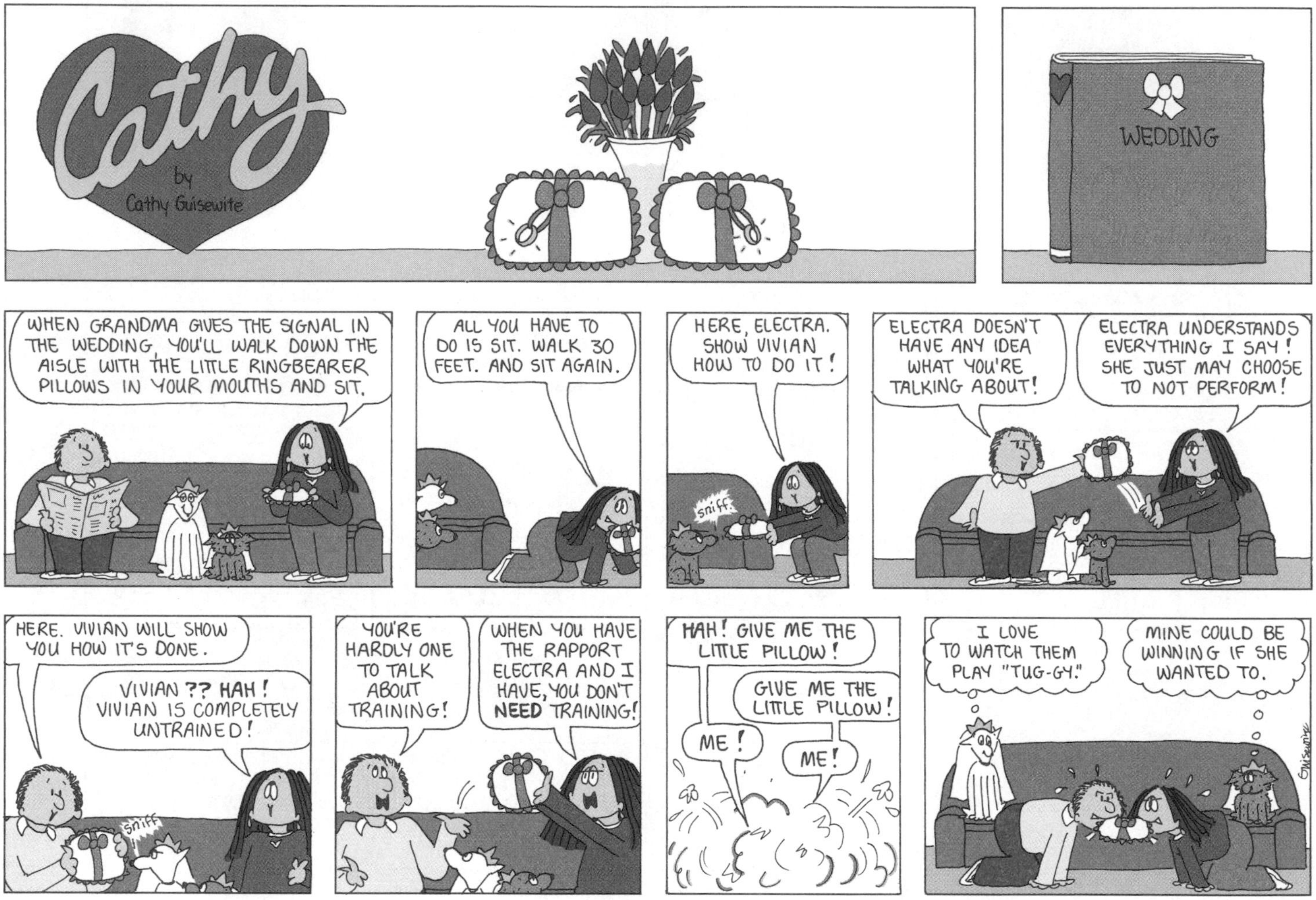

Cathy
by
Cathy Guisewite
WEDDING
WHEN GRANDMA GIVES THE SIGNAL IN THE WEDDING, YOU'LL WALK DOWN THE AISLE WITH THE LITTLE RINGBEARER PILLOWS IN YOUR MOUTHS AND SIT.
ALL YOU HAVE TO DO IS SIT. WALK 30 FEET. AND SIT AGAIN.
HERE, ELECTRA. SHOW VIVIAN HOW TO DO IT!
sniff.
ELECTRA DOESN'T HAVE ANY IDEA WHAT YOU'RE TALKING ABOUT!
ELECTRA UNDERSTANDS EVERYTHING I SAY! SHE JUST MAY CHOOSE TO NOT PERFORM!
HERE. VIVIAN WILL SHOW YOU HOW IT'S DONE.
sniff
VIVIAN ?? HAH! VIVIAN IS COMPLETELY UNTRAINED!
YOU'RE HARDLY ONE TO TALK ABOUT TRAINING!
WHEN YOU HAVE THE RAPPORT ELECTRA AND I HAVE, YOU DON'T NEED TRAINING!
HAH! GIVE ME THE LITTLE PILLOW!
GIVE ME THE LITTLE PILLOW!
ME!
ME!
I LOVE TO WATCH THEM PLAY "TUG-GY."
MINE COULD BE WINNING IF SHE WANTED TO.

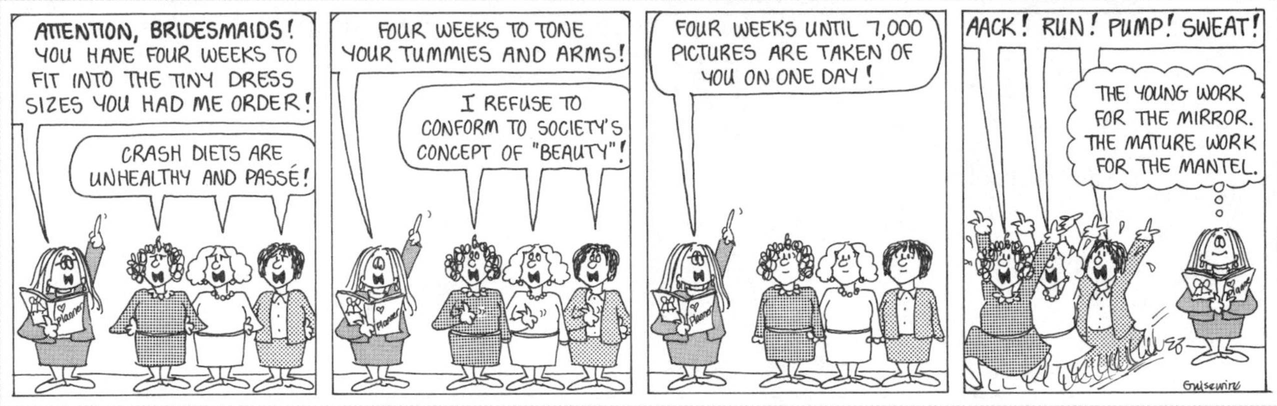
ATTENTION, BRIDESMAIDS! YOU HAVE FOUR WEEKS TO FIT INTO THE TINY DRESS SIZES YOU HAD ME ORDER!
CRASH DIETS ARE UNHEALTHY AND PASSÉ!
FOUR WEEKS TO TONE YOUR TUMMIES AND ARMS!
I REFUSE TO CONFORM TO SOCIETY'S CONCEPT OF "BEAUTY"!
FOUR WEEKS UNTIL 7,000 PICTURES ARE TAKEN OF YOU ON ONE DAY!
AACK! RUN! PUMP! SWEAT!
THE YOUNG WORK FOR THE MIRROR. THE MATURE WORK FOR THE MANTEL.

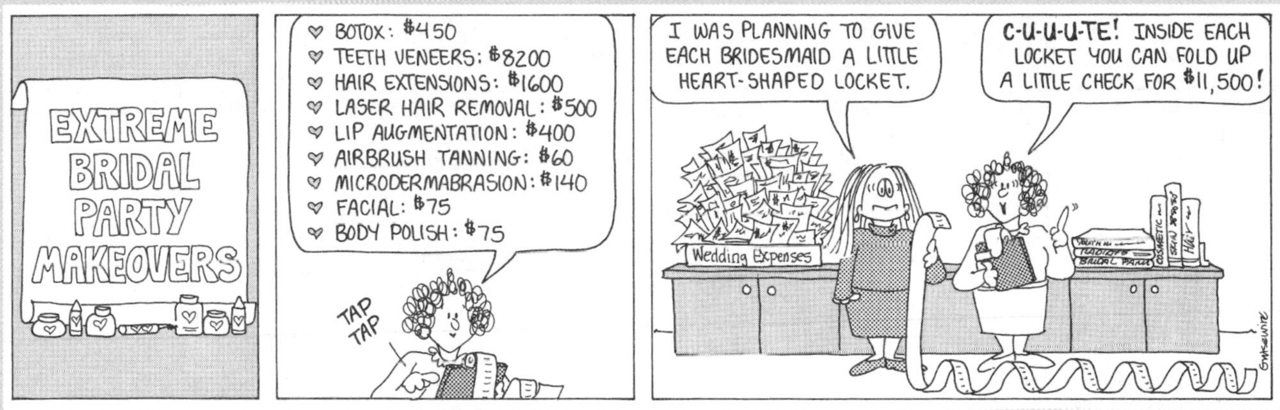
EXTREME BRIDAL PARTY MAKEOVERS
♡ BOTOX: $450
♡ TEETH VENEERS: $8200
♡ HAIR EXTENSIONS: $1600
♡ LASER HAIR REMOVAL: $500
♡ LIP AUGMENTATION: $400
♡ AIRBRUSH TANNING: $60
♡ MICRODERMABRASION: $140
♡ FACIAL: $75
♡ BODY POLISH: $75
TAP TAP
I WAS PLANNING TO GIVE EACH BRIDESMAID A LITTLE HEART-SHAPED LOCKET.
C-U-U-U-TE! INSIDE EACH LOCKET YOU CAN FOLD UP A LITTLE CHECK FOR $11,500!
Wedding Expenses

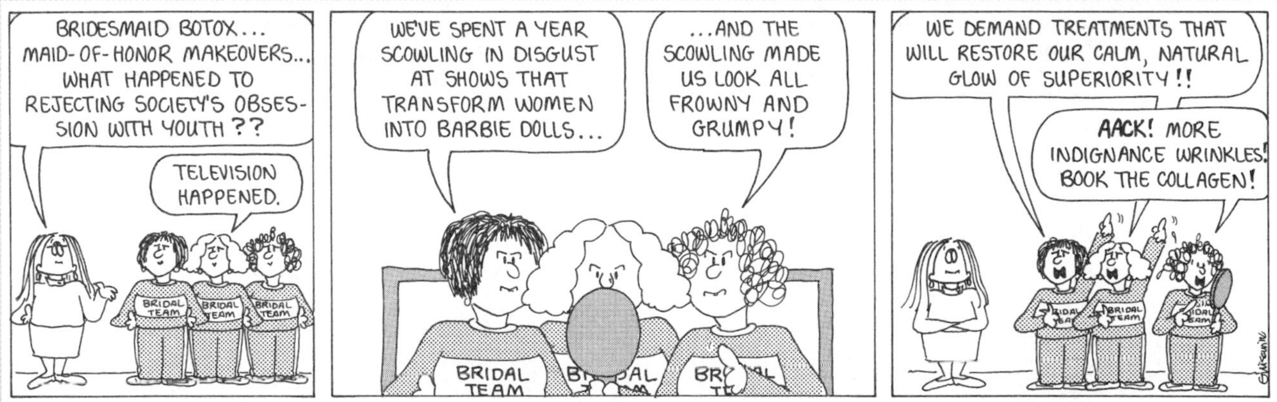
BRIDESMAID BOTOX... MAID-OF-HONOR MAKEOVERS... WHAT HAPPENED TO REJECTING SOCIETY'S OBSESSION WITH YOUTH??
TELEVISION HAPPENED.
BRIDAL TEAM
WE'VE SPENT A YEAR SCOWLING IN DISGUST AT SHOWS THAT TRANSFORM WOMEN INTO BARBIE DOLLS...
...AND THE SCOWLING MADE US LOOK ALL FROWNY AND GRUMPY!
WE DEMAND TREATMENTS THAT WILL RESTORE OUR CALM, NATURAL GLOW OF SUPERIORITY!!
AACK! MORE INDIGNANCE WRINKLES! BOOK THE COLLAGEN!

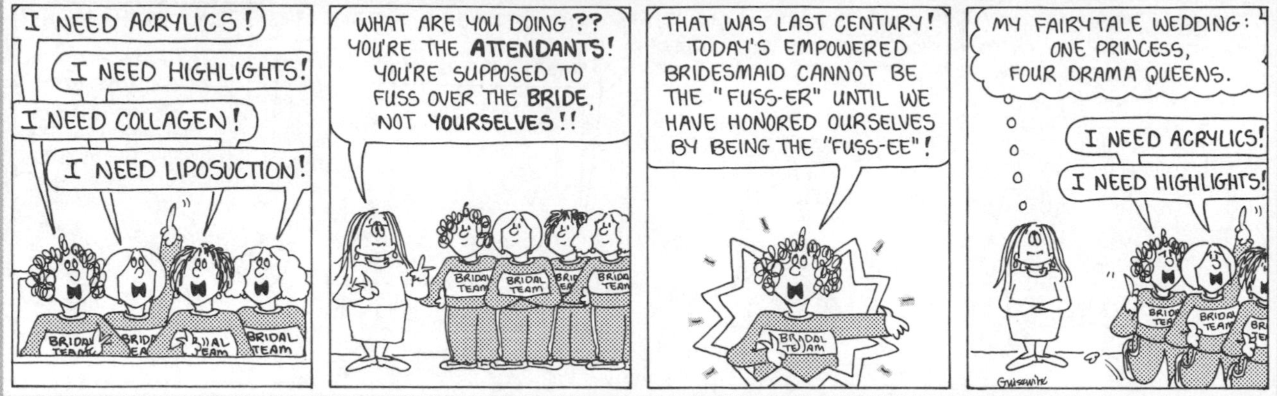
I NEED ACRYLICS!
I NEED HIGHLIGHTS!
I NEED COLLAGEN!
I NEED LIPOSUCTION!
WHAT ARE YOU DOING?? YOU'RE THE ATTENDANTS! YOU'RE SUPPOSED TO FUSS OVER THE BRIDE, NOT YOURSELVES!!
THAT WAS LAST CENTURY! TODAY'S EMPOWERED BRIDESMAID CANNOT BE THE "FUSS-ER" UNTIL WE HAVE HONORED OURSELVES BY BEING THE "FUSS-EE"!
MY FAIRYTALE WEDDING: ONE PRINCESS, FOUR DRAMA QUEENS.
I NEED ACRYLICS!
I NEED HIGHLIGHTS!

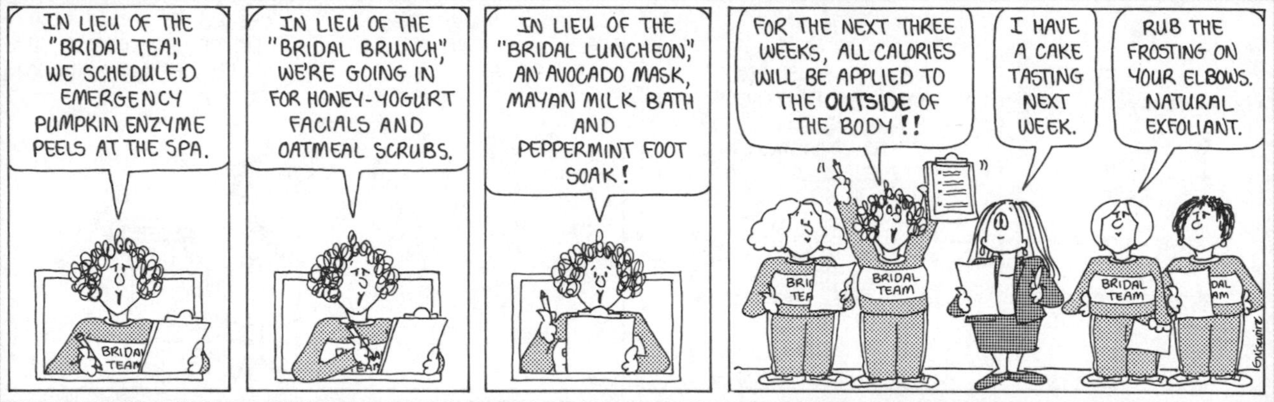
IN LIEU OF THE "BRIDAL TEA," WE SCHEDULED EMERGENCY PUMPKIN ENZYME PEELS AT THE SPA.
IN LIEU OF THE "BRIDAL BRUNCH," WE'RE GOING IN FOR HONEY-YOGURT FACIALS AND OATMEAL SCRUBS.
IN LIEU OF THE "BRIDAL LUNCHEON," AN AVOCADO MASK, MAYAN MILK BATH AND PEPPERMINT FOOT SOAK!
FOR THE NEXT THREE WEEKS, ALL CALORIES WILL BE APPLIED TO THE OUTSIDE OF THE BODY!!
I HAVE A CAKE TASTING NEXT WEEK.
RUB THE FROSTING ON YOUR ELBOWS. NATURAL EXFOLIANT.

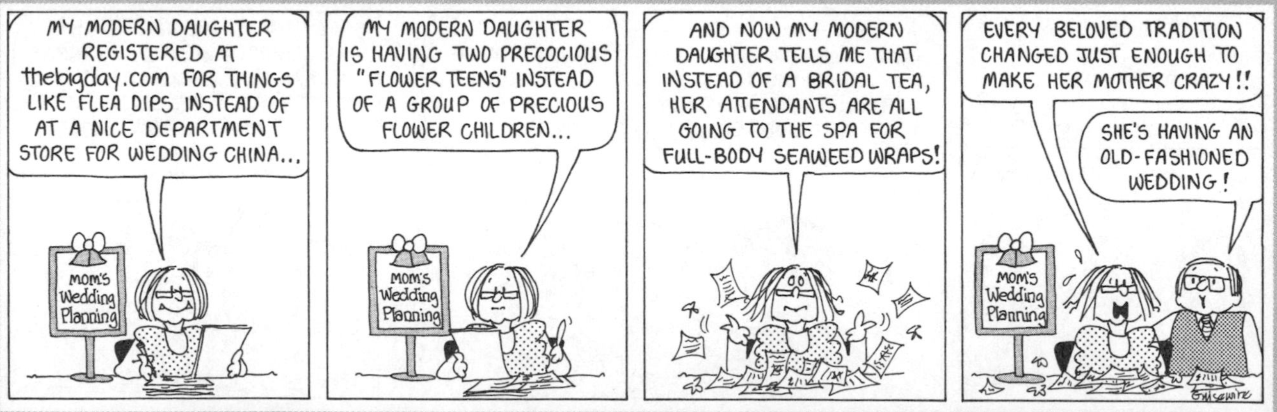
MY MODERN DAUGHTER REGISTERED AT thebigday.com FOR THINGS LIKE FLEA DIPS INSTEAD OF AT A NICE DEPARTMENT STORE FOR WEDDING CHINA...
Mom's Wedding Planning
MY MODERN DAUGHTER IS HAVING TWO PRECOCIOUS "FLOWER TEENS" INSTEAD OF A GROUP OF PRECIOUS FLOWER CHILDREN...
Mom's Wedding Planning
AND NOW MY MODERN DAUGHTER TELLS ME THAT INSTEAD OF A BRIDAL TEA, HER ATTENDANTS ARE ALL GOING TO THE SPA FOR FULL-BODY SEAWEED WRAPS!
EVERY BELOVED TRADITION CHANGED JUST ENOUGH TO MAKE HER MOTHER CRAZY!!
SHE'S HAVING AN OLD-FASHIONED WEDDING!
Mom's Wedding Planning

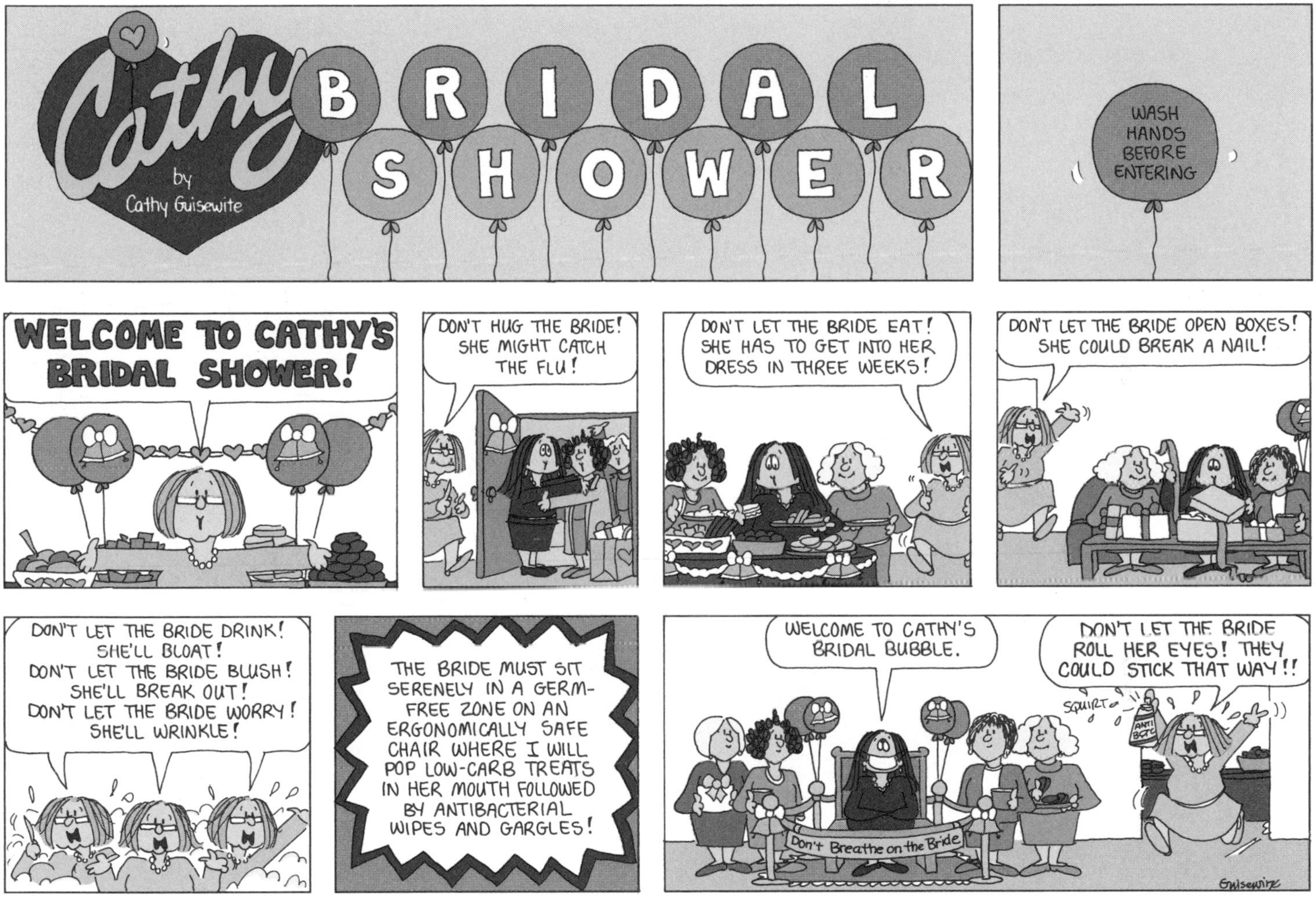
Cathy
by Cathy Guisewite
BRIDAL SHOWER
WASH HANDS BEFORE ENTERING
WELCOME TO CATHY'S BRIDAL SHOWER!
DON'T HUG THE BRIDE! SHE MIGHT CATCH THE FLU!
DON'T LET THE BRIDE EAT! SHE HAS TO GET INTO HER DRESS IN THREE WEEKS!
DON'T LET THE BRIDE OPEN BOXES! SHE COULD BREAK A NAIL!
DON'T LET THE BRIDE DRINK! SHE'LL BLOAT! DON'T LET THE BRIDE BLUSH! SHE'LL BREAK OUT! DON'T LET THE BRIDE WORRY! SHE'LL WRINKLE!
THE BRIDE MUST SIT SERENELY IN A GERM-FREE ZONE ON AN ERGONOMICALLY SAFE CHAIR WHERE I WILL POP LOW-CARB TREATS IN HER MOUTH FOLLOWED BY ANTIBACTERIAL WIPES AND GARGLES!
WELCOME TO CATHY'S BRIDAL BUBBLE.
DON'T LET THE BRIDE ROLL HER EYES! THEY COULD STICK THAT WAY!!
SQUIRT
Don't Breathe on the Bride
Guisewite

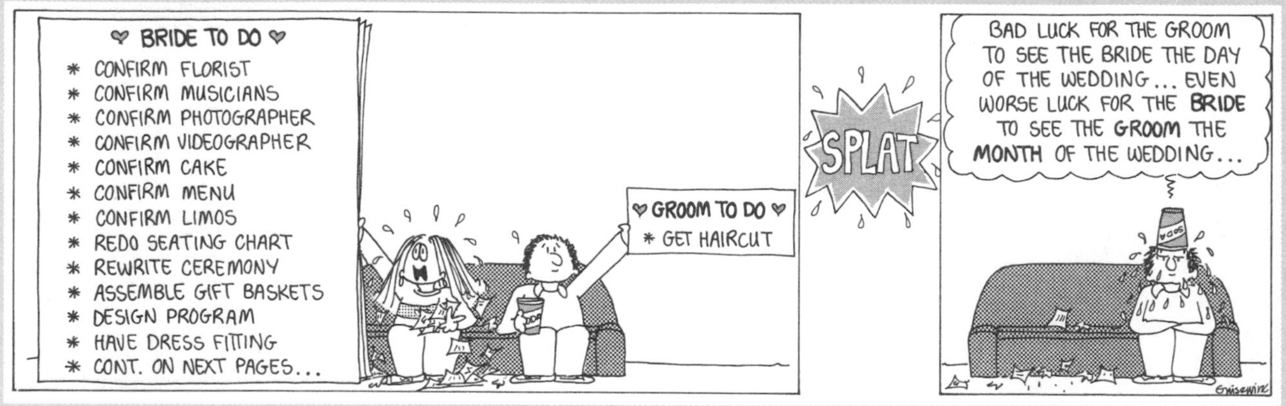
♥ BRIDE TO DO ♥
* CONFIRM FLORIST
* CONFIRM MUSICIANS
* CONFIRM PHOTOGRAPHER
* CONFIRM VIDEOGRAPHER
* CONFIRM CAKE
* CONFIRM MENU
* CONFIRM LIMOS
* REDO SEATING CHART
* REWRITE CEREMONY
* ASSEMBLE GIFT BASKETS
* DESIGN PROGRAM
* HAVE DRESS FITTING
* CONT. ON NEXT PAGES...
♥ GROOM TO DO ♥
* GET HAIRCUT
SPLAT
BAD LUCK FOR THE GROOM TO SEE THE BRIDE THE DAY OF THE WEDDING... EVEN WORSE LUCK FOR THE BRIDE TO SEE THE GROOM THE MONTH OF THE WEDDING...

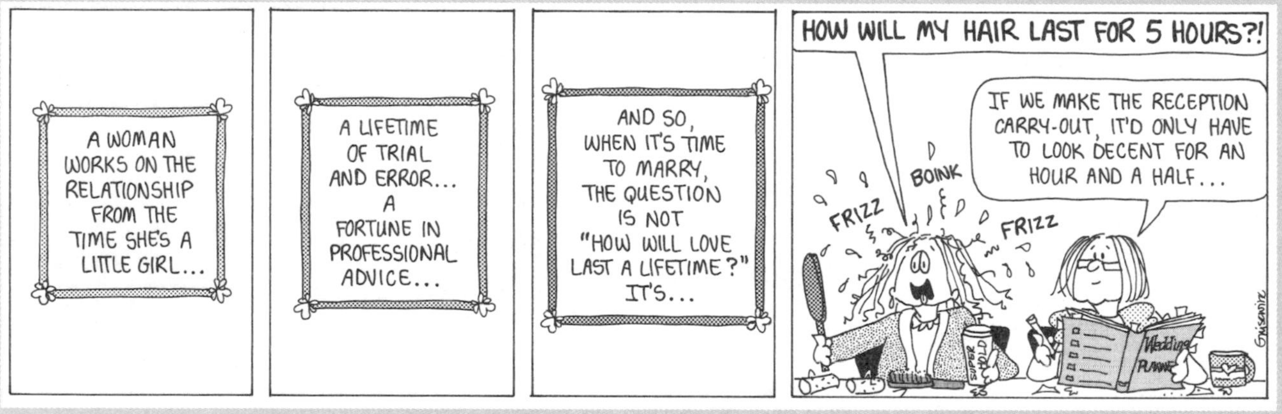
A WOMAN WORKS ON THE RELATIONSHIP FROM THE TIME SHE'S A LITTLE GIRL...
A LIFETIME OF TRIAL AND ERROR... A FORTUNE IN PROFESSIONAL ADVICE...
AND SO, WHEN IT'S TIME TO MARRY, THE QUESTION IS NOT "HOW WILL LOVE LAST A LIFETIME?" IT'S...
HOW WILL MY HAIR LAST FOR 5 HOURS?!
FRIZZ
BOINK
FRIZZ
IF WE MAKE THE RECEPTION CARRY-OUT, IT'D ONLY HAVE TO LOOK DECENT FOR AN HOUR AND A HALF...

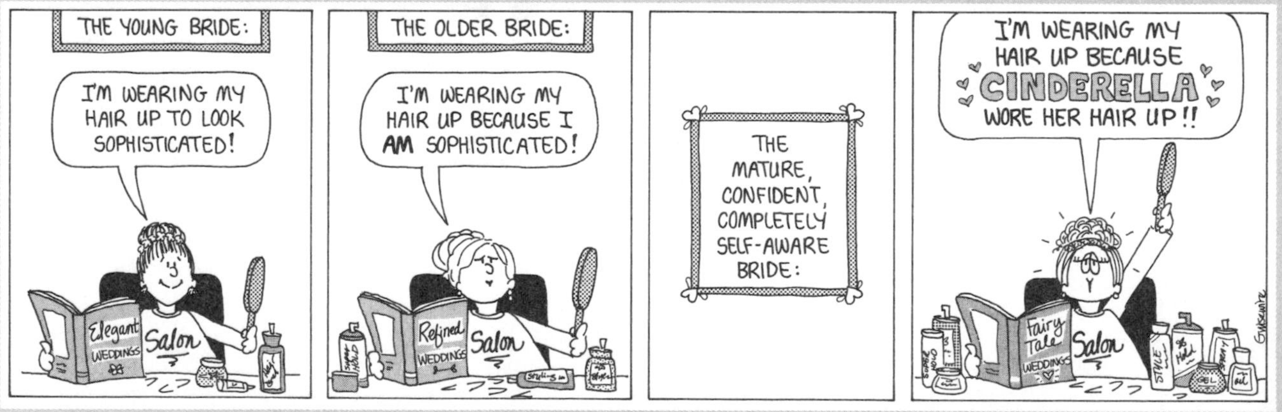
THE YOUNG BRIDE:
I'M WEARING MY HAIR UP TO LOOK SOPHISTICATED!
Elegant WEDDINGS
Salon
THE OLDER BRIDE:
I'M WEARING MY HAIR UP BECAUSE I AM SOPHISTICATED!
Refined WEDDINGS
Salon
THE MATURE, CONFIDENT, COMPLETELY SELF-AWARE BRIDE:
I'M WEARING MY HAIR UP BECAUSE CINDERELLA WORE HER HAIR UP!!
Fairy Tale WEDDINGS
Salon

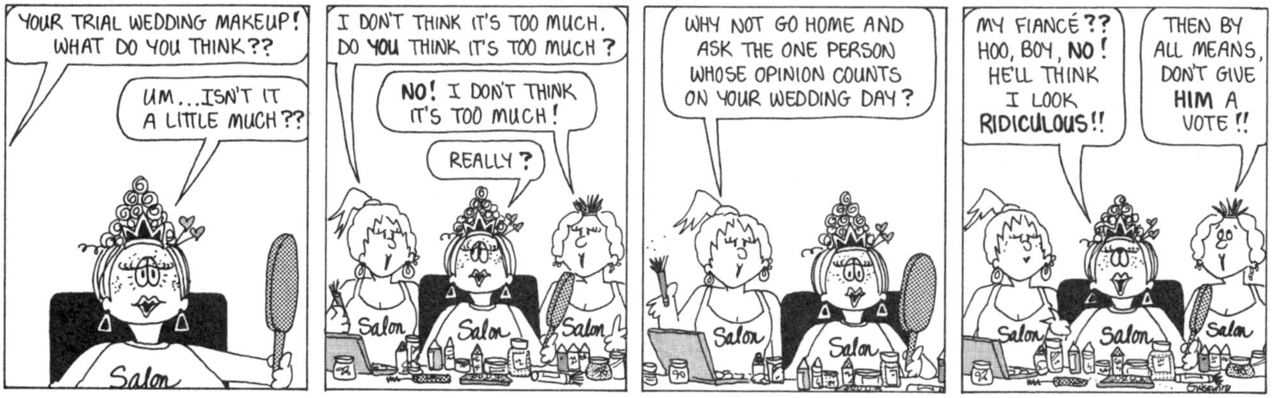
YOUR TRIAL WEDDING MAKEUP! WHAT DO YOU THINK??
UM...ISN'T IT A LITTLE MUCH??
Salon
I DON'T THINK IT'S TOO MUCH. DO **YOU** THINK IT'S TOO MUCH?
NO! I DON'T THINK IT'S TOO MUCH!
REALLY?
Salon
WHY NOT GO HOME AND ASK THE ONE PERSON WHOSE OPINION COUNTS ON YOUR WEDDING DAY?
Salon
MY FIANCÉ?? HOO, BOY, **NO**! HE'LL THINK I LOOK **RIDICULOUS**!!
THEN BY ALL MEANS, DON'T GIVE **HIM** A VOTE!!
Salon

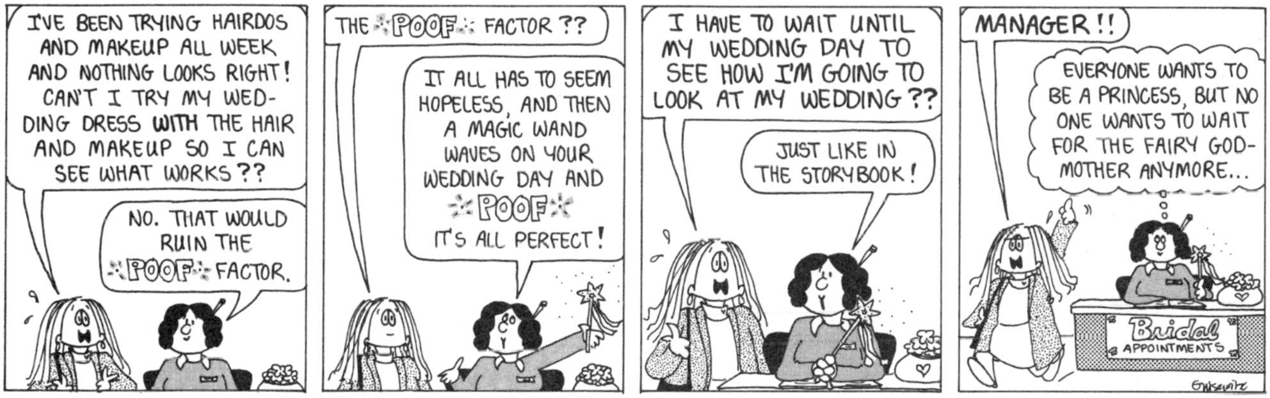
I'VE BEEN TRYING HAIRDOS AND MAKEUP ALL WEEK AND NOTHING LOOKS RIGHT! CAN'T I TRY MY WEDDING DRESS **WITH** THE HAIR AND MAKEUP SO I CAN SEE WHAT WORKS??
NO. THAT WOULD RUIN THE POOF FACTOR.
THE POOF FACTOR??
IT ALL HAS TO SEEM HOPELESS, AND THEN A MAGIC WAND WAVES ON YOUR WEDDING DAY AND POOF IT'S ALL PERFECT!
I HAVE TO WAIT UNTIL MY WEDDING DAY TO SEE HOW I'M GOING TO LOOK AT MY WEDDING??
JUST LIKE IN THE STORYBOOK!
MANAGER!!
EVERYONE WANTS TO BE A PRINCESS, BUT NO ONE WANTS TO WAIT FOR THE FAIRY GODMOTHER ANYMORE...
Bridal APPOINTMENTS

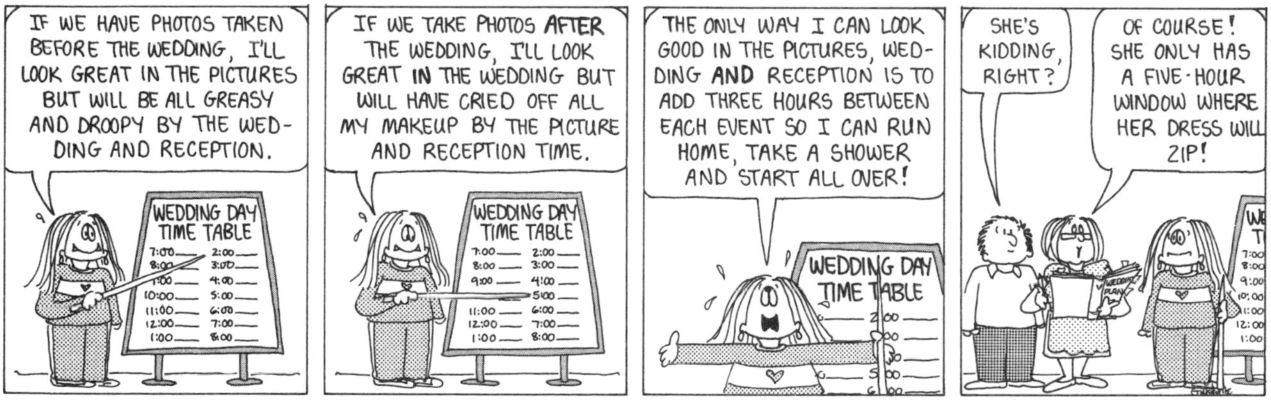
IF WE HAVE PHOTOS TAKEN BEFORE THE WEDDING, I'LL LOOK GREAT IN THE PICTURES BUT WILL BE ALL GREASY AND DROOPY BY THE WEDDING AND RECEPTION.
WEDDING DAY TIME TABLE
IF WE TAKE PHOTOS **AFTER** THE WEDDING, I'LL LOOK GREAT **IN** THE WEDDING BUT WILL HAVE CRIED OFF ALL MY MAKEUP BY THE PICTURE AND RECEPTION TIME.
WEDDING DAY TIME TABLE
THE ONLY WAY I CAN LOOK GOOD IN THE PICTURES, WEDDING **AND** RECEPTION IS TO ADD THREE HOURS BETWEEN EACH EVENT SO I CAN RUN HOME, TAKE A SHOWER AND START ALL OVER!
WEDDING DAY TIME TABLE
SHE'S KIDDING, RIGHT?
OF COURSE! SHE ONLY HAS A FIVE-HOUR WINDOW WHERE HER DRESS WILL ZIP!

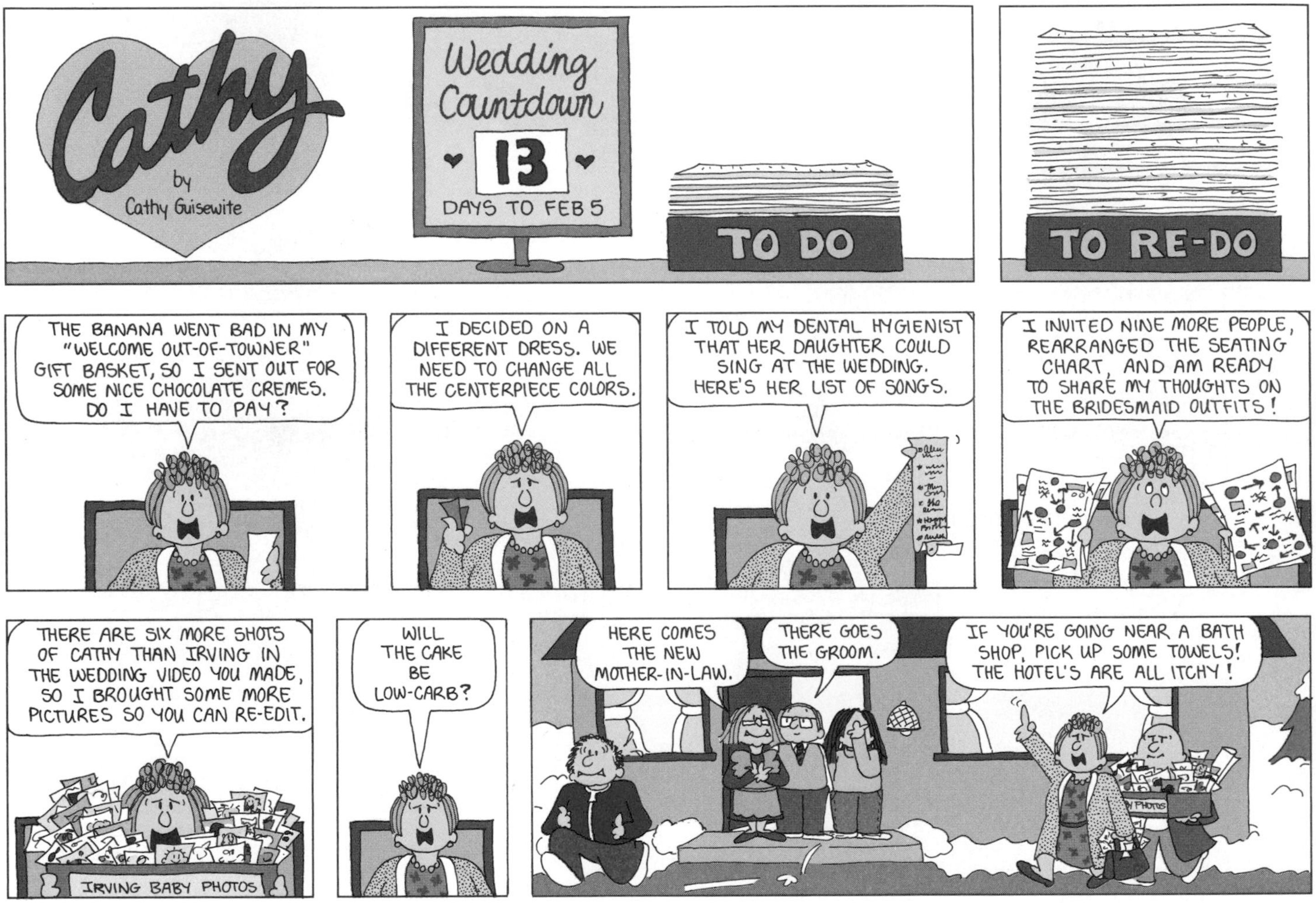
Cathy
by
Cathy Guisewite
Wedding Countdown
13
DAYS TO FEB 5
TO DO
TO RE-DO
THE BANANA WENT BAD IN MY "WELCOME OUT-OF-TOWNER" GIFT BASKET, SO I SENT OUT FOR SOME NICE CHOCOLATE CREMES. DO I HAVE TO PAY?
I DECIDED ON A DIFFERENT DRESS. WE NEED TO CHANGE ALL THE CENTERPIECE COLORS.
I TOLD MY DENTAL HYGIENIST THAT HER DAUGHTER COULD SING AT THE WEDDING. HERE'S HER LIST OF SONGS.
I INVITED NINE MORE PEOPLE, REARRANGED THE SEATING CHART, AND AM READY TO SHARE MY THOUGHTS ON THE BRIDESMAID OUTFITS!
THERE ARE SIX MORE SHOTS OF CATHY THAN IRVING IN THE WEDDING VIDEO YOU MADE, SO I BROUGHT SOME MORE PICTURES SO YOU CAN RE-EDIT.
IRVING BABY PHOTOS
WILL THE CAKE BE LOW-CARB?
HERE COMES THE NEW MOTHER-IN-LAW.
THERE GOES THE GROOM.
IF YOU'RE GOING NEAR A BATH SHOP, PICK UP SOME TOWELS! THE HOTEL'S ARE ALL ITCHY!

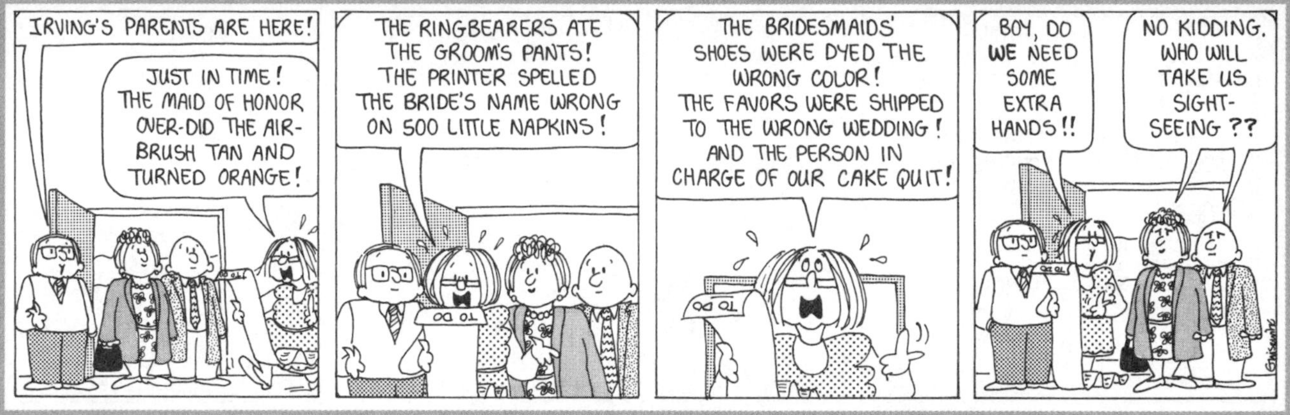
IRVING'S PARENTS ARE HERE!
JUST IN TIME! THE MAID OF HONOR OVER-DID THE AIR-BRUSH TAN AND TURNED ORANGE!
THE RINGBEARERS ATE THE GROOM'S PANTS! THE PRINTER SPELLED THE BRIDE'S NAME WRONG ON 500 LITTLE NAPKINS!
TO DO
THE BRIDESMAIDS' SHOES WERE DYED THE WRONG COLOR! THE FAVORS WERE SHIPPED TO THE WRONG WEDDING! AND THE PERSON IN CHARGE OF OUR CAKE QUIT!
BOY, DO WE NEED SOME EXTRA HANDS!!
NO KIDDING. WHO WILL TAKE US SIGHT-SEEING??

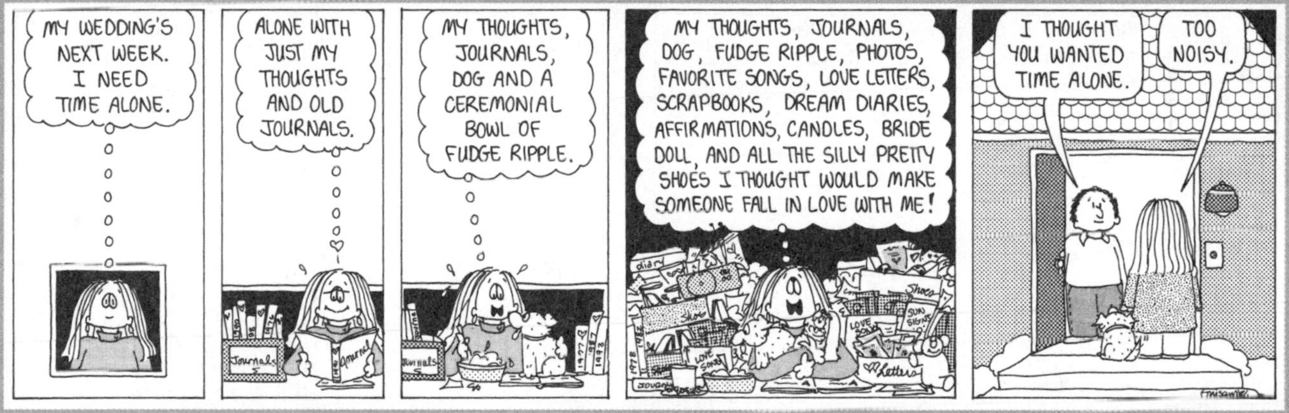
MY WEDDING'S NEXT WEEK. I NEED TIME ALONE.
ALONE WITH JUST MY THOUGHTS AND OLD JOURNALS.
Journals
MY THOUGHTS, JOURNALS, DOG AND A CEREMONIAL BOWL OF FUDGE RIPPLE.
MY THOUGHTS, JOURNALS, DOG, FUDGE RIPPLE, PHOTOS, FAVORITE SONGS, LOVE LETTERS, SCRAPBOOKS, DREAM DIARIES, AFFIRMATIONS, CANDLES, BRIDE DOLL, AND ALL THE SILLY PRETTY SHOES I THOUGHT WOULD MAKE SOMEONE FALL IN LOVE WITH ME!
I THOUGHT YOU WANTED TIME ALONE.
TOO NOISY.

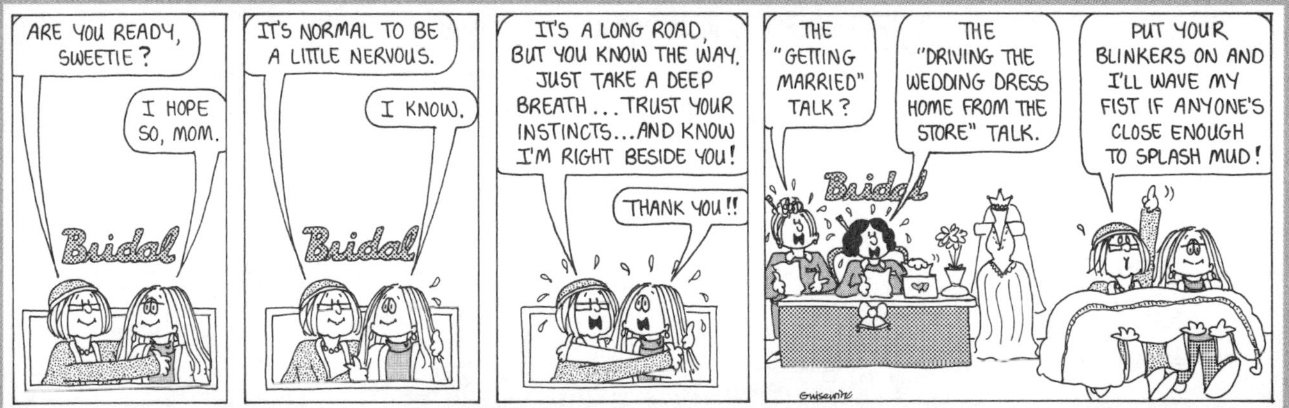
ARE YOU READY, SWEETIE?
I HOPE SO, MOM.
Bridal
IT'S NORMAL TO BE A LITTLE NERVOUS.
I KNOW.
IT'S A LONG ROAD, BUT YOU KNOW THE WAY. JUST TAKE A DEEP BREATH... TRUST YOUR INSTINCTS... AND KNOW I'M RIGHT BESIDE YOU!
THANK YOU!!
THE "GETTING MARRIED" TALK?
THE "DRIVING THE WEDDING DRESS HOME FROM THE STORE" TALK.
PUT YOUR BLINKERS ON AND I'LL WAVE MY FIST IF ANYONE'S CLOSE ENOUGH TO SPLASH MUD!

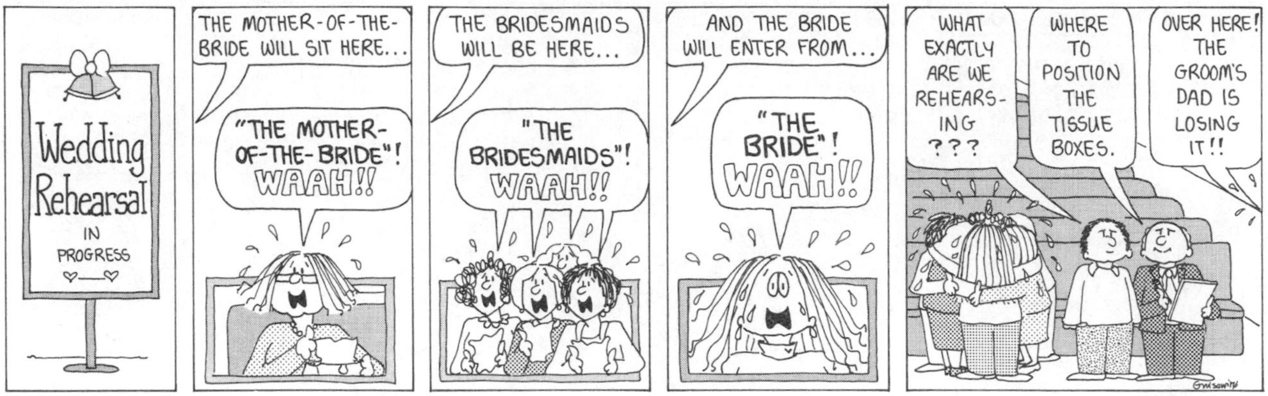
Wedding Rehearsal IN PROGRESS
THE MOTHER-OF-THE-BRIDE WILL SIT HERE...
"THE MOTHER-OF-THE-BRIDE"! WAAH!!
THE BRIDESMAIDS WILL BE HERE...
"THE BRIDESMAIDS"! WAAH!!
AND THE BRIDE WILL ENTER FROM...
"THE BRIDE"! WAAH!!
WHAT EXACTLY ARE WE REHEARSING ???
WHERE TO POSITION THE TISSUE BOXES.
OVER HERE! THE GROOM'S DAD IS LOSING IT!!

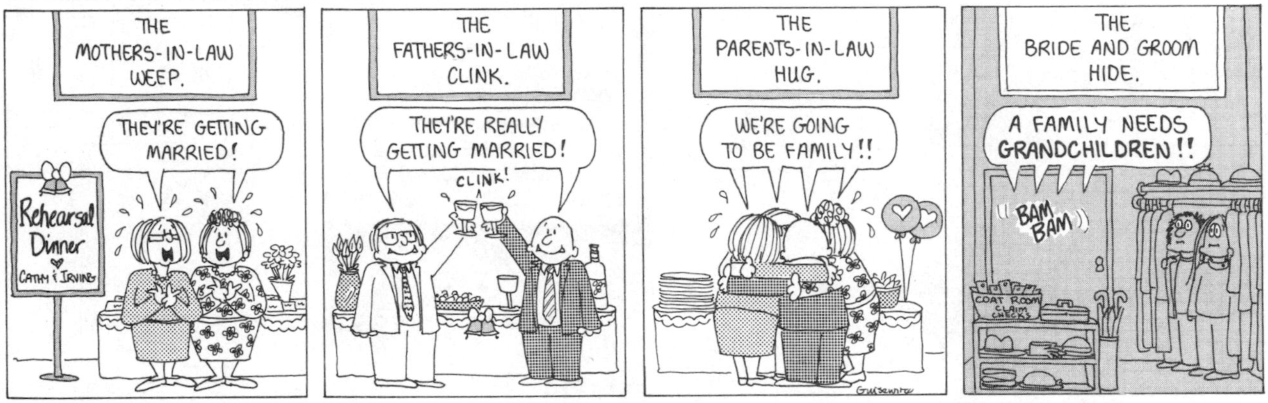
THE MOTHERS-IN-LAW WEEP.
Rehearsal Dinner CATHY & IRVING
THEY'RE GETTING MARRIED!
THE FATHERS-IN-LAW CLINK.
THEY'RE REALLY GETTING MARRIED!
CLINK!
THE PARENTS-IN-LAW HUG.
WE'RE GOING TO BE FAMILY!!
THE BRIDE AND GROOM HIDE.
A FAMILY NEEDS GRANDCHILDREN!!
BAM BAM
COAT ROOM CLAIM CHECKS

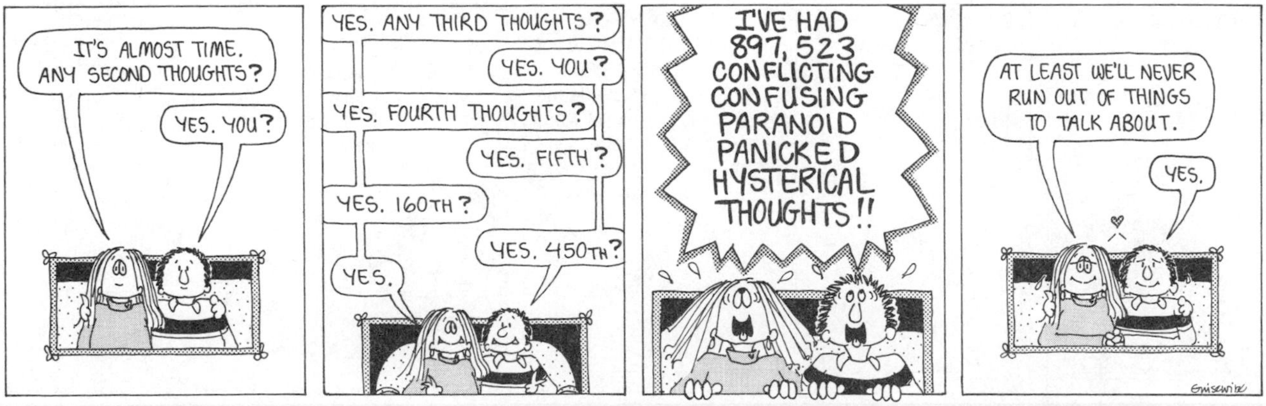
IT'S ALMOST TIME. ANY SECOND THOUGHTS?
YES. YOU?
YES. ANY THIRD THOUGHTS?
YES. YOU?
YES. FOURTH THOUGHTS?
YES. FIFTH?
YES. 160TH?
YES. 450TH?
YES.
I'VE HAD 897,523 CONFLICTING CONFUSING PARANOID PANICKED HYSTERICAL THOUGHTS!!
AT LEAST WE'LL NEVER RUN OUT OF THINGS TO TALK ABOUT.
YES.

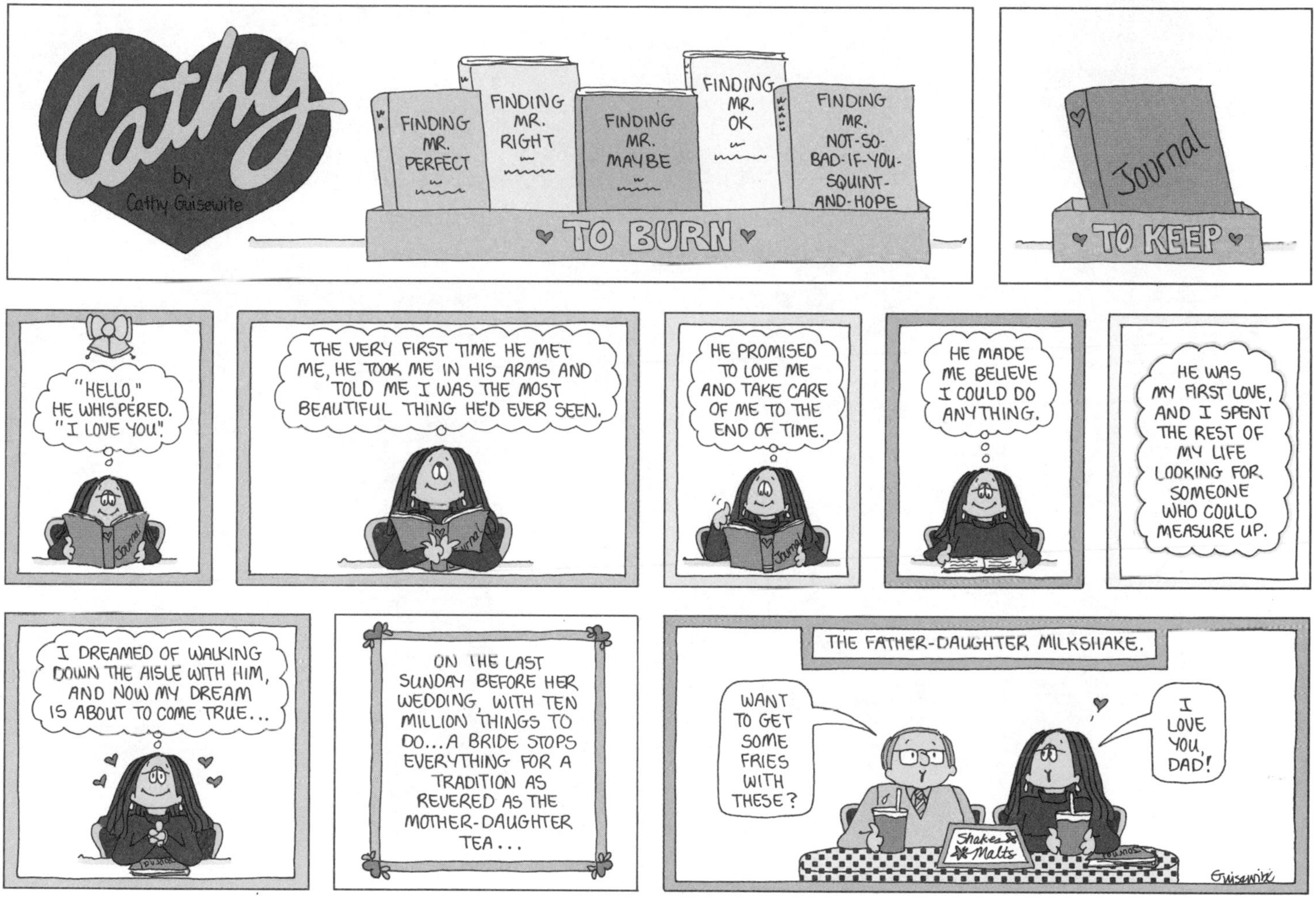
Cathy
by Cathy Guisewite
FINDING MR. PERFECT
FINDING MR. RIGHT
FINDING MR. MAYBE
FINDING MR. OK
FINDING MR. NOT-SO-BAD-IF-YOU-SQUINT-AND-HOPE
TO BURN
Journal
TO KEEP
"HELLO," HE WHISPERED. "I LOVE YOU."
THE VERY FIRST TIME HE MET ME, HE TOOK ME IN HIS ARMS AND TOLD ME I WAS THE MOST BEAUTIFUL THING HE'D EVER SEEN.
HE PROMISED TO LOVE ME AND TAKE CARE OF ME TO THE END OF TIME.
HE MADE ME BELIEVE I COULD DO ANYTHING.
HE WAS MY FIRST LOVE, AND I SPENT THE REST OF MY LIFE LOOKING FOR SOMEONE WHO COULD MEASURE UP.
I DREAMED OF WALKING DOWN THE AISLE WITH HIM, AND NOW MY DREAM IS ABOUT TO COME TRUE...
ON THE LAST SUNDAY BEFORE HER WEDDING, WITH TEN MILLION THINGS TO DO... A BRIDE STOPS EVERYTHING FOR A TRADITION AS REVERED AS THE MOTHER-DAUGHTER TEA...
THE FATHER-DAUGHTER MILKSHAKE.
WANT TO GET SOME FRIES WITH THESE?
I LOVE YOU, DAD!
Shakes Malts
Guisewite

The Wedding

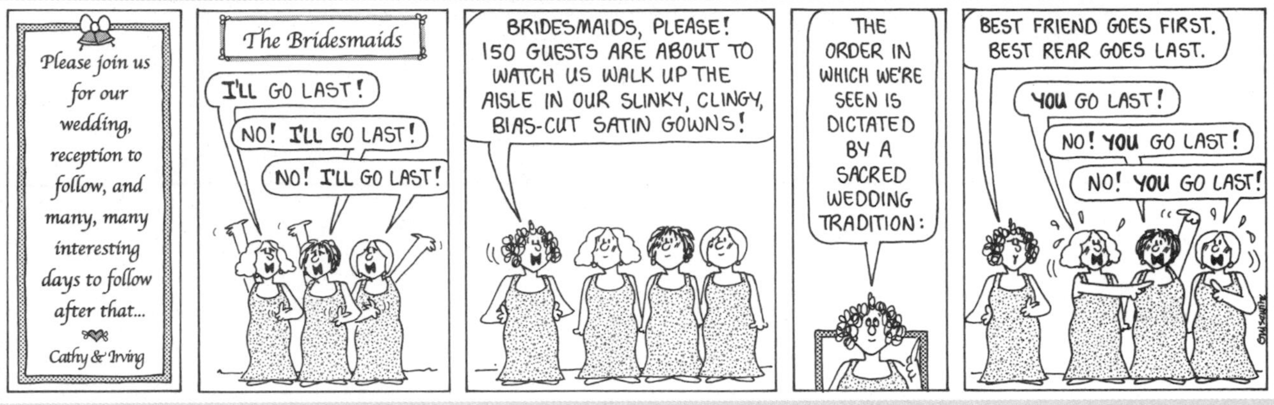
Please join us for our wedding, reception to follow, and many, many interesting days to follow after that...
Cathy & Irving
The Bridesmaids
I'LL GO LAST!
NO! I'LL GO LAST!
NO! I'LL GO LAST!
BRIDESMAIDS, PLEASE! 150 GUESTS ARE ABOUT TO WATCH US WALK UP THE AISLE IN OUR SLINKY, CLINGY, BIAS-CUT SATIN GOWNS!
THE ORDER IN WHICH WE'RE SEEN IS DICTATED BY A SACRED WEDDING TRADITION:
BEST FRIEND GOES FIRST. BEST REAR GOES LAST.
YOU GO LAST!
NO! YOU GO LAST!
NO! YOU GO LAST!

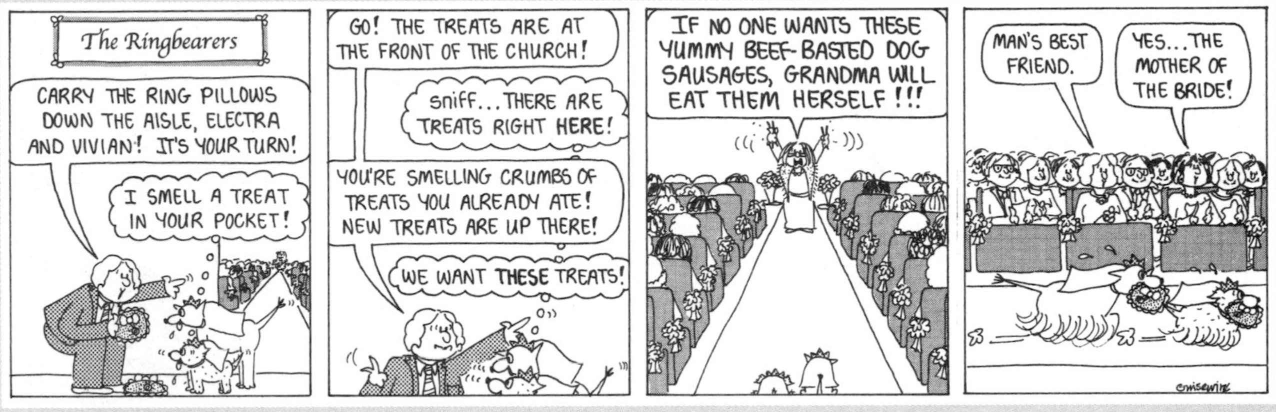
The Ringbearers
CARRY THE RING PILLOWS DOWN THE AISLE, ELECTRA AND VIVIAN! IT'S YOUR TURN!
I SMELL A TREAT IN YOUR POCKET!
GO! THE TREATS ARE AT THE FRONT OF THE CHURCH!
sniff... THERE ARE TREATS RIGHT HERE!
YOU'RE SMELLING CRUMBS OF TREATS YOU ALREADY ATE! NEW TREATS ARE UP THERE!
WE WANT THESE TREATS!
IF NO ONE WANTS THESE YUMMY BEEF-BASTED DOG SAUSAGES, GRANDMA WILL EAT THEM HERSELF!!!
MAN'S BEST FRIEND.
YES... THE MOTHER OF THE BRIDE!

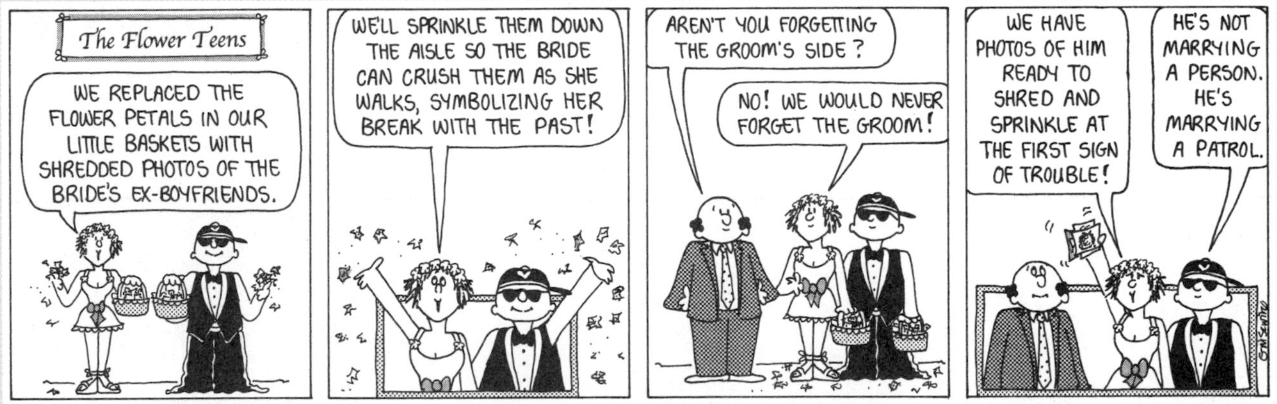
The Flower Teens
WE REPLACED THE FLOWER PETALS IN OUR LITTLE BASKETS WITH SHREDDED PHOTOS OF THE BRIDE'S EX-BOYFRIENDS.
WE'LL SPRINKLE THEM DOWN THE AISLE SO THE BRIDE CAN CRUSH THEM AS SHE WALKS, SYMBOLIZING HER BREAK WITH THE PAST!
AREN'T YOU FORGETTING THE GROOM'S SIDE?
NO! WE WOULD NEVER FORGET THE GROOM!
WE HAVE PHOTOS OF HIM READY TO SHRED AND SPRINKLE AT THE FIRST SIGN OF TROUBLE!
HE'S NOT MARRYING A PERSON. HE'S MARRYING A PATROL.

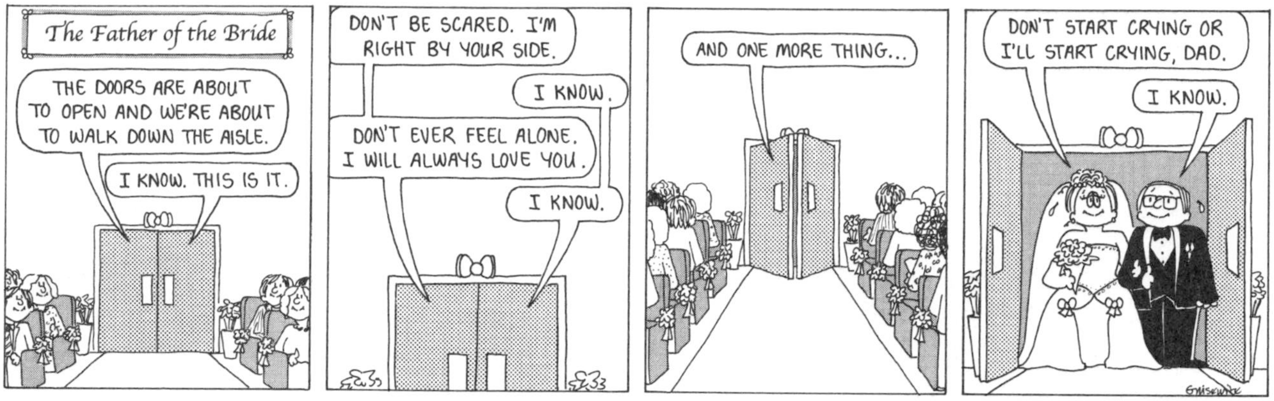
The Father of the Bride
THE DOORS ARE ABOUT TO OPEN AND WE'RE ABOUT TO WALK DOWN THE AISLE.
I KNOW. THIS IS IT.
DON'T BE SCARED. I'M RIGHT BY YOUR SIDE.
I KNOW.
DON'T EVER FEEL ALONE. I WILL ALWAYS LOVE YOU.
I KNOW.
AND ONE MORE THING...
DON'T START CRYING OR I'LL START CRYING, DAD.
I KNOW.

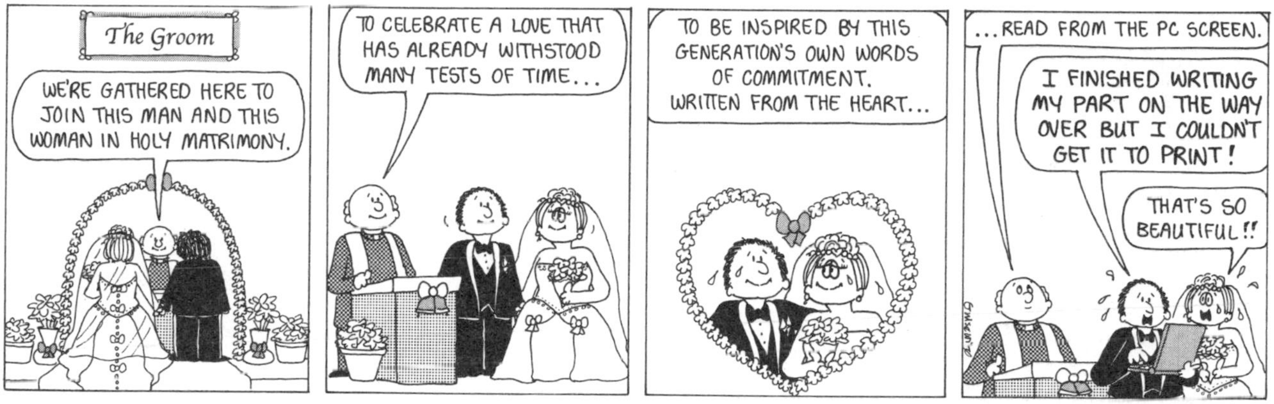
The Groom
WE'RE GATHERED HERE TO JOIN THIS MAN AND THIS WOMAN IN HOLY MATRIMONY.
TO CELEBRATE A LOVE THAT HAS ALREADY WITHSTOOD MANY TESTS OF TIME...
TO BE INSPIRED BY THIS GENERATION'S OWN WORDS OF COMMITMENT. WRITTEN FROM THE HEART...
...READ FROM THE PC SCREEN.
I FINISHED WRITING MY PART ON THE WAY OVER BUT I COULDN'T GET IT TO PRINT!
THAT'S SO BEAUTIFUL!!

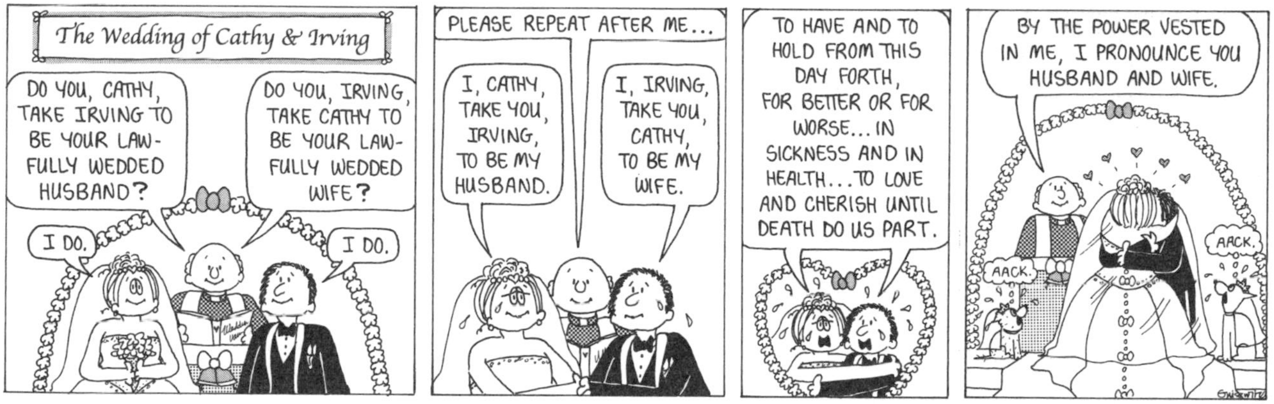
The Wedding of Cathy & Irving
DO YOU, CATHY, TAKE IRVING TO BE YOUR LAW-FULLY WEDDED HUSBAND?
DO YOU, IRVING, TAKE CATHY TO BE YOUR LAW-FULLY WEDDED WIFE?
I DO.
I DO.
PLEASE REPEAT AFTER ME...
I, CATHY, TAKE YOU, IRVING, TO BE MY HUSBAND.
I, IRVING, TAKE YOU, CATHY, TO BE MY WIFE.
TO HAVE AND TO HOLD FROM THIS DAY FORTH, FOR BETTER OR FOR WORSE... IN SICKNESS AND IN HEALTH... TO LOVE AND CHERISH UNTIL DEATH DO US PART.
BY THE POWER VESTED IN ME, I PRONOUNCE YOU HUSBAND AND WIFE.
AACK.
AACK.

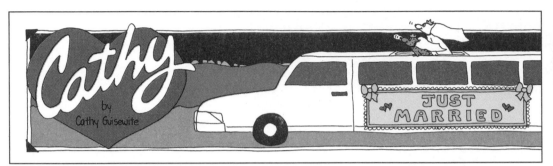

Cathy
by Cathy Guisewite

JUST MARRIED

The Reception

Cathy & Irving
2-5-05

The Bridesmaids and Groomsmen

IT WAS SO BEAUTIFUL!!

THERE GOES THE MAKEUP AGAIN! IT'LL TAKE AN HOUR TO GET THIS PICTURE TAKEN!

The Bride and Her Ring

I'M MARRIED! AACK! I'M MARRIED! AACK!

The Groom and His Laptop

A TOAST TO MY BEAUTIFUL...WAIT. CURSOR'S FROZEN ...HOLD ON...SCREEN WENT BLANK...I...

The Parents and In-Laws

EVERY-THING'S JUST PERFECT!

CAN'T HEAR YOU! MUSIC'S TOO LOUD!

The Bride and Her Dad

DID YOU CONFIRM YOUR FLIGHT? UNPLUG ALL APPLIANCES? TRIPLE-CHECK YOUR HOTEL??

NICE TO SEE YOU CAN FINALLY RELAX, DAD.

The Ringbearers and the Bouquet

I CAUGHT IT! NO! I CAUGHT IT!

The Bride and Groom

I LOVE YOU!

The Mother and Her Maker

HALLELUJAH!

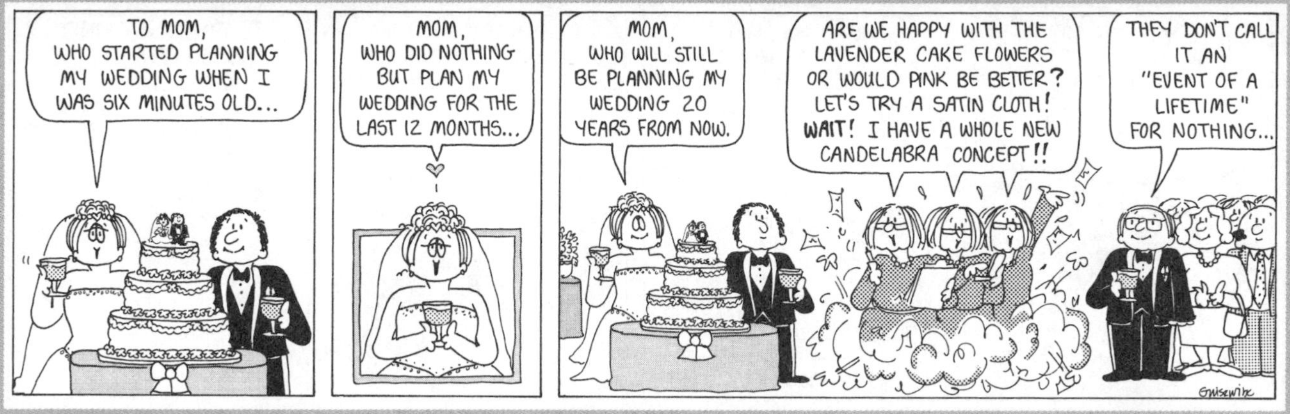
TO MOM, WHO STARTED PLANNING MY WEDDING WHEN I WAS SIX MINUTES OLD...
MOM, WHO DID NOTHING BUT PLAN MY WEDDING FOR THE LAST 12 MONTHS...
MOM, WHO WILL STILL BE PLANNING MY WEDDING 20 YEARS FROM NOW.
ARE WE HAPPY WITH THE LAVENDER CAKE FLOWERS OR WOULD PINK BE BETTER? LET'S TRY A SATIN CLOTH! WAIT! I HAVE A WHOLE NEW CANDELABRA CONCEPT!!
THEY DON'T CALL IT AN "EVENT OF A LIFETIME" FOR NOTHING...
GUISEWITE

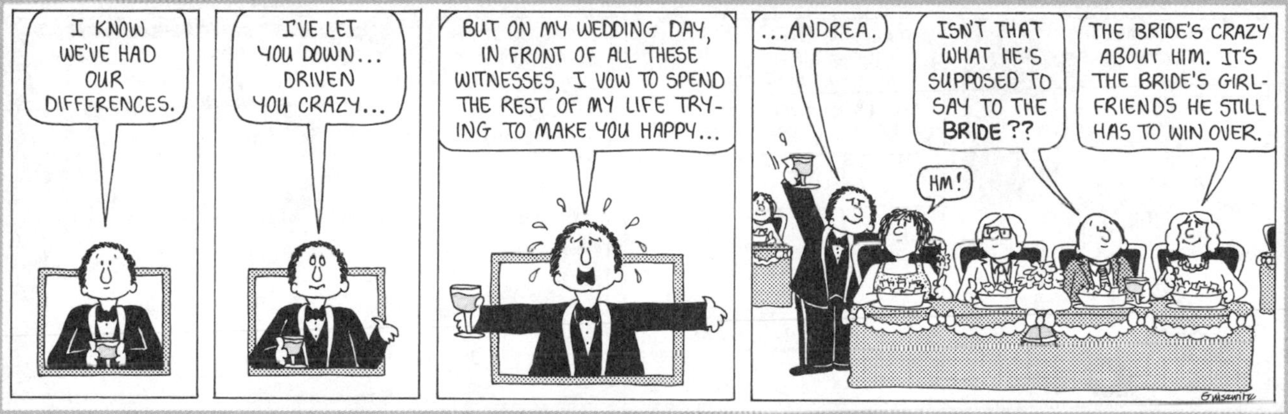
I KNOW WE'VE HAD OUR DIFFERENCES.
I'VE LET YOU DOWN... DRIVEN YOU CRAZY...
BUT ON MY WEDDING DAY, IN FRONT OF ALL THESE WITNESSES, I VOW TO SPEND THE REST OF MY LIFE TRYING TO MAKE YOU HAPPY...
...ANDREA.
HM!
ISN'T THAT WHAT HE'S SUPPOSED TO SAY TO THE BRIDE??
THE BRIDE'S CRAZY ABOUT HIM. IT'S THE BRIDE'S GIRLFRIENDS HE STILL HAS TO WIN OVER.
GUISEWITE

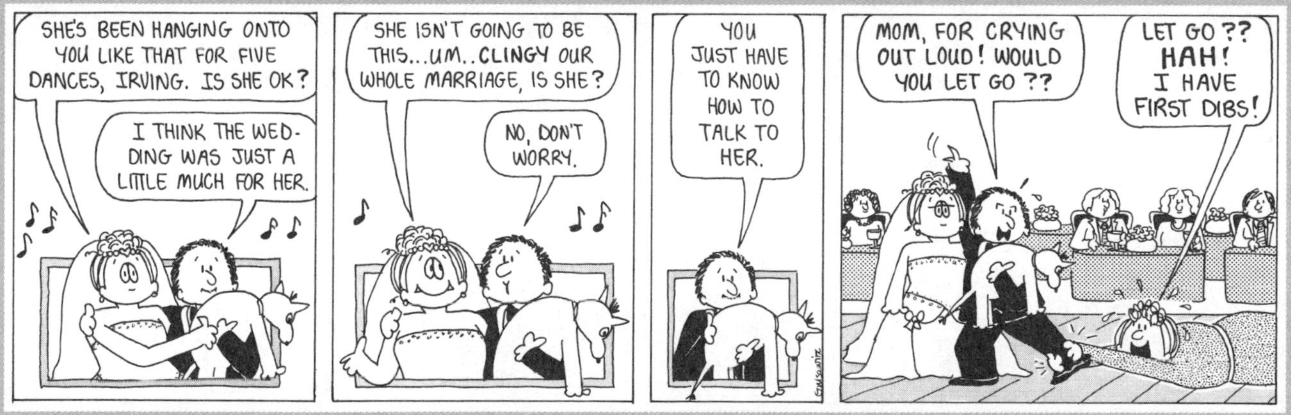
SHE'S BEEN HANGING ONTO YOU LIKE THAT FOR FIVE DANCES, IRVING. IS SHE OK?
I THINK THE WEDDING WAS JUST A LITTLE MUCH FOR HER.
SHE ISN'T GOING TO BE THIS...UM..CLINGY OUR WHOLE MARRIAGE, IS SHE?
NO, DON'T WORRY.
YOU JUST HAVE TO KNOW HOW TO TALK TO HER.
GUISEWITE
MOM, FOR CRYING OUT LOUD! WOULD YOU LET GO??
LET GO?? HAH! I HAVE FIRST DIBS!

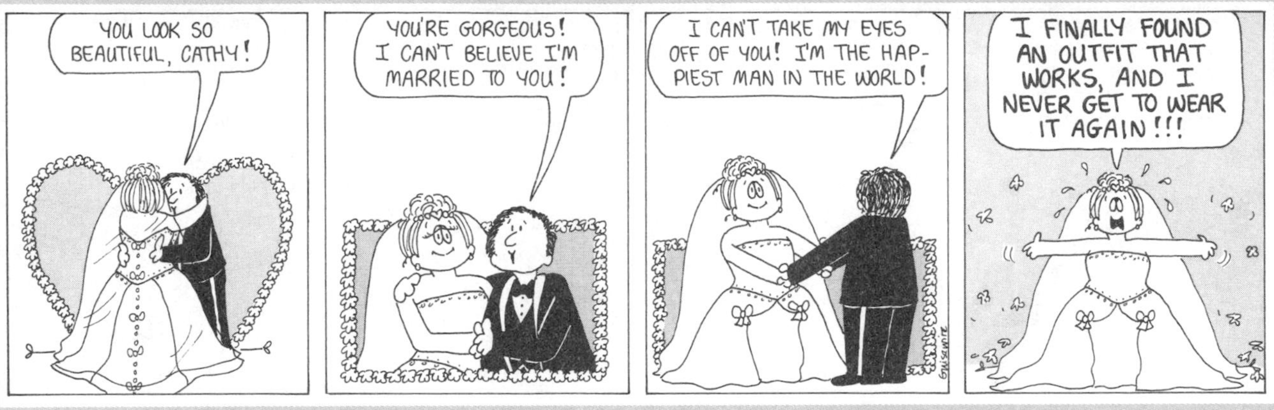
YOU LOOK SO BEAUTIFUL, CATHY!
YOU'RE GORGEOUS! I CAN'T BELIEVE I'M MARRIED TO YOU!
I CAN'T TAKE MY EYES OFF OF YOU! I'M THE HAPPIEST MAN IN THE WORLD!
I FINALLY FOUND AN OUTFIT THAT WORKS, AND I NEVER GET TO WEAR IT AGAIN!!!

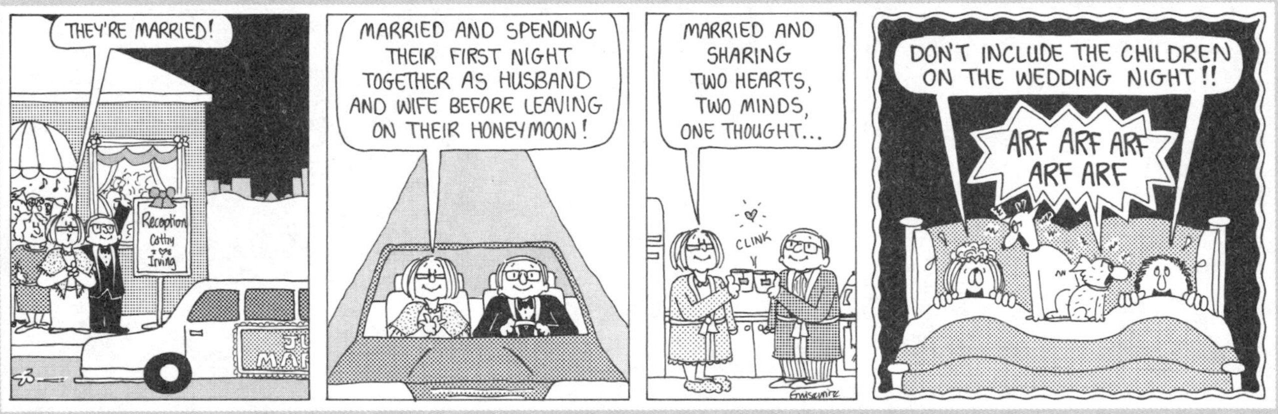
THEY'RE MARRIED!
Reception
Cathy & Irving
MARRIED AND SPENDING THEIR FIRST NIGHT TOGETHER AS HUSBAND AND WIFE BEFORE LEAVING ON THEIR HONEYMOON!
MARRIED AND SHARING TWO HEARTS, TWO MINDS, ONE THOUGHT...
CLINK
DON'T INCLUDE THE CHILDREN ON THE WEDDING NIGHT!!
ARF ARF ARF ARF ARF

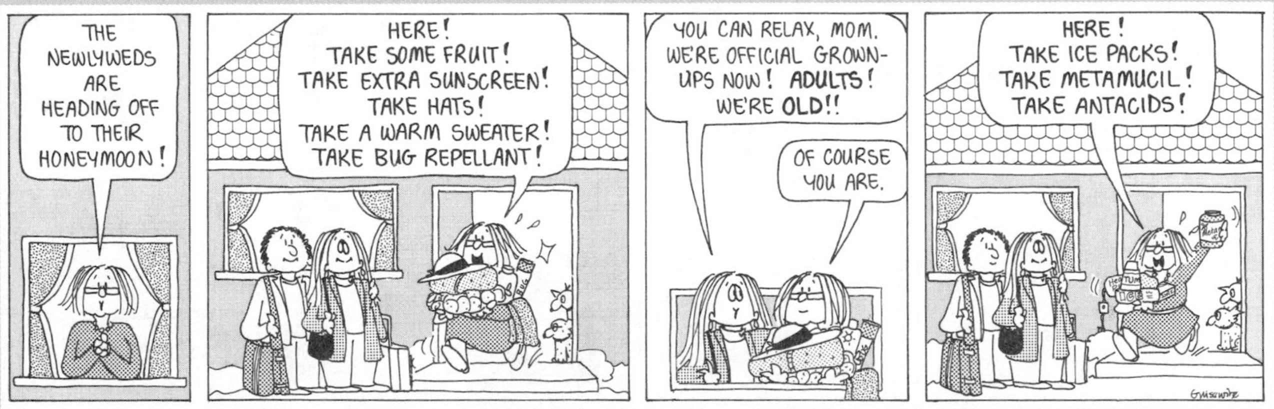
THE NEWLYWEDS ARE HEADING OFF TO THEIR HONEYMOON!
HERE! TAKE SOME FRUIT! TAKE EXTRA SUNSCREEN! TAKE HATS! TAKE A WARM SWEATER! TAKE BUG REPELLANT!
YOU CAN RELAX, MOM. WE'RE OFFICIAL GROWN-UPS NOW! ADULTS! WE'RE OLD!!
OF COURSE YOU ARE.
HERE! TAKE ICE PACKS! TAKE METAMUCIL! TAKE ANTACIDS!

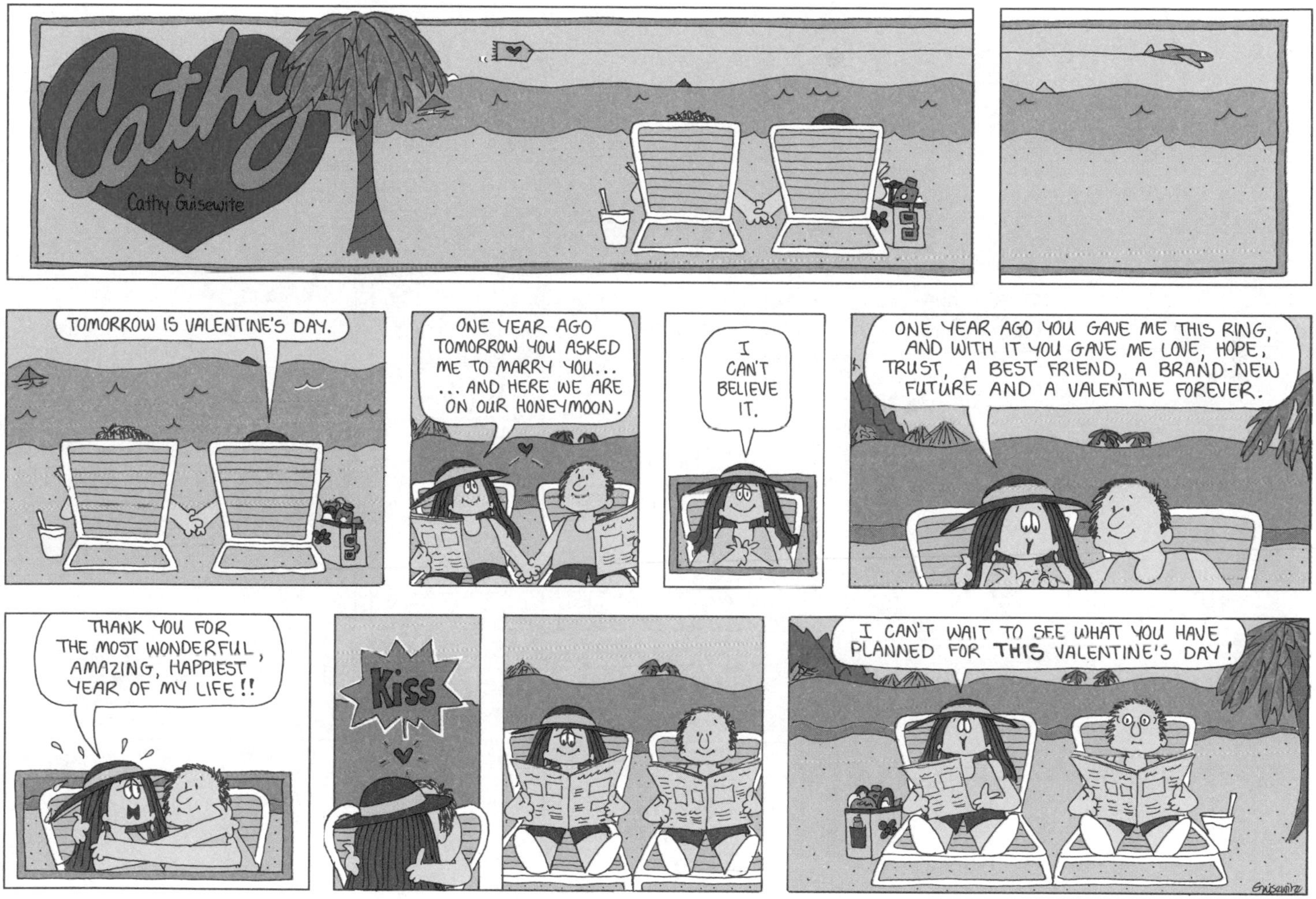
Cathy
by
Cathy Guisewite
TOMORROW IS VALENTINE'S DAY.
ONE YEAR AGO TOMORROW YOU ASKED ME TO MARRY YOU... ...AND HERE WE ARE ON OUR HONEYMOON.
I CAN'T BELIEVE IT.
ONE YEAR AGO YOU GAVE ME THIS RING, AND WITH IT YOU GAVE ME LOVE, HOPE, TRUST, A BEST FRIEND, A BRAND-NEW FUTURE AND A VALENTINE FOREVER.
THANK YOU FOR THE MOST WONDERFUL, AMAZING, HAPPIEST YEAR OF MY LIFE!!
KISS
I CAN'T WAIT TO SEE WHAT YOU HAVE PLANNED FOR THIS VALENTINE'S DAY!
Guisewite

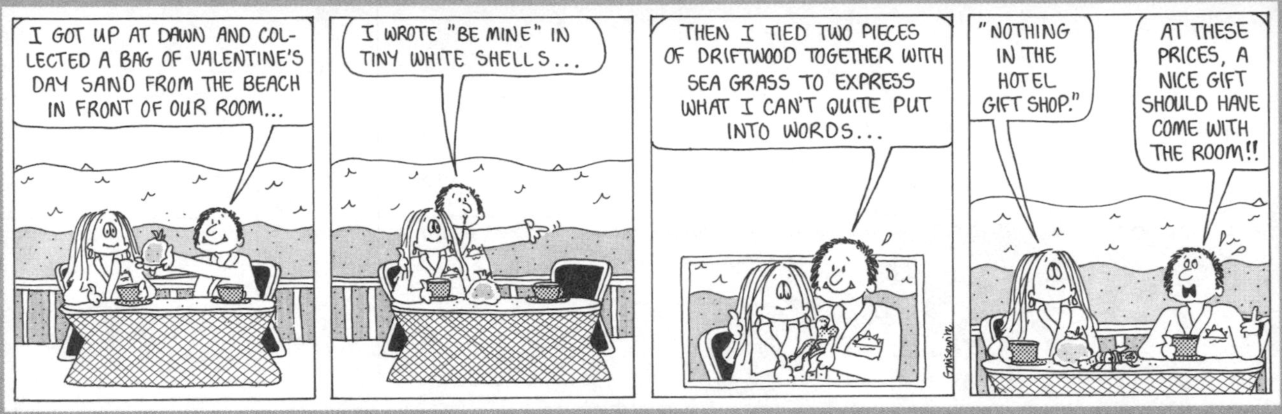
I GOT UP AT DAWN AND COLLECTED A BAG OF VALENTINE'S DAY SAND FROM THE BEACH IN FRONT OF OUR ROOM...
I WROTE "BE MINE" IN TINY WHITE SHELLS...
THEN I TIED TWO PIECES OF DRIFTWOOD TOGETHER WITH SEA GRASS TO EXPRESS WHAT I CAN'T QUITE PUT INTO WORDS...
"NOTHING IN THE HOTEL GIFT SHOP."
AT THESE PRICES, A NICE GIFT SHOULD HAVE COME WITH THE ROOM!!

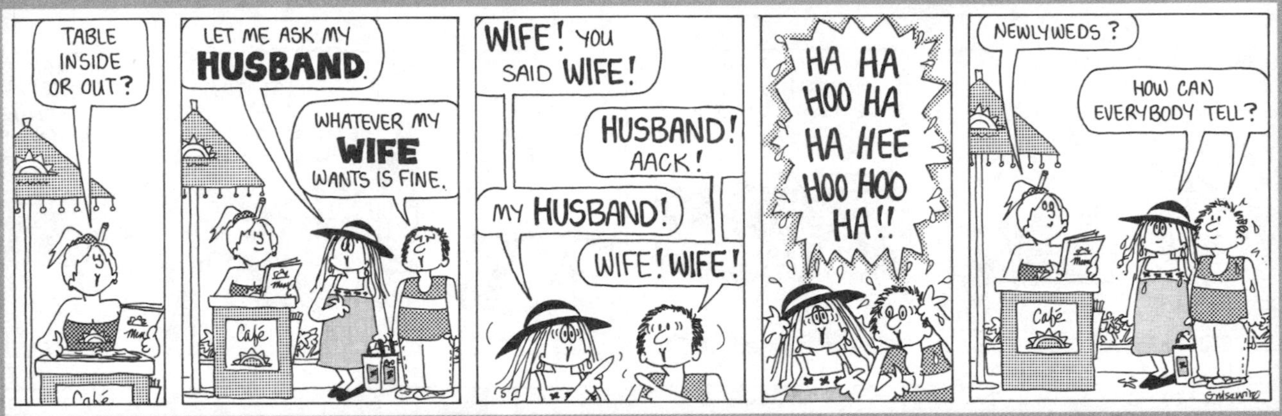
TABLE INSIDE OR OUT?
LET ME ASK MY HUSBAND.
WHATEVER MY WIFE WANTS IS FINE.
WIFE! YOU SAID WIFE!
HUSBAND! AACK!
MY HUSBAND!
WIFE! WIFE!
HA HA HOO HA HA HEE HOO HOO HA!!
NEWLYWEDS?
HOW CAN EVERYBODY TELL?

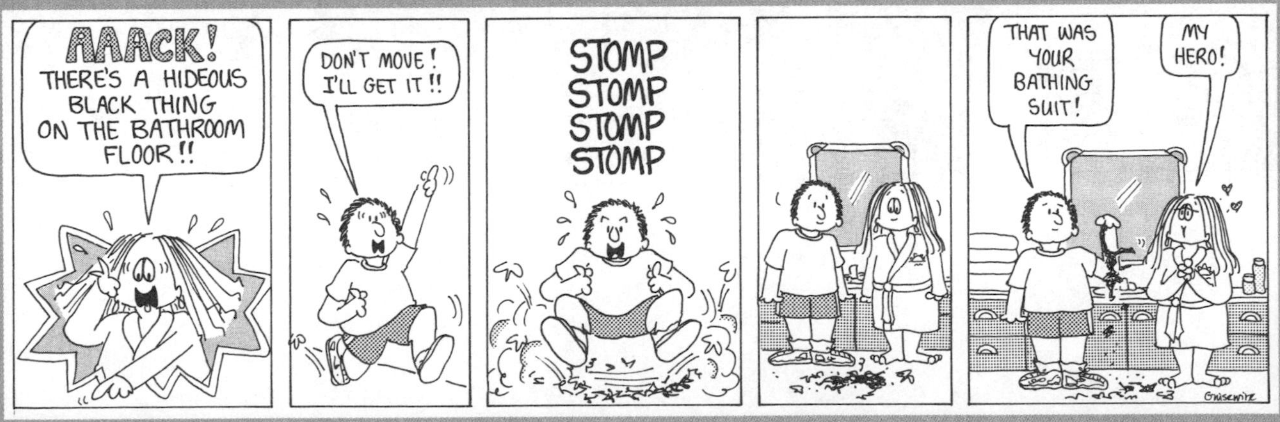
AAACK! THERE'S A HIDEOUS BLACK THING ON THE BATHROOM FLOOR!!
DON'T MOVE! I'LL GET IT!!
STOMP STOMP STOMP STOMP
THAT WAS YOUR BATHING SUIT!
MY HERO!

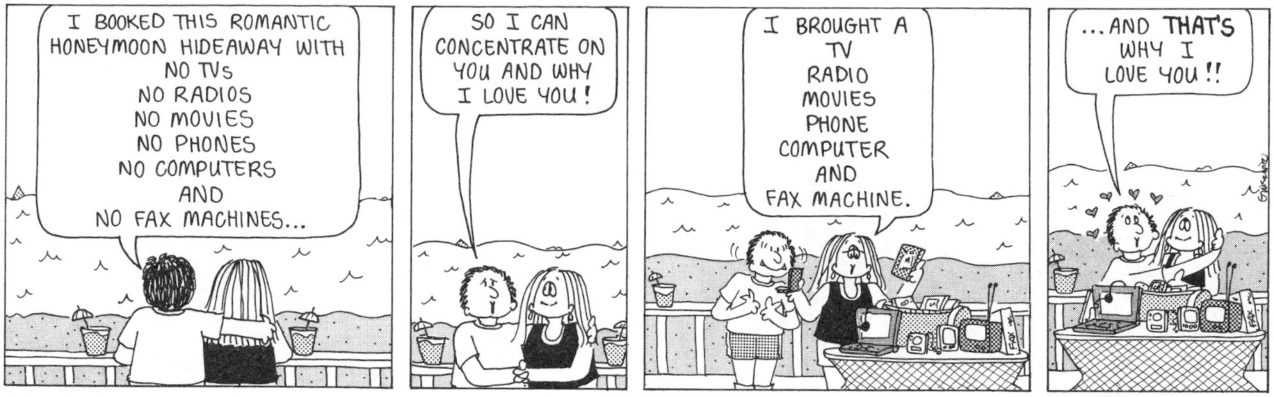
I BOOKED THIS ROMANTIC HONEYMOON HIDEAWAY WITH NO TVs NO RADIOS NO MOVIES NO PHONES NO COMPUTERS AND NO FAX MACHINES...
SO I CAN CONCENTRATE ON YOU AND WHY I LOVE YOU!
I BROUGHT A TV RADIO MOVIES PHONE COMPUTER AND FAX MACHINE.
...AND THAT'S WHY I LOVE YOU!!

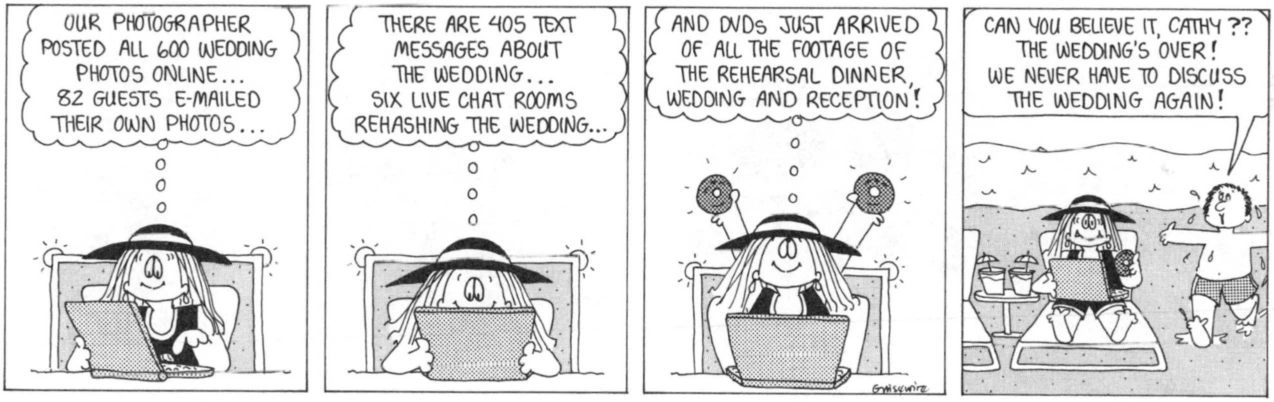
OUR PHOTOGRAPHER POSTED ALL 600 WEDDING PHOTOS ONLINE... 82 GUESTS E-MAILED THEIR OWN PHOTOS...
THERE ARE 405 TEXT MESSAGES ABOUT THE WEDDING... SIX LIVE CHAT ROOMS REHASHING THE WEDDING...
AND DVDs JUST ARRIVED OF ALL THE FOOTAGE OF THE REHEARSAL DINNER, WEDDING AND RECEPTION!
CAN YOU BELIEVE IT, CATHY?? THE WEDDING'S OVER! WE NEVER HAVE TO DISCUSS THE WEDDING AGAIN!

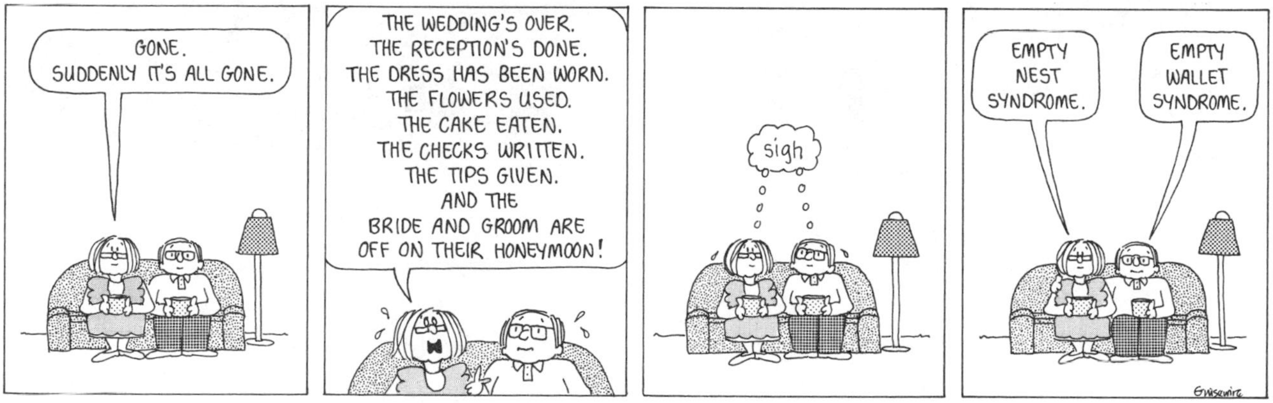
GONE. SUDDENLY IT'S ALL GONE.
THE WEDDING'S OVER. THE RECEPTION'S DONE. THE DRESS HAS BEEN WORN. THE FLOWERS USED. THE CAKE EATEN. THE CHECKS WRITTEN. THE TIPS GIVEN. AND THE BRIDE AND GROOM ARE OFF ON THEIR HONEYMOON!
sigh
EMPTY NEST SYNDROME.
EMPTY WALLET SYNDROME.

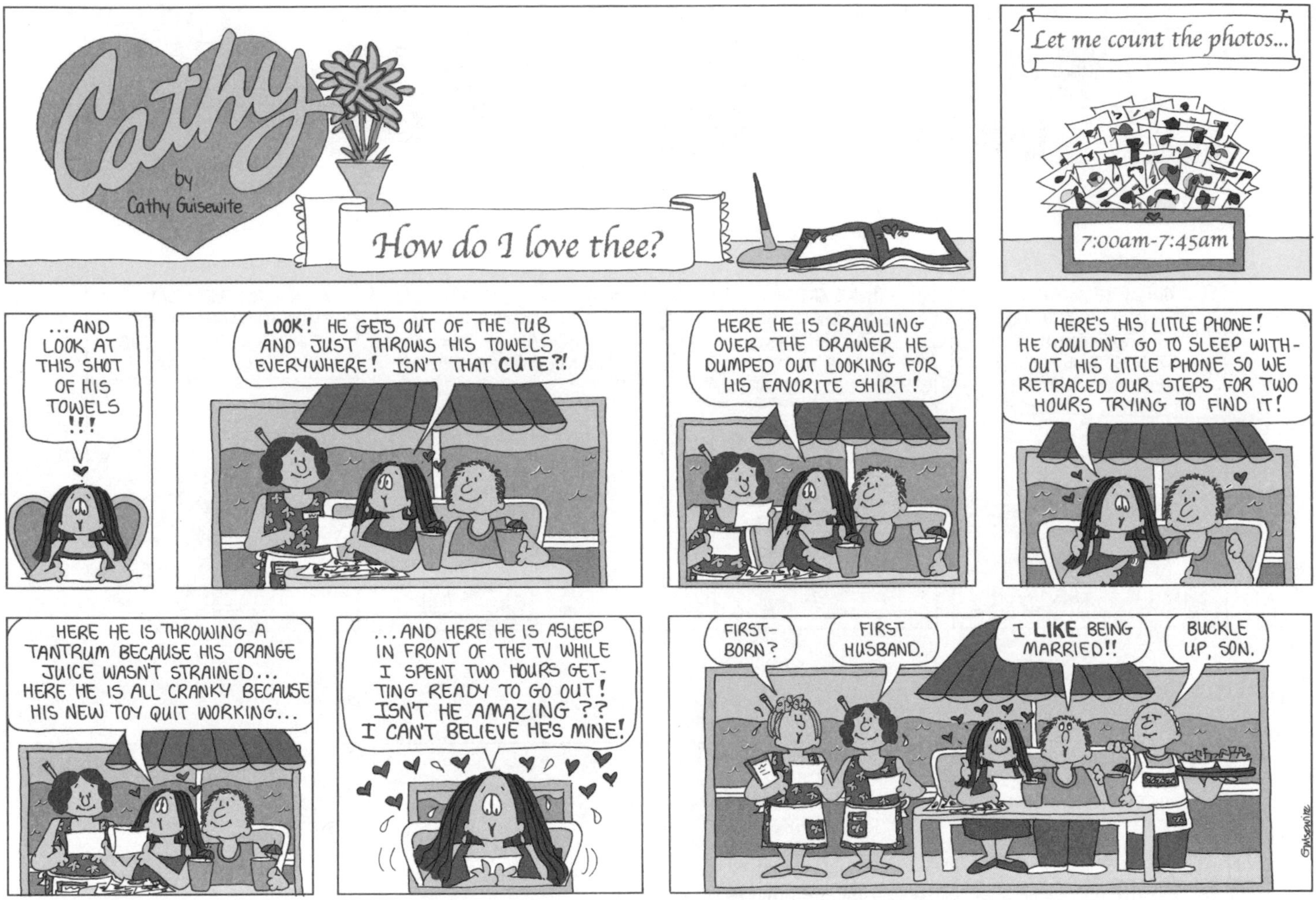
Cathy
by
Cathy Guisewite
How do I love thee?
Let me count the photos...
7:00am-7:45am
...AND LOOK AT THIS SHOT OF HIS TOWELS !!!
LOOK! HE GETS OUT OF THE TUB AND JUST THROWS HIS TOWELS EVERYWHERE! ISN'T THAT CUTE?!
HERE HE IS CRAWLING OVER THE DRAWER HE DUMPED OUT LOOKING FOR HIS FAVORITE SHIRT!
HERE'S HIS LITTLE PHONE! HE COULDN'T GO TO SLEEP WITH-OUT HIS LITTLE PHONE SO WE RETRACED OUR STEPS FOR TWO HOURS TRYING TO FIND IT!
HERE HE IS THROWING A TANTRUM BECAUSE HIS ORANGE JUICE WASN'T STRAINED... HERE HE IS ALL CRANKY BECAUSE HIS NEW TOY QUIT WORKING...
...AND HERE HE IS ASLEEP IN FRONT OF THE TV WHILE I SPENT TWO HOURS GET-TING READY TO GO OUT! ISN'T HE AMAZING ?? I CAN'T BELIEVE HE'S MINE!
FIRST-BORN?
FIRST HUSBAND.
I LIKE BEING MARRIED!!
BUCKLE UP, SON.
GUISEWITE

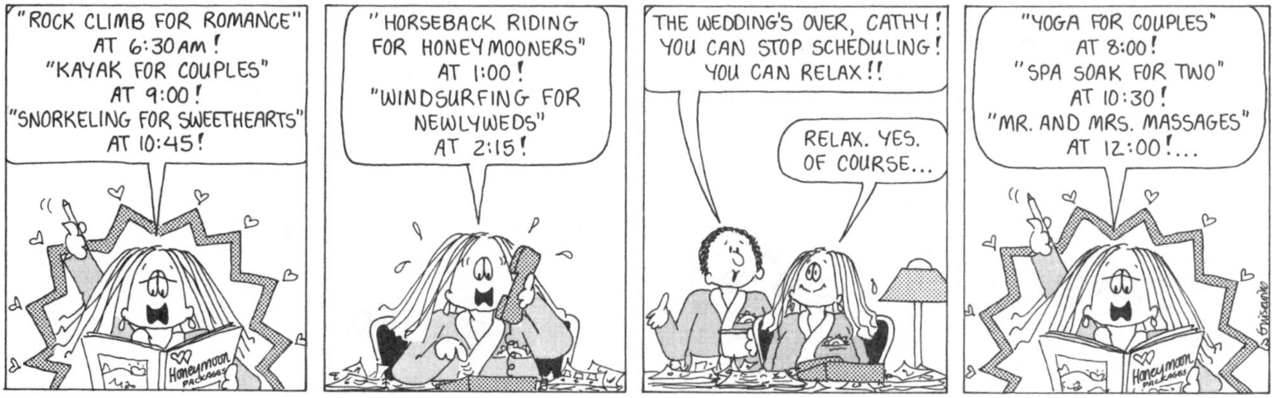
"ROCK CLIMB FOR ROMANCE" AT 6:30 AM! "KAYAK FOR COUPLES" AT 9:00! "SNORKELING FOR SWEETHEARTS" AT 10:45!
Honeymoon PACKAGES
"HORSEBACK RIDING FOR HONEYMOONERS" AT 1:00! "WINDSURFING FOR NEWLYWEDS" AT 2:15!
THE WEDDING'S OVER, CATHY! YOU CAN STOP SCHEDULING! YOU CAN RELAX!!
RELAX. YES. OF COURSE...
"YOGA FOR COUPLES" AT 8:00! "SPA SOAK FOR TWO" AT 10:30! "MR. AND MRS. MASSAGES" AT 12:00!...
Honeymoon PACKAGES

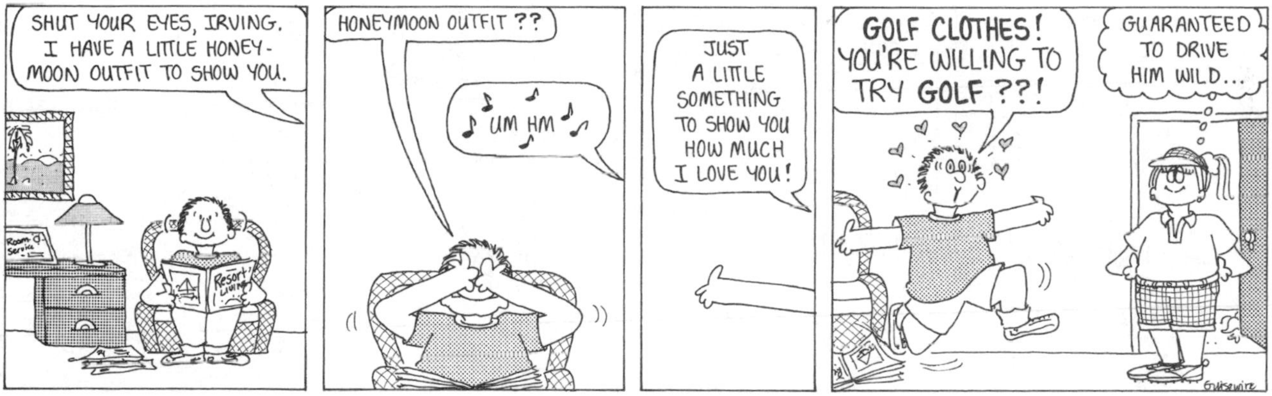
SHUT YOUR EYES, IRVING. I HAVE A LITTLE HONEY-MOON OUTFIT TO SHOW YOU.
Resort LIVING
HONEYMOON OUTFIT??
UM HM
JUST A LITTLE SOMETHING TO SHOW YOU HOW MUCH I LOVE YOU!
GOLF CLOTHES! YOU'RE WILLING TO TRY GOLF??!
GUARANTEED TO DRIVE HIM WILD...

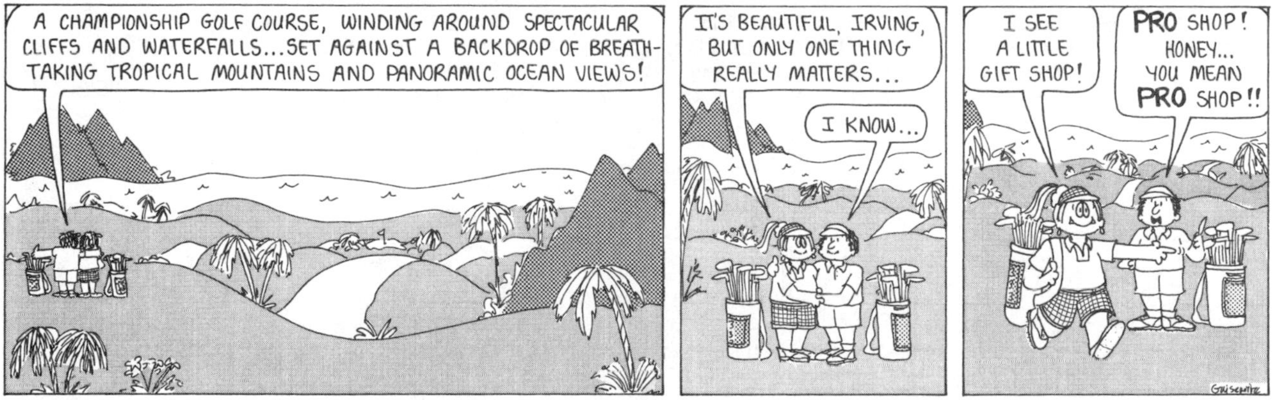
A CHAMPIONSHIP GOLF COURSE, WINDING AROUND SPECTACULAR CLIFFS AND WATERFALLS...SET AGAINST A BACKDROP OF BREATH-TAKING TROPICAL MOUNTAINS AND PANORAMIC OCEAN VIEWS!
IT'S BEAUTIFUL, IRVING, BUT ONLY ONE THING REALLY MATTERS...
I KNOW...
I SEE A LITTLE GIFT SHOP!
PRO SHOP! HONEY... YOU MEAN PRO SHOP!!

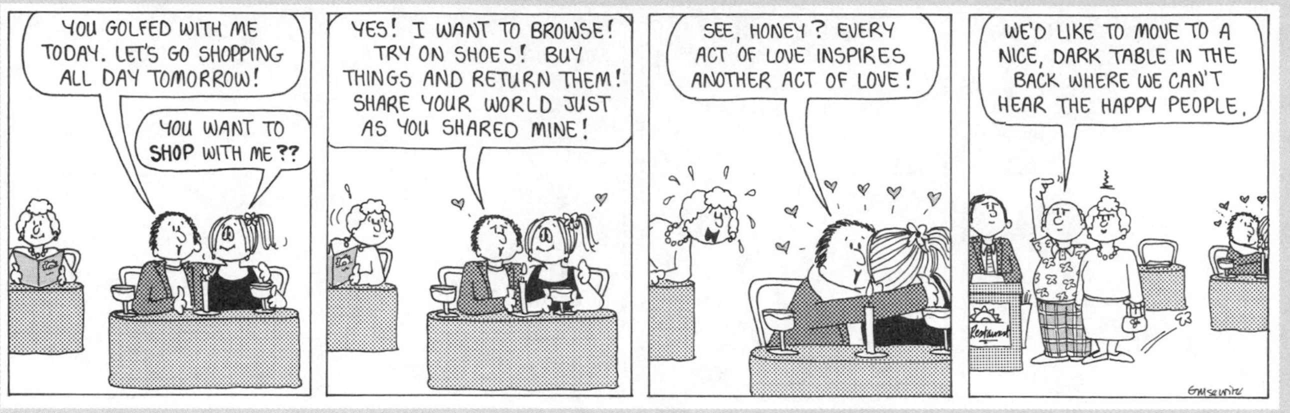
YOU GOLFED WITH ME TODAY. LET'S GO SHOPPING ALL DAY TOMORROW!
YOU WANT TO SHOP WITH ME??
YES! I WANT TO BROWSE! TRY ON SHOES! BUY THINGS AND RETURN THEM! SHARE YOUR WORLD JUST AS YOU SHARED MINE!
SEE, HONEY? EVERY ACT OF LOVE INSPIRES ANOTHER ACT OF LOVE!
WE'D LIKE TO MOVE TO A NICE, DARK TABLE IN THE BACK WHERE WE CAN'T HEAR THE HAPPY PEOPLE.

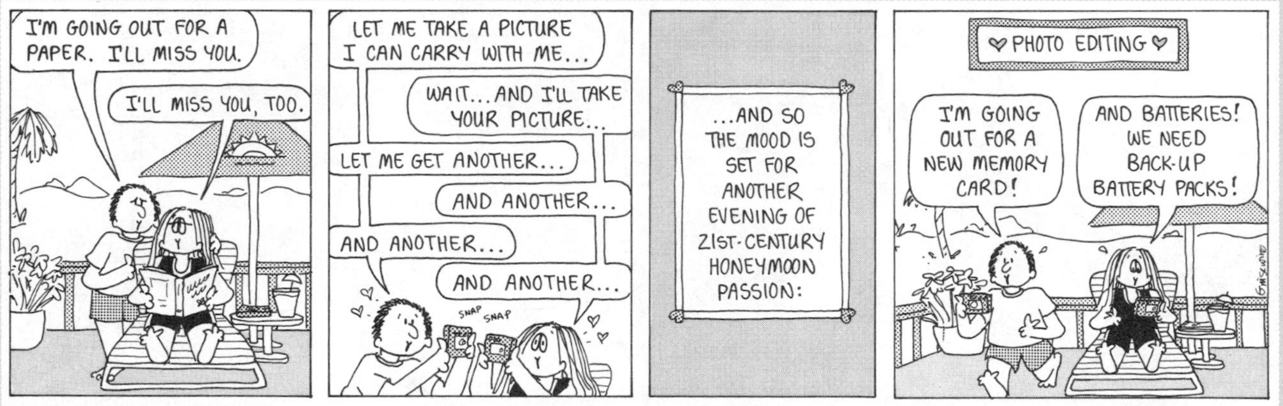
I'M GOING OUT FOR A PAPER. I'LL MISS YOU.
I'LL MISS YOU, TOO.
LET ME TAKE A PICTURE I CAN CARRY WITH ME...
WAIT... AND I'LL TAKE YOUR PICTURE...
LET ME GET ANOTHER...
AND ANOTHER...
AND ANOTHER...
AND ANOTHER...
SNAP
SNAP
...AND SO THE MOOD IS SET FOR ANOTHER EVENING OF 21ST-CENTURY HONEYMOON PASSION:
PHOTO EDITING
I'M GOING OUT FOR A NEW MEMORY CARD!
AND BATTERIES! WE NEED BACK-UP BATTERY PACKS!

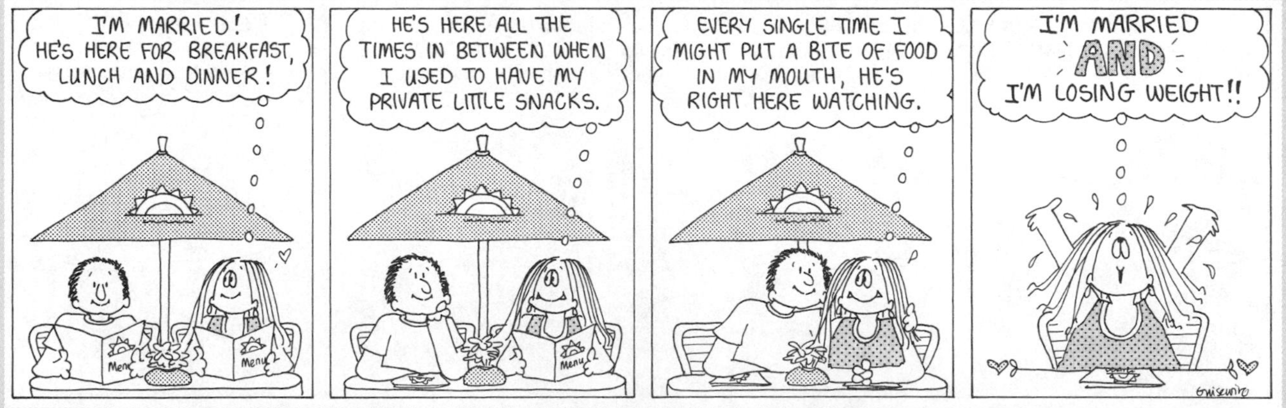
I'M MARRIED! HE'S HERE FOR BREAKFAST, LUNCH AND DINNER!
HE'S HERE ALL THE TIMES IN BETWEEN WHEN I USED TO HAVE MY PRIVATE LITTLE SNACKS.
EVERY SINGLE TIME I MIGHT PUT A BITE OF FOOD IN MY MOUTH, HE'S RIGHT HERE WATCHING.
I'M MARRIED AND I'M LOSING WEIGHT!!

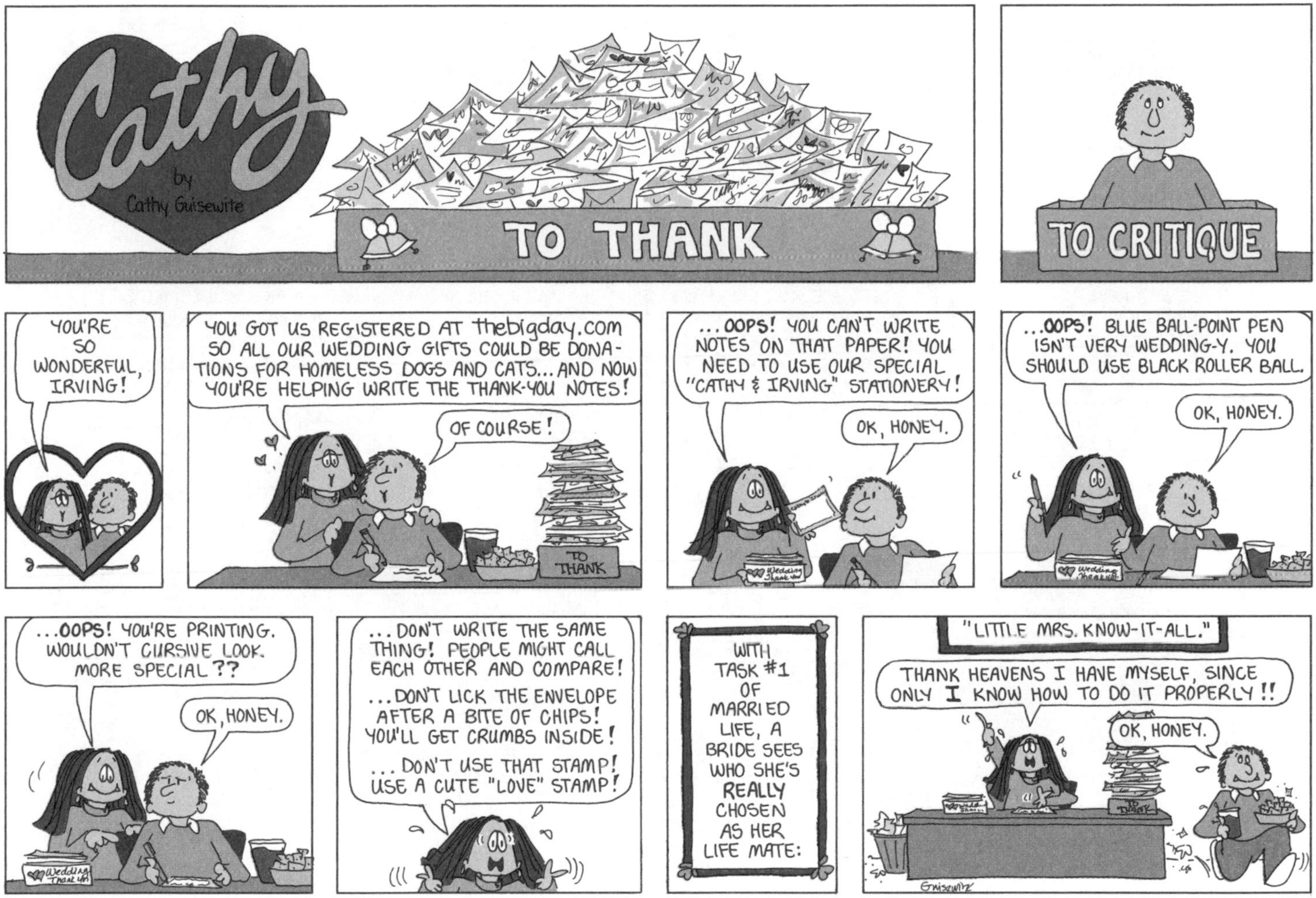
Cathy
by
Cathy Guisewite
TO THANK
TO CRITIQUE
YOU'RE SO WONDERFUL, IRVING!
YOU GOT US REGISTERED AT thebigday.com SO ALL OUR WEDDING GIFTS COULD BE DONATIONS FOR HOMELESS DOGS AND CATS... AND NOW YOU'RE HELPING WRITE THE THANK-YOU NOTES!
OF COURSE!
TO THANK
...OOPS! YOU CAN'T WRITE NOTES ON THAT PAPER! YOU NEED TO USE OUR SPECIAL "CATHY & IRVING" STATIONERY!
OK, HONEY.
...OOPS! BLUE BALL-POINT PEN ISN'T VERY WEDDING-Y. YOU SHOULD USE BLACK ROLLER BALL.
OK, HONEY.
...OOPS! YOU'RE PRINTING. WOULDN'T CURSIVE LOOK MORE SPECIAL??
OK, HONEY.
...DON'T WRITE THE SAME THING! PEOPLE MIGHT CALL EACH OTHER AND COMPARE!
...DON'T LICK THE ENVELOPE AFTER A BITE OF CHIPS! YOU'LL GET CRUMBS INSIDE!
...DON'T USE THAT STAMP! USE A CUTE "LOVE" STAMP!
WITH TASK #1 OF MARRIED LIFE, A BRIDE SEES WHO SHE'S REALLY CHOSEN AS HER LIFE MATE:
"LITTLE MRS. KNOW-IT-ALL."
THANK HEAVENS I HAVE MYSELF, SINCE ONLY I KNOW HOW TO DO IT PROPERLY!!
OK, HONEY.
Guisewite

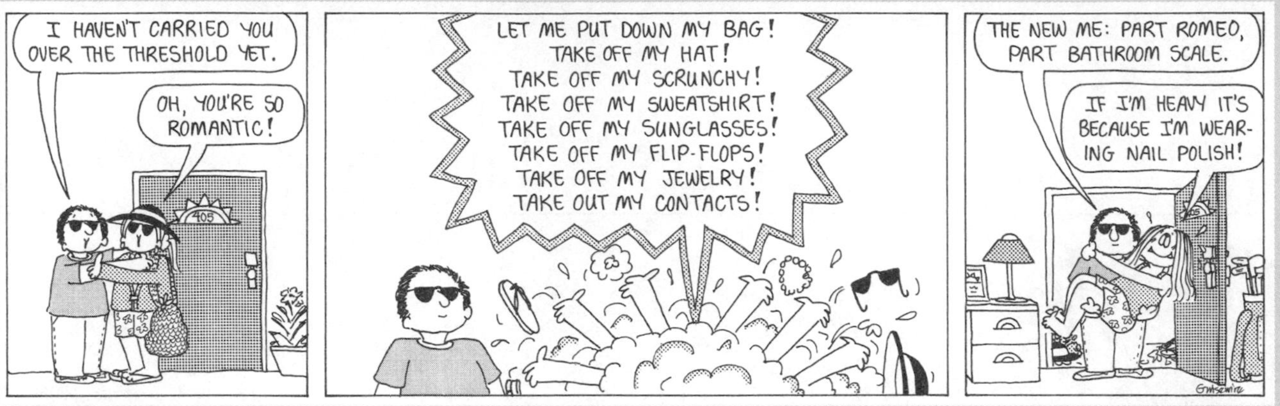
I HAVEN'T CARRIED YOU OVER THE THRESHOLD YET.
OH, YOU'RE SO ROMANTIC!
405
LET ME PUT DOWN MY BAG! TAKE OFF MY HAT! TAKE OFF MY SCRUNCHY! TAKE OFF MY SWEATSHIRT! TAKE OFF MY SUNGLASSES! TAKE OFF MY FLIP-FLOPS! TAKE OFF MY JEWELRY! TAKE OUT MY CONTACTS!
THE NEW ME: PART ROMEO, PART BATHROOM SCALE.
IF I'M HEAVY IT'S BECAUSE I'M WEARING NAIL POLISH!

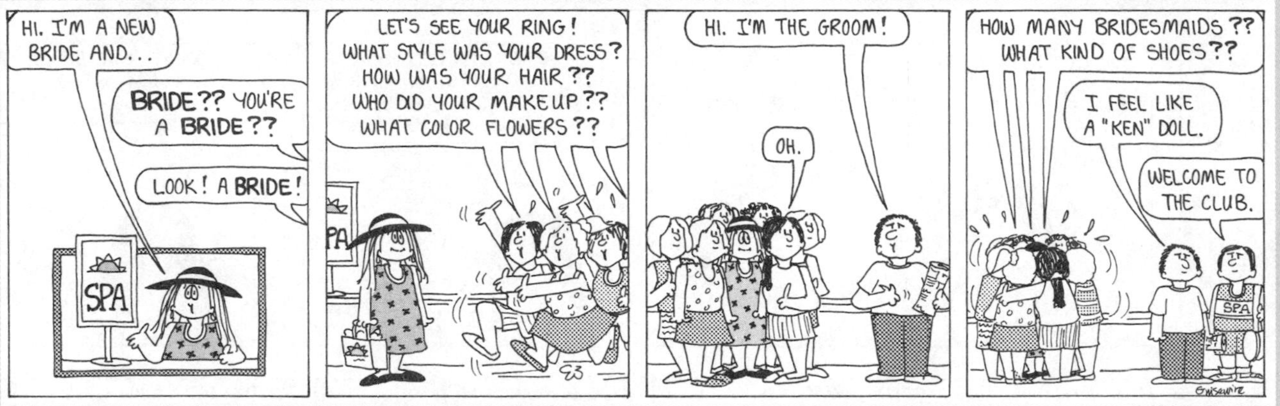
HI. I'M A NEW BRIDE AND...
BRIDE?? YOU'RE A BRIDE??
LOOK! A BRIDE!
SPA
LET'S SEE YOUR RING! WHAT STYLE WAS YOUR DRESS? HOW WAS YOUR HAIR?? WHO DID YOUR MAKEUP?? WHAT COLOR FLOWERS??
HI. I'M THE GROOM!
OH.
HOW MANY BRIDESMAIDS?? WHAT KIND OF SHOES??
I FEEL LIKE A "KEN" DOLL.
WELCOME TO THE CLUB.
SPA

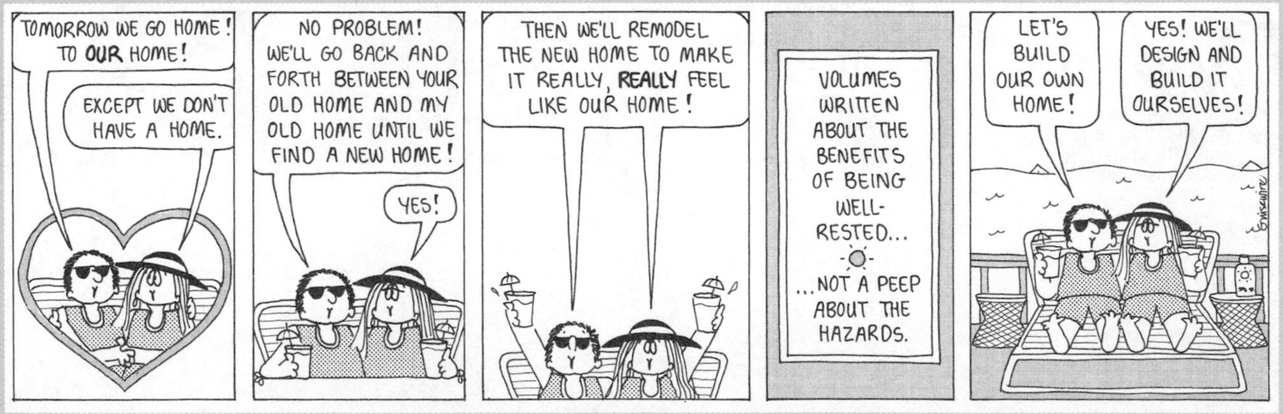
TOMORROW WE GO HOME! TO OUR HOME!
EXCEPT WE DON'T HAVE A HOME.
NO PROBLEM! WE'LL GO BACK AND FORTH BETWEEN YOUR OLD HOME AND MY OLD HOME UNTIL WE FIND A NEW HOME!
YES!
THEN WE'LL REMODEL THE NEW HOME TO MAKE IT REALLY, REALLY FEEL LIKE OUR HOME!
VOLUMES WRITTEN ABOUT THE BENEFITS OF BEING WELL-RESTED...
...NOT A PEEP ABOUT THE HAZARDS.
LET'S BUILD OUR OWN HOME!
YES! WE'LL DESIGN AND BUILD IT OURSELVES!

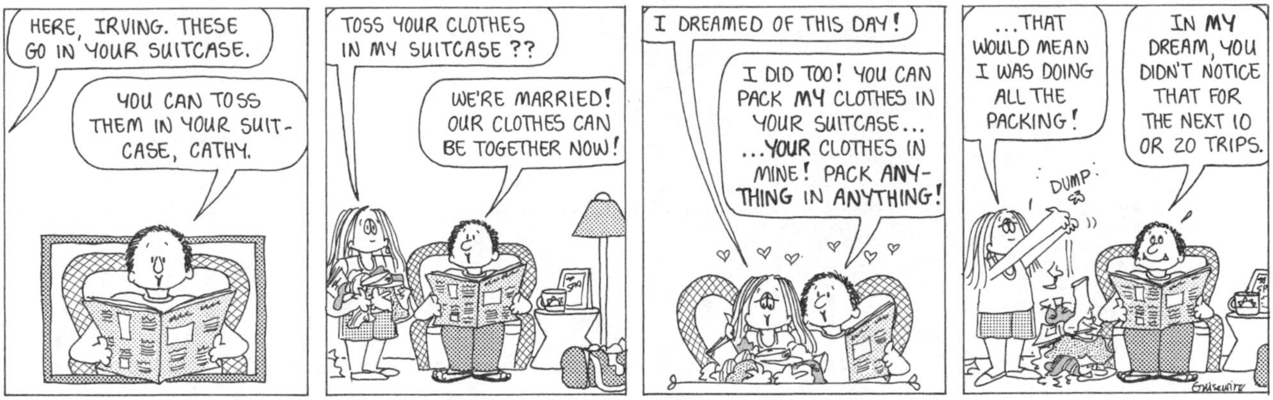
HERE, IRVING. THESE GO IN YOUR SUITCASE.
YOU CAN TOSS THEM IN YOUR SUIT-CASE, CATHY.
TOSS YOUR CLOTHES IN MY SUITCASE??
WE'RE MARRIED! OUR CLOTHES CAN BE TOGETHER NOW!
I DREAMED OF THIS DAY!
I DID TOO! YOU CAN PACK MY CLOTHES IN YOUR SUITCASE... ...YOUR CLOTHES IN MINE! PACK ANY-THING IN ANYTHING!
...THAT WOULD MEAN I WAS DOING ALL THE PACKING!
DUMP
IN MY DREAM, YOU DIDN'T NOTICE THAT FOR THE NEXT 10 OR 20 TRIPS.

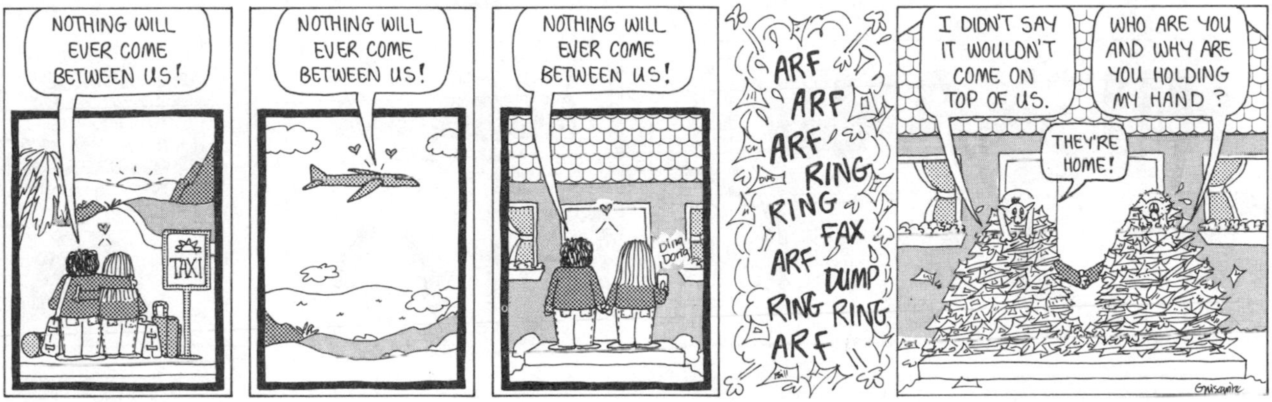
NOTHING WILL EVER COME BETWEEN US!
TAXI
NOTHING WILL EVER COME BETWEEN US!
NOTHING WILL EVER COME BETWEEN US!
Ding Dong
ARF ARF ARF RING RING FAX ARF DUMP RING RING ARF
I DIDN'T SAY IT WOULDN'T COME ON TOP OF US.
WHO ARE YOU AND WHY ARE YOU HOLDING MY HAND?
THEY'RE HOME!

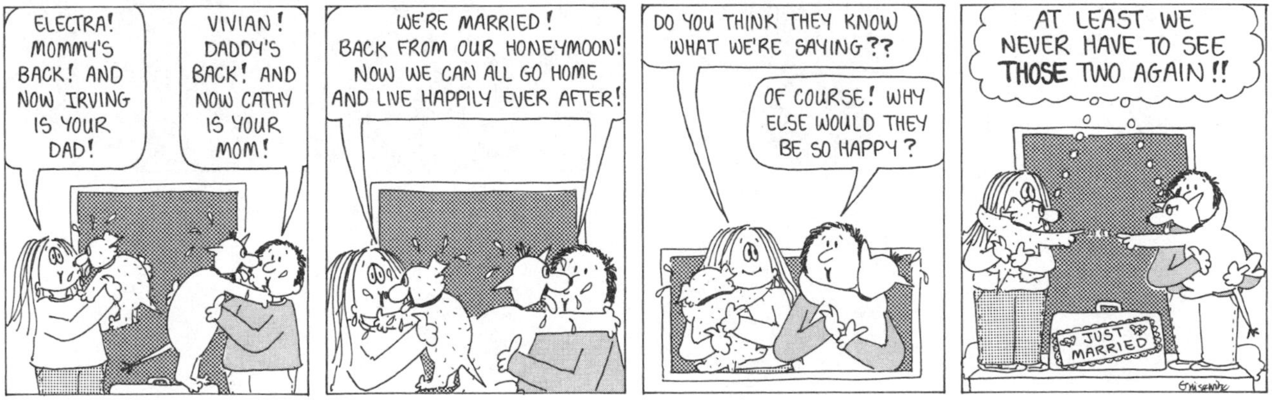
ELECTRA! MOMMY'S BACK! AND NOW IRVING IS YOUR DAD!
VIVIAN! DADDY'S BACK! AND NOW CATHY IS YOUR MOM!
WE'RE MARRIED! BACK FROM OUR HONEYMOON! NOW WE CAN ALL GO HOME AND LIVE HAPPILY EVER AFTER!
DO YOU THINK THEY KNOW WHAT WE'RE SAYING??
OF COURSE! WHY ELSE WOULD THEY BE SO HAPPY?
AT LEAST WE NEVER HAVE TO SEE THOSE TWO AGAIN!!
JUST MARRIED

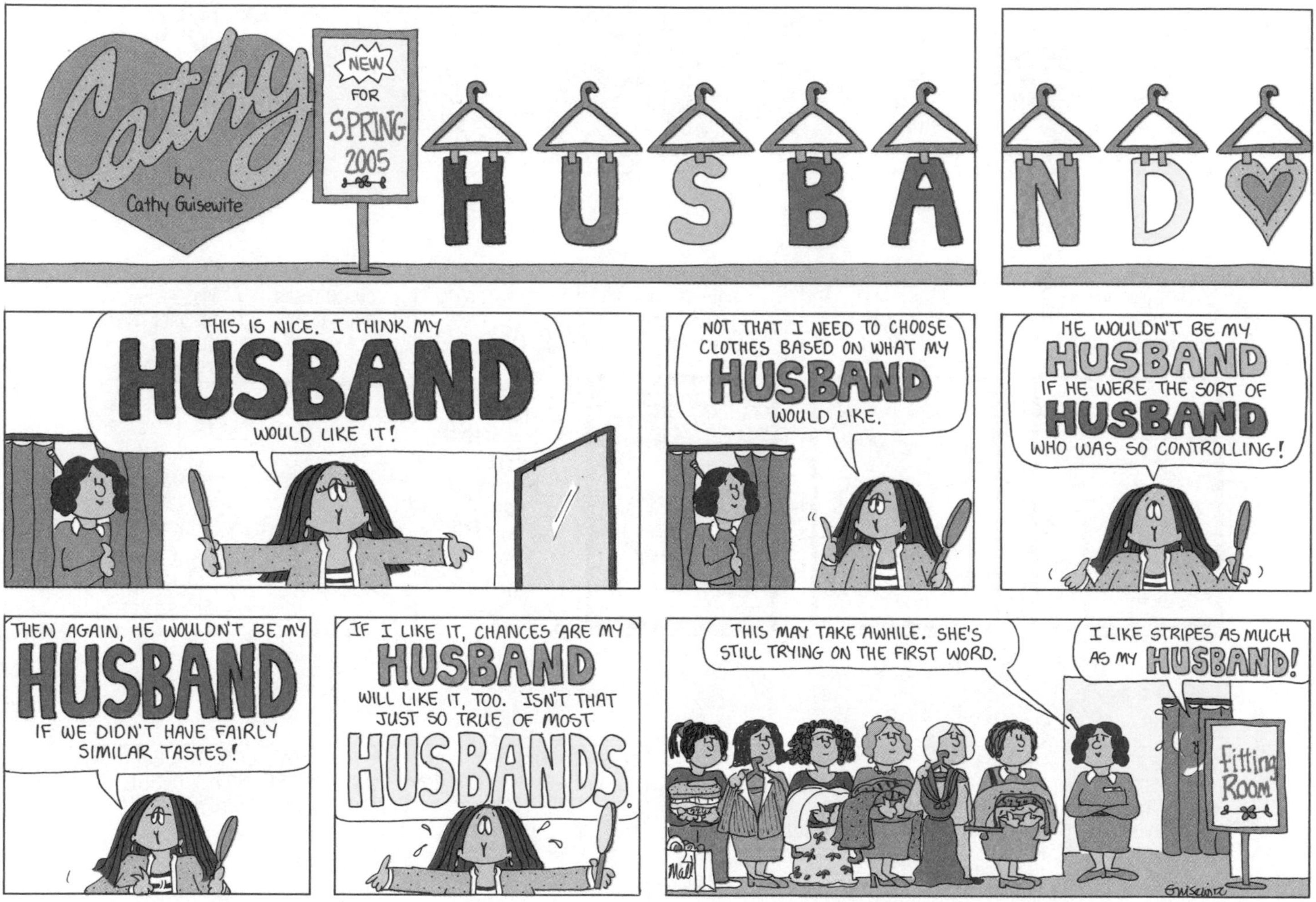
Cathy
by
Cathy Guisewite
NEW FOR SPRING 2005
HUSBAND
THIS IS NICE. I THINK MY HUSBAND WOULD LIKE IT!
NOT THAT I NEED TO CHOOSE CLOTHES BASED ON WHAT MY HUSBAND WOULD LIKE.
HE WOULDN'T BE MY HUSBAND IF HE WERE THE SORT OF HUSBAND WHO WAS SO CONTROLLING!
THEN AGAIN, HE WOULDN'T BE MY HUSBAND IF WE DIDN'T HAVE FAIRLY SIMILAR TASTES!
IF I LIKE IT, CHANCES ARE MY HUSBAND WILL LIKE IT, TOO. ISN'T THAT JUST SO TRUE OF MOST HUSBANDS.
THIS MAY TAKE AWHILE. SHE'S STILL TRYING ON THE FIRST WORD.
I LIKE STRIPES AS MUCH AS MY HUSBAND!
Fitting Room
Mall
Guisewite

Scenes from a 27-Year Courtship

Why?
Why him?
Why now?
Why not someone nice and new with better hair?
I ask myself the same questions.
And then I look through their history.
Little glimpses of all the phases they survived.
I'm moved by how hard they tried to connect, how completely they failed.
How much they changed because of and in spite of each other.
I get reminded of how it felt in the beginning.
Of all the reasons people keep coming back.
For better or for worse,
For richer or for poorer,
In sickness and in health,
Life was always just a little more interesting when Irving was in the picture.

The Getting to Know You Phase

November 22, 1976—The world's first peek at Cathy, empowered woman of 1976

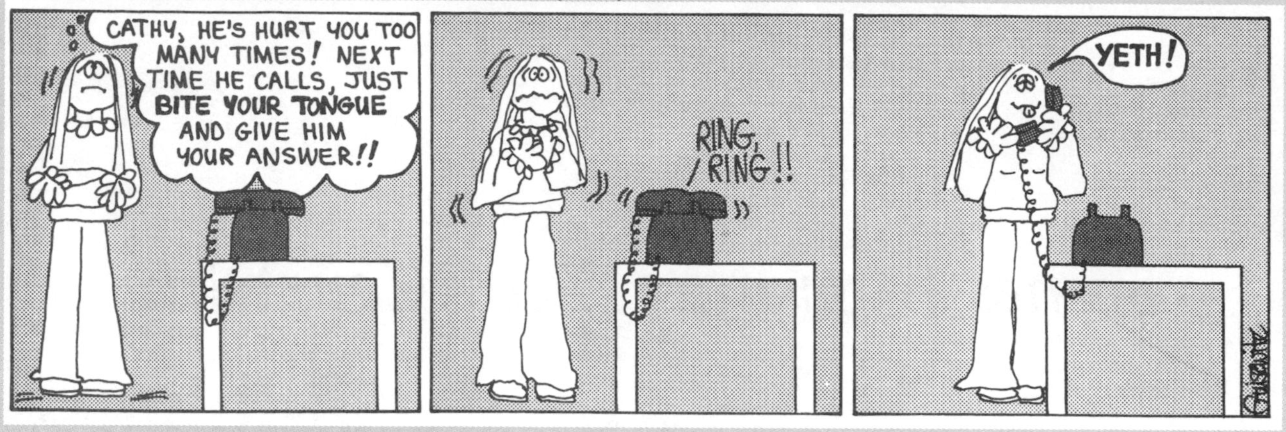
CATHY, HE'S HURT YOU TOO MANY TIMES! NEXT TIME HE CALLS, JUST BITE YOUR TONGUE AND GIVE HIM YOUR ANSWER!!
RING, RING!!
YETH!

November 27, 1976—Irving's first appearance

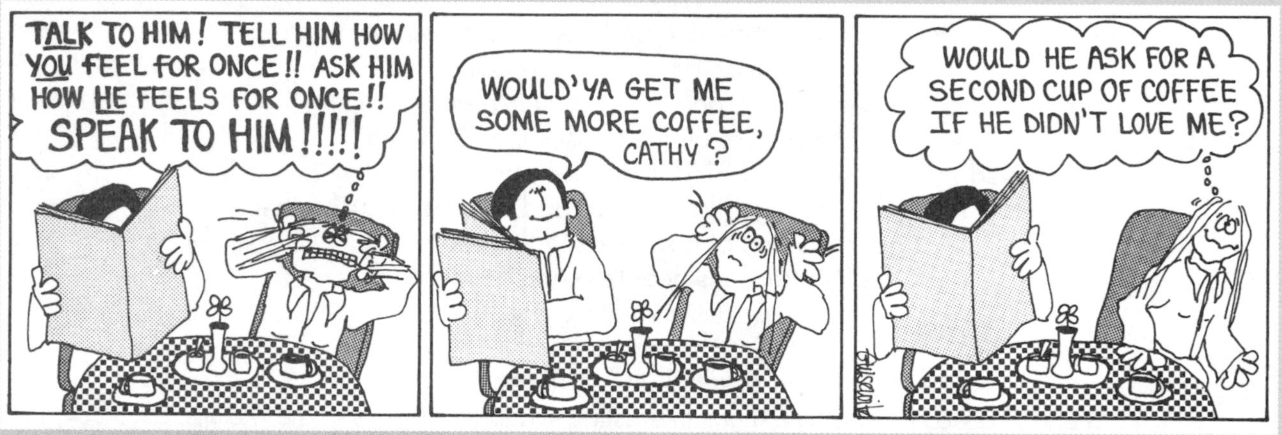
TALK TO HIM! TELL HIM HOW YOU FEEL FOR ONCE!! ASK HIM HOW HE FEELS FOR ONCE!! SPEAK TO HIM!!!!!
WOULD'YA GET ME SOME MORE COFFEE, CATHY?
WOULD HE ASK FOR A SECOND CUP OF COFFEE IF HE DIDN'T LOVE ME?

December 13, 1976—Irving's first disappearance

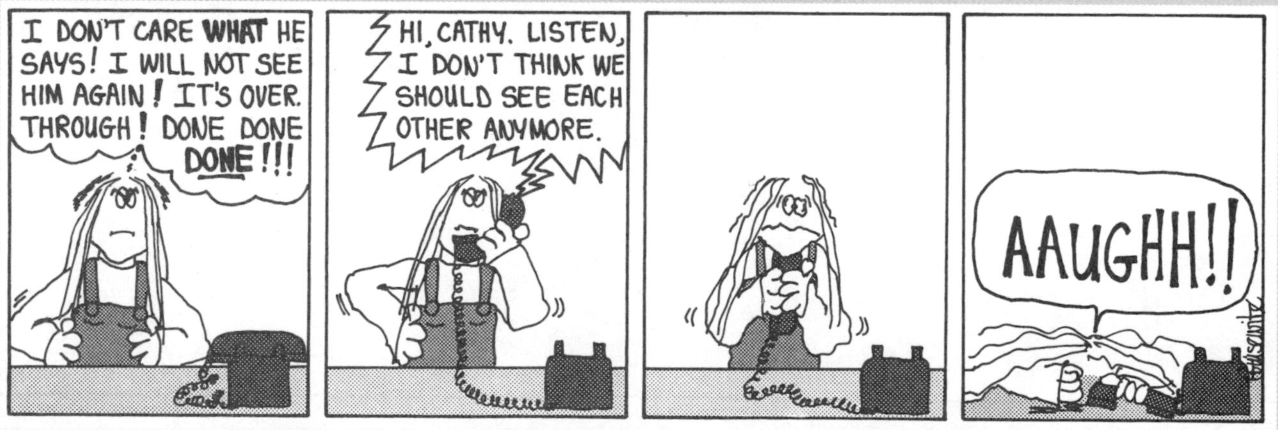
I DON'T CARE WHAT HE SAYS! I WILL NOT SEE HIM AGAIN! IT'S OVER. THROUGH! DONE DONE DONE!!!
HI, CATHY. LISTEN, I DON'T THINK WE SHOULD SEE EACH OTHER ANYMORE.
AAUGHH!!

The Trying to Establish a Meaningful Relationship While Rebelling Against Monogamy and Redefining the Roles of Men and Women in Society Phase

1977

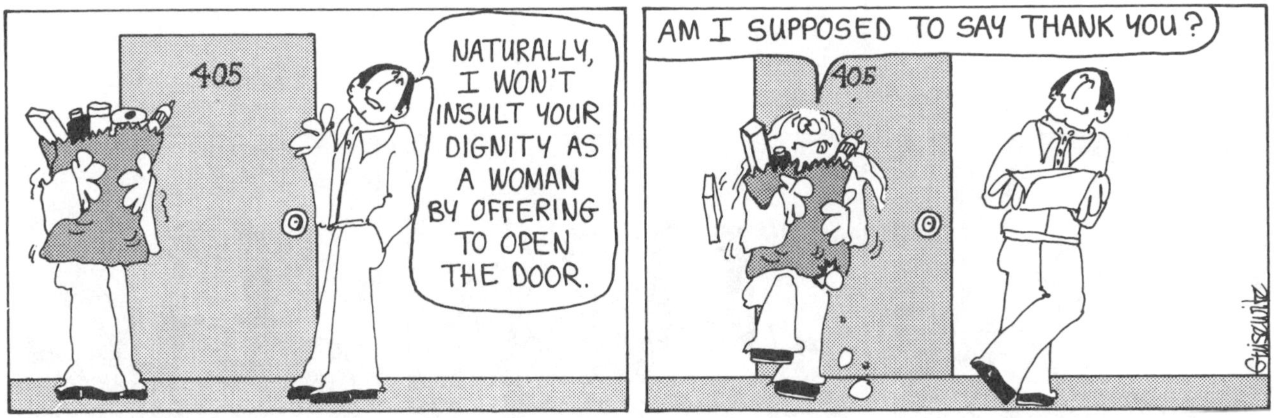
405
NATURALLY, I WON'T INSULT YOUR DIGNITY AS A WOMAN BY OFFERING TO OPEN THE DOOR.
AM I SUPPOSED TO SAY THANK YOU?

1977

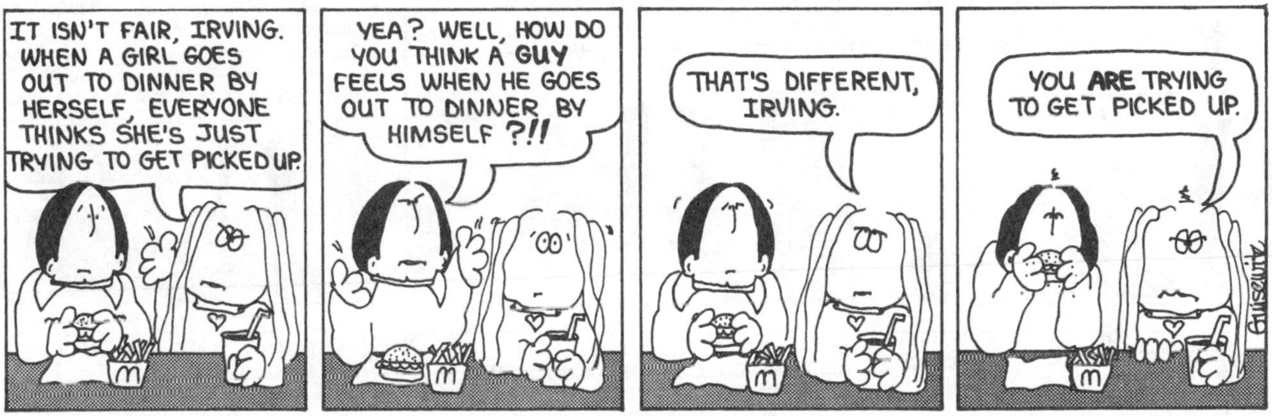
IT ISN'T FAIR, IRVING. WHEN A GIRL GOES OUT TO DINNER BY HERSELF, EVERYONE THINKS SHE'S JUST TRYING TO GET PICKED UP.
YEA? WELL, HOW DO YOU THINK A GUY FEELS WHEN HE GOES OUT TO DINNER BY HIMSELF ?!!
THAT'S DIFFERENT, IRVING.
YOU ARE TRYING TO GET PICKED UP.

1979

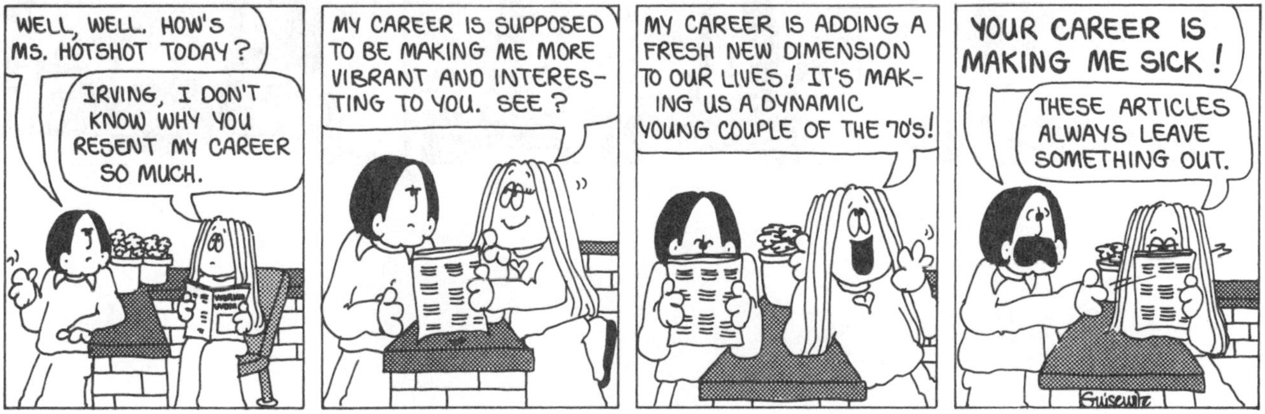
WELL, WELL. HOW'S MS. HOTSHOT TODAY?
IRVING, I DON'T KNOW WHY YOU RESENT MY CAREER SO MUCH.
MY CAREER IS SUPPOSED TO BE MAKING ME MORE VIBRANT AND INTERESTING TO YOU. SEE?
MY CAREER IS ADDING A FRESH NEW DIMENSION TO OUR LIVES! IT'S MAKING US A DYNAMIC YOUNG COUPLE OF THE 70'S!
YOUR CAREER IS MAKING ME SICK!
THESE ARTICLES ALWAYS LEAVE SOMETHING OUT.

cathy

by Cathy Guisewite

I CAN'T DO IT.

HERE'S A HYPOTHETICAL SITUATION, IRVING... SAY I BROUGHT HOME ALL THESE JELLY BEANS AND THE BLACK ONES WERE YOUR FAVORITES. WHAT WOULD YOU DO?

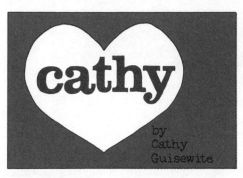

I'D EAT THEM.

RIGHT. AS A MAN, YOU WERE BROUGHT UP THAT WAY.

BUT AS A WOMAN, I WAS BROUGHT UP BELIEVING THAT EVEN IF I LIKED BLACK JELLY BEANS AS MUCH AS YOU, I SHOULD GIVE THEM ALL TO YOU. MY HAPPINESS WAS SUPPOSED TO COME FROM MAKING **YOU** HAPPY.

NOW, INTELLECTUALLY I KNOW THAT CAN'T BE RIGHT. AT THE VERY LEAST, WE SHOULD SHARE THE BLACK JELLY BEANS. BUT EMOTIONALLY, I CAN'T HELP MYSELF.

DEEP DOWN, I STILL WANT YOU TO HAVE ALL THE BLACK JELLY BEANS. IRVING, I WANT YOU TO HAVE **ALL** THE JELLY BEANS!!

NAH, I THINK I'LL TAKE THE...

GET YOUR HANDS OFF MY MARSHMALLOW RABBIT.

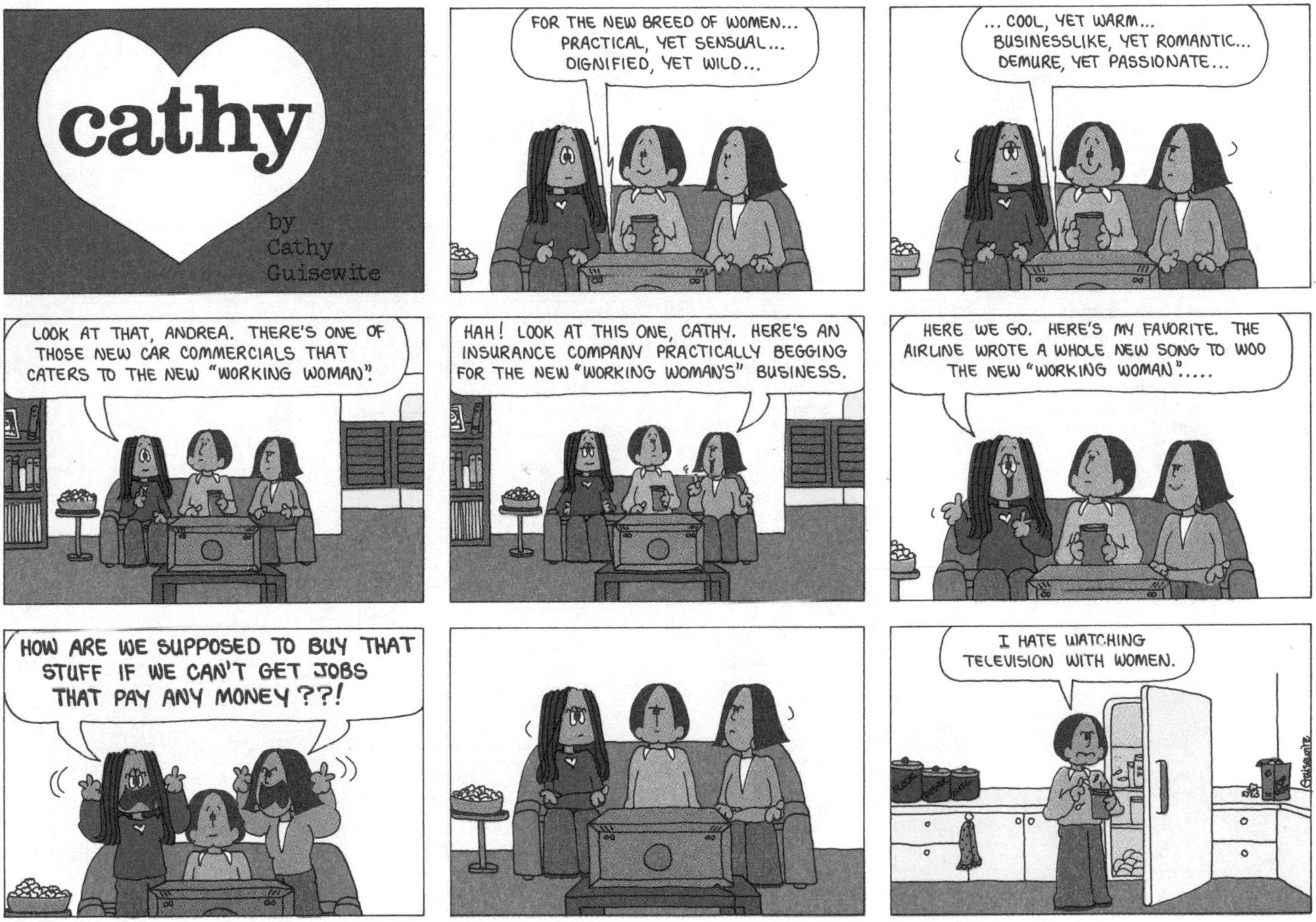
cathy
by
Cathy
Guisewite
FOR THE NEW BREED OF WOMEN... PRACTICAL, YET SENSUAL... DIGNIFIED, YET WILD...
...COOL, YET WARM... BUSINESSLIKE, YET ROMANTIC... DEMURE, YET PASSIONATE...
LOOK AT THAT, ANDREA. THERE'S ONE OF THOSE NEW CAR COMMERCIALS THAT CATERS TO THE NEW "WORKING WOMAN".
HAH! LOOK AT THIS ONE, CATHY. HERE'S AN INSURANCE COMPANY PRACTICALLY BEGGING FOR THE NEW "WORKING WOMAN'S" BUSINESS.
HERE WE GO. HERE'S MY FAVORITE. THE AIRLINE WROTE A WHOLE NEW SONG TO WOO THE NEW "WORKING WOMAN".....
HOW ARE WE SUPPOSED TO BUY THAT STUFF IF WE CAN'T GET JOBS THAT PAY ANY MONEY??!
I HATE WATCHING TELEVISION WITH WOMEN.
Guisewite

1981

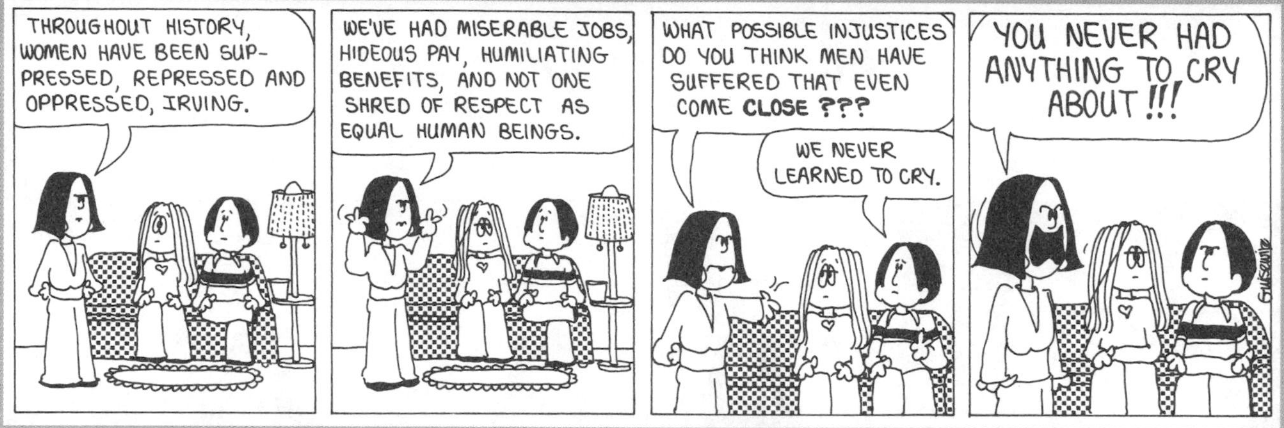
THROUGHOUT HISTORY, WOMEN HAVE BEEN SUP-PRESSED, REPRESSED AND OPPRESSED, IRVING.
WE'VE HAD MISERABLE JOBS, HIDEOUS PAY, HUMILIATING BENEFITS, AND NOT ONE SHRED OF RESPECT AS EQUAL HUMAN BEINGS.
WHAT POSSIBLE INJUSTICES DO YOU THINK MEN HAVE SUFFERED THAT EVEN COME CLOSE ???
WE NEVER LEARNED TO CRY.
YOU NEVER HAD ANYTHING TO CRY ABOUT !!!

1981

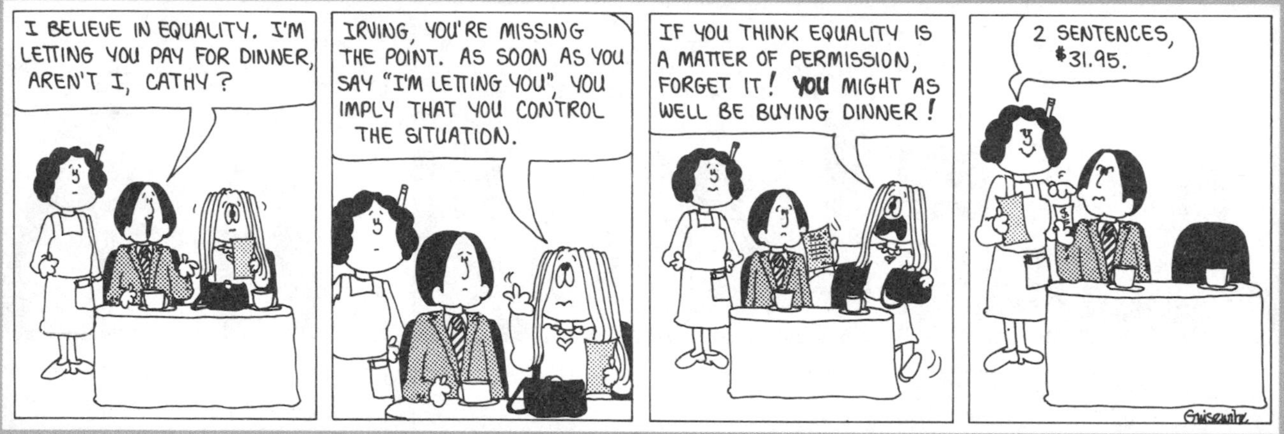
I BELIEVE IN EQUALITY. I'M LETTING YOU PAY FOR DINNER, AREN'T I, CATHY ?
IRVING, YOU'RE MISSING THE POINT. AS SOON AS YOU SAY "I'M LETTING YOU", YOU IMPLY THAT YOU CONTROL THE SITUATION.
IF YOU THINK EQUALITY IS A MATTER OF PERMISSION, FORGET IT! YOU MIGHT AS WELL BE BUYING DINNER!
2 SENTENCES, $31.95.

1982

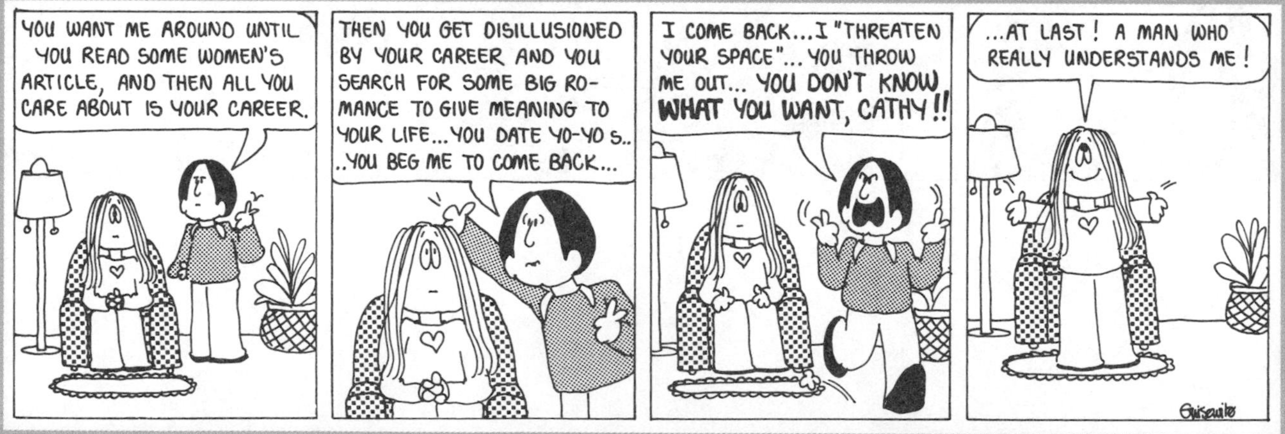
YOU WANT ME AROUND UNTIL YOU READ SOME WOMEN'S ARTICLE, AND THEN ALL YOU CARE ABOUT IS YOUR CAREER.
THEN YOU GET DISILLUSIONED BY YOUR CAREER AND YOU SEARCH FOR SOME BIG RO-MANCE TO GIVE MEANING TO YOUR LIFE...YOU DATE YO-YO S.. ..YOU BEG ME TO COME BACK...
I COME BACK...I "THREATEN YOUR SPACE"... YOU THROW ME OUT... YOU DON'T KNOW WHAT YOU WANT, CATHY!!
...AT LAST! A MAN WHO REALLY UNDERSTANDS ME!

The Committing to Anything Except Another Human Phase

1983

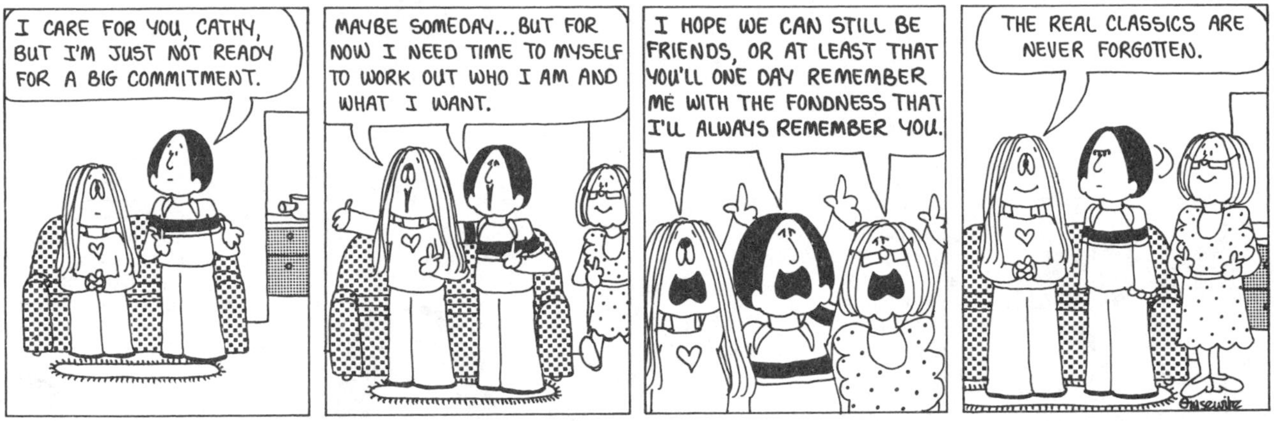
I CARE FOR YOU, CATHY, BUT I'M JUST NOT READY FOR A BIG COMMITMENT.
MAYBE SOMEDAY... BUT FOR NOW I NEED TIME TO MYSELF TO WORK OUT WHO I AM AND WHAT I WANT.
I HOPE WE CAN STILL BE FRIENDS, OR AT LEAST THAT YOU'LL ONE DAY REMEMBER ME WITH THE FONDNESS THAT I'LL ALWAYS REMEMBER YOU.
THE REAL CLASSICS ARE NEVER FORGOTTEN.

1983

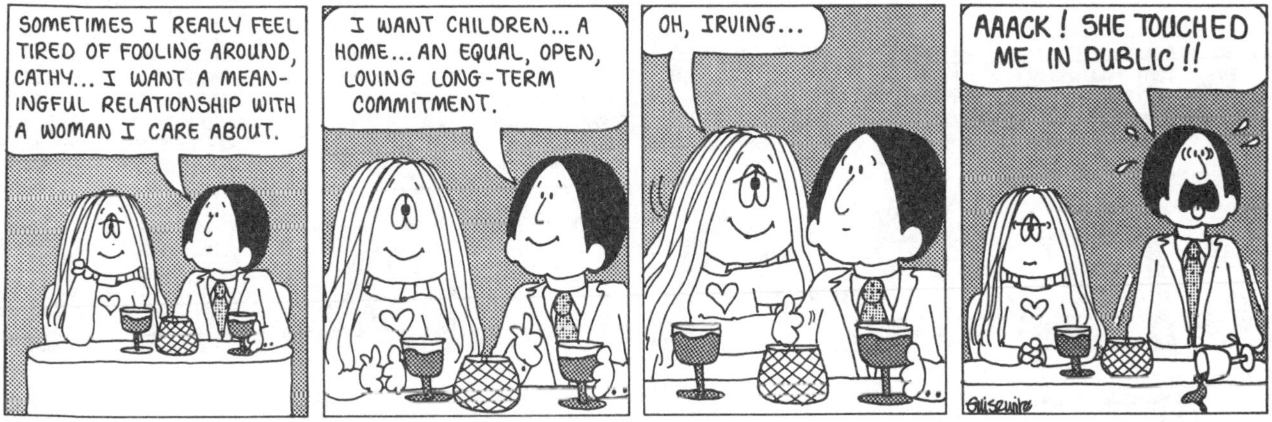
SOMETIMES I REALLY FEEL TIRED OF FOOLING AROUND, CATHY... I WANT A MEANINGFUL RELATIONSHIP WITH A WOMAN I CARE ABOUT.
I WANT CHILDREN... A HOME... AN EQUAL, OPEN, LOVING LONG-TERM COMMITMENT.
OH, IRVING...
AAACK! SHE TOUCHED ME IN PUBLIC!!

1987

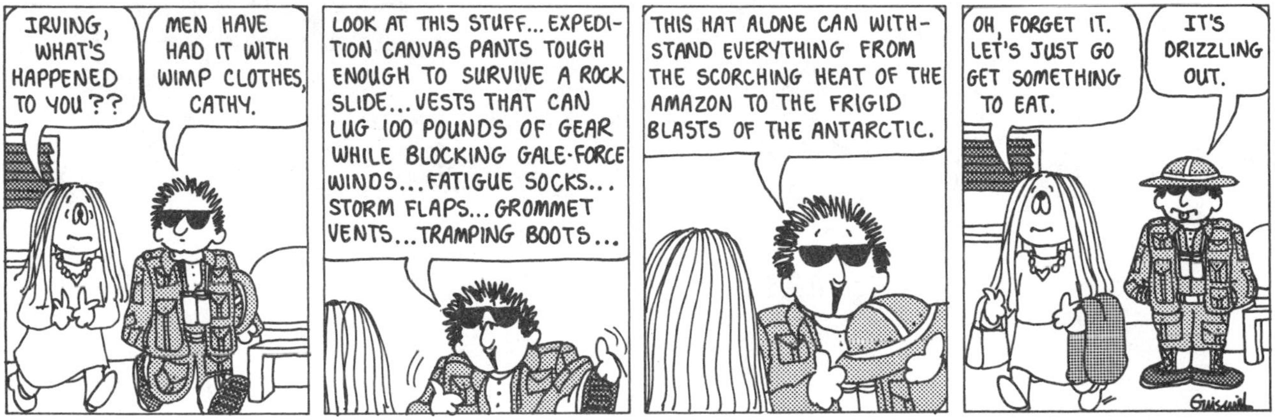
IRVING, WHAT'S HAPPENED TO YOU??
MEN HAVE HAD IT WITH WIMP CLOTHES, CATHY.
LOOK AT THIS STUFF... EXPEDITION CANVAS PANTS TOUGH ENOUGH TO SURVIVE A ROCK SLIDE... VESTS THAT CAN LUG 100 POUNDS OF GEAR WHILE BLOCKING GALE-FORCE WINDS... FATIGUE SOCKS... STORM FLAPS... GROMMET VENTS... TRAMPING BOOTS...
THIS HAT ALONE CAN WITHSTAND EVERYTHING FROM THE SCORCHING HEAT OF THE AMAZON TO THE FRIGID BLASTS OF THE ANTARCTIC.
OH, FORGET IT. LET'S JUST GO GET SOMETHING TO EAT.
IT'S DRIZZLING OUT.

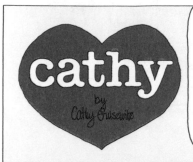

cathy by Cathy Guisewite

ANODIZED ALUMINUM MULTI-LENS THREE-BEAM MINI EXCAVATION SPOTLIGHT THAT WILL LIVE ITS LIFE IN THE JUNK DRAWER WITH DEAD BATTERIES.

HIGH-TECH, EPOXY-FINISHED, HEAVY-GAUGE STEEL GRID HANGING UNIT FOR HOME REPAIR TOOLS THAT REQUIRED TWO CARPENTERS TO INSTALL, AND IS NOW USED AS A SCARF RACK.

SAFARI CLOTHES THAT WILL NEVER BE NEAR A JUNGLE.

AEROBIC FOOTGEAR THAT WILL NEVER SET FOOT IN AN AEROBICS CLASS.

DEEP-SEA DIVE WATCH THAT WILL NEVER GET DAMP.

KEYS TO A 4-WHEEL-DRIVE VEHICLE THAT WILL NEVER EXPERIENCE A HILL.

PROFESSIONAL DESIGNER'S MAGNIFYING DRAFTING LAMP THAT WILL NEVER BE IN A ROOM WITH AN IDEA.

INDUSTRIAL STAINLESS STEEL PASTA VAT THAT WILL NEVER SEE A NOODLE OR A GROUP.

ARCHITECTURAL MAGAZINES WE DON'T READ FILLED WITH PICTURES OF FURNITURE WE DON'T LIKE.

10-FUNCTION ANSWERING MACHINE WITH ANTI-TAP DEVICE FOR A TELEPHONE THAT NEVER RINGS.

27-TIME-ZONE INTERNATIONAL CLOCK IN AN INDESTRUCTIBLE MOLDED ALLOY BRIEFCASE THAT WILL NEVER LEAVE OUR ZIP CODE.

FINANCIAL STRATEGY SOFTWARE KEYED TO A CHECKBOOK THAT'S LOST SOMEWHERE UNDER A COMPUTER NO ONE KNOWS HOW TO WORK.

ART POSTER FROM AN EXHIBIT WE NEVER WENT TO OF AN ARTIST WE NEVER HEARD OF.

Leon Bozzolini

HAUTE GALLERIE
22 OCT 1985

ABSTRACT MATERIALISM HAS ARRIVED.

WE'VE MOVED PAST THE THINGS WE WANT AND NEED AND ARE BUYING THOSE THINGS THAT HAVE NOTHING TO DO WITH OUR LIVES.

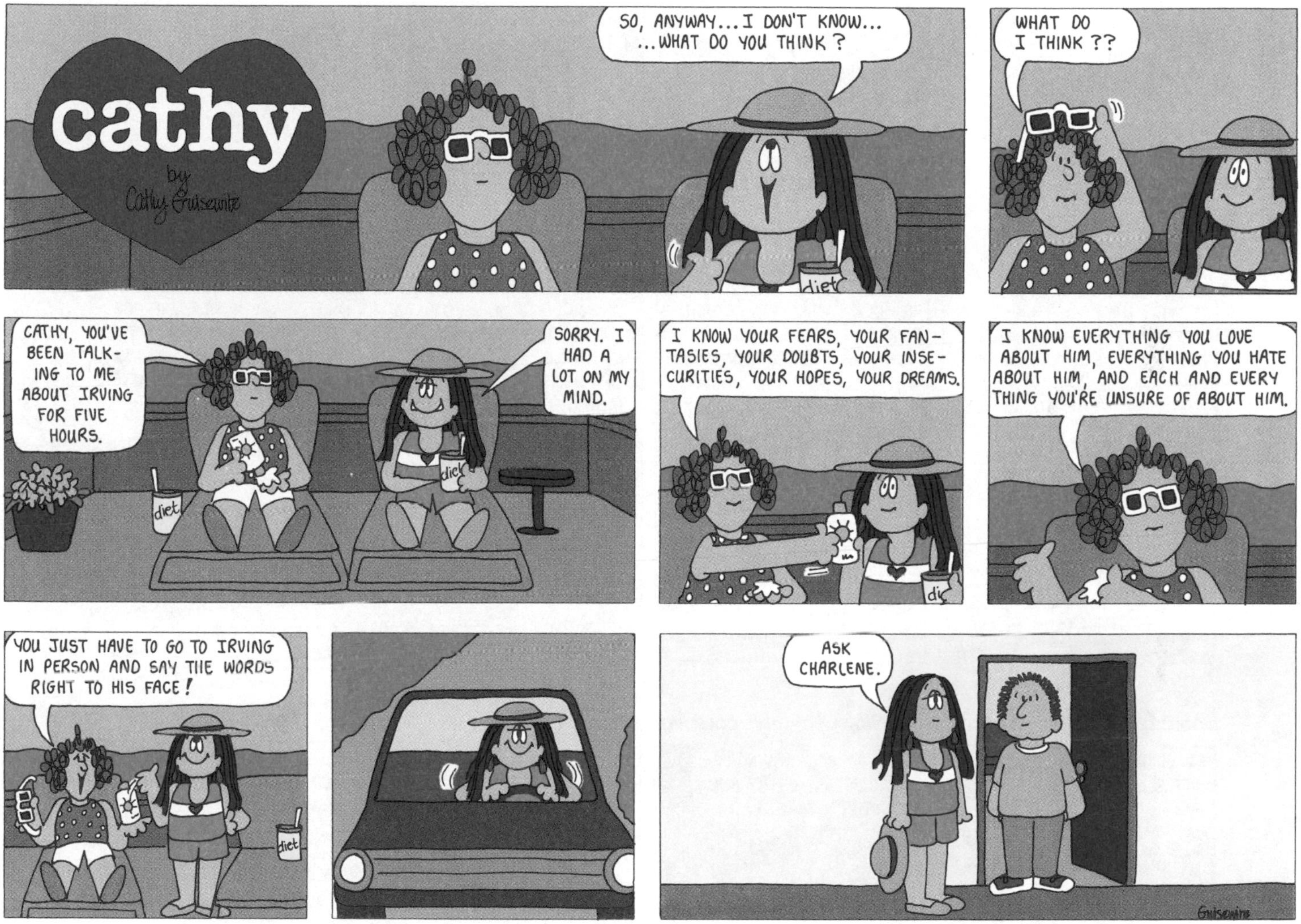
cathy
by Cathy Guisewite
SO, ANYWAY... I DON'T KNOW... ...WHAT DO YOU THINK?
WHAT DO I THINK??
CATHY, YOU'VE BEEN TALKING TO ME ABOUT IRVING FOR FIVE HOURS.
SORRY. I HAD A LOT ON MY MIND.
I KNOW YOUR FEARS, YOUR FANTASIES, YOUR DOUBTS, YOUR INSECURITIES, YOUR HOPES, YOUR DREAMS.
I KNOW EVERYTHING YOU LOVE ABOUT HIM, EVERYTHING YOU HATE ABOUT HIM, AND EACH AND EVERY THING YOU'RE UNSURE OF ABOUT HIM.
YOU JUST HAVE TO GO TO IRVING IN PERSON AND SAY THE WORDS RIGHT TO HIS FACE!
ASK CHARLENE.
Guisewite

The Meeting of the Parents

August 2, 1977—Irving meets Cathy's parents

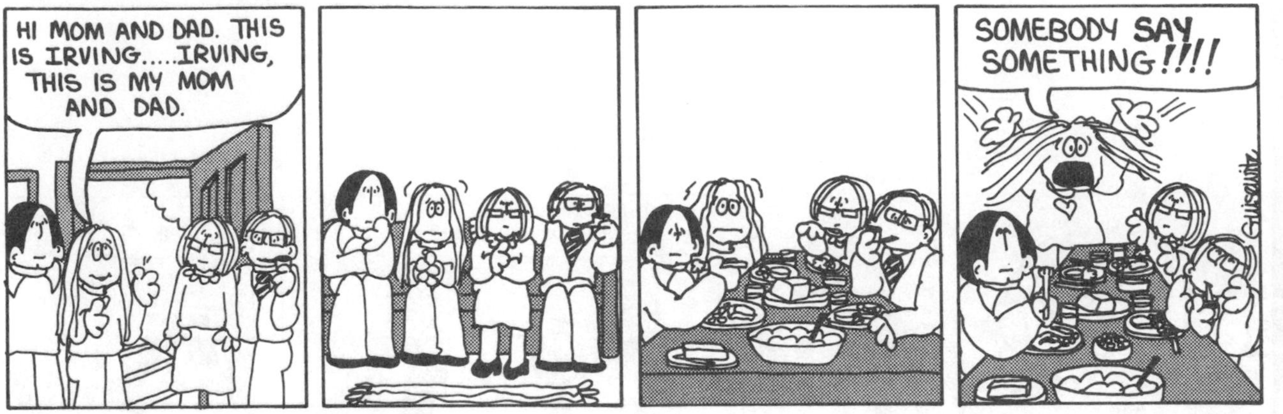
HI MOM AND DAD. THIS IS IRVING.....IRVING, THIS IS MY MOM AND DAD.
SOMEBODY SAY SOMETHING!!!!

February 7, 1985—Cathy meets Irving's parents

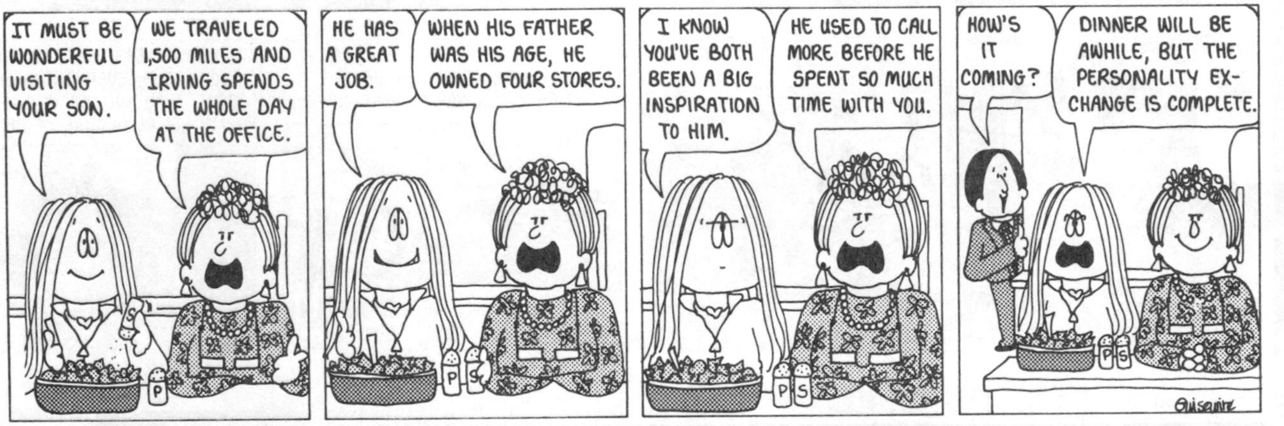
IT MUST BE WONDERFUL VISITING YOUR SON.
WE TRAVELED 1,500 MILES AND IRVING SPENDS THE WHOLE DAY AT THE OFFICE.
HE HAS A GREAT JOB.
WHEN HIS FATHER WAS HIS AGE, HE OWNED FOUR STORES.
I KNOW YOU'VE BOTH BEEN A BIG INSPIRATION TO HIM.
HE USED TO CALL MORE BEFORE HE SPENT SO MUCH TIME WITH YOU.
HOW'S IT COMING?
DINNER WILL BE AWHILE, BUT THE PERSONALITY EX-CHANGE IS COMPLETE.

December 3, 1987—Cathy's parents meet Irving's parents

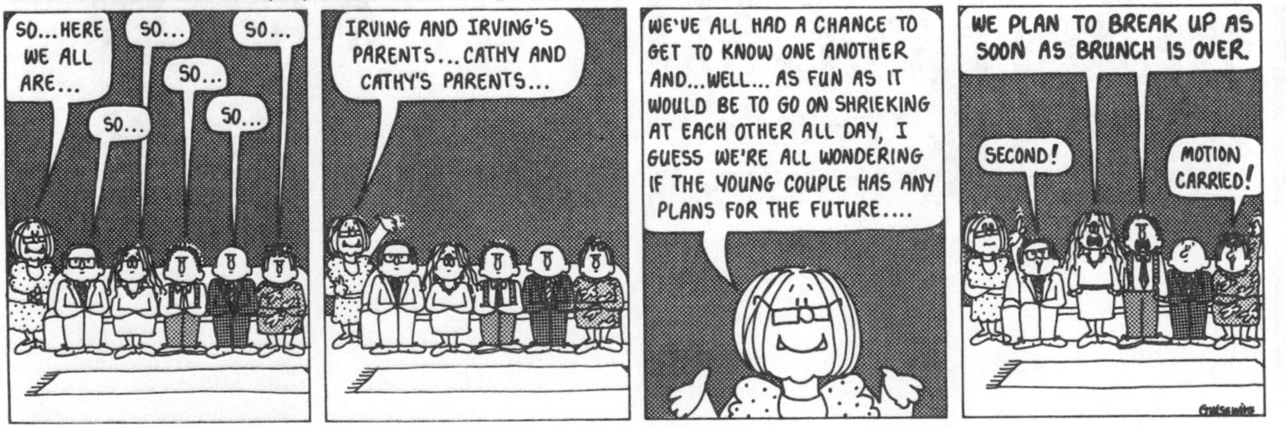
SO...HERE WE ALL ARE...
SO...
SO...
SO...
SO...
SO...
IRVING AND IRVING'S PARENTS...CATHY AND CATHY'S PARENTS...
WE'VE ALL HAD A CHANCE TO GET TO KNOW ONE ANOTHER AND...WELL... AS FUN AS IT WOULD BE TO GO ON SHRIEKING AT EACH OTHER ALL DAY, I GUESS WE'RE ALL WONDERING IF THE YOUNG COUPLE HAS ANY PLANS FOR THE FUTURE....
WE PLAN TO BREAK UP AS SOON AS BRUNCH IS OVER.
SECOND!
MOTION CARRIED!

October 10, 1988—Irving meets Electra

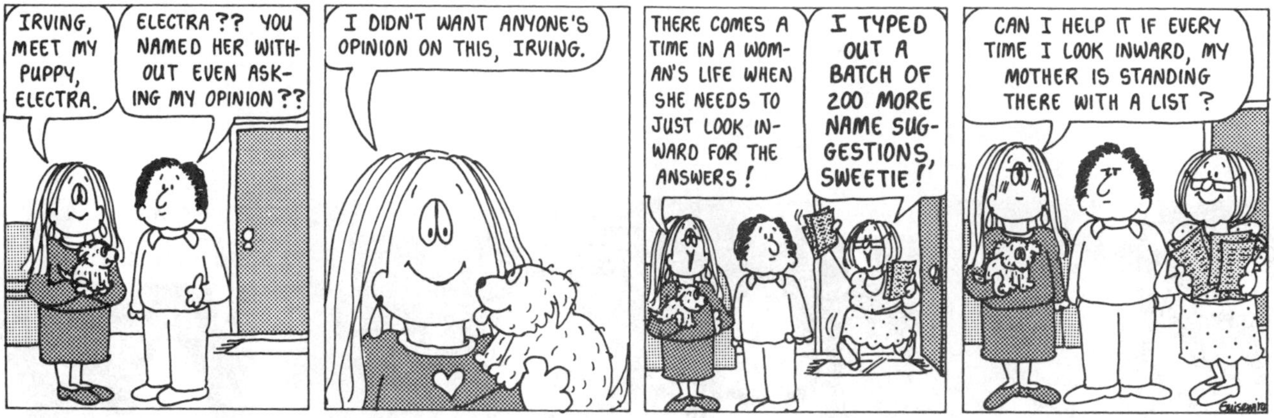
IRVING, MEET MY PUPPY, ELECTRA.
ELECTRA?? YOU NAMED HER WITHOUT EVEN ASKING MY OPINION??
I DIDN'T WANT ANYONE'S OPINION ON THIS, IRVING.
THERE COMES A TIME IN A WOMAN'S LIFE WHEN SHE NEEDS TO JUST LOOK INWARD FOR THE ANSWERS!
I TYPED OUT A BATCH OF 200 MORE NAME SUGGESTIONS, SWEETIE!
CAN I HELP IT IF EVERY TIME I LOOK INWARD, MY MOTHER IS STANDING THERE WITH A LIST?

1989—Unconditional Love

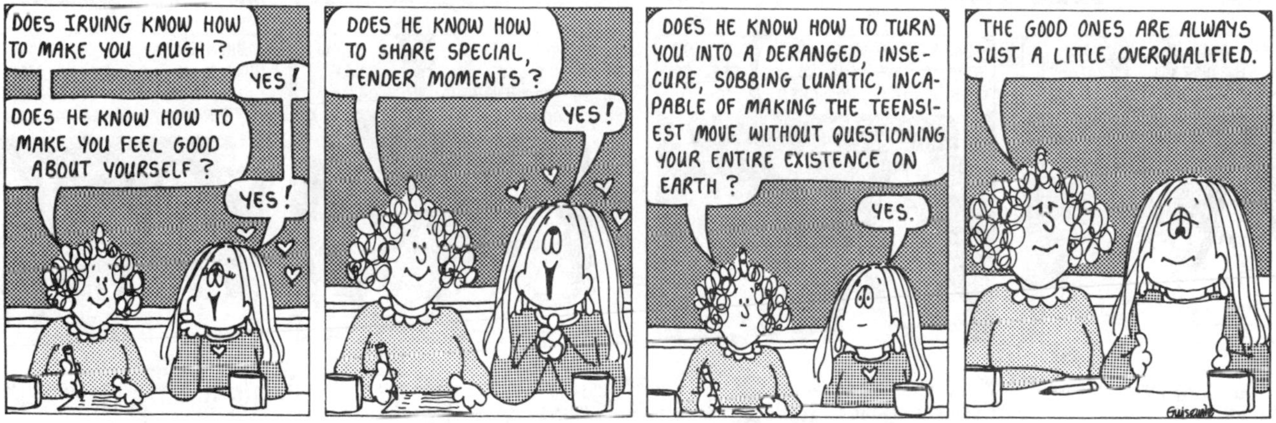
DOES IRVING KNOW HOW TO MAKE YOU LAUGH?
YES!
DOES HE KNOW HOW TO MAKE YOU FEEL GOOD ABOUT YOURSELF?
YES!
DOES HE KNOW HOW TO SHARE SPECIAL, TENDER MOMENTS?
YES!
DOES HE KNOW HOW TO TURN YOU INTO A DERANGED, INSECURE, SOBBING LUNATIC, INCAPABLE OF MAKING THE TEENSIEST MOVE WITHOUT QUESTIONING YOUR ENTIRE EXISTENCE ON EARTH?
YES.
THE GOOD ONES ARE ALWAYS JUST A LITTLE OVERQUALIFIED.

1989—Unsuccessful Breakup

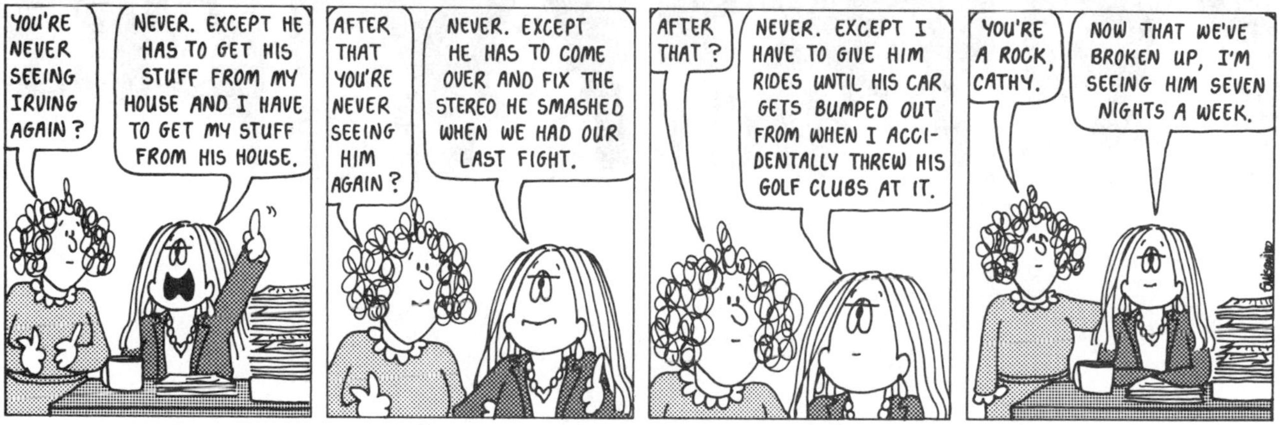
YOU'RE NEVER SEEING IRVING AGAIN?
NEVER. EXCEPT HE HAS TO GET HIS STUFF FROM MY HOUSE AND I HAVE TO GET MY STUFF FROM HIS HOUSE.
AFTER THAT YOU'RE NEVER SEEING HIM AGAIN?
NEVER. EXCEPT HE HAS TO COME OVER AND FIX THE STEREO HE SMASHED WHEN WE HAD OUR LAST FIGHT.
AFTER THAT?
NEVER. EXCEPT I HAVE TO GIVE HIM RIDES UNTIL HIS CAR GETS BUMPED OUT FROM WHEN I ACCIDENTALLY THREW HIS GOLF CLUBS AT IT.
YOU'RE A ROCK, CATHY.
NOW THAT WE'VE BROKEN UP, I'M SEEING HIM SEVEN NIGHTS A WEEK.

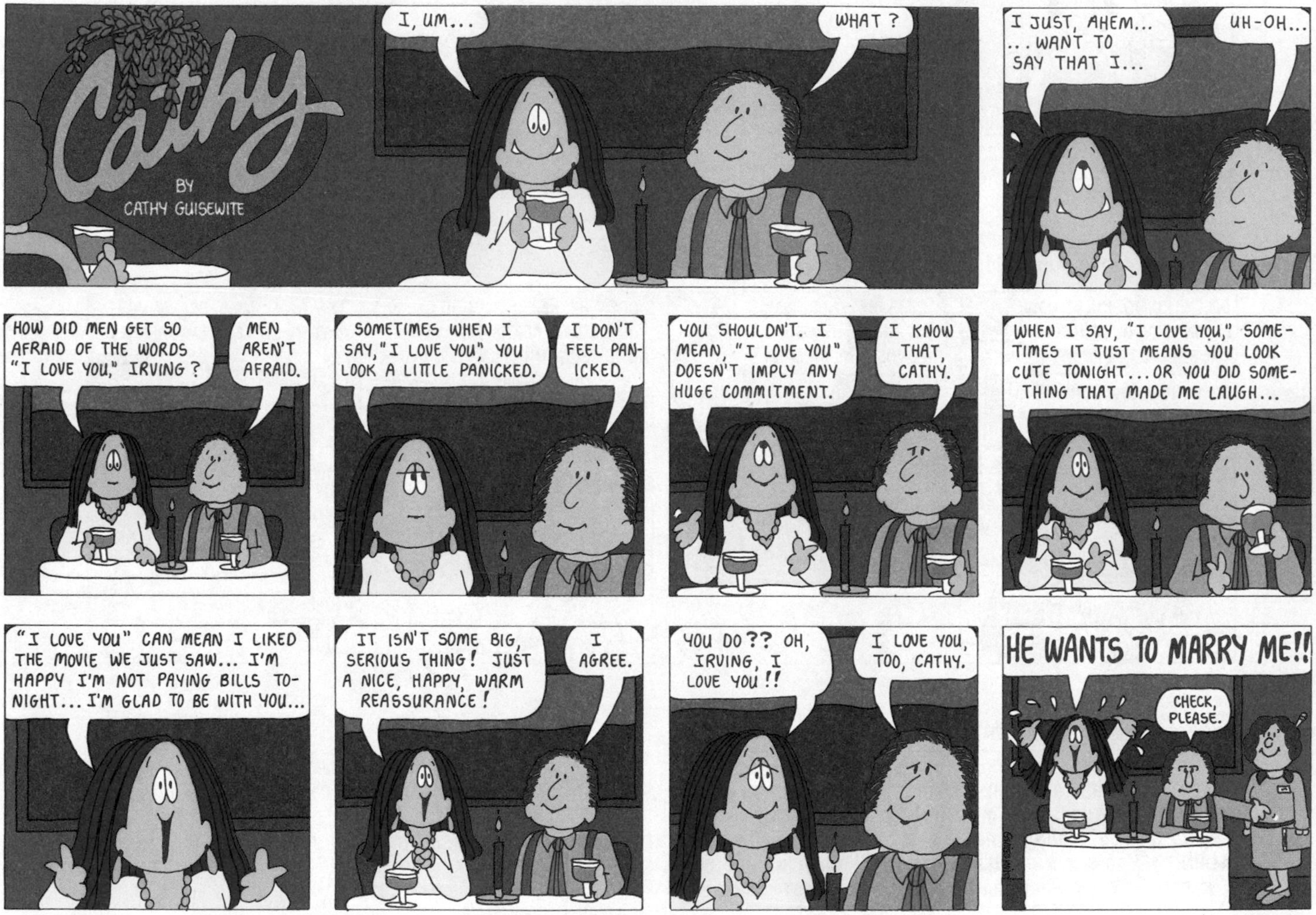
Cathy
BY CATHY GUISEWITE
I, UM...
WHAT?
I JUST, AHEM... ...WANT TO SAY THAT I...
UH-OH...
HOW DID MEN GET SO AFRAID OF THE WORDS "I LOVE YOU," IRVING?
MEN AREN'T AFRAID.
SOMETIMES WHEN I SAY, "I LOVE YOU," YOU LOOK A LITTLE PANICKED.
I DON'T FEEL PANICKED.
YOU SHOULDN'T. I MEAN, "I LOVE YOU" DOESN'T IMPLY ANY HUGE COMMITMENT.
I KNOW THAT, CATHY.
WHEN I SAY, "I LOVE YOU," SOMETIMES IT JUST MEANS YOU LOOK CUTE TONIGHT... OR YOU DID SOMETHING THAT MADE ME LAUGH...
"I LOVE YOU" CAN MEAN I LIKED THE MOVIE WE JUST SAW... I'M HAPPY I'M NOT PAYING BILLS TONIGHT... I'M GLAD TO BE WITH YOU...
IT ISN'T SOME BIG, SERIOUS THING! JUST A NICE, HAPPY, WARM REASSURANCE!
I AGREE.
YOU DO?? OH, IRVING, I LOVE YOU!!
I LOVE YOU, TOO, CATHY.
HE WANTS TO MARRY ME!!
CHECK, PLEASE.

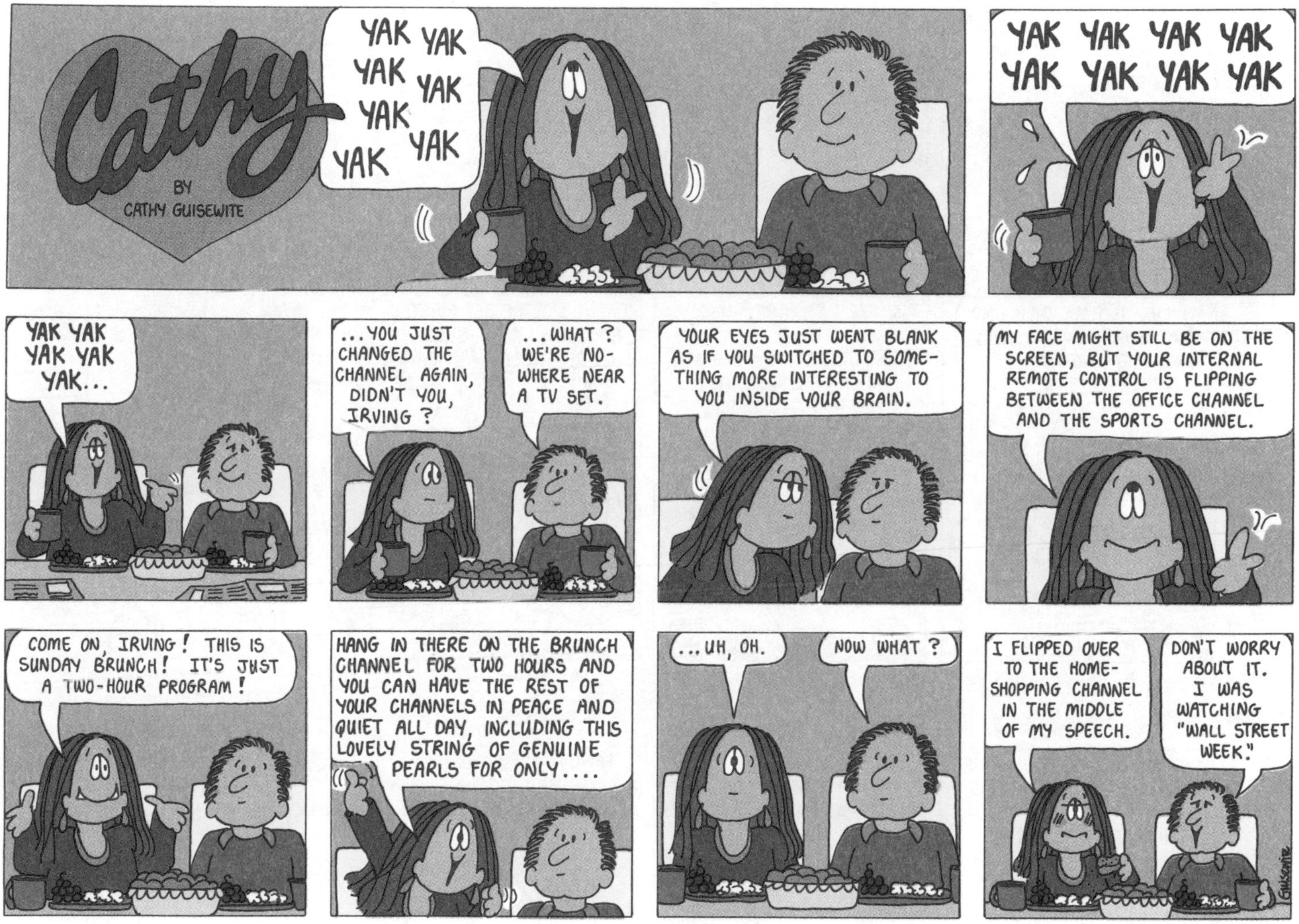

Cathy
BY CATHY GUISEWITE
YAK YAK YAK YAK YAK YAK YAK YAK
YAK YAK YAK YAK YAK YAK YAK YAK
YAK YAK YAK YAK YAK...
...YOU JUST CHANGED THE CHANNEL AGAIN, DIDN'T YOU, IRVING ?
...WHAT ? WE'RE NO-WHERE NEAR A TV SET.
YOUR EYES JUST WENT BLANK AS IF YOU SWITCHED TO SOME-THING MORE INTERESTING TO YOU INSIDE YOUR BRAIN.
MY FACE MIGHT STILL BE ON THE SCREEN, BUT YOUR INTERNAL REMOTE CONTROL IS FLIPPING BETWEEN THE OFFICE CHANNEL AND THE SPORTS CHANNEL.
COME ON, IRVING! THIS IS SUNDAY BRUNCH! IT'S JUST A TWO-HOUR PROGRAM!
HANG IN THERE ON THE BRUNCH CHANNEL FOR TWO HOURS AND YOU CAN HAVE THE REST OF YOUR CHANNELS IN PEACE AND QUIET ALL DAY, INCLUDING THIS LOVELY STRING OF GENUINE PEARLS FOR ONLY....
...UH, OH.
NOW WHAT ?
I FLIPPED OVER TO THE HOME-SHOPPING CHANNEL IN THE MIDDLE OF MY SPEECH.
DON'T WORRY ABOUT IT. I WAS WATCHING "WALL STREET WEEK."

The Extremely Unhappy Birthday Phase

1990

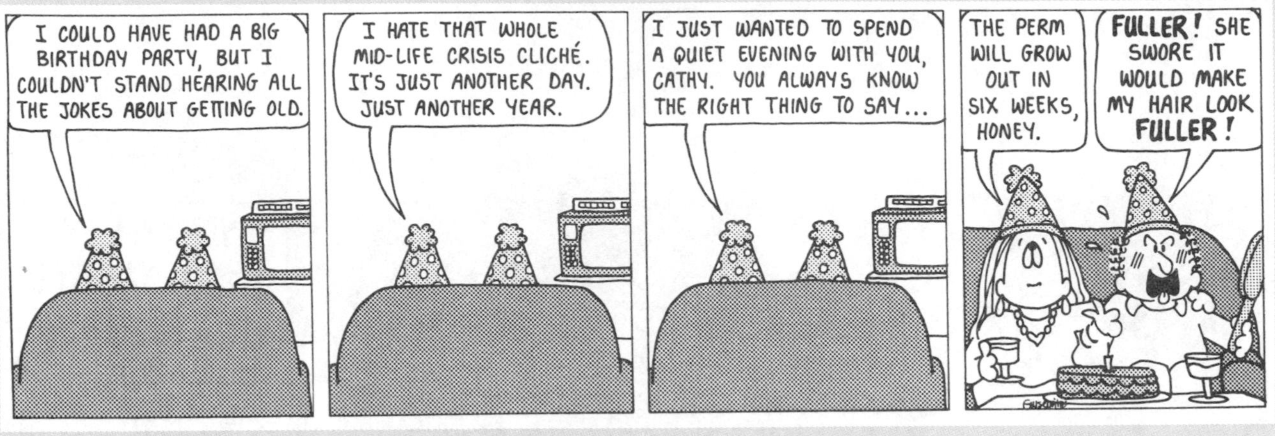
I COULD HAVE HAD A BIG BIRTHDAY PARTY, BUT I COULDN'T STAND HEARING ALL THE JOKES ABOUT GETTING OLD.
I HATE THAT WHOLE MID-LIFE CRISIS CLICHÉ. IT'S JUST ANOTHER DAY. JUST ANOTHER YEAR.
I JUST WANTED TO SPEND A QUIET EVENING WITH YOU, CATHY. YOU ALWAYS KNOW THE RIGHT THING TO SAY...
THE PERM WILL GROW OUT IN SIX WEEKS, HONEY.
FULLER! SHE SWORE IT WOULD MAKE MY HAIR LOOK FULLER!

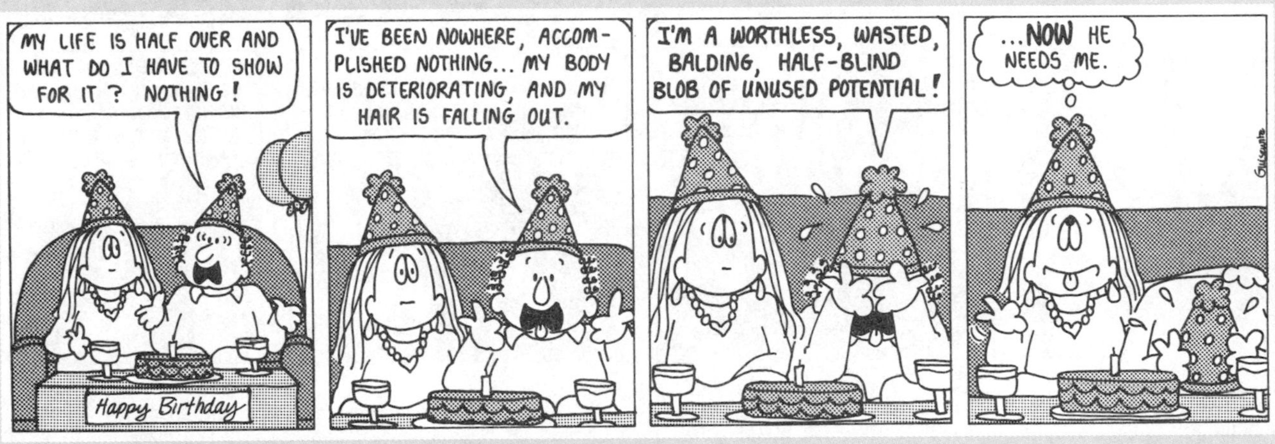
MY LIFE IS HALF OVER AND WHAT DO I HAVE TO SHOW FOR IT? NOTHING!
Happy Birthday
I'VE BEEN NOWHERE, ACCOMPLISHED NOTHING... MY BODY IS DETERIORATING, AND MY HAIR IS FALLING OUT.
I'M A WORTHLESS, WASTED, BALDING, HALF-BLIND BLOB OF UNUSED POTENTIAL!
...NOW HE NEEDS ME.

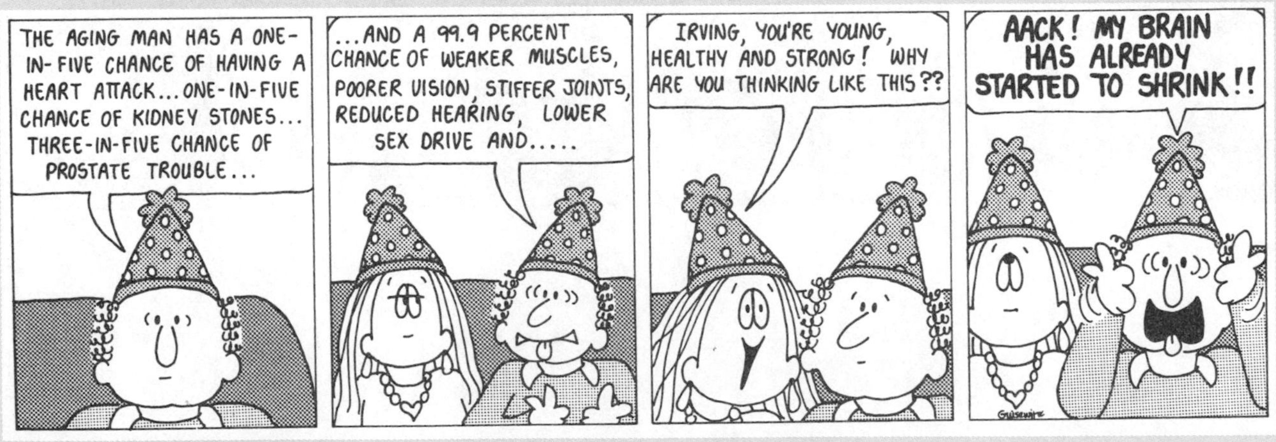
THE AGING MAN HAS A ONE-IN-FIVE CHANCE OF HAVING A HEART ATTACK... ONE-IN-FIVE CHANCE OF KIDNEY STONES... THREE-IN-FIVE CHANCE OF PROSTATE TROUBLE...
...AND A 99.9 PERCENT CHANCE OF WEAKER MUSCLES, POORER VISION, STIFFER JOINTS, REDUCED HEARING, LOWER SEX DRIVE AND.....
IRVING, YOU'RE YOUNG, HEALTHY AND STRONG! WHY ARE YOU THINKING LIKE THIS??
AACK! MY BRAIN HAS ALREADY STARTED TO SHRINK!!

The Looking Inward and Finding a Golfer Phase

1991

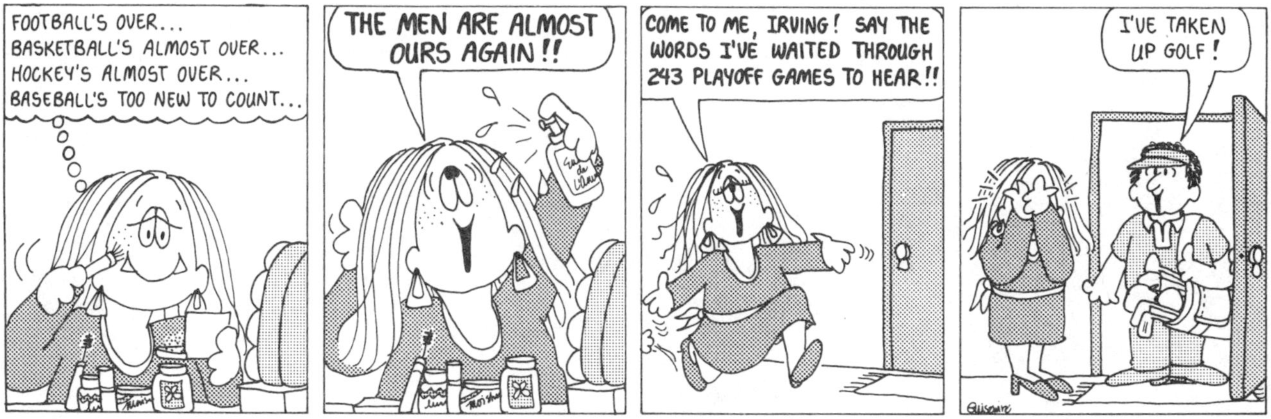

FOOTBALL'S OVER... BASKETBALL'S ALMOST OVER... HOCKEY'S ALMOST OVER... BASEBALL'S TOO NEW TO COUNT...
THE MEN ARE ALMOST OURS AGAIN!!
COME TO ME, IRVING! SAY THE WORDS I'VE WAITED THROUGH 243 PLAYOFF GAMES TO HEAR!!
I'VE TAKEN UP GOLF!

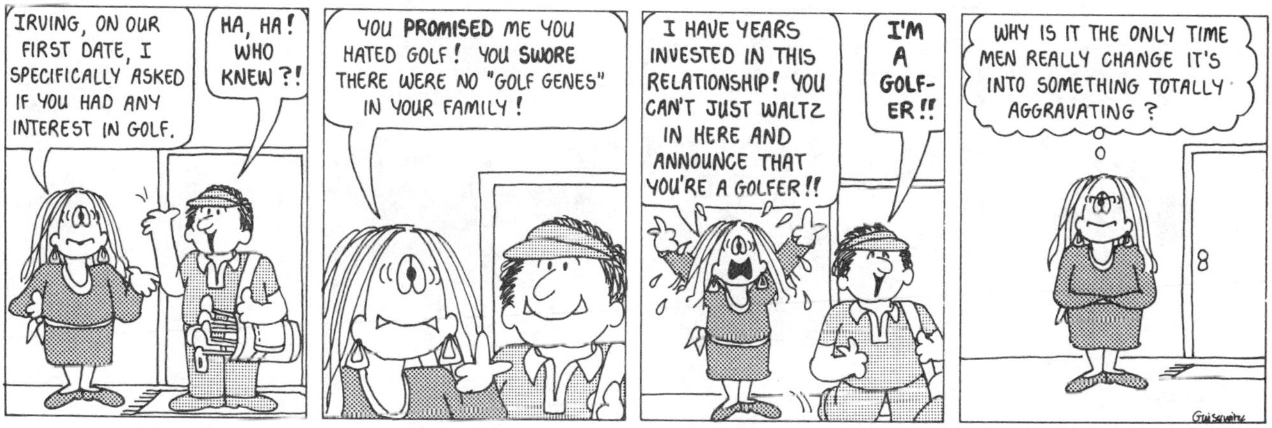

IRVING, ON OUR FIRST DATE, I SPECIFICALLY ASKED IF YOU HAD ANY INTEREST IN GOLF.
HA, HA! WHO KNEW?!
YOU PROMISED ME YOU HATED GOLF! YOU SWORE THERE WERE NO "GOLF GENES" IN YOUR FAMILY!
I HAVE YEARS INVESTED IN THIS RELATIONSHIP! YOU CAN'T JUST WALTZ IN HERE AND ANNOUNCE THAT YOU'RE A GOLFER!!
I'M A GOLF-ER!!
WHY IS IT THE ONLY TIME MEN REALLY CHANGE IT'S INTO SOMETHING TOTALLY AGGRAVATING?

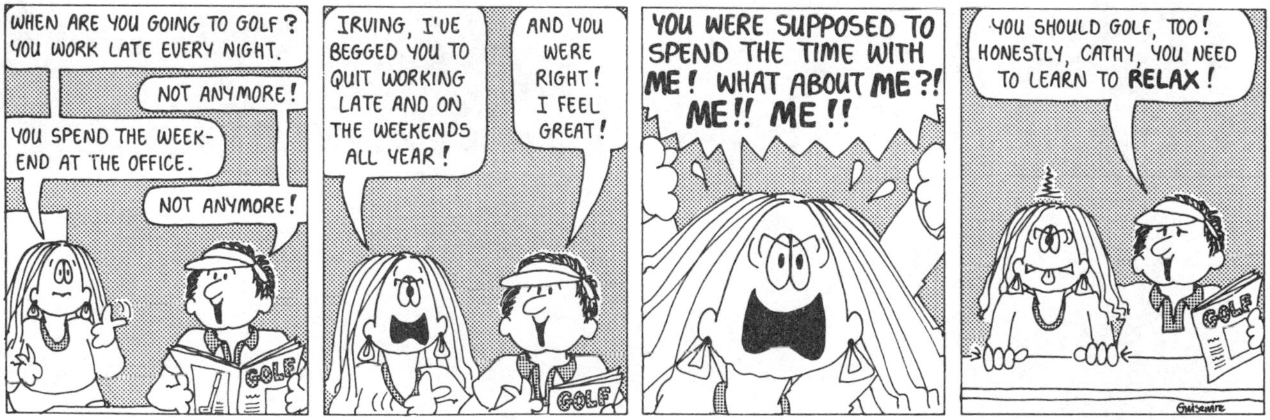

WHEN ARE YOU GOING TO GOLF? YOU WORK LATE EVERY NIGHT.
NOT ANYMORE!
YOU SPEND THE WEEK-END AT THE OFFICE.
NOT ANYMORE!
GOLF
IRVING, I'VE BEGGED YOU TO QUIT WORKING LATE AND ON THE WEEKENDS ALL YEAR!
AND YOU WERE RIGHT! I FEEL GREAT!
GOLF
YOU WERE SUPPOSED TO SPEND THE TIME WITH ME! WHAT ABOUT ME?!
ME!! ME!!
YOU SHOULD GOLF, TOO! HONESTLY, CATHY, YOU NEED TO LEARN TO RELAX!
GOLF

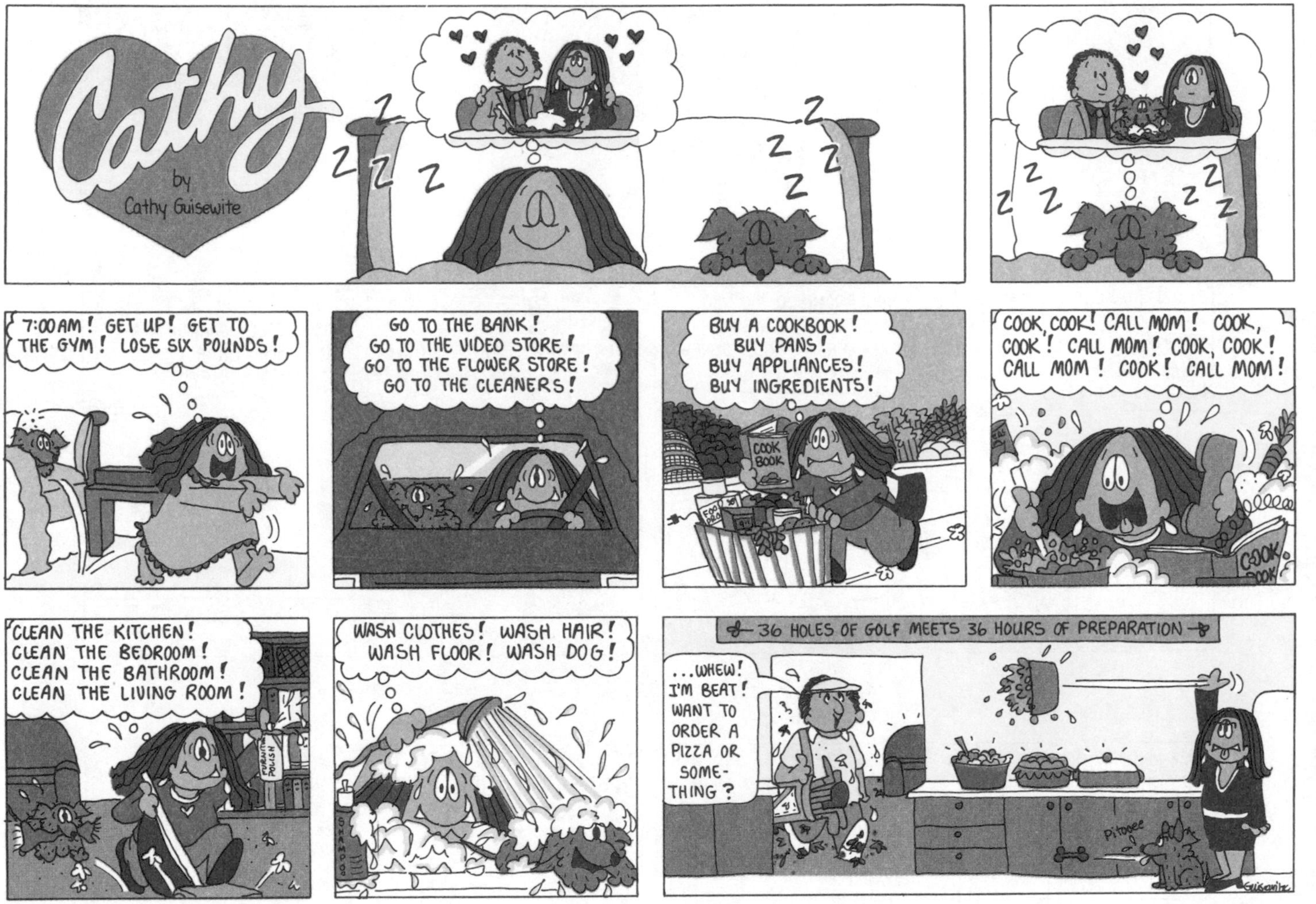
Cathy
by
Cathy Guisewite
Z Z Z Z
Z Z Z Z
Z Z Z Z Z
7:00AM! GET UP! GET TO THE GYM! LOSE SIX POUNDS!
GO TO THE BANK! GO TO THE VIDEO STORE! GO TO THE FLOWER STORE! GO TO THE CLEANERS!
BUY A COOKBOOK! BUY PANS! BUY APPLIANCES! BUY INGREDIENTS!
COOK BOOK
COOK, COOK! CALL MOM! COOK, COOK! CALL MOM! COOK, COOK! CALL MOM! COOK! CALL MOM!
CLEAN THE KITCHEN! CLEAN THE BEDROOM! CLEAN THE BATHROOM! CLEAN THE LIVING ROOM!
FURNITURE POLISH
WASH CLOTHES! WASH HAIR! WASH FLOOR! WASH DOG!
SHAMPOO
36 HOLES OF GOLF MEETS 36 HOURS OF PREPARATION
...WHEW! I'M BEAT! WANT TO ORDER A PIZZA OR SOME-THING?
Pitooee
Guisewite

The Looking Inward and Not Finding a Golfer Phase

1992

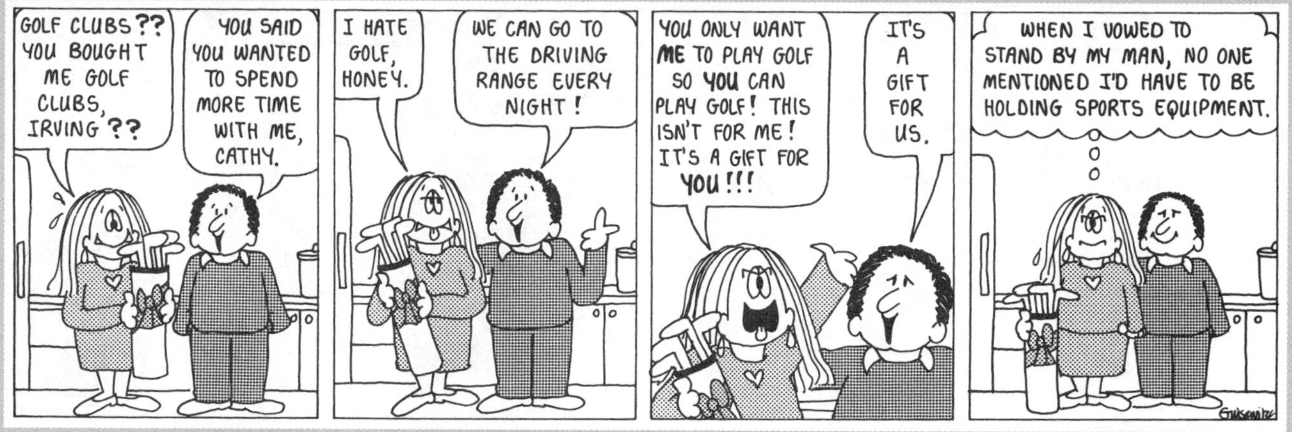
GOLF CLUBS?? YOU BOUGHT ME GOLF CLUBS, IRVING??
YOU SAID YOU WANTED TO SPEND MORE TIME WITH ME, CATHY.
I HATE GOLF, HONEY.
WE CAN GO TO THE DRIVING RANGE EVERY NIGHT!
YOU ONLY WANT ME TO PLAY GOLF SO YOU CAN PLAY GOLF! THIS ISN'T FOR ME! IT'S A GIFT FOR YOU!!!
IT'S A GIFT FOR US.
WHEN I VOWED TO STAND BY MY MAN, NO ONE MENTIONED I'D HAVE TO BE HOLDING SPORTS EQUIPMENT.

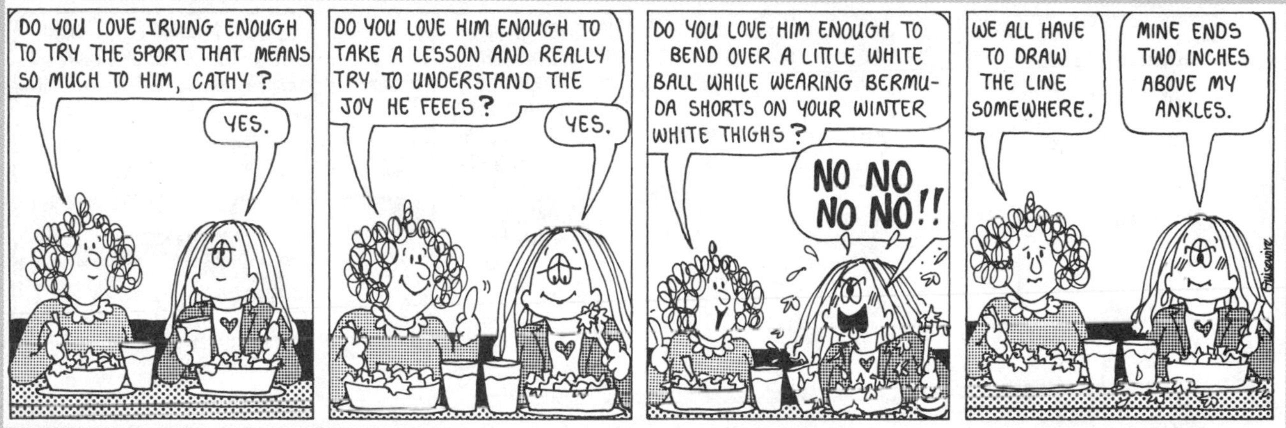
DO YOU LOVE IRVING ENOUGH TO TRY THE SPORT THAT MEANS SO MUCH TO HIM, CATHY?
YES.
DO YOU LOVE HIM ENOUGH TO TAKE A LESSON AND REALLY TRY TO UNDERSTAND THE JOY HE FEELS?
YES.
DO YOU LOVE HIM ENOUGH TO BEND OVER A LITTLE WHITE BALL WHILE WEARING BERMUDA SHORTS ON YOUR WINTER WHITE THIGHS?
NO NO NO NO!!
WE ALL HAVE TO DRAW THE LINE SOMEWHERE.
MINE ENDS TWO INCHES ABOVE MY ANKLES.

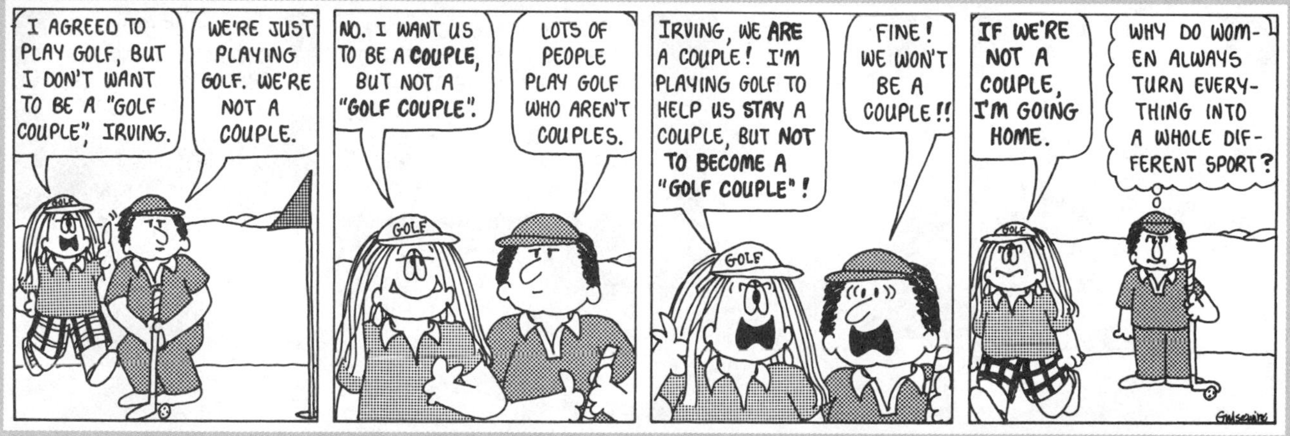
I AGREED TO PLAY GOLF, BUT I DON'T WANT TO BE A "GOLF COUPLE," IRVING.
WE'RE JUST PLAYING GOLF. WE'RE NOT A COUPLE.
GOLF
NO. I WANT US TO BE A COUPLE, BUT NOT A "GOLF COUPLE".
LOTS OF PEOPLE PLAY GOLF WHO AREN'T COUPLES.
GOLF
IRVING, WE ARE A COUPLE! I'M PLAYING GOLF TO HELP US STAY A COUPLE, BUT NOT TO BECOME A "GOLF COUPLE"!
FINE! WE WON'T BE A COUPLE!!
GOLF
IF WE'RE NOT A COUPLE, I'M GOING HOME.
WHY DO WOMEN ALWAYS TURN EVERYTHING INTO A WHOLE DIFFERENT SPORT?

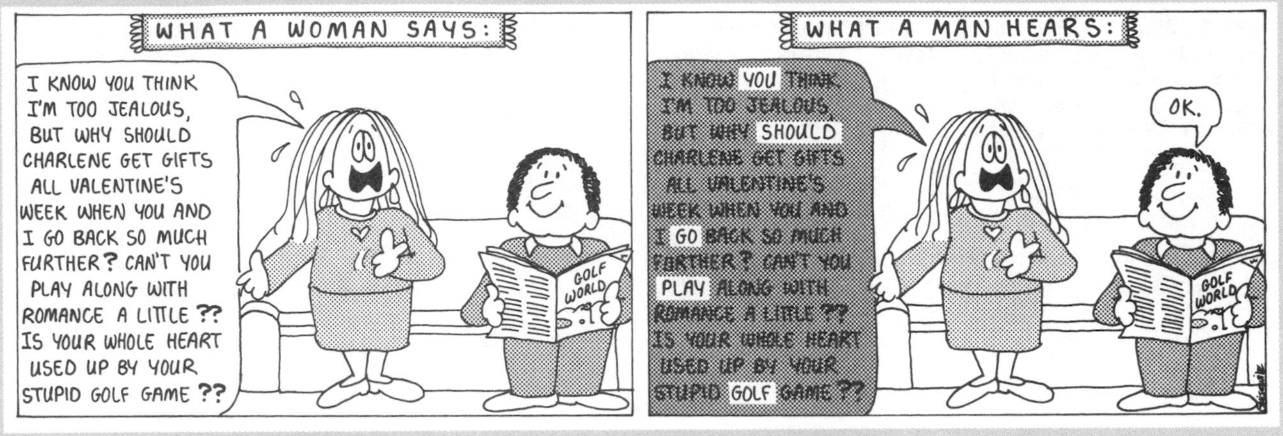
WHAT A WOMAN SAYS:
I KNOW YOU THINK I'M TOO JEALOUS, BUT WHY SHOULD CHARLENE GET GIFTS ALL VALENTINE'S WEEK WHEN YOU AND I GO BACK SO MUCH FURTHER? CAN'T YOU PLAY ALONG WITH ROMANCE A LITTLE?? IS YOUR WHOLE HEART USED UP BY YOUR STUPID GOLF GAME??
GOLF WORLD
WHAT A MAN HEARS:
I KNOW YOU THINK I'M TOO JEALOUS, BUT WHY SHOULD CHARLENE GET GIFTS ALL VALENTINE'S WEEK WHEN YOU AND I GO BACK SO MUCH FURTHER? CAN'T YOU PLAY ALONG WITH ROMANCE A LITTLE?? IS YOUR WHOLE HEART USED UP BY YOUR STUPID GOLF GAME??
OK.
GOLF WORLD

1992—Meaningful Dialogues

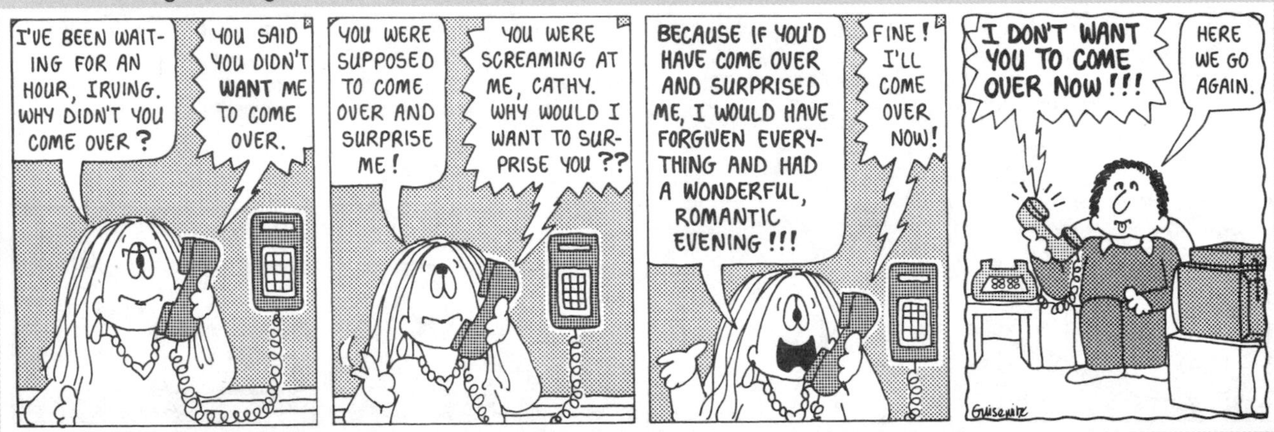
I'VE BEEN WAITING FOR AN HOUR, IRVING. WHY DIDN'T YOU COME OVER?
YOU SAID YOU DIDN'T WANT ME TO COME OVER.
YOU WERE SUPPOSED TO COME OVER AND SURPRISE ME!
YOU WERE SCREAMING AT ME, CATHY. WHY WOULD I WANT TO SURPRISE YOU??
BECAUSE IF YOU'D HAVE COME OVER AND SURPRISED ME, I WOULD HAVE FORGIVEN EVERYTHING AND HAD A WONDERFUL, ROMANTIC EVENING!!!
FINE! I'LL COME OVER NOW!
I DON'T WANT YOU TO COME OVER NOW!!!
HERE WE GO AGAIN.

1994—Meaningful Monologues

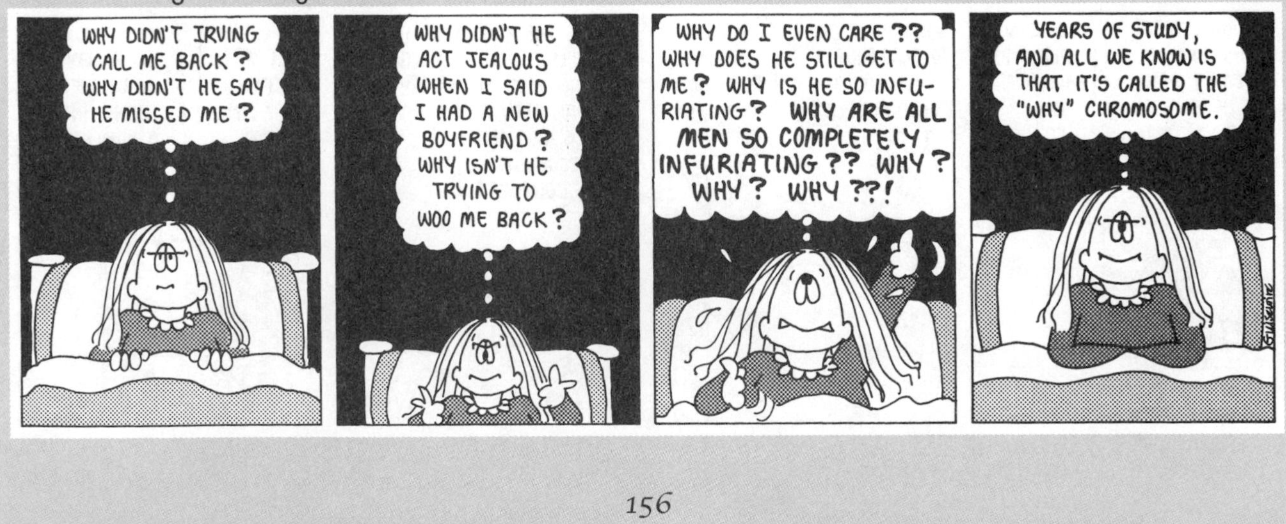
WHY DIDN'T IRVING CALL ME BACK? WHY DIDN'T HE SAY HE MISSED ME?
WHY DIDN'T HE ACT JEALOUS WHEN I SAID I HAD A NEW BOYFRIEND? WHY ISN'T HE TRYING TO WOO ME BACK?
WHY DO I EVEN CARE?? WHY DOES HE STILL GET TO ME? WHY IS HE SO INFURIATING? WHY ARE ALL MEN SO COMPLETELY INFURIATING?? WHY? WHY? WHY??!
YEARS OF STUDY, AND ALL WE KNOW IS THAT IT'S CALLED THE "WHY" CHROMOSOME.

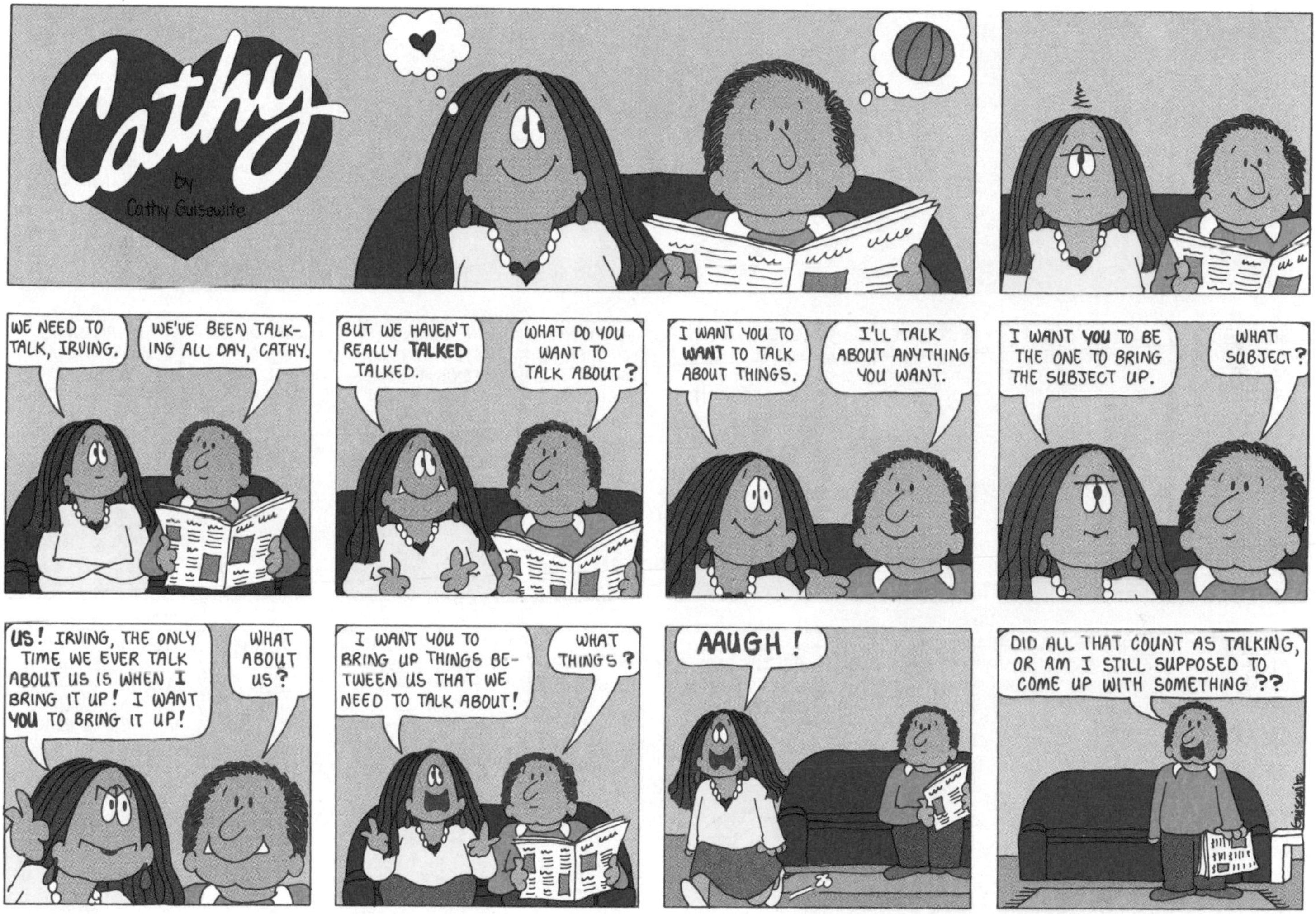
Cathy
by
Cathy Guisewite
WE NEED TO TALK, IRVING.
WE'VE BEEN TALKING ALL DAY, CATHY.
BUT WE HAVEN'T REALLY **TALKED** TALKED.
WHAT DO YOU WANT TO TALK ABOUT?
I WANT YOU TO **WANT** TO TALK ABOUT THINGS.
I'LL TALK ABOUT ANYTHING YOU WANT.
I WANT **YOU** TO BE THE ONE TO BRING THE SUBJECT UP.
WHAT SUBJECT?
US! IRVING, THE ONLY TIME WE EVER TALK ABOUT US IS WHEN **I** BRING IT UP! I WANT **YOU** TO BRING IT UP!
WHAT ABOUT US?
I WANT YOU TO BRING UP THINGS BETWEEN US THAT WE NEED TO TALK ABOUT!
WHAT THINGS?
AAUGH!
DID ALL THAT COUNT AS TALKING, OR AM I STILL SUPPOSED TO COME UP WITH SOMETHING??
Guisewite

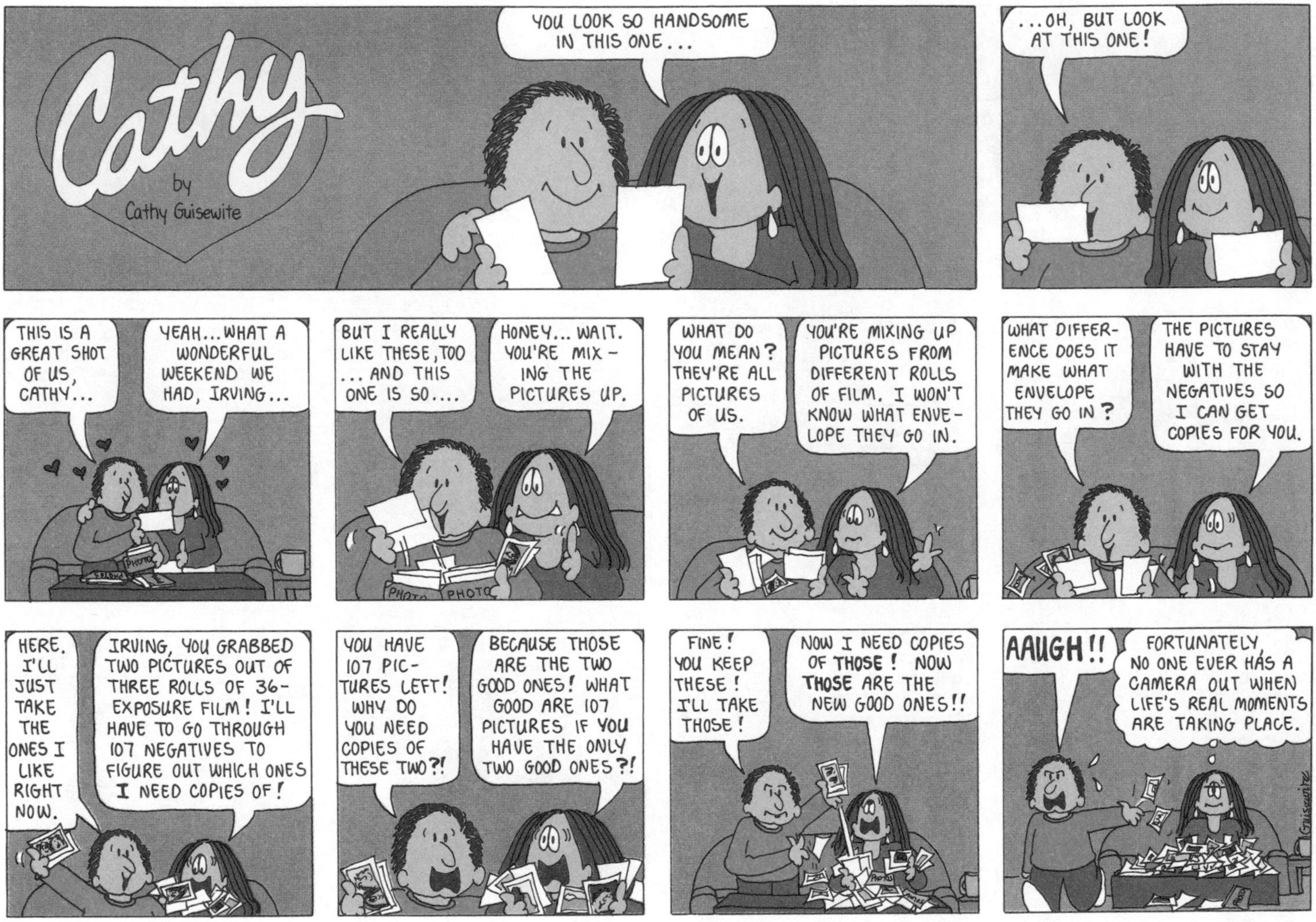
Cathy
by
Cathy Guisewite
YOU LOOK SO HANDSOME IN THIS ONE...
...OH, BUT LOOK AT THIS ONE!
THIS IS A GREAT SHOT OF US, CATHY...
YEAH... WHAT A WONDERFUL WEEKEND WE HAD, IRVING...
BUT I REALLY LIKE THESE, TOO ... AND THIS ONE IS SO....
HONEY... WAIT. YOU'RE MIX - ING THE PICTURES UP.
WHAT DO YOU MEAN? THEY'RE ALL PICTURES OF US.
YOU'RE MIXING UP PICTURES FROM DIFFERENT ROLLS OF FILM. I WON'T KNOW WHAT ENVE - LOPE THEY GO IN.
WHAT DIFFER - ENCE DOES IT MAKE WHAT ENVELOPE THEY GO IN?
THE PICTURES HAVE TO STAY WITH THE NEGATIVES SO I CAN GET COPIES FOR YOU.
HERE. I'LL JUST TAKE THE ONES I LIKE RIGHT NOW.
IRVING, YOU GRABBED TWO PICTURES OUT OF THREE ROLLS OF 36-EXPOSURE FILM! I'LL HAVE TO GO THROUGH 107 NEGATIVES TO FIGURE OUT WHICH ONES I NEED COPIES OF!
YOU HAVE 107 PIC - TURES LEFT! WHY DO YOU NEED COPIES OF THESE TWO?!
BECAUSE THOSE ARE THE TWO GOOD ONES! WHAT GOOD ARE 107 PICTURES IF YOU HAVE THE ONLY TWO GOOD ONES?!
FINE! YOU KEEP THESE! I'LL TAKE THOSE!
NOW I NEED COPIES OF THOSE! NOW THOSE ARE THE NEW GOOD ONES!!
AAUGH!!
FORTUNATELY, NO ONE EVER HAS A CAMERA OUT WHEN LIFE'S REAL MOMENTS ARE TAKING PLACE.
Guisewite

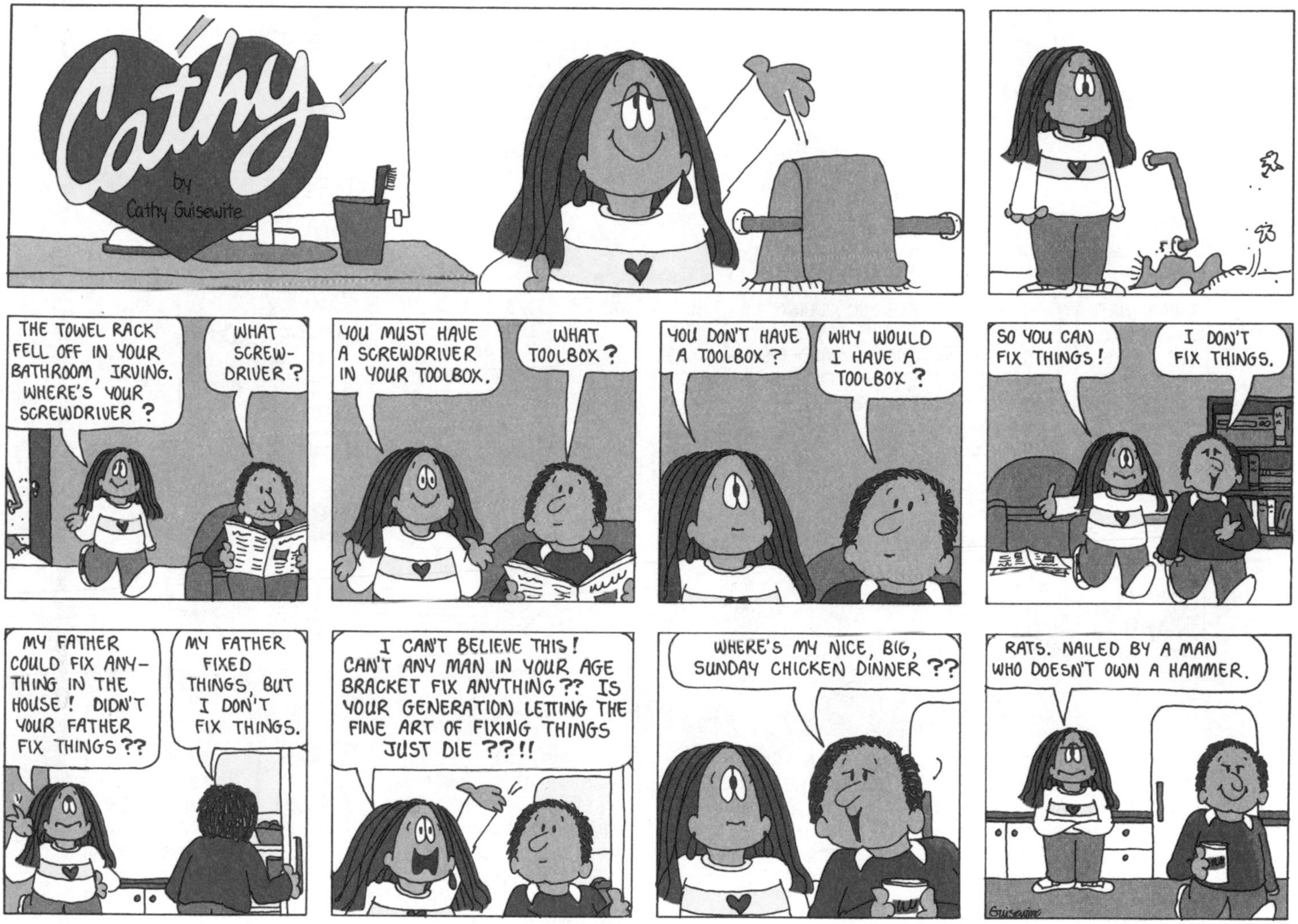
Cathy
by
Cathy Guisewite
THE TOWEL RACK FELL OFF IN YOUR BATHROOM, IRVING. WHERE'S YOUR SCREWDRIVER ?
WHAT SCREW-DRIVER ?
YOU MUST HAVE A SCREWDRIVER IN YOUR TOOLBOX.
WHAT TOOLBOX ?
YOU DON'T HAVE A TOOLBOX ?
WHY WOULD I HAVE A TOOLBOX ?
SO YOU CAN FIX THINGS !
I DON'T FIX THINGS.
MY FATHER COULD FIX ANY-THING IN THE HOUSE ! DIDN'T YOUR FATHER FIX THINGS ??
MY FATHER FIXED THINGS, BUT I DON'T FIX THINGS.
I CAN'T BELIEVE THIS ! CAN'T ANY MAN IN YOUR AGE BRACKET FIX ANYTHING ?? IS YOUR GENERATION LETTING THE FINE ART OF FIXING THINGS JUST DIE ??!!
WHERE'S MY NICE, BIG, SUNDAY CHICKEN DINNER ??
RATS. NAILED BY A MAN WHO DOESN'T OWN A HAMMER.
Guisewite

The Downsizing Phase

1997—Irving resurfaces after a three-year absence to oust Cathy from her job

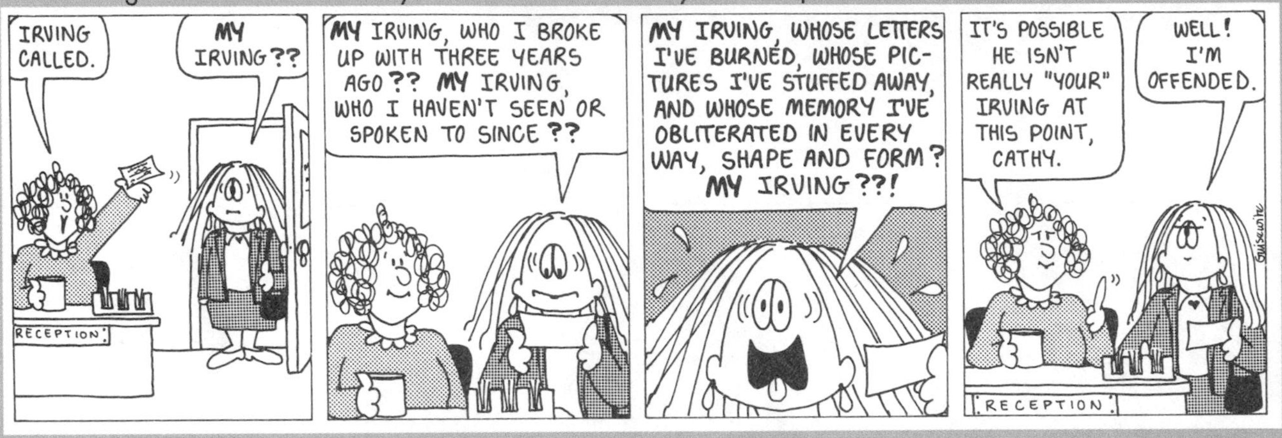

IRVING CALLED.
MY IRVING??
MY IRVING, WHO I BROKE UP WITH THREE YEARS AGO?? MY IRVING, WHO I HAVEN'T SEEN OR SPOKEN TO SINCE??
MY IRVING, WHOSE LETTERS I'VE BURNED, WHOSE PICTURES I'VE STUFFED AWAY, AND WHOSE MEMORY I'VE OBLITERATED IN EVERY WAY, SHAPE AND FORM? MY IRVING??!
IT'S POSSIBLE HE ISN'T REALLY "YOUR" IRVING AT THIS POINT, CATHY.
WELL! I'M OFFENDED.
RECEPTION

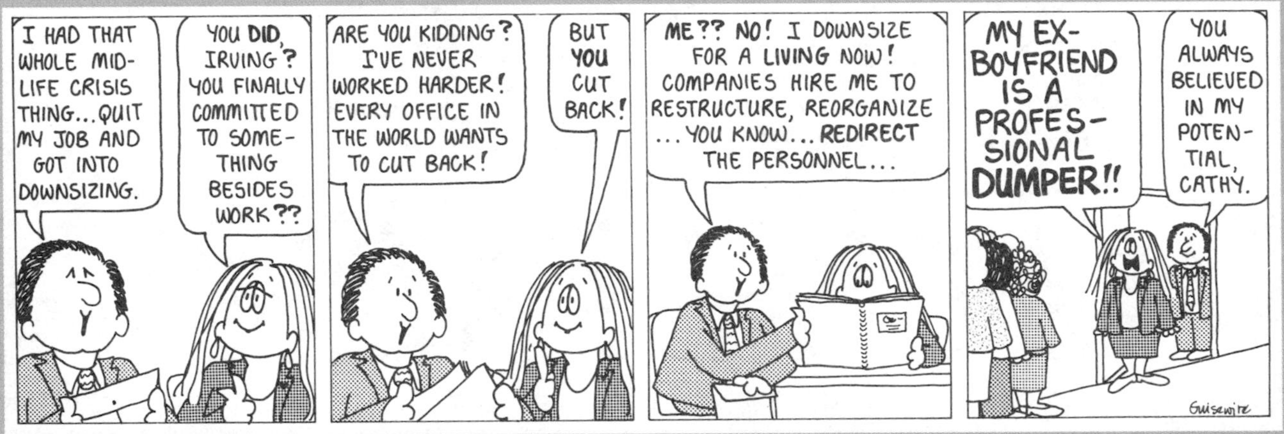

I HAD THAT WHOLE MID-LIFE CRISIS THING... QUIT MY JOB AND GOT INTO DOWNSIZING.
YOU DID, IRVING? YOU FINALLY COMMITTED TO SOMETHING BESIDES WORK??
ARE YOU KIDDING? I'VE NEVER WORKED HARDER! EVERY OFFICE IN THE WORLD WANTS TO CUT BACK!
BUT YOU CUT BACK!
ME?? NO! I DOWNSIZE FOR A LIVING NOW! COMPANIES HIRE ME TO RESTRUCTURE, REORGANIZE ... YOU KNOW... REDIRECT THE PERSONNEL...
MY EX-BOYFRIEND IS A PROFESSIONAL DUMPER!!
YOU ALWAYS BELIEVED IN MY POTENTIAL, CATHY.
Guisewite

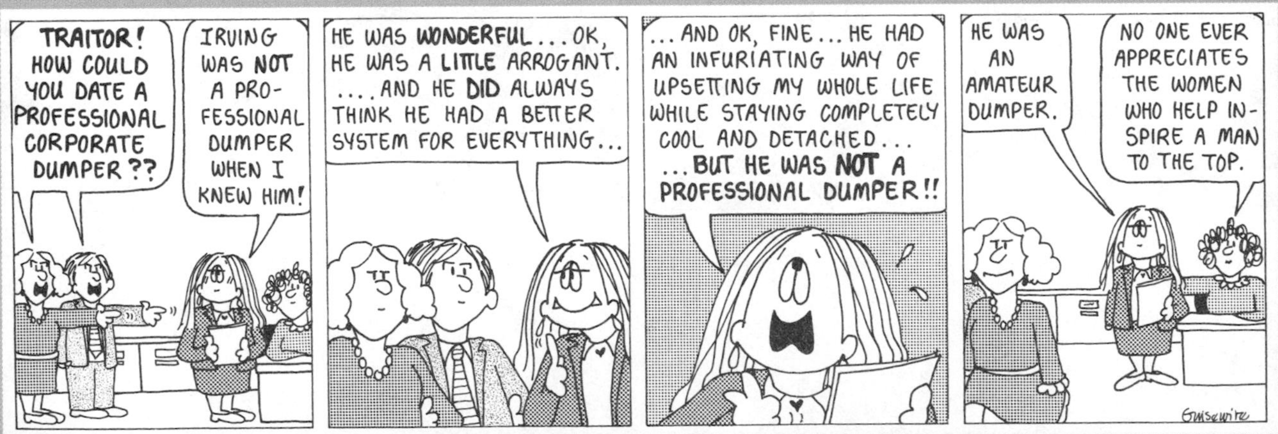

TRAITOR! HOW COULD YOU DATE A PROFESSIONAL CORPORATE DUMPER??
IRVING WAS NOT A PROFESSIONAL DUMPER WHEN I KNEW HIM!
HE WAS WONDERFUL... OK, HE WAS A LITTLE ARROGANT. ....AND HE DID ALWAYS THINK HE HAD A BETTER SYSTEM FOR EVERYTHING...
...AND OK, FINE... HE HAD AN INFURIATING WAY OF UPSETTING MY WHOLE LIFE WHILE STAYING COMPLETELY COOL AND DETACHED... ...BUT HE WAS NOT A PROFESSIONAL DUMPER!!
HE WAS AN AMATEUR DUMPER.
NO ONE EVER APPRECIATES THE WOMEN WHO HELP INSPIRE A MAN TO THE TOP.
Guisewite

The Human Resources Facilitator Phase

1998—Irving resurfaces months later to woo Cathy back to her job

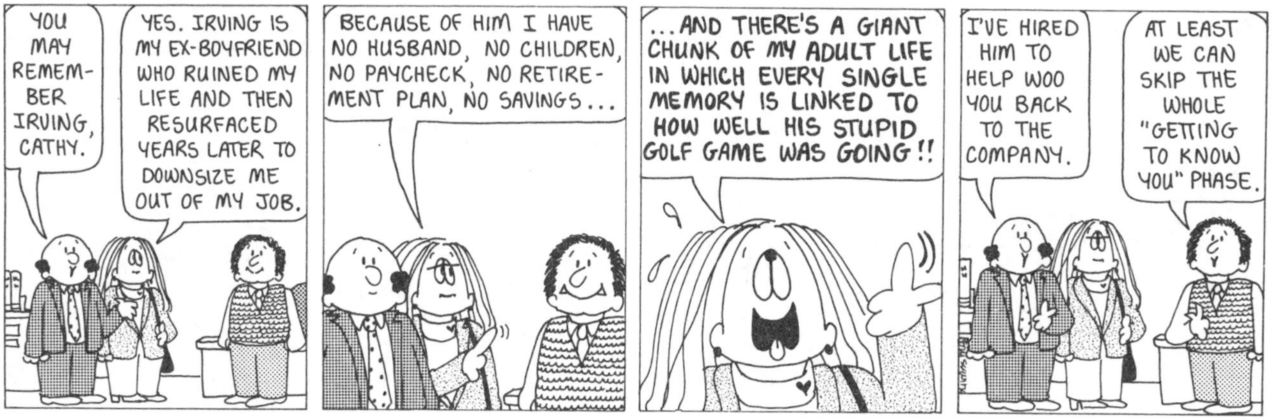

YOU MAY REMEMBER IRVING, CATHY.
YES. IRVING IS MY EX-BOYFRIEND WHO RUINED MY LIFE AND THEN RESURFACED YEARS LATER TO DOWNSIZE ME OUT OF MY JOB.
BECAUSE OF HIM I HAVE NO HUSBAND, NO CHILDREN, NO PAYCHECK, NO RETIREMENT PLAN, NO SAVINGS...
...AND THERE'S A GIANT CHUNK OF MY ADULT LIFE IN WHICH EVERY SINGLE MEMORY IS LINKED TO HOW WELL HIS STUPID GOLF GAME WAS GOING!!
I'VE HIRED HIM TO HELP WOO YOU BACK TO THE COMPANY.
AT LEAST WE CAN SKIP THE WHOLE "GETTING TO KNOW YOU" PHASE.

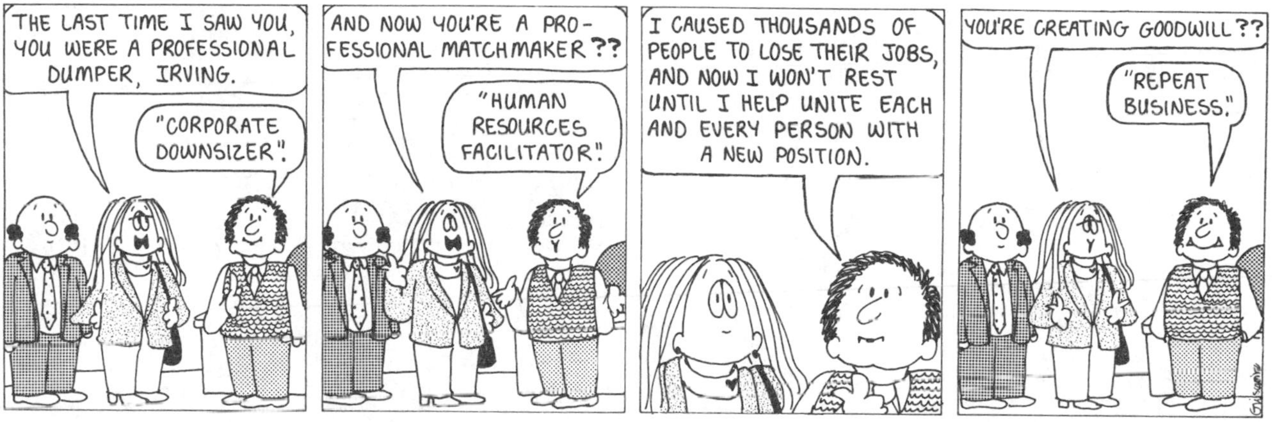

THE LAST TIME I SAW YOU, YOU WERE A PROFESSIONAL DUMPER, IRVING.
"CORPORATE DOWNSIZER".
AND NOW YOU'RE A PROFESSIONAL MATCHMAKER??
"HUMAN RESOURCES FACILITATOR".
I CAUSED THOUSANDS OF PEOPLE TO LOSE THEIR JOBS, AND NOW I WON'T REST UNTIL I HELP UNITE EACH AND EVERY PERSON WITH A NEW POSITION.
YOU'RE CREATING GOODWILL??
"REPEAT BUSINESS."

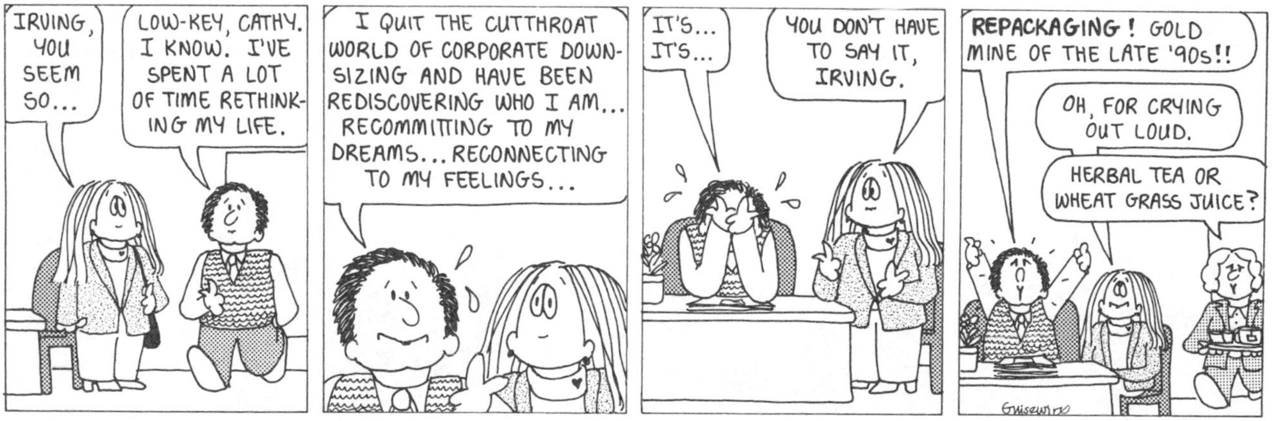

IRVING, YOU SEEM SO...
LOW-KEY, CATHY. I KNOW. I'VE SPENT A LOT OF TIME RETHINKING MY LIFE.
I QUIT THE CUTTHROAT WORLD OF CORPORATE DOWNSIZING AND HAVE BEEN REDISCOVERING WHO I AM... RECOMMITTING TO MY DREAMS... RECONNECTING TO MY FEELINGS...
IT'S... IT'S...
YOU DON'T HAVE TO SAY IT, IRVING.
REPACKAGING! GOLD MINE OF THE LATE '90s!!
OH, FOR CRYING OUT LOUD.
HERBAL TEA OR WHEAT GRASS JUICE?

The Great Equalizer Phase

1999—Irving resurfaces a year later with a broken heart

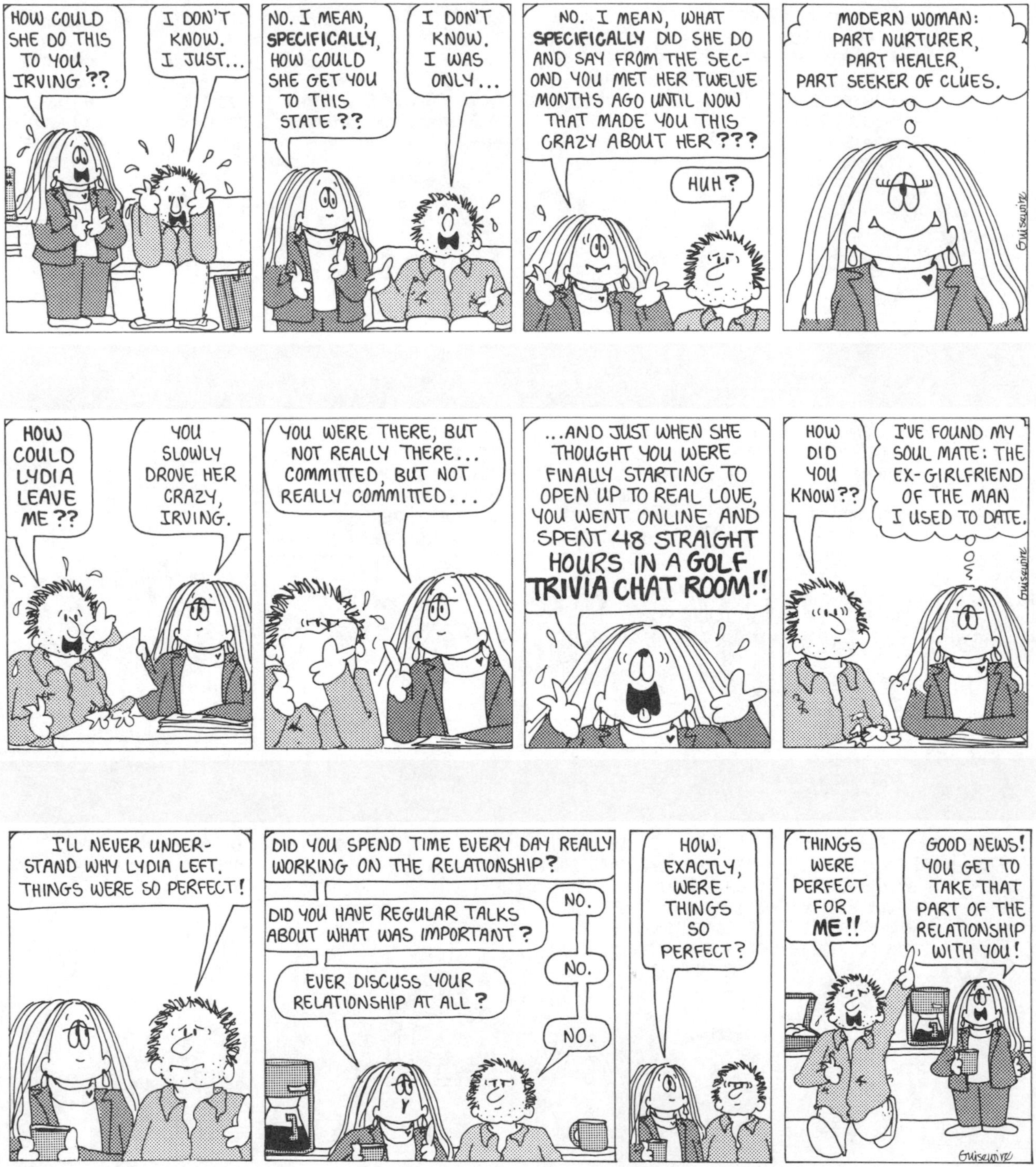

HOW COULD SHE DO THIS TO YOU, IRVING??
I DON'T KNOW. I JUST...
NO. I MEAN, SPECIFICALLY, HOW COULD SHE GET YOU TO THIS STATE??
I DON'T KNOW. I WAS ONLY...
NO. I MEAN, WHAT SPECIFICALLY DID SHE DO AND SAY FROM THE SECOND YOU MET HER TWELVE MONTHS AGO UNTIL NOW THAT MADE YOU THIS CRAZY ABOUT HER???
HUH?
MODERN WOMAN: PART NURTURER, PART HEALER, PART SEEKER OF CLUES.
HOW COULD LYDIA LEAVE ME??
YOU SLOWLY DROVE HER CRAZY, IRVING.
YOU WERE THERE, BUT NOT REALLY THERE... COMMITTED, BUT NOT REALLY COMMITTED...
...AND JUST WHEN SHE THOUGHT YOU WERE FINALLY STARTING TO OPEN UP TO REAL LOVE, YOU WENT ONLINE AND SPENT 48 STRAIGHT HOURS IN A GOLF TRIVIA CHAT ROOM!!
HOW DID YOU KNOW??
I'VE FOUND MY SOUL MATE: THE EX-GIRLFRIEND OF THE MAN I USED TO DATE.
I'LL NEVER UNDERSTAND WHY LYDIA LEFT. THINGS WERE SO PERFECT!
DID YOU SPEND TIME EVERY DAY REALLY WORKING ON THE RELATIONSHIP?
NO.
DID YOU HAVE REGULAR TALKS ABOUT WHAT WAS IMPORTANT?
NO.
EVER DISCUSS YOUR RELATIONSHIP AT ALL?
NO.
HOW, EXACTLY, WERE THINGS SO PERFECT?
THINGS WERE PERFECT FOR ME!!
GOOD NEWS! YOU GET TO TAKE THAT PART OF THE RELATIONSHIP WITH YOU!

The Platonic Friendship Phase

1999

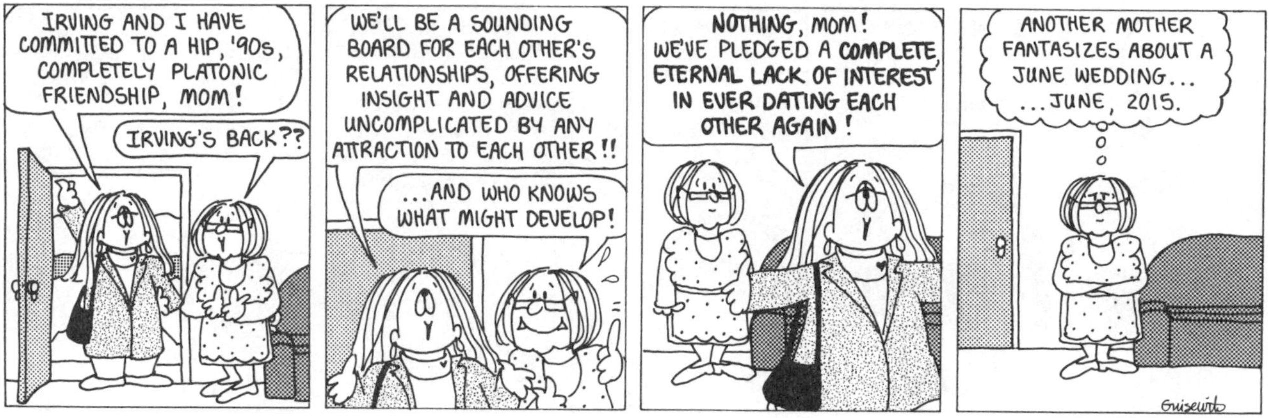
IRVING AND I HAVE COMMITTED TO A HIP, '90s, COMPLETELY PLATONIC FRIENDSHIP, MOM!
IRVING'S BACK??
WE'LL BE A SOUNDING BOARD FOR EACH OTHER'S RELATIONSHIPS, OFFERING INSIGHT AND ADVICE UNCOMPLICATED BY ANY ATTRACTION TO EACH OTHER!!
...AND WHO KNOWS WHAT MIGHT DEVELOP!
NOTHING, MOM! WE'VE PLEDGED A COMPLETE, ETERNAL LACK OF INTEREST IN EVER DATING EACH OTHER AGAIN!
ANOTHER MOTHER FANTASIZES ABOUT A JUNE WEDDING... ...JUNE, 2015.
Guisewite

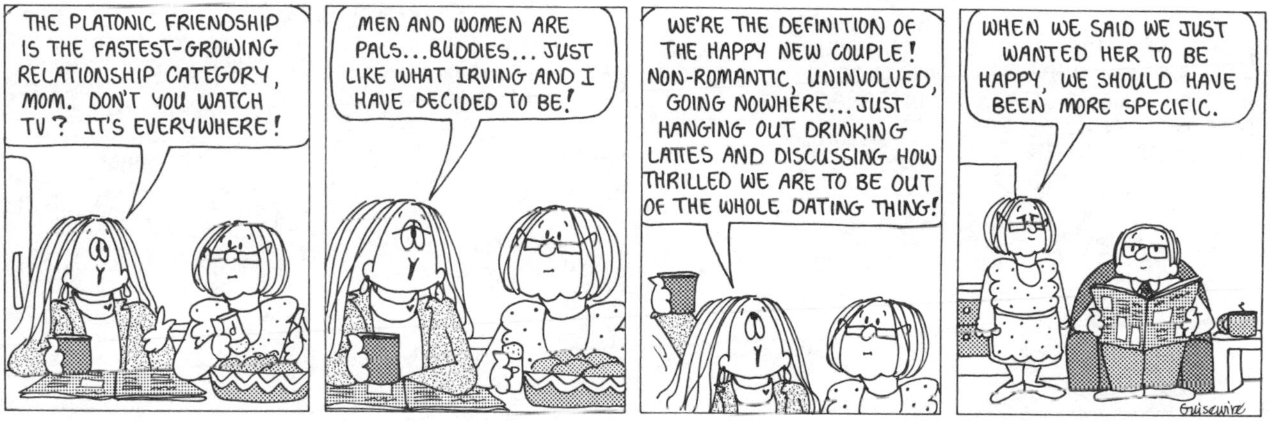
THE PLATONIC FRIENDSHIP IS THE FASTEST-GROWING RELATIONSHIP CATEGORY, MOM. DON'T YOU WATCH TV? IT'S EVERYWHERE!
MEN AND WOMEN ARE PALS...BUDDIES... JUST LIKE WHAT IRVING AND I HAVE DECIDED TO BE!
WE'RE THE DEFINITION OF THE HAPPY NEW COUPLE! NON-ROMANTIC, UNINVOLVED, GOING NOWHERE...JUST HANGING OUT DRINKING LATTES AND DISCUSSING HOW THRILLED WE ARE TO BE OUT OF THE WHOLE DATING THING!
WHEN WE SAID WE JUST WANTED HER TO BE HAPPY, WE SHOULD HAVE BEEN MORE SPECIFIC.
Guisewite

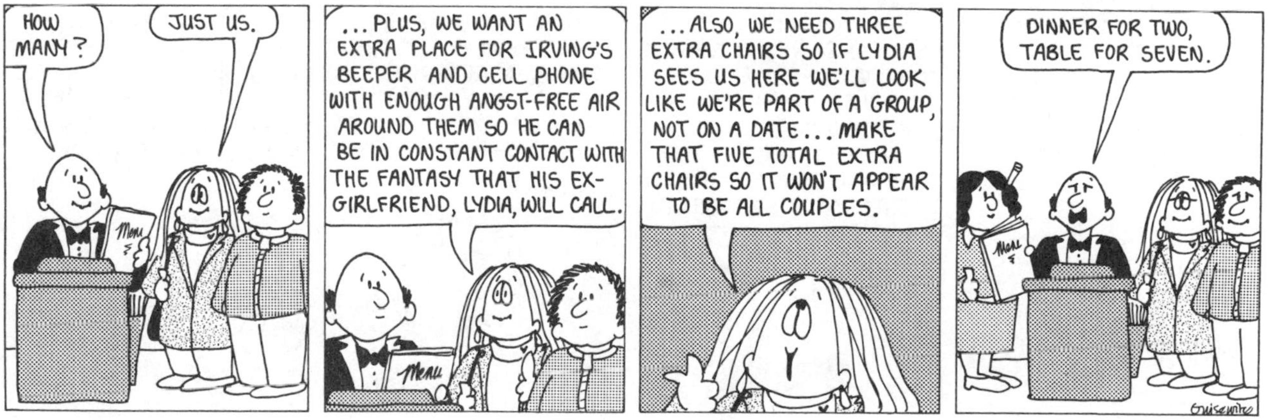
HOW MANY?
JUST US.
...PLUS, WE WANT AN EXTRA PLACE FOR IRVING'S BEEPER AND CELL PHONE WITH ENOUGH ANGST-FREE AIR AROUND THEM SO HE CAN BE IN CONSTANT CONTACT WITH THE FANTASY THAT HIS EX-GIRLFRIEND, LYDIA, WILL CALL.
...ALSO, WE NEED THREE EXTRA CHAIRS SO IF LYDIA SEES US HERE WE'LL LOOK LIKE WE'RE PART OF A GROUP, NOT ON A DATE... MAKE THAT FIVE TOTAL EXTRA CHAIRS SO IT WON'T APPEAR TO BE ALL COUPLES.
DINNER FOR TWO, TABLE FOR SEVEN.
Guisewite

1999

Panel 1: IT'S THE NEW ME, CATHY, **MILLENNIUM MAN!**

Panel 2: NET-SAVVY, HDTV-READY, 100% Y2K COMPLIANT!

Panel 3: I GOT MY LEASE AT 8%... MY MORTGAGE AT 6%... AND MY AMAZON.COM STOCK AT $20!

Panel 4: AND JUST IN CASE IT ALL GOES BELLY-UP, I KEEP A THREE-MONTH SUPPLY OF FAT-FREE SURVIVAL RATIONS STRAPPED TO ME AT ALL TIMES.

Panel 5: I, FOR ONE, WILL BE RUNNING FULL SPEED ON JANUARY 1, 2000!

THIS CENTURY'S DOUBLE ESPRESSOS WON'T HAVE WORN OFF YET...

Panel 6: LIKE OUR COMPUTERS, MEN BORN IN THE 1950s WERE PROGRAMMED WITH AN OPERATING SYSTEM THAT ONLY LET US ACCEPT A LIMITED DATE FIELD.

Panel 7: BUT MY BREAKUP WITH LYDIA THIS YEAR FORCED ME TO DO AN AGONIZING INTERNAL OVERHAUL.

Panel 8: I'M UPGRADED, CATHY! Y2K-PRIMED! READY FOR ANY DATE THE MILLENNIUM HAS TO OFFER!

MARRIAGE IN 00.

Panel 9: 00? 00? 00? AACK. 00?

FULL SYSTEM FAILURE.

GOOD TO DO A FEW TEST RUNS BEFORE DECEMBER 31.

Panel 10: YOU'RE A "Y2K CONSULTANT" NOW, IRVING?

IT'S MY DUTY, CATHY. NO ONE KNOWS WHAT "00" WILL BRING.

Panel 11: WILL THE MICROCHIP EMBEDDED IN YOUR TOASTER MAKE IT REFUSE TO HEAT UP A FROZEN WAFFLE ON JANUARY 1?... OR WILL THE WHOLE CITY LOSE WATER, ELECTRICITY AND THE CARTOON NETWORK?

Panel 12: LIKE SO MANY INVOLVED, CARING MEMBERS OF THE BABY BOOM GENERATION, BEING PREPARED IS MORE THAN A WAY OF LIFE TO ME!

Panel 13: IT'S A WAY TO MAKE MONEY.

WHICH I'LL BE STASHING IN MY MATTRESS IN CASE THE BANK'S COMPUTER GOES BERSERK.

The New Age of Commitment Phase

1999—Commitment to gizmos

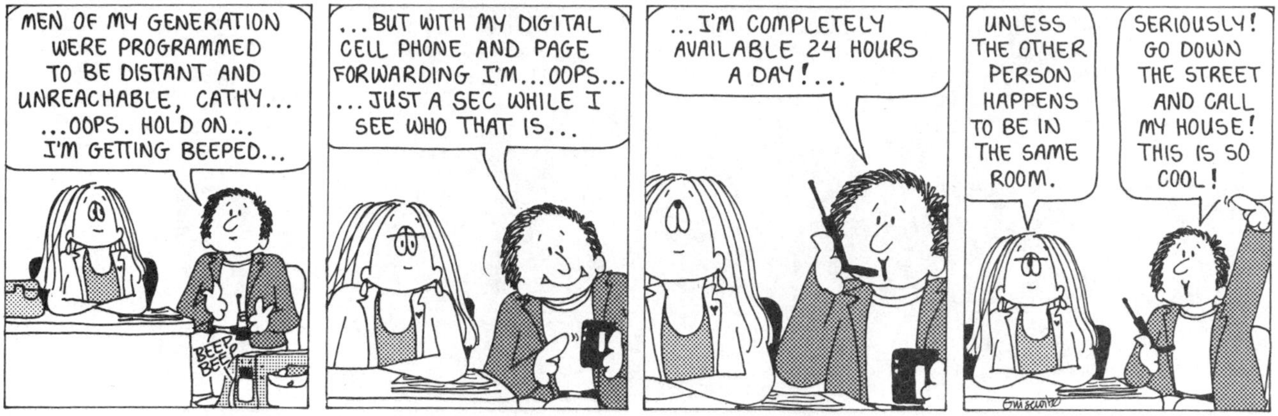
MEN OF MY GENERATION WERE PROGRAMMED TO BE DISTANT AND UNREACHABLE, CATHY... ...OOPS. HOLD ON... I'M GETTING BEEPED...
BEEP BEEP
...BUT WITH MY DIGITAL CELL PHONE AND PAGE FORWARDING I'M...OOPS... ...JUST A SEC WHILE I SEE WHO THAT IS...
...I'M COMPLETELY AVAILABLE 24 HOURS A DAY!...
UNLESS THE OTHER PERSON HAPPENS TO BE IN THE SAME ROOM.
SERIOUSLY! GO DOWN THE STREET AND CALL MY HOUSE! THIS IS SO COOL!

1999—Commitment to the culinary arts

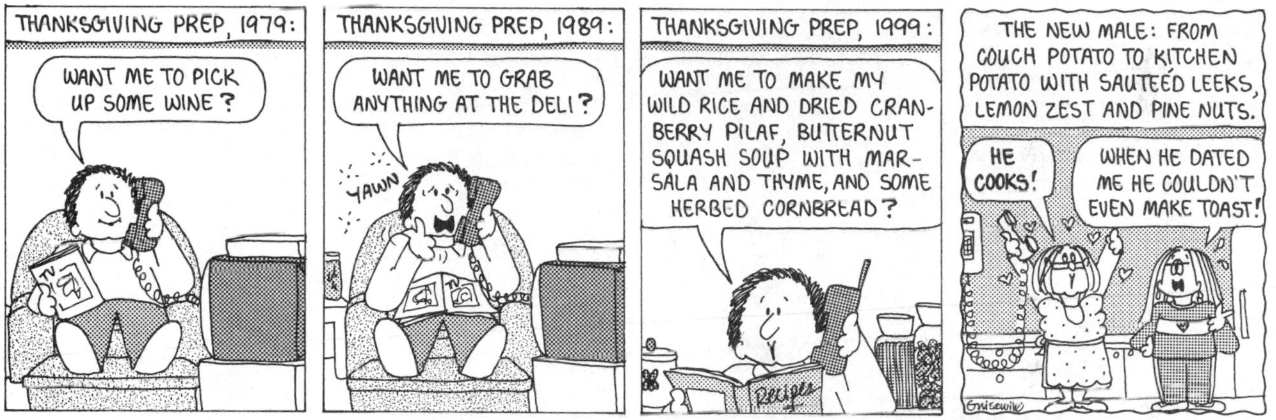
THANKSGIVING PREP, 1979:
WANT ME TO PICK UP SOME WINE?
TV
THANKSGIVING PREP, 1989:
WANT ME TO GRAB ANYTHING AT THE DELI?
YAWN
TV
THANKSGIVING PREP, 1999:
WANT ME TO MAKE MY WILD RICE AND DRIED CRANBERRY PILAF, BUTTERNUT SQUASH SOUP WITH MARSALA AND THYME, AND SOME HERBED CORNBREAD?
Recipes
THE NEW MALE: FROM COUCH POTATO TO KITCHEN POTATO WITH SAUTEÉD LEEKS, LEMON ZEST AND PINE NUTS.
HE COOKS!
WHEN HE DATED ME HE COULDN'T EVEN MAKE TOAST!

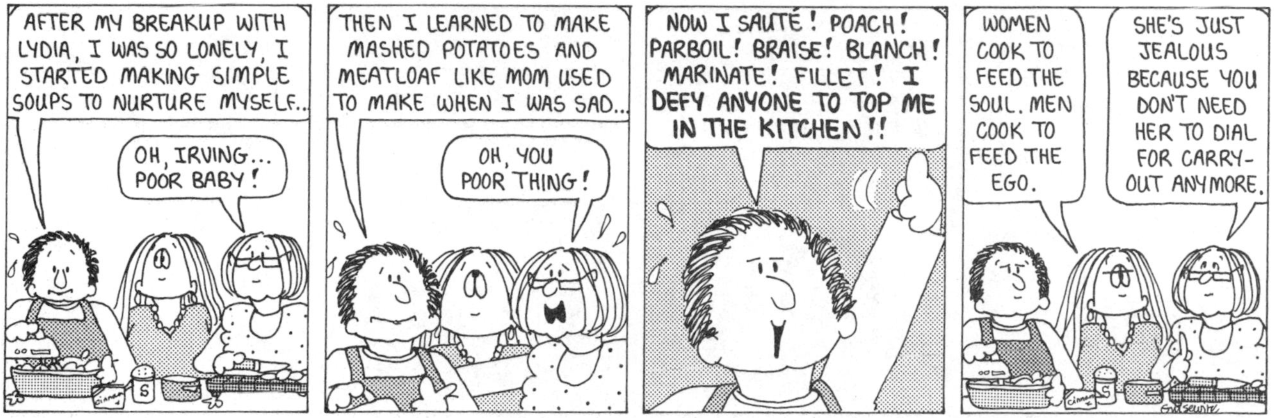
AFTER MY BREAKUP WITH LYDIA, I WAS SO LONELY, I STARTED MAKING SIMPLE SOUPS TO NURTURE MYSELF...
OH, IRVING... POOR BABY!
THEN I LEARNED TO MAKE MASHED POTATOES AND MEATLOAF LIKE MOM USED TO MAKE WHEN I WAS SAD...
OH, YOU POOR THING!
NOW I SAUTÉ! POACH! PARBOIL! BRAISE! BLANCH! MARINATE! FILLET! I DEFY ANYONE TO TOP ME IN THE KITCHEN!!
WOMEN COOK TO FEED THE SOUL. MEN COOK TO FEED THE EGO.
SHE'S JUST JEALOUS BECAUSE YOU DON'T NEED HER TO DIAL FOR CARRY-OUT ANYMORE.

2000—Commitment to becoming an Internet millionaire

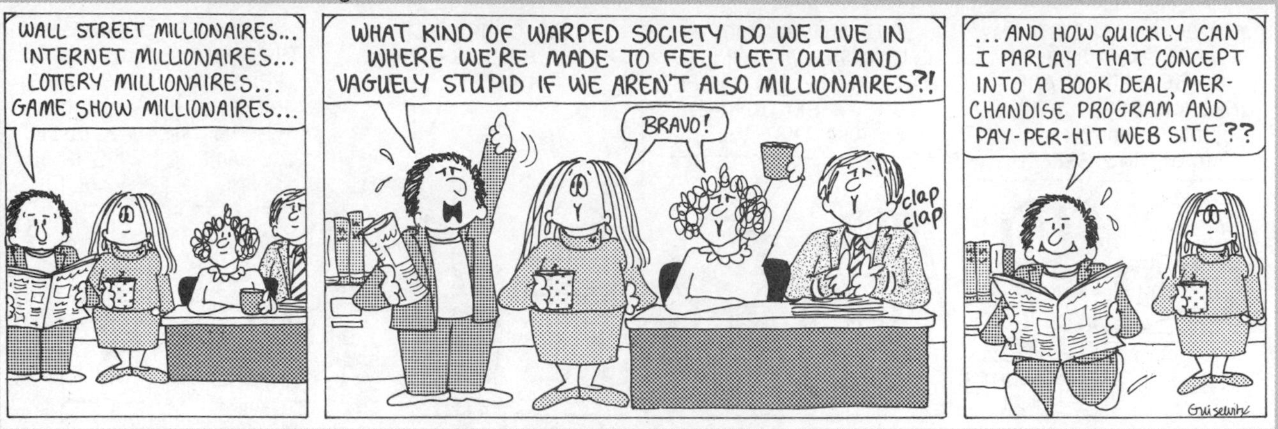
WALL STREET MILLIONAIRES... INTERNET MILLIONAIRES... LOTTERY MILLIONAIRES... GAME SHOW MILLIONAIRES...
WHAT KIND OF WARPED SOCIETY DO WE LIVE IN WHERE WE'RE MADE TO FEEL LEFT OUT AND VAGUELY STUPID IF WE AREN'T ALSO MILLIONAIRES?!
BRAVO!
clap clap
...AND HOW QUICKLY CAN I PARLAY THAT CONCEPT INTO A BOOK DEAL, MERCHANDISE PROGRAM AND PAY-PER-HIT WEB SITE??
Guisewite

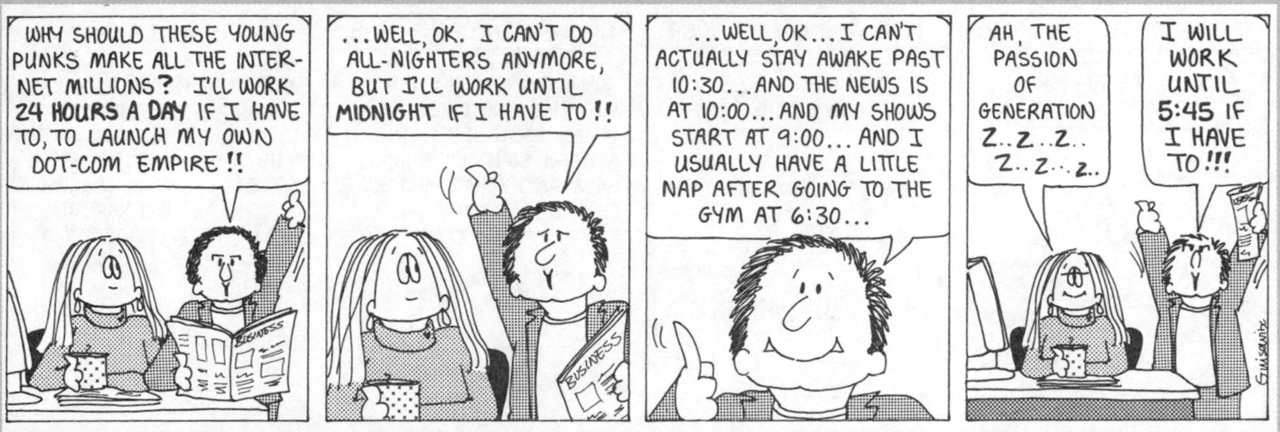
WHY SHOULD THESE YOUNG PUNKS MAKE ALL THE INTERNET MILLIONS? I'LL WORK 24 HOURS A DAY IF I HAVE TO, TO LAUNCH MY OWN DOT-COM EMPIRE!!
BUSINESS
...WELL, OK. I CAN'T DO ALL-NIGHTERS ANYMORE, BUT I'LL WORK UNTIL MIDNIGHT IF I HAVE TO!!
BUSINESS
...WELL, OK... I CAN'T ACTUALLY STAY AWAKE PAST 10:30... AND THE NEWS IS AT 10:00... AND MY SHOWS START AT 9:00... AND I USUALLY HAVE A LITTLE NAP AFTER GOING TO THE GYM AT 6:30...
AH, THE PASSION OF GENERATION Z..Z..Z.. Z..Z..Z..
I WILL WORK UNTIL 5:45 IF I HAVE TO!!!
Guisewite

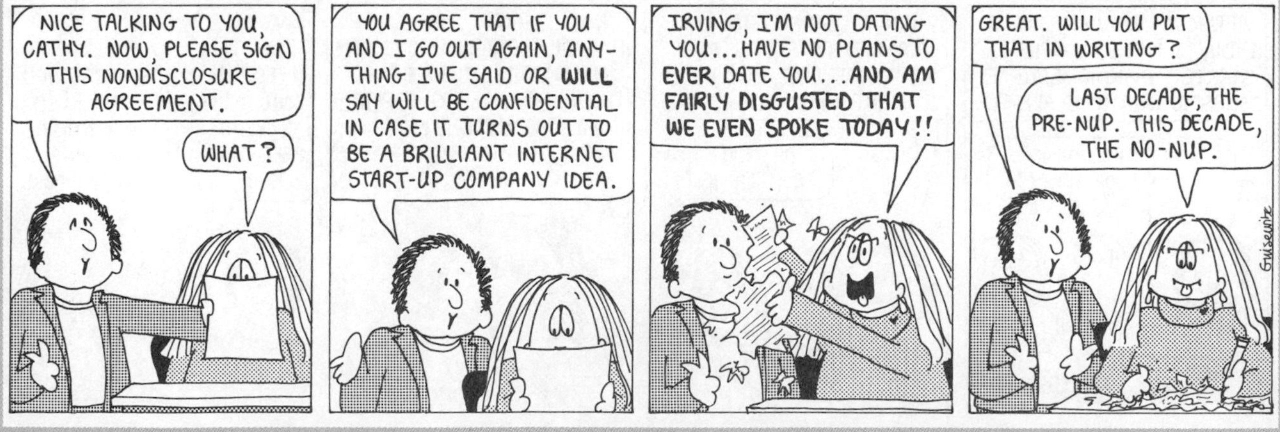
NICE TALKING TO YOU, CATHY. NOW, PLEASE SIGN THIS NONDISCLOSURE AGREEMENT.
WHAT?
YOU AGREE THAT IF YOU AND I GO OUT AGAIN, ANYTHING I'VE SAID OR WILL SAY WILL BE CONFIDENTIAL IN CASE IT TURNS OUT TO BE A BRILLIANT INTERNET START-UP COMPANY IDEA.
IRVING, I'M NOT DATING YOU... HAVE NO PLANS TO EVER DATE YOU... AND AM FAIRLY DISGUSTED THAT WE EVEN SPOKE TODAY!!
GREAT. WILL YOU PUT THAT IN WRITING?
LAST DECADE, THE PRE-NUP. THIS DECADE, THE NO-NUP.
Guisewite

The Identity Crisis Phase

2000—Irving voluntarily shops for the first time

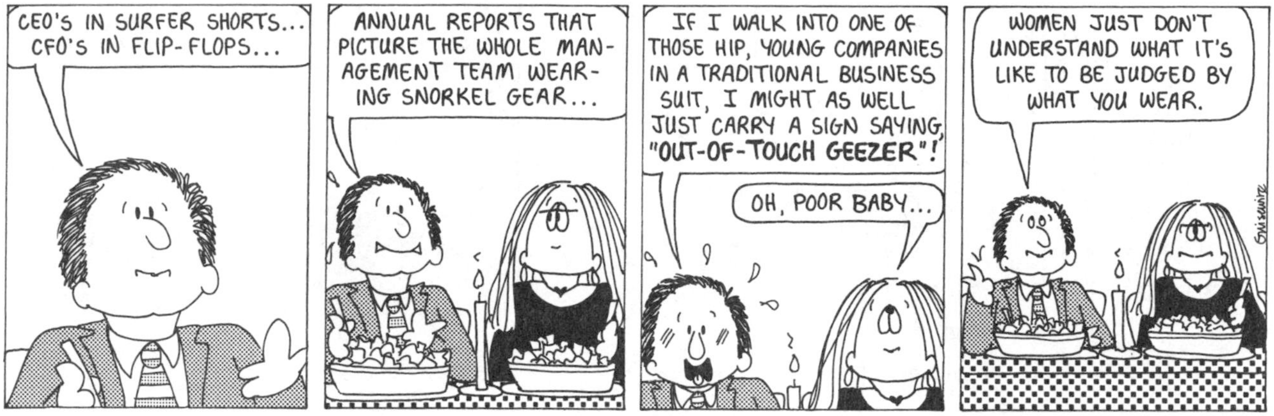

CEO'S IN SURFER SHORTS... CFO'S IN FLIP-FLOPS...
ANNUAL REPORTS THAT PICTURE THE WHOLE MANAGEMENT TEAM WEARING SNORKEL GEAR...
IF I WALK INTO ONE OF THOSE HIP, YOUNG COMPANIES IN A TRADITIONAL BUSINESS SUIT, I MIGHT AS WELL JUST CARRY A SIGN SAYING, "OUT-OF-TOUCH GEEZER"!
OH, POOR BABY...
WOMEN JUST DON'T UNDERSTAND WHAT IT'S LIKE TO BE JUDGED BY WHAT YOU WEAR.

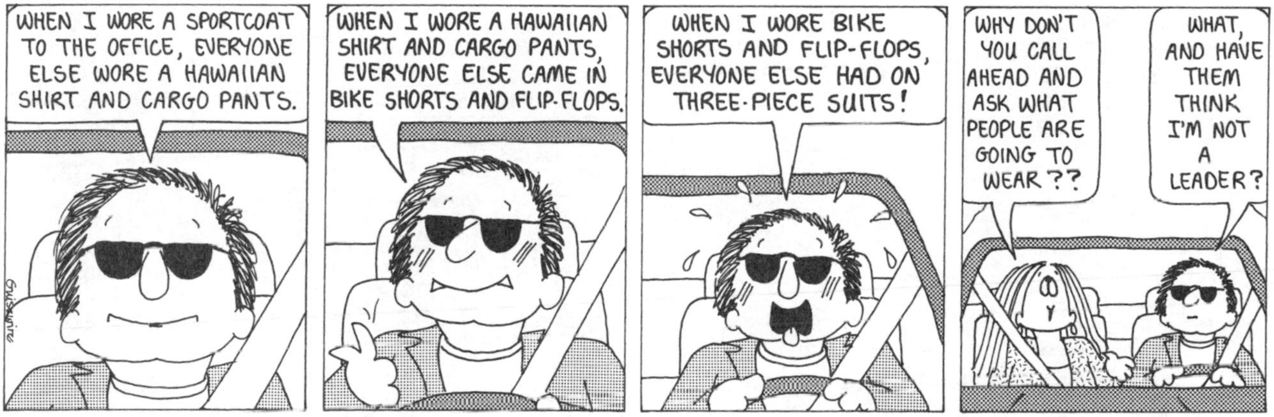

WHEN I WORE A SPORTCOAT TO THE OFFICE, EVERYONE ELSE WORE A HAWAIIAN SHIRT AND CARGO PANTS.
WHEN I WORE A HAWAIIAN SHIRT AND CARGO PANTS, EVERYONE ELSE CAME IN BIKE SHORTS AND FLIP-FLOPS.
WHEN I WORE BIKE SHORTS AND FLIP-FLOPS, EVERYONE ELSE HAD ON THREE-PIECE SUITS!
WHY DON'T YOU CALL AHEAD AND ASK WHAT PEOPLE ARE GOING TO WEAR??
WHAT, AND HAVE THEM THINK I'M NOT A LEADER?

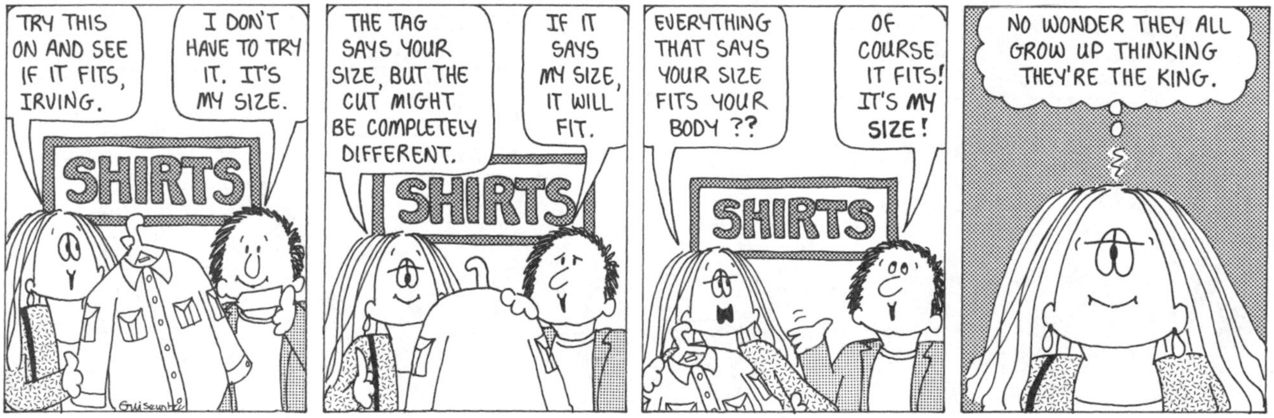

TRY THIS ON AND SEE IF IT FITS, IRVING.
I DON'T HAVE TO TRY IT. IT'S MY SIZE.
SHIRTS
THE TAG SAYS YOUR SIZE, BUT THE CUT MIGHT BE COMPLETELY DIFFERENT.
IF IT SAYS MY SIZE, IT WILL FIT.
SHIRTS
EVERYTHING THAT SAYS YOUR SIZE FITS YOUR BODY??
OF COURSE IT FITS! IT'S MY SIZE!
SHIRTS
NO WONDER THEY ALL GROW UP THINKING THEY'RE THE KING.

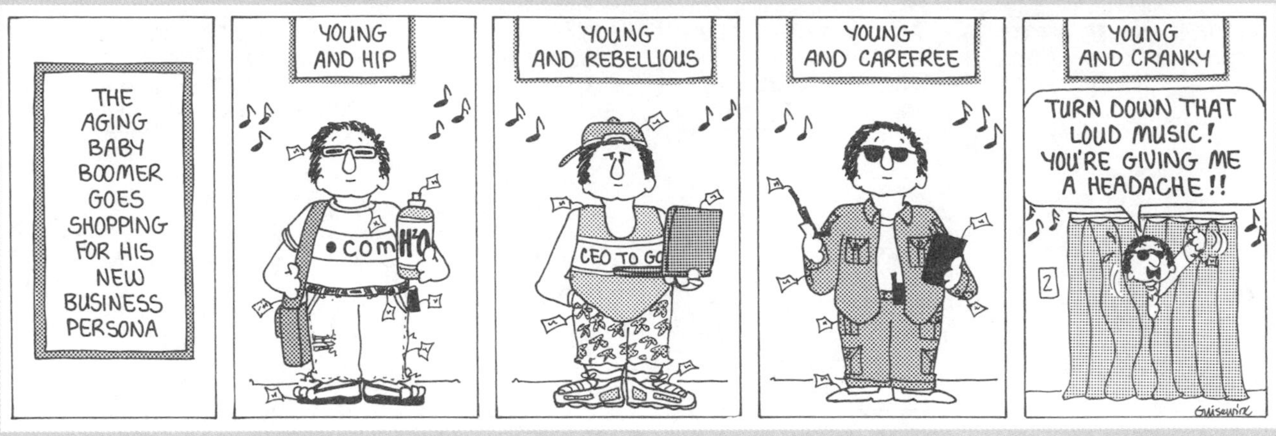
THE AGING BABY BOOMER GOES SHOPPING FOR HIS NEW BUSINESS PERSONA
YOUNG AND HIP
•COM
H2O
YOUNG AND REBELLIOUS
CEO TO GO
YOUNG AND CAREFREE
YOUNG AND CRANKY
TURN DOWN THAT LOUD MUSIC! YOU'RE GIVING ME A HEADACHE!!
2

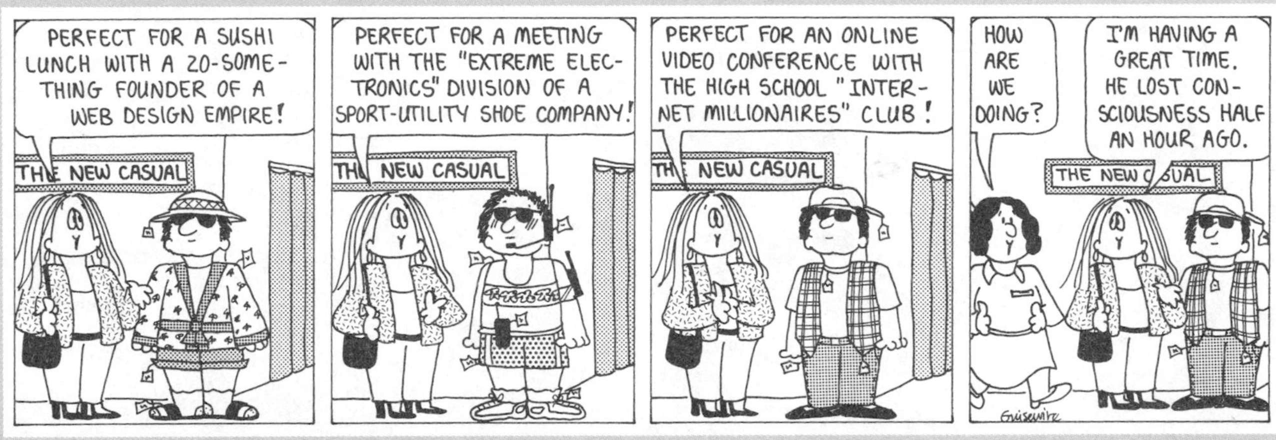
PERFECT FOR A SUSHI LUNCH WITH A 20-SOMETHING FOUNDER OF A WEB DESIGN EMPIRE!
THE NEW CASUAL
PERFECT FOR A MEETING WITH THE "EXTREME ELECTRONICS" DIVISION OF A SPORT-UTILITY SHOE COMPANY!
THE NEW CASUAL
PERFECT FOR AN ONLINE VIDEO CONFERENCE WITH THE HIGH SCHOOL "INTERNET MILLIONAIRES" CLUB!
THE NEW CASUAL
HOW ARE WE DOING?
I'M HAVING A GREAT TIME. HE LOST CONSCIOUSNESS HALF AN HOUR AGO.

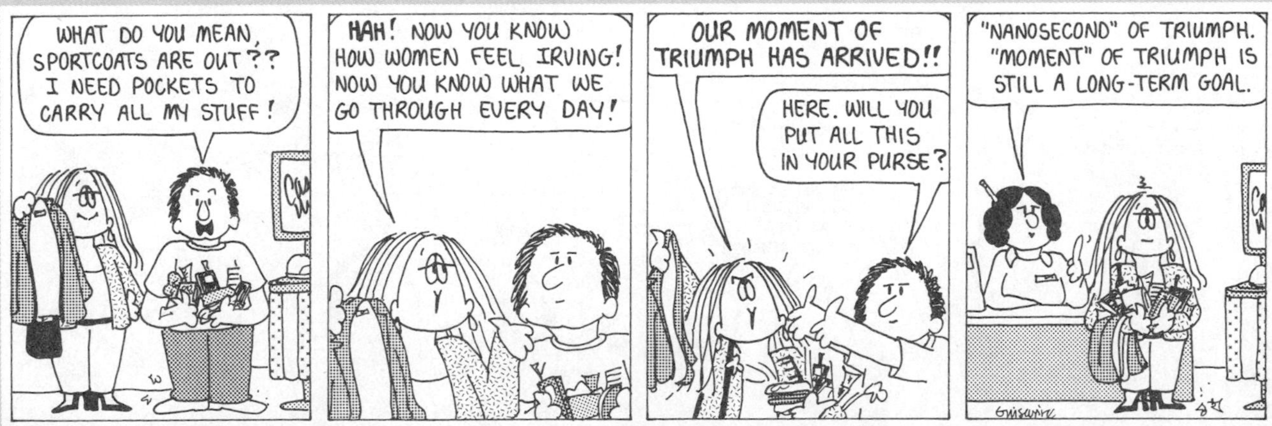
WHAT DO YOU MEAN, SPORTCOATS ARE OUT?? I NEED POCKETS TO CARRY ALL MY STUFF!
HAH! NOW YOU KNOW HOW WOMEN FEEL, IRVING! NOW YOU KNOW WHAT WE GO THROUGH EVERY DAY!
OUR MOMENT OF TRIUMPH HAS ARRIVED!!
HERE. WILL YOU PUT ALL THIS IN YOUR PURSE?
"NANOSECOND" OF TRIUMPH. "MOMENT" OF TRIUMPH IS STILL A LONG-TERM GOAL.

The Perfect Harmony Phase

2000

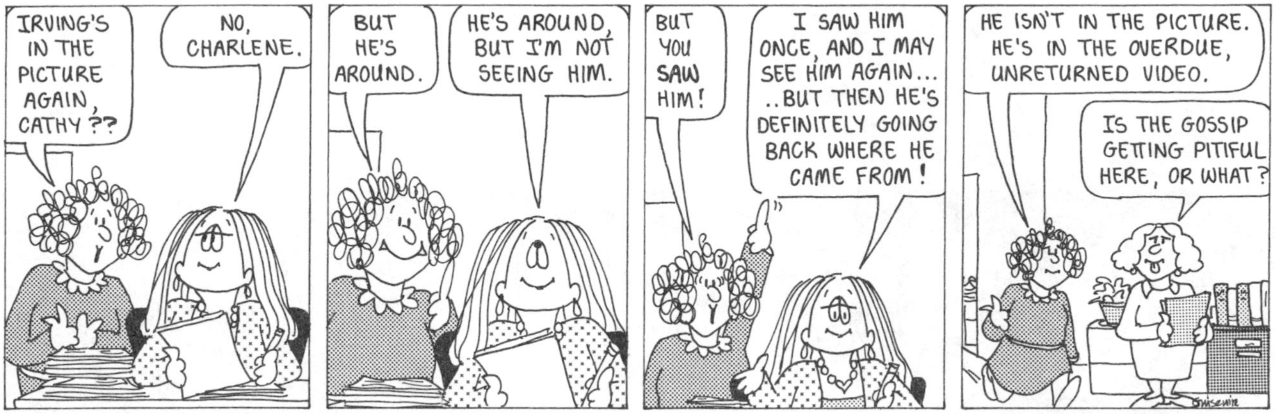
IRVING'S IN THE PICTURE AGAIN, CATHY??
NO, CHARLENE.
BUT HE'S AROUND.
HE'S AROUND, BUT I'M NOT SEEING HIM.
BUT YOU SAW HIM!
I SAW HIM ONCE, AND I MAY SEE HIM AGAIN... ..BUT THEN HE'S DEFINITELY GOING BACK WHERE HE CAME FROM!
HE ISN'T IN THE PICTURE. HE'S IN THE OVERDUE, UNRETURNED VIDEO.
IS THE GOSSIP GETTING PITIFUL HERE, OR WHAT?

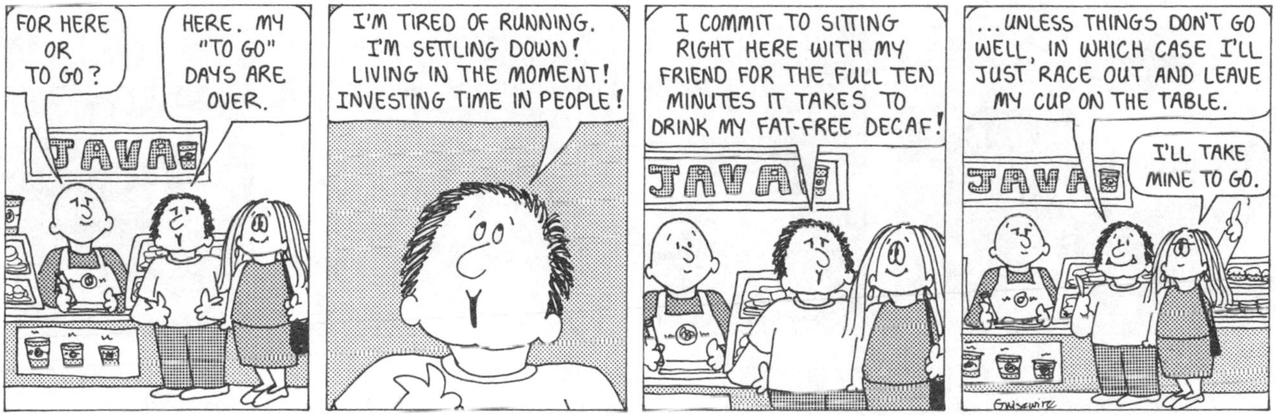
FOR HERE OR TO GO?
HERE. MY "TO GO" DAYS ARE OVER.
JAVA
I'M TIRED OF RUNNING. I'M SETTLING DOWN! LIVING IN THE MOMENT! INVESTING TIME IN PEOPLE!
I COMMIT TO SITTING RIGHT HERE WITH MY FRIEND FOR THE FULL TEN MINUTES IT TAKES TO DRINK MY FAT-FREE DECAF!
...UNLESS THINGS DON'T GO WELL, IN WHICH CASE I'LL JUST RACE OUT AND LEAVE MY CUP ON THE TABLE.
I'LL TAKE MINE TO GO.

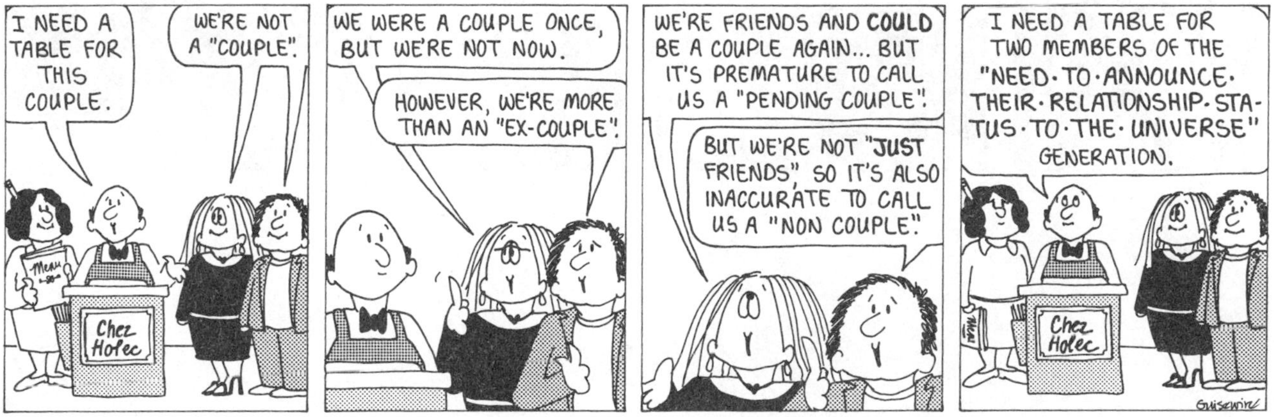
I NEED A TABLE FOR THIS COUPLE.
WE'RE NOT A "COUPLE".
Menu
Chez Holec
WE WERE A COUPLE ONCE, BUT WE'RE NOT NOW.
HOWEVER, WE'RE MORE THAN AN "EX-COUPLE".
WE'RE FRIENDS AND COULD BE A COUPLE AGAIN... BUT IT'S PREMATURE TO CALL US A "PENDING COUPLE".
BUT WE'RE NOT "JUST FRIENDS", SO IT'S ALSO INACCURATE TO CALL US A "NON COUPLE".
I NEED A TABLE FOR TWO MEMBERS OF THE "NEED·TO·ANNOUNCE·THEIR·RELATIONSHIP·STATUS·TO·THE·UNIVERSE" GENERATION.

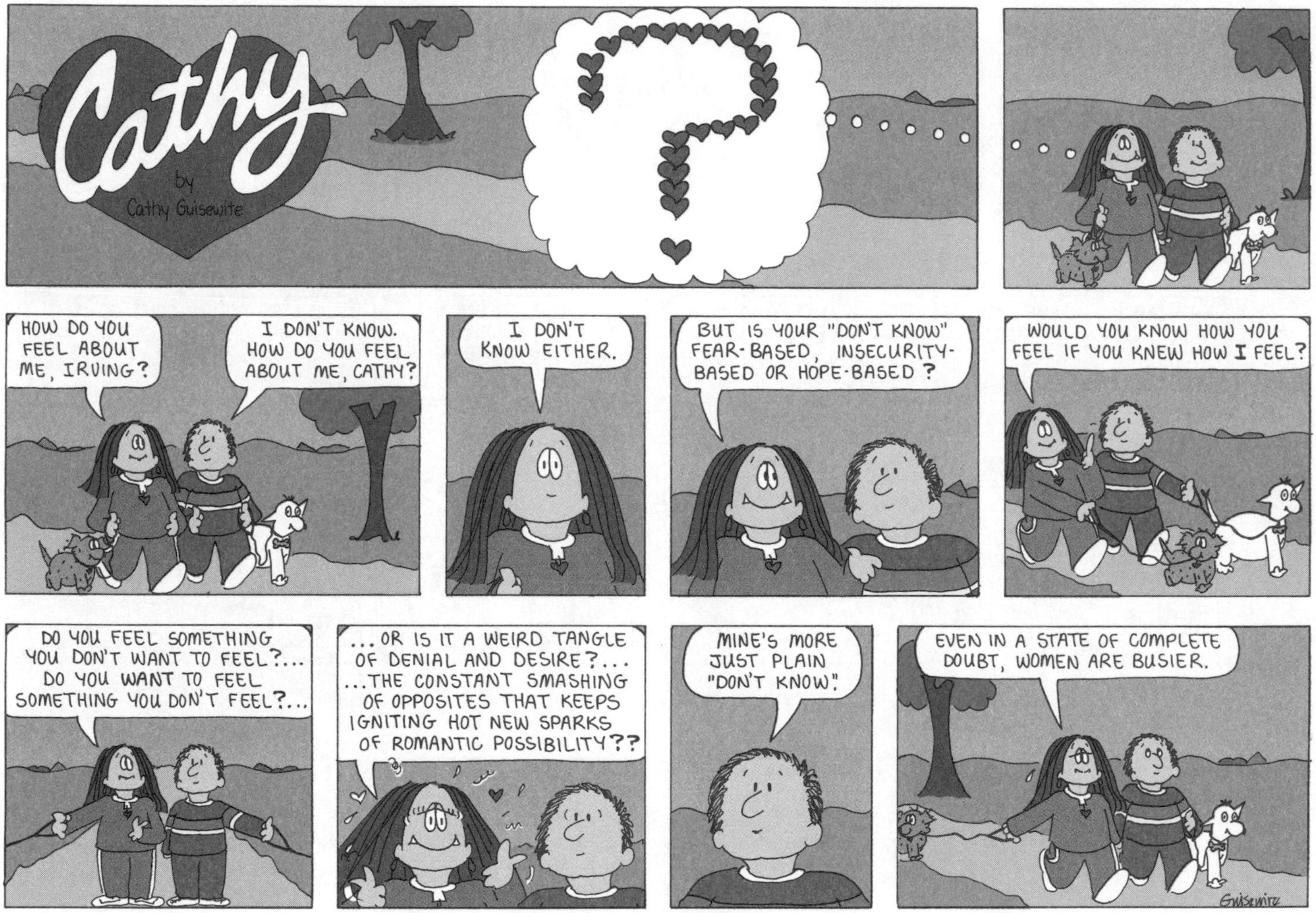
Cathy
by
Cathy Guisewite
HOW DO YOU FEEL ABOUT ME, IRVING?
I DON'T KNOW. HOW DO YOU FEEL ABOUT ME, CATHY?
I DON'T KNOW EITHER.
BUT IS YOUR "DON'T KNOW" FEAR-BASED, INSECURITY-BASED OR HOPE-BASED?
WOULD YOU KNOW HOW YOU FEEL IF YOU KNEW HOW I FEEL?
DO YOU FEEL SOMETHING YOU DON'T WANT TO FEEL?... DO YOU WANT TO FEEL SOMETHING YOU DON'T FEEL?...
...OR IS IT A WEIRD TANGLE OF DENIAL AND DESIRE?... ...THE CONSTANT SMASHING OF OPPOSITES THAT KEEPS IGNITING HOT NEW SPARKS OF ROMANTIC POSSIBILITY??
MINE'S MORE JUST PLAIN "DON'T KNOW".
EVEN IN A STATE OF COMPLETE DOUBT, WOMEN ARE BUSIER.
Guisewite

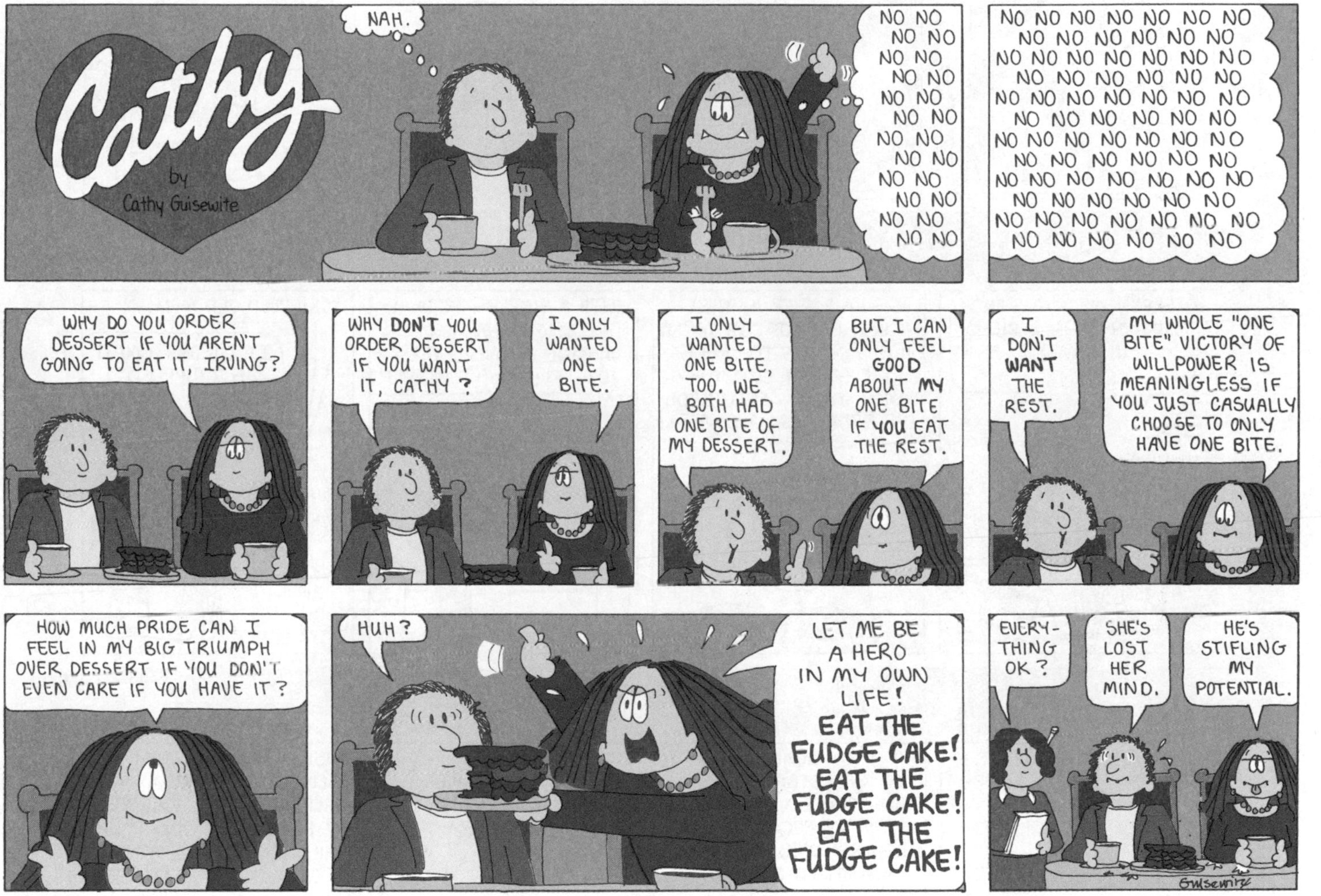
Cathy
by
Cathy Guisewite
NAH.
NO NO NO NO NO NO NO NO NO NO NO NO NO NO NO NO NO NO NO NO NO NO NO NO
NO NO NO NO NO NO NO NO NO NO NO NO NO NO NO NO NO NO NO NO NO NO NO NO NO NO NO NO NO NO NO NO NO NO NO NO NO NO NO NO NO NO NO NO NO NO NO NO NO NO NO NO NO NO NO NO NO NO NO NO NO NO NO NO NO NO NO NO
WHY DO YOU ORDER DESSERT IF YOU AREN'T GOING TO EAT IT, IRVING?
WHY **DON'T** YOU ORDER DESSERT IF YOU WANT IT, CATHY ?
I ONLY WANTED ONE BITE.
I ONLY WANTED ONE BITE, TOO. WE BOTH HAD ONE BITE OF MY DESSERT.
BUT I CAN ONLY FEEL **GOOD** ABOUT **MY** ONE BITE IF **YOU** EAT THE REST.
I DON'T **WANT** THE REST.
MY WHOLE "ONE BITE" VICTORY OF WILLPOWER IS MEANINGLESS IF YOU JUST CASUALLY CHOOSE TO ONLY HAVE ONE BITE.
HOW MUCH PRIDE CAN I FEEL IN MY BIG TRIUMPH OVER DESSERT IF YOU DON'T EVEN CARE IF YOU HAVE IT?
HUH?
LET ME BE A HERO IN MY OWN LIFE! **EAT THE FUDGE CAKE! EAT THE FUDGE CAKE! EAT THE FUDGE CAKE!**
EVERY-THING OK ?
SHE'S LOST HER MIND.
HE'S STIFLING MY POTENTIAL.
GUISEWITE

The Inner Child Phase

2000—Irving resurfaces as an athlete

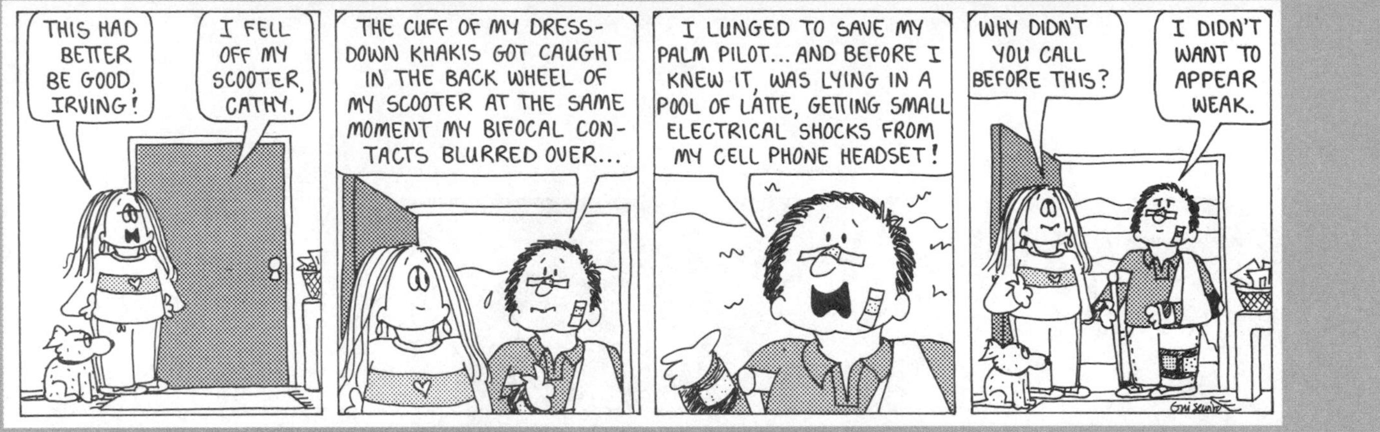
THIS HAD BETTER BE GOOD, IRVING!
I FELL OFF MY SCOOTER, CATHY.
THE CUFF OF MY DRESS-DOWN KHAKIS GOT CAUGHT IN THE BACK WHEEL OF MY SCOOTER AT THE SAME MOMENT MY BIFOCAL CONTACTS BLURRED OVER...
I LUNGED TO SAVE MY PALM PILOT... AND BEFORE I KNEW IT, WAS LYING IN A POOL OF LATTE, GETTING SMALL ELECTRICAL SHOCKS FROM MY CELL PHONE HEADSET!
WHY DIDN'T YOU CALL BEFORE THIS?
I DIDN'T WANT TO APPEAR WEAK.

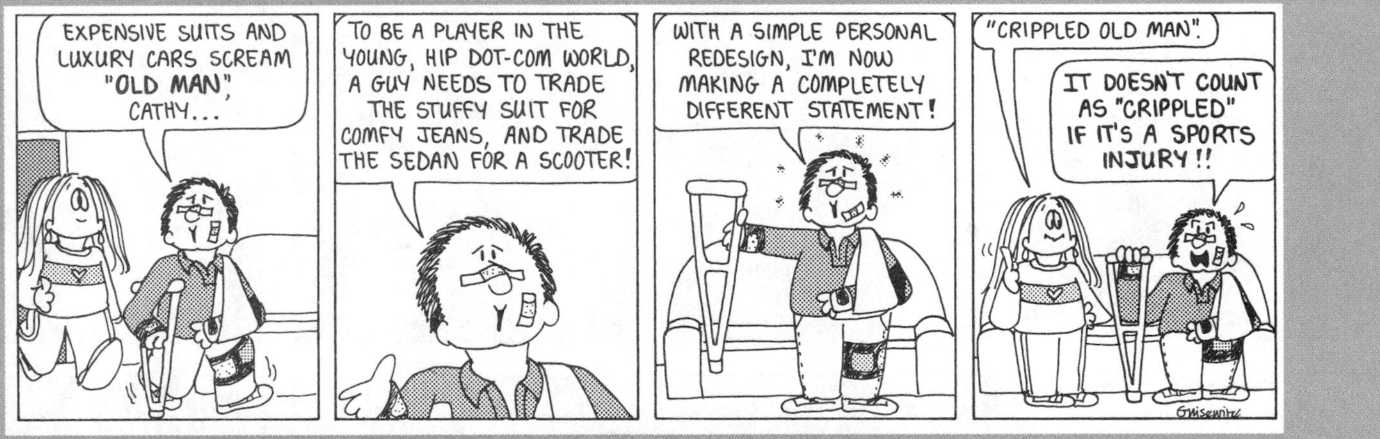
EXPENSIVE SUITS AND LUXURY CARS SCREAM "OLD MAN", CATHY...
TO BE A PLAYER IN THE YOUNG, HIP DOT-COM WORLD, A GUY NEEDS TO TRADE THE STUFFY SUIT FOR COMFY JEANS, AND TRADE THE SEDAN FOR A SCOOTER!
WITH A SIMPLE PERSONAL REDESIGN, I'M NOW MAKING A COMPLETELY DIFFERENT STATEMENT!
"CRIPPLED OLD MAN".
IT DOESN'T COUNT AS "CRIPPLED" IF IT'S A SPORTS INJURY!!

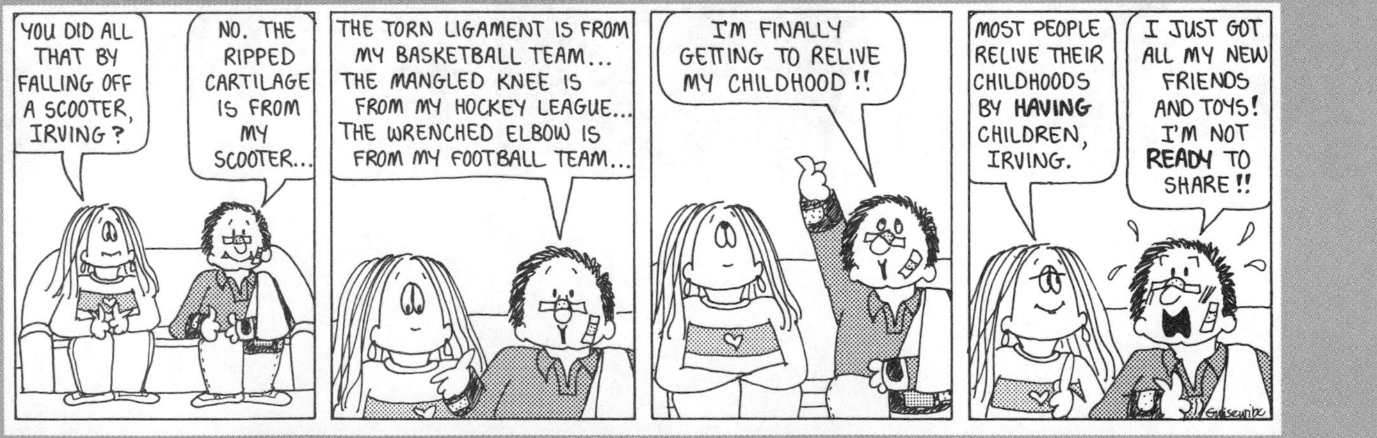
YOU DID ALL THAT BY FALLING OFF A SCOOTER, IRVING?
NO. THE RIPPED CARTILAGE IS FROM MY SCOOTER...
THE TORN LIGAMENT IS FROM MY BASKETBALL TEAM... THE MANGLED KNEE IS FROM MY HOCKEY LEAGUE... THE WRENCHED ELBOW IS FROM MY FOOTBALL TEAM...
I'M FINALLY GETTING TO RELIVE MY CHILDHOOD!!
MOST PEOPLE RELIVE THEIR CHILDHOODS BY HAVING CHILDREN, IRVING.
I JUST GOT ALL MY NEW FRIENDS AND TOYS! I'M NOT READY TO SHARE!!

The Inner Father Phase

2000—Irving finds true love at the animal shelter

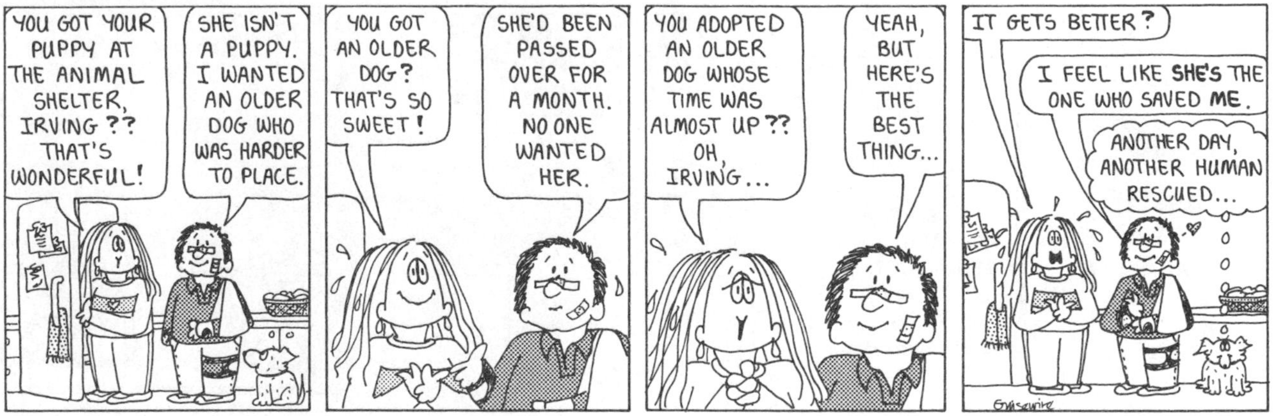

YOU GOT YOUR PUPPY AT THE ANIMAL SHELTER, IRVING ?? THAT'S WONDERFUL!
SHE ISN'T A PUPPY. I WANTED AN OLDER DOG WHO WAS HARDER TO PLACE.
YOU GOT AN OLDER DOG? THAT'S SO SWEET!
SHE'D BEEN PASSED OVER FOR A MONTH. NO ONE WANTED HER.
YOU ADOPTED AN OLDER DOG WHOSE TIME WAS ALMOST UP ?? OH, IRVING...
YEAH, BUT HERE'S THE BEST THING...
IT GETS BETTER?
I FEEL LIKE **SHE'S** THE ONE WHO SAVED **ME**.
ANOTHER DAY, ANOTHER HUMAN RESCUED...

Cathy meets Vivian

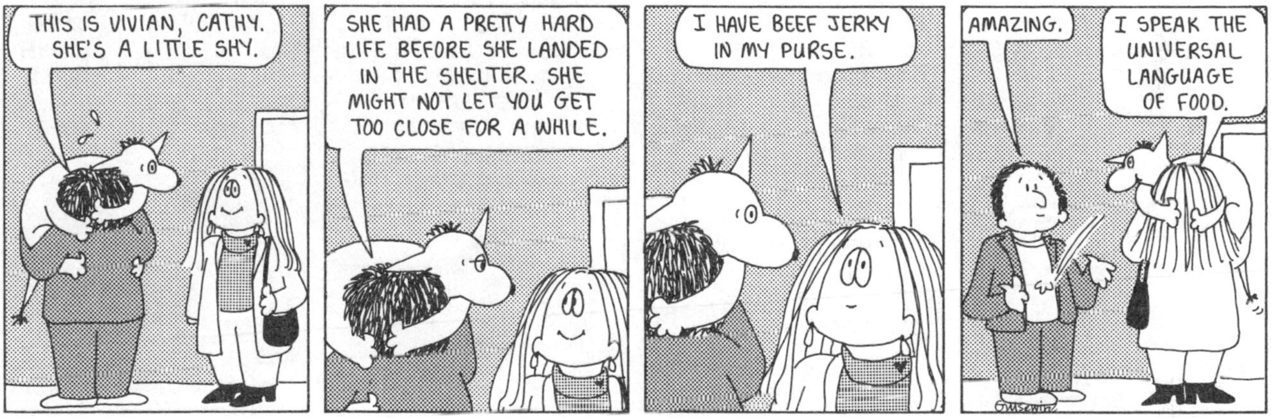

THIS IS VIVIAN, CATHY. SHE'S A LITTLE SHY.
SHE HAD A PRETTY HARD LIFE BEFORE SHE LANDED IN THE SHELTER. SHE MIGHT NOT LET YOU GET TOO CLOSE FOR A WHILE.
I HAVE BEEF JERKY IN MY PURSE.
AMAZING.
I SPEAK THE UNIVERSAL LANGUAGE OF FOOD.

Electra meets Vivian

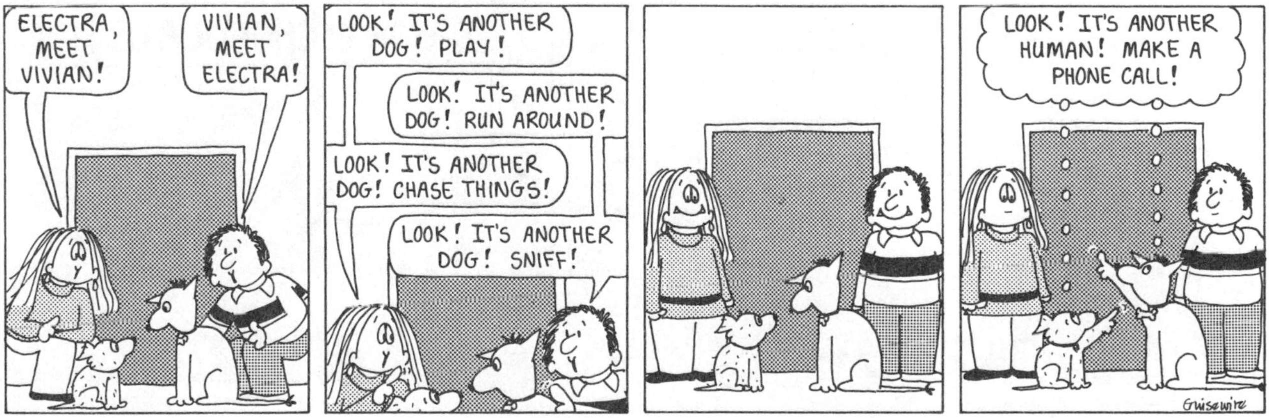

ELECTRA, MEET VIVIAN!
VIVIAN, MEET ELECTRA!
LOOK! IT'S ANOTHER DOG! PLAY!
LOOK! IT'S ANOTHER DOG! RUN AROUND!
LOOK! IT'S ANOTHER DOG! CHASE THINGS!
LOOK! IT'S ANOTHER DOG! SNIFF!
LOOK! IT'S ANOTHER HUMAN! MAKE A PHONE CALL!

The Outer Old Man Phase

2001—Irving gets his first good look at the old man in the mirror

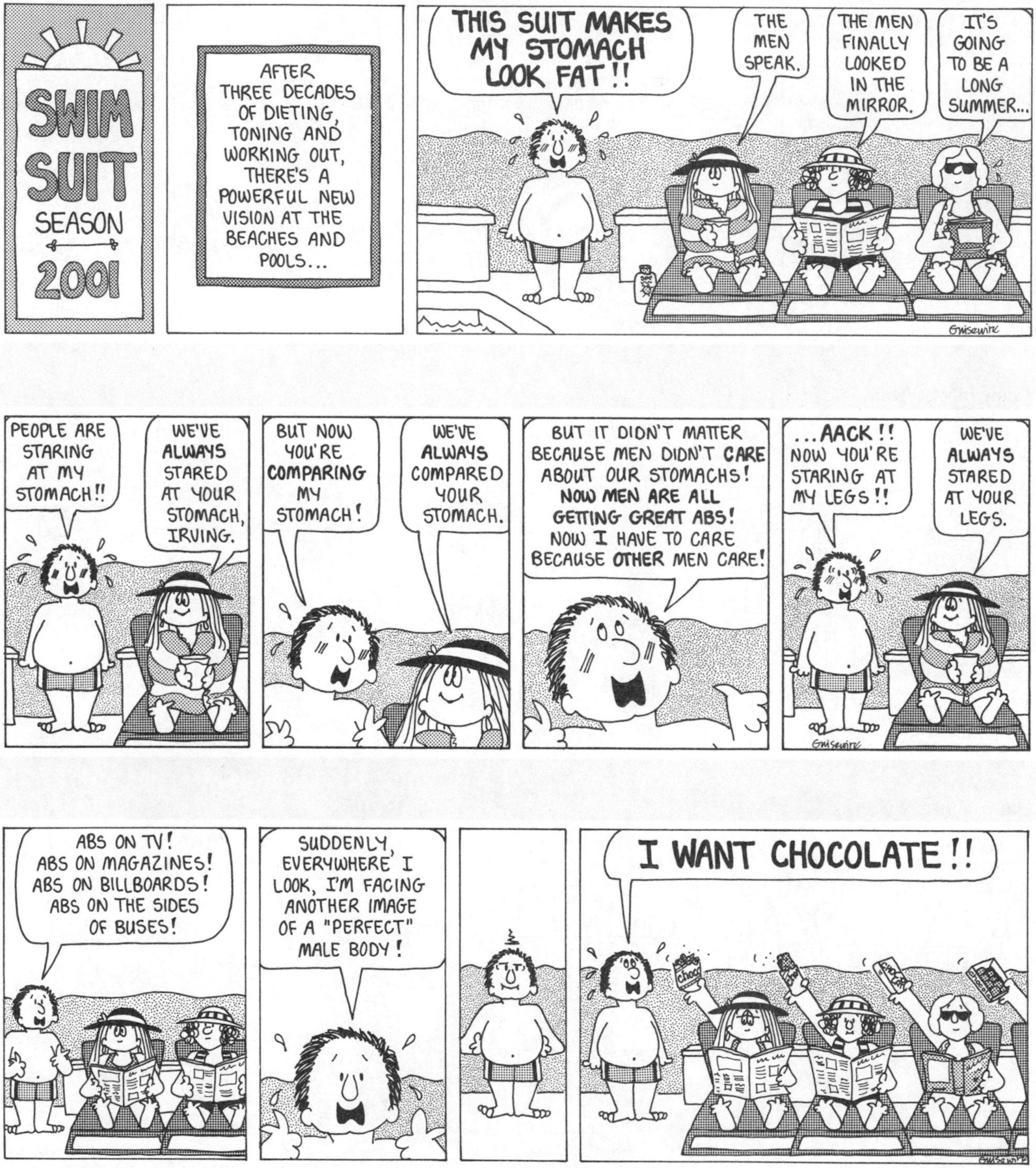
SWIM SUIT SEASON 2001
AFTER THREE DECADES OF DIETING, TONING AND WORKING OUT, THERE'S A POWERFUL NEW VISION AT THE BEACHES AND POOLS...
THIS SUIT MAKES MY STOMACH LOOK FAT!!
THE MEN SPEAK.
THE MEN FINALLY LOOKED IN THE MIRROR.
IT'S GOING TO BE A LONG SUMMER...
Guisewite
PEOPLE ARE STARING AT MY STOMACH!!
WE'VE ALWAYS STARED AT YOUR STOMACH, IRVING.
BUT NOW YOU'RE COMPARING MY STOMACH!
WE'VE ALWAYS COMPARED YOUR STOMACH.
BUT IT DIDN'T MATTER BECAUSE MEN DIDN'T CARE ABOUT OUR STOMACHS! NOW MEN ARE ALL GETTING GREAT ABS! NOW I HAVE TO CARE BECAUSE OTHER MEN CARE!
...AACK!! NOW YOU'RE STARING AT MY LEGS!!
WE'VE ALWAYS STARED AT YOUR LEGS.
Guisewite
ABS ON TV! ABS ON MAGAZINES! ABS ON BILLBOARDS! ABS ON THE SIDES OF BUSES!
SUDDENLY, EVERYWHERE I LOOK, I'M FACING ANOTHER IMAGE OF A "PERFECT" MALE BODY!
I WANT CHOCOLATE!!
Guisewite

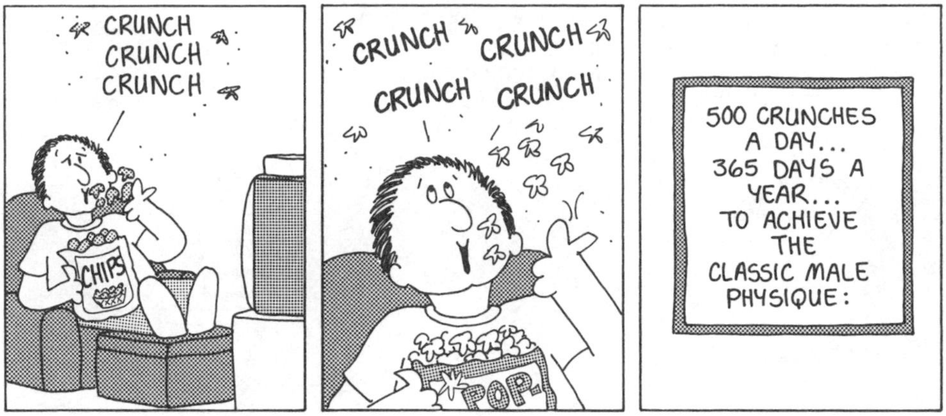
CRUNCH CRUNCH CRUNCH
CHIPS
CRUNCH CRUNCH
CRUNCH CRUNCH
POP-
500 CRUNCHES A DAY... 365 DAYS A YEAR... TO ACHIEVE THE CLASSIC MALE PHYSIQUE:
THE 36-PACK.
Guisewite

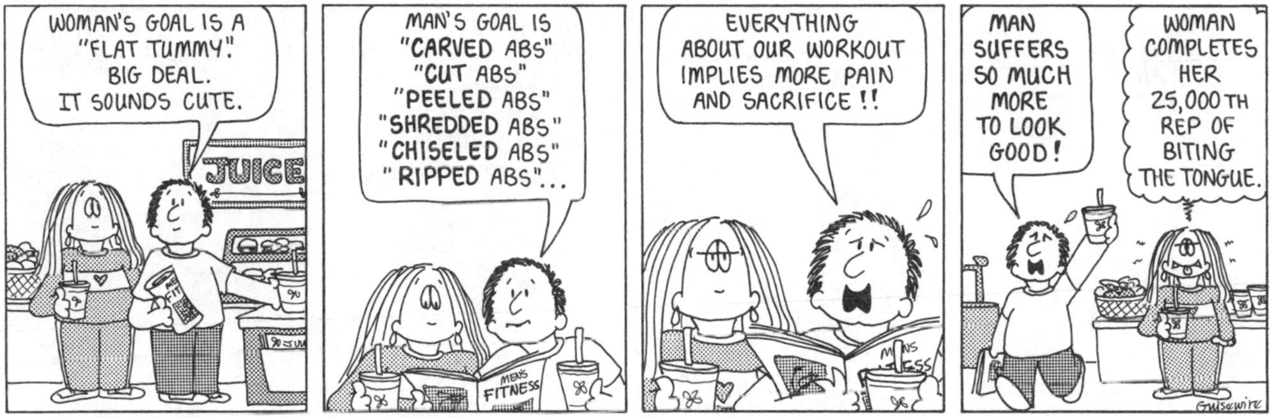
WOMAN'S GOAL IS A "FLAT TUMMY." BIG DEAL. IT SOUNDS CUTE.
JUICE
MAN'S GOAL IS "CARVED ABS" "CUT ABS" "PEELED ABS" "SHREDDED ABS" "CHISELED ABS" "RIPPED ABS"...
MEN'S FITNESS
EVERYTHING ABOUT OUR WORKOUT IMPLIES MORE PAIN AND SACRIFICE!!
MAN SUFFERS SO MUCH MORE TO LOOK GOOD!
WOMAN COMPLETES HER 25,000TH REP OF BITING THE TONGUE.
Guisewite

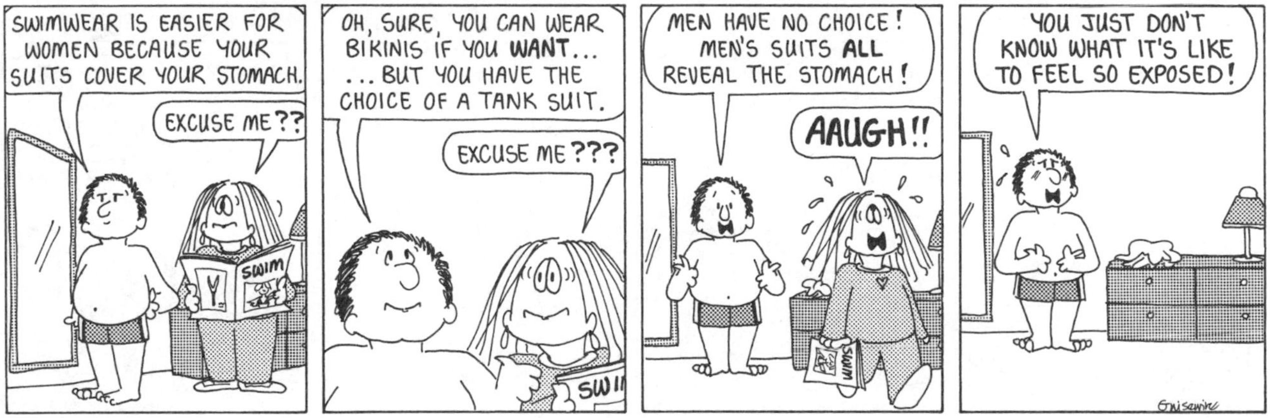
SWIMWEAR IS EASIER FOR WOMEN BECAUSE YOUR SUITS COVER YOUR STOMACH.
EXCUSE ME??
SWIM
OH, SURE, YOU CAN WEAR BIKINIS IF YOU WANT... ...BUT YOU HAVE THE CHOICE OF A TANK SUIT.
EXCUSE ME???
MEN HAVE NO CHOICE! MEN'S SUITS ALL REVEAL THE STOMACH!
AAUGH!!
YOU JUST DON'T KNOW WHAT IT'S LIKE TO FEEL SO EXPOSED!
Guisewite

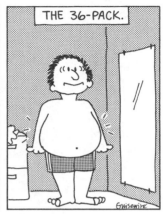

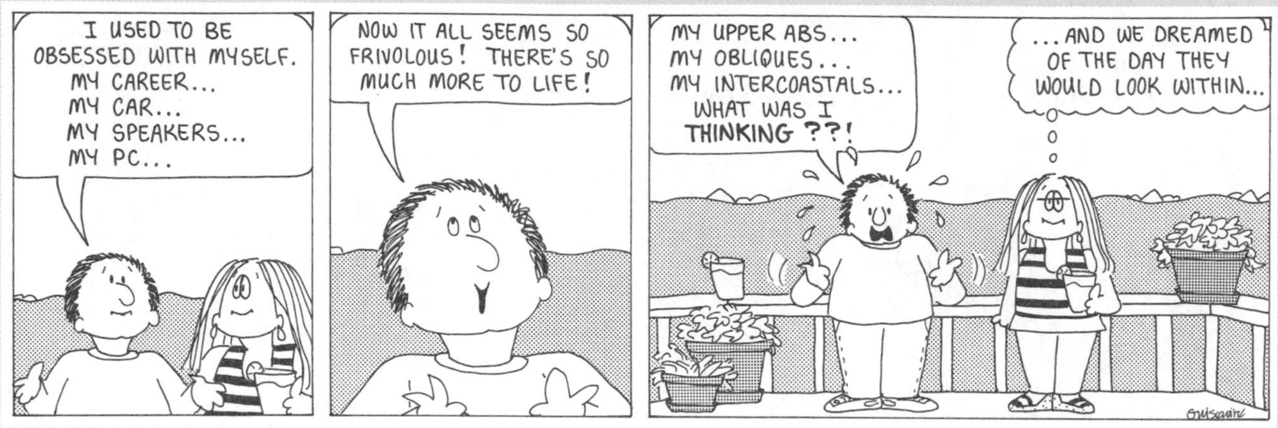
I USED TO BE OBSESSED WITH MYSELF. MY CAREER... MY CAR... MY SPEAKERS... MY PC...
NOW IT ALL SEEMS SO FRIVOLOUS! THERE'S SO MUCH MORE TO LIFE!
MY UPPER ABS... MY OBLIQUES... MY INTERCOASTALS... WHAT WAS I THINKING ??!
...AND WE DREAMED OF THE DAY THEY WOULD LOOK WITHIN...

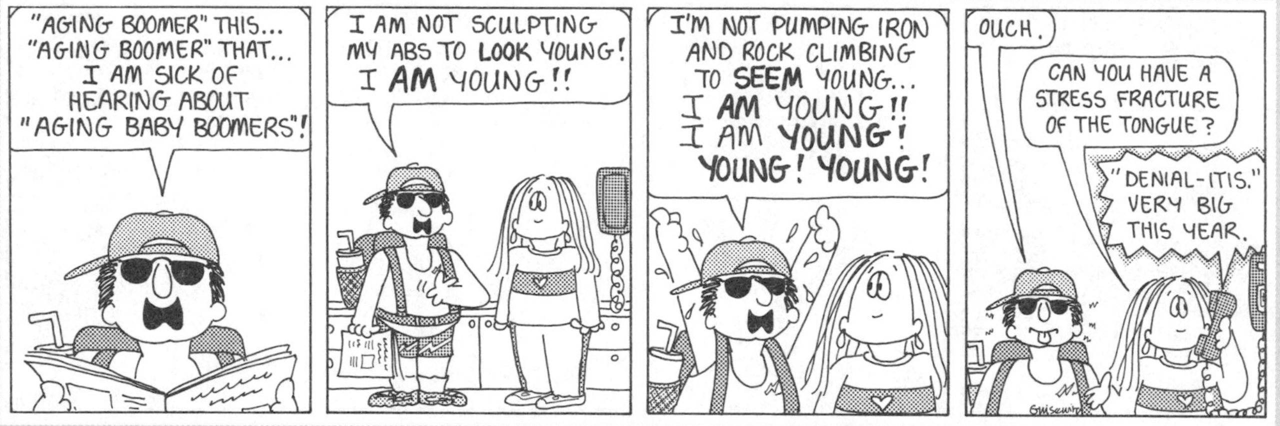
"AGING BOOMER" THIS... "AGING BOOMER" THAT... I AM SICK OF HEARING ABOUT "AGING BABY BOOMERS"!
I AM NOT SCULPTING MY ABS TO LOOK YOUNG! I AM YOUNG!!
I'M NOT PUMPING IRON AND ROCK CLIMBING TO SEEM YOUNG... I AM YOUNG!! I AM YOUNG! YOUNG! YOUNG!
OUCH.
CAN YOU HAVE A STRESS FRACTURE OF THE TONGUE?
"DENIAL-ITIS." VERY BIG THIS YEAR.

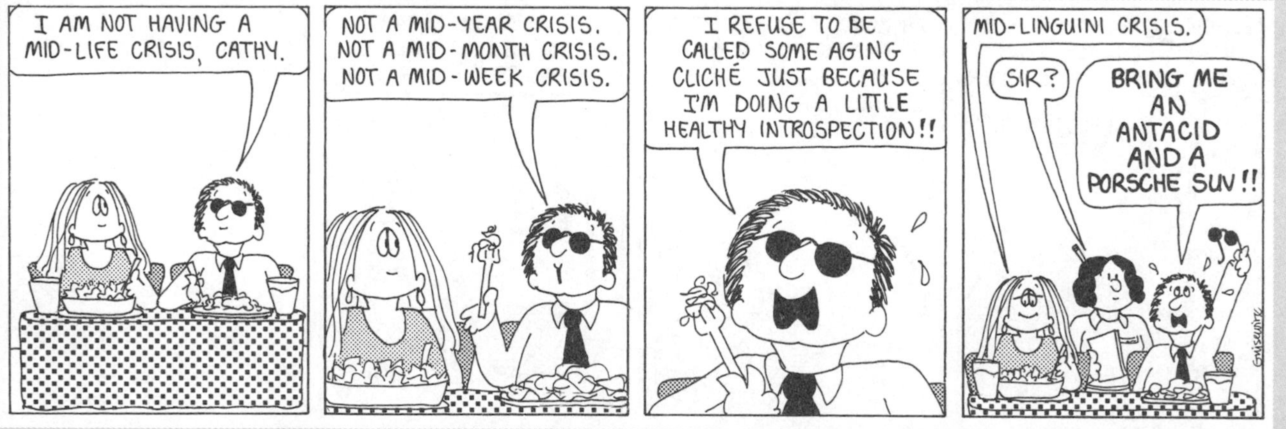
I AM NOT HAVING A MID-LIFE CRISIS, CATHY.
NOT A MID-YEAR CRISIS. NOT A MID-MONTH CRISIS. NOT A MID-WEEK CRISIS.
I REFUSE TO BE CALLED SOME AGING CLICHÉ JUST BECAUSE I'M DOING A LITTLE HEALTHY INTROSPECTION!!
MID-LINGUINI CRISIS.
SIR?
BRING ME AN ANTACID AND A PORSCHE SUV!!

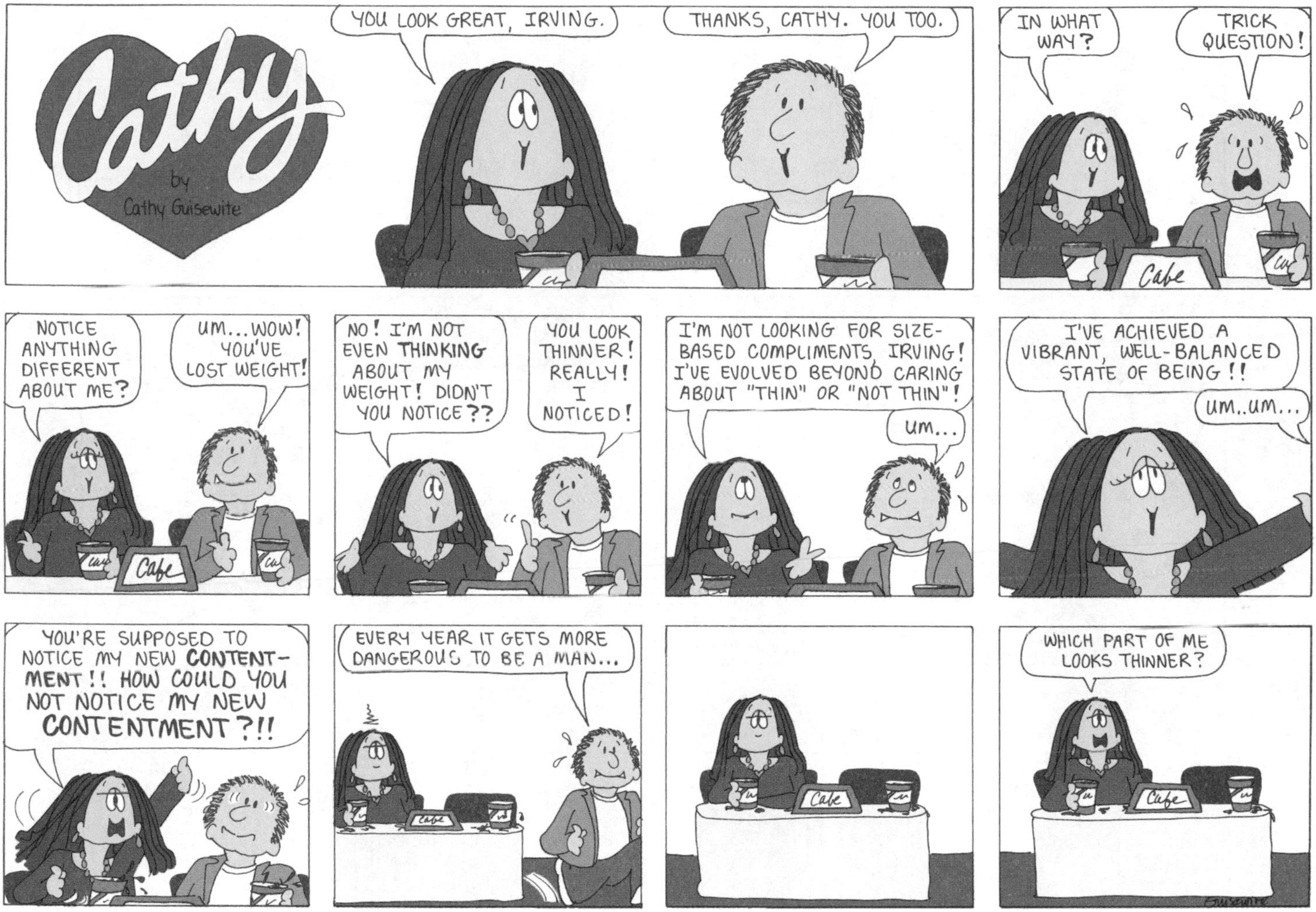
Cathy
by
Cathy Guisewite
YOU LOOK GREAT, IRVING.
THANKS, CATHY. YOU TOO.
IN WHAT WAY?
TRICK QUESTION!
NOTICE ANYTHING DIFFERENT ABOUT ME?
UM...WOW! YOU'VE LOST WEIGHT!
NO! I'M NOT EVEN THINKING ABOUT MY WEIGHT! DIDN'T YOU NOTICE??
YOU LOOK THINNER! REALLY! I NOTICED!
I'M NOT LOOKING FOR SIZE-BASED COMPLIMENTS, IRVING! I'VE EVOLVED BEYOND CARING ABOUT "THIN" OR "NOT THIN"!
UM...
I'VE ACHIEVED A VIBRANT, WELL-BALANCED STATE OF BEING!!
UM..UM...
YOU'RE SUPPOSED TO NOTICE MY NEW CONTENTMENT!! HOW COULD YOU NOT NOTICE MY NEW CONTENTMENT?!!
EVERY YEAR IT GETS MORE DANGEROUS TO BE A MAN...
WHICH PART OF ME LOOKS THINNER?

The Hair-free Phase

2001—Irving resurfaces with a slick new confidence

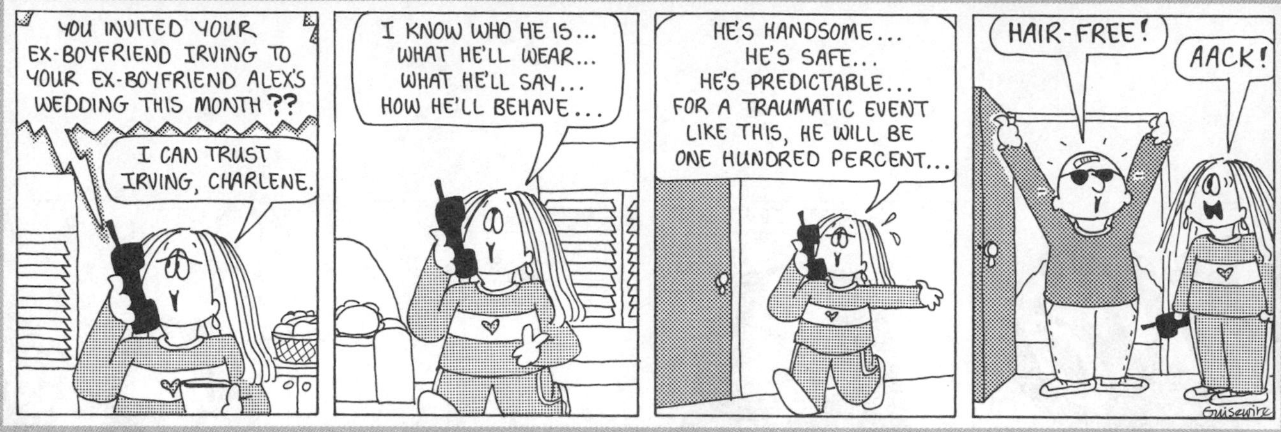

YOU INVITED YOUR EX-BOYFRIEND IRVING TO YOUR EX-BOYFRIEND ALEX'S WEDDING THIS MONTH??
I CAN TRUST IRVING, CHARLENE.
I KNOW WHO HE IS... WHAT HE'LL WEAR... WHAT HE'LL SAY... HOW HE'LL BEHAVE...
HE'S HANDSOME... HE'S SAFE... HE'S PREDICTABLE... FOR A TRAUMATIC EVENT LIKE THIS, HE WILL BE ONE HUNDRED PERCENT...
HAIR-FREE!
AACK!

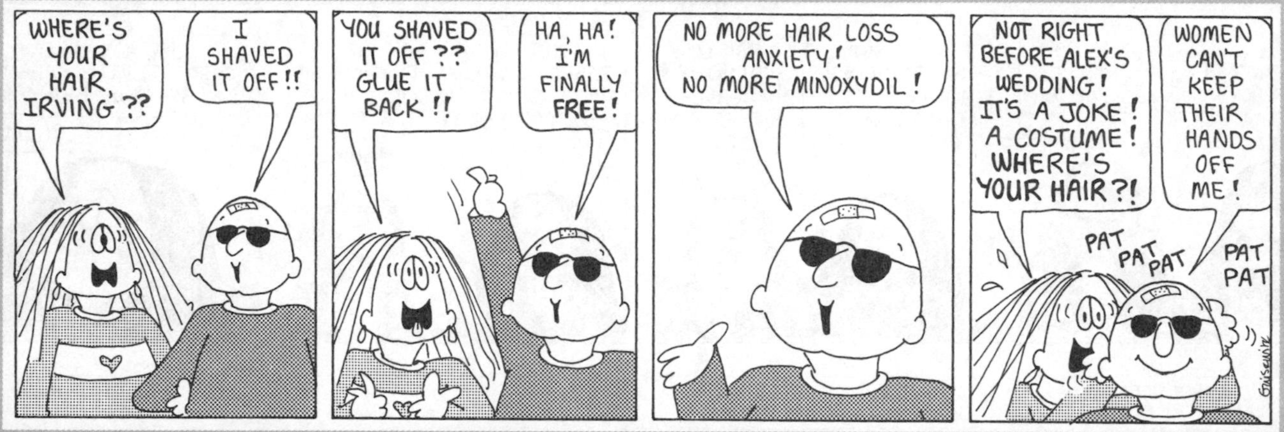

WHERE'S YOUR HAIR, IRVING??
I SHAVED IT OFF!!
YOU SHAVED IT OFF?? GLUE IT BACK!!
HA, HA! I'M FINALLY FREE!
NO MORE HAIR LOSS ANXIETY! NO MORE MINOXYDIL!
NOT RIGHT BEFORE ALEX'S WEDDING! IT'S A JOKE! A COSTUME! WHERE'S YOUR HAIR?!
WOMEN CAN'T KEEP THEIR HANDS OFF ME!
PAT PAT PAT
PAT PAT

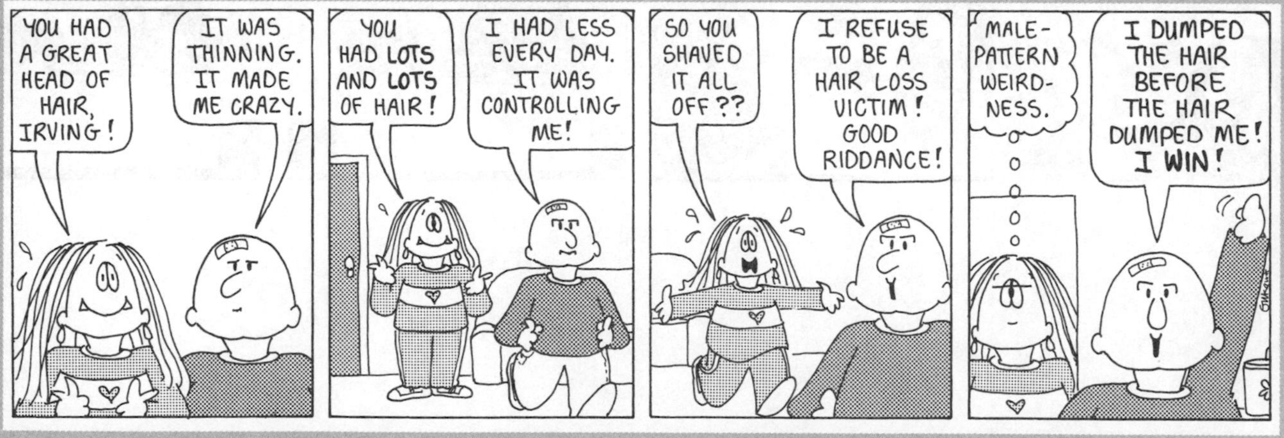

YOU HAD A GREAT HEAD OF HAIR, IRVING!
IT WAS THINNING. IT MADE ME CRAZY.
YOU HAD LOTS AND LOTS OF HAIR!
I HAD LESS EVERY DAY. IT WAS CONTROLLING ME!
SO YOU SHAVED IT ALL OFF??
I REFUSE TO BE A HAIR LOSS VICTIM! GOOD RIDDANCE!
MALE-PATTERN WEIRD-NESS.
I DUMPED THE HAIR BEFORE THE HAIR DUMPED ME! I WIN!

Panel 1:
THERE'S ALEX, IRVING.

HIM?? THAT'S THE HANDSOME EX-BOYFRIEND ???

Panel 2:
HE'S GREAT-LOOKING... BUT HE DOESN'T SEEM **THAT** MUCH YOUNGER OR MORE BUFF THAN I AM! HAH!

Panel 3:
WHAT IS IT WITH WOMEN AND YOUR OBSESSIVE INSECURITIES ??!

Panel 4:
...NO. THAT'S HIS FATHER. ALEX IS **THAT** ONE.

DID YOU BRING SUN BLOCK? MY SCALP IS WRINKLING.

Panel 5:
I HAD A FEELING YOU AND IRVING WOULD WIND UP TOGETHER, CATHY!

WE'RE NOT TOGETHER.

Panel 6:
YOU'RE **HERE** TOGETHER!

YES, BUT WE WEREN'T TOGETHER BEFORE, AND WE WON'T BE TOGETHER AFTER.

Panel 7:
WE'RE ONLY TOGETHER FOR THE TIME IT TOOK TO GET HERE, BE HERE AND DRIVE HOME FROM HERE!

Panel 8:
MY LOVE LIFE: THE CARPOOLING YEARS.

THAT'S HOW **WE** STARTED!

TAXI!!

Panel 9:
YOUR EX-BOYFRIEND LOOKS SO...

YOUNG? ATHLETIC? HANDSOME?

Panel 10:
NO! SO...

LOVING? EMOTIONALLY OPEN? ACCESSIBLE?

Panel 11:
NO!! LOOK AT HIM! HE'S JUST SO... SO...

STRONG? VIBRANT? TONED? CONFIDENT? BLOND?

Panel 12:
DORKY! HE'S SO DORKY!!

THE GREEN-EYED MONSTER: NOW SPORTING HIS NICE NEW TRIFOCAL PRESCRIPTION SHADES.

The Confidence-Free Phase

2002—Irving and his future greet Irving and his past

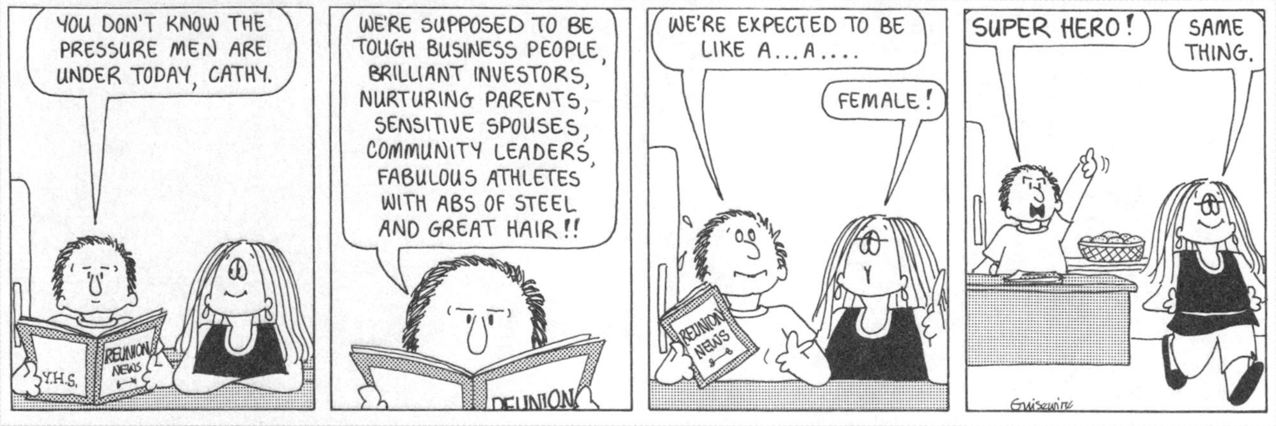

YOU DON'T KNOW THE PRESSURE MEN ARE UNDER TODAY, CATHY.
Y.H.S. REUNION NEWS
WE'RE SUPPOSED TO BE TOUGH BUSINESS PEOPLE, BRILLIANT INVESTORS, NURTURING PARENTS, SENSITIVE SPOUSES, COMMUNITY LEADERS, FABULOUS ATHLETES WITH ABS OF STEEL AND GREAT HAIR!!
REUNION
WE'RE EXPECTED TO BE LIKE A...A....
FEMALE!
REUNION NEWS
SUPER HERO!
SAME THING.

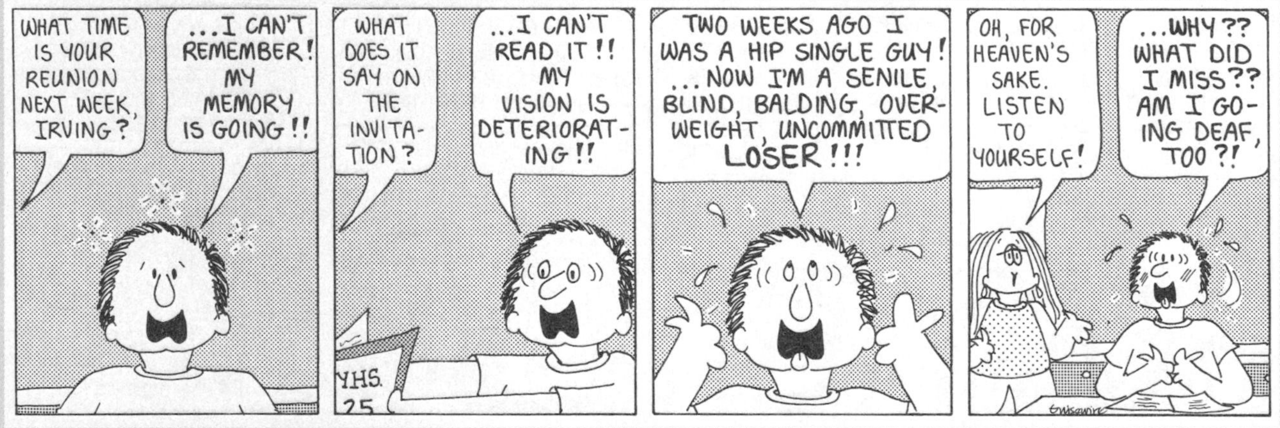

WHAT TIME IS YOUR REUNION NEXT WEEK, IRVING?
...I CAN'T REMEMBER! MY MEMORY IS GOING!!
WHAT DOES IT SAY ON THE INVITATION?
...I CAN'T READ IT!! MY VISION IS DETERIORATING!!
YHS. 25
TWO WEEKS AGO I WAS A HIP SINGLE GUY! ...NOW I'M A SENILE, BLIND, BALDING, OVERWEIGHT, UNCOMMITTED LOSER!!!
OH, FOR HEAVEN'S SAKE. LISTEN TO YOURSELF!
...WHY?? WHAT DID I MISS?? AM I GOING DEAF, TOO?!

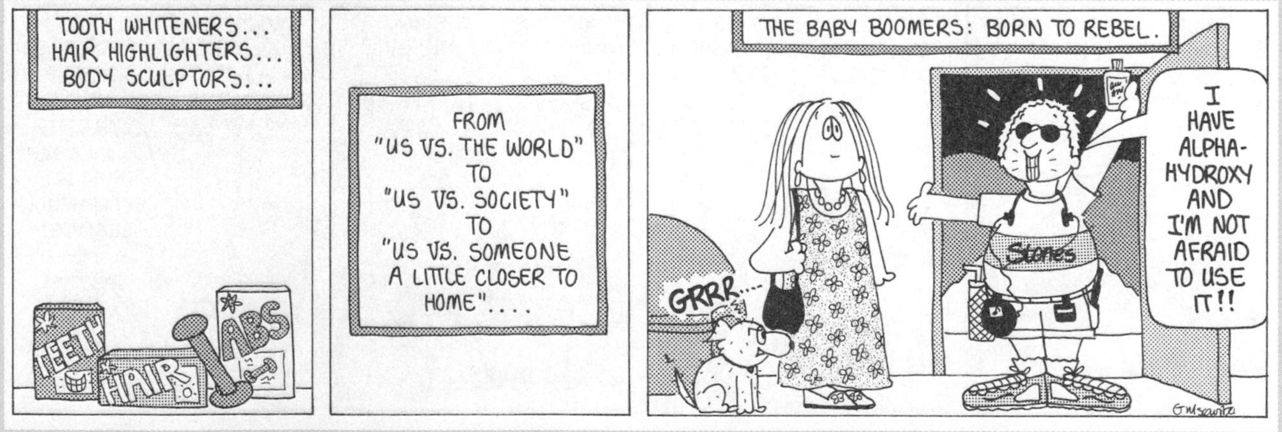

TOOTH WHITENERS... HAIR HIGHLIGHTERS... BODY SCULPTORS...
TEETH
HAIR
ABS
FROM "US VS. THE WORLD" TO "US VS. SOCIETY" TO "US VS. SOMEONE A LITTLE CLOSER TO HOME"....
THE BABY BOOMERS: BORN TO REBEL.
GRRR....
Stones
I HAVE ALPHA-HYDROXY AND I'M NOT AFRAID TO USE IT!!

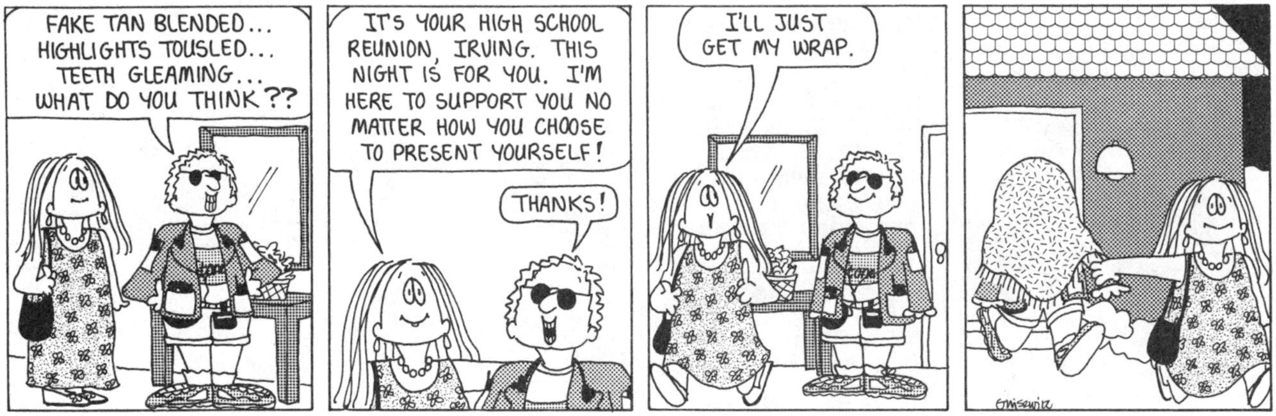
FAKE TAN BLENDED... HIGHLIGHTS TOUSLED... TEETH GLEAMING... WHAT DO YOU THINK??
IT'S YOUR HIGH SCHOOL REUNION, IRVING. THIS NIGHT IS FOR YOU. I'M HERE TO SUPPORT YOU NO MATTER HOW YOU CHOOSE TO PRESENT YOURSELF!
THANKS!
I'LL JUST GET MY WRAP.

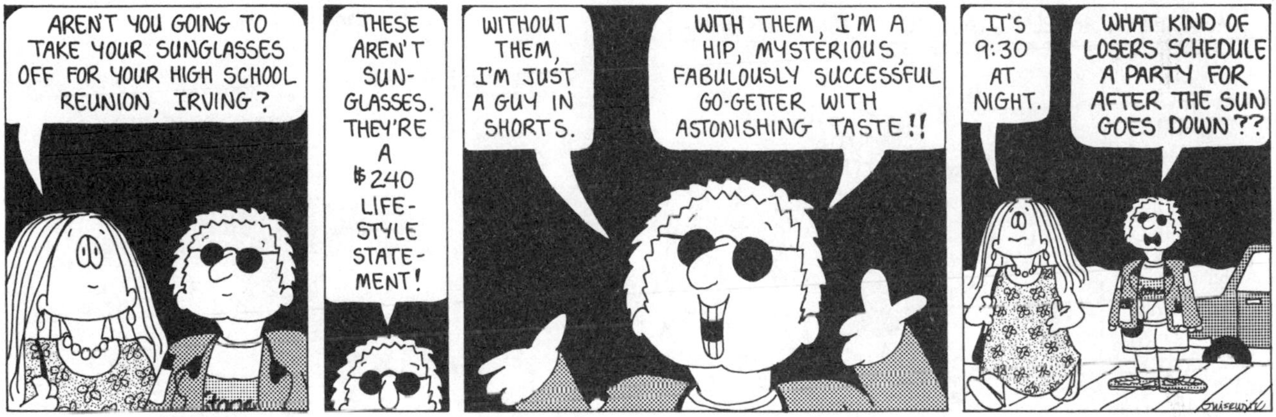
AREN'T YOU GOING TO TAKE YOUR SUNGLASSES OFF FOR YOUR HIGH SCHOOL REUNION, IRVING?
THESE AREN'T SUN-GLASSES. THEY'RE A $240 LIFE-STYLE STATE-MENT!
WITHOUT THEM, I'M JUST A GUY IN SHORTS.
WITH THEM, I'M A HIP, MYSTERIOUS, FABULOUSLY SUCCESSFUL GO-GETTER WITH ASTONISHING TASTE!!
IT'S 9:30 AT NIGHT.
WHAT KIND OF LOSERS SCHEDULE A PARTY FOR AFTER THE SUN GOES DOWN??

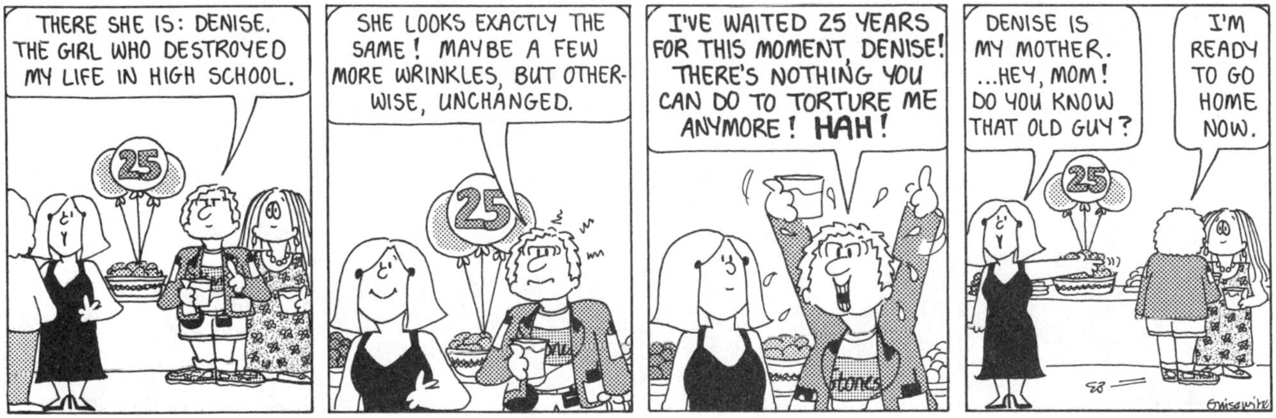
THERE SHE IS: DENISE. THE GIRL WHO DESTROYED MY LIFE IN HIGH SCHOOL.
SHE LOOKS EXACTLY THE SAME! MAYBE A FEW MORE WRINKLES, BUT OTHER-WISE, UNCHANGED.
I'VE WAITED 25 YEARS FOR THIS MOMENT, DENISE! THERE'S NOTHING YOU CAN DO TO TORTURE ME ANYMORE! HAH!
DENISE IS MY MOTHER. ...HEY, MOM! DO YOU KNOW THAT OLD GUY?
I'M READY TO GO HOME NOW.

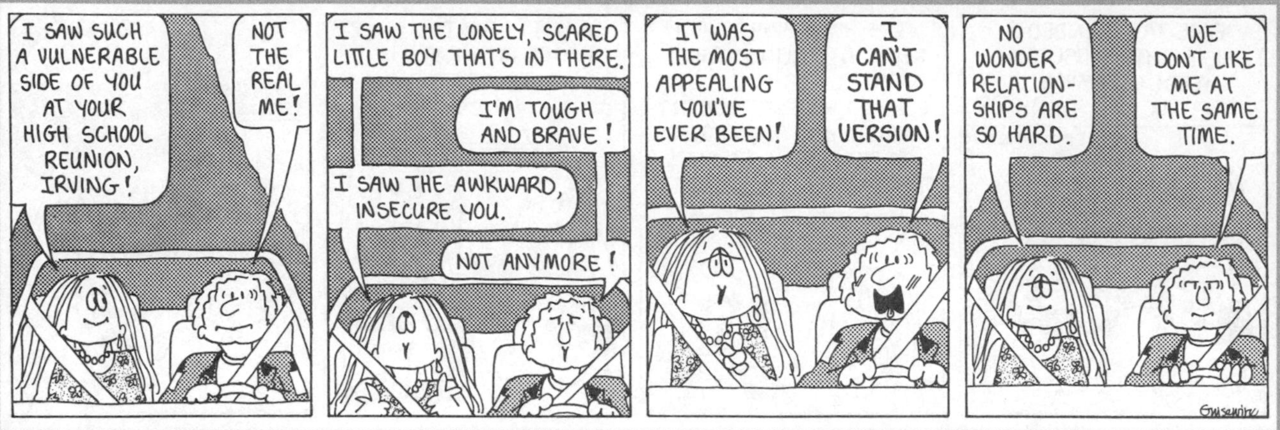
I SAW SUCH A VULNERABLE SIDE OF YOU AT YOUR HIGH SCHOOL REUNION, IRVING!
NOT THE REAL ME!
I SAW THE LONELY, SCARED LITTLE BOY THAT'S IN THERE.
I'M TOUGH AND BRAVE!
I SAW THE AWKWARD, INSECURE YOU.
NOT ANYMORE!
IT WAS THE MOST APPEALING YOU'VE EVER BEEN!
I CAN'T STAND THAT VERSION!
NO WONDER RELATIONSHIPS ARE SO HARD.
WE DON'T LIKE ME AT THE SAME TIME.
Guisewite

2002—Relationship skills progress report: Him

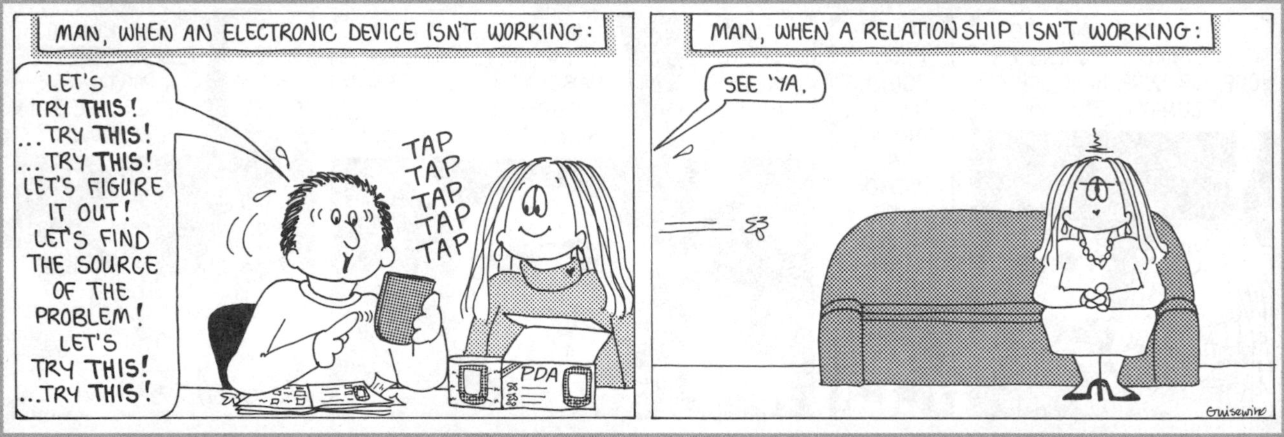
MAN, WHEN AN ELECTRONIC DEVICE ISN'T WORKING:
LET'S TRY THIS! ...TRY THIS! ...TRY THIS! LET'S FIGURE IT OUT! LET'S FIND THE SOURCE OF THE PROBLEM! LET'S TRY THIS! ...TRY THIS!
TAP TAP TAP TAP TAP
PDA
MAN, WHEN A RELATIONSHIP ISN'T WORKING:
SEE 'YA.
Guisewite

2003—Relationship skills progress report: Her

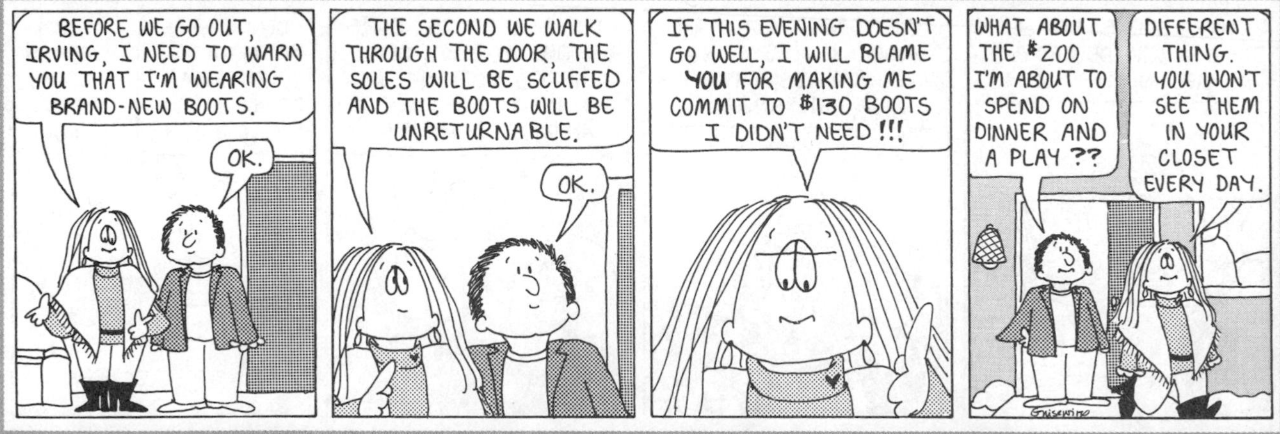
BEFORE WE GO OUT, IRVING, I NEED TO WARN YOU THAT I'M WEARING BRAND-NEW BOOTS.
OK.
THE SECOND WE WALK THROUGH THE DOOR, THE SOLES WILL BE SCUFFED AND THE BOOTS WILL BE UNRETURNABLE.
OK.
IF THIS EVENING DOESN'T GO WELL, I WILL BLAME YOU FOR MAKING ME COMMIT TO $130 BOOTS I DIDN'T NEED!!!
WHAT ABOUT THE $200 I'M ABOUT TO SPEND ON DINNER AND A PLAY??
DIFFERENT THING. YOU WON'T SEE THEM IN YOUR CLOSET EVERY DAY.
Guisewite

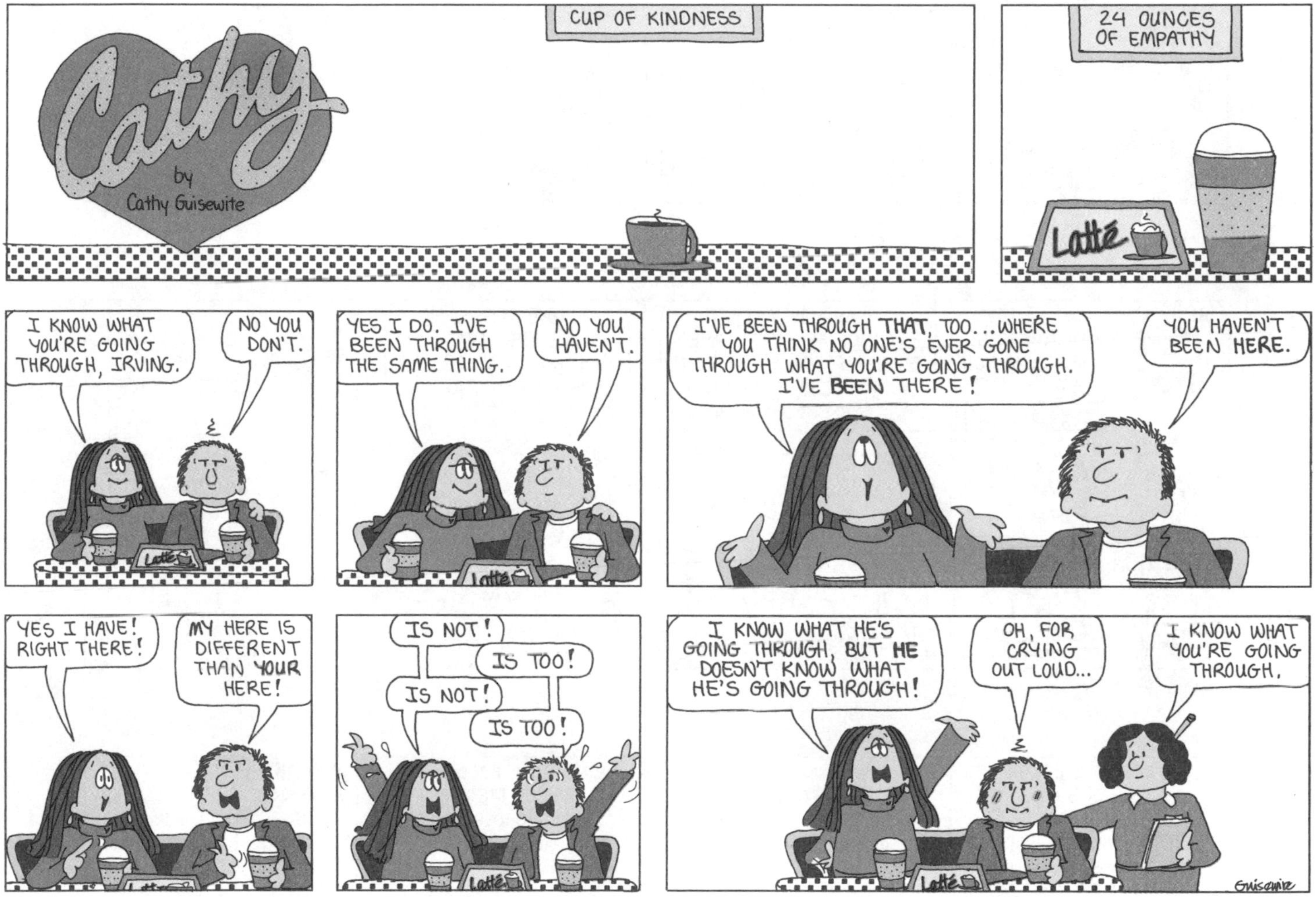

Cathy
by
Cathy Guisewite
CUP OF KINDNESS
24 OUNCES OF EMPATHY
Latté
I KNOW WHAT YOU'RE GOING THROUGH, IRVING.
NO YOU DON'T.
YES I DO. I'VE BEEN THROUGH THE SAME THING.
NO YOU HAVEN'T.
I'VE BEEN THROUGH THAT, TOO...WHERE YOU THINK NO ONE'S EVER GONE THROUGH WHAT YOU'RE GOING THROUGH. I'VE BEEN THERE!
YOU HAVEN'T BEEN HERE.
YES I HAVE! RIGHT THERE!
MY HERE IS DIFFERENT THAN YOUR HERE!
IS NOT!
IS TOO!
IS NOT!
IS TOO!
I KNOW WHAT HE'S GOING THROUGH, BUT HE DOESN'T KNOW WHAT HE'S GOING THROUGH!
OH, FOR CRYING OUT LOUD...
I KNOW WHAT YOU'RE GOING THROUGH.
Guisewite

The "Mr. Perfect" Phase

2003—Irving resurfaces—and is rejected—as the dream guy

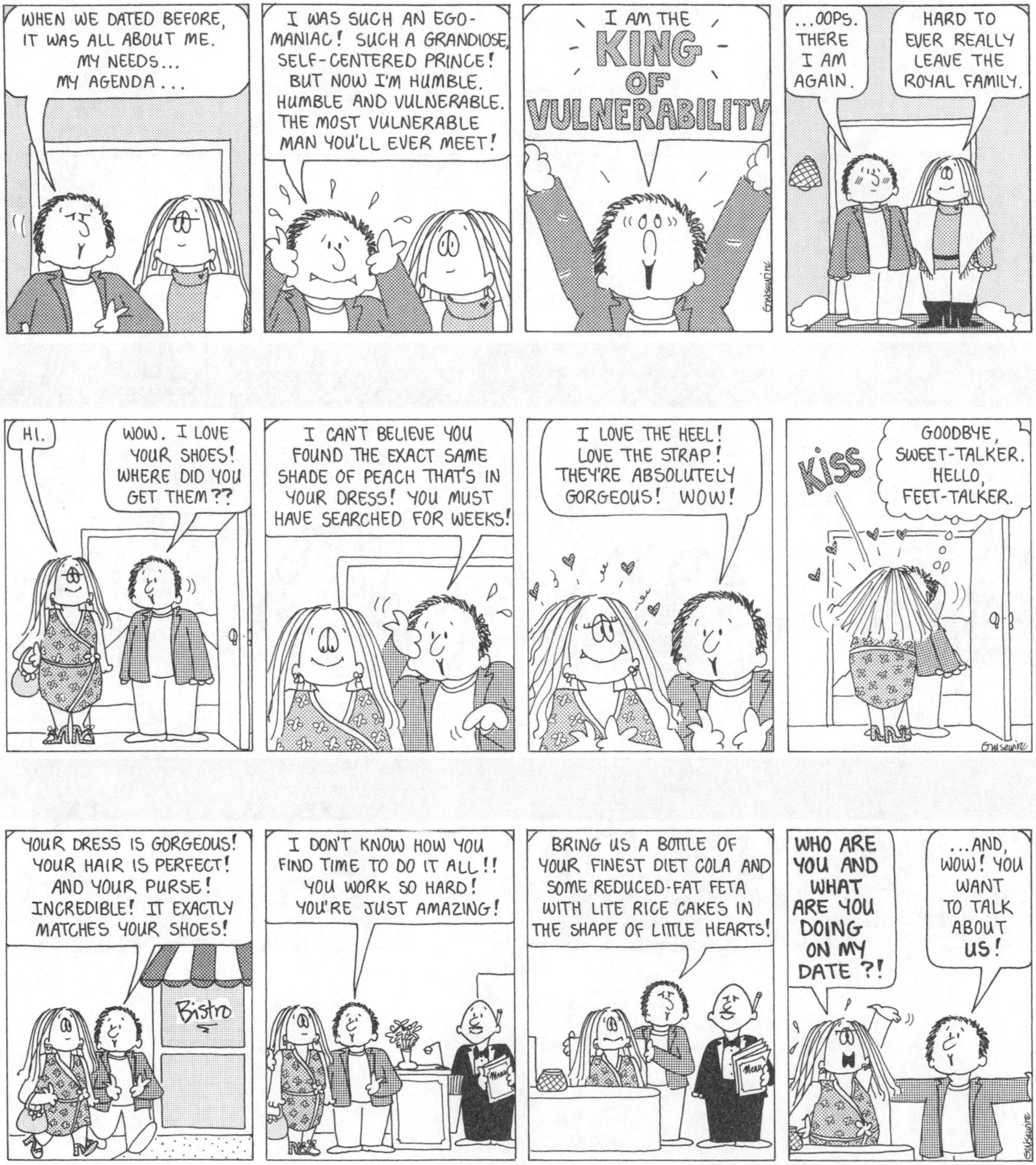
WHEN WE DATED BEFORE, IT WAS ALL ABOUT ME. MY NEEDS... MY AGENDA...
I WAS SUCH AN EGO-MANIAC! SUCH A GRANDIOSE, SELF-CENTERED PRINCE! BUT NOW I'M HUMBLE. HUMBLE AND VULNERABLE. THE MOST VULNERABLE MAN YOU'LL EVER MEET!
I AM THE KING OF VULNERABILITY
...OOPS. THERE I AM AGAIN.
HARD TO EVER REALLY LEAVE THE ROYAL FAMILY.
HI.
WOW. I LOVE YOUR SHOES! WHERE DID YOU GET THEM??
I CAN'T BELIEVE YOU FOUND THE EXACT SAME SHADE OF PEACH THAT'S IN YOUR DRESS! YOU MUST HAVE SEARCHED FOR WEEKS!
I LOVE THE HEEL! LOVE THE STRAP! THEY'RE ABSOLUTELY GORGEOUS! WOW!
KISS
GOODBYE, SWEET-TALKER. HELLO, FEET-TALKER.
YOUR DRESS IS GORGEOUS! YOUR HAIR IS PERFECT! AND YOUR PURSE! INCREDIBLE! IT EXACTLY MATCHES YOUR SHOES!
Bistro
I DON'T KNOW HOW YOU FIND TIME TO DO IT ALL!! YOU WORK SO HARD! YOU'RE JUST AMAZING!
Menu
BRING US A BOTTLE OF YOUR FINEST DIET COLA AND SOME REDUCED-FAT FETA WITH LITE RICE CAKES IN THE SHAPE OF LITTLE HEARTS!
Menu
WHO ARE YOU AND WHAT ARE YOU DOING ON MY DATE?!
...AND, WOW! YOU WANT TO TALK ABOUT US!

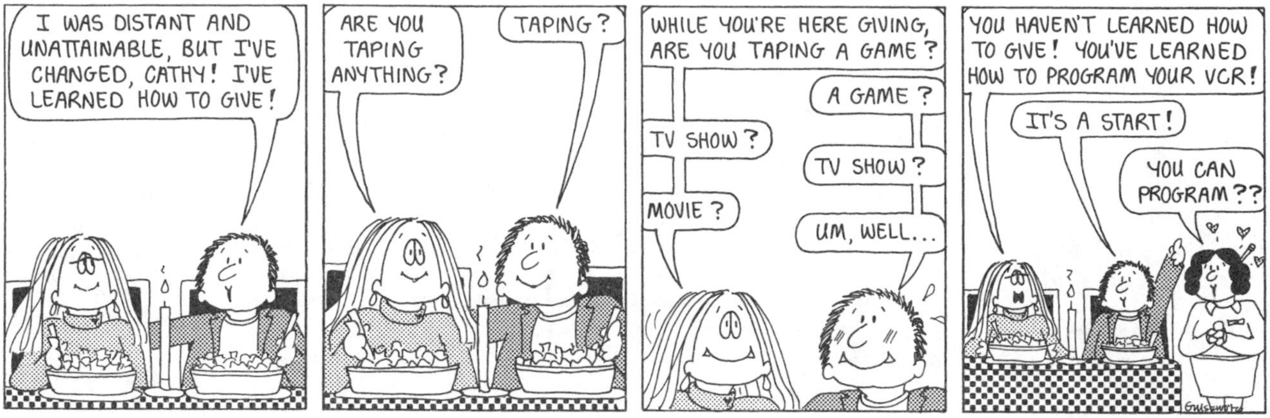
I WAS DISTANT AND UNATTAINABLE, BUT I'VE CHANGED, CATHY! I'VE LEARNED HOW TO GIVE!
ARE YOU TAPING ANYTHING?
TAPING?
WHILE YOU'RE HERE GIVING, ARE YOU TAPING A GAME?
A GAME?
TV SHOW?
TV SHOW?
MOVIE?
UM, WELL...
YOU HAVEN'T LEARNED HOW TO GIVE! YOU'VE LEARNED HOW TO PROGRAM YOUR VCR!
IT'S A START!
YOU CAN PROGRAM??

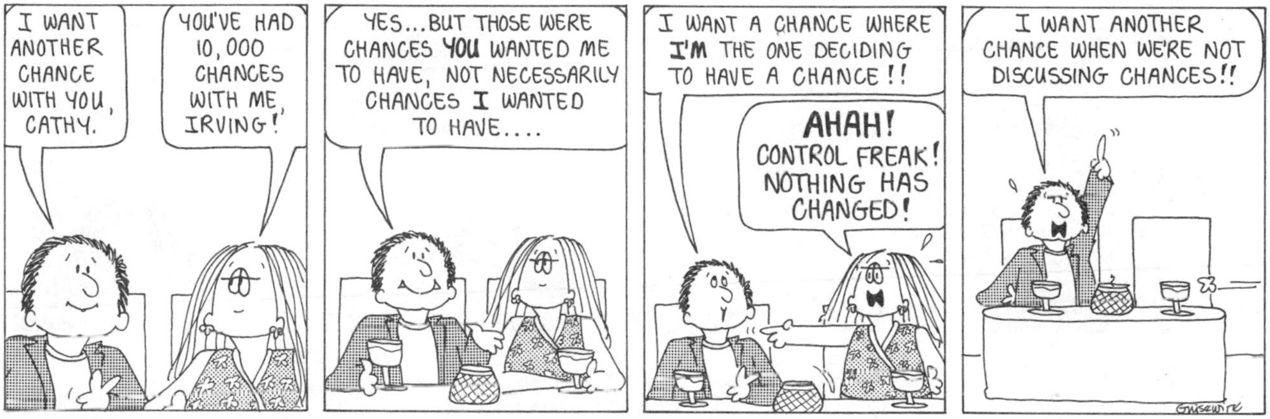
I WANT ANOTHER CHANCE WITH YOU, CATHY.
YOU'VE HAD 10,000 CHANCES WITH ME, IRVING!
YES...BUT THOSE WERE CHANCES YOU WANTED ME TO HAVE, NOT NECESSARILY CHANCES I WANTED TO HAVE....
I WANT A CHANCE WHERE I'M THE ONE DECIDING TO HAVE A CHANCE!!
AHAH! CONTROL FREAK! NOTHING HAS CHANGED!
I WANT ANOTHER CHANCE WHEN WE'RE NOT DISCUSSING CHANCES!!

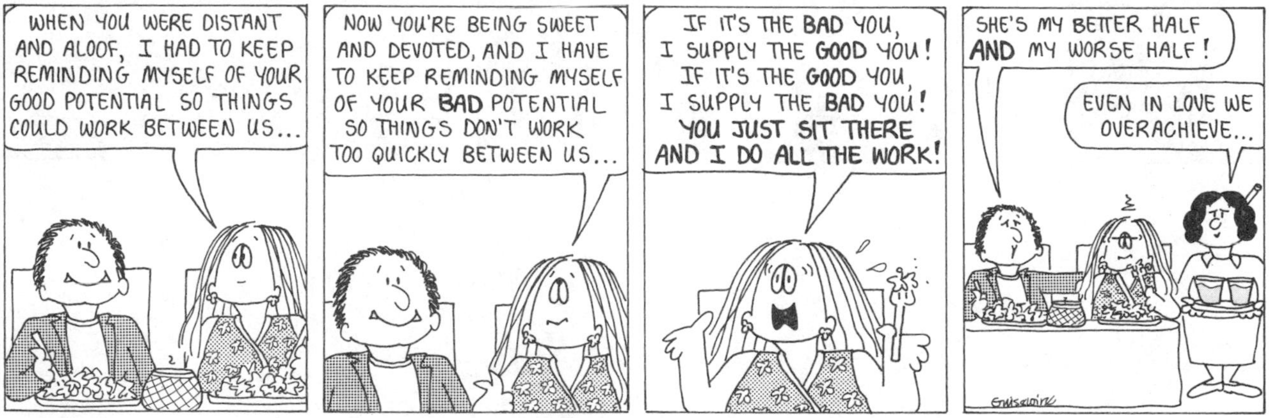
WHEN YOU WERE DISTANT AND ALOOF, I HAD TO KEEP REMINDING MYSELF OF YOUR GOOD POTENTIAL SO THINGS COULD WORK BETWEEN US...
NOW YOU'RE BEING SWEET AND DEVOTED, AND I HAVE TO KEEP REMINDING MYSELF OF YOUR BAD POTENTIAL SO THINGS DON'T WORK TOO QUICKLY BETWEEN US...
IF IT'S THE BAD YOU, I SUPPLY THE GOOD YOU! IF IT'S THE GOOD YOU, I SUPPLY THE BAD YOU! YOU JUST SIT THERE AND I DO ALL THE WORK!
SHE'S MY BETTER HALF AND MY WORSE HALF!
EVEN IN LOVE WE OVERACHIEVE...

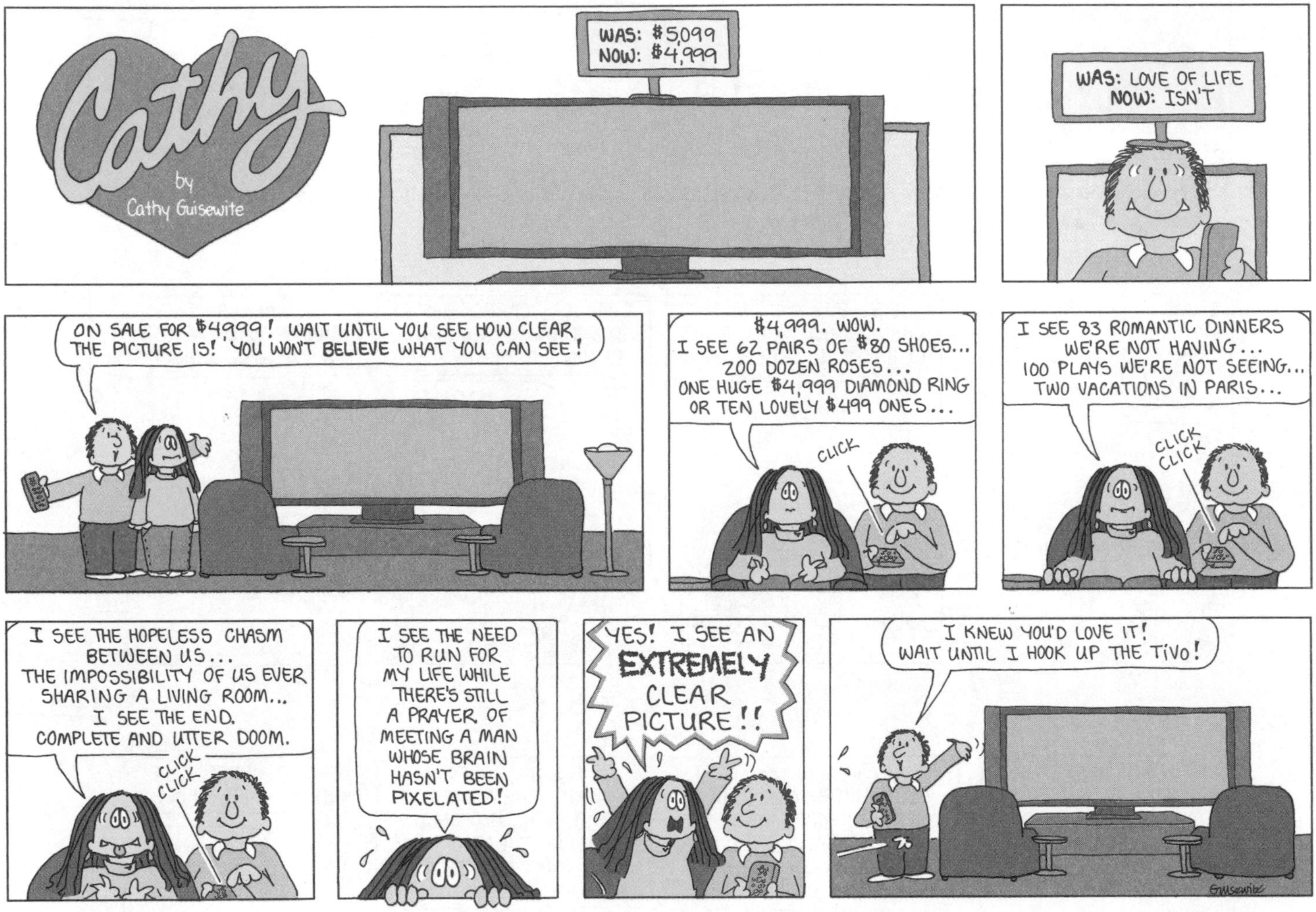
Cathy
by
Cathy Guisewite
WAS: $5,099
NOW: $4,999
WAS: LOVE OF LIFE
NOW: ISN'T
ON SALE FOR $4999! WAIT UNTIL YOU SEE HOW CLEAR THE PICTURE IS! YOU WON'T BELIEVE WHAT YOU CAN SEE!
$4,999. WOW. I SEE 62 PAIRS OF $80 SHOES... 200 DOZEN ROSES... ONE HUGE $4,999 DIAMOND RING OR TEN LOVELY $499 ONES...
CLICK
I SEE 83 ROMANTIC DINNERS WE'RE NOT HAVING... 100 PLAYS WE'RE NOT SEEING... TWO VACATIONS IN PARIS...
CLICK CLICK
I SEE THE HOPELESS CHASM BETWEEN US... THE IMPOSSIBILITY OF US EVER SHARING A LIVING ROOM... I SEE THE END. COMPLETE AND UTTER DOOM.
CLICK CLICK
I SEE THE NEED TO RUN FOR MY LIFE WHILE THERE'S STILL A PRAYER OF MEETING A MAN WHOSE BRAIN HASN'T BEEN PIXELATED!
YES! I SEE AN EXTREMELY CLEAR PICTURE!!
I KNEW YOU'D LOVE IT! WAIT UNTIL I HOOK UP THE TiVo!
GUISEWITE

The Dieting Together Phase

2003—Irving pops the question

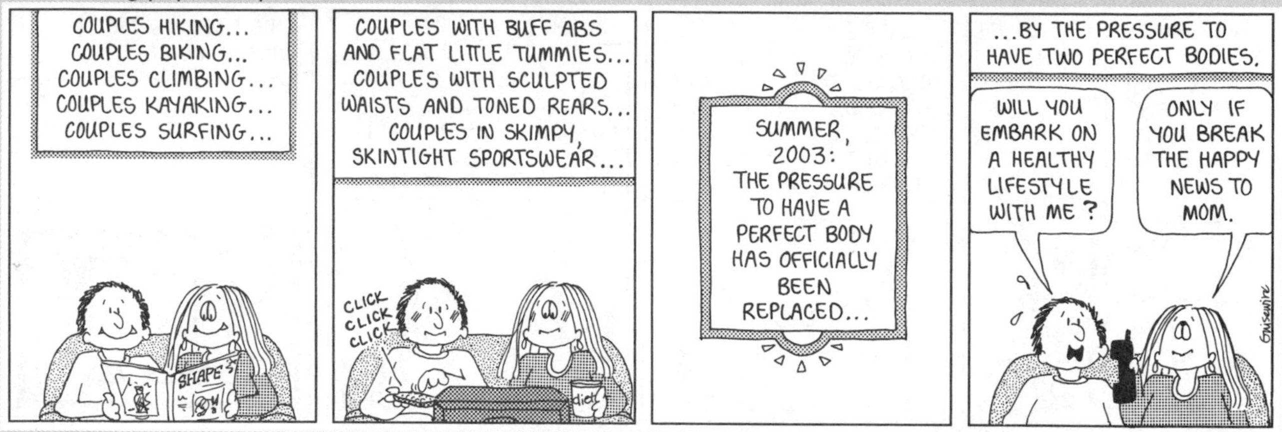
COUPLES HIKING... COUPLES BIKING... COUPLES CLIMBING... COUPLES KAYAKING... COUPLES SURFING...
SHAPE
COUPLES WITH BUFF ABS AND FLAT LITTLE TUMMIES... COUPLES WITH SCULPTED WAISTS AND TONED REARS... COUPLES IN SKIMPY, SKINTIGHT SPORTSWEAR...
CLICK CLICK CLICK
diet
SUMMER, 2003: THE PRESSURE TO HAVE A PERFECT BODY HAS OFFICIALLY BEEN REPLACED...
...BY THE PRESSURE TO HAVE TWO PERFECT BODIES.
WILL YOU EMBARK ON A HEALTHY LIFESTYLE WITH ME?
ONLY IF YOU BREAK THE HAPPY NEWS TO MOM.
GUISEWITE

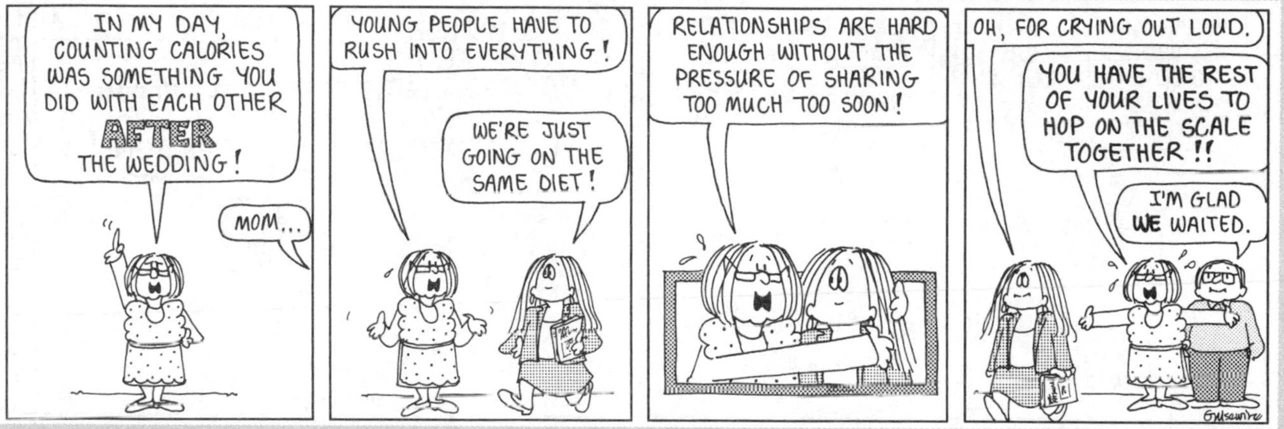
IN MY DAY, COUNTING CALORIES WAS SOMETHING YOU DID WITH EACH OTHER AFTER THE WEDDING!
MOM...
YOUNG PEOPLE HAVE TO RUSH INTO EVERYTHING!
WE'RE JUST GOING ON THE SAME DIET!
RELATIONSHIPS ARE HARD ENOUGH WITHOUT THE PRESSURE OF SHARING TOO MUCH TOO SOON!
OH, FOR CRYING OUT LOUD.
YOU HAVE THE REST OF YOUR LIVES TO HOP ON THE SCALE TOGETHER!!
I'M GLAD WE WAITED.
GUISEWITE

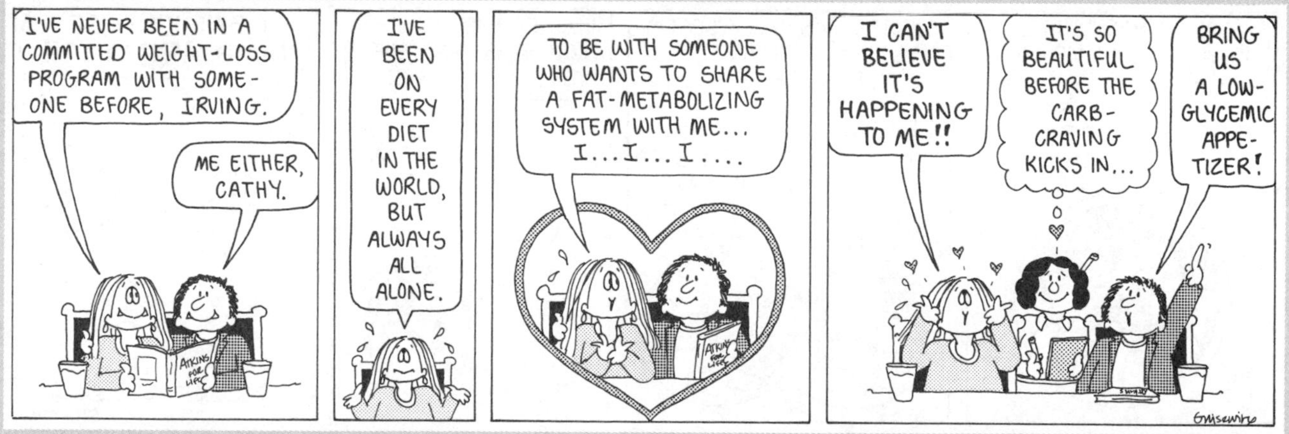
I'VE NEVER BEEN IN A COMMITTED WEIGHT-LOSS PROGRAM WITH SOME-ONE BEFORE, IRVING.
ME EITHER, CATHY.
ATKINS FOR LIFE
I'VE BEEN ON EVERY DIET IN THE WORLD, BUT ALWAYS ALL ALONE.
TO BE WITH SOMEONE WHO WANTS TO SHARE A FAT-METABOLIZING SYSTEM WITH ME... I...I...I....
I CAN'T BELIEVE IT'S HAPPENING TO ME!!
IT'S SO BEAUTIFUL BEFORE THE CARB-CRAVING KICKS IN...
BRING US A LOW-GLYCEMIC APPE-TIZER!
GUISEWITE

The "Family" Vacation

2003—Irving pops another question

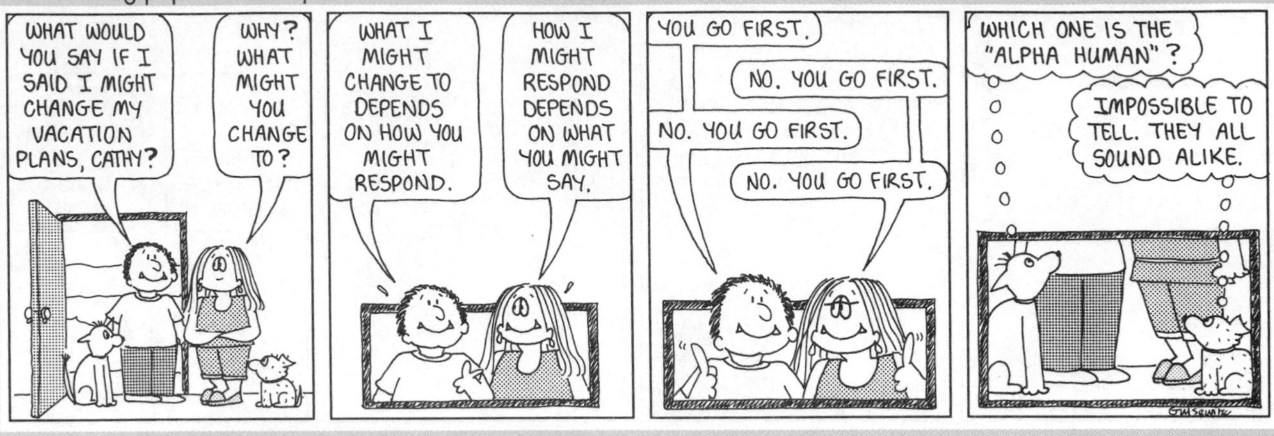
WHAT WOULD YOU SAY IF I SAID I MIGHT CHANGE MY VACATION PLANS, CATHY?
WHY? WHAT MIGHT YOU CHANGE TO?
WHAT I MIGHT CHANGE TO DEPENDS ON HOW YOU MIGHT RESPOND.
HOW I MIGHT RESPOND DEPENDS ON WHAT YOU MIGHT SAY.
YOU GO FIRST.
NO. YOU GO FIRST.
NO. YOU GO FIRST.
NO. YOU GO FIRST.
WHICH ONE IS THE "ALPHA HUMAN"?
IMPOSSIBLE TO TELL. THEY ALL SOUND ALIKE.

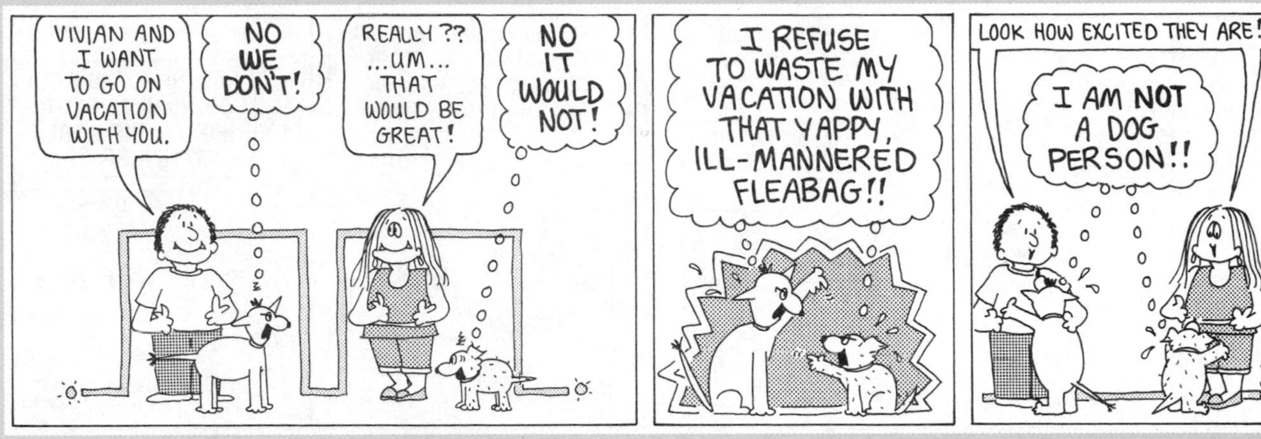
VIVIAN AND I WANT TO GO ON VACATION WITH YOU.
NO WE DON'T!
REALLY?? ...UM... THAT WOULD BE GREAT!
NO IT WOULD NOT!
I REFUSE TO WASTE MY VACATION WITH THAT YAPPY, ILL-MANNERED FLEABAG!!
LOOK HOW EXCITED THEY ARE!
I AM NOT A DOG PERSON!!

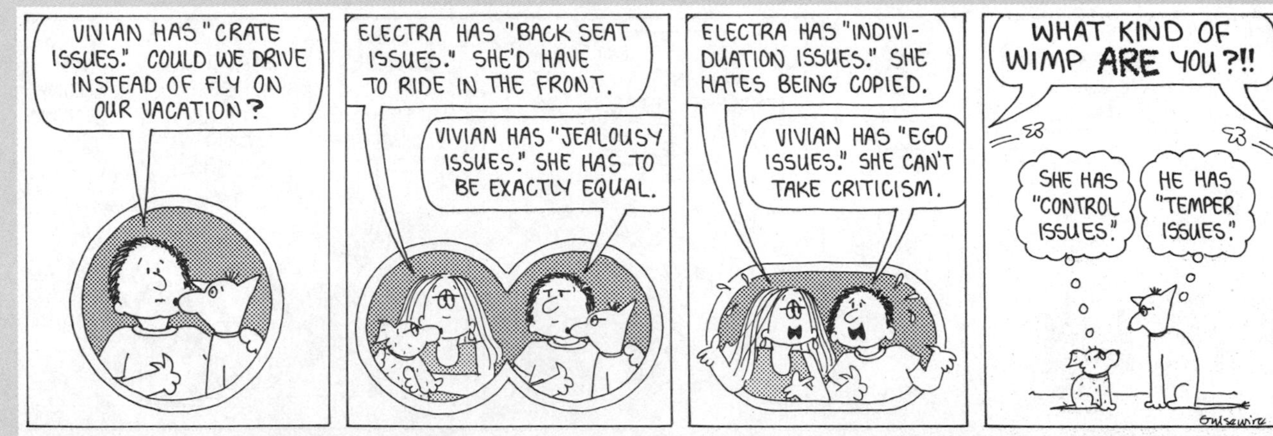
VIVIAN HAS "CRATE ISSUES." COULD WE DRIVE INSTEAD OF FLY ON OUR VACATION?
ELECTRA HAS "BACK SEAT ISSUES." SHE'D HAVE TO RIDE IN THE FRONT.
VIVIAN HAS "JEALOUSY ISSUES." SHE HAS TO BE EXACTLY EQUAL.
ELECTRA HAS "INDIVIDUATION ISSUES." SHE HATES BEING COPIED.
VIVIAN HAS "EGO ISSUES." SHE CAN'T TAKE CRITICISM.
WHAT KIND OF WIMP ARE YOU?!!
SHE HAS "CONTROL ISSUES."
HE HAS "TEMPER ISSUES."

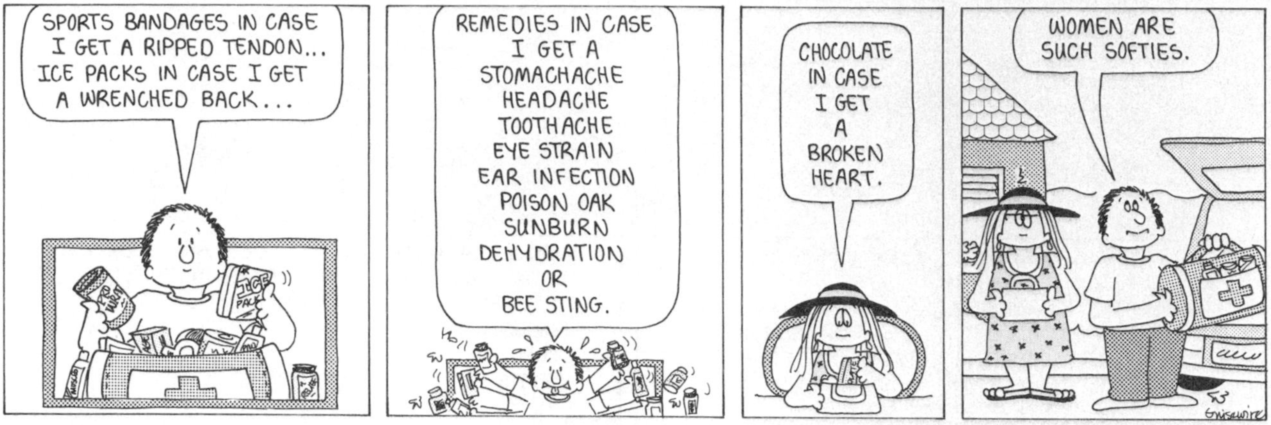
SPORTS BANDAGES IN CASE I GET A RIPPED TENDON... ICE PACKS IN CASE I GET A WRENCHED BACK...
REMEDIES IN CASE I GET A STOMACHACHE HEADACHE TOOTHACHE EYE STRAIN EAR INFECTION POISON OAK SUNBURN DEHYDRATION OR BEE STING.
CHOCOLATE IN CASE I GET A BROKEN HEART.
WOMEN ARE SUCH SOFTIES.

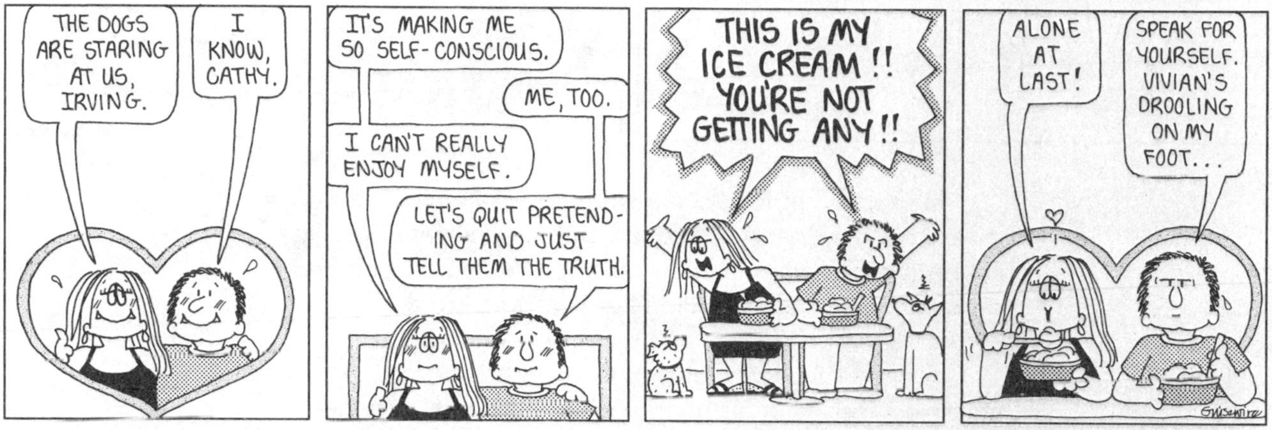
THE DOGS ARE STARING AT US, IRVING.
I KNOW, CATHY.
IT'S MAKING ME SO SELF-CONSCIOUS.
ME, TOO.
I CAN'T REALLY ENJOY MYSELF.
LET'S QUIT PRETENDING AND JUST TELL THEM THE TRUTH.
THIS IS MY ICE CREAM!! YOU'RE NOT GETTING ANY!!
ALONE AT LAST!
SPEAK FOR YOURSELF. VIVIAN'S DROOLING ON MY FOOT...

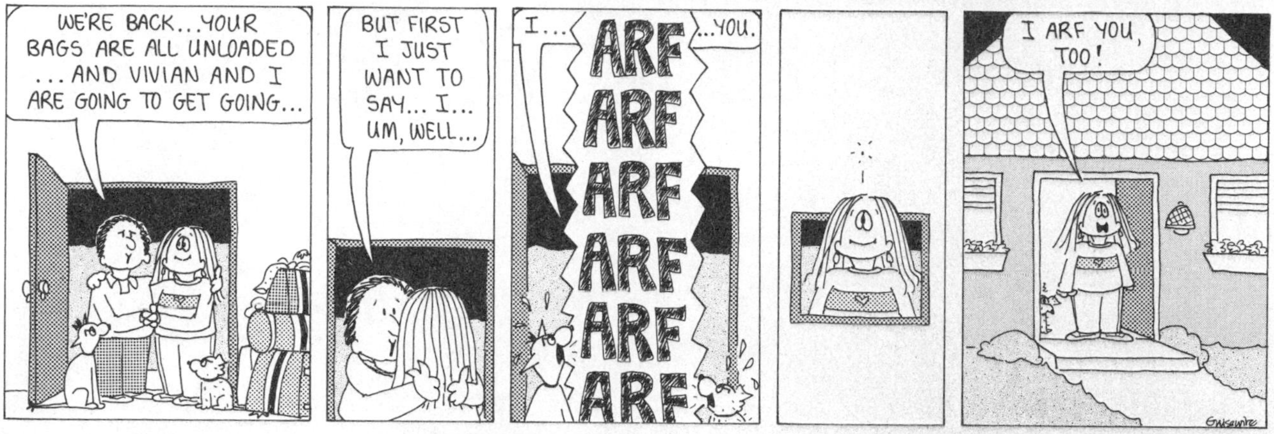
WE'RE BACK... YOUR BAGS ARE ALL UNLOADED ... AND VIVIAN AND I ARE GOING TO GET GOING...
BUT FIRST I JUST WANT TO SAY... I... UM, WELL...
I...
ARF ARF ARF ARF ARF ARF
...YOU.
I ARF YOU, TOO!

IRVING AND I REALLY GOT TO KNOW EACH OTHER ON OUR TRIP, MOM.
YOU'RE HAPPY?
VERY HAPPY.
GOING STEADY HAPPY? SERIOUSLY DATING HAPPY? ENGAGED HAPPY?
WE'RE-COMMITTED-TO-EXPLORING-THE-POSSIBILITY-OF-DISCUSSING-THE-CONCEPT-OF-A-FUTURE HAPPY!
DOES ANY JEWELRY COME WITH THAT??
Guisewite

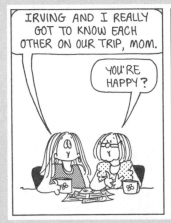

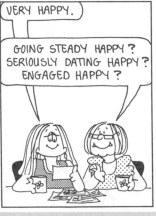

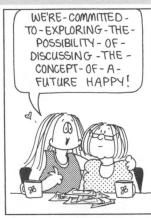

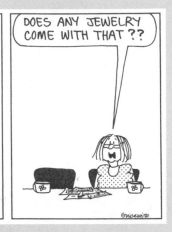

Jewelry did, in fact, come with that. Unbeknownst to anyone except me, Irving had taken an engagement ring with him on the trip with the intention of proposing. For one reason or another, he just couldn't get the words out.

On one of the last nights of the trip, he had a fully rehearsed speech in his head, love in his heart, and the engagement ring in his pocket. With the aid of the dogs and me, he chickened out.

THE DOGS ARE EXHAUSTED. WE CAN FINALLY HAVE A FEW MINUTES TO OURSELVES.
Z Z Z
Z Z Z
I'VE HAD SUCH A WONDERFUL TIME WITH YOU, CATHY.
ME, TOO.
I'M SO GLAD WE'RE HERE TOGETHER.
ME, TOO.
YOU'RE JUST SO... SO...
ARF
ARF
ARF
ARF
ARF
YOU WERE SOUND ASLEEP!!!
WE HEARD A PACKAGE OF SWEET NOTHINGS BEING OPENED.

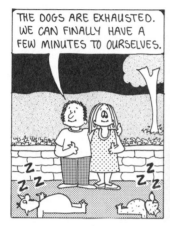

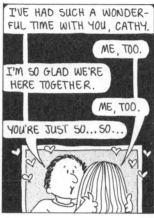

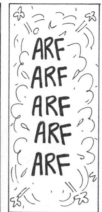

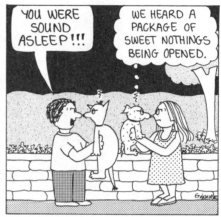

The ring came home in the gym bag Irving had taken on the trip and stayed, forgotten, at the bottom when he unpacked. Normal life took over again . . . the relief of not having proposed settled in . . . the gym bag was taken back and forth to the driving range . . . and was finally left at Cathy's one day, where it stayed for the next five months.

Stayed until that fateful day a week before Valentine's Day, 2004, when Cathy was purging all traces of Irving from her home and flung his gym bag on the "out" heap . . .